The Handbook of Japanese

Blackwell Handbooks in Linguistics

This outstanding multi-volume series covers all the major subdisciplines within linguistics today and, when complete, will offer a comprehensive survey of linguistics as a whole.

Already published:

The Handbook of Japanese Linguistics

Edited by

Natsuko Tsujimura

Copyright © Blackwell Publishers Ltd 1999, 2002

First published 1999
First published in paperback 2002

Blackwell Publishers Inc.
350 Main Street
Malden, Massachusetts 02148
USA

Blackwell Publishers Ltd
108 Cowley Road
Oxford OX4 1JF
UK

Library of Congress Cataloging-in-Publication Data

The handbook of Japanese linguistics / edited by Natsuko Tsujimura.
    p. cm. — (Blackwell handbooks in linguistics)
   Includes bibliographical references and index.
    ISBN 0–631–20504–7 (hc : alk. paper)—ISBN 0–631–23494–2 (pb : alk. paper)
    1. Japanese language.   I. Tsujimura, Natsuko.   II. Series.
  PL523.H26 1999
  495.6'5—dc21   99–10380
                                      CIP

British Library Cataloguing in Publication Data

A CIP catalogue record for this book is available from the British Library.

Typeset in 10 on 12 pt Palatino
By Graphicraft Limited., Hong Kong
Printed in Great Britain by T. J. International Ltd., Padstow, Cornwall

This book is printed on acid-free paper.

To my mother

Contents

Notes on Contributors

Takako Aikawa
Microsoft

Shosuke Haraguchi
Institute of Modern Languages and Cultures, University of Tsukuba

Junko Hibiya
International Center, Keio University

Hiroto Hoshi
School of Oriental and African Studies, University of London

Sachiko Ide and Megumi Yoshida
Faculty of Humanities Department of English, Japan Women's University

Junko Itô and Armin Mester
Department of Linguistics, University of California at Santa Cruz

Taro Kageyama
School of Humanities, Kwansei Gakuin University

Haruo Kubozono
Department of Linguistics, Kobe University

Senko Maynard
Department of East Asian Languages and Cultures, Rutgers University

Shigeru Miyagawa
Department of Linguistics, Department of Foreign Languages and
Literatures, MIT

Mineharu Nakayama
Department of East Asian Languages and Literatures, Ohio State University

Naoko Nemoto
Asian Studies Program, Mt Holyoke College

Taisuke Nishigauchi
Institute for Linguistic Sciences, Kobe Shoin Women's University

Toshiyuki Ogihara
Department of Linguistics, University of Washington

Yukio Otsu
Institute of Cultural and Linguistic Studies, Keio University

Natsuko Tsujimura
Department of East Asian Languages and Cultures, Indiana University

Preface

Since the inception of the generative approach to linguistic research, the field of theoretical linguistics has made tremendous progress. Various theories have been proposed and developed to account for the universality of the human language faculty. At the same time and to the same end, researchers have made a remarkable contribution to this progress by investigating a wider range of languages, far beyond English and others in the Indo-European family. The field of Japanese linguistics has certainly followed this trend for the last thirty years. Japanese has become one of the most closely examined languages, and serves as a testing ground for theoretical developments in virtually all areas of linguistics. The examination of Japanese has revealed its differences from and similarities to other languages, and this indeed has contributed to the elucidation of linguistic phenomena at the descriptive level, and has led to developments and improvements at the theoretical level. As an example from phonology, the study of Japanese accentual patterns played an important role in the development of autosegmental theory. Moreover, numerous syntactic phenomena such as scrambling, pronominal reference, and passives received different treatments over the years, and a new perspective has emerged that Japanese phrase structure is not as drastically different from English as it was perceived as being before. Given the extent to which Japanese has contributed and continues to contribute to the field as a whole, it is timely to compile a volume summarizing the depth and breadth of the research that has made Japanese linguistics a thriving field.

This *Handbook* has come into existence in an attempt to bring together major aspects of Japanese linguistics, presenting an overview of relevant topics. The areas included in the *Handbook* are phonology, syntax, morphology, semantics, language acquisition, sentence processing, pragmatics, and sociolinguistics. Chapters 1–4 deal with phonology including autosegmental theory, optimality theory, and phonological variation. Chapters 5–8 examine several topics in syntax that have made significant contributions to the development of syntactic theories. Chapters 9–12 present interface areas with aspects of syntax, semantics, and morphology. Chapters 13–14 introduce psycholinguistics research ranging from first language acquisition to sentence processing. Chapters 15–16 consider discourse analysis and sociological aspects of the Japanese language. Each chapter contains an overview of the topic, current concerns, and future directions. Due to space limitations and unforeseeable predicaments beyond our control, we were unable to incorporate important topics including historical linguistics and various issues in syntax like pronominal reference and phrase structure matters. This *Handbook* is for those who are familiar with the topic at the basic level and wish to investigate it in more detail, but it is also to be used as a language-specific and typological reference.

In putting this volume together, I have received an enormous amount of professional support from my colleagues. I would like to thank Stuart Davis, Masayo Iida, Senko Maynard, Shigeru Miyagawa, Mineharu Nakayama, Peter Sells, and Mamoru Saito for helping me select topics and contributors and giving me valuable suggestions as to how the *Handbook* should be organized. Their expertise contributed to shaping up an otherwise chaotic volume. Karen Baertsch did a remarkable job in compiling references and index. Her calm way of handling such tedious work was indeed a lifesaver during the summer and fall of 1998. I owe thanks to the East Asian Studies Center at Indiana University for its generous support through a publication subvention grant. I have received a tremendous amount of assistance from experts at Blackwell: Selina Norman, Beth Remmes, Mary Riso, and Steve Smith all patiently helped me get through this project in a timely manner. Fiona Sewell did a superb job in copy-editing the entire manuscript. Her eagle eyes and meticulous editing skills demonstrate true finesse. Finally, special thanks go to Stuart Davis, who not only spent a tremendous amount of his time in reading several chapters but also made sure that I remained with this project, keeping my sanity by his ridiculous sense of humor. This book is dedicated to my mother, who never fails to believe that I am doing something meaningful and brags about me to her neighbors.

Acknowledgments

The authors of chapter 16, editor, and publisher gratefully acknowledge the following for permisssion to reproduce copyright material:

Mouton de Gruyter for figure 16.1 (reprinted from Ide, S. (1989). Formal forms and discernment: two neglected aspects of Japanese linguistic politeness. *Multilingua*, 8, 223–48), figure 16.4 (reprinted from Ide, S., Hill, B., Carnes, Y. M., Ogino, T., and Kawasaki, A. (1992). The concept of politeness: an empirical study of American English and Japanese. In R. J. Watts, S. Ide, and K. Ehlich (eds), *Politeness in Language: Studies in its History, Theory and Practice* (pp. 281–97)), figures 16.5 and 16.9 (reprinted from Ide, S., Hori, M., Kawasaki, A., Ikuta, S., and Haga, H. (1986). Sex difference and politeness in Japanese. *International Journal of the Sociology of Language*, 58, 25–36), and figures 16.7 and 16.8 (reprinted from Ogino, T. (1986). Quantification of politeness based on the usage patterns of honorific expressions. *International Journal of the Sociology of Language*, 58, 37–8); Elsevier Science for figures 16.2 and 16.3 (reprinted from *Journal of Pragmatics*, 10, Hill, B. Ide, S., Ikuta, S., Kawasaki, A., and Ogino, T., 'Universals of linguistic politeness: quantitative evidence from Japanese and American English', 347–71, © (1986), with permission from Elsevier Science).

1 Accent

SHOSUKE HARAGUCHI

0 Introduction

The study of Japanese accent has a long history, during the course of which a large number of data have been accumulated by numerous Japanese linguists.[1] Japanese consists of a great number of different dialects, which have their own phonetic peculiarities. The accentual phenomena of these dialects differ from one another in at least some respects. However, dialects can be classified into a number of types in terms of their accentual patterns and tonal melodies.

Within the framework of generative phonology, J. D. McCawley (1968b) and Shibatani (1972), among others, have attracted the attention of many linguists to Japanese accentual phenomena by their penetrating analyses. Following their pioneering work, Haraguchi (1977, 1979a, 1979b, 1991), Okuda (1971), Kubozono (1993), and many others have further contributed to our understanding of Japanese accent and the advancement of phonological theory. In this chapter, I will draw upon all these previous efforts in order to shed light on a variety of the characteristics of Japanese accent and tonal systems.

Despite the variety of Japanese dialects, I will focus attention in this chapter on two dialects: Tokyo Japanese and Osaka Japanese. One of the reasons why I limit discussion to these two dialects is that they are representative accentual systems with one and two basic tone melodies. Also a good number of accentual data for these dialects are available, since they have been well studied by a number of phonologists. Another reason is simply that space is limited and thus it is next to impossible to cover all of the various accentual and tonal systems in Japanese.

Before going on to the discussion of these two dialects, let us first outline briefly the accentual and tonal varieties of Japanese dialect. The survey will be helpful to understand the schematic picture of Japanese "accentual patterns."

Japanese accentual and tonal systems are divided into two types: accentual systems and unaccentual ones. The former are divided into subtypes in terms of the number of both underlying and surface accentual patterns (n, n+1, n+2, etc.) and the latter into tonal systems and unaccented or intonational systems. Both the accentual and unaccentual systems can be further classified into a number of subtypes in terms of the number and type of tonal melodies (e.g. 1 Basic Tone Melody (1BTM), 2BTM, 3BTM, etc.). This is schematically represented in (1).

In (1), accentual type n means that words with n moras have n-accentual patterns, which implies that all words are accented; accentual type n+1 means that words with n moras have n+1 accentual patterns, which implies that words are divided into unaccented and n-mora accented; accentual type n+2 means that the dialect has n+1 accentual patterns with one more additional accentual class. nBTM refers to the number of basic tone melodies in the language or dialect; for example, 1BTM means that there is one basic tone melody.

(1)

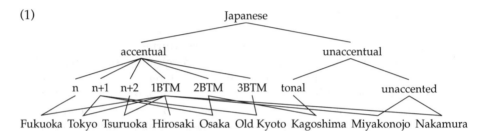

Tokyo Japanese, for example, is an n+1 accentual type dialect with one basic tone melody (HL). Osaka Japanese is virtually identical to Tokyo Japanese in that it has an n+1 accentual pattern for each melody, but it is different from Tokyo Japanese in that it has two basic tone melodies (HL and LHL). Old Kyoto Japanese manifests the richest surface tonal melodies due to the fact that it has three basic tone melodies (HL, LHL, and LH), while the underlying tonal pattern is n+1, just like that of Tokyo Japanese and Osaka Japanese.

Accentual systems of Japanese dialects have a number of characteristics. In almost all dialects, verbs and adjectives are divided into two classes in one of two ways: either accented and unaccented (e.g. Tokyo Japanese) or into two different melodies (e.g. HL and LHL in Osaka Japanese, LHL and LH in Kagoshima Japanese, etc.). The former normally has accent on the penultimate mora, which is equivalent to the stem-final mora/syllable V in (2). See section 1 for more discussion on this point.

(2) $\text{CV(C)]}_{\text{stem}} \left(\genfrac{}{}{0pt}{}{(r)u]_{\text{verb}}}{i]_{\text{adj}}} \right)$

[hasir]u   [tabe]ru
[aka]i   [naga]i

Nouns, on the other hand, tend to have more accentual varieties than verbs and adjectives, depending on the surface accentual/tonal realization. Consider (3), which contains some systems frequently observed in Japanese dialects.

(3)		No. of surface tonal patterns	Analysis/system
みやこのじょう	a.	1	one-melody unaccentual system
鹿古島	b.	2	two-melody unaccentual system
くみ	c.	3	accentual system
	d.	n	accented words only
	e.	n+1	accented words and unaccented ones
鶴岡	f.	n+2	accented and unaccented words + Accent Shift
関西	g.	2n+1 (n+1; n)	two-melody system
	h.	3n+2 (n+1; n+1; n)	three-melody system

If a dialect has only one or two tonal patterns, the system is interpreted as a one-melody unaccentual system or a two-melody unaccentual system respectively. Miyakonojo Japanese and Izumi Japanese are examples of (3a). Kagoshima Japanese is a celebrated example of (3b). Both of these patterns differ from the remaining ones in that they are unaccentual systems whereas the rest are accentual systems. Kumi Japanese is an example of (3c).

The n-accentual or tonal pattern type as witnessed in Fukuoka Japanese can be found in accentual systems only. The n+1 accentual or tonal patterns are the most common in Japanese dialects. The existence of an n+2 accentual pattern type is rather amazing in that the largest logical possibility should be n+1. It is shown in Haraguchi (1977, 1979a, 1979b, 1998) that Tsuruoka Japanese, which is an example of (3f), can be analyzed as having an underlying n+1 accentual system.

Systems incorporating 2n+1 accentual or tonal patterns, as in (3g), are analyzed as consisting of two-melody systems. Most of the Kansai dialects, including Osaka Japanese, belong to this class. What is interesting with respect to this class is that there is no dialect with 2n patterns or 2n+2 patterns. Furthermore, systems with 3n+2 accentual or tonal patterns, as in (3h), are analyzed as having three-melody systems. The only dialect which belongs to this class is the Old Kyoto dialect. Notice that within the three-melody class, there are no cases with 3n patterns, 3n+1 patterns, or 3n+3 patterns.

Japanese dialects can also be classified into a number of types in terms of tonal systems. The most complicated dialect is that of the Old Kyoto Japanese as found in *The Ruizyuumyougisyou*. This dialect is peculiar in that it has three tonal melodies for nouns: HL/LH/LHL. To the best of my knowledge, there seems to be no accentual Japanese dialect with any other logically possible combination of tonal melodies, such as H/HL/L, or H/LH/LHL, or L/HL/LH.

Interestingly enough, some Japanese dialects have a smaller number of tonal melodies. There are a number of contemporary Japanese dialects with two tonal melodies. Thus, the so-called Kansai-type dialects, such as Kyoto Japanese, Osaka Japanese, Kameyama Japanese, and Kochi Japanese, have two tonal melodies: HL and LHL. Another type of dialect with two tonal melodies is Kagoshima Japanese, which has LH and LHL melodies. For some unknown reason, there is no Japanese dialect with HL and LH melodies. I suspect that this gap is accidental, and not systematic.

Japanese dialects belonging to the accentual system are divided into three types: the HL melody class, the LH melody class, and the LHL melody class. A large number of the Tokyo-type dialects have the HL melody system. Only a limited number of accentual dialects have the LH melody system. Hirosaki Japanese and Shizukuishi Japanese belong to this class. Other dialects have an LHL melody system, to which Narada Japanese, Kumi Japanese, Tsuruoka Japanese, etc. belong. There seems to be no accentual dialect with an H melody or an L melody, or an M (Mid) melody for that matter.

In contrast, dialects which are classified as unaccentual are either LH, HL, M, or have no perceivable melodic shape. Miyakonojo Japanese, spoken in an area located near that where Kagoshima Japanese (which has LH and LHL melodies) is spoken, has an LH melody system. Another well-known unaccentual dialect is Sendai Japanese, which is analyzed as having an HL melody system. As shown by Haraguchi (1977), Uchiko Japanese has an M melody system. It is widely recognized that a fair number of Japanese unaccentual dialects do not have a fixed melodic system. Thus, their melody can change depending on certain circumstances.

The observations above can be summarized in the following diagram.

(4) a. 3-melody system: HL, LH, LHL --------------- Old Kyoto Japanese
     b. 2-melody system: (i)   HL, LHL ------------- Kansai-type dialects
                           (ii)   LH, LHL ------------- Kagoshima Japanese
                           (iii) HL, LH -------------- Gap
     c. 1-melody system: (i)   HL (accentual) ------ Tokyo-type Japanese
                                  (unaccentual) -- Sendai Japanese
                           (ii)   LH (accentual) ------ Hirosaki,
                                                        Shizukuishi Japanese
                                  (unaccentual) -- Miyakonojo Japanese
                           (iii) LHL ----------------- Kumi, Narada,
                                                        Nakamura Japanese,
                                                        etc.
                           (iv)   M --------------------- Uchiko Japanese
                           (v)   H --------------------- ? Gap
                           (vi)   L --------------------- ? Gap
                           (vii) No fixed melody --- Other unaccentual
                                                        Japanese

The characteristics of the Japanese melodic systems in (4) will be made clearer if we compare them to the melodic systems of tonal languages such as Chinese or Mende.

(5) a. Chinese: 4-melody system: H, L, HL, and LH
     b. Mende: 5-melody system: H, L, HL, LH, and LHL

A comparison of (4) and (5) shows clearly that Japanese dialects use a subset of the melodic systems permitted in other languages. In addition to this, a large number of Japanese dialects make use of accentual information to distinguish lexical differences.

With this much background information in mind, let us now turn to the analysis of two typical Japanese dialects: Tokyo Japanese and Osaka Japanese. The remainder of this chapter is organized as follows: section 1 discusses the accentual and tonal system of Tokyo Japanese. Section 2 is devoted to a detailed discussion of the accentual and tonal system of Osaka Japanese. Section 3 is a brief summary and conclusion.

1 Accentual and Tonal System of Tokyo Japanese

1.1 *Introduction*

Tokyo Japanese is a typical dialect with a pitch accent system. Words can be distinguished only by accent, as is illustrated by the examples in (6). Notice that the location of the accent corresponds to the mora before the pitch drop: that is, the accent is on the H immediately before L.

(6)　　*Nouns*　　　*Glosses*　　　　　*Analyses*
　　a.　ka'ki (-ga)　"oyster"+Nom　　o' o (o): initial-accented
　　　　H L　 L
　　b.　kaki' (-ga)　"fence"+Nom　　 o o' (o): final-accented
　　　　L H　 L
　　c.　kaki (-ga)　"persimmon"+Nom　o o (o): unaccented
　　　　L H　 H
　　　　(where the diacritic mark (') indicates that the immediately preceding syllable (o) has an accent.)

In isolation, *kaki* in (b) and (c) have the same melody, LH. However, they are distinguished when followed by, for example, the Nominative morpheme *ga*. Thus, they should be analyzed as different in terms of accent, as indicated in (6).

Tokyo Japanese has a number of accentual and tonal characteristics, some of which are summarized as follows:

(7)　a.　It has n+1 accentual patterns for n-mora words.
　　　b.　Words are divided into two classes: accented and unaccented (more than 50 percent of nouns are unaccented).
　　　c.　Approximately 75 percent of accented nouns have an accent on the head of the syllable head containing the antepenultimate mora.
　　　d.　The basic tone melody is HL.
　　　e.　It has a number of tonal and accentual rules.
　　　f.　Present forms of accented verbs and adjectives have an accent on the penultimate mora.

In what follows, I will discuss these characteristics, on the basis of a number of examples.

1.2   *The accentual pattern of Tokyo Japanese*

Dialects of type (3e) above are different from those of (3d) in that they have unaccented words in addition to n accented words. A well-known example of this type of dialect is Tokyo Japanese, which has the tonal surface melodies for nouns.

(8)

	Unaccented	*Initial-accented*	*Second-accented*	*Third-accented*	*Fourth-accented*
1.	e-ga	e'-ga			
	L H	H L			
	"handle"-Nom	"picture"-Nom			
2.	hasi (-ga)	ha'si (-ga)	hasi' (-ga)		
	LH H	H L L	LH L		
	"edge"-Nom	"chopstick"-Nom	"bridge"-Nom		
3.	sakura (-ga)	ka'rasu (-ga)	koko'ro (-ga)	otoko' (-ga)	
	L HH H	H L L L	L H L L	LH H L	
	"cherry"-Nom	"crow"-Nom	"heart"-Nom	"man"-Nom	
4.	kamigata (-ga)	se'kitan (-ga)	asa'gao (-ga)	aozo'ra (-ga)	kaminari' (-ga)
	L HHH H	H LLL L	LH LL L	LHH L L	L HHH L
	"hair style"-Nom	"coal"-Nom	"morning-glory"-Nom	'blue sky"-Nom	"thunder"-Nom

(where the diacritic mark (') stands for accent on the immediately preceding mora.)

Tokyo Japanese is peculiar in that we cannot predict where the H to L falling tone occurs. Thus, we need lexical information regarding where the fall in tone (i.e. the accent) appears. According to traditional analyses of this dialect, the words of the first column, which do not have a fall in pitch even when they are followed by the Nominative morpheme *ga*, are analyzed as unaccented, while the words of the other columns are accented as indicated in (8).

Almost all of the Tokyo-type dialects consist of n+1 accentual systems, while they are divided into a number of different subtypes depending on their basic tonal melody. I will omit the discussion of these differences in this chapter.

1.3   *The tonal system of Tokyo Japanese*

Most works on Japanese accent begins with a discussion of the tonal system of Tokyo Japanese. This is because Tokyo Japanese is virtually equivalent to so-called Standard Japanese or Common Japanese. In addition to this, Tokyo Japanese has been examined extensively and the accumulated data are detailed and numerous. Furthermore, there are a number of accent dictionaries for Tokyo Japanese.

1.3.1 *The tonal melody of nouns*

Let us begin with a discussion of nouns. The accentual pattern of Tokyo Japanese is, as discussed in section 1.2, considered to be a typical n+1 type; i.e. it has n+1 accentual variations for n-syllable words.

The largest number of words (approximately 55 percent) are unaccented. Among the accented words, approximately 75 percent have accent on the antepenultimate mora (see J. D. McCawley 1968b, Haraguchi 1991, E. Yamada 1990, and others for discussion concerning this point). Based on this observation, Haraguchi (1991) proposes that Tokyo Japanese has an accentual system virtually parallel to that of the English stress system. This finding is rather surprising taking into consideration the fact that Tokyo Japanese and English are not related to each other in terms of origin and language typology.

How do we decide the basic tone melody of Tokyo Japanese? Examination of the tonal melodies in (8) above suggests that the L tone on the initial syllable is automatically accounted for. What we need to assume is a dissimilation process schematically shown in (9), which is commonly referred to as initial lowering.

(9) Dissimilation (Tokyo Japanese):
     #H H → L H

Notice, as pointed out by Hattori (1954, 1960), that this dissimilation does not apply in natural speech when the word-initial syllable is heavy, i.e. it is CVV or CVC. Thus, consider the following samples.

(10) a. kooban   "police station"
          HHHH
      b. kondan   "familiar talk"
          HHHH

The lowering of the initial H tone on the initial mora will be possible only if the word is uttered in a slow, careful, unnatural fashion. In addition, initial lowering is not applicable if there is no preceding pause. A pause indicates the accentual phrase boundary. This observation shows that this dissimilation process is phonetic in nature and is dependent on factors such as the speed of speech, style of pronunciation, and others. For detailed discussion, see Haraguchi (1977) and the reference cited therein.

We can thus exclude the initial L tone from consideration when we determine the basic tonal melody of Tokyo Japanese. The tonal melody common to unaccented words and final-accented words is H whereas the tonal melody of all the other accented words is HL. These two melodies can be unified into the HL melody if we assume that the final moras of unaccented and final-accented words are associated with the H tone of the HL melody, leaving the L tone unassociated with the final mora of the word in question. On the basis of this observation, I conclude that the basic tone melody of Tokyo Japanese is HL.

Let us now discuss some of the tonal phenomena related to phrases. The enclitic *ma'de* "even" and the predicate *de'su* "be" have their own accent on the initial mora. What happens when these morphemes are attached to nouns? As illustrated in (11), the left accent wins and the H tone of the HL melody is associated with the accent.

(11) a.   sakura-ma'de   b.   otoko'-ma'de
          L HH H L   LH H L L
          "cherry"-even   "man"-even
      c.   koko'ro-ma'de   d.   ka'rasu-ma'de
          L H L L L   H LL L L
          "heart"-even   "crow"-even

After the association of the HL melody to all the tone-bearing units, initial lowering applies and the initial H tone is turned into an L tone if it is followed by another H tone.

It is well known that the genitive morpheme *no* causes the accent on the final syllable to be deleted if the final-accented noun has two moras or more. To see this, examine the cases in (12) and (13).

(12)		Noun	Gloss	Noun+Gen	Noun+Obj
	a.	uti'wa	"fan"	uti'wa-no	uti'wa-wo
		LH L		LH L L	LH L L
	b.	iro'gami	"color paper"	iro'gami-no	iro'gami-wo
		LH L L		LH L L L	LH L L L
	c.	a'rasi	"storm"	a'rasi-no	a'rasi-wo
		H LL		HLL L	HLL L

(13)		Noun	Gloss	Noun+Gen	Noun+Obj
	a.	kawa'	"river"	kawa-no	kawa'-wo
		L H		L H H	L H L
	b.	atama'	"head"	atama-no	atama'-wo
		LH H		LH H H	LH H L
	c.	niho'n	"Japan"	nihon-no	niho'n-wo
		LHL		LHH H	LHL L
	d.	kino'o	"yesterday"	kinoo-no	kino'o-wo
		LHL		LHH H	LHL L

A comparison of (12) and (13) indicates that accent deletion applies only when accent is on the final syllable of a noun followed by the genitive morpheme. Thus, the accent on the other syllables is preserved when *no* is attached to a noun.

Furthermore, compare the examples in (13) to those in (14). The examples in (13) undergo accent deletion, while those in (14) do not.

(14)

	Noun	Gloss	Noun+Gen	Noun+Obj
a.	ha'	"teeth"	ha'-no	ha'-wo
	H		H L	H L
b.	kyo'o	"today"	kyo'o-no	kyo'o-wo
	HL		HL L	HL L
c.	ho'n	"today"	ho'n-no	ho'n-wo
	H L		H L L	H L L

Where does this difference in accent loss come from? Notice that the examples in (14) are monosyllabic while those in (13) are polysyllabic. Thus, we can summarize the above observation as follows:

(15)   Accent is deleted when a polysyllabic noun with accent on the final syllable is followed by the Genitive *no*.

This generalization can be put differently, if we note the fact that the examples in (14) can be interpreted as either initial-accented or final-accented, while those in (13) can only be interpreted as final-accented.

(15)′   Accent is deleted when a noun which is uniquely interpreted as having accent on the final syllable is followed by the Genitive *no*.

I have nothing to say here about whether these two generalizations are merely notational variants or whether they are qualitatively different conceptualizations and thus have theoretically independent implications.

In contrast to accent deletion, Tokyo Japanese has at least one case of accent insertion. A typical case is the insertion of accent on the initial mora of a noun when the word is preceded by the honorific prefix *o*. Consider the following samples.

(16)

	Noun	Gloss	o+noun
a.	huro'	"bath"	o-hu'ro
	L H		L H L
b.	susi'	"sushi"	o-su'si
	L H		L H L
c.	ha'si	"chopsticks"	o-ha'si
	H L		L H L

(17)

	Noun	Gloss	o+noun
a.	tegami	"letter"	o-te'gami
	L H H		L H L L
b.	sentaku	"washing"	o-se'ntaku
	LHH H		L H LL L

Irrespective of the presence or absence of accent, accent is assigned to the initial mora of the noun to which honorific *o* has been attached. This accent assignment is, as suggested in Haraguchi (1977), interpreted as a type of compound formation in Tokyo Japanese.

1.3.2 Tonal patterns of verbs

Consider now verbal patterns in Tokyo Japanese. As mentioned briefly in the introduction of this section, verbs are divided into two types: accented and unaccented. Consider the data in (18).

(18) Verbal classes in Tokyo Japanese:

		Unaccented		*Accented*		
(i)	a.	wur-u L H	"sell"	ka't-u H L	"win"	consonant-ending verb
	b.	ki-ru L H	"wear"	mi'-ru H L	"see"	vowel-ending verb
(ii)	a.	susum-u L H H	"advance"	kaku's-u L H L	"hide"	consonant-ending verb
	b.	kari-ru LH H	"borrow"	tate'-ru L H L	"build"	vowel-ending verb
(iii)	a.	utagaw-u L H H H	"doubt"	yoroko'b-u L H H L	"be glad"	consonant-ending verb
	b.	narabe-ru LH H H	"line up"	kakure'-ru L H H L	"hide"	vowel-ending verb

Taking into consideration the analysis of the tonal patterns of nouns, the surface LH melody class is analyzed as unaccented and the surface (L) H (H) L melody class is analyzed as penultimate-accented (or stem-final-accented).

Let us examine in more detail some verbal forms of Tokyo Japanese. As representatives of accented and unaccented verbs, consider various forms of the verbs in (18ii) shown in (19) and (20).

(19)

		Present	*Gloss*	*Imperative*[2]	*Causative*	*V+want*
	a.	susum-u L H H	"advance"	susum-e L H H	susum-ase-ru L H HH H	susum-i-ta-i L H HHH
	b.	kari-ru LH H	"borrow"	kari-ro LH H	kari-sase-ru LH HH H	kari-ta-i LHHH

(20)

		Present	*Gloss*	*Imperative*	*Causative*	*V+want*
	a.	kaku's-u L H L	"hide"	kaku's-e L H L	kakus-ase'-ru L H HH L	kakus-i-ta'-i L H HHL
	b.	tate'-ru LH L	"build"	tate'-ro L H L	tate-sase'-ru LH HH L	tate-ta'-i L H HL

Imperative forms, Causative forms, and V+*want* forms are all parallel to the Present forms in that unaccented verbs are unaccented and accented verbs are penultimate-accented. Accent is assigned by the same mechanism as that of the Present form.

Consider now what happens when the morphemes *(y)o'o* "let" and *ma'su* "Polite-Present" are attached to these verbs.

(21)		*Present*		*(y)o'o "let"*	*ma'su "Polite-Present"*
	a.	susum-u	"advance"	susum-o'o	susumi-ma's-u
		L H H		L H HL	L H H H L
	b.	kari-ru	"borrow"	kari-yo'o	kari-ma's-u
		LHH		LH HL	LH H L
(22)	a.	kaku's-u	"hide"	kakus-o'o	kakusi-ma's-u
		L H L		L H HL	L HH H L
	b.	tate'-ru	"build"	tate-yo'o	tate-ma's-u
		LH L		L H HL	LH H L

Examination of (21) and (22) shows that these morphemes remove the accent of the accented verbs and their own accent is realized on the penultimate mora.

Consider next Negative and Preverbal forms.

(23)		*Present*		*Negative*	*Preverbal*
	a.	susum-u	"advance"	susum-a-na-i	susun-de
		L H H		L H H HH	L HHH
	b.	kari-ru	"borrow"	kari-na-i	kari-te
		LHH		LH HH	LHH
(24)	a.	kaku's-u	"hide"	kakus-a'-na-i	kaku'si-te
		L H L		L H H LL	L HLL
	b.	tate'-ru	"build"	tate'-na-i	ta'te-te
		LH L		LH LL	H L L

With the exception of some segmental variation, nothing happens when the negative morpheme *na-i* or the connective morpheme *te* is attached to unaccented verbs. When these forms are attached to accented verbs, the final mora becomes extratonal or invisible and accent is assigned to the penultimate mora of the visible part; that is, accent is placed on the antepenultimate mora. Note that the negative morpheme *-nai*, which is an adjective, is assigned accent by the mechanism of accent assignment for adjectives.

Consider finally Conditional forms and Past forms.

(25)		*Present*		*Conditional*	*Past*
	a.	susum-u	"advance"	susum-e'-ba	susu'n-da
		L H H		L H H L	L HLL
	b.	kari-ru	"borrow"	karir-e'-ba	kari'-ta
		LHH		LHH L	LH L

(26) a. kaku's-u   "hide"   kaku's-e-ba   kaku'si-ta
          L H L   L H L L   L H L L
      b. tate'-ru   "build"   tate'-re-ba   ta'te-ta
          LH L   LH L L   H L L

It seems that the Conditional morpheme *(r)e-ba* and the Past morpheme *ta* assign accent on the penultimate mora when they are attached to unaccented verbs, while they assign accent on the antepenultimate mora when they are attached to accented verbs. One possible way to interpret these facts is that the final mora of Conditional forms and Past forms becomes extrametrical or invisible when the morphemes in question are attached to accented verbs.

Another possible interpretation is to assume that the Conditional and Past morphemes are extratonal or invisible to tone association of the HL melody and that accent is assigned to the penultimate mora of accented verbs just like the Present form. Thus the derivations would be as illustrated in (27), where extratonality is represented by < >.

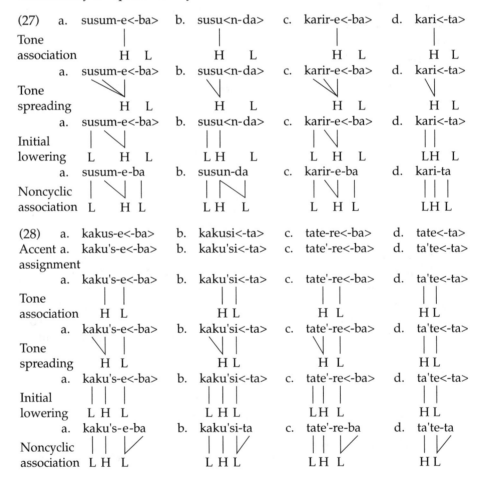

The merit of this analysis is that there is no need to introduce an accent assignment rule for unaccented forms.

The observations above show that verbal suffixes are classified into three types in Tokyo Japanese. One type, such as *(r)u* and *te*, is unaccented in itself and forms a single prosodic word together with the preceding verbal root. A second type of verbal suffix, such as *yo'o* and *ma'su*, asserts its accentual integrity; i.e. the compound forms are accented, assigning accent to the penultimate mora. A third type of verbal affix, including the morphemes *(y)oo*, *te*, and *(r)e-ba*, makes the final mora extratonal or invisible when attached to verbs.

1.3.3 *The tonal patterns of adjectives*

Adjectives in Tokyo Japanese are also divided into two tonal classes: accented and unaccented. Accented adjectives have accent on the penultimate mora in the Present form.

(29) Adjectival classes in Tokyo Japanese:

	Unaccented		*Accented*	
a.	aka-i L HH	"red"	siro'-i LH L	"white"
b.	tumeta-i L HHH	"cold"	tanosi'-i L HHL	"happy"
c.	namanuru-i L H HHH	"lukewarm"	omosiro'-i L HHHL	"interesting"

The fact that accented adjectives have penultimate accent is parallel to the situation with verbs, as demonstrated above. Let us now examine some of the inflectional forms of adjectives. Consider first the following cases.

(30)

		Unaccented			*Accented*	
	a.	aka-i L HH	"red"	b.	siro'-i LH L	"white"
Preverbal		aka-ku LH H			si'ro-ku HL L	
Nominal		aka-sa LH H			si'ro-sa HL L	
	c.	tumeta-i L HHH	"cold"	d.	tanosi'-i L HHL	"happy"
Preverbal		tumeta-ku L HH H			tano'si-ku L HL L	
Nominal		tumeta-sa L HH H			tano'si-sa L HL L	

Unaccented cases remain unaccented and accented cases with *ku* and *sa* have accent on the antepenultimate mora. The antepenultimate accent is analyzed as the consequence of the extrametricality of *ku* and *sa* and the ensuing accent assignment on the penultimate mora. Note that the extrametricality of these cases is restricted to the level of accent assignment only.

Consider now the following cases of adjectival forms.

(31)		*Unaccented*			*Accented*	
	a.	aka-i	"red"	b.	siro'-i	"white"
		L HH			LH L	
. . . *ku + wa*		aka-ku-wa			si'ro-ku-wa	
		LH L L			H L L L	
Past		aka-kat-ta			si'ro-kat-ta	
		LH LL L			H L LL L	
Conditional		aka-kere-ba			si'ro-kere-ba	
		LH LL L			H L LL L	
	c.	tumeta-i	"cold"	d.	tanosi'-i	"happy"
		L HHH			L HHL	
. . . *ku + wa*		tumeta-ku-wa			tano'si-ku-wa	
		L HH L L			L H L L L	
Past		tumeta-kat-ta			tano'si-kat-ta	
		L HH L L			L H L LLL	
Conditional		tumeta-kere-ba			tano'si-kere-ba	
		L HH LL L			L H L LL L	

I assume that *-ku-wa*, *-kat-ta*, and *kere-ba* are all noncyclic or extratonal and thus they are irrelevant to accent assignment and tone association. Thus, the H tone of the HL melody is associated with the final mora of unaccented stems in (31) and accent is assigned to the penultimate mora of the visible part of each accented verb. Everything else is handled with virtually the same mechanisms as were necessary in the derivations illustrated in (27) and (28).

Notice that the *ku-wa* forms, the Past form *kat-ta* and the Conditional form *kere-ba* all appear to assign accent to the stem-final mora when they are attached to unaccented adjectives. However, as noted in the preceding paragraph, there is no need to resort to accent assignment to account for these unaccented cases. All we need is to simply assume that the morphemes *ku-wa*, *kat-ta*, and *kere-ba* are either noncyclic or extratonal, both in unaccented and accented cases. Notice also that the extratonality works at the level of accent assignment and tone association, whereas the extrametricality mentioned above works at the level of accent assignment. Thus, these two notions must be distinguished from each other.

Some sample derivations follow, where X stands for either *ku-wa*, *kat-ta*, or *kere-ba*.

(32)

	Unaccented	*Unaccented*	*Accented*	*Accented*
Extratonal accent assignment	aka-X aka<-X> n/a	tumeta-X tumeta<-X> n/a	siro-X siro<-X> si'ro<-X>	tanosi-X tanosi<-X> tano'si<-X>
Tone association	aka<-X> | H L	tumeta<-X> | H L	si'ro<-X> | | H L	tano'si<-X> | | H L
Tone spreading	aka<-X> \\\| H L	tumeta<-X> \\\\\| H L	si'ro<-X> | | H L	tano'si<-X> \\\| | H L
Initial lowering	aka<-X> | | L H L	tumeta<-X> | \\\| L H L	si'ro<-X> | | H L	tano'si<-X> | | | L H L
Noncyclic association	aka-X | | | L H L	tumeta-X | \\\| | H H L	si'ro-X | |/ H L	tano'si-X | | |/ L H L

The derivations of the first two columns above show clearly that what appears to be accent assignment to unaccented cases is actually a result of extratonality of the relevant suffixes. In addition, accent assignment to the penultimate mora of the visible parts of accented cases is based on the same accent assignment process as is required for the accent assignment to the Present forms.

In the discussion so far, I have ignored the existence of marked cases. This is partly because marked irregularities are not important to the discussion of general properties of accentual phenomena of adjectives, and partly because I do not have enough space to go into the details of a variety of Japanese accentual phenomena that are described elsewhere. There are a number of dictionaries and papers on Japanese accent whose primary concern is a detailed description of accentual facts.

To briefly summarize this section, I have examined accentual and tonal properties of Tokyo Japanese, with special emphasis on the identification of the basic tone melody, and carefully analyzed a number of aspects of tonal and accentual phenomena of nouns, verbs, and adjectives.

2 The Accentual and Tonal System of Osaka Japanese

2.1 Introduction

The so-called Kansai-type dialects all have two melodies. In this section, I will explain Osaka Japanese as a representative of two melody Kansai-type dialects.

Some of the characteristics of the accentual and tonal system of this dialect can be summarized as follows.

(i)   It has 2n+1 surface tonal classes.
(ii)   It has two basic tone melodies: HL and LHL.
(iii)   It has n+1 accentual patterns for nouns.
(iv)   Verbs and adjectives are divided into two classes: unaccented HL melody class and unaccented LHL melody class.
(v)   Application of the accent deletion rule for *no*-phrases is dependent on melodic class.
(vi)   It is mora-based and not syllable-based.
(vii)   The surface tonal melody of a compound is determined by the left member of the compound.

These characteristics will be illustrated below on the basis of a variety of data.

2.2.1   Nouns in Osaka

Let us first examine tonal melodies of nouns. Nouns in Osaka Japanese have 2n+1 surface tonal classes. Comparing the tonal system of nouns in this dialect with those of Old Kyoto Japanese, which had three basic tone melodies, HL, LHL, and LH, reveals that Osaka Japanese has one fewer melody: That is, Osaka Japanese lost the LH melody found in Old Kyoto Japanese in the course of historical change.

Consider the following examples of Osaka nouns. Recall that the diacritic mark (') stands for accent on the immediately preceding mora.

(33)

	Sample	*~+ga*	*Melody*	*Analysis*
1a.[3]	ee "handle" HH	ee-ga HHH	HL	unaccented
1b.	na'a "name" HL	na'a-ga HL L	HL	initial-accented
1c.	ee "picture" LH	ee-ga LL H	LHL	unaccented
1d.	(o' o: gap1) H L	(o'o-ga: gap1) HL L	LHL	initial-accented
2a.	take "bamboo" H H	take-ga H H H	HL	unaccented
2b.	ya'ma "mountain" H L	ya'ma-ga H L L	HL	initial-accented
2c.	(o o': gap2) HH L	(o o'-ga: gap2) HH L	HL	final-accented
2d.	sora "sky" L H	sora-ga L L H	LHL	unaccented
2e.	(o' o: gap3) H L	(o'o-ga: gap3) HL L	LHL	initial-accented

2f.	ame' "rain" LHL	ame'-ga L H L	LHL	final-accented
3a.	sakura "cherry tree" H HH	sakura-ga H HH H	HL	unaccented
3b.	i'noti "life" H LL	i'noti-ga H LL L	HL	initial-accented
3c.	oto'ko "man" HH L	oto'ko-ga HH L L	HL	second-accented
3d.	(o o o' gap4) HHH L	(o o o'-ga gap4) HHH L	HL	final-accented
3e.	suzume "sparrow" L L H	suzume-ga L L L H	LHL	unaccented
3f.	(o' o o: gap5) H LL	(o'o o-ga: gap5) HL L L	LHL	initial-accented
3g.	kabu'to "helmet" L H L	kabu'to-ga L H L L	LHL	second-accented
3h.	matti' "match" LLHL	matti'-ga LLH L	LHL	final-accented
4a.	niwatori "chicken" H HHH	niwatori-ga H HHH H	HL	unaccented
4b.	u'guisu "nightingale" H LLL	u'guisu-ga H LLL L	HL	initial-accented
4c.	ben'too "lunch" HH LL	ben'too-ga HH LL L	HL	second-accented
4d.	kamina'ri "thunder" H HH L	kamina'ri-ga H HH L L	HL	third-accented
4e.	(o o o o' gap6) HHHHL	(o o o o'-ga gap6) H HHH L	HL	final-accented
4f.	tukemono "pickles" L L L H	tukemono-ga L L L L H	LHL	unaccented
4g.	(o' o o o: gap7) H LLL	(o' o o o-ga: gap7) H LLL L	LHL	initial-accented
4h.	bita'min "vitamin" LH LL	bita'min-ga LH LL L	LHL	second-accented
4i.	nokogi'ri "saw" L L HL	nokogi'ri-ga L L HL L	LHL	third-accented
4j.	(o o o o' gap8) L L L HL	(o o o o'-ga gap8) L L L H L	LHL	final-accented

Comparison of this list with (8), from Tokyo Japanese, shows that the accentual and tonal patterns of Osaka Japanese are more complicated than those of Tokyo Japanese. This is due to the fact that Osaka Japanese has two basic tone melodies, HL and LHL, while Tokyo Japanese has one basic tone melody, HL. Notice that one-mora nouns of the Osaka dialect undergo lengthening due to a constraint on minimal words, which forces all words to have at least one foot or two moras: [M M]$_F$.

When we consider the examples in (33), we will immediately notice some of the characteristics of Osaka Japanese:

(A)   As in Tokyo Japanese, unaccented nouns do not have a pitch fall.
(B)   For both HL and LHL melody nouns, the accent is on the mora before the pitch fall.
(C)   There are no final-accented HL melody nouns in Osaka Japanese (see gaps 2, 4, and 6).
(D)   Osaka Japanese is unique in that it has no initial-accented LHL melody class (see gaps 1, 3, 5, and 7).
(E)   Osaka Japanese permits a falling tone observed in the two- and three-mora LHL nouns.

(C) seems to be an accident. (D) seems to be due to the fact that the surface tonal melody of this class cannot be distinguished from that of the initial-accented HL melody class.

It is widely recognized that the basic prosodic unit that can carry accent in Osaka Japanese is a mora. This will be clear if we look at the following examples.

(34)   a.   ben'too   "lunch"   on'na   "woman"
            HHLL   HHL
       b.   sen'dati   "pioneer"   san'zi "three o'clock"
            L HL L   L HL

(35)   a.   ee'si   "the rich"
            LHL
       b.   roo'zi   "alley"
            LH L
       c.   kyuu'sibai   "old drama"
            LH L LL

The examples in (34) indicate that the so-called moraic nasal *n* can carry accent, which is impossible in Tokyo Japanese. Those in (35) illustrate that the second member of the VV sequence can carry accent, which is also different from Tokyo Japanese.

Notice furthermore that there are a number of minimal pairs showing that Osaka Japanese is a mora system (examples due to Shin-ichi Tanaka, personal communication):

(36) (i)   a.   ko'oko   "archaeology"   (ii)   a.   se'ndo   "degree of freshness"
                HL L   HL L
           b.   koo'ko   "pickles"   b.   sen'do   "last time"
                LH L   L HL

The (a) examples in (36) are accented on the first mora, which means that the left member of the initial syllable is accented, while the (b) examples are accented on the second mora, which consists of the right member of the initial syllable.

Let us now turn to tonal melodies of compound nouns. Consider the following examples, which are cited from Wada (1942) and Haraguchi (1977).

(37) a. ya'ma   +   sakura   >   yama-za'kura
          H L   H HH   H H H L L
          "mountain"   "cherry tree"
      b. asa'   +   sakura   >   asa-za'kura
          LHL   H HH   L L H L L
          "morning"   "cherry tree"

(38) a. tuki'mi   +   dango   >   tukimi-da'ngo
          HH L   LLH   H H H HL L
          "appreciation of the moon"   "dumpling"
      b. kabu'to   +   dango   >   kabuto-da'ngo
          L H L   LLH   L LL HL L
          "helmet"   "dumpling"

Examination of these cases suggests that the surface tonal melody of a compound is determined by the left member of the compound in the following way.

(39) *Selection of a tonal melody for the whole compound:*
      If the left member of the compound belongs to the LHL melody class,
      the whole compound has a surface LHL melody; and if it belongs to the
      HL melody class, the whole compound has a surface HL melody
      (Haraguchi 1977).

Notice that this principle of melody selection governing compounds is also
valid in the case of compound verbs. This is clear from the following examples
of compound verb formation.

(40)   *Left member*   *Right member*   *Compound verb*
      a.   mak-u   +   naos-u   >   mak-i naos-u
           H H   HH H   H H HH H
           "wind"   "fix"   "wind again, rewind"
      b.   hor-u   +   das-u   >   hor-i-das-u
           H H   L H   H H H H
           "throw"   "take out"   "throw out"

(41)   *Left member*   *Right member*   *Compound verb*
      a.   mak-u   +   naos-u   >   mak-i naos-u
           L H   HH H   L L LL H
           "sow"   "fix"   "sow again"
      b.   hor-u   +   das-u   >   hor-i-das-u
           L H   L H   L L L H
           "dig"   "take out"   "dig out"

The Present forms of Osaka verbs are all unaccented and their melodies are either the HL or LHL. In (40) and (41), the left members of the compound verbs decide the melodic class of the whole compound, irrespective of the melodic difference in the right members.

Accent assignment for nouns is, according to Wada (1942), dependent on the length of the right member of the compound. Thus, the rule can be summarized as follows.

(42) *Accent assignment for a compound:*
   a. If the right member of a compound consists of three or four moras, and its left member consists of either two, three, four, or five moras, then (i) the accent is, in principle, assigned to the initial mora of the right member; (ii) no accent is placed on any mora.
   b. If the right member of a compound consists of two moras, then there are three cases:
       (i)   accent is placed on the initial mora of the right member of the compound;
       (ii)   accent is placed on the final mora of the left member of the compound;
       (iii) no accent is placed on any mora.
   c. If the right member of a compound consists of only one mora, then there are two cases:
       (i)   accent is placed on the final mora of the left member of the compound;
       (ii)   no accent is placed on any mora.

Notice that (42a), (42bi), (42bii), and (42ci) conspire to assign the accent on either the preantepenultimate, antepenultimate, or penultimate mora. What is remarkable with respect to (42) is that it never places an accent on the final mora of a compound. This rule seems to be responsible for the lack of final-accented nouns of at least four moras, for almost all long nouns are compounds in this dialect.

2.3.2   Accent deletion before the Genitive morpheme no

What is interesting with respect to *no*-phrases in Osaka Japanese is that the accent in the *no*-phrase is deleted if its head noun belongs to the HL melody class (Okuda, 1971: 26ff). This is illustrated by the following examples.

(43) a. kaga'mi + no   ana   >   kagami-no ana
          HH L   L H   HH H HL H
          "mirror" "Gen" "hole"
      b. huro?o'ke + no   ana   >   huro?oke-no ana
          HHH L   L H   HHH H HL H
          "bathtub" "Gen" "hole"
          (Here and below "?" stands for a glottal stop.)

The all-H tone on the *no*-phrases in (43) shows that the accent on the penulti-mate mora is lost.

In contrast to this, the accent of LHL melody nouns is preserved before the morpheme *no*, as is clear from the following examples.

(44) a. hata'ke   + no   tu'ti   >   hata'ke-no tu'ti
          LH L   HL   LH L L H L
          "field"   "Gen"   "soil"
      b. toka'ge   + no   mee   >   toka'ge-no mee
          L H L   LH   LH L L LH
          "lizard"   "Gen"   "eyes"

These facts show that Deaccenting applies to the HL melody class only, exclud-ing the LHL melody class from the domain of this process. This implies that this dialect has a process dependent on a tonal melodic class.

This observation shows that Deaccenting in Osaka Japanese is different from that in the so-called Tokyo-type dialects, which only applies to nouns with final accent (see section 1.3.1).

Taking these facts into consideration, we can show that the initial-accented nouns are of the HL melody class. Consider the following examples from Okuda (1971).

(45) a. ha'na   + no   miyako   >   hana-no miyako
          H L   HH H   H H H HH H
          "flower"   "Gen"   "capital"   "glorious capital"
                                             cf.   *hana-no miyako
                                                    L L H HH H
      b. hi'kari   + no   haya'sa   >   hikari-no haya'sa
          H L L   L H L   HHH H L H L
          "light"   "Gen"   "speed"
                                                    *hikari-no haya'sa
                                                    L LL H L H L

The very fact that Deaccenting applies to initial-accented nouns, and that the resultant surface melody is all H tone, indicates that these initial-accented classes belong to the HL melody class.

2.3.3 *Accentual patterns of verbs*

In Japanese, verbs tend to be divided into two classes. I suggested above that verbs in Osaka Japanese are of two types: the HL melody type and the LHL melody type.

(46)   *HL*   *LHL*
      (i)   a. wur-u   "sell"   kat-u   "win"
                 H H   L H
             b. ki-ru   "wear"   mi-ru   "see"
                 H H   L H

(ii)	a.	susum-u	"advance"	kakus-u	"hide"
		H H H		L L H	
	b.	kari-ru	"borrow"	tate-ru	"build"
		HH H		L L H	
(iii)	a.	yorokob-u	"be glad"	? gap	
		HHH H		L L L H	
	b.	narabe-ru	"line up"	kakure-ru	"hide"
		HH H H		L L L H	

These examples indicate that all verbs are unaccented and are classified in terms of melodic classes.

In (46), the (a) verbs end in a consonant and the (b) verbs end in a vowel. For reasons that are not clear to me, there seems to be a gap in (46): there are no consonant-ending LHL melody verbs with four moras or more. To put it another way, all verbs of this type seem to be restricted to the HL melody class. Of course we can find a number of LHL melody verbs with four moras or more, if the verbs are vowel-ending, as exemplified in (46iii).

These two classes of verbs correspond basically to the unaccented and accented verbs of Tokyo Japanese, as is clear from the following data.

(47)   Verbal classes in Tokyo Japanese:

		Unaccented		*Accented*	
(i)	a.	wur-u	"sell"	ka't-u	"win"
		L H		H L	
	b.	ki-ru	"wear"	mi'-ru	"see"
		L H		H L	
(ii)	a.	susum-u	"advance"	kaku's-u	"hide"
		L H H		L H L	
	b.	kari-ru	"borrow"	tate'-ru	"build"
		LH H		LH L	
(iii)	a.	yoroko'b-u	"be glad"	(odoro'k-u	"be surprised")
		L H H L		L HH L	
	cf.	wutagaw-u	"doubt"		
		LHH H			
	b.	narabe-ru	"line up"	kakure'-ru	"hide"
		LH H H		L HH L	

Verbs of the HL melody class in Osaka Japanese correspond to those of the unaccented class in Tokyo Japanese, and those of the LHL melody class in Osaka Japanese correspond to those of the accented class in Tokyo Japanese, with a number of lexical exceptions like (47iiia). For a detailed analysis of the tonal melodies of verbs in Tokyo Japanese, see section 1.3.2.

Consider now the Past tense form of Osaka verbs. Let us begin with HL melody consonant-ending verbs. Present and Past forms are illustrated in (48).

(48)   *Present*   *Past*

    I   a.   wur-u   "sell"   wu't-ta
               H H   HH L

        b.   tir-u   "scatter"   ti't-ta
               H H   HHL

    II   ?azaker-u "mock at" ?azake't-ta
               HH H H   HHHH L

    III a.   kanasim-u "feel sad" kanasi'n-da
               H HH H   H HHL L

        b.   yorokob-u "be glad"   yoroko'n-da
               HH H H   HH HL L

The Past tense forms of all of these verbs with two moras or more have accent on the penultimate mora of the stems excluding the past tense morpheme *ta* (or its allophonic form *da*). This accent is assigned by the following rule, which assigns accent based on the left-headed binary constituent structure (see Halle and Vergnaud 1987 and Haraguchi 1991, among others, for discussion of these notions and their theoretical background).

(49)   *

      (* *) – <ta>

      (where < > indicates that the Past morpheme *ta* is extrametrical or invisible.)

What is puzzling in (48II) is that the mora consisting of the geminate consonant only is regarded as having an H tone.

    Let us now turn to the HL melody vowel-ending verbs in (50).

(50)   *Present*   *Past*

    IV a.   ne-ru   "sleep"   ne'-ta
               H H   H L

        b.   ki-ru   "wear"   ki'-ta
               H H   H L

    V   a.   ?ake-ru   "dawn"   ?a'ke-ta
               H H H   H L L

        b.   kari-ru   "borrow"   ka'ri-ta
               HH H   H L L

    VI a.   ?ata?e-ru "give"   ?ata'?e-ta
               HHH H   HH L L

        b.   narabe-ru "line up"   nara'be-ta
               HH H H   HH L L

These verbs also have accent on the penultimate mora (or on the final mora) of the verb stem, excluding the Past morpheme *ta*. Rule (49) applies to these cases with virtually no change. Notice that the HL melody verbs preserve the melody in the Past forms.

Let us now consider the Past forms of the LHL melody verbs, the behavior of which is rather complicated. Examination of the following verbs shows that the LHL melody is preserved in their Past forms too.

(51) | | | *Present* | | *Past* |
|---|---|---|---|---|
| VII | a. | kat-u | "win" | kat-ta |
| | | L H | | LL H |
| | b. | nom-u | "drink" | non-da |
| | | L H | | L L H |
| VIII | a. | ?oki-ru | "get up" | ?oki'-ta |
| | | L L H | | L H L |
| | b. | tate-ru | "build" | tate'-ta |
| | | L L H | | L H L |
| IX | | ?asob-u | "play" | ?aso'n-da |
| | | L L H | | L HL L |

LHL melody verbs are peculiar in that accent is not assigned to the Past forms of the VII class verbs and that it is assigned to the stem-final mora of the VIII class verbs. The IX class verbs undergo the accent assignment rule in (49).

Now consider the following LHL melody verbs.

(52) | | *Present* | | *Past* |
|---|---|---|---|
| a. | ku-ru | "come" | ki'-ta |
| | L H | | H L |
| b. | de-ru | "go out" | de'-ta |
| | L H | | H L |
| c. | mi-ru | "see" | mi'-ta |
| | L H | | H L |

The surface melody of these Past forms is apparently identical to that of HL melody nouns. However, note that the HL melody in (52) should be analyzed as a realization of the LHL melody with the initial accent. This is because the melody of all other verbs is kept even after the addition of the Past morpheme *ta*.

Finally, consider the following verbs, which are rather different from the other verbs in that they insert the stem vowel *i* and that consonant-ending *g* and *k* are deleted in the relevant Past forms.

(53) | | | *Present* | | *Past* |
|---|---|---|---|---|
| X | a. | ?ok-u | "place" | ?o'i-ta |
| | | H H | | HL L |
| | b. | sak-u | "bloom" | sa'i-ta |
| | | H H | | HL L |
| | c. | ?aruk-u | "walk" | ?aru'i-ta |
| | | L L H | | L HL L |
| | d. | ?odorok-u | "be surprised" | ?odoro'i-ta |
| | | H HH H | | H HHL L |

XI	a.	kas-u	"lend"	ka'si-ta
		H H		H L L
	b.	kakus-u	"hide"	kaku'si-ta
		L L H		L H L L
	c.	?arawas-u	"represent"	?arawa'si-ta
		HH H H		HH H L L

In other respects these verbs are the same as most of the other HL and LHL melody verbs: the Past forms of these verbs preserve the tonal melody of the Present forms and the accent assignment rule in (49) applies to the Past forms of these verbs.

2.3.4 *Accentual patterns of adjectives*

Adjectives in Osaka Japanese are also divided into two classes, HL and LHL, as a cursory look at the following Present tense forms suggests.

(54)

			Present	Gloss
(i)	a.		ee < yo-i	"good"
			LH	
	b.		su'-i	"sour"
			H L	
(ii)	a.		ta'ka-i	"high"
			H LL	
	b.		?a'ka-i	"red"
			H LL	
(iii)	a.		?ure'si-i	"glad"
			HH LL	
	b.		kana'si-i	"sad"
			H H LL	
(iv)			?omosi'ro-i	"interesting"
			H HH LL	

It should be clear that the two-mora adjective *ee*, which is derived from the underlying form /yo-i/, should be of the LHL melody class. All the other adjectives appear to belong to the HL melody class. Is this really the case? To answer this question, consider the following Past forms and nominal forms of the adjectives in (54iii) and (54iv).

(55)

			Past forms	
(iii)	a.		?uresi'-kat-ta	"was glad"
			HHH LL L	
	b.		kanasi'-kat-ta	"was sad"
			H HH LL L	
(iv)	a.		?omosiro'-kat-ta	"was interesting"
			H HHH L L L	

(56)   *Nominals*
  (iii) a. ?uresi-sa   "gladness"
            H HH H
         b. kanasi-sa   "sadness"
            H HH H
  (iv)   a. ?omosiro-sa   "interest"
            H HHH H

Past forms in (55) and nominals in (56) confirm that the corresponding adjectives in (54iii) and (54iv) belong to the HL melody class.

Consider now the Past forms and nominals of the adjectives of (54i).

(57)   *Past forms*   *Nominals*
  (i)   a. yo'-kat-ta   "was good"   yo-sa "goodness"
           H LL L   L H
        b. suu'-kat-ta "was sour"   su-sa "sourness"
           HH LL L   H H

It should be clear that, on the basis of the tonal melodies of the Past forms and the nominals in (57ib), the adjective *sui* "sour" belongs to the HL melody class. In contrast, the tonal melodies of the Present forms in (54i) and the nominals in (57ia) indicate that the adjective *ee* (*yo-i*) belongs to the LHL melody class. This compels us to interpret the surface HLLL melody of the Past form in (57ia) as a realization of the LHL melody of the initial-accented verb.

Keeping the discussion above in mind, consider now the HLL melody adjectives in (54ii). If we take the corresponding Past forms and nominals into consideration, we can say that this melody is also a surface realization of the LHL melody.

(58)   *Past forms*
  (ii) a. taka'-kat-ta   "was high"
           L H LL L
        b. ?aka'-kat-ta   "was red"
           L H LL L

(59)   *Nominals*
  (ii) a. taka-sa   "height"
           L L H
        b. ?aka-sa   "redness"
           L L H

The surface tonal melodies of the Past forms in (58) and the nominals in (59) are those of a typical LHL melody class. Thus we can conclusively answer the question whether the HLL melody adjectives in (53ii) belong to the HL melody class: they do not.

Assuming that this line of argument is sound, we are forced to regard the absence of initial-accented LHL melody nouns in Osaka Japanese, or more generally in the Kansai-type dialects, as characteristic to nouns. This gap is not applicable to adjectives. This finding is noteworthy because the absence of the initial-accented LHL melody class nouns in Osaka Japanese, or in the Kansai-type dialects in general, is nothing but accidental and not systematic in nature.

3   Concluding Remarks

Up to now, I have discussed accent in Tokyo Japanese and Osaka Japanese in terms both of the types of accentual patterns and the tonal systems. I would like to summarize briefly what has been shown.

(60)

	Tokyo Japanese	*Osaka Japanese*
surface tonal classes	n+1	2n+1
basic tone melody	1BTM: HL	2BTM: HL and LHL
Initial Lowering	Yes	No
Deaccenting of *no*-phrases	applicable to final accent only	applicable to the HL melody only
verbs and adjectives	accented and unaccented	HL melody and LHL melody
Contour tone	not permitted	permitted on the final mora
Vowel lengthening for one-mora words	No	Yes

Note that we can deduce a number of characteristics from the discussion above.

(61)   a.   If a dialect has n+1 surface melodies for n-mora (or n-syllable) words (or accentual phrases) as in Tokyo Japanese, it has an accentual system with one basic tone melody.

b.   If a dialect has 2n+1 surface melodies as in Osaka Japanese, it is a two-melody system with n+1 accentual patterns.

c.   Japanese dialects select their own basic tone melody or melodies from the universally permitted melodic set.

A large number of Japanese dialects have accentual systems, while some dialects have a tonal system. The accentual systems of these accentual dialects consist of a pitch accent system, which is handled in a way parallel to the stress accent systems of languages such as English, Spanish, Polish, etc. at a deeper level.

Japanese accentual and tonal properties can be schematically shown as follows.

(62)	Type of BTM					
No. of AP	HL/LH/LHL	HL/LHL	LH/LHL	LHL	HL	LH
1	n/a	n/a	n/a		Sendai	Miyakonojo
2	n/a		Kagoshima	n/a	n/a	n/a
3				Kumi		
n				Fukuoka		
n+1				Narada	Tokyo	Hirosaki
n+2				Tsuruoka		
2n+1		Kansai-type				
3n+2	Old Kyoto					

(BTM stands for the "basic tone melody," and AP for "accentual patterns.")

Most Japanese dialects have richer accentual properties for nouns than for verbs and adjectives. Tokyo-type Japanese and Osaka Japanese (or more generally Kansai-type Japanese) have two accentual or tonal distinctions for verbs and adjectives, while Kumi Japanese is peculiar in that it has three accentual distinctions for nouns and verbs (see Haraguchi 1998 for discussion on this point). The melodic and/or accentual selection for compounds is determined by the left-hand member of the compound in question.

Due to limitations of time and space, I have to omit discussion of other dialects listed in (62). See Haraguchi (1977, 1979a, 1979b, 1991, and 1998) for discussion of these and other dialects, as well as more detailed discussion of theoretical implications of the analyses above.

Before closing the discussion of Japanese accent in this chapter, I would like to mention briefly some remaining problems and directions for future research, including both observational/descriptive and theoretical/explanatory aspects. More descriptive work is needed to obtain more detailed, abundant, and systematic data with high quality and reliability; whereas explanation is the main concern of theoretical phonologists.

To gather good accentual data, a fieldworker should, on the one hand, be well trained as a phonetician and have a fair knowledge of theoretical problems. On the other hand, good and accurate data are indispensable when trying to solve theoretical problems and to improve existing theories or even to develop an entirely new theory with greater explanatory adequacy.

I suggest that we need more large-scale joint enterprises by theoretical phonologists and fieldworkers in order to collect abundant data of good quality which are profitable to theoretical research. Most, if not all, of the accentual data collected by traditional linguists are, for example, devoid not only of accentual information on long words, compound words, verbal inflectional forms, and adjectival inflectional forms, but also of accentual information on phrases and sentences. Since long and compound words, for example, often turn out to be indispensable for determining the underlying accentual pattern of a language or a dialect, we must have access to such data in order to make clear the whole picture of the accentual system of the language or the dialect. The need for systematic accentual data is growing due to the advancement and deepening of theoretical investigations and typological studies.

Past efforts by Haraguchi (1991), E. Yamada (1990), Kubozono and Ohta (1998), and others have made it clear that the pitch accent system of Tokyo Japanese and the stress accent system of English have common properties. This is an amazing finding taking into consideration the fact that these two languages have no common ancestral relations and that they are typologically diagonal to each other. This is also theoretically interesting in that it illustrates that truly deep analyses based on a well-developed theory make it possible to bring to light underlying similarities which are often hidden by apparent surface differences. To reach a deeper and more insightful understanding of a variety of accentual systems, we must pursue more systematic and profound comparative and contrastive inquiries into various accentual systems.

From the perspective of theoretical investigation, the accentual systems of a number of Japanese dialects contribute to determining some of the theoretical controversies. These systems provide us with good data to test several tenets of the existing prosodic theories, such as the stress theory proposed by Halle and Idsardi (1995), Idsardi (1992), and Haraguchi (1991), and Optimality Theory, proposed by McCarthy and Prince (1993b), Prince and Smolensky (1993), and others. The systems also play an important role in improving existing theories and even in developing new and more appealing ones.

Comparative studies of Japanese and Korean accentual systems and contrastive studies of the accentual systems of genetically and typologically different languages must be done on a more systematic and larger scale. Such studies will be helpful to distinguish accentual properties common to languages from those particular to each language. This distinction is no doubt essential to the correct understanding of accentual properties.

Finally, I would like to draw the reader's attention to the fact that we must conduct thorough investigation of the relation between accent and properties of consonants and vowels, intonation, meaning, various pragmatic properties, and so on. Though past effects undoubtedly made it possible for us to attain a fair amount of insight on Japanese accentual phenomena, there still spreads a vast ocean of accentual problems before us, awaiting to be uncovered.

NOTES

*   This chapter was in part supported by the Monbusho under Grant-in-Aid for Scientific Research (A) No. 07401015 and Grant-in-Aid for COE Research No. 08CE1001, and the Special Research Project for the Investigation of Languages and Cultures of the East and West

of the University of Tsukuba.
I am grateful to Roger Martin,
Joseph Johnson, Robyne Tiedeman,
and Natsuko Tsujimura for many
helpful comments and suggestions
on an earlier draft of this
chapter.

1   This survey of Japanese accent has
benefited enormously from the
findings of phonologists, whose work
is mainly conducted by traditional
Japanese linguists, with a fair number
of recent insights provided by
generative phonologists and
government phonologists. Most of
these works are published only in
Japanese.

2. Note that the imperative suffix of a
consonant-ending verb is *e* and that
of a vowel-ending verb is *ro*. Note
also that the Causative morpheme
ase is selected for a consonant-ending
verb and *sase* is selected for a vowel-
ending verb. When the morpheme
-*tai* is attached to a consonant-ending
verb, the stem vowel *i* is inserted to
the end of the verb root.

3   In Kansai-type dialects, one-mora
nouns undergo lengthening
obligatorily in isolation and
optionally with an enclitic *ga*. This
lengthening is due to the constraint
on minimal words that requires two
moras for prosodic words.

2 Mora and Syllable

HARUO KUBOZONO

0 Introduction

In his classical typological study Trubetzkoy (1969) proposed that natural languages fall into two groups, "mora languages" and "syllable languages," according to the smallest prosodic unit that is used productively in that language. Tokyo Japanese is classified as a "mora" language whereas Modern English is supposed to be a "syllable" language. The mora is generally defined as a unit of duration in Japanese (Bloch 1950), where it is used to measure the length of words and utterances. The three words in (1), for example, are felt by native speakers of Tokyo Japanese as having the same length despite the different number of syllables involved. In (1) and the rest of this chapter, mora boundaries are marked by hyphens /-/, whereas syllable boundaries are marked by dots /./. All syllable boundaries are mora boundaries, too, although not vice versa.[1]

(1) a. to-o-kyo-o "Tokyo"   b. a-ma-zo-n "Amazon"
         too.kyoo   a.ma.zon
     c. a-me-ri-ka "America"
         a.me.ri.ka

The notion of "mora" as defined in (1) is equivalent to what Pike (1947) called a "phonemic syllable," whereas "syllable" in (1) corresponds to what he referred to as a "phonetic syllable." Pike's choice of terminology as well as Trubetzkoy's classification may be taken as implying that only the mora is relevant in Japanese phonology and morphology. Indeed, the majority of the literature emphasizes the importance of the mora while essentially downplaying the syllable (e.g. Sugito 1989, Poser 1990, Tsujimura 1996b). This symbolizes the importance of the mora in Japanese, but it remains an open question whether the syllable is in fact irrelevant in Japanese and, if not, what role this second unit actually plays in the language. Moreover, it remains an important question which aspects of the mora phenomena in Japanese are language-specific and which are universal.

With these fundamental questions in mind, this chapter attempts to examine the role of the mora and the syllable in Japanese from a cross-linguistic perspective. It is laid out as follows. The next section (section 1) describes various roles played by the mora in Japanese phonetics, phonology, and morphology. This includes the roles played by "bimoraic foot," which presupposes the existence of the mora. Section 2 examines the role which the syllable plays in Japanese and demonstrates that this second prosodic unit, too, is indispensable for generalizing a wide range of phenomena from word accent and loanword phonology to morphological patterning. The final section (section 3) summarizes the main discussion of this chapter as well as some interesting questions that must be addressed in the future. In what follows, the term "Japanese" refers to Tokyo Japanese unless otherwise specified.

1   Relevance of Mora

The mora in Japanese can be defined in four ways according to its roles: (i) as a basic unit of temporal regulation, (ii) as a unit by which phonological distance is defined, (iii) as a segmentation unit whereby words/speech are broken into discrete chunks in speech production, and (iv) as a segmentation unit used in speech perception. All these roles, with the possible exception of the second one, seem to be specific to Japanese as a mora language.

1.1   *Temporal regulation*

The crucial reason which compels linguists to posit the mora and not the syllable as a basic prosodic unit in Japanese is that several elements serve as an independent unit although they do not form a syllable on their own. These elements fall into four kinds: (a) a moraic nasal, which occupies the coda position of the syllable; (b) a moraic obstruent, or the first half of a geminate consonant; (c) the second half of long vowels; and (d) the second half of diphthongal vowel sequences. These are exemplified in (2a–d), respectively.

(2)   a.   ro-*n*.do-*n*   "London"   a.ma.zo-*n*   "Amazon"
       b.   ki-*t*.te   "stamp"   ni-*p*.po-n   "Japan"
       c.   kyo-*o*.to   "Kyoto"   to-*o*.kyo-*o*   "Tokyo"
       d.   ge-n.da-*i*   "modern times"   ra-*i*.to   "right, light"

These elements, generally known as "special moras," "moraic phonemes," or "non-syllabic moras," serve as an independent timing unit just as CV moras that constitute a syllable by themselves. Let us first consider traditional verse forms such as *haiku* and *tanka*, which are characterized by the number of moras contained in each phrase. *Haiku* is made up of a sequence of three phrases in which a seven-mora phrase is flanked by five-mora phrases, i.e. 5–7–5. *Tanka* is a slightly extended version with two seven-mora phrases added to the basic form of *haiku*, i.e. 5–7–5–7–7. In the *haiku* in (3a), for example, the final phrase consists of three units by syllable count but five units by mora count. Likewise, the poem in (3b) involves a trimoraic personal name, *Issa*, which forms a standard seven-mora phrase together with the preceding word *makeruna*; this uniformity would not result if the phonological form of the poem should be defined in terms of the syllable.

(3)   a.   ka.ki.ku.e.ba   ka.ne.ga.na.ru.na.ri   ho-o.ryu-u.zi
          "I heard the bell of Horyuji Temple toll as I ate a persimmon"
      b.   ya.se.ga.e.ru   ma.ke.ru.na.i-s.sa   ko.re.ni.a.ri
          "Never give up, thin frog; Issa is here with you"

The mora's role as a timing unit also shows itself in the text–tune relationship in music (Vance 1987). In traditional Japanese songs, mora and note usually have a one-to-one correspondence, with every mora assigned to an independent note and vice versa. In (4), for example, the second moras of the bimoraic syllables, ma*i* and tya*n*, are counted as an independent timing unit.

(4)   Inuno Omawarisan "Policeman, the Dog"
      4/4 ## | ♪♪♪ ♪   ♪♪♪ ♪ | ♪ ♪ ♪ ♪ᵌ |
                 ma-i.go.no   ma-i.go.no   ko.ne.ko.tya-n
                 "lost, lost little kitten"

More general evidence for the mora as a timing unit comes from the literature on speech rhythm. Japanese is generally characterized as a language with a mora-timed rhythm, where each mora is supposed to take an equal duration of time. Thus four-mora words are said to be twice as long as bimoraic words, whereas nine-mora phrases are three times as long as trimoraic phrases (Homma 1981, Port et al. 1987, Han 1994; see M. E. Beckman 1982 for a critical view, and Nagano-Madsen 1992 and Han 1994 for a review of the literature). This is in accordance with native speakers' intuition on the length of words, which says that four-mora words such as those in (1) take roughly the same duration of time irrespective of the differences they might involve in syllable structure. The isochronous nature of the mora in Japanese can probably be demonstrated in spontaneous connected speech too, in a physical sense as well as in a psychological sense (Sugito 1989).

The mora's role as a timing unit also shows itself in temporal compensation *within* the syllable. Many languages, including English, exhibit a temporal compensation effect between the nuclear vowel and the coda consonant. For example, other things being equal, vowels are phonetically shorter in closed syllables than in open syllables, which is a phenomenon known as "closed syllable vowel shortening" (Maddieson 1985). Similarly, vowels tend to be phonetically shorter when they precede an intrinsically long consonant, e.g. a voiceless stop, than when preceding an intrinsically short consonant, e.g. a voiced stop (see Port 1981, and other references cited in Maddieson 1985). These durational variations are suggestive of a tight relationship between the syllable nucleus and the coda consonant(s) whose combined durations are to be kept constant. Temporal compensation of this kind is attested in a wide range of languages, but not in Japanese. In Japanese, vowel duration is independent of the difference in syllable structure, i.e. closed syllables vs. open syllables (Han 1962, Homma 1981). Moreover, there is experimental evidence suggestive of a temporal compensation between the onset and the nuclear vowel (Han 1962, Campbell and Sagisaka 1991). These exceptional temporal patterns shown by Japanese can be properly accounted for if the mora is posited as a unit of temporal organization in the language. Namely, closed syllables (CVC) are bimoraic and, hence, take twice as much time as open syllables (CV), which are monomoraic. Moreover, temporal compensation occurs within the domain of the mora rather than within the syllable.[2]

1.2   *Phonological length*

A second function of the mora in Japanese concerns the phonological length of words and phrases to which phonological and morphological rules refer. Just as poets and composers measure the length of words and phrases by counting the number of moras, various linguistic processes count the number of moras to measure phonological distance.

1.2.1   *Accent and mora*

A typical case measuring phonological distance in moras is found in the rules of accentuation. The loanword accent rule, for example, places the accent on the antepenultimate mora, or the third mora counted from the end of the word. Thus, the pitch drops suddenly immediately after the antepenultimate mora in a majority of loanwords including those in (5); the accent is marked by the diacritic ('), placed immediately after the accented mora.

(5)   a.   bi'.ru.ma   "Burma"   o-o.su.to'.ri.a   "Austria"
           o-o.su.to.ra'.ri.a   "Australia"
      b.   de-n.ma'-a.ku   "Denmark"   a-i.ru.ra'-n.do   "Ireland"
           re.ba'.no-n   "Lebanon"

 The mora plays a similar role in compound accentuation. Compound nouns in Japanese generally form one accentual unit, or prosodic word, by deaccenting their first member (N1), if it is lexically accented at all, and reassigning a compound accent (CA) in or immediately before the second member (N2).[3] A classical account (Hirayama 1960, J. D. McCawley 1968b) divides noun–noun compounds into two groups according to the unmarked location of the CA, (i) those accented on the final position of N1 and (ii) those accented on the initial position of N2. These two patterns can be predicted by the mora length of N2 in such a way that monomoraic and bimoraic N2s yield the first pattern, whereas three-mora and four-mora N2s yield the second. They are illustrated in (6), where /=/ denotes a compound-internal word boundary.

(6) a. kyo'oto + si'   → kyooto' = si   "Kyoto City"
        ka'buto + musi   → kabuto' = musi   "helmet, bug; beetle"
    b. so'romon + o'ozi   → soromon = o'ozi   "Solomon, prince; Prince Solomon"

    minami + amerika → minami = a'merika   "south, America; South America"

Kubozono and Mester (1995) and Kubozono et al. (1997) have developed this traditional analysis one step further to point out that a new CA pattern emerges if N2 is longer than four moras. Specifically, compound nouns with an N2 of five or six moras generally keep the accentuation, i.e. accentedness and accent location, of N2 while deaccenting N1. This results in unaccented compounds when N2 is originally unaccented, as shown in (7a), or, otherwise, in compounds accented on N2, as in (7b).

(7) a. nyu'u + karedonia   → nyuu = karedonia   "New Caledonia"
        minami + kariforunia → minami = kariforunia   "south California"
        nankyoku + tankentai → nankyoku = tankentai   "South Pole expedition team"
    b. iso'ppu + monoga'tari → isoppu = monoga'tari   "The Fable of Aesop"

    tiho'o + saibansyo'   → tihoo = saibansyo'   "district, law court; district court"

The mora's role as a basic unit of phonological measurement is probably not language-specific. Recent phonological work shows that word accent/stress rules in English and many other languages can be generalized with the mora as a basic unit of description (e.g. Hayes 1995). For example, accentuation in Latin and the accentuation of nouns in English place an accent/stress on the penultimate syllable if it is bimoraic, or otherwise on the antepenultimate syllable. In these and other accentuation rules, the mora plays a crucial role as a unit by which the length of the syllable is defined. This function of the mora naturally leads to that of "syllable weight," in which the notion of mora is integrated with that of syllable. This will be discussed in section 2.3.

1.2.2 Compensatory lengthening

Another interesting phonological process for which the mora is indispensable is that of compensatory lengthening. In Tokyo Japanese, diphthongs are frequently monophthongized, especially in colloquial, casual speech. However, this change in vowel quality is usually accompanied by vowel lengthening, which results in an alternation between a diphthong and a long vowel as shown in (8).[4]

(8) a. daikon ~ deekon   "radish"
     b. hai ~ hee   "Yes, I got it"
     c. ikanai ~ ikanee   "(I) won't go"
     d. omae ~ omee   "you!"
     e. sugoi ~ sugee   "wonderful"

In (8a), for example, the diphthongal vowel sequence of the first syllable /dai/ is amalgamated into a monophthong but retains the bimoraic length of the entire syllable by lengthening the nuclear vowel. In other words, vowel lengthening compensates for a segmental loss which would otherwise result in the reduction of a mora. Compensatory lengthening of this kind is not a phenomenon specific to Japanese. Many quantity-sensitive languages, i.e. languages with a contrast in vowel and/or consonant length, exhibit a similar phenomenon (Hayes 1989).

    Interestingly, compensatory lengthening does not occur in syllable-based dialects of Japanese. For example, in the Kagoshima Dialect spoken in the south of Japan, vowel monophthongization is not accompanied by vowel lengthening, as shown in (9a–f); moreover, there are instances where long vowels are simply shortened, as in (9f–h). These processes create an alternation between a long/diphthongal vowel in careful speech and a short monophthongal vowel in casual speech.

(9) a. dai.kon ~ de.kon   "radish"
     b. hai ~ he   "ash"
     c. hae ~ he   "a fly"
     d. tai.gai ~ te.ge   "approximately"
     e. ti.gau ~ ti.go   "wrong, not true"
     f. kyoo.dai ~ kyo.de   "brother"
     g. see.bo ~ se.bo   "end-of-the-year present"
     h. zii.san ~ zi.san   "grandfather, elderly man"

    A similar situation is found in Classical Japanese, whose system is believed to have had no contrast in vowel length and have been syllable-based rather than mora-based.[5] In this system, monophthongization of diphthongal vowel sequences as in (10a) as well as vowel deletion as in (10b–c) was not accompanied by vowel lengthening (K. Kindaichi 1976).

(10) a. na.ga + i.ki → na.ge.ki, *na.gee.ki   "long, breath; lament"
      b. na.ga + a.me → na.ga.me, *na.gaa.me   "long, rain; long spell of rainy weather"
      c. a.ra + i.so → a.ri.so, *a.rii.so   "wilderness, coast; a reefy coast"

1.2.3 Word formation and mora

It is not just accentuation and other phonological rules that require reference to the mora in measuring phonological distance or the length of words. Some morphological rules, too, exert an effect that can only be generalized by the mora. A typical example of this is the blending rule which, as exemplified in (11), produces new words by combining the initial portion of one word with the final portion of another (Kubozono 1990).

(11) a. go.(ri.ra)   / (ku).zi.ra   → go.zi.ra
          "gorilla"   "whale"   "godzilla, an imaginary monster"
      b. kya.be.(tu)   / (ni-n).zi-n   → kya.be.zi-n
          "cabbage"   "carrot"   (name of a medicine)
      c. ba-i.(ba-i)   / (sa.yo).na.ra → ba-i.na.ra
          "bye-bye"   "good-bye"   "good-bye (colloquial)"
      d. ba.to.(mi-n.to-n) / (pi-n).po-n   → ba.to.po-n
          "badminton"   "ping-pong"   (name of a toy)

One important principle underlying this word formation process is that the resultant word has the same phonological length as the right-hand source word, i.e. the source word that leaves its final portion. While this length relationship appears to be universal (Kubozono 1990), it can be defined by the mora in Japanese: the blend word consists of the same number of moras as the right-hand source word. Thus, *gozira* in (11a) is a trimoraic word just like *kuzira*, whereas *kyabezin*, *bainara*, and *batopon* in (11b–d) are four moras long as are *ninzin*, *sayonara*, and *pinpon*. This length relationship cannot be captured by measuring the phonological length of words in terms of the syllable. Thus the trisyllabic blend forms in (11c–d), i.e. *bainara* and *batopon*, have the same syllable length as neither of the source words.

Not surprisingly, this mora-based length rule applies as well to blend errors that are produced in spontaneous speech (Kubozono 1989). This is illustrated in (12).

(12) a. to.ma.(re) "stop!"   / (su.to)-p.pu "stop" → to.ma-p.pu
      b. hi-(i.ta-a) "heater" / (su).to-o.bu "stove" → hi.to-o.bu

The notion of mora is indispensable for accounting for the regularity underlying other morphological processes as well. This will be discussed in more detail in sections 1.5 and 2.

1.3 Segmentation unit

The mora also enables us to account for the segmentation pattern observed in Japanese. Consider the spontaneous speech errors in (13)–(14) (Kubozono 1985, 1996a).

(13)   Metathesis errors
    a.   a.ra.*bu*.*zi*-n   → a.ra.zi.bu-n   "Arabic"
    b.   *ke*.*tya*-p.pu   → tya.ke-p.pu   "ketchup"
    c.   *te*-k.ki-n. *ko*-n.ku.ri-i.to → ko-k.ki-n te-n.ku.ri-i.to "ferroconcrete"
    d.   e.*re*.*be*-e.ta-a   → e.be.re-e.ta-a   "elevator"

(14)   Blend errors
    a.   (=12a) to.ma.(re) "stop!" / (su.to)-p.pu "stop"   → to.ma-p.pu
    b.   (=12b) hi-(i.ta-a) "heater" / (su).to-o.bu "stove"   → hi.to-o.bu
    c.   syu-(u.zi) "penmanship" / (syo).do-o "calligraphy"   → syu.do-o
    d.   pe.ni-(i) "penny"   / (pe-n).su "pence"   → pe.ni.su
    e.   ba-(i.ba-i) "bye-bye"   / (a).ku.syu "handshaking" → ba.ku.syu

The most important fact about these errors is that words are segmented at a mora boundary, very often at a syllable-internal mora boundary. In the metathesis (transposition) error given in (13a), for example, the word-final syllable, *zin*, is split into *zi* and *n*, of which the first mora is subsequently interchanged with its preceding mora. Similarly, word blend errors in (14) split and subsequently conjoin the two source words at a corresponding mora boundary: e.g. between the first and second moras in each source word in (14b, 14c, 14e) and between the second and third moras in (14a, 14d).

Essentially the same segmentation strategy is employed in substitution errors such as those in (15).

(15)   Substitution errors
    a.   ge-n.*ba*.ku *do*-o.mu   → ge-n.*do*.ku do-o.mu   "Atomic Bomb Dome"
    b.   ku-*u*.bo mi-*d*.do.we-e → ku-*b*.bo mi-d.do.we-e "aircraft carrier Midway"
    c.   ku.da-*n* ka-*i*.ka-n   → ku.da-*i* ka-i.ka-n   "Kudan Hall"

The error in (15b) represents an interesting case where the second half of a long vowel has been replaced with the first part of a geminate consonant. Here the second mora of the bimoraic syllable, *kuu*, has been replaced with the corresponding mora of a following bimoraic syllable, *mid*.[6] Vowel-consonant interactions of this kind are almost never observed in English and related languages (Fromkin 1973), where the most typical error pattern involves the interaction of the onset consonant of one word with the onset of another. Some typical examples are given in (16).

(16)   a.   Metathesis: *Ch*om.sky and *H*al.le   → Hom.sky and Chal.le
      b.   Blend: Ch(om.sky) / (H)al.le   → Chal.le
      c.   Substitution: *Ch*om.sky and *H*al.le → Hom.sky and Hal.le

Not surprisingly, many speech errors in Japanese are ambiguous with respect to the segmentation point implied. The error in (13d), for example, can also be interpreted as a segmental error whereby the onset of one syllable, *re*, changes its position with the onset of the following syllable, *bee*. A similar ambiguity may be pointed out with the errors in (14e) and (15c) too.

(17) a. (=13d) e.*re.be*-e.ta-a   → e.be.re-e.ta-a
      b. (=14e) b(a-i.ba-i) / a.ku.syu → ba.ku.syu
      c. (=15c) ku.d*a-n* k*a-i*.ka-n   → ku.da-i ka-i.ka-n

It is worth emphasizing, however, that almost all of these ambiguous instances can be interpreted as a moraic error, too, as already shown in (13)–(15). More importantly, there are quite a few instances such as those in (13a–c), (14a–d), and (15a–b) that can only be interpreted as cases in which one mora interacted with another mora. These errors, after all, call for a mora-based analysis and eventually argue for the importance of the mora as a behavioral unit in Japanese.

It is important to point out here that speech errors are not an isolated source of evidence from performance data for the mora in Japanese. Exactly the same segmentation strategy is seen in the process of speech disfluency known as stuttering (Ujihira and Kubozono 1994). Adult stutterers of Japanese typically exhibit the disfluency pattern shown in (18a), where the word-initial mora is repeated, often separated from the rest of the word at a syllable-internal mora boundary. This disfluency pattern contrasts sharply with the pattern illustrated in (18b), which is typically shown by stutterers in English.

(18) a. do do do do do-mo-ri   "stuttering"
          ro ro ro ro ro-n-do-n   "London"
      b. s s s s stuttering
          m m m m member

1.4   Perceptual unit

The mora plays a crucial role in speech perception just as it does in the various speech production processes outlined in the preceding section. Kubozono (1995b) conducted a word blend experiment in which native speakers of Japanese were presented with pairs of monosyllabic English words as auditory stimuli and were asked to blend them into a new one. The purpose of this experiment was to see where the subjects segment the source words, i.e. whether they segment the words before the nuclear vowel, as in (19a), or after it, as in (19b). The result of this experiment showed that native speakers of Japanese choose the response in (19b). This result contrasts sharply with the results of Treiman's (1986) similar experiments with native speakers of English, who predominantly preferred the response in (19a). Kubozono interpreted this interesting cross-linguistic difference as suggesting that Japanese speakers make a CV-based, i.e. mora-based, segmentation when they hear words – namely, that they segment auditory stimuli mora by mora.

(19)   Source words: Dick,   fog
       Response: (a) dog   (b) dig

More sophisticated perceptual experiments were conducted by Hayashi and
Kakehi (1990) and Otake et al. (1993). Hayashi and Kakehi measured the time
that Japanese listeners needed to respond to certain targets in speech. They
concluded that Japanese listeners respond to mora-sized units (i.e. CVs) more
quickly than segments or phonemes. Using a similar target-monitoring task,
Otake et al. demonstrated that Japanese listeners respond to mora-sized units
more readily than syllable-sized units.

1.5   Relevance of foot

The argument for the mora in Japanese can be reinforced by the evidence for
foot structure. Many phonological and morphological structures of Japanese
can be generalized if a sequence of two moras is thought to form a larger (or
higher) prosodic unit. A typical example of this is the morphological process of
compound clipping, whereby long compound nouns and phrases are shortened.
The unmarked phonological pattern of this morphological process is the one
illustrated in (20), where the first two moras of each member are combined to
form a four-mora word. What is important here is that syllable structure is
not directly relevant: The first two moras can be either monosyllabic or bisyllabic and, moreover, bimoraic syllables may be split if they happen to involve
the second and third moras of the word, e.g. ri.*mo*(o.to). This basic pattern
can be defined in a simple manner if sequences of two moras are thought to
form a prosodic unit, or "foot." On this analysis, the morphological process is
defined as combining the initial foot of each component word: [ ] denotes a
foot boundary.[7]

(20) a. se.ku.syu.a.ru ha.ra.su.me-n.to
                             → [se.ku][ha.ra]   "sexual harassment"
      b. ri.mo-o.to ko-n.to.ro-o.ru   → [ri.mo][ko-n]   "remote control"
      c. ha-n.ga-a su.to.ra-i.ki   → [ha-n][su.to]   "hunger strike"
      d. ha-n.bu-n do-n.ta.ku   → [ha-n][do-n]   "a half day off (= a
                                                         half + holiday)"

The notion of bimoraic foot plays an important role in hypocoristic (nick-
name) formation too (R. A. Mester 1990, Poser 1990). The unmarked pattern
of this word formation process is that of creating a bimoraic base out of the
source word (a given name) and adding an ending, *tyan* or *kun*, to it. The base
is usually the initial two moras of the source word as in (21a), but it can also
be formed by lengthening the initial mora as in (21b) or by adding a non-
syllabic mora to it as in (21c). Note that the most productive pattern, i.e. (21a),
often combines two moras across a morpheme boundary in the source word,
e.g. *mi#sa.to* → *[mi.sa].tya-n*. All the changes in (21a–c) conspire to yield a

bimoraic base form, which suggests that base forms of a monomoraic length are ill formed. An analogous constraint is observed in the interesting morphological process found in the formation of a secret language (Tateishi 1989b, Itô et al. 1996).

(21) ma.sa.ru → (a) [ma.sa].ku-n, (b) [ma-a].ku-n, *ma.ku-n
      mi.sa.to → (a) [mi.sa].tya-n, (b) [mi-i].tya-n, (c) [mi-t].tya-n, *mi.tya-n
      no.ri.ko → (a) [no.ri].tya-n, (c) [no-n].tya-n, *no.tya-n
      a-i.ko   → (a) [a-i].tya-n, *a.tya-n

This analysis leads to the idea of word minimality, a constraint by which the minimal length of words is defined. In Japanese as in many other languages (Hayes 1995), this constraint is defined in terms of bimoraic foot. This constraint shows itself very clearly when words are morphologically shortened. When numerals were shortened in the course of the history of Japanese, for example, the resultant forms became bimoraic or longer as exemplified in (22). The most productive pattern is shown in (22a), where the word-initial monomoraic syllable is lengthened.[8,9] In (22b), in contrast, two moras are taken from the beginning of the word, whereas no shortening takes place in the forms in (22c).

(22) a. hi-i (<hi.to.tu) "one," hu-u (<hu.ta.tu) "two," mi-i (<mi.tu) "three,"
          yo-o (<yo.tu) "four," mu-u (<mu.tu) "six," ya-a (<ya.tu) "eight"
      b. i.tu (<i.tu.tu) "five," na.na (<na.na.tu) "seven"
      c. ko.ko.no.tu "nine," to-o "ten"

It seems difficult to predict which word exhibits which pattern in (22). However, it is important to point out that the resultant forms are never monomoraic. An analogous situation is found in the process of loanword clipping to be discussed in section 2.2.[10]

The notion of foot plays a crucial role in word accent phenomena, too. Poser (1990) proposed that the accentuation of noun–noun compounds described in (6) above can be stated more simply if the foot is incorporated as a basic unit of accentuation. According to this analysis, compound nouns in (6a) and (6b) can be defined as containing an N2 of one foot and two feet, respectively. Note that the definition of foot here is slightly different from the one used in the morphological processes described in (20)–(22) in that in compound accentuation feet are formed within each morpheme. What this means is that every morpheme will form at least one foot – or, equivalently, monomoraic morphemes form an independent foot on their own.

Kubozono and Mester (1995) and Kubozono (1995a) critically extended this analysis in two crucial ways. First, the CA patterns described in (6a–b) can now be generalized as a pattern whereby a CA is placed on the penultimate foot, or on the nonfinal, rightmost foot, to be more precise. Secondly, the same foot-based analysis can be extended to cover the compound nouns with a longer N2, i.e. those in (7): this class of compound nouns can now be defined as compounds with an N2 of three feet. All these foot-based analyses have been further elaborated by Kubozono et al. (1997), who propose that noun–noun compounds in Japanese generally fall into three classes according to the phonological length of N2 and the typical phonological pattern it yields. These are summarized in (23).

(23) a. (= 6) N2 = 1 or 2 feet
        ka'buto + [musi]   → kabuto'] = [musi]
        minami + [ame][rika]   → minami] = [a'me][rika]
    b. (= 7) N2 = 3 feet
        nankyoku + [tan][ken][tai]   → nankyoku] = [tan][ken][tai]
        minami + [kari][foru][nia]   → minami] = [kari][foru][nia]
        tiho'o + [sai][ban][syo']   → tihoo] = [sai][ban][syo']
    c. N2 ≧ 4 feet
        ni'tibei + [an][po][zyo'o][yaku] → [ni'ti][bei] [an][po][zyo'o][yaku]
        "Japan–US Security Treaty"
        to'oa + [koku][nai][ko'o][kuu] → [to'o][a] [koku][nai][ko'o][kuu]
        "Toa Domestic Airlines"

If N2 is one or two feet long as in (23a), a default CA falls on the penultimate foot while N1 is deaccented (if it is accented at all). If N2 consists of three feet as in (24b), then it retains its own accent pattern, i.e. its accentedness and accent location, while deaccenting N1. The crucial difference between (23a) and (23b) is that N2 loses its prosodic independence in (23a) but not in (23b), whereas N1 loses its independence in both cases. Finally, if N2 consists of four or more feet, both N1 and N2 retain their prosodic independence, i.e. their own accent pattern, and, consequently, result in two prosodic words. This last pattern is identical to the accent pattern of phrasal constructions, which do not change the accentuation of their components: e.g. *ao'i tora'kku* → *ao'i tora'kku* "blue truck"; *ao'i enpitu* → *ao'i enpitu* "blue pencil." In more general terms, the three accent patterns sketched in (23) represent a prosodic continuum from the accentuation of the compound word to that of the phrase, with (23b) representing an intermediate prosodic stage between the two. The essence of the analysis described in (23), then, is that this prosodic continuum can be defined essentially in terms of the phonological length of N2 which, in turn, is to be defined in terms of the prosodic unit "foot."

There is still room for discussion about the principle of foot formation in Japanese (see section 3.2). It is nevertheless worth emphasizing that the complexities of the CA rules can be reduced to a very simple picture if one adopts the notion of foot, which is bimoraic in unmarked cases.

2   Relevance of Syllable

The discussion so far has abundantly shown the importance of "mora" and, furthermore, of the notion "foot" based thereon. Arguments along this line may and in fact have led to the claim that Japanese does not need a unit equivalent to the syllable. This claim is challenged in this section, where it is shown that the conception of the mora as an indispensable unit in a language is not incompatible at all with the idea that the syllable too plays a certain role in the same system.

2.1 Word accent

2.1.1 Bearer of word accent

The first evidence for the syllable in Japanese comes from the facts about word accent. Many Japanese accent rules refer to the mora structure of the word and, thereby, determine the location of word accent by counting the number of moras. Recall, for example, that the loanword accent rule sketched in (5) places an accent on the antepenultimate mora, i.e. the third mora counted from the end of the word. This rule, however, fails to account for the accent patterns of words as in (24), which are accented one mora leftward. In most cases the antepenultimate mora of these words is one of the nonsyllabic moras described in (2).

(24) a. mya'-n.ma-a "Myanmar," ro'-n.do-n "London,"
     wa.si'-n.to-n "Washington"
   b. sa'-i.pa-n "Saipan," su.pa'-i.da-a "spider," de.za'-i.na-a "designer"
   c. sa'-a.ka.su "circus," pe'-e.pa-a "paper," pi'-i.na.tu "peanut"
   d. so'-k.ku.su "socks," de.ra'-k.ku.su "deluxe," pi'-t.tya-a "pitcher"

The best way to generalize this pattern with the antepenultimate pattern described in (5) is to assume that the syllable is the bearer of the accent (Shibatani 1990). The antepenultimate rule sketched in (5) will then be reformulated as in (25) (J. D. McCawley 1978).

(25) Loanword accent rule: Place an accent on the *syllable containing the antepenultimate mora*.

The conception of Tokyo Japanese as being a "mora-counting, syllable language" (J. D. McCawley 1978) allows us to generalize accent variations found in other accentual phenomena.[11] Compound accentuation, for example, exhibits the pattern in (26) as a variant of (6a). This variant pattern can be generalized with the regular pattern if the syllable is regarded as the bearer of the accent. That is, the accent patterns in (6a) and (26) can be attributed to a rule which places the CA on the final *syllable* of N1.

(26) se'ndai + si'   → senda'i = si   "Sendai City"
     itoo + si'   → ito'o = si   "Ito City"
     so'romon + o'o   → soromo'n = oo   "Solomon, king; King Solomon"
     cf. (6a) kyo'oto + si' → kyooto' = si "Kyoto City"

Another interesting case in which the syllable plays a role as the bearer of accent is that of a personal name *zi'roo*. This noun exhibits an exceptional but highly predictable CA behavior when combined with a prefix-like element, to form a larger personal name (see Akinaga 1981 for a traditional analysis). Unlike the ordinary noun–noun compounds such as those in (6) and (7), the accentuation of X-ziroo compounds is determined by the lefthand member (N1). If N1 is monomoraic as in (27a), it yields an unaccented word. If N1 is bimoraic as in (27b) and (27b′), it attracts a CA on its final position. Finally, if N1 contains more than two moras as in (27c), the CA falls on the initial mora of N2 (*zi'roo*) – or, equivalently, the lexical accent of N2 is preserved in the resultant compound. Only this final case can be accounted for by the general CA rule described in (6b) and (23a).

(27) a. ko   "little" + zi'roo   →   ko = ziroo
      b. kane   "money" + zi'roo   →   kane' = ziroo
      b′. ki'n   "gold" + zi'roo   →   ki'n = ziroo
      c. tikara' "power" + zi'roo   →   tikara = zi'roo
          karee   "curry" + zi'roo   →   karee = zi'roo

The three accent patterns described in (27) can basically be generalized in terms of the mora. Namely, bimoraic, monosyllabic N1 such as *kin* patterns with the bimoraic, bisyllabic form *kane* and not with the monosyllabic form *ko*. Moreover, trimoraic, bisyllabic N1 like *karee* patterns with trimoraic, trisyllabic forms like *tikara*, not with bimoraic, bisyllabic forms such as *kane*. However, it is necessary to refer to the syllable structure of the output in order to generalize the patterns in (27b) and (27b′), where the CA is placed on the final syllable of N1: *Kane' = ziroo* and *ki'n = ziroo* would appear to exhibit different CA patterns under a purely mora-based analysis.

We need information on syllable structure to generalize not only the output of phonological rules but their input forms as well. A classical case to demonstrate this is the "pre-*no* deaccenting rule" (Akinaga 1981, Poser 1984), which has the effect of deaccenting finally accented nouns followed by the genitive particle *no*. This rule is subject to two major constraints, both of which require information on syllable structure. One of them requires the noun undergoing the rule to be accented on the final syllable. Thus the rule readily applies to nouns accented on the final bimoraic syllable, as in (28b), as well as those accented on the final monomoraic syllable, as in (28a).

(28) a. uma' + no   →   umano   "of the horse"
          otoko' + no   →   otokono   "of the man"
      b. niho'n + no   →   nihonno   "of Japan"
          kino'o + no   →   kinoono   "of yesterday"
          cf. koko'ro + no →   koko'rono   "of the heart"
      c. me' + no   →   me'no   "of the eye"
          ki' + no   →   ki'no   "of the tree"
      d. kyo'o + no   →   kyo'ono   "of today"
          ka'i + no   →   ka'ino   "of the shellfish"

A second constraint on the deaccenting rule requires that the word be more than one syllable long in order for it to undergo the rule. Thus monosyllables do not undergo the deaccenting rule irrespective of whether they are monomoraic as in (28c) or bimoraic as in (28d).

So far we have presented evidence that the syllable rather than the mora is the bearer of word accent in Japanese. This finding itself may not be surprising in the context of general linguistic theory since the syllable plays the same role in a large number of languages in the world – so many so that Hayes (1995) proposes that this is universally true. What is truly interesting about accent phenomena in Japanese is that the syllable plays some other crucial roles in this putatively mora-based system and that most of these roles are also found in the syllable-based systems of other languages.

2.1.2 Other accentual phenomena

In addition to the role as the bearer of the accent, the syllable plays an indispensable role in various accentual phenomena in Japanese. Consider compound accentuation, which was outlined in (23) above. If the second member (N2) is one foot long, a default CA falls on the final syllable of N1, which is contained in the penultimate foot of the entire compound noun: e.g. kabuto'] = [musi] in (23a). A major exception to this is the case where N2 is bisyllabic and originally accented on its non-final syllable. In this particular case, N2 very often retains its accent in the resultant compound, as shown in (29a). This contrasts sharply with the case where N2 is originally accented on the final monomoraic syllable as in (29b) as well as with the case where N2 is an accented monosyllable as in (29c). In these latter cases the accent of N2 almost never survives as the CA and, consequently, a default CA appears on the penultimate foot just as it does in (29d), where N2 is originally unaccented.[12]

(29) a. pe'rusya + ne'ko → perusya][ne'ko] "Persian cat"
          ti'izu + pi'za   → tiizu][pi'za]   "cheese pizza"
      b. a'kita + inu'   → akita'][inu]   "Akita dog"
      c. sakura + ka'i   → sakura'][gai]   "cherry shell"
          ne'kutai + pi'n   → nekuta'i][pin]   "necktie pin"
      d. ka'buto + musi   → kabuto'][musi]   "beetle"

The seemingly peculiar contrast between (29a) and (29b–c) can be attributed to the general principle of Nonfinality, whereby word-final accents are disfavored (Prince and Smolensky 1993). In the particular case under consideration, this principle can be defined as a constraint prohibiting a CA on the final *syllable* of the compound (Kubozono 1995a, 1997).

Another interesting accentuation rule that requires information on syllable structure concerns compound nouns whose second member is a personal name *ta'roo*, e.g. *kin = taroo*, *momo' = taroo* and *tikara = ta'roo*. Just like *zi'roo* discussed in (27), *ta'roo* exhibits an exceptional CA behavior when combined with a prefix-like element, or N1, in that its CA patterns cannot be accounted for by the

general CA rule described in (6b) and (23a). However, like *zi'roo*, its CA behavior
is highly predictable on the basis of the phonological length of N1 (see Akinaga
1981 for a traditional mora-based account). X-taroo compounds exhibit identical
accent patterns with the X-ziroo compounds described in (27) above except that
they require information on syllable structure as well as mora structure. Specifically, *ta'roo* exhibits two different CA patterns when combined with a bimoraic
N1: monosyllabic N1 in (30b) yields an unaccented compound just as the monomoraic N1 in (30a), whereas bisyllabic N1 attracts a CA on the final syllable, as
illustrated in (30c). Here, the distinction of bimoraic sequences in terms of
their syllable structure turns out to be crucial just as it did in compound accentuation described in (29). Curiously, the third CA pattern described in (30), i.e.
(30d), can be defined in terms of the mora, and not the syllable, as bisyllabic,
trimoraic N1 such as *karee* patterns with trisyllabic, trimoraic forms like *tikara*.

(30) a. ki "devil" + ta'roo   →   ki = taroo
          ne "sleeping" + ta'roo   →   ne = taroo
      b. ki'n "gold" + ta'roo   →   kin = taroo
          ma'n "ten thousand" + ta'roo   →   man = taroo
          kyu'u "Q" + ta'roo   →   kyuu = taroo
      c. momo "peach" + ta'roo   →   momo' = taroo
          kane "money" + ta'roo   →   kane' = taroo
      d. tikara' "power" + ta'roo   →   tikara = ta'roo
          karee "curry" + ta'roo   →   karee = ta'roo
          urutora'man "superman" + ta'roo   →   urutoraman = ta'roo

The argument for syllable structure is further reinforced by the data of loanword accentuation. A vast majority of loanwords are accented according to the
rule described in (25) above, but about 10 percent of loanwords are unaccented.
Interestingly, a majority of these unaccented loanwords have two common
features: They are four moras long and end with a sequence of two monomoraic
syllables (Kubozono 1996b). (31) lists some typical examples of placenames.

(31) a.me.ri.ka "America," e.zi.pu.to "Egypt," sa-n.ho.ze "San Jose,"
      ho.no.ru.ru "Honolulu," yo.se.mi.te "Yosemite," a.ri.zo.na "Arizona,"
      a-i.da.ho "Idaho," a-i.o.wa "Iowa"

That the above generalization is correct can be borne out by the accentuation
of nonsense words. The words in (32a–b), for example, obey the rule in (25),
thereby attracting an accent on the syllable containing the antepenultimate
mora. In contrast, nonsense words in (32c) do not follow this rule but tend to
be unaccented.[13] The most crucial difference between the two groups is that
only the latter end with a sequence of monomoraic syllables.

(32) a. re.ba'.no-n, re.no'.ba-n
      b. re.ba'-n.no, re.no'-n.ba
      c. re-n.ba.no, re-n.no.ba

Another aspect of loanword accentuation in which syllable structure plays a crucial part concerns an exceptional accent pattern shown by some trimoraic loanwords. Most trimoraic loanwords are accented on the antepenultimate mora, as correctly predicted by the rule in (25). Some examples are given in (33a–b). However, some words such as those in (33c) are accented on the penultimate mora. Careful analysis of the data reveals that these words almost always end with a bimoraic syllable preceded by an epenthetic vowel (Kubozono 1996b). The trimoraic forms in (33a) involve an epenthetic vowel in the initial syllable but do not end with a bimoraic syllable. Those in (33b) end with a bimoraic syllable but do not contain an epenthetic vowel in the initial syllable. Trimoraic words in (33c) satisfy both of these conditions.

(33) a. pu'.ra.su "plus," gu'.ra.su "glass," do'.re.su "dress," to'.ri.o. "trio"
      b. ha'.wa-i "Hawaii," ri'.re-e "relay," i'.ra-n "Iran," se'.da-n "sedan"
      c. do.ra'-i "dry," bu.ru'-u "blue," su.ri'-i "three," tu.i'-n "twin"

In sum, all of the accentual phenomena described in (29)–(33) can be properly accounted for if the syllable is incorporated as a basic unit of description.

2.2 Word formation

Morphological processes, too, require reference to the syllable structure of words. Consider the process of loanword clipping illustrated in (34) (Itô 1990). Loanwords in Japanese are generally very long as a result of the vowel epenthesis which takes place during the borrowing process. Once borrowed into Japanese, these relatively long words are often shortened to the length of two to four moras, as illustrated in (34a–c) respectively: ( ) shows the truncated portion.

(34) a. de.mo(-n.su.to.re-e.syo-n) "demonstration," su.to.(ra-i.ki) "strike"
      b. te.re.bi.(zyo-n) "television," a.ni.me-(e.syo-n) "animation"
      b'. pa-n.hu.(re-t.to) "pamphlet," pa-a.ma.(ne-n.to) "permanent wave"
      c. ri.su.to.ra.(ku.tya.ri-n.gu) "restructuring,"
          i.ra.su.to.(re-e.syo-n) "illustration"

This process is interesting in two respects. First, it embodies the minimality constraint discussed in section 1.5: the resultant word must consist of at least one foot, i.e. two moras, as shown in (34a). A second fact, which is of interest here, is that the resultant form must be at least *bisyllabic*. This can be seen by the comparison of the clipped forms in (34a) and those in (34b'). In (34a), all the resultant forms are bimoraic and bisyllabic. In (34b'), in contrast, the original loanwords begin with a bimoraic syllable and result in a trimoraic form when shortened, e.g. *pa-n.hu*, **pa-n* for *pa-n.hu.re-t.to*. This difference is suggestive of a constraint by which the resultant word must be more than one syllable long.[14] This second constraint cannot be defined by the mora alone but requires information on the syllable structure of the source word. Four-mora forms such as those in (34c) satisfy both the moraic and syllabic constraints discussed here.[15]

2.3   Syllable weight

In addition to the various phenomena discussed in the preceding section, there are many more linguistic processes for which the notion of syllable seems indispensable. Many of these processes can be defined in terms of "syllable weight" or "syllable quantity," a notion which has been proposed to account for the phonological length of syllables (Allen 1973).

Syllables generally fall into two or three categories according to their phonological weight and their characteristic phonological behavior: light syllables, heavy syllables, and superheavy syllables. Generally speaking, short vowels count as one phonological unit, whereas long vowels and diphthongs count as two units. Coda consonants often serve as an independent unit so that closed syllables with a short vowel (CVC) count as being as long as open syllables with a long vowel or diphthong (CVV). Closed syllables with a long vowel or diphthong (CVVC) count as three units and are longer than any other syllable type. Onset consonants do not contribute to syllable weight so that the presence or absence of an onset does not change the weight of the particular syllable.

The notion of syllable weight is closely related to the phonological notion of "mora" discussed in section 1.2. Syllable weight, in fact, is a notion in which the two notions, "syllable" and "mora," are integrated: namely, light syllables (V or CV) are monomoraic, heavy syllables ((C)VV or (C)VC) are bimoraic, and superheavy syllables ((C)VVC) are trimoraic.

2.3.1   Compensatory lengthening

The first case in which "syllable weight" plays a crucial role is that of compensatory lengthening discussed in section 1.2.2 above. As illustrated in (8), Tokyo Japanese exhibits vowel lengthening occurring concomitantly with vowel monophthongization. A global effect of this process is to keep intact the total length of words as measured in terms of the mora. Seen from the viewpoint of syllable weight, it can be redefined as a process whereby the phonological length of the relevant syllable is kept intact. In the *daikon* ~ *deekon* alternation stated in (8a), for example, the first syllable, *dai*, keeps its bimoraic length as the monophthongized vowel, [e], is lengthened. Compensatory lengthening in Tokyo Japanese always occurs within the domain of the syllable, which implies that the primary motivation of the process is to preserve the phonological length of syllables.[16]

2.3.2 Generality of accent rules

The notion of syllable weight also enables us to understand the general linguistic nature of accent rules in Japanese. Consider, for example, the antepenultimate accent rule in (25). This rule would produce the outputs in (35) should it be interpreted in terms of syllable weight: "H" and "L" stand for heavy (bimoraic) and light (monomoraic) syllables, respectively.

(35) a. ...LH'L#   b. ...LH'H#   c. ...HH'L#   d. ...HH'H#
      e. ...L'LL#   f. ...LL'H#   g. ...H'LL#   h. ...HL'H#

The effects described in (35) look quite similar to those of the accent rule of classical Latin and many other languages including modern English. The accent rule of Latin is claimed to be sensitive to the weight of the penultimate syllable in a straightforward manner (Prince and Smolensky 1993, Hayes 1995).

(36) Latin accent rule: Place an accent on the penultimate syllable if it is heavy and on the antepenultimate syllable if it is light.

This rule yields the results in (37).

(37) a. ...LH'L#   b. ...LH'H#   c. ...HH'L#   d. ...HH'H#
      e. ...L'LL#   f. ...L'LH#   g. ...H'LL#   h. ...H'LH#

The similarity between (35) and (37) is obvious: they differ in just two out of the eight phonological environments, i.e. (f) and (h). More interestingly, modern Japanese exhibits a striking variation in these two environments (Kubozono 1996b, Kubozono and Ohta 1998). Thus loanwords in (38) yield the patterns in (35f, 35h), whereas those in (39) exhibit somewhat new patterns which are identical to those shown in (37f, 37h). Moreover, words in (40) show a fluctuation between the old patterns in (38) and the new patterns in (39). In a historical perspective, the lexical variation between (38) and (39) and the fluctuation in (40) represent an ongoing accentual change whereby the traditional mora-based rule in (25) seems to develop into the Latin-type rule in (36), which is primarily syllable-based.

(38) a. ...LL'H#   i.e'.me-n "Yemen" bi.ta'.mi-n "vitamin"
                     e.su.ki'.moo "Eskimo"
      b. ...HL'H#   ka-n.ga'.ru-u "kangaroo" ba-a.be'.kyu-u "BBQ"

(39) a. ...L'LH#   to'.ro.fi-i "trophy" a'.ma.zo-n "Amazon"
                     te'.ne.si-i "Tennessee"
      b. ...H'LH#   i'-n.ta.byu-u "interview" ba'-a.ku.re-e "Berkeley"

(40) a. ...LLH#   re.ba'.no-n ~ re'.ba.no-n "Lebanon"
                     do.ra'.go-n ~ do'.ra.go-n "dragon"
                     e.ne.ru'.gi-i ~ e.ne'.ru.gi-i "energy"

b.   ...HLH#   myu-u.zi'.sya-n ~ myu'-u.zi.sya-n "musician"
                  e-n.de'.ba-a ~ e'-n.de.ba-a "(Space Shuttle) Endeavor"
                  ha-n.ga'.ri-i ~ ha'-n.ga.ri-i "Hungary"

In sum, the basic similarity between the Japanese loanword accent rule in (25) and the Latin-type accent rule in (36) can be revealed if the mora-based rule in (25) is reinterpreted in the light of syllable weight. Moreover, the general linguistic nature of the synchronic lexical variation described in (38)–(40) can best be understood if syllable weight is adopted as a relevant descriptive notion. Since "syllable weight" presupposes the notion of syllable, all these observations clearly demonstrate the importance of the syllable in Japanese.

2.3.3   Trimoraic syllable ban

A more convincing argument for syllable weight in Japanese comes from the analysis of trimoraic syllables. Trimoraic syllables are reported to be disfavored in a number of languages including English and other Germanic languages (Árnason 1980), Koya and Fula (Sherer 1994), and Pali (Zec 1995), to mention just a few. This constraint, as formulated in (41), provides a principled account of many phonological processes including the vowel length alternation in English illustrated in (42). Traditionally interpreted as vowel shortening in closed syllables (Myers 1987),[17] this process can be reinterpreted, as shown in (43), as a case where trimoraic syllables are converted into bimoraic ones to satisfy the constraint in (41).

(41) $*\sigma_{\mu\mu\mu}$

(σ = syllable, μ = mora.)

(42)   a.   keep-kept, wise-wis.dom, house-hus.band
       b.   go-gone, do-done, say-said

(43) $\sigma_{\mu\mu\mu} \to \sigma_{\mu\mu}$

Interestingly, the constraint in (41) has been shown to play a role in the phonology of other Indo-European languages including Latin and most Germanic languages (Árnason 1980, Sherer 1994). To make the matter more interesting, there are several independent pieces of evidence which suggest that the constraint on the well-formedness of syllable weight restricts Japanese phonology, too. Japanese has traditionally been an open-syllable language and, hence, did not originally have such a complex syllable structure as /CVVC/. However, an analysis of loanword phonology reveals that Japanese makes every effort to avoid creating such a syllable structure in the process of borrowing. To begin with, let us consider the vowel shortening phenomenon known as "pre-nasal shortening (PNS)" (Lovins 1975): /N/ denotes a moraic nasal, which normally appears in the coda of a syllable.[18]

(44) a. range   → /re-N.zi/, */re-i-N.zi/
          change   → /tye-n.zi/, */tye-i-N.zi/
          stainless   → /su.te-N.re.su/, */su.te-i-N.re.su/;
          stained glass → /su.te-N.do.gu.ra.su/, */su.te-i-N.do.gu.ra.su/
      b. ground   → /gu.ra-N.do/, *?/gu.ra-u-N.do/;
          foundation   → /fa-N.de-e.syo-N/, */fa-u-N.de-e.syo-N/
      c. machine   → /ma.si-N/, */ma.si-i-N/
          cornbeef   → /ko-N.bi-i.hu/, */ko-o-N.bi-i.hu/
          ice cream   → /a-i.su.ku.ri-N/, */a-i.su.ku.ri-i-N/

In (44), the second half of long vowels and diphthongs has dropped when it appears before a nasal which is to be borrowed as a moraic nasal. The most revealing case is that of the word *ice cream* in (44c), which permits two forms in Japanese. If the word-final nasal is adopted as a moraic nasal in Japanese, the form with a short vowel, i.e. /a-i.su.ku.ri-N/, results. If, on the other hand, the nasal is adopted as the onset of a new syllable, then the original bimoraic length of the vowel is retained to produce the form /a-i.su.ku.ri-i.mu/. This second form is the standard form in modern Japanese, whereas the form with a shortened vowel is an archaic or dialectal one. What is most interesting here is the fact that a third form, /a-i.su.ku.ri-i-N/, has never been attested. This indicates that Japanese permits the parsing of either the original vowel length or the coda nasal; if the original bimoraic vowel length is to be maintained as in the contemporary form, the word-final consonant cannot be parsed as the coda of the same syllable; if the original coda nasal is to be parsed as a coda consonant as in the archaic/dialectal form, the original bimoraicity of the vowel must be abandoned. This trade-off between vowel length and the coda consonant embodies exactly the same syllable weight constraint that yields the English vowel alternations stated in (42).

The constraint responsible for the vowel shortening in (44) also accounts for coda deletion in (45). This phenomenon might look entirely different from the vowel shortening in (44) but, seen from the viewpoint of syllable structure, it can be attributed to the constraint that prohibits creating trimoraic syllables.

(45) entertainment   → /e-N.ta-a.te-i.me-N.to/, ??/e-N.ta-a.te-i-N.me-N.to/
      alignment   → /a.ra-i.me-N.to/, *?/a.ra-i-N.me-N.to/
      cf. eight   → /e-i.to/, right → /ra-i.to/,
           entertainer → /e-N.ta-a.te-i.na-a/, */e-n.ta-a.te.na-a/

The constraint prohibiting trimoraic syllables accounts for an antigemination effect in loanword phonology, too. Obstruents in the coda position are often geminated in Japanese, yielding bimoraic syllables as illustrated in (46a). This gemination process is invariably blocked, however, if the obstruent is preceded by a long vowel or diphthong. This antigemination effect is illustrated in (46b).

(46)   a.   cut → /ka-t.to/, */ka.to/; hip → /hi-p.pu/, */hi.pu/
     b.   cart → /ka-a.to/, */ka-a-t.to/; kite → /ka-i.to/, */ka-i-t.to/

The gemination–antigemination contrast in (46) reveals a trading relationship between vowel length and consonant gemination. This relationship can be explained by the ban on trimoraic syllables, although, again, the phonotactic effect of the phenomenon itself seems to have little in common with the effects of the phenomena in (44)–(45).

Another interesting phenomenon arguably attributable to the syllable weight constraint in (41) is that of compound accentuation. There are quite a few loanwords in contemporary Japanese which seem to form exceptions to the processes described in (44)–(46) and, hence, to the constraint in (41). The words given in (47), for example, contain a sequence of segments which apparently forms a superheavy syllable of the form /CVVN/.

(47)   a.   /aiN/   ra-i-N "line, Rhine," de.za-i-N "design,"
                   ba.re-N.ta-i-N "Valentine"
     b.   /auN/   ta-u-N "town," da-u-N "down," ka-u-N.ta-a "counter"
     c.   /eiN/   su.pe-i-N "Spain"
     d.   /oiN/   ko-i-N "coin," po-i-n.to "point"
     e. $/V_i V_i N/$ ri-N.ka-a-N "Lincoln," tye-e-N "chain," ku.re-e-N "crane"

An accentual analysis of these words, however, suggests that the /CVVN/ sequences in question actually form a sequence of two syllables. As mentioned in (6a), the CA rule in Japanese places a default CA on the final syllable of the first member (N1) if the second member (N2) is either monomoraic or bimoraic. This rule correctly predicts the CA pattern in (48), where the CA docks onto the nucleus of the final syllable of N1.

(48)   a.   te'.mu.zu + ka.wa'   → te.mu.zu' = ga.wa "the Thames River"
     b.   a'.ma.zo-N + ka.wa'   → a.ma.zo'-N = ga.wa "the Amazon River"
     c.   ka'.ga.ku + ha'.ku   → ka.ga.ku' = ha.ku "Science Exposition"
     d.   mi'.ra-i + ha'.ku   → mi.ra'-i = ha.ku "Future Exposition"
     e.   ha.ya.ri' + ka.ze   → ha.ya.ri' = ka.ze "epidemic, cold; influenza"
     f.   ho-N.ko'-N + ka.ze   → ho-N.ko'-N = ka.ze "Hong Kong Flu"

However, the words in (47) show an unexpected behavior when they form the N1 of a compound noun. In such compounds, the CA generally docks onto the penultimate mora of N1, not on the antepenultimate mora. This is shown in (49), where the trimoraic sequences in question are tentatively assumed to form one syllable, i.e. a trimoraic syllable.[19]

(49)   a.   ra'-i-N + ka.wa'   → ra-i'-N = ga.wa, *ra'-i-N = ga.wa
                      "the Rhine River"
     b.   de.za'-i-n + ha'.ku   → de.za-i'-N = ha.ku, *de.za'-i-N = ha.ku
                      "Design Exposition"

c. ba.re-N.ta-i-N + de'-e → ba.re-N.ta-i'-N = de-e, ?ba.re-N.ta'-i-N = de-e
"Valentine's Day"

d. ta'-u-N + si → ta-u'-N = si, *ta'-u-N = si
"a local magazine"

e. su.pe'-i-N + ka.ze → su.pe-i'-N = ka.ze, *su.pe'-i-N = ka.ze
"Spain Flu"

f. ko'-i-N + syo'-o → ko-i'-N = syo-o, *ko'-i-N = syo-o
"coin dealer"

g. ri-N.ka'-a-N + ha'-i → ri-N.ka-a'-N = ha-i, ?ri-N.ka'-a-N = ha-i
"Lincoln Cup"

What appears to be a mysterious CA pattern in (49) can be properly accounted for if one assumes that the trimoraic sequences in question actually consist of two syllables with a syllable boundary between the first and second moras, i.e. /CV.VN/. This analysis allows us to represent the CA in (49) as in (50), which can now be generalized with the regular CA pattern in (48).

(50) a. ra'.i-N + ka.wa' → ra.i'-N = ga.wa, *ra'.i-N = ga.wa
b. de.za'.i-n + ha'.ku → de.za.i'-N = ha.ku, *de.za'.i-N = ha.ku
c. ba.re-N.ta.i-N + de'-e → ba.re-N.ta.i'-N = de-e, ?ba.re-N.ta'.i-N = de-e
d. ta'.u-N + si → ta.u'-N = si, *ta'.u-N = si
e. su.pe'.i-N + ka.ze → su.pe.i'-N = ka.ze, *su.pe'.i-N = ka.ze
f. ko'.i-N + syo'-o → ko.i'-N = syo-o, *ko'.i-N = syo-o
g. ri-N.ka'.a-N + ha'-i → ri-N.ka.a'-N = ha-i, ?ri-N.ka'.a-N = ha-i

Another revealing case for the bisyllabic status of the trimoraic sequences in question is the accentuation of the word /deza'iN/ "design" and its related words. These are shown in (51), where only mora boundaries are given to avoid confusion.

(51) a. de-za'-i-N "design"
b. (= 24b) de-za'-i-na-a "designer"
c. (= 50b) de-za-i'-N = ha-ku "Design Exposition"

The word /de-za'-i-N/ in (51a) attracts an accent on its antepenultimate mora, as correctly predicted by the loanword accent rule stated in (25). Note that this accent pattern alone does not reveal the syllable structure of the trimoraic sequence /za-i-N/, since the loanword accent rule determines the basic docking site of accent by counting the number of moras. /de-za-'i-na-a/ in (51b), in contrast, attracts an accent on the fourth mora from the end. This, too, can be accounted for by the loanword accent rule in (25), which predicts that the accent will dock on /za'i/, or the syllable containing the antepenultimate mora. What is relevant here is the fact that the second half of the vowel sequence, i.e. /i/ in /ai/, does not form the nucleus of the syllable. However, this is not always the case, as clearly demonstrated by the accent pattern of the word in (51c), which, by the CA rule described in (26), should be accented on the final syllable of the first member, /dezain/. This word contains the same vowel sequence /ai/, but actually attracts a CA on /i/ rather than on /a/. The comparison of (51b) and (51c) reveals that the second half of the vowel sequence /ai/ functions as a syllable nucleus in (51c), but not in (51b), which, in turn, suggests that /ai/ forms one integral syllable in (51b) but is divided into two syllables in (51c). In more general terms, vowel sequences like /ai/ generally form one syllable except when they are followed by another non-syllabic mora such as the moraic nasal /N/. This otherwise mysterious behavior of vowel sequences can be explained by the constraint in (41) in a straight-forward manner.

Similarly, what appears to be a peculiar contrast in compound accentuation between the words in (52a) and (52b) below can also be accounted for by the constraint prohibiting trimoraic syllables. With a monomoraic or bimoraic second member, these compound nouns are expected to be accented on the final syllable of the first member, just as are the compound nouns in (48). However, they are actually accented on different loci: e.g. /roNdo'N=basi/ is accented on the penultimate mora of /roN.doN/, whereas /roNdoN'k=ko/ is generally accented on the final mora of the same word, namely, on the moraic nasal.

(52)   a.   ro-N.do-N + ha.si' → ro-N.do'-N = ba.si
                          "London, bridge; London Bridge"
        ge-N.da-i + zi'-N   → ge-N.da'-i = zi-N
                          "modern, people; the moderns"
    b.   ro-N.do-N + ko   → ro-N.do.N'-k = ko, *?ro-N.do'-N-k = ko
                          "London, child; Londoner"
        ge-N.da-i + ko   → ge-N.da.i'-k = ko, *?ge-N.da'-i-k = ko
                          "modern children"

The CA difference illustrated in (52) can be attributed to the fact that the onset consonant of the second member is geminated in (52b) but not in (52a). Since gemination adds an extra mora to the preceding syllable, the compound noun in (52b) comes to involve a trimoraic sequence, i.e. /CVNC/ or /CVVC/, at the end of its first member. In view of syllable weight, this is comparable to the situation illustrated in (49), where the first component word ends with a trimoraic sequence which, from a purely phonotactic point of view, would seem to form a trimoraic syllable. What happens in (52b) is that the final mora of N1, i.e. the moraic nasal or the second half of a diphthongal vowel sequence, becomes a syllable nucleus and thereby attracts an accent on itself. Obviously, this is triggered by the gemination of the following heterosyllabic consonant, which has created an extra nonsyllabic mora at the end of the first component word. In short, the accentual difference between (52a) and (52b) can be attributed to a difference in syllable structure, which, in turn, is attributable to the presence or absence of an extra mora at the end of the first component word. This whole story, too, can be accounted for by the constraint on syllable weight in (41).

To summarize, many seemingly independent phenomena conspire to avoid creating trimoraic syllables in Japanese. Stated conversely, postulating a constraint prohibiting trimoraic syllables as in (41) allows us to generalize a number of phonological phenomena in Japanese which would otherwise appear to be totally unrelated to each other. Since the same constraint has been shown to constrain the phonology of English and many other languages, positing the same syllable well-formedness constraint in Japanese phonology also leads us to understand the general linguistic basis of syllable weight phenomena in the language. All these arguments for the existence of the syllable weight constraint reinforce the argument developed throughout this section, namely, that the syllable is a unit no less indispensable than the mora in Japanese.

3 Summary and Future Work

3.1 *Summary*

In this chapter we have considered various roles played by the mora and the syllable in Japanese. Japanese has traditionally been labeled a "mora language" as opposed to a "syllable language." In the first half of this chapter we saw a wide range of phenomena – phonetic, phonological, and morphological – for which the notion of "mora" is indispensable. We considered functions played by the mora from four different viewpoints: (i) as a phonetic unit to define temporal organization of speech, (ii) as a phonological unit by which phonological distance or length is defined, (iii) as a segmentation unit in speech production, and (iv) as a perceptual unit relevant in speech perception processes. In addition to these four roles, the mora plays an important role in defining the notion of phonological "foot," which allows us to generalize a number of seemingly unrelated phenomena in the same language. It was suggested that the second function of the mora and the role of the foot which derives from it may be observed in other languages as well, whereas all the other functions seem to be characteristic of Japanese as a "mora language" in Trubetzkoy's classical sense.

In the second half of this chapter we challenged the traditional view that the syllable plays little or no role in the putatively mora-based system. Starting with the classical role of the syllable as the bearer of word accent, we demonstrated that many accent-related phenomena can be generalized by positing the syllable as a basic unit of description. Particularly important is the distinction of bimoraic words in terms of their syllable structure, i.e. monosyllabic vs. bisyllabic. The arguments for syllable and syllable structure in Japanese have been reinforced by evidence for syllable weight, a notion that is used to define the phonological weight or length of syllables. This new notion provides a principled account of a number of phenomena from vowel shortening and anti-gemination in loanwords to peculiar accentuation in compounds. All these data provide strong evidence that the syllable forms an integral part of Japanese phonology, quite contrary to Pike's (1947) characterization of the unit as simply a "phonetic syllable."

The arguments developed in this chapter as a whole challenge the claim implicitly assumed in the classical literature, namely, that the syllable and the mora are mutually exclusive in a single prosodic system. Our arguments demonstrated, quite contrary to this traditional hypothesis, that both the mora and the syllable are indispensable for generalizing linguistic phenomena in Japanese and, indeed, for understanding their true meanings in the context of general linguistic theory.

3.2   Future agenda

We have seen in section 1 various kinds of evidence for the centrality of the mora in Japanese. Unlike the evidence for the syllable, the evidence for the mora is more or less language specific, i.e. specific to Japanese as a "mora language." Given this characterization of the mora phenomena in Japanese, it is quite natural to ask why Japanese is unique in this respect. This question can be tackled from two different perspectives, one from a phonological viewpoint and the other from the viewpoint of language acquisition.

Considered from a phonological viewpoint, the mora phenomena we have seen prompt the question of how they can be related to the prosodic organization of speech or, more specifically, to the organization of the syllable. Particularly interesting in this respect is the proposal of Moraic Phonology (Hyman 1985, Kubozono 1985, Hayes 1989, Katada 1990) that the mora is an integral part of the syllable. According to this theory, the mora (μ) rather than the unit known as the "rhyme" forms a constituent of the syllable (σ). This is illustrated in (53) with the Japanese word /tookyoo/ "Tokyo."[20]

(53)

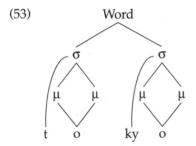

This analysis provides a very straightforward account of the phonological function discussed in section 1.2 above, namely, that the mora serves as a basic unit of phonological length in Japanese and many other languages. It also seems to explain the evidence described in sections 1.3 and 1.4 showing that the mora serves as a segmentation unit in speech production and perception in Japanese. However, it fails to explain the crucial differences between

Japanese and English (and other languages) with respect to the roles of the mora described in sections 1.1, 1.3, and 1.4. These inter-language differences seem to suggest the need to distinguish Japanese as a truly mora-based system from English and other languages, where the mora is only partially relevant. These differences will also require serious attention when we attempt to develop the analysis illustrated in (53) – or any analysis related to syllable structure – in our future work.

Turning to the acquisition side of the mora phenomena, there are several hypotheses to account for mora phenomena in Japanese, including those phenomena which seem to be specific to the language (see Kubozono 1995b, 1996a, for details). One such hypothesis is that native speakers of Japanese acquire the prosodic unit of mora under the influence of the essentially mora-based writing system. Two of the three writing systems used in Japanese, namely, *hiragana* and *katakana*, are mora-based systems in which each letter corresponds to a mora.[21] Notably, all the nonsyllabic moras described in (2) are written with independent letters. This orthography-based hypothesis may account for the peculiar phenomena Japanese exhibits with respect to temporal regulation and speech segmentation, although the details need to be considered more carefully.

This said, it must be emphasized that not all the mora phenomena discussed in section 1 can be attributed directly to the orthographic systems. It is highly implausible that the mora evidence from speech errors, for example, is a direct result of orthography, since this kind of performance data is produced by an unconscious process which should in principle be independent of orthography. If the mora evidence could be linked to orthography at all, it would probably mean that the basic structure of the writing system is somehow integrated into the phonological competence of the speakers, which then shows itself in linguistic phenomena.

In connection with this, it is probably worth adding that some of the linguistic evidence putatively supporting the mora in Japanese may well simply reflect the speakers' explicit knowledge of orthography. This probably includes raw data from various word games such as *siritori* and *babibu* languages (Katada 1990, Haraguchi 1996). Unlike speech errors and other data discussed in section 1, linguistic data from word games seem explicitly dependent on the speakers' knowledge of orthography and, therefore, may only be evidence that the Japanese writing system is mora-based. These data can be used as independent linguistic evidence for the mora itself if and only if the mora hypothesis has successfully been tested with preliterate children. In order to avoid methodological problems of this kind, we must carefully examine the processes in which Japanese-speaking children come to acquire the prosodic unit of mora. This is indeed a very important line of research to pursue in the future.[22]

In addition to the questions directly related to the mora, there are a number of important issues that are indirectly related to this prosodic unit. The formation of "foot," for example, raises many interesting questions: e.g. whether it proceeds from left to right or from right to left, whether (or when) it permits a monomoraic (i.e. degenerate) foot, whether an unfooted syllable may be allowed, and whether it is entirely independent of syllable structure as assumed by Poser (1990). None of these questions has been settled in the literature.

A more fundamental question may be raised concerning the nature of the foot itself. As discussed in section 1.5, the notion of bimoraic foot plays important roles in Japanese phonology and morphology. However, it remains largely unanswered why bimoraic form functions as an optimal structure at all. Note that the notion of foot binarity as proposed by Prince and Smolensky (1993) does not answer this question; it is no more than a restatement of the observation that bimoraic foot serves as an unmarked foot form in a number of languages. This question naturally leads us to ask whether bimoraic foot is a phonological notion at all. Given the fact that bimoraicity can readily be attained by simply lengthening monomoraic syllables at the phonetic level as shown in (22a), it may not be so unrealistic to suspect that what is truly relevant is a bimoraic phonetic duration, and not the bimoraic configuration in phonological representation (Kubozono 1995d). This is another interesting topic for future research.

Finally, the second prosodic unit discussed in this chapter, i.e. syllable, raises as many questions as the mora. The biggest question of all concerns the range of linguistic phenomena which can be generalized in terms of this prosodic unit. Given the several different kinds of evidence for this unit in section 2, it is highly probable that a new analysis based on this unit should provide a more satisfactory and principled account of a wider range of phenomena in Japanese. The key to this new stage of research hinges crucially upon how successfully we can free ourselves of the conventional idea that the mora and the syllable are incompatible with each other in a single prosodic system.

NOTES

1   The traditional phonemic transcriptions known as *kunreisiki* are used throughout this chapter: e.g. /si/ for [ʃi], /zi/ for [dʒi], /ti/ for [tʃi], /sya/ for [ʃa], and /ky/ for the onset of *Kyoto*.

2   A phonological process which seems fundamentally similar to this phonetic process of temporal compensation is that of vowel epenthesis in loanword phonology. A language with a very simple syllable structure, Japanese inserts a vowel wherever necessary when it borrows words from a foreign language with a more complex syllable structure. Interestingly, the value of the epenthetic vowel is determined by the phonetic quality of the preceding consonant (Lovins 1975), suggesting a tight relationship within the unit of CV: (i) /i/ is epenthesized after [tʃ] and [dʒ] (e.g. *match* → [mat.tʃi], *edge* → [ed.dʒi]) and marginally after /k/ (e.g. *ink* → /in.ki/, *strike* "industrial action" → /su.to.rai.ki/); (ii) /o/ is epenthesized after /t/ and /d/

(e.g. *pet* → /pet.to/, *bed* → /bed.do/), and (iii) /u/ is epenthesized elsewhere (e.g. *box* → /bok.ku.su/). The same cohesiveness between the onset and the vowel also shows itself in the phonetic assimilation of consonants. Namely, an onset consonant tends to assimilate to the quality of the following vowel, not of the preceding vowel. Thus /s/ shows an allophonic variation between [ʃ] (before /i/) and [s] (before any other vowel), and /h/ exhibits an alternation between [ç] (before /i/), [Φ] (before /u/), and [h] (elsewhere). This contrasts with the assimilation of consonants to their preceding vowel which is observed in many languages; in German, for example, the voiceless velar fricative /x/ assimilates to [ç] when it appears after a front vowel, e.g. *ich* [iç] vs. *Buch* [bux].

3 The vocabulary of Japanese falls into two classes, accented and unaccented words. Unaccented words are defined as words which have a flat pitch, i.e. no abrupt pitch drop, at the phonetic output. The accentedness of a particular item is largely lexical and is not readily predictable on the basis of its linguistic information (some exceptions are discussed in section 2.1.2). A statistical study cited in Hayashi (1982: 331) shows that unaccentedness is not exceptional but actually accounts for a majority of Japanese words, especially words of native and Sino-Japanese origins. This chapter employs the conventional notation whereby unaccented words are not marked by a diacritic or anything equivalent to it.

4 This lengthening process is often apparently blocked in sentence-final positions, where vowel length may be neutralized by an independent

vowel shortening process: e.g. /itai/ → /ite:/ ~ /ite/ "ouch!"

5 Classical Japanese had only CV syllables except in word-initial position, where an onsetless syllable was also allowed.

6 This mora-based change can be understood more easily if the moraic obstruent is represented by an abstract symbol (/Q/ in the following transcription): i.e. kuu.bo miQ.do.wee → kuQ.bo miQ.do.wee.

7 Exceptions to this generalization include trimoraic forms such as *so.re-n* (<so.(bi.e.to) re-n.(po-o) "Soviet Union") and *da-n.pa* (<da-n.(su) pa-(a.ti-i) "dance party") as well as the unusual bimoraic form of *be.a* (<be-(e.su) a-(p.pu) "base-up").

8 The bisyllabic input forms in (22a) have a geminate consonant in modern Japanese: e.g. mit.tu (<mi.tu), yot.tu (<yo.tu).

9 Essentially the same situation is found in the citation of modern numerals. Thus monomoraic forms, e.g. /ni/ "two" and /go/ "five," are lengthened to attain bimoraic length and, moreover, bimoraic forms such as /yon/ "four" and /kyuu/ "nine" are chosen in preference to their monomoraic variants, /si/ "four" and /ku/ "nine" (Itô 1990). Similarly, the minimal bimoraic length is kept when the twelve horary signs in the traditional calendar are pronounced in sequence: i.e. [nee, usi, tora, uu, tatu, mii, uma, hituzi, saru, tori, inu, ii] for /ne, usi, tora, u, tatu, mi, uma, hituzi, saru, tori, inu, i/ "mouse, ox, tiger, rabbit, dragon, snake, horse, sheep, monkey, chicken, dog, wild boar."

10 A crucial difference between (Tokyo) Japanese and other languages with a minimality

constraint is that underived words in Japanese are exempt from this constraint: Japanese permits monomoraic content words such as /te/ "hand" and /ka/ "mosquito." In other words, the minimality constraint applies only to derived words, or words produced via a productive word formation process in Japanese. Note that this distinction between derived and underived words may not be necessary in Kinki Japanese spoken in Kyoto and Osaka, where monosyllabic CV words are generally lengthened to bimoraic length: e.g. [te:] for /te/ and [ka:] for /ka/. In this dialect, the minimality constraint applies to all the vocabulary just as it does in many other languages sensitive to a similar constraint.

11 The same typology by J. D. McCawley (1978) would classify Kinki (Osaka/Kyoto) Japanese as a "mora-counting, mora language." A crucial difference between Tokyo Japanese and Kinki Japanese is that moraic nasals and other special moras often bear an accent on their own in the latter: for example, in such words as *on'gaku* "music" and *kin'tetu* "Kinki Railways" only the moraic nasal bears a high tone. It remains a question, however, whether the syllable is totally irrelevant in the description of this dialect.

12 There are some exceptions to the regularity described in (29a): e.g. ni'ngyo + hi'me → ningyo'][hime] "mermaid, princess; Little Mermaid;" yoyaku + se'ki → yoyaku'][seki] "reservation, seat; reserved seat" (Kubozono 1997). Note that the existence of these exceptions does not constitute evidence against the Nonfinality constraint described here.

13 Hypothetical words of the syllable structure in (32a) often permit a variant pattern whereby an accent is located one mora leftward: e.g. re'.ba.no-n and re'.no.ba-n. This reflects a new accent pattern illustrated in (39) in section 2.3.2 below.

14 The same constraint is seen to operate in the less productive cases of loanword clipping where the word-initial portion is truncated: (he.ru).me-t.to "helmet," (a.ru).ba-i.to "Arbeit, part-time job," (a.do).bai.zaa "adviser." Note that the last example cannot be reduced to the monosyllabic form, *zaa*.

15 See Haraguchi (1996) for additional morphological evidence for the syllable in Japanese.

16 Apart from compensatory lengthening, the notion of syllable weight provides a unified and insightful account of many processes which have hitherto been described as segmental and/or moraic phenomena. These include the historical process of *onbin* and the structure of children's language or "motherese:" see Kubozono (1995c) for a new analysis of these phenomena.

17 The lefthand member of the pairs in (42a) was originally bisyllabic and was stressed on the initial open syllable: e.g. *wí.se*. The righthand member of the same pairs, on the other hand, had a closed stressed syllable throughout the history of English: e.g. *wís.dom*.

18 This shortening process is quite productive in the loanword phonology of Japanese and can be differentiated from many sporadic instances involving vowel shortening such as /po.su.to/, */pou.su.to/ "post" and /fi.ru.daa/, */fii.ru.daa/ "fielder."

19 Some speakers of Tokyo Japanese accept the pronunciation in which the CA docks onto the final mora of N1, or the moraic nasal in these compound expressions: e.g. /raiN' = ga.wa/, /de.zaiN' = ha.ku/. These speakers usually place a CA on the final mora in other compound nouns such as those in (48) too, e.g. /amazoN' = gawa/, which implies that the moraic nasal has established itself as a syllable nucleus in their grammar. However, the existence of this variant accent pattern does not invalidate the argument here: what is relevant is the fact that the CA almost never docks onto the initial mora of the trimoraic sequences, i.e. */ra'iN = ga.wa/, */de.za'iN = ha.ku/.

20 Opinions differ on whether the onset consonant(s) belongs to the mora (Hyman 1985, Kubozono 1985, Itô 1989) or directly to the syllable (Hayes 1989).

21 The sole exception to this is in writing moras involving a consonant-glide sequence in the onset position, e.g. /to-o.*kyo*-o/, which is represented with two letters, one of which is a subscript.

22 This is a research area largely unexplored. See Mazuka et al. (1996) and Ito and Tatsumi (1997) for experimental work on this topic.

3 The Phonological Lexicon*

JUNKO ITÔ AND ARMIN MESTER

0 Introduction: Stratification and Lexical Subsetting

This chapter presents some recent results on a central aspect of Japanese phonology, namely, the structure of the phonological lexicon. The issue here is the fundamental division of the lexicon into different strata: native (or Yamato), Sino-Japanese, and Western loans at various stages of assimilation. An understanding of such stratification patterns not only is a prerequisite for serious analytical work in Japanese phonology (and elsewhere), but enables us to raise the question of what, if anything, the existence of lexical strata might tell us about the organization of the phonology (and ultimately, the grammar) as a whole. Within Optimality Theory (Prince and Smolensky 1993), as we will see, this issue is intimately connected to the form and function of faithfulness constraints.

In virtually all languages whose grammars have been explored to any degree of detail, the lexicon shows evidence for some internal stratification. Such different lexical strata are usually referred to with terms like "native vocabulary," "assimilated loans," "foreign vocabulary," or by labels identifying the loan source: "Arabic," "Latinate," "Sanskrit," "Spanish," "Sino-Korean," "Swahili," "Portuguese," etc. While the ultimate origin of a given lexical item consists of etymological information without any relevance for the synchronic grammar, such classifications often have synchronic impact in that they reflect, more or less accurately, an overall partitioning of the total set of lexical items into distinct subsets whose members behave alike with respect to several different criteria within the grammar, including observance of morpheme structure constraints, morpheme combinatorics, and morphophonemic alternations.

For Japanese, there is a well-established tradition[1] of distinguishing between *yamato-kotoba* "native (Yamato) vocabulary" (1a), *kan-go* "Sino-Japanese vocabulary" (1b), *gairai-go* "foreign vocabulary" (1c), and *gisei-/gitai-go* "onomatopoetic/ mimetic vocabulary" (1d).[2]

(1) Examples of vocabulary items from:
    a. *Native (Yamato) stratum:*

kotoba	"word, language"
oto	"sound"
hanaši	"talk"
kuruma	"wheel, car"

    b. *Sino-Japanese stratum:*

geŋ-go-gaku	"linguistics"	(speak-word-study)
oN-in-roN	"phonology"	(sound-rhyme-theory)
deN-wa	"telephone"	(electric-speak)
ǰi-dō-ša	"automobile"	(self-moving-vehicle)

    c. *Foreign stratum:*

raŋgēǰi-raboratorī	"language laboratory"
saN-tora	"sound track"[3]
terefoN-kādo	"telephone card"
pato-kā	"patrol car, police car"[4]

    d. *Onomatopoetic/Mimetic stratum:*

pera-pera	"(speak) fluently"
kori-kori	"crisply"
sui-sui	"lightly and quietly"
mota-mota	"slowly, inefficiently"

This stratification corresponds in kind to the distinction in English between the Germanic versus the Latinate vocabulary, but is more accessible and conscious to the nonspecialists because of its reflection in the writing system.[5] It is also more elaborate in that four different morpheme classes need to be recognized. *Yamato-kotoba* forms the native stratum (1a), corresponding to the Germanic/Anglo-Saxon vocabulary in English. Analogous to the Latinate/Greek stratum in English, *kan-go* (1b) constitutes the vast technical and learned vocabulary of the language, and appears mostly as compounds consisting of bound roots. Taking over the role of Sino-Japanese as the main source of new technical vocabulary are the *gairai-go*, the ever-increasing loanwords of the foreign stratum (1c). The examples in (1a–c) were chosen to illustrate cases in which items from different morpheme classes share some core meaning.

Alongside these three strata (Yamato, Sino-Japanese, and foreign), there is the substantial class of *gisei-go* and *gitai-go* (1d), mimetic or sound-symbolic vocabulary items that play a much more important role in the overall system than corresponding words in English.[6] As J. D. McCawley (1968b: 64) points out, mimetics "function syntactically as manner adverbs and may refer to just any aspect (visual, emotional, etc.) of the activity involved, rather than just its sound."

If such morpheme classifications were nothing more than a record of etymological history, they would be of little linguistic interest.[7] However, as is familiar from the classical linguistic literature on the subject, they require explicit synchronic recognition if, and as far as, they continue to play a role in the grammar.[8] As has been shown in numerous cases, morpheme classes demarcate the areas of the lexicon where certain phonological regularities hold (segmental alternations and structural constraints), and they serve to restrict morpheme combinatorics.[9] Occasional hybrid formations aside, Latinate suffixes tend to attach to Latinate stems, Sino-Japanese roots compound only with other Sino-Japanese roots, etc.

While the factual existence of stratification can hardly be in doubt, its appropriate place in the theory has remained unclear. After some early influential work in Praguean phonology,[10] there have only been very few studies focusing on the question of what the existence of lexical strata might mean for the theory of the lexicon and for the organization of the grammar.[11] The topic emerged on a larger scale in early generative phonology, where the serious analysis of the morphophonemics of English and other languages required a systematic way of referring to lexical strata (Chomsky and Halle 1968 and related work).

An initial idea might be that stratification can be depicted as in (2), where the lexicon is partitioned into parallel sublexica containing native items, loan items, etc.

(2)

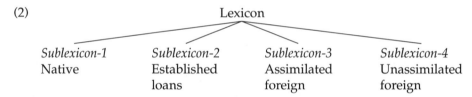

	Lexicon		
Sublexicon-1	*Sublexicon-2*	*Sublexicon-3*	*Sublexicon-4*
Native	Established loans	Assimilated foreign	Unassimilated foreign

However, a significant finding of Kiparsky (1968), taken up and extended in Saciuk (1969), is that a model like (2) misses two central and interrelated features of lexical structure – the *gradual* and *hierarchical* character of lexical stratification. Lexical items do not come neatly packaged into groups labeled [±foreign]; rather, different degrees of nativization among foreign words are commonplace.[12] Instead of a partitioning into parallel and disjoint [+foreign] and [–foreign] sublexica, we have "a hierarchy of foreignness, with exceptions to one rule always being exceptions to another rule, but not vice versa" (Kiparsky 1968: 20).

On the basis of a detailed investigation of the phonological lexicon of contemporary Japanese, Itô and Mester (1995a, 1995b) take up this idea and argue for a model of the phonological lexicon in which this kind of hierarchy among lexical items plays a central role. In this conception, which is to be further developed and motivated below, the central notion is that of a "lexical constraint domain;" that is, analyzing lexical stratification means analyzing the inclusion and overlap relations between constraint domains. The main result is that lexical items are organized in terms of an overall *core–periphery structure* that can be depicted as in (3).[13]

(3)

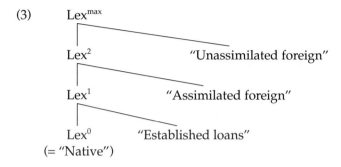

Lex^{max}

Lex^2 "Unassimilated foreign"

Lex^1 "Assimilated foreign"

Lex^0 "Established loans"
(= "Native")

In this model, the relevant structural organization of the lexicon is set inclusion, leading from the innermost lexical core Lex^0 to the most inclusive set Lex^{max} comprising all lexical items. In this set inclusion hierarchy Lex$^0 \subset$ Lex^1 $\subset$ Lex$^2 \subset \ldots \subset$ Lex^{max}, Lex^0 corresponds to what is usually called the "native stratum," Lex^1 includes "native" and "established loans," and so on. Crucially different from the sublexicon model in (2), the (higher) lexical strata do not directly correspond to Lex^1, Lex^2, etc., but are defined by set complementation, following the general schema Lex^i – Lex^{i-1} (i.e. Lex^i minus Lex^{i-1}). Thus the stratum of established loans in (3) is the set Lex^1 – Lex^0, etc. More inclusive sets can be read off the diagram in an analogous way: the set of all non-native items is Lex^{max} – Lex^0, the complement of Lex^0, etc. The elements of Lex^0 fulfill lexical constraints in the maximal way and form the core of the lexicon. Moving outwards from the core, we encounter items that violate more and more constraints until we encounter, at the periphery, items fulfilling only a small subset of the constraints. These constraints are truly fundamental in the sense that they define the basic syllable canons and other central aspects of the language.

Structures as in (3) are built out of a network of implicational relations involving lexical items and phonological constraints of the following kind: items that are subject to constraint A are also always subject to constraint B, but not all items subject to B are also subject to A. This makes A a constraint with a more restricted domain than B – in fact, A's domain is properly included in B's domain, as schematically shown in (4).

(4)

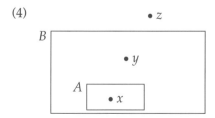

$\bullet z$

B

$\bullet y$

A

$\bullet x$

Here x is in the domain of A and of B, y is in the domain of B, but not of A, and z is in the domain of neither A nor B. It is not possible for an item to be in the domain of A without being in the domain of B. If lexical items and constraints consistently pattern in this way, it makes sense to talk about core–periphery relations, with *x* being closer to the lexical core than *y*, *z* occupying the periphery, etc.

The rest of this chapter is organized as follows. After exploring the core–periphery relations of the various constraints whose interaction gives rise to some of the characteristics of the Japanese sound pattern (section 1), we turn to the formal analysis of the constraint domains in Optimality Theory (section 2), test the model's predictions and expand it further by exploring the development of stratified grammars (section 3), and conclude with a discussion of some further theoretical issues regarding stratification and faithfulness constraints (appendix).

1   Phonological Constraints: Canonical Patterns, Alternations, and Domains

We see clear instances of core–periphery relations when we consider how the different classes of lexical items discussed above (see (1)) behave with respect to the constraints in (5) (taken from Itô and Mester 1995a, 1995b) operative in the phonological lexicon of Japanese.

(5) a. SYLLSTRUC: Syllable structure constraints (see below)
     b. NOVOICEDGEM (NO-DD):   "No voiced obstruent geminates" (*bb, *dd, *gg, etc.)
     c. NOVOICELESSLAB (NO-P): "No singleton-*p*": a constraint against nongeminate [p]
     d. NONAS⌢VOICELESS (NO-NT): "Post-nasal obstruents must be voiced" (*nt, *mp, *ŋk)

The set of basic syllable constraints of Japanese collectively referred to as SYLLSTRUC includes, among others, *COMPLEX (disallowing complex onsets and complex codas) and CODACOND (limiting codas to place-linked consonants or segments without consonantal place (= nasal glide N)).[14] These constraints are responsible for the well-known verbal paradigm alternations (6), where the gerundive form shows gemination (6a) or epenthesis (6b) to avoid high-ranking CODACOND or *COMPLEX violations.

(6) a. tor-u "take-Present"   tot-te   "take-Gerundive"   *tor-te
     b. kas-u "lend-Present"   kaši-te "lend-gerundive"   *kas-te

The pattern is not limited to the verbal paradigm, but is productively found in verbal root compounds (7), where the unsyllabifiable input cluster *kt* is either split by epenthesis or geminated.

(7) fuk- "blow"   tob- "fly"
     fuki-tobu, fut-tobu "blow-away"   *fuk-tobu

The constraint against voiced geminates (No-DD) also plays an active role in verbal root compounding. As shown in (8), the prefixal roots *ow-* and *tsuk-* induce gemination of the following consonant (*ok-kakeru*, *tsut-tatsu*). When this consonant is a voiced obstruent, the result is not a geminate (**od-dasu*, **tsud-dasu*) but rather a homorganic nasal + voiced obstruent sequence (*on-dasu*, *tsun-dasu*).

(8)

ow-	"chase"	kake-	"run"	ok-kakeru	"run after"[15]
		tsuk-	"arrive"	ot-tsuku	"overtake"
		das-	"put out"	on-dasu, *od-dasu	"drive out"
tsuk-	"stab"	kom-	"be full"	tsuk-komu	"cram"
		tat-	"stand"	tsut-tatsu	"stand straight"
		nomer-	"lean"	tsun-nomeru	"lunge forward"
		das-	"put out"	tsun-dasu, *tsud-dasu	"thrust out"

As shown in (9), similar patterns are observed for intensive *-ri* adverbs with internal gemination.[16] The corresponding single consonants are found in the base forms, which occur as reduplicated adverbs (e.g. *zabu-zabu*), or as stems of other lexical formations (*hiso-ka* = adj., *nobi-ru* = verb, etc.).

(9) a.

uka(-uka)	ukka(-ri)		"absentmindedly"
biku(-biku)	bikku(-ri)		"surprising, frightening"
šito(-šito)	šitto(-ri)		"wet, rainy"
hiso(-ka)	hisso(-ri)		"secretly"
gusa(-ri)	gussa(-ri)		"plunging in (with a dagger)"
hono(-ka)	honno(-ri)		"dimly, faintly"
šimi(-ǰimi)	šimmi(-ri)		"deeply, heartily"

b.

zabu(-zabu)	zambu(-ri)	*zabbu(-ri)	"raining heavily"
šobo(-šobo)	šombo(-ri)	*šobbo(-ri)	"lonely"
koga(-su)	koŋga(-ri)	*kogga(-ri)	"toasted, roasted"
nobi(-ru)	nombi(-ri)	*nobbi(-ri)	"leisurely"
nodo(-ka)	nondo(-ri)	*noddo(-ri)	"tranquil, calm"

The voiceless labial restriction (No-P) rules out any *p* that is exclusively linked to onset position (henceforth, "singleton-*p*").[17] An underlying singleton-*p* is debuccalized to [h] and appears allophonically as bilabial [ɸ] and palatal [ç] before high back and high front vowels, respectively. Following standard transcriptional practice, we render these as [fu] and [hi]. Besides the well-known variants *nippoɴ* and *nihoɴ* "Japan" and the adverb *yappari~yahari* "after all," we find numerous instances of the *p~h* alternation, some of which are listed in (10)–(12).[18]

(10) Verbal root compounding (cf. (8) above):

hik-	"pull"	har-	"stretch"	hip-paru	"pull strongly"
ow-	"chase"	haǰime-	"start"	op-paǰimeru	"really start"
tsuk-	"stab"	hašir-	"run"	tsup-paširu	"dash, race"

(11) *ma-* prefixation:

	hiruma	"daytime"		map-piruma	"broad daylight"
	hadaka	"naked"		map-padaka	"stark naked"
cf.	kuro	"black"		mak-kuro	"pitch black"
	naka	"center"		man-naka	"dead center"

(12) Sino-Japanese compounding:[19]

hatsu-bai	"sale"		šup-patsu	"departure"
hai-tatsu	"distribution"		šim-pai	"worry"
tai-fuu	"typhoon"		top-puu	"sudden wind"

By adding a voicing feature, Rendaku gives rise to *h~b* alternations in Yamato word compounding.[20]

(13)

hana	"flower"		ike-bana	"flower arrangement"
hata	"side, bank"		kawa-bata	"river bank"
fue	"flute"		kuči-bue	"mouth flute, whistle"
hito	"person"		tabi-bito	"traveller"

Finally, the constraint against nasal⌢voiceless sequences (No-NT) (5d)[21] is responsible for a widespread and fully regular alternation in verbs involving the gerundive ending *-te* and the past tense ending *-ta* (14).[22]

(14)

	Base	*Gerundive*	*Past*	
	šin-	šin-de	šin-da	"die"
	in-[23]	in-de	in-da	"leave"
	yom-	yon-de	yon-da	"read"
	susum-	susun-de	susun-da	"progress"
	hasam-	hasan-de	hasan-da	"put between"
cf.	mi-	mi-te	mi-ta	"see"
	hašir-	hašit-te	hašit-ta	"run"
	kaw-	kat-te	kat-ta	"buy"

Verbal root compounding also shows ample evidence for a postnasal voicing alternation, as illustrated in (15), where the first verbal root *fum-* "to step on" ends in a nasal.

(15)

tsukeru	"attach"		fun-dzukeru	*fun-tsukeru	"trample on"
haru	"stretch"		fum-baru	*fum-paru	"resist"
kiru	"cut"		fuŋ-giru	*fuŋ-kiru	"give up"
šibaru	"tie"		fun-jibaru	*fun-šibaru	"immobilize"

While the formal structure of these constraints and their phonetic grounding are an interesting topic deserving further exploration, the focus of this chapter is a different one, namely, their systematic patterning in the various lexical strata. Besides leading to a large number of morpheme alternations in Yamato and Sino-Japanese items (see (6)–(15)), the constraints in (5) leave their mark on the phonological lexicon as a whole in a less direct, but equally significant way. They result in static restrictions on morpheme shape, independent of any alternations. The way in which these restrictions are distributed over the lexicon reveals the details of its stratal structure.

The syllable constraints of Japanese collectively referred to as SYLLSTRUC in (5a) are observed in all lexical strata. An item such as *trot*, with a complex onset and non-place-linked consonantal place in the coda, is simply not a viable lexical item in Japanese. While No-DD (5b) is observed in most of the lexicon, violations are encountered in the unassimilated foreign vocabulary (e.g. *roddo* "rod" or *nobbu* "knob;" cf. the nativized variant *nobu*). No-P (5c) is frequently violated in all kinds of foreign items (e.g. *peepaa* "paper"), including cases showing effects of nativization (e.g. *sepaado* "German shepherd dog").[24] Finally, while No-NT (5d) is observed in the Yamato vocabulary, violations are freely found elsewhere in the lexicon, not only in the foreign stratum (e.g. *kompyuutaa* "computer," *santa* "Santa"), but also in Sino-Japanese items (e.g. *sampo* "walk," *hantai* "opposite").[25]

All of this may strike the casual observer as nothing but a collection of random facts and idiosyncracies; in reality, we are dealing with an instance of a simple generalization holding for every stratified lexicon. The table in (16) reveals the systematicity of the pattern, in the form of hierarchical inclusion relations between the domains in the phonological lexicon where the various constraints are active.

(16)

	SYLLSTRUC	No-DD	No-P	No-NT
Yamato	✓	✓	✓	✓
Sino-Japanese	✓	✓	✓	violated
Assimilated foreign	✓	✓	violated	violated
Unassimilated foreign	✓	violated	violated	violated

The situation seen in (16) is an instance of the abstract pattern shown in (4). Everything subject to No-DD is also subject to SYLLSTRUC, but not vice versa; everything subject to No-P is also subject to No-DD, but not vice versa, etc. Given the cross-linguistic frequency of such patterns, it is natural to hypothesize that some fundamental property of lexical constraint systems must be at work here. The nesting of constraint domains is depicted in (17), where in Japanese "Native" is instantiated by Yamato and "Established loans" by Sino-Japanese.

(17)

$$
\begin{array}{llll}
\text{SYLLSTRUC} & \text{Lex}^{\text{max}} & & \\
& | & \longleftarrow \text{Lex}^{\text{max}} - \text{Lex}^2 & = \text{"Unassimilated foreign"} \\
\text{No-DD} & \text{Lex}^2 & & \\
& | & \longleftarrow \text{Lex}^2 - \text{Lex}^1 & = \text{"Assimilated foreign"} \\
\text{No-P} & \text{Lex}^1 & & \\
& | & \longleftarrow \text{Lex}^1 - \text{Lex}^0 & = \text{"Established loans"} \\
\text{No-NT} & \text{Lex}^0 & & \\
& & \longleftarrow \text{Lex}^0 & = \text{"Native"}
\end{array}
$$

Several observations can be made about this kind of model. First, viewed as a large set of elements, the whole lexicon is organized as a structure with more and more inclusive subsets: a member of Lex^i is also a member of Lex^{i+1} in that it fulfills all the constraints of Lex^{i+1}.

Second, a consistent pattern of set inclusion of this kind entails the existence of an innermost domain included in all the larger domains – in other words, a core area governed by the maximum set of lexical constraints (and hence "unmarked").

Third, the fundamental structural characteristic of the lexicon is the set-inclusion structure, and not the existence of large, homogeneous, and well-defined strata, which is a secondary phenomenon. It is certainly true that some traditional vocabulary strata emerge as lexical areas that stand out in virtue of serving as the domains for a number of different constraints, somewhat reminiscent of the bundles of isoglosses defining dialect areas in a traditional dialect map. In Japanese, this holds true for Yamato and Sino-Japanese; such groupings constitute genuine morphological classes in the sense of Aronoff (1994), which can be referred to as such in the grammar.[26] On the other hand, a closer inspection (Itô and Mester 1995a: 198–205) also supports the cross-linguistic finding that the class of foreign items does not constitute a uniform stratum, but is best thought of as the cumulative totality of the items occupying less and less central areas of the lexicon.[27] In (17) and elsewhere in this chapter, this nonuniformity is acknowledged by the split into "unassimilated" and "assimilated" foreign items. In reality, many finer distinctions are hidden beneath this coarse classification: the less nativized an item is, the more it disobeys lexical constraints, i.e. the more it falls outside of various constraint domains and is located towards the periphery of the lexical space.

While we continue to use historicizing terms like "native," "loan," "foreign," etc., because they are firmly established in this area, it is very important to understand them in a synchronic-structural sense. Some items are historically speaking "native" in that they are not borrowed from any other language, but they are still peripheral in a synchronic-structural sense. Examples of non-borrowed peripheral items include exclamations like [če?][28] and certain contractions, such as the syncopated form *anta*[29] (from *anata* "you") with an -*nt*- cluster. On the other hand, there are also historically borrowed items with core behavior. A case in point is the Portuguese loan *karuta*, which is treated as a core item with respect to Rendaku voicing in *hana-garuta* "flower card game." Similar behavior is found with certain Sino-Japanese items, such as *keŋka* "quarrel" in *oyako-geŋka* "quarrel between parent and child," or *teŋka* "empire" in *onna-deŋka* "petticoat government."[30] The last examples, which exhibit a mixture of native characteristics (Rendaku) with non-native characteristics (-*ŋk* – clusters), also show that non-homogeneity is not restricted to the foreign stratum, but is also found in other areas of the lexicon, albeit to a much lesser extent. The demarcation lines for the different constraints characterizing, for example, the native stratum do not always exactly coincide, resulting in the occurrence of items with mixed behavior. The existence of such elements supports an important claim of our proposal: namely, that it is the individual constraint domains that are primary, not the stratal structure that emerges from them as a secondary generalization.[31] At the same time, a small set of items with mixed behavior does not alter the overwhelming generalization that structural properties show stratal clustering.

2 Optimality Theory and Lexical Core–Periphery Relations

Up to this point, our usage of the term "constraint" has been an informal, pretheoretic one. It is now time to be more precise in this respect. In particular, we need to clarify what it means for a given constraint to be "out of force" in certain areas of the lexicon. In Optimality Theory, the traditional notion of a parametrized constraint – something that can be turned "on" or "off" in grammars – is replaced by the notion that a grammar literally consists in imposing a ranking order on a given set of universal and violable constraints.[32] In this view, constraints are universal, uniformly present in all grammars; the effects of a given constraint differ from grammar to grammar depending on the placement of the constraint within the overall ranking. The "on/off" settings approach of earlier theories can be seen as a rough approximation to a more accurate theory based on the notions of ranking and violability.

For the case at hand, the question becomes how the core–periphery structure in (17) can be obtained with a uniform constraint set: how do the various areas of the lexicon differ, if they do not differ in terms of which constraints are "on" and which are "off"? The obvious suggestion is that they differ in the way the constraints are *ranked*. In pursuing this line of investigation, familiar considerations of restrictiveness suggest that we explore the possibility that there are strict limits on such lexicon-internal rerankings.[33] In Optimality Theory crucial aspects of the role of a particular constraint are determined by the way it is ranked with respect to the faithfulness constraints, including the three subfamilies prohibiting segment deletion (MAX), segment insertion (DEP), and change in feature value (IDENT).[34]

For a given wellformedness constraint (say, NOCODA), being ranked above some conflicting faithfulness constraints is roughly equivalent to being "on" in terms of traditional parameter setting; being ranked below all conflicting faithfulness constraints is roughly equivalent to being "off." In Optimality Theory, the "underlying inventory" of a certain language (segments, clusters, syllable types, etc.) is determined indirectly. Inputs themselves are not directly regulated; anything at all can in principle serve as an input; the grammar, as a system of ranked constraints, determines how, if at all, the input gets parsed.

Let us start with Prince and Smolensky's (1993) assumption of strict domination: every optimality-theoretic grammar imposes a total order on the set of constraints. Given constraints A and B, either $A \gg B$ or $B \gg A$ must hold.

Taking a cue from the relation between the domains seen above in (16) and
(17), it is natural to hypothesize that the four constraints under discussion are
ranked as in (18).

(18)   SYLLSTRUC

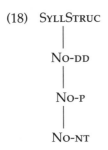

In order to focus on the essential point, we abstract away from the differentiation between various Input/Output (henceforth, IO) constraints and con-
solidate the family of faithfulness conditions into a single unit (abbreviated as
"FAITH"). Ranking FAITH below some constraint C means that C can command
violations of faithfulness – at least one of the relevant faithfulness constraints
is ranked below C. Likewise, ranking FAITH above some constraint C means
that C cannot command violations of faithfulness – none of the relevant faithfulness constraints is ranked below C.[35]

The hierarchy in (18) suggests a very simple hypothesis about lexical stratification, namely, that it comes about through different rankings of faithfulness
within a fixed hierarchy of structural wellformedness constraints. Consider the
four wellformedness constraints under discussion. With their relative ranking
fixed as in (18) above, there are five niches where FAITH can in principle be
located, marked as FAITH$_1$ through FAITH$_5$ in (19). As indicated, FAITH$_1$–FAITH$_4$
indeed characterize the four vocabulary strata of Japanese under discussion.[36]

(19)

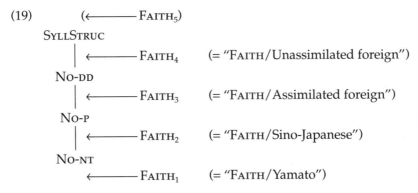

Working within the original version of Optimality Theory as developed in
Prince and Smolensky (1993), Itô and Mester (1995a) conceive of FAITH$_1$–FAITH$_5$
as different rankings of the same block of IO- faithfulness constraints. Different
strata involve slightly different grammars, and stratification is thus a form of
linguistic variation. A variant of this proposal couched within Correspondence

Theory (McCarthy and Prince 1995) posits the different rankings of IO-FAITH as distinct replicas of IO-FAITH, each indexed for a vocabulary stratum (i.e. FAITH/Yamato, etc.). We will here present the theory in the indexed-FAITH format, and will later return to general questions raised by FAITH₁, etc.[37]

FAITH/Yamato ranks below all four wellformedness constraints in (19), with the consequence that it cannot interfere with their demands. When a faithfulness violation is preferred over violations of segmental, sequential, or syllabic well-formedness, we have core behavior: in Japanese, a characteristic of Yamato items.[38]

At the other end of the spectrum, top-ranking FAITH/Unassimilated foreign in (19) is subordinate to general syllable structure constraints. For example, Japanese disallows complex onsets and adheres to a very strict coda condition (see above) – hence the appearance of epenthetic vowels in loanwords where the loan source has a consonant cluster or a final coda. But since FAITH/Unassimilated foreign dominates the other three structural wellformedness constraints, faithfulness demands will be met at their cost. As shown in (20), *beddo*, *petto*, and *tento*, while taking a final epenthetic vowel[39] to meet syllable structure demands, faithfully preserve their voiced geminate, singleton-*p*, and nasal + voiceless obstruent cluster, respectively, in violation of the lower-ranking structural constraints.

(20)   Unassimilated foreign:
      beddo "bed"   petto "pet"   tento "tent"
      (violation of No-DD) (violation of No-P) (violation of No-NT)

		SYLLSTRUC	FAITH/ Unassimilated foreign	No-DD	:	No-P	:	No-NT	:
/bed/	[bed]	*!							
Unassimilated foreign	☞ [beddo]		* (DEP)	*					
	[betto]		**! (DEP, IDENT-F)						
/pet/	[pet]	*!				*			
Unassimilated foreign	☞ [petto]		* (DEP)			*			
	[hetto]		**! (DEP, IDENT-F)						
/tent/	[tent]	*!						*	
Unassimilated foreign	☞ [tento]		* (DEP)					*	
	[tendo]		**! (DEP, IDENT-F)						

The candidate [beddo] is more faithful to /bed/ than [betto], which has an IDENT (i.e. change of feature value) violation in addition to a DEP (epenthesis) violation.[40]

As Katayama (1998) points out for similar cases, nothing much hinges on the choice of underlying forms. Besides /bed/, /pet/, and /tent/, another possibility is /beddo/, /petto/, /tento/, i.e. with lexically encoded epenthetic vowels, as shown in (21). In the absence of alternations, a version of lexicon optimization that puts a higher value on input–output similarity than on input simplicity in fact selects the latter set as the optimal input forms.[41]

(21)

		SyllStruc	Faith/ Unassimilated foreign	No-DD	:	No-P	:	No-NT	:
/beddo/ Unassimilated foreign	☞ [beddo]			*					
	[betto]		*! (Ident-F)						
/petto/ Unassimilated foreign	☞ [petto]					*			
	[hetto]		*! (Ident-F)						
/tento/ Unassimilated foreign	☞ [tento]							*	
	[tendo]		*! (Ident-F)						

One step down the ladder in (19), we find Faith/Assimilated foreign, which differs from Faith/Unassimilated foreign only in being subordinate to the voiced geminate obstruent constraint No-DD. Avoidance of voiced obstruent geminates is therefore a high priority, as far as the nativization of loanwords is concerned.[42] The result is illustrated in (22).

(22)   Unassimilated foreign: beddo   Assimilated foreign: (hando)bakku
       "bed"   "handbag"[43]
       (violation of No-DD)   (no violation of No-DD, violation of
                                             Faith/Assimilated foreign)

		Faith/ Unassimilated foreign	No-DD	Faith/ Assimilated foreign	No-P	:	No-NT	:
/beddo/ Unassimilated foreign	☞ [beddo]		*					
	[betto]	*! (Ident-F)						
/baggu/ Assimilated foreign	[baggu]		*!					
	☞ [bakku]			*! (Ident-F)				
/pabbu/ Assimilated foreign	[pabbu]		*!		*			
	☞ [pabu]			* (Ident-μ)	*			
	[habu]			**! (Ident-F,μ)				
	[habbu]		*!	* (Ident-F)				

With respect to the other two constraints, No-p and No-nt, Faith/ Assimilated foreign remains dominant, thus forestalling any changes leading to the avoidance of singleton-*p* or of nasal+voiceless obstruent clusters. This is illustrated in (22) for the loanword *pabu* "pub" with its possible input /pabbu/: while parsing the *b* non-moraically, which is one way of avoiding the otherwise expected geminate, is legitimized by this ranking of Faith, debuccalizing *p* to *h*, which would lead to a more fully nativized form *habu*, is forestalled by faithfulness.

In (23), we define the individual faithfulness constraints violated in the tableaux above.

(23) Let *s* and *s'* be two segments that are correspondents of each other, and let *P(x)* denote the specification status of segment *x* with respect to some property *P* (e.g. [+continuant], [−continuant], or [0continuant]; [0μ], [1μ], or [2μ], etc.).[44]

    a. IDENT-F: *F(s) = F(s')*. "Correspondent segments have identical specifications for feature F."

    b. IDENT-μ: μ(s) = μ(s'). "Correspondent segments have the same moraicity."

Returning to the hierarchy of indexed Faith (19), we find Faith/Sino-Japanese ranked below SyllStruc, No-dd, and No-p, but still above No-nt. This means that an input sequence like /...nt.../ will be parsed as such in the output, in violation of No-nt, but the other three constraints can all command violations of Faith/Sino-Japanese. In particular, singleton-*p* cannot surface in Sino-Japanese.

(24) Assimilated foreign: paN "bread"   Sino-Japanese: haN "group"
                      (violation of No-p)   (no violation of No-p)

		⋮	No-DD	FAITH/ Assimilated foreign	No-P	FAITH/ Sino-Japanese	No-NT	⋮
/paN/ Assimilated foreign	☞ [paN]				*			
	[haN]			*!				
/paN/ Sino-Japanese	[paN]				*!			
	☞ [haN]					*		

Thus the word for *bread* surfaces as [paN] (cf. Portuguese *pão*), but the Sino-Japanese morpheme /paN/ "group" is realized as [haN] (cf. *ippaN* "group one," *sampaN* "group 3").

Finally, (25) contrasts Sino-Japanese and Yamato items with respect to the low-ranking constraint No-nt.

(25)   Sino-Japanese: šin-tai "body"   Yamato: šin-de "die-Gerund"
            (violation of No-NT)   (no violation of No-NT)

	⋮	No-DD	⋮	No-P	FAITH/ Sino-Japanese	*No-NT	FAITH/ Yamato
/šiN-tai/ ☞ [šiNtai]						*	
Sino-Japanese [šiNdai]					*!		
/šiN-te/ [šiNte]						*!	
Yamato ☞ [šiNde]							*

Stepping back from the details of this sketch of the stratal grammar of Japanese, we see that the simple hypothesis that stratal variation is due to the ranking of faithfulness and nothing else appears to provide enough descriptive flexibility to account for the empirical facts of stratification while at the same time imposing tight limits on the types of divergence allowed between strata. Ranked and violable faithfulness constraints are essential for this enterprise, just as in other areas. Optimality Theory allows us to reduce what looks like a haphazard application of constraints in different strata to a simple model, viz. a single phonology with a unique set of ranked structural constraints, with stratally indexed faithfulness constraints interleaved at different points.[45]

3   Developing Grammars and Stratification

The theory advocated here receives further support from the predictions it makes regarding possible nativizations. In this section, we first lay out the evidence and its implications (section 3.1). Building on these findings and recent results in Optimality Theory, we consider how stratification arises in the development of a grammar with diversified faithfulness, starting from an initial state where all faithfulness constraints are ranked below all markedness constraints (section 3.2).

3.1   Possible and impossible nativizations

There are significant restrictions on the ways in which native and non-native properties can be combined in partial nativizations, as shown in several studies, including Holden (1976) for Russian and Itô and Mester (1995a: 201–4) for Japanese. As the latter authors note, given a particular grammar and hence a specific ranking of the structural constraints, impossible nativization patterns constitute a crucial argument for the optimality-theoretic approach to stratification advocated here.

A concrete example from Itô and Mester (1995b: 832–3) illustrates the basic point about impossible nativizations. The palatalization constraints on fricatives and plosives of Japanese (here informally abbreviated as *SI and *TI; see the work cited for formal statements) result in the replacements *si → ši* and *ti → či*, giving rise to well-known alternations, e.g. *kas-e* "lend-Imperative," *kaš-i* "a loan;" *kat-e* "win-Imperative," *kač-i* "a win." However, there is one crucial difference between the two palatalization constraints: whereas the fricative-targeting constraint *SI is enforced in practically all recent loans, the plosive-targeting version *TI is not. Thus "sea" is *šii* and not **sii*, but "party" is *paatii* and not **paačii*. Palatalizing the fricative is more important than palatalizing the plosive, or in optimality-theoretic terms, the ranking must be as in (26), with other constraint(s) crucially intervening.

(26)   *SI
        ⋮
        *TI

Given (26) and the input form /siti/, with both consonants nonpalatalized, the system correctly predicts that *siti*, *šiti*, and *šiči*, but not *siči*, are possible nativizations of "city." The outcome depends on the stratum and its concomitant FAITH, as shown in (27). The second is the one usually encountered, as in the name *šitibaŋku* "Citibank."

(27)

		FAITH/X	*SI	FAITH/Y	*TI	FAITH/Z
a. /siti/ [stratum: Z]	☞ [šiči]					**
	[šiti]				*!	*
	[siti]		*!		*	
	[siči]		*!			*
b. /siti/ [stratum: Y]	[šiči]			**!		
	☞ [šiti]			*	*	
	[siti]		*!		*	
	[siči]		*!	*		
c. /siti/ [stratum: X]	[šiči]	**!				
	[šiti]	*!			*	
	☞ [siti]		*		*	
	[siči]	*!	*			

X, Y, and Z roughly correspond to "unassimilated," "assimilated," and "native," respectively. When the input is indexed for FAITH/Z, which is positioned below both *si and *ti, we get the fully nativized *šiči* (27a), with double palatalization. This is found, for example, in the brand-name "Citizen," whose proper pronunciation is *šičizuN*. When the input is indexed for FAITH/X, which is positioned above both markedness constraints, the unassimilated *siti* wins (27c), without any palatalization; and when it is indexed for FAITH/Y, which intervenes between the two constraints, the partially assimilated *šiti* emerges victorious (27b), with mixed palatalization behavior. Crucially, the candidate *siči*, which shows the other possible mix of palatalization properties, can never be the winner, given the input /siti/. In fact, in (27a–c) *siči* is not just non-optimal in individual competitions, but is a perpetual loser – it is always bettered by some other candidate. Because of the ranking of the sequential markedness constraints *si ≫ *ti, there is no way to rank some FAITH/α in such a way that *siči* wins at stratum α. The input–output pairing /siti/~[siči] is therefore harmonically bounded (cf. Prince and Smolensky 1993: 176–8), and is impossible as a nativization of a form containing both *si* and *ti*. In order for a winning output candidate to contain *s* before *i*, it must be the case that FAITH/X ≫ *si. Given *si ≫ *ti, this implies FAITH/X ≫ *ti by transitivity. In other words, once the sequence *si* is protected by faithfulness, *ti* is protected as well. By similar reasoning we determine that once *ti* is ruled out by markedness, so is *si* (*si ≫ *ti ≫ FAITH/Z). The sequences *ti* and *si* can be treated differently only in the way instantiated by *šiti* (*si ≫ FAITH/Y ≫ *ti). Given the central hypothesis of the core–periphery model, viz. that there is only a stratal replication of faithfulness and no stratal replication of structural constraints in the lexicon, no ranking selects *siči* as the best way of parsing /siti/, since this would require *ti ≫ FAITH/W ≫ *si – which cannot coexist with *si ≫ . . . ≫ *ti.

The *siči*-effect is a concrete illustration of a point made earlier (see (3) and (16)), namely, that the optimality-theoretic core–periphery model captures the implicational relations holding within the phonological lexicon.[46] Comparable to *siči* as an impossible nativization on the basis of the input /siti/ is the form *habbu* considered earlier in (22) as an output candidate at the Assimilated foreign stratum for the input /pabbu/ "pub." With preservation of the voiced obstruent geminate and debuccalization of *p* to *h* in order to avoid a singleton-*p*, the input–output pairing /pabbu/~[habbu] resembles /siti/~[siči] in showing an ill-fated combination of properties. Given No-DD ≫ No-P, there is no place in the hierarchy where some FAITH/α could be ranked so that *habbu* wins at stratum α – in other words, different from the other candidates (*pabu, pabbu, habu*), *habbu* is impossible as a nativization relative to the input /pabbu/.[47]

Impossible nativizations are useful as a test for different theories of stratal organization. Let us compare the stratal indexation model developed here with an approach which attempts to distinguish strata exclusively by means of input (pre)specification vs. underspecification for a given property.[48] If the core–periphery status of an item is formally expressed by degree of specification, this means, roughly speaking, that peripheral items need more specifications to counteract feature- and structure-filling defaults. Whether in a classic rule-based setting or in an optimality-theoretic environment, such a model can certainly express the core–periphery distribution of individual properties within the lexicon. However, since (pre/under)specification in one place is independent of (pre/under)specification in another place, the higher-level task of accounting for implicational dependencies *between* properties (e.g. the **siči*-effect) remains unsolved and would require extra machinery.[49] This shortcoming, which we will now exemplify more concretely, is a by-product of the independence of specifications, which introduces too many degrees of freedom into the system.

Let us assume, for concreteness, that nonpalatalizability of consonants is expressed by specifying [+anterior] in the input. The actual feature or structure that is used does not matter for the purpose of the argument; what matters is that the input specifications must be protected by faithfulness. All relevant faithfulness constraints must rank above the markedness constraints concerned with the ban against [+anterior] coronals preceding high front vowels, schematically: FAITH ≫ {*SI, *TI, . . . }. For the example under discussion, we have now the four representations in (28), where capital letters denote segments not specified for the feature anterior.[50]

(28)

a.	b. [+ant]	c. [+ant] [+ant]	d. [+ant]
S i T i	S i T i	S i T i	S i T i
[šiči]	[šiti]	[siti]	[siči]

(29)

		FAITH	*SI	*TI
a. /S i T i/	☞ [šiči]	**		
	[šiti]	**		*!
	[siti]	**	*!	*
	[siči]	**	*!	
b. [+ant] over /S i T i/	[šiči]	**!		
	☞ [šiti]	*		*
	[siti]	*	*!	*
	[siči]	**!	*	
c. [+ant] [+ant] over /S i T i/	[šiči]	*!*		
	[šiti]	*!*		*
	☞ [siti]		*!	*
	[siči]	*!*	*!	

(29)	d. [+ant] | /S i T i/	[šiči]	**!		
		[šiti]	**!		*
		☞ [siti]	*	*	*!
		[siči]	*	*	

The trouble is with representation (28d), which leads directly to the impossible nativization *siči*, as tableau (29d) verifies.[51] We cannot remedy the problem by ranking FAITH between *SI and *TI: *SI ≫ FAITH ≫ *TI, since this would not work for the native stratum, where palatalization of *t* before *i* is obligatory as well. One could try to overcome this problem by differentiating faithfulness in terms of strata: *SI ≫ FAITH/Y ≫ *TI ≫ FAITH/Z. But this move amounts to conceding the point that is at issue, viz. that input (pre/under)specification is insufficient to express stratal structure in the lexicon. In addition, the crucial dependency is still not expressed: whenever the sequence [si] is tolerated in a possible nativization, the sequence [ti] is as well, but not necessarily vice versa. In order to account for this, FAITH/X has to be added at the top of the hierarchy, replicating the entire ranking in (27). The analytical burden has shifted entirely to the stratal faithfulness constraints and their ranking, and (pre/under)specification ([+anterior] vs. [0anterior]) no longer plays a decisive role in distinguishing strata.[52]

On the other hand, in the model with stratum-indexed faithfulness constraints advocated here, such dependencies, and the resulting distinction between possible and impossible nativizations, are a consequence of a fundamental property of optimality-theoretic grammars, namely, the strict ranking of constraints.

3.2   *The initial state, ranking conservatism, and ranking consistency*

The details of the analysis of the multi-stratal vocabulary of Japanese raise some further important theoretical questions pertaining to the formal structure of faithfulness constraints. One of the central points of this chapter is that stratification in the lexicon shows an interesting subset structure. Strata are arrayed in a core–periphery manner, such that given two strata *A* and *B*, either the structures possible at *A* form a proper subset of the structures possible at *B*, or vice versa. This empirical generalization follows directly from our optimality-theoretic conception of the lexicon, which understands stratification as the result of different rankings of a block of FAITH constraints within a fixed hierarchy of structural constraints.

The specific account presented so far makes one simplifying assumption about the ranking of faithfulness constraints: all faithfulness constraints relevant to the markedness constraints NO-DD, NO-P, etc., such as IDENT-μ (checking the moraic value of correspondent segments), IDENT-PLACE (enforcing place feature identity between correspondent segments), are taken to be consolidated in Faith/X, etc. (where X is a lexical class), so that strata are carved out by uniform indexations of the whole block of faithfulness constraints.

(30) Input: /pabbu/
Ranking: Output

a. No-DD $\gg$ No-P $\gg$ "Faith/$_A$":   [habu]
$\begin{Bmatrix} \text{Id-Pl}/_A \\ \text{Id-}\mu/_A \end{Bmatrix}$(etc.)

b. No-DD $\gg$ "Faith/$_B$": $\gg$ No-P   [pabu]
$\begin{Bmatrix} \text{Id-Pl}/_B \\ \text{Id-}\mu/_B \end{Bmatrix}$(etc.)

c. "Faith/$_C$": $\gg$ No-DD $\gg$ No-P   [pabbu]
$\begin{Bmatrix} \text{Id-Pl}/_C \\ \text{Id-}\mu/_C \end{Bmatrix}$(etc.)

Let us now remove this "faithfulness block" idealization, which is not as harmless as it might appear, and assume that the various indexed instantiations of the individual micro-constraints, such as Ident-Place (enforcing place feature identity between correspondent segments) and Ident-μ (checking the moraic value of correspondent segments), are independently rankable, as shown in (31), where the rankings are sorted by the output form that they select. The ranking of the markedness constraints is fixed as No-DD $\gg$ No-P, as before, and the additional rankings common to each group are given in the leftmost column.

(31) Ranking of markedness constraints fixed as: No-DD $\gg$ No-P
Input: /pabbu/

a.	No-DD $\gg$ Id-$\mu/_A$ Id-Pl/$_A$ $\gg$ No-P	i.	No-DD	Id-$\mu/_A$	Id-Pl/$_A$	No-P	☞ pabu
		ii.	No-DD	Id-Pl/$_A$	Id-$\mu/_A$	No-P	☞ pabu
		iii.	No-DD	Id-Pl/$_A$	No-P	Id-$\mu/_A$	☞ pabu
		iv.	Id-Pl/$_A$	No-DD	Id-$\mu/_A$	No-P	☞ pabu
		v.	Id-Pl/$_A$	No-DD	No-P	Id-$\mu/_A$	☞ pabu
b.	Id-$\mu/_B$ $\gg$ No-DD Id-Pl/$_B$ $\gg$ No-P	i.	Id-$\mu/_B$	No-DD	Id-Pl/$_B$	No-P	☞ pabbu
		ii.	Id-$\mu/_B$	Id-Pl/$_B$	No-DD	No-P	☞ pabbu
		iii.	Id-Pl/$_B$	Id-$\mu/_B$	No-DD	No-P	☞ pabbu
c.	No-DD $\gg$ Id-$\mu/_C$ No-P $\gg$ Id-Pl/$_C$	i.	No-DD	Id-$\mu/_C$	No-P	Id-Pl/$_C$	☞ habu
		ii.	No-DD	No-P	Id-Pl/$_C$	Id-$\mu/_C$	☞ habu
		iii.	No-DD	No-P	Id-$\mu/_C$	Id-Pl/$_C$	☞ habu
d.	Id-$\mu/_D$ $\gg$ No-DD No-P $\gg$ Id-Pl/$_D$	i.	Id-$\mu/_D$	No-DD	No-P	Id-Pl/$_D$	☞ habbu

Table (31) demonstrates two important points. First, the ranking of the four constraints is to a considerable degree undetermined since three of the four mappings can be obtained with more than one ranking: *pabu* (31a) is derived by five rankings, *pabbu* (31b) and *habu* (31c) by three each. Second, besides the structurally possible realizations (from least to most nativized) *pabbu*, *pabu*, and *habu* (31a–c) for the input /pabbu/, the system now also produces the impossible nativization *habbu* (31d) (cf. (22) above, and the discussion in section 3.1 in connection with the *siči*-effect).

The latter result is a serious problem since it deprives the model of its central empirical prediction (namely, the existence of a characteristic core–periphery structure). It is therefore important for future research to consider ways to preserve the theory's predictive power. The explosive growth of ranking possibilities comes about through the step of individualizing the faithfulness component into separate and mutually independent micro-constraints. However, reverting to the simplicity of (30) by consolidating all faithfulness into a single monolithic unit (i.e. in effect denying the diversification of faithfulness constraints) is unlikely to be successful. Attractive though it might seem from the perspective of conceptual restrictiveness, it is incompatible with the collective results of recent analytical work in Optimality Theory, which demonstrate quite clearly that the faithfulness component of the constraint system needs a considerable amount of flexibility.[53]

In this situation, it might be useful to ask the more modest question of what must minimally be true about the relative ranking of indexed faithfulness constraints in order for the situation in (31) not to arise. The task is therefore to secure the results regarding possible and impossible nativizations while maintaining full diversification of the faithfulness component. Since this topic is clearly beyond the scope of this chapter, we will here restrict our remarks to a few pointers in the direction of future research in the remainder of this section. Our proposal consists of three elements: (i) a requirement demanding ranking consistency for IO-faithfulness constraints (32), (ii) an M ≫ F structure for the initial state of the grammar ((35) and Smolensky 1996), and (iii) Ranking Conservatism (36) as a guiding principle for successive stages of a developing grammar. As will be seen, the core–periphery model can be significantly enhanced by embedding it in the context of learnability and grammar development considerations.

First, we impose a consistency condition on the relative rankings of the different stratal representatives of individual faithfulness constraints.[54]

(32)   *Ranking Consistency:*
       Let F and G be two types of IO-faithfulness constraints (e.g. IDENT-
       PLACE and IDENT-µ).
       Then the relative rankings of the indexed versions of F and G are the
       same across all strata: $\forall AB\ (F/_A \gg G/_A) \Rightarrow (F/_B \gg G/_B)$.

Thus, if $F/_A \gg G/_A$ holds for some stratum A, then $F/_B \gg G/_B$ must hold for every stratum B. In other words, there is a sense in which the ranking of the various types of faithfulness constraints is fixed across all indexed instantiations, just as the ranking of structural constraints – namely, insofar as the ranking of faithfulness constraints with respect to each other is concerned.[55] This is schematically shown in (33).

(33) $R(Con_M)$: $M^1 \gg M^2 \gg M^3 \gg M^4$ $R(Con_F)$: $F^1 \gg F^2 \gg F^3$

Variation is confined to the ranking of individual faithfulness constraints with respect to individual structural constraints. In this view, instead of thinking of a grammar as a ranking R(Con) of a universal constraint set Con, it is more adequate to conceive of it as comprising (i) a ranking $R(Con_F)$ of a universal set of faithfulness constraint types Con_F, (ii) a ranking $R(Con_M)$ of a universal set of structural markedness constraints Con_M, and (iii) different inter-calations of the faithfulness constraint hierarchy $R(Con_F)$ with the structural constraint hierarchy $R(Con_M)$. Each such intercalation defines a stratum, con-sisting of $R(Con_M)$ and indexed copies of the faithfulness constraints in Con_F, respecting the ranking in $R(Con_F)$.[56]

(34) $R(Con_M)$: $M^1 \gg M^2 \gg M^3 \gg M^4$ $R(Con_F)$: $F^1 \gg F^2 \gg F^3$

a. Stratum X:

$$M^1 \gg M^2 \gg M^3 \gg M^4$$
$$\gg F^1 \gg F^2 \gg F^3$$

conflated into a single hierarchy:

$$\boxed{M^1 \gg M^2 \gg M^3 \gg M^4 \gg F_X^1 \gg F_X^2 \gg F_X^3}$$

b. Stratum Y:

$$M^1 \gg M^2 \quad M^3 \quad M^4$$
$$\gg F^1 \gg \gg F^2 \gg \gg F^3$$

conflated into a single hierarchy:

$$\boxed{M^1 \gg M^2 \gg F_Y^1 \gg M^3 \gg F_Y^2 \gg M^4 \gg F_Y^3}$$

c. all strata conflated into a single hierarchy:

$$\boxed{M^1 \gg M^2 \gg F_Y^1 \gg M^3 \gg F_Y^2 \gg M^4 \gg F_Y^3, F_X^1 \gg F_X^2 \gg F_X^3}$$

The second ingredient of our proposal is Smolensky's (1996) hypothesis that in the initial state $\mathcal{H}_0$ of grammar acquisition all faithfulness constraints are subordinated to all markedness constraints, as schematically expressed in (35).[57]

(35) *Initial State* $\mathcal{H}_0$: $M \gg F$ (Markedness $\gg$ Faithfulness)

Finally, we assume that in developing and expanding a grammar, the domi-nance relations of each state are preserved as much as possible in the next state, i.e. grammar change is minimal. This is expressed as the principle of Ranking Conservatism in (36).

(36)   *Ranking Conservatism:*
In expanding the grammar (for example, by diversifying faithfulness constraints by stratal indexation), dominance relations of the current state $\mathcal{H}_i$ are maximally preserved in the subsequent state $\mathcal{H}_{i+1}$.

In (37), we formulate a special application of Ranking Conservatism which concerns the ranking of stratally indexed versions of some faithfulness constraint F.

(37)   *Ranking Inheritance* (a special case of Ranking Conservatism):
The stratal representatives $F/_A, \ldots, F/_Z$ in state $\mathcal{H}_{i+1}$ corresponding to an undiversified faithfulness F in state $\mathcal{H}_i$ each maximally inherit F's ranking relations with respect to other constraints.

The main idea behind the overall proposal, consisting of Ranking Consistency (32), an initial state with $M \gg F$ (35), and Ranking Conservatism (36), is the following: conservatism with respect to the initial state $\mathcal{H}_0$ entails that a later state $\mathcal{H}_i$, even though deviating from the original $M \gg F$ pattern, still inherits, as the residue of $\mathcal{H}_0$'s subordination of *every* faithfulness constraint to *every* markedness constraints, a general low ranking of faithfulness constraints with respect to markedness constraints (*ceteris paribus*, i.e. except where contradicted by overt evidence and possibly other ranking principles). For $\mathcal{H}_i$, this singles out a specific articulation of the constraint hierarchy (among other possibilities that are also compatible with the data under consideration), with induced M–M dominance relations between different markedness constraints and F–F dominance relations between different faithfulness constraints. Through Ranking Conservatism (36) and Ranking Consistency (32), these relations become a fixed property of the grammar. Certain unattested rankings are in this way excluded, and we will see that this makes many input–output mappings unreachable as nativization patterns.

In order to illustrate the proposal with a concrete example, we take up the markedness constraints and faithfulness constraints discussed earlier in (30)–(31). For the four constraints under consideration (though not for others), we can, for purposes of presentation, identify the core grammar of Japanese with the initial state $\mathcal{H}_0$, with markedness constraints reigning supreme. This is shown in (38), where the M-constraints (No-DD and No-P) are ranked higher than F-constraints (ID-μ, ID-PL).

(38) $\mathcal{H}_0$:   {No-DD, No-P}

$\gg$

{ID-μ,   ID-PL}

The four separate dominance relations asserted in (38), individually listed in (39a–d), are more explicitly depicted in (40).

(39) a. No-DD ≫ Id-μ
      b. No-DD ≫ Id-Pl
      c. No-p ≫ Id-Pl
      d. No-p ≫ Id-μ

(40) $\mathcal{H}_0$: No-DD   No-p   (Markedness)

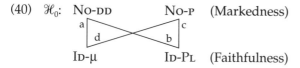

      Id-μ   Id-Pl   (Faithfulness)

With the initial state grammar (40), the mapping /pabbu/ → [habu] emerges
due to high-ranking No-p and No-DD.
   Now suppose that, in the process of expanding the grammar so as to deal
with loan vocabulary and other peripheral items, additional mappings have to
be mastered that lead to more faithful (and hence in general more marked)
outputs. In order to keep things simple, we will use /pabbu/ → [pabu] to
represent such mappings. In cases of a stratally organized lexicon, as discussed
in earlier sections, the acquisition of such more faithful mappings does not
lead to a wholescale overwriting of the core grammar, as it exists up to this
point. New mappings are instead accommodated by the addition of a separate
stratum, leaving the more central areas of the lexicon unaffected. Put in classical phonemic terms (see C. C. Fries and Pike 1949), it is a fallacy to conclude
from the fact that "*x* is a phoneme" holds for foreign loans in Japanese that
"*x* is a phoneme" must be true everywhere in Japanese.[58]
   Stratal diversification of the faithfulness system means that the coexistence of
the two mappings in (41) has to be dealt with (where /pabbu/$_N$ and /pabbu/$_{AF}$
are schematic examples of input forms of different lexical items, belonging to
the native and the assimilated foreign stratum, respectively).

(41) a. /pabbu/$_N$ → [habu]   b. /pabbu/$_{AF}$ → [pabu]

In order to select [pabu] as the output for /pabbu/$_{AF}$, it must be the case that in
the grammar of the new state $\mathcal{H}_1$ in (42), faithfulness to the place feature Ident-
Pl$_{AF}$ dominates No-p (42c′), different from the situation in $\mathcal{H}_0$ (see (42c) and (39)).

(42) a. No-DD ≫ Id-μ
      b. No-DD ≫ Id-Pl
      c. ~~No-p ≫ Id-Pl~~   c′. Ident-Pl$_{AF}$ ≫ No-p
      d. No-p ≫ Id-μ

We have already seen in (31) that several overall rankings are able to produce the mapping /pabbu/ → [pabu]. Among these, Ranking Conservatism
(36) singles out one ranking for the AF stratum, namely the ranking that is
maximally similar to $\mathcal{H}_0$ (repeated in (43) for ease of comparison).[59] The rankings
relevant for the new stratum in (44) preserve the $\mathcal{H}_0$-rankings (43a–b, 43d),
but (42c′) Ident-Pl$_{AF}$ ≫ No-p takes the place of (42c) No-p ≫ Id-Pl.

(43) $\mathcal{H}_0$:   No-DD   No-P   (44)   No-DD

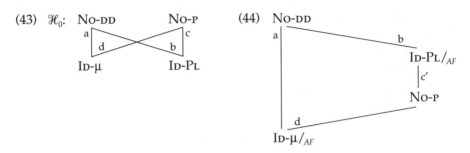

(44) is equivalent to the strict ranking in (45), which incorporates the two new induced ranking relations in (46). Id-Pl$/_{AF}$ ≫ No-p (44c′) and No-p ≫ Id-μ$/_{AF}$ (44d) give rise to the induced FF-ranking Id-Pl$/_{AF}$ ≫ Id-μ$/_{AF}$ (46b), and No-DD ≫ Id-Pl$/_{AF}$ (44b) and Id-Pl$/_{AF}$ ≫ No-p (44c′) given rise to the induced MM-ranking No-DD ≫ No-p (both by transitivity).

(45)   Rankings relevant for AF-stratum:

No-DD

Id-Pl$/_{AF}$

No-p

Id-μ$/_{AF}$

(46)   Induced ranking relations:
   a.   MM-ranking: No-DD ≫ No-p
   b.   FF-ranking   Id-Pl$/_{AF}$ ≫ Id-μ$/_{AF}$

(46a) highlights an advance of the new theory over the version presented earlier in this chapter. Instead of having to postulate MM-rankings such as No-DD ≫ No-p as givens, they are now seen to emerge in a systematic way in the process of grammar development. The crucial factor is that mappings of the type /pabbu/ → [pabu], which preserve singleton-p in the winning output, while not part of the core lexicon, appear reasonably early in the process of grammar development (presumably, due to the statistical frequency of such forms in contemporary Japanese) – earlier than unassimilated foreign mappings such as /pabbu$/_{UF}$ → [pabbu] which preserve the voiced obstruent geminate in the output. This order of events is eminently plausible, given the truly marginal status of voiced obstruent geminates in the sound pattern of Japanese, but, needless to say, the point deserves further empirical scrutiny.

As for the ranking relation between the two faithfulness constraints in (46b), Consistency (32) projects it to all strata, as in (47), which must hold for all strata X, including X = Native. Combining the AF-ranking for the assimilated foreign stratum in (45) with the earlier $\mathcal{H}_0$ state for the core lexicon in (43) (from the current viewpoint, an N-ranking), we obtain (48) as the $\mathcal{H}_1$ state of the full grammar.

(47) ID-PL/$_X$ ≫ ID-µ/$_X$ (48) $\mathcal{H}_1$:

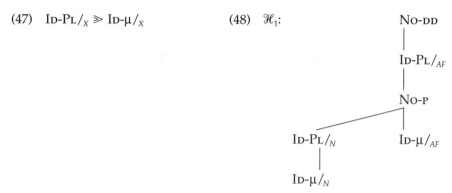

The next step is the acquisition of a third stratum for unassimilated foreign items ("UF"), here schematically represented by the hyper-faithful mapping /pabbu/$_{UF}$ → [pabbu]. In the overall language, we have a coexistence of three mappings (49).

(49) a. /pabbu/$_N$ → [habu]   b. /pabbu/$_{AF}$ → [pabu]
      c. /pabbu/$_{UF}$ → [pabbu]

(49c) means that UF-faithfulness must allow voiced obstruent geminates to be faithfully parsed, calling for ID-µ/$_{UF}$ ≫ NO-DD. We know already from (47) that ID-PL/$_X$ ≫ ID-µ/$_X$ must hold for all strata X, including X = UF. These considerations together dictate the subhierarchy (50) for the unassimilated foreign stratum. Combining this with the $\mathcal{H}_1$-grammar in (48), we obtain the $\mathcal{H}_2$-grammar in (51) for the full language.

(50) ID-PL/$_{UF}$

      ID-µ/$_{UF}$

      NO-DD

(51) $\mathcal{H}_2$:

      ID-PL/$_{UF}$

      ID-µ/$_{UF}$

      NO-DD

      ID-PL/$_{AF}$

      NO-P

      ID-PL/$_N$ ID-µ/$_{AF}$

      ID-µ/$_N$

Let us now return to our central issue, namely, impossible nativizations. Continuing with our example, we will show that, once the system has been modified so as to accommodate the mapping /pabbu/$_{AF}$ → [pabu], it is *not* (or only at a considerable cost) able to accommodate mappings of the kind /pabbu/$_X$ → [habbu], for some stratum X.

The two crucial rankings necessary to achieve the mapping /pabbu/$_X$ → [habbu] are given in (52).

(52) ID-μ/$_X$ ≫ No-DD   (to preserve the voiced geminate)
      No-P ≫ ID-PL/$_X$ (to change the labial place specification).

Among the 4! = 24 rankings of the four constraints {No-P, ID-PL, ID-μ, No-DD}, 6 rankings are compatible with (52). They are listed in (53).

(53) Rankings resulting in the mapping /pabbu/$_X$ → [habbu]:
      a. ID-μ ≫ No-DD ≫ No-P ≫ ID-PL } incompatible with ID-PL ≫ ID-μ
      b. No-P ≫ ID-PL ≫ ID-μ ≫ No-DD } incompatible with No-DD ≫
                                              No-P
      c. ID-μ ≫ No-P ≫ ID-PL ≫ No-DD ⎤
      d. ID-μ ≫ No-P ≫ No-DD ≫ ID-PL ⎥ incompatible with both ID-PL ≫
      e. No-P ≫ ID-μ ≫ ID-PL ≫ No-DD ⎥ ID-μ and No-DD ≫ No-P
      f. No-P ≫ ID-μ ≫ No-DD ≫ ID-PL ⎦

However, as seen in (46), the acquisition of assimilated foreign mapping /pabbu/$_{AF}$ → [pabu] earlier in the grammar development process has fixed the MM-ranking between the two markedness constraints and the FF-ranking between the two faithfulness constraints as No-DD ≫ No-P and ID-PL ≫ ID-μ, respectively. Each one of the six rankings in (53) is incompatible with at least one of these rankings: (53a) is incompatible with the faithfulness ranking, (53b) with the markedness ranking, and (53c–f) with both rankings. Ranking Consistency thus predicts that, given the prior establishment of the rankings yielding the mapping /pabbu/ → [pabu], there is no simple stratal extension of a grammar yielding the mapping /pabbu/ → [habbu]. The latter is thus not possible as a nativizing mapping in the sense of section 3.1.[60] In this way, given a few general assumptions about the initial state and the course of grammar development, early steps in the acquisition process automatically impose limitations on all subsequent steps, explaining the phenomenon of "impossible nativizations."

4   Summary and Directions for Future Research

This chapter has presented an overview of the organization of the phonological lexicon of Japanese, focusing on questions relating to the segment inventory (such as the occurrence of singleton-*p*) and sequential conditions (such as postnasal voicing or palatalization). As in earlier work on this topic, the traditional subdivisions (such as Yamato, Sino-Japanese, and Western loans with various degrees of assimilation) are seen to play a major role. Generalizing over many individual cases and phenomena, an overall core–periphery picture emerges which calls for a systematic account in the context of a coherent theory.

After a brief critical examination of earlier theories, a general optimality-theoretic model of the phonological lexicon is put forth which aims to account for differences between strata within a unitary constraint system. The central hypothesis asserts that stratum-specific input–output faithfulness constraints are necessary and sufficient to account for the stratal organization of a language's lexicon. We show that stratally indexed faithfulness, but not alternative input specification/underspecification approaches, is able to capture crucial higher-level implicational relations between nativization effects, thus deriving the existence of a core–periphery structure in the lexicon from basic tenets of Optimality Theory, without additional mechanisms.

Finally, the chapter attempts to point out some avenues for further research by recasting the issues within the context of recent optimality-theoretic work on the acquisition and development of grammars. Such a move makes it possible to sharpen the proposal and to derive important generalizations and restrictions regarding the rankings of individual stratum-specific faithfulness constraints. If pursued further, it promises to lead to a deeper understanding of the factors and principles involved in lexical stratification. For example, the stratal distinctions in the accentual system investigated by a number of researchers (Katayama 1995, 1998, Kubozono 1997, among others) cast additional light on these acquisition issues. Are the results of previous investigation compatible with the approach advocated here, and do they lead to new insights in this regard? Related questions concern forms that are stratal hybrids (Fukazawa et al. 1998, R. Walker 1998): when faithfulness constraints relating to different strata conflict with each other, is their competition resolved in the correct way through their independently established ranking? How does it interact with the FAITH(Root) ≫ FAITH(Affix) scheme of McCarthy and Prince (1995)? Certain details of the stratal organization of Japanese also remain to be worked out. Interesting issues arise, for example, regarding the proper treatment of mimetic items (Fukazawa 1998, Itô and Mester 1995a, 1995b, Spaelti 1998): do they constitute a separate stratum, or do they belong to the Yamato stratum? If the latter, what are the crucial factors that make the distinction? The issue is not merely a descriptive one since it bears on the general question of the limits of stratal organization (Inkelas et al. 1997): at what point does stratal structure become opaque, leading to a reduction of strata? The general answer must be that the point of restructuring is determined by general principles of grammar simplicity and optimization (see Kiparsky 1965 and later work). Fleshing out this general idea through concrete case studies is an important task for future work.

Appendix: Faithfulness Schemata and Instantiations

The question to be addressed in this appendix is why only faithfulness constraints – and not structural constraints – can be indexed to a particular lexical class or lexical item. Within current Optimality Theory, this is little more than a stipulation. There is no principled reason why stratal indexation could not be extended to structural markedness constraints, resulting in special versions of, for example, NoCoda or No-p such as NoCoda/Foreign or No-p/Sino-Japanese, with their own special ranking.[61]

Replication of faithfulness constraints, and the nonreplicability of structural constraints, are of course not unique properties of the core–periphery model of the lexicon, but rather reflect a general feature of the correspondence model of Optimality Theory. The most important and influential case involves Base-Reduplicant (BR) faithfulness (McCarthy and Prince 1995, etc.), where the distinction between Faith-IO and Faith-BR has provided key insights into the workings of prosodic morphological phenomena.[62] For example, the ban against codas having tangible effects only in the reduplicant is accounted for by the "Emergence-of-the-Unmarked" schema in (54a) (McCarthy and Prince 1994a, 1995, Spaelti 1997, etc.), sandwiching the NcCoda constraint between the two faithfulness constraints. Non-replicability of structural constraints is important since the same effects could otherwise in principle be achieved by having an additional specialized NoCoda constraint applying only to the reduplicant (i.e. NoCoda/R), and sandwiching undifferentiated faithfulness between specialized and general NoCoda (54b).

(54)   a.   Faith-IO ≫ NoCoda ≫ Faith-BR
       b.   NoCoda/R ≫ Faith ≫ NoCoda

Codalessness in the reduplicant could then be due to either the EoU-schema (54a) or the alternative indexed account (54b), seriously undermining the explanatory level achieved by the theory. The issue here goes beyond redundancy: in unpublished work, Prince (1996) has given a cogent argument showing that templatic constraints such as NoCoda/R or R = MinWd, while not conceptually incompatible with the theory of reduplicative overapplication of McCarthy and Prince (1995), lead to empirically absurd results, such as reduplicating hypothetical *wakari* as *waka-waka* (instead of the expected *waka-wakari* or *wakari-kari*), with back-copying of the templatic property due to the ranking R = MinWd, Max-BR ≫ Max-IO. Extending the argument of Prince (1996), Spaelti (1997) demonstrates that theories operating with general templatic constraints such as Affix syllable (see McCarthy and Prince 1994b: 10, among others) suffer from the same back-copying problem, and goes on to develop a fully a-templatic model of reduplication (see also McCarthy and Prince 1998 for similar arguments). A templatic NoCoda/R constraint would fall to the same criticism, as shown by the unattested back-copying of reduplicative codalessness into the base, as shown in (55).

(55)

RED + *warum*	*No-Coda/R*	*Max-BR*	*Max-IO*	*NoCoda*
warum + warum	*!			**
waru + warum		m!		*
☞ waru + waru			m	

That properties like codalessness are apparently never back-copied makes sense, if they are strictly due to the Emergence-of-the-Unmarked schema, which cannot coexist with the overcopying ranking for one and the same structural constraint. This in turn implies that the theory must not admit indexed structural constraint such as NoCoda/R.

From the analytical-empirical side, then, there is a need for faithfulness constraints to be indexable to various dimensions of grammatical derivation (such as truncation, reduplication, etc.) and also to strata in the lexicon. There is no such need for structural constraints – in fact, the opposite is suggested by the back-copying argument. Where does this prolific character of faithfulness constraints stem from, and why do structural constraints not share it? The answer should ideally come from the form and function of faithfulness constraints. Faithfulness is different from structural wellformedness in that faithfulness is always faithfulness *to* something, whereas NoCoda is not NoCoda to something. A candidate cannot be faithful *tout court*, in a way in which it has a coda or lacks an onset. Faithfulness constraints involve two linguistic representations and assess how similar one is to the other. In Correspondence Theory as developed in McCarthy and Prince (1995) and related work, faithfulness constraints are literally conceived of as constraints on a pair of corresponding representations. Taking up this proposal and developing it in a slightly different way, we start with a fundamental division between constraints that take a single representation as their argument (56a) and constraints that take two representations as their arguments (56b).

(56) a. *One-argument constraints:*
A given representation is judged in terms of its intrinsic harmony, irrespective of other representations. One-argument constraints are defined strictly on outputs (output candidates produced by GEN), and are the structural, wellformedness, and markedness constraints in the broadest sense, including segmental markedness constraints, sequential constraints, prosodic form constraints relating to syllables and feet, etc.

b.   *Two-argument constraints:*
     A given representation (an input or output representation, or a specific subpart of an output representation, such as a reduplicant) is judged by measuring it against a second representation (another input or output representation, or another part of the same output representation). These are the faithfulness constraints.

More formally, optimality-theoretic constraints can be thought of as devices that assign violation marks to representations (see Prince and Smolensky 1993: 68–71). Starting with a structural constraint S, S is a function that takes a candidate output representation o as its argument and assigns it a (possibly empty) list of violation marks for S as a value, as illustrated in (57).

(57) $S(o) = List\ of\ violations$
   e.g.: $S(o) = (\emptyset)$ o is assigned no violation mark for constraint S
          $S(o) = (*S)$ o is assigned one violation mark for constraint S
          $S(o) = (*S, *S)$ o is assigned two violation marks for constraint S, etc.

Some concrete examples are given in (58). The representation .*kaf*. is assigned a list consisting of one violation mark *NoCoda, and the representation .*kaf.tan*. is mapped to the list (*NoCoda, *NoCoda). The representation .*ka.ta*. consisting of two open syllables is assigned no violation mark by NoCoda (i.e. it is assigned the empty list as a value). The other examples follow the same pattern.

(58) a.   NoCoda (.*kaf*.)   = (*NoCoda)
           NoCoda (.*kaf.tan*.) = (*NoCoda, *NoCoda)
           NoCoda (.*ka.ta*.)   = ($\emptyset$)
      b.   No-DD (.*bed.do*.)   = (*No-DD)
           No-DD (.*bet.to*.)   = ($\emptyset$)
      c.   No-P (.*paN*.)   = (*No-P)
           No-P (.*haN*.)   = ($\emptyset$)
      d.   No-NT (.*tom.po*.)   = (*No-NT)
           No-NT (.*tom.bo*.)   = ($\emptyset$)

Faithfulness constraints, on the other hand, require a different format, as shown in (59). Every faithfulness constraint F needs two arguments: besides a representation o to be judged, there is also a representation i serving as the model against which o is measured (o and i, even though mnemonic of "output" and "input," can also stand for subrepresentations of a single representation, such as reduplicant and base).

(59) $F(i)(o) = List\text{-}of\text{-}violations$

Rewriting (59) in a form similar to (57), i.e. as a function of one argument returning a list of marks as value, we have (60b). What corresponds to the structural constraint S (60a) is not F, but rather the complex $[F(i)]$.

(60) a. Structural constraint: $S(o)$ $= List\text{-}of\text{-}violations$
      b. Faithfulness constraint: $[F(i)](o) = List\text{-}of\text{-}violations$

This small change expresses a conceptual unification: just like structural constraints, faithfulness constraints are functions that are strictly defined on outputs. In a formal sense, this is a return to the original model of Optimality Theory in Prince and Smolensky (1993) in that all constraints apply to output representations. This version of Optimality Theory relied on the principle of containment (so named in McCarthy and Prince 1993b) in order to make phonological outputs rich enough for the computation of all faithfulness violations by requiring every output to *contain* the input. This model turned out to lack the degree of generality necessary to handle central aspects of phonology and prosodic morphology, such as the featural filling of epenthetic structure, reduplicant–base relations, etc., leading to the current correspondence-based conception. In the proposal made here, strict output-orientation for all constraints is made possible by enriching the internal structure of faithfulness constraints by correspondence, with a distinction between constraint schemata (F, e.g. MAX) and instantiated constraints (F(i), e.g. MAX (/kaftan/) in (61)). The new conception is illustrated in (61) for the constraint schemata MAX and IDENT, instantiated for the inputs /kaftan/ and /paN/.[63]

(61) a. [MAX (/kaftan/)] (kaftan) = (ø)
          [MAX (/kaftan/)] (kafta) = (*MAX)
          [MAX (/kaftan/)] (kata)   = (*MAX, *MAX)
      b. [IDENT (/paN/)] (paN)   = (ø)
          [IDENT (/paN/)] (haN)   = (*IDENT)

In other words, MAX, DEP, IDENT, and other types of faithfulness are by themselves not constraints that could apply to an output candidate; rather, they are constraint schemata which, when applied to an input i related to an output candidate o by correspondence, yield (as its value) an *instantiated constraint* $F(i)$, which in turn applies to o to yield a list of violations of F by o relative to i. This entails that there is an instantiated faithfulness constraint for each lexical item. Instantiated faithfulness constraints are not elementary constraints, but rather derived within individual grammars by composing a universal constraint schema F with the elements of a lexical correspondence network. In the unmarked case, we assume that all instantiated constraints $F(i)$ for a given constraint schema F occupy the same position in the ranking (notated in tableaux by the usual "MAX-IO," "DEP-IO," etc.). However, different from structural constraints, faithfulness constraints are by necessity specialized, with a separate instantiation for each input item. This opens up the possibility of ranking different instantiated faithfulness constraints in different positions, and this formal option is exploited in lexical stratification – for various functional reasons that are not the concern of the cognitive system dealing with formal grammar. In stratification, this takes the form of indexed faithfulness constraints, as shown in (62). Here the instantiations of a given faithfulness constraint schema for items belonging to two different strata I and J are ranked differently with respect to some constraint C.

(62) $F(i) \gg C \gg F(j)$,   where $i \in I$, $j \in J$, and I, J are vocabulary strata.

For structural constraints the formal possibility of differential ranking simply does not arise because they do not have instantiations. Different from other approaches, this conception of faithfulness thus makes sense of the fundamental dichotomy between structural markedness and faithfulness, as far as indexability is concerned.[64]

NOTES

* This work was partially supported by faculty senate grants from the University of California at Santa Cruz and by the National Science Foundation under grant SBR-9510868. The names of the authors appear in alphabetical order. We are grateful to Dan Karvonen, Kazutaka Kurisu, Jaye Padgett, Philip Spaelti, and Natsuko Tsujimura for detailed comments on a previous version that resulted in many improvements.

1 See S. E. Martin (1952), J. D. McCawley (1968b), Vance (1987), Shibatani (1990), Kubozono (1995c), among others.

2 We follow standard transcriptional practice, which is largely equivalent to the Hepburn style of Romanization used by the leading dictionaries, with some minor modifications. Thus for the palato-alveolar obstruent series, we use [š, č, ǰ], rather than {sh, ch, j}. For moraic nasal glides, we use [N] (i.e. if word-final or preceding a vowel or glide); and for assimilated nasals, [m, n, ŋ].

3 Shortened from *sauNdo torakku*. For a phonological analysis of such shortenings, see Itô (1990) and Itô and Mester (1992).

4 Shortened from *patorooru kaa*.

5 Roughly speaking, *hiragana* and *kanji* are used for the native forms, *kanji* for the Sino-Japanese vocabulary, and *katakana* for the foreign vocabulary. For discussion of the writing system and its linguistic significance, see Miller (1967), S. Martin (1972), and references cited there.

6 For a detailed discussion of the phonological properties of mimetics, see Hamano (1986).

7 In fact, it is well known that the synchronic classifications, as evidenced by the overt behavior of speakers, in numerous cases

diverge from the true etymological origin of the items in question. Thus certain Yamato items, such as *fude* "brush" or *uma* "horse," are probably very early (and nowadays unrecognizable) borrowings from Chinese, mediated through Korean (see Sansom, 1928: 29–30). Even some older Western loans, like *tabako* "cigarettes, tobacco" and *karuta* "(playing) cards" (sixteenth-century, from Portuguese), are nowadays treated as native, and are written in *hiragana* and *kanji*.

8 For discussion, see e.g. Chomsky and Halle (1968: 174, 373), J. D. McCawley (1968b: 62–75), Postal (1968: 120–39), Saciuk (1969: 505–12).

9 See Itô and Mester (1995b) for examples, with references to the extensive literature on the topic.

10 See Mathesius (1929), among others.

11 C. C. Fries and Pike (1949) is an example.

12 See, for example, Holden (1976) and Lightner (1972) on Russian, and Nessly (1971) on English.

13 For further developments, see C. Paradis and Lebel (1994) on Quebec French, Cohn and McCarthy (1994) on Indonesian stress, Pater (1995) on English stress, Davidson and Noyer (1997) on Huave loan phonology, Kubozono (1997) on Japanese compound accent, Shinohara (1997) and Katayama (1998) on Japanese segment inventories and pitch accent, and Karvonen (1998) on Finnish loanwords.

14 Together with most researchers, we are assuming that the complex of conditions collectively referred to as the "Coda Condition" since Itô (1986) need further analysis. An approach that makes the required distinctions (i.e. disallowing non-place-linked codas while permitting geminates and place-assimilated nasals) is the alignment proposal in Itô and Mester (1994, 1998). In light of more recent work, a further reduction to a conjunction of more elementary factors is perhaps feasible – for example, to structural markedness locally conjoined with segmental markedness, as we have argued for coda-devoicing languages like German in other work (see Itô and Mester, 1997c: 130–2), building on Smolensky (1995). Related proposals have been made in Positional Faithfulness Theory, as in the work of J. N. Beckman (1998), Lombardi (to appear), Padgett (1995), and others.

15 Some of these forms have alternants without gemination (*oikakeru*, *oitsuku*, *oidasu*).

16 For further details regarding the gemination of other sonorant consonants, resulting in forms like *huɴwari* or *hiɴyari* (phonetically, [huw̃wari] and [hiỹyari]), see A. Mester and Itô (1989: 275).

17 Historically speaking, in forms nowadays pronounced with initial [h] some feature of labial articulation must have persisted until recent times. Thus in the early 1500s the future emperor Gonara is reported to have posed the following riddle:

(i) *haha ni wa ni-do aitare-do mo, čiči ni wa iči-do mo awazu*
     "for mother (*haha*) they meet twice, for father (*čiči*) not even once"

The intended answer is *kučibiru* "(the) lips," which only makes sense if *haha* was still pronounced somewhat like [ɸaɸa]. S. E. Martin (1987: 11) comments: "It would seem that in the mainstream of the language, centering on the capital cities, the syllable *ha* was pronounced *Fa* from as early as 800 till as late as 1600, at least initially."

18   See Poser (1984) for an illuminating discussion of double-verb compounding (10) and *ma*-prefixation (11), and see Itô and Mester (1996) and works cited there for many other examples of Sino-Japanese compounding (12).

19   For optimality-theoretic analyses of Sino-Japanese compounding, see Sakai (1994), Nasu (1996), and Kurisu (1998).

20   For further examples and discussion, see Itô and Mester (1986).

21   See Itô et al. (1995), Padgett (1995), Suzuki (1995), Pater (1996), and Hayes (1996) for different views regarding the constraints involved in the postnasal voicing syndrome. In order to sidestep unnecessary complications, we simplify the exposition of the analysis by means of the ad hoc constraint NO-NT. Similar remarks hold for No-P and No-DD, which can each be reduced to more elementary constraints.

22   See Davis and Tsujimura (1991) for an autosegmental analysis of the verbal alternations.

23   This root is felt to be archaic. Except for *šin-* "die," other *n*-final roots appear almost exclusively with stem-extensions in contemporary Japanese, e.g. *kasan-ar-u* "pile up," *sokon-er-u* "harm" for older †*kasan-u*, †*sokon-u*.

24   This form violates No-P but obeys the sequential constraint disallowing the sequence *še* (or more generally, "palatal consonant + front mid vowel"). See Itô and Mester (1995a, 1995b) for further analysis and discussion of these sequential restrictions.

25   See the end of this section for some discussion of borderline cases.

26   See Itô and Mester (1995a, 1995b) and Tateishi (1989a) for details, and S. E. Martin (1952) and J. D. McCawley (1968b) for earlier comprehensive studies.

27   Cf. Saciuk's (1969) [–homogeneous] class.

28   See Itô and Mester (1995b: 830).

29   Cited in Rice (1997: 545). For other examples of contractions, see Itô and Mester (1995b: 837, n. 20) and references cited there.

30   These examples are discussed in Itô and Mester (1986: 54, 1995b: 830, 1997a: 427). Rice (1997: 554) adds further examples to this category.

31   Rice (1997) has critically argued against the approach advocated by Itô and Mester (1995a, 1995b) and Itô et al. (1995), basing her argumentation on the incorrect assumption that there are no alternations associated with the constraints that are involved in lexical stratification. Itô et al. (1998) show in detail that this criticism is invalid, cf. the alternations associated with No-NT, No-DD, and No-P (see the examples in (8)–(15)).

32   See Prince and Smolensky (1993) as well as the large subsequent literature.

33   For a discussion of the limits on positing different "cophonologies" within the same grammar, see Inkelas et al. (1997).

34   We adopt here the correspondence-theoretic version of faithfulness, as developed by McCarthy and Prince (1995).

35   With respect to a more elaborate analysis differentiating between the various aspects of faithfulness, FAITH marks the position of the lowest-ranking relevant faithfulness constraint (MAX, DEP, etc.). See section 3.2 and the appendix for further discussion.

36 Top-ranked FAITH₅, which overrides even basic syllable constraints, appears to play no stratificatory role in Japanese, but see Itô and Mester (1995a: 198).

37 The indexed-FAITH format was first used by Pater (1995) for the English lexicon. Later applications include Prince (1996) and Fukazawa (1998) for Japanese. While the two versions of the theory are conceptually quite distinct, we are unaware of any decisive empirical differences between the two versions. As Rachel Walker (personal communication) has pointed out, hybrid formations, such as the cooccurrence of fixed affixes with alternating affixes in Tuyuca discussed and analyzed in R. Walker (1998: 116–38), are interesting in this regard: here simultaneous access to two rankings would be required (see also Fukazawa et al. 1998 for a case in Japanese) – a situation dealt with straightforwardly in the indexed faithfulness account, but calling for some imaginative development of the technical aspects of the original reranking proposal in Itô and Mester 1995a. Putting aside matters of execution and the technicalia of Correspondence Theory, the larger question for linguistic theory is whether variation *within* a single language is entirely different from – or related to – variation *between* languages, which must be the result of a difference in grammars, i.e. of differential constraint ranking.

38 Instead of FAITH/Yamato, it might be more adequate to make use of general, unindexed, IO-faithfulness. An indexed FAITH/Yamato family for core behavior is in danger of missing the point that core– periphery patterns show "Elsewhere" organization.

39 We are not concerned here with the quality of epenthetic vowels, which are mostly *u*, but *o* after coronal plosives where *u* would trigger major allophony (hence *beddo* instead of *beddzu*), and *i* after *k* in some older loans like *sutoraiki* "labor strike" (vs. *sutoraiku* "a strike in a baseball game").

40 The degeminating candidate [bedo] violates another higher-ranking constraint, either ALIGN-R (STEM, σ), requiring that the right edge of a stem and a syllable coincide (Kitahara 1996), or a sympathetic faithfulness constraint requiring the coronal /d/ to maintain its syllable role (here: as a coda, see Katayama (1998)).

41 See Prince and Smolensky (1993) and Itô et al. (1995) for further discussion.

42 Among early loans from Western languages, there are a few cases of *p*-replacement, such as the word *batereɴ* "padre" (modern *paadoru*) from Portuguese, and in some documents from the late Tokugawa period the last name of Commander Perry appears as *heruri*. But such cases are sporadic.

43 It is unsurprising that we find a considerable amount of variation in this area of the lexicon, with some speakers treating the loanword for "bed" as Assimilated foreign (i.e. *betto*), and the loanword for "bag" as Unassimilated foreign (i.e. *baggu*).

44 Further differentiation is of course possible and arguably required in terms of individual features, feature values, specification/ underspecification, insertion/ deletion, zero-, mono-, and bimoraicity, consonantal vs. vocalic moras, etc.

45 For the strata appearing in this model of the phonological

lexicon, the term "cophonologies" (see Inkelas et al. (1997)) is therefore misleading. Just as for reduplication and other areas where special faithfulness relations are involved, we are dealing with a single grammar and a single phonology.

46   Cf. Kiparsky's (1968) "hierarchy of foreignness," and see Itô and Mester (1995a: 191–2, 201–2) for other examples.

47   As given here, the argument from impossible nativizations rests on the simplifying assumption that all faithfulness constraints are, for purposes of stratal indexation, consolidated into a single monolithic "FAITH." Once property-specific faithfulness constraints are distinguished, such as IDENT-F and IDENT-μ in (23), further ranking options arise, such as IDENT-μ$_{/X}$ ≫ No-DD ≫ No-P ≫ IDENT-PLACE$_{/X}$, prima facie a way of deriving pseudo-nativizations like *habbu* at some stratum X. This loophole will be closed in section 3.2 by tightening the overall theory of constraint ranking.

48   A concrete proposal of this kind is advocated in Inkelas et al. (1997).

49   Or else the theory gives up altogether on characterizing the notion "possible nativization." Notice that pointing to the history of the language as holding the key to an explanation in this case amounts to a reversal of logic. Even though it is unpredictable whether, and when, some foreign item enters a language, the nativization course of an item, once acquired, is not at all arbitrary, but to a large extent determined by structural and markedness factors – precisely what we are trying to understand in the first place. There is thus no explanation of structure through history here; there is rather

an explanation of (some aspects of) history through structure.

50   The example is modeled after the discussion of Turkish obstruent voicing in Inkelas et al. (1997: 408–10).

51   As in the work referred to, the tableau marks a violation of faithfulness for every [0anterior] segment acquiring a specification for [anterior] in the output. This is not a necessary assumption: Even if such feature filling were assumed not to violate faithfulness, the same winners would emerge – but the first column would contain one fewer asterisk in each cell.

52   Needless to say, in a general sense input specifications continue to remain central to the enterprise. Without input, no output will be derived, and marked segments, marked sequences, and marked structures will never emerge without being posited in the input. In this sense, there is no Optimality Theory without "prespecification." It is a different matter whether the "input" is best viewed as consisting of classical underlying representations or of surface representations of some kind, as suggested in some recent work (Flemming 1995, Ní Chiosáin and Padgett 1997, among others).

53   One could attempt to get around the problem by climbing up to some level of meta-markedness and assert that it is the unmarked state for a system to have all faithfulness constraints clustering together in the ranking (i.e. literally occupying, as a group, the rank informally marked as FAITH/X in our tableaux).

54   This version assumes that constraints are totally ordered (see Tesar and Smolensky 1998 for recent discussion). Under partial ordering, it is minimally necessary

to avoid ranking reversals: if $F/_A \gg G/_A$ for some stratum A, then there is no stratum B such that $G/_B \gg F/_B$: $\neg\exists AB\ (F/_A \gg G/_A \wedge G/_B \gg F/_B)$. As formulated in (32), the IO-Ranking Consistency condition is a minimal condition, stronger versions are conceivable and perhaps justified. Thus one might consider strengthening it into a parallelism requirement (a reformulation along such lines appears in Fukazawa et al. 1998).

55 Going beyond IO-faithfulness constraints and their various stratally indexed incarnations, an important issue to consider is whether ranking consistency (32) can be generalized as in (i), linking IO-faithfulness to other dimensions of faithfulness in the grammar, such as base–reduplicant identity, output–output analogy, and opacity-inducing sympathy.

(i) *Generalized Ranking Consistency*: Let F and G be two types of faithfulness constraints (IDENT, MAX, etc.) and A and B types of correspondence (input–output, output–output, base–reduplicant, base–truncatum, etc.). Then the relative rankings of the indexed versions of F and G are the same across all faithfulness dimensions: $\forall AB\ (F/_A \gg G/_A) \Rightarrow (F/_B \gg G/_B)$.

Although it is conceivable that different dimensions of faithfulness will turn out to deviate from each other in such a way that (i) does not hold, it is difficult to construct a scenario in which, e.g. the IO- and BR-versions of a particular faithfulness constraint F are ranked differently with respect to a certain structural constraint M, and hence to each other. A prime example of exactly this type would seem to

arise between IO-faithfulness and BR-faithfulness, when Emergence-of-the-Unmarked effects rely on the ranking $F/_{IO} \gg M \gg F/_{BR}$, for some faithfulness constraint F, and overapplication requires M, $G/_{BR} \gg G/_{IO}$ for some faithfulness constraint G. This does not constitute a ranking inconsistency in the sense of (i), since $F \neq G$. What is needed is a situation requiring $F/_{IO} \gg M \gg G/_{IO}$ in the IO-dimension and simultaneously $G/_{BR} \gg M \gg F/_{BR}$ in the BR-dimension. It is at present unknown whether an empirically convincing case can be made demonstrating that the faithfulness apparatus of Optimality Theory needs this kind of descriptive power. Until such cases are found, familiar considerations of restrictiveness recommend (i) as a general condition on faithfulness ranking.

56 Insofar as Ranking Consistency (32) governs the relation of the various versions of indexed IO-faithfulness constraints to each other, it recaptures the idea embodied in the earlier version of our theory (Itô and Mester 1995a), namely, that there is an underlying unity behind the various stratal incarnations of a given faithfulness constraint. This unity goes beyond their relatedness through the general schemata of Correspondence Theory (McCarthy and Prince 1995), which say nothing about the ranking of the pairs F_A/G_A and F_B/G_B in (32).

57 Smolensky (1996: 6–7) attributes the original proposal to Alan Prince.

58 In the case of Japanese, this result is facilitated by the rich system of alternations supported by the core grammar (see Itô et al. 1998 for discussion).

59 Here and in what follows, we make the simplifying assumption that the maximally "faithful" ranking

is always uniquely determined. For cases where ambiguities arise, a further refinement of the theory will be called for, which we leave for future development.

60   In order to admit such a mapping, a more radical revision of the grammar (or alternatively, a violation of Ranking Consistency) would be necessary, exacting a considerable cost.

61   Some analysts have indeed taken this step, which results in a less restrictive model of lexical stratification in which no consistent lexical subset structure, as in (16) and (17), is predicted to emerge. See Pater (1995) for an analysis of regular and exceptional secondary stress in English, where, alongside the faithfulness constraint STRESSIDENT, the structural constraint STRESSWELL ("No stressed syllable may be adjacent to the head syllable of the Prosodic Word") is indexed to a particular subset of the lexicon).

62   Others include FAITH-BT (Base–Truncatum) for truncation processes (Benua 1995), FAITH-BA (Base–Argot) for language games (Itô et al. 1996), level-specific faithfulness (level 1 vs. level 2 faithfulness for English (Benua 1997)), and surface

analogy (Steriade 1997, Burzio 1997, Itô and Mester 1997a). Most recently, sympathetic faithfulness has been proposed by McCarthy (1997), and an analysis using sympathy has been proposed by Itô and Mester (1997b) for the Japanese *gagyō* alternation and by Katayama (1995, 1998) for recent loanwords in Japanese.

63   Cf. also Russell (1995) and Hammond (1997) for proposals that are in some respects similar to the one made here.

64   From this vantage point, the criticism raised in Benua (1997) against the faithfulness reranking model of Itô and Mester (1995a), while well taken, is seen not to go far enough. It is true that the theory does not provide an explanation for why only faithfulness constraints can be reranked – but the very same criticism can be leveled against standard Correspondence Theory, where the absence of NOCODA/R, etc. is simply a tacit assumption about the model, and does not follow from any more general principles. On the other hand, the proposal made here attempts an explanation by deriving replicability from the internal structure of constraints.

4 Variationist Sociolinguistics

JUNKO HIBIYA

0 Introduction

The present chapter is intended to provide a synthesis of the field called variationist sociolinguistics that began in the 1960s. Within the framework proposed by Weinreich et al. (1968), attempts have been made to study linguistic change and variation in different speech communities around the world with a perspective which views the linguistic system in a fundamentally different way from any of the preceding models (Labov 1963, 1966). In this research tradition, the most important development towards an understanding of linguistic change has been made by recognizing that historical change in progress is manifested as synchronic variation.

Variationist research conducted in the past thirty years has shown that variation found in linguistic data is highly systematic and furthermore variation which occurs in the speech of individuals exhibits a regular pattern. Viewed from a traditional standpoint, linguistic variation might be regarded as mere chaos. Labov and his associates, on the other hand, have proposed the notion of orderly heterogeneity. In this school of linguistic analysis, it is believed that the investigation of the linguistic analysis of individuals within their speech community is directly relevant to diachronic linguistics.

The next section begins with the discussion of the standard methodology. The section describes the data collection procedures and reviews the study of /-t, d/ deletion phenomenon in English as a concrete example of what has been conducted in the field. Section 2 presents the results of the quantitative analyses of voiced velar nasalization in Japanese as it is spoken in Tokyo. The section concludes with a discussion of how diachronic and synchronic variation observed in Tokyo Japanese can be represented in a theoretical framework. Section 3 summarizes the chapter and outlines directions for further research.

1   Methodological Principles

1.1   *Overview*

The field of sociolinguistics probably is best defined in terms of its methods and goals, rather than its subject matter. Thus, in this section, we will review the progress which has been made in the area of methodology in the course of a number of studies of sound change in progress in the past three decades (Abdel-Jawad 1981, Bailey 1973, Baugh 1979, Cedergren 1973, Cofer 1972, Guy 1981, Haeri 1991, Harris 1985, Herold 1990, Hindle 1980, Hong 1991, Laberge 1977, Labov et al. 1972, 1980, Lavandera 1975, Lennig 1978, MacCaulay 1977, L. Milroy 1980, Modaressi 1978, C. Paradis 1985, Payne 1976, Poplack 1979, Tarallo 1983, Trudgill 1974).

The success of the study of language in its social context depends heavily on selecting appropriate methods of data collection and analysis. The traditional field methods developed in dialect geography are inappropriate for studying natural speech. Chambers (1992: 674) states:

> Dialect geography studied regional speech patterns qualitatively, and concentrating on the speech of nonmobile, older, rural, predominantly male consultants – known acronymically as NORMs – elicited relatively stable, regionally distinctive, highly differentiated speech samples. Variability was peripheral, and only occasionally drew comment from the investigators.

Technological progress in sound recording in the past several decades has enabled the student of language variation to take a different methodological path. Instead of asking the informant, she or he can record spontaneous speech and capture its systematicity.

Previous research has shown that the vernacular is the best database to reveal the most systematic and regular character of language. Labov (1984: 29) states the reasons for preferring the vernacular used in casual and spontaneous interaction to more formal styles as follows:

> The vernacular is defined as that mode of speech that is acquired in pre-adolescent years. Its highly regular character is an empirical observation. The vernacular includes inherent variation, but the rules governing that variation appear to be more regular than those operating in the more formal "superposed" styles that are acquired later in life. Each speaker has a vernacular form in at least one language; this may be the prestige dialects (as in the case of "RP"), or a non-standard variety.

In his New York City study (Labov 1966), Labov conducted a series of face-to-face, tape-recorded interviews with individuals based on a random sample. Although one can get a representative sample of a speech community most efficiently by this method, it does not facilitate the elicitation of vernacular for two reasons: first, the setting in which an informant is being interviewed by a stranger is more likely to elicit careful style; second, we can get no view of the interaction of speakers since each individual is isolated from his or her social networks. To overcome the problem of direct interviewing, Labov first attempted to minimize the constraints of the setting which may promote speakers' consciousness of their speech style based on topic; general interview topics such as place of birth, residential history, education, and occupation are considered to elicit relatively careful and formal style, while a specific set of topics such as danger of death, childhood rhymes, and customs (and any speech outside the formal interview, with a third person, or not in direct response to questions) override the negative effects of the interview situation and are likely to lead the interaction to the other end of the spectrum, i.e. casual and informal style. This approach, however, is not always a successful means of approximating the ideal; it sometimes fails to enable researchers to elicit an unreflecting way of speaking.

In their Harlem study, Labov and his associates took a completely different approach: participant observation techniques and group sessions (Labov et al. 1968). A number of pre-existing peer groups were located and their members were recorded as a group. This way of obtaining data is superior to an individual interview, for the undesirable effect of observation and recording is reduced by the control of social interaction. The method of eliciting data through group sessions, however, lacks representativeness. No one can claim that the speech collected through this method is representative of the entire speech community. Labov et al. (1968) overcame this shortcoming by supplementing the data from the group interviews with material collected from individual interviews with each member of these groups as well as with interview data obtained from a random sample of the community.

The Project on Linguistic Change and Variation (Labov et al. 1980) was an attempt to aim at both depth and breadth by combining both methods. It incorporated a telephone survey, which is comparable to a conventional random sample survey, and a series of neighborhood studies, through which a large number of linguistic and social data on the major social networks of the neighborhoods under investigation are obtained. No one method can be perfect in all respects. Labov (1984: 50) lists seven criteria to rate the methods of collecting data:

> the possibility of obtaining a representative sample; the demographic data obtained; the comparability of the data obtained; success in minimizing the effects of observation; the quality of the sound recorded; the volume of data obtained; and the feasibility of including field experiments.

Either of the methods employed in the Project on Linguistic Change and Variation has its own strengths and weaknesses, and hence, agreement in the results provided the basis for confidence in the findings of the project and presented a well-balanced view of linguistic change in progress.[1]

1.2   /-t, d/ deletion in English

The field of variationist sociolinguistics originally started from an interest in diachronic change. Labov (1963, 1966) analyzed primarily the effect of social factors such as age, gender, socioeconomic status, and ethnic or other characteristics of the speakers on linguistic variables which represent linguistic change in progress. The variationist approach has been modified in a significant way by recognizing that a particular variation is maintained across many generations with no sign of change. The case which brought this home is the /-t, d/ deletion phenomenon in English. It is characterized by the absence of change.

The /-t, d/ deletion is a phonological process which results in the absence of a final apical stop (/-t/ or /-d/) when it is the last member of a consonant cluster. The variable omission of /-t, d/ yields pronunciations such as *didn'* *wan' us* (< didn't want us) and *the firs' chil'* (< the first child). It is the best-known variable process that has been studied in the variationist paradigm of socioliguistic studies.

Three decades of empirical research carried out for a wide variety of English dialects has repeatedly shown that the variable process of /-t, d/ deletion is constrained not only by the social factors but also by the linguistic internal constraints (Bayley 1991, 1994, Fasold 1972, Guy 1980, 1991a, 1991b, 1993, 1994, 1997, Guy and Boyd 1990, Hibiya 1997, Labov 1975, 1989, Labov et al. 1968, Neu 1980, Patrick 1991, 1992, Roberts 1994, Romaine 1984, Santa Ana 1991, 1992, Wolfram 1969, 1972, Wolfram and Christian 1976). The linguistic constraints include the following:

(1)   a.   whether the syllable containing /-t, d/ is stressed or not:
  e.g.   different, island, thousand, interest > hard-working
      b.   consonant cluster length:
  e.g.   next > list
      c.   the phonetic features of the segment preceding /-t, d/:
  /s/ > stops > nasals > other fricatives > liquids
  e.g.   first > except > recent > left > bolt
      d.   the phonetic features of the segment following /-t, d/:
  obstruents > liquids > glides > vowels
  e.g.   didn't go > didn't learn > didn't watch > didn't eat
      e.   the grammatical feature of /-t, d/:
  part of -n't morpheme > part of stem > irregular verb
  past tense or past participial form which are marked by both suffixation and ablaut > regular past tense or past participial suffix
  e.g.   isn't > mist > felt > missed
      f.   whether the segments preceding and following /-t, d/ agree in voicing or not:
  homovoiced > heterovoiced
  e.g.   except swimming > except running

Among them, the effects of (1d) and (1e) have been unanimously found to be the most important in every dialect. The relative ranking of the two varies from dialect to dialect: in European American English dialects (1e) is more signifi- cant (Neu 1980) while in the so-called ethnic or minority varieties, i.e. African American, Puerto Rican, Chicano, Appalachian, and Japanese-Canadian English, (1d) is stronger (Labov et al. 1968, Wolfram 1972, Santa Ana 1991, Wolfram and Christian 1976, Hibiya 1997).

Let us examine these two constraints in detail. For (1d), the deletion is pro- moted in the following order: obstruents > liquids > glides > vowels. In other words, when a segment which follows the final /-t, d/ is lower in sonority, the /-t, d/ is likely to be deleted. Interestingly, the effect of a following pause is dialect-specific (Guy 1980, Hibiya 1997).

With respect to (1e), the /-t/ of *-n't* produced by negative contraction is deleted most frequently. The deletion is promoted to a larger extent when the /-t, d/ is part of the stem, as in *past, mist* (M-words), than when it is the regular past tense or past participial suffix, as in *passed, missed* (P-verbs). The final /-t, d/ of verb forms like *left* and *sold* (S-verbs) fall between these two in deletion rate.

Two different hypotheses have been proposed to account for the ranking. The first one is in functional terms. According to this hypothesis, the /-t/ of *missed* is deleted less frequently than the /-t/ of *mist* since the former is an inflectional suffix that carries the grammatical feature of past tense. In other words, semantically relevant information is more likely to be retained (Kiparsky 1971, 1982). The second one is based on lexical phonology (Kiparsky 1982, 1985, Mohanan 1986). In this theory, lexical derivation is organized into two principal levels, i.e. lexical and postlexical. The lexicon consists of at least two ordered levels. At each level, the morphological and phonological processes alternate with each other. It is possible for rules to apply at more than one level. In the case of the /-t, d/ deletion phenomenon, M-words have their final consonant clusters underlyingly. S-verbs acquire their final /-t, d/ by under- going affixation at level 1 of the lexicon while the regular inflectional affixes are attached at level 2. Adopting the theoretical framework of lexical phonol- ogy, Guy (1991a) proposes that /-t, d/ deletion is a variable phonological rule that applies both within the lexicon and in the postlexical level whenever its structural descriptions are met. M-words undergo deletion three times whereas S-verbs twice and P-verbs do so only once each. Therefore, the difference in derivational history accounts for the ranking M-words > S-verbs > P-verbs.

The deletion is subject to stylistic and social factors as well. Earlier studies have repeatedly found that in formal speech /t/ and /d/ tend to be retained. The gender, socioeconomic status, and educational background of speakers also constrain the variable process.

As has been mentioned at the beginning of this section, the /-t, d/ deletion is a typical case of a stable variable which shows no sign of change, and among the linguistic variables examined so far, stable ones are relatively common. The field of linguistics has been concerned with invariance for a long time; but the analyses of this phenomenon have established the notion that variation is the fundamental problem of synchronic linguistics which is worthy of systematic study.

2 The Tokyo Project

The /-t, d/ deletion has been considered as a showcase variable of inherent variation which is constrained by both social and linguistic internal factors. Studies of /-t, d/ deletion in English have set standards for the detailed analysis of variation. This section presents the results of the quantitative investigation of one variable in Japanese (Hibiya 1988). It is an attempt to describe the language as it is spoken in Tokyo. The study was carried out with the purpose of building upon the progress which had been made since the 1960s in the area of data collection and analysis.

2.1 Background

The purpose of this subsection is to discuss the methodology used in this study. I will describe in detail the specific methods used for: (1) selecting informants in such a way that the sample would provide both detail and representativeness of linguistic behavior; and (2) eliciting data which would illustrate the informants' full range of speech behavior. Let us first describe the speech community under investigation.

Tokyo (previously Edo), one of the major urban centers of the world, has been inhabited since 2500 BC. It used to be a peripheral village until Tokugawa Ieyasu established a feudal government in Edo in 1603. Since then, the city has developed greatly as a political center of the country. By the end of the eighteenth century, it had grown into a city with a population of 1,200,000. During the Edo era (1603–1868), the city was inhabited by members of the samurai "military" class, merchants, and artisans. In 1868, the emperor defeated the Tokugawas and regained power. Since then, it has been the capital of the country. The city was renamed Tokyo, which means "eastern capital."

Its importance as the political, commercial, financial, and cultural center of Japan has steadily increased. Although Tokyo was badly damaged by the earthquake of 1923 and air raids during World War II, the city was rebuilt within a short period of time after the destruction.

Tokyo is divided into two subareas, *yamanote* "uptown" and *shitamachi* "downtown." The former consists of middle- and upper-class residential areas, whereas the latter is mostly a commercial or industrial area where the lower middle-class and blue-collar workers live. Historically, *yamanote* was inhabited by the samurai class, and *shitamachi* by merchants and artisans during the Edo era. This social difference resulted in the development of two different versions of the dialect.

Today standard Japanese is based on a variety of the Tokyo dialect typical of educated, middle-class natives of the *yamanote* area. It is the language of the government, education, and media. The *yamanote* dialect is considered to have more prestige than the *shitamachi* dialect (Vance 1987).

The main target speech community of Hibiya (1988) was one neighborhood in Tokyo named Nezu. It is a typical *shitamachi* neighborhood located on the border between the two subareas. At the time of data collection (1986), the population was 7,514, and the number of households was 2,913 (census data).

In Nezu, a total of 97 people were interviewed.[2] The first major source of data came from a neighborhood study. We entered the community in July 1986, to establish contacts and develop relationships with members who later allowed us to make tape-recordings. The Nezu neighborhood study began in mid-July 1986 with a series of interviews with a peer group of retired people, which lasted for three months. All of the interviews with old men and women were conducted in the center for retired people run by Bunkyo Ward. During this period, the interviews with other peer groups and individuals from different generations of the area were carried out at their homes.

In the neighborhood study, we interviewed a total of nine people, five males and four females, ranging in age from 16 to 83 years old. Because they were few in number and the procedures employed to select them were not adequate to achieve representativeness, the results from this study would not be considered as typical of the neighborhood as a whole.

In addition to the above neighborhood study, we carried out a random sample survey of the population to evaluate the data from the neighborhood study. This second sample consisted of 88 people. There were 41 males and 47 females. The sampling procedure was as follows. First, we selected one out of every 15 people from the list of residents kept at the Nezu branch of Bunkyo Ward Office, yielding a sample of 402. We then excluded 50 who were below 10 years of age, reducing the sample to 352 people. It turned out that 42 had moved out of the neighborhood, and 16 could not be interviewed because they were sick or handicapped. Of the remaining 294, we were able to carry out standard sociolinguistic interviews with 88 residents: 30 refused to be interviewed, while 176 were never located although we tried to reach each one as many as three times. Among the 88, the speech of 62 speakers was analyzed. They were native speakers of the dialect; 48 were born in Nezu, while 14 grew up in other areas of the city. They ranged in age between 14 and 81 years old at the time of the data collection (1986). Table 4.1 shows the distribution of the informants by age and sex.

A supplementary group of ten native speakers from other areas of Tokyo (five males and five females) was contacted in the course of data collection. For this series of interviews, we worked with families; the two home sites made it possible to obtain data across three generations. The informants ranged in age from 15 to 81.

Each individual interview in the neighborhood study consisted of several modules of questions referred to as Q-GEN-II, which were developed at the

Table 4.1   Distribution of informants by age and sex

Sex	10–19	20–9	30–9	40–9	50–9	60–9	70+	Total
Male	7	5	2	9	6	1	1	31
Female	5	2	7	4	5	4	4	31
Total	12	7	9	13	11	5	5	62

University of Pennsylvania. It is a network of modules covering a wide range of topics which is designed to allow the interviewer to get at speakers' areas of major interest. Each module contains a dozen questions which are meant to be open-ended. Questions were adapted to the speech communities in Tokyo.

The individual interview of the Nezu random sample survey included readings of texts and words and a short interview. The recordings were made using a Sony TCM 5000 EV tape recorder and a Sony ECM 150 lavaliere microphone.

2.2   *Voiced velar nasalization as a linguistic variable*

The study of variation and change over the past 30 years has focused on the social context of language use, the linguistic constraints of variation and change, or both. In this section, we will discuss the interaction between linguistic and social processes, focusing on one well-known linguistic variable in Tokyo Japanese: voiced velar nasalization.

2.2.1   *Facts*

In the conservative dialect of Tokyo Japanese, voiced velar plosives are nasalized word-medially. Some examples are listed in (2). (The symbol [¥] represents a voiced velar nasal.)

(2)   *Word-initial [g]:*   *Word-medial [¥]:*

gin	"silver"	hi¥asi	"east"
geki	"play"	ka¥e	"shadow"
gan	"cancer"	ka¥i	"key"
goma	"sesame"	iti¥o	"strawberry"
gun	"county"	hu¥u	"blowfish"

As a first approximation, it can be stated that for speakers of this dialect, underlying /g/ is realized as [g] in word-initial position, but as [¥] in other positions; in other words, [g] and [¥] are in complementary distribution. However, there are several systematic exceptions where word-internal [¥] must or may be blocked (Sakuma 1929, S. E. Martin 1987, Arisaka 1959, Vance 1987). These exceptions will be discussed in detail later.

The pronunciation with consistent use of non-initial [¥] has been considered to be standard and has official status. Before World War II, it was an emphasized point of elementary school education that /g/ should be realized as [¥] in non-initial position. Today, many trained television and radio broadcasters use non-initial [¥].

2.2.2 *Variation in apparent and real time: social aspects*

It has widely been observed that the non-initial nasal [¥] is undergoing a change and being pronounced as a plosive [g] (Hibiya 1988, 1995a). For speakers of this newer dialect of Tokyo Japanese, voiced velar plosives are never nasalized regardless of their position within a word.

Figure 4.1 shows the temporal distribution of word-internal [g]. For each speaker of the Nezu random sample survey, the number of [g] tokens were counted and their percentage was plotted against age individually. A clear pattern of age stratification emerges. Among the speakers in their teens and twenties, the [g] variant is predominant while the percentage of [g] drops off as age increases. The correlation is highly significant ($R^2 = 0.651$, $p < .001$).

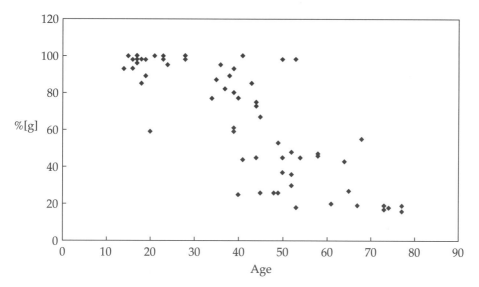

Figure 4.1   Age distribution of [g]
Source: Hibiya 1995a: 144

When a clear correlation between a given linguistic variable and age is found, it is assumed to reflect a linguistic change, in this case a shift from word-internal [¥] toward [g]. This way, the trajectory of linguistic change within a community can be followed in apparent time. Correlation with age, however, may be a case of age-grading, a pattern which repeats in each generation instead of a sign of change (Hockett 1950). To determine whether a given relationship between age and the linguistic variable represents change in progress or age-grading, real-time observations have to be consulted. Differences among sets of data collected at discrete points in time can confirm that a true change has occurred (Labov 1994).

For the linguistic variable under consideration, there are a number of concrete sources of real-time data (Hibiya 1995b). In early nineteenth-century literature (Ukiyoburo written by Shikitei Samba), it is specifically mentioned that speakers in Edo had the nasal word-internally while rural speakers had the plosive. The descriptions of the language by foreigners who came to Japan in the late nineteenth century (Hepburn 1872, Chamberlain 1888) also indicate that the native speakers then had the initial [g] and internal [¥].

A study carried out in 1941 by Kindaichi bears directly on this phenomenon (H. Kindaichi 1967). By means of a word list, he examined how 70 native middle-school students who were 14–15 years of age pronounced underlying /g/. The results showed that about one-third of the informants had consistent use of word-internal [¥], and about another one-third had consistent use of word-internal [g]. The rest used both variably. Although he did not include any speakers from other age groups in his study, he also mentioned that native speakers over 30 at that time all had consistent use of word-internal [¥]. His results and observation clearly show that the shift from an older variant to a newer one was in progress more than five decades ago.

In addition to these written records, we were able to locate two different sets of earlier tape-recordings. In the 1950s, NHK (Japan Broadcasting Association) carried out a project in which it located a few aged informants from each major dialect area of the country and recorded their natural conversation. The tape prepared in 1952 for the Tokyo dialect included the speech of two native speakers: a man born in 1868 and a woman born in 1891. The examination of the recording shows that both of them had word-internal [¥]. Interestingly, they overtly talked about voiced velar nasalization during their taped conversation; both agreed that the word-internal [g] which was occasionally heard in their daily life then was not typical of genuine Tokyo dialect. This kind of comment indicates that the people were aware of the change.

The second set is a collection of recordings of a series from a radio program. Seventeen speakers who were born between 1875 and 1888 were interviewed at home for the program in the 1940s and 1950s. They acquired their vernacular in the late nineteenth century when the above-mentioned foreigners were describing the language. Everyone had the pattern which was consistent with the rules and their exceptions for voiced velar nasal of the conservative dialect.

The analyses of the real-time data have all indicated that native speakers had word-internal [¥] until at least the late nineteenth century. The change must have started in the early twentieth century and is headed toward completion in the youngest generation of today.

As compared to the age stratification which has been discussed, the gender difference is not so striking. Both male and female speakers participated in the variation in a similar way.

Among the social factors, the degree of one's contact with *yamanote* has also turned out to be important in constraining the variability and change. As described earlier, the city consists of two subareas: *yamanote* and *shitamachi*. According to the study conducted by Kindaichi, it was the natives of the former that were leading the change 50 years ago. An examination of the speech of the Nezu random sample survey shows that not only those who were born and brought up in the *yamanote* area but also those who had daily contact with *yamanote* in their adolescence definitely favored word-internal [g]. As can be seen in figure 4.1, there are three informants who use [g] almost categorically among the speakers between 40 and 59 years of age. They use [g] much more frequently than the rest of the same age group. What these three have in common is that they all went to high school in the *yamanote* area. In figure 4.2, all speakers that have had an extensive contact with *yamanote* are coded as [+*yamanote*]. These speakers favor [g], and this pattern holds for all age groups but the youngest, in which this factor does not have an effect.

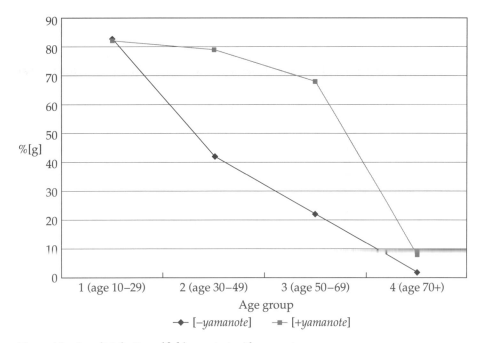

Figure 4.2   Age distribution of [g] by contact with *yamanote*

The results of these analyses, along with the earlier findings and observations, show that the change of word-internal [¥] to [g] in Tokyo Japanese originated in *yamanote* in the early twentieth century and has spread to the entire Tokyo speech community. An overall increase in the use of word-internal [g] in the vernacular is observed over several decades. The change is near completion, and the word-internal [¥] has been replaced by [g] at a very rapid rate within three generations.

2.2.3   *Linguistic internal factors*

As is clear from figure 4.1, except for some speakers in the youngest age group, there are only few who have categorical word-internal [g]. In this subsection, the effect of various linguistic internal factors will be analyzed and inter- and intra-speaker variation will be examined. The data used for the analyses of linguistic internal factors were drawn from the neighborhood studies in Nezu and other areas: a large body of vernacular speech from each speaker was obtained.

As mentioned earlier, there are several systematic exceptions to voiced velar nasalization in the conservative dialect. There are items for which the nasalization is blocked, and word-internal [g] occurs (Vance 1987).

The /g/ in relatively recent loanwords such as (3a) is pronounced as [g], while older ones including (3b) are more likely to have [¥].

(3)   a.   yooguruto   "yogurt"
       b.   i¥irisu   "England"

In the corpus, there were 56 loanword tokens; the percentage of [g] for this category is 77 percent. This result clearly shows that loanwords favor the [g] realization.

The reduplicated /g/ at the beginning of the second part in mimetic forms is always realized as [g].

(4)   gara-gara   "rattle-rattle"

In the corpus, there were 21 mimetic tokens; the percentage of [g] for this category is 100 percent.

Earlier research has indicated that morphological structuring plays a crucial role in determining whether nasalization is obligatory or not. In compound words consisting of two elements, there is a tendency for medial [g] to appear in initial position of the second element. This is almost categorical when the second element is a loanword,

(5)   doku#gasu   "poison gas"

or consists of two Sino-Japanese morphemes. In what follows, the tokens which belong to this category are classified as "#compound."

(6)   sekai#ginkoo   "World Bank"

It should be noted that these second elements (e.g. gasu, ginkoo) also occur with [g] in isolation because they will be in the word-initial position.

When the second element is a single Sino-Japanese bound root, however, the root-initial /g/ is realized as [¥]. The tokens of this type are referred to as "+compound."

(7)   ho+¥o   "protection"

Based on the description of several pronunciation dictionaries, Vance (1987) observed that [¥] is favored when the word-internal voiced velar is induced by sequential voicing. These tokens are abbreviated as "voicing."

(8)   hana+¥asa   "flower umbrella"
      *hana+kasa

Finally, it should be noted that there is a very strong tendency for the nominative case particle -*ga*, which marks the subject, to be pronounced [¥] (Hibiya 1988). This type is classified as "nom." The tokens belonging to this category make up 44 percent of the neighborhood study database. Only 14 percent of them were pronounced [g].

In the following, we will select six individuals from the neighborhood study and examine their data in detail; a substantial number of tokens were obtained from each of them. Since they belong to different age groups, some are typical speakers of the conservative dialect whereas some exhibit a wide range of variation in their voiced velar nasalization. From the analyses below, the loanword and mimetic tokens are excluded because the effect of these factors is obvious. Consider table 4.2.

For each speaker, the percentage of [g] tokens was calculated. As is expected from their age, the first two individuals, speakers 1 and 2, are consistent [¥] speakers. [g] appeared in word-initial position or in compounds of which the second element is either a loanword or consists of two Sino-Japanese morphemes, while [¥] appeared in all other cases.

Let us now examine the results of speakers 3 and 4. They pronounced "#compound" /g/s as [g] almost categorically. Those which belong to the other four categories, i.e. "+compound," "voicing," "no boundary," and "nom," however, were not always realized as [¥].

Speakers 5 and 6 use [g] much more often. This tendency is especially clear for speaker 6, who pronounced /g/s as [g] almost categorically except for "nom" and "no boundary" tokens.

The foregoing analyses show that the levels of the [g] usage increase steadily as age decreases. Linguistic internal factors strongly influence the pronunciation of /g/. The plosive pronunciation appears least often with "nom" tokens.

Table 4.2 Effects of linguistic factors

	#compound	+compound	Voicing	No boundary	Nom	Total
Speaker 1 (male, 80s):						
[g]/N	26/32	4/88	0/17	1/122	1/308	32/567
[g]%	81	5	0	1	0	6
Speaker 2 (male, 70s):						
[g]/N	8/10	0/106	0/1	3/124	4/303	15/544
[g]%	80	0	0	2	1	3
Speaker 3 (female, 40s):						
[g]/N	10/10	16/60	0/10	23/109	14/191	53/380
[g]%	100	27	0	23	7	14
Speaker 4 (female, 30s):						
[g]/N	10/11	15/44	5/15	18/46	33/137	81/253
[g]%	91	34	33	39	24	32
Speaker 5 (male, 20s):						
[g]/N	3/3	20/32	4/5	48/70	49/75	124/185
[g]%	100	63	80	69	65	67
Speaker 6 (female, 10s)						
[g]/N	3/3	38/39	3/3	38/43	41/52	123/140
[g]%	100	97	100	88	79	79

2.3 An optimality-theoretic approach to variation and change

As is obvious from the discussion of the /-t, d/ deletion phenomenon in English in section 1.2, the variationist approach has benefited greatly from formal linguistic theory. Over the past several decades, the field has formulated the findings of variation studies in terms of the Sound Pattern of English format and the lexical phonology.

The present section is another attempt to account for the quantitative data by a particular formal model. The theory and analysis of variationist sociolinguistics in the 1990s have been enriched in a significant way by drawing on the current emergence of Optimality Theory (McCarthy and Prince 1993a, 1993b, Prince and Smolensky 1993, Reynolds 1994, Reynolds and Nagy 1994, Nagy 1996, Sells et al. 1996, Nagy and Reynolds 1996, 1997, Zubritskaya 1994, 1997). Optimality Theory is a constraint-based approach and a number of constraints are relevant for the realization of the voiced velar. As will be shown, these constraints are ranked and violable, as is standard in Optimality Theory.

Adopting the framework of McCarthy and Prince (1995), Itô and Mester (1997a: 4) have proposed the following three constraints to account for the voiced velar nasalization among words consisting of a single element in the conservative dialect. The abbreviations which will be used for these constraints in this section are given in parentheses.

¥ is prohibited in word-initial position (*[¥). The form [geki] satisfies this constraint because the initial sound is [g], while the form [¥eki] does not because it starts with [¥].

Voiced dorsal obstruents are prohibited (*g). [¥eki] and [ka¥e] satisfy this constraint because they do not contain [g]. Given the choice between [geki] and [¥eki], or [kage] and [ka¥e], this constraint chooses the latter forms.

The underlying form and surface form are identically specified for [nasal] (IDENTLS). When the input forms are /geki/ and /kage/, [geki] and [kage] satisfy this constraint while [¥eki] and [ka¥e] do not.

Another constraint is necessary to account for both the optionality of voiced velar nasalization in certain compounds, i.e. words consisting of two free elements (*hana-gara* and *hana-¥ara* "flower pattern"), and the obligatory nasalization of bound stems (*doku¥a* "poison fang"). The bound form of a stem must be segmentally identical with its corresponding free form (IDENTSS).

In Itô and Mester (1997a), these four constraints are ranked in the following hierarchy. The place for IDENTSS is exactly the same as *g (free ranking).

(9)   1   *[¥
        2   *g
            IDENTSS
        3   IDENTLS

/hana-gara/ Surf [gara]	*[¥	IDENTSS	*g	IDENTLS
→ [hanagara]			*	
[hana¥ara]		*!		*

/hana-gara/ Surf [gara]	*[¥	*g	IDENTSS	IDENTLS
[hanagara]		*!		
→ [hana¥ara]			*	*

Given the choice between [hanagara] and [hana¥ara], the former is the winner with the 1 *[¥, 2 IDENTSS, 3 *g, and 4 IDENTLS ranking, since it satisfies the second constraint. On the other hand, if the ranking is 1 *[¥, 2 *g, 3 IDENTSS, and 4 IDENTLS, the latter is selected because avoiding the voiced velar [g] is more important. In the case of *dokuga*, [doku¥a] is chosen with either ranking. This candidate satisfies *g. IDENTSS is irrelevant here because, being a bound form, [-¥a] does not have a corresponding free form.

Finally, Itô and Mester (1997a) have proposed one more constraint. In a compound word, the second element must begin with a [+voice] segment (SEQ VOI). For instance, [iro+kami] "colored paper" does not satisfy this constraint, whereas both [iro+gami] and [iro+¥ami] do. No other constraint dominates SEQ VOI. Since it is a constraint regarding the noninitial element, *[¥ becomes irrelevant whenever SEQ VOI plays a role in determining the winning candidate. This is illustrated by the vertical line between *[¥ and SEQ VOI. The final constraint ranking is given in (10):

(10) 1 *[¥ | SEQ VOI
    2 *g
       IDENTSS
    3 IDENTLS

Itô and Mester (1997a) have specifically included no social and geographic variation in their analyses by focusing on the conservative dialect. How can the inherent inter- and intra-speaker variability found in the speech community be accounted for within the framework of Optimality Theory?

Reynolds (1994) summarizes three ways for Optimality Theory in its current state to handle variation. (1) Multiple candidates may be equally optimal because more than one form satisfies exactly the same constraints; (2) several different rankings may exist within a given language; or (3) two or more constraints may be unranked with respect to each other.

In order to account for the patterns of diachronic change, Reynolds (1994) has added the notion of Floating Constraint (FC) to Optimality Theory. FCs are those which can appear anywhere within its domain on the constraint hierarchy. The ranking of normal constraints is fixed while that of FCs may vary in a principled manner. The addition of FCs produces several different rankings under which different forms may be optimal.

Let us adopt this approach to account for the variation and change discussed in the above sections. The constraints are ranked as (11) for the single stem word:

(11) 1   *[¥

     2    $\left\{ \begin{matrix} \text{*g} \\ \text{IDENTLS} \end{matrix} \right\}$

*[¥ is anchored and always ranked over the other two constraints, while *g and IDENTLS are FCs which can appear in any position with each other. As has been seen, *g is ranked above IDENTLS in the conservative dialect. The relative ranking of these two constraints is reversed in the newer dialect and IDENTLS is ranked above *g.[3] Consider /kage/ as an example. Neither [kage] nor [ka¥e] violates *[¥. [kage], not [ka¥e], is selected because it does not violate IDENTLS.

Let us include IDENTSS and SEQ VOI in the constraint hierarchy.

(12) 1   *[¥ | SEQ VOI

     2    $\left[\begin{matrix} ...... & \text{IDENTSS} & ...... \\ & \left\{ \begin{matrix} \text{*g} \\ \text{IDENTLS} \end{matrix} \right\} & \end{matrix} \right]$

IDENTSS is also an FC which can appear in any position within its domain. As has been stated, *g and IDENTLS are FCs with respect to each other. This hierarchy, consisting of both ranked and floating constraints, thus produces different hierarchical orders. The newer dialect has the order shown in (13), which makes the right prediction for the words with three different types of morphological structuring. Tableaux for /hana+gara/, /doku-ga/, and /iro+kami/ are given in (14), (15), and (16) respectively.

(13)   1   *[¥ | SEQ VOI
      2   IDENTSS
      3   IDENTLS
      4   *g

(14)   /hana+gara/

Surf [gara]	*[¥ | SEQ VOI	IDENTSS	IDENTLS	*g
→ [hanagara]				*
[hana¥ara]		*!	*	

(15)   /doku-ga/

Surf –	*[¥ | SEQ VOI	IDENTSS	IDENTLS	*g
→ [doku ga]				*
[doku ¥a]			*!	

(16)   /iro+kami/

Surf [kami]	*[¥ | SEQ VOI	IDENTSS	IDENTLS	*g
[irogami]		*	*	*!
→ [iro¥ami]		*	*	
[irokami]	*!			

First let us examine /hana+gara/. *[¥ and Seq Voi are irrelevant. The form [hana-gara] is the winning candidate because [hana-¥ara] violates IdentSS. In the case of /doku-ga/, for which *[¥ and Seq Voi are again irrelevant, neither [doku ga] nor [doku ¥a] violates IdentSS. IdentLS is crucial in selecting [doku ga]. For /iro+kami/, [iro-kami] is excluded because it violates Seq Voi. IdentSS is violated both by [iro-gami] and [iro-¥ami], because neither is identical with /iro+kami/. IdentLS cannot distinguish between the two either. Finally, [iro-¥ami] is selected because it is the only candidate that fulfills *g.

The third case is particularly interesting in that it accounts for the data presented in table 4.2. Both speakers 3 and 4 disfavor the [g] pronunciation more when /g/ is induced by sequential voicing than when it occurs at nonboundary position. However, there are too few "voicing" tokens from speakers 5 and 6 to support a detailed analysis of this constraint.

The change from [g] to [¥] which has been discussed earlier in this chapter can be accounted for by positing that (1) IdentSS floats at the higher end of its domain, i.e. right below *[¥|Seq Voi; and (2) IdentLS is ranked higher than *g in the grammar of the newer dialect.

3   Synthesis: Variationist Approach to Linguistic Heterogeneity

In the development of theoretical linguistics, it has generally been assumed that language is homogeneous and that linguistic variation falls outside the scope of the field. Variationist research carried out in the past three decades, however, has shown that variation found within spontaneous speech exhibits a highly regular pattern whether it represents a change in progress or not. The systematic nature of inherent variation has repeatedly been shown in numerous studies. The voiced velar nasalization alternation can be viewed as another supporting evidence for the notion of "orderly heterogeneity."

In review, the analyses of the natural conversation data have shown that in Tokyo Japanese the word-internal /g/ is undergoing a change from [¥] to [g]. This diachronic change is manifested as synchronic variation, which is constrained by both social and linguistic factors. Among the former, the effect of two factors, i.e. age and one's contact with *yamanote*, have been crucial. As to the latter, the variation is constrained by the environments in which /g/ is found.

The goal of variationist sociolinguistics is to give an answer to the question about where and how variation is located in speakers' grammars. In the present investigation, we have shown that one way of solving this problem is to adopt Optimality Theory enhanced with FCs, in analyzing the data obtained by means of the methodology which has been developed within the tradition of variationist sociolinguistics. This approach to heterogeneity, which attempts to account for phonological variation in terms of constraint ranking, has proved fruitful. It provides new ways for relating quantitative patterns to the formal principles and will link empirical studies of variation and formal linguistic theory.

In the present chapter, I have discussed several assumptions underlying the framework first proposed by Weinreich et al. (1968) and recognized the value of variationist sociolinguistics. The data on which the findings in this investigation are based have mostly been collected in one neighborhood in Tokyo. It is desirable that similar projects which rely on comparable methodological principles be carried out at different sites.

To conclude, a few suggestions can be made for future research. In the history of Japanese phonology, pitch accent is by far the most widely studied topic. Like most phonological aspects, it changes over time. The wealth of material collected within the field of traditional dialectology serves as a starting point in searching for variables to be investigated in detail.

Traditionally it has been said that adjectives are divided into two classes in Tokyo Japanese: accented and unaccented. The former has a lexical accent on the penultimate mora in the present tense form; the latter does not.

(17)   *Accented*   *Unaccented*
    ao'i   "blue"   akai   "red"
    uresi'i   "happy"   akarui   "bright"
    omosiro'i "interesting"   muzukasii "difficult"

All the conjugational forms of the former have an accent on the penultimate vowel of the stem while only some of the latter have an accent on the final vowel of the stem.

(18)   *Accented*   *Unaccented*
    stem   aok-   akak-
    preverbal   a'oku   akaku
    past   a'okatta   aka'katta

Preliminary analyses (Hibiya 1990, 1991, 1993, Nakao et al. 1997) show the apparent and real-time evidence for the loss of this distinction.

(19)   *Accented*   *Unaccented*
    present tense ao'i   aka'i
    preverbal   ao'ku   aka'ku
    past   ao'katta aka'katta

Vowel devoicing is another topic for future investigation. In some regional dialects, high vowels are devoiced when they occur between two voiceless consonants, or at the end of the word and preceded by a voiceless consonant. The process interacts in an interesting way with accent (Nakao et al. 1997). It applies only when the syllables containing high vowels are unaccented.

In order to avoid an accent on a devoiced syllable, accent shift occurs as in (20) and (21).

(20)   compound noun tookyooti'hoo   "Tokyo region"
           →   tookyootiho'o (accent shift)

(21)   present tense   ayasi'i (accented adjective) "dubious"
       preverbal   ayasi'ku   →   aya'siku (accent shift)

Recent observations, however, have found that the accent shift has been dis-appearing in Tokyo Japanese (tookyooti'hoo, ayasi'ku). More analyses are called for to account for these changes.

   Recent studies (Labov 1989, Guy and Boyd 1990, Kerswill and Williams 1992, Roberts 1994, 1996, 1997a, 1997b, Kerswill 1996, Roberts and Labov 1995) have illuminated the acquisition of variation by young children. Among them, Labov (1989), Guy and Boyd (1990), and Roberts (1994, 1997b) have shown that first-language speakers as young as 3 or 4 years of age acquire variable constraints on /-t, d/ deletion, discussed in section 1.2. This is an area which should have attracted more attention in the history of variationist sociolinguistics. More studies on this topic will give us some clue to the problem of how constraints on variables are transmitted from generation to generation.

NOTES

1   Until recently most research of the field has relied on random sampling in a speech community under investigation. Two different approaches, namely social network analysis (L. Milroy 1980, 1987, J. Milroy 1992) and principal components analysis (Horvath 1985), have been proposed as alternatives to the conventional methodology.

2   The fieldwork was conducted by the author and Kenjiro Matsuda in 1986. His cooperation is much appreciated.

3   This ranking is exactly the same as lexically marked ranking, which Itô and Mester (1997a: 23) have proposed to account for nonnasalized g in loanwords.

5 Scrambling

NAOKO NEMOTO

0 Introduction

In Japanese, word order is flexible: the verb must come at the end of the sentence, but the order of the other phrases are free. For example, all the sentences in (1) are perfectly grammatical and mean virtually the same.[1]

(1) a. Taroo-ga   ano mise-de hon-o   katta (koto)
        Taro-Nom that store-at book-Acc bought
        "Taro bought a book at that store"
    b. Hon-o   Taroo-ga   ano mise-de katta (koto)
       book-Acc Taro-Nom that store-at bought
    c. Ano mise-de Taroo-ga   hon-o   katta (koto)
       that store-at Taro-Nom book-Acc bought
    d. Hon-o   ano mise-de Taroo-ga   katta (koto)
       book-Acc that store-at Taro-Nom bought
    e. Taroo-ga   hon-o   ano mise-de katta (koto)
       Taro-Nom book-Acc that store-at bought
    f. Ano mise-de hon-o   Taroo-ga   katta (koto)
       that store-at book-Acc Taro-Nom bought

The flexible word order phenomenon has been one of the major issues in Japanese linguistics in conjunction not only with the theory of movement but also with phrase structure and Case assignment, among others.

In this chapter, we consider two basic questions regarding the flexible word order phenomenon: (i) are all the sentences (1a–f) base-generated or are (1b–f) derived from (1a) by movement?; (ii) if the word order change in (1) is due to movement, what kind of characteristic does this movement exhibit?

1   Word Order in Japanese

We first examine whether any of the orders in (1) can be considered as the basic order in Japanese.

1.1   *Configurational vs. nonconfigurational dichotomy*

In the early 1980s, K. Hale proposed the configurationality parameters (see Hale 1980, 1982, 1983).[2] Hale (1980) and Farmer (1980, 1984) categorize Japanese as a typical example of a nonconfigurational language (see also Whitman 1979 and Miyagawa 1980). One of the motivations for analyzing Japanese as a nonconfigurational language is its flexible word order. Hale (1980) and Farmer (1980, 1984) propose to generate all the sentences in (1) by means of a phrase structure rule like (2), without appealing to a movement rule.

(2) $x' \rightarrow x'^* \, x$

(2) expresses that Japanese is a head-final language. The symbol x stands for a head and x' is a higher level than x. x'^* means any number of xs.

As noted in Saito (1985), this nonconfigurational analysis of Japanese crucially depends on the hypothesis that Japanese lacks VP (see Hinds 1973 and Fukui 1986). This is because crossing of phrase-marker branches as illustrated in (3) is not allowed.[3]

(3)

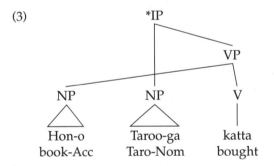

If we assume VP and a phrase structure rule IP → NP VP, we also assume the basic word order in Japanese is SOV.

We may, however, say that since Japanese allows the OSV order, a verb and its object need not be a constituent. Under this hypothesis, (1a) has the following structure. Notice that there is no VP in (4).

(4)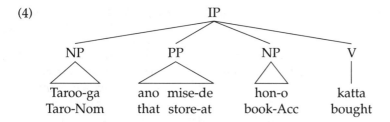

Saito and Hoji (1983), Saito (1985), and Hoji (1985, 1987), on the other hand, argue that Japanese has VP. With a VP node, (1a) has the following structure.[4]

(5)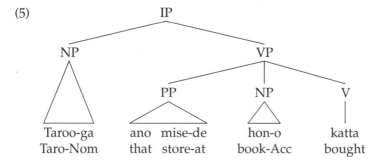

1.2 Evidence for the VP node

Since the existence of VP is crucial to argue for the configurationality of Japanese as noted above, we now examine Saito's (1985) arguments for the VP node in Japanese.

1.2.1 Pronominal coreference

Saito (1985) argues for VP in Japanese appealing to a subject/object asymmetry in pronominal coreference (see also Whitman 1982/87, Huang 1982, and Saito 1983). Let us first observe a paradigm in English in (6). Note that the intended reading where *John* and *he* are coindexed is not available in (6b). Note also the grammaticality of (6d) indicates that the crucial notion in binding is not precedence (Reinhart 1976).[5]

(6) a. John$_i$ loves his$_i$ mother
     b. *He$_i$ loves John$_i$'s mother
     c. John$_i$'s mother loves him$_i$
     d. His$_i$ mother loves John$_i$

This paradigm can be accounted for by Binding Theory (N. Chomsky 1981a). We can simply state the following.

(7)   A pronoun cannot c-command its antecedent. (Saito, 1985: 36)[6]

Note that the existence of VP is crucial to account for this paradigm in terms of (7): without a VP node, in (6c), the pronoun *him* would c-command *John* and the grammaticality difference between (6b) and (6c) cannot be accounted for.

Whitman (1982/87) and Saito (1985) show that Japanese exhibits exactly the same paradigm as (6) with respect to pronominal coreference. Let us observe the Japanese paradigm cited from Saito (1985: 37).[7] (8d) indicates that the crucial notion in binding is not precedence in Japanese.

(8)   a.   John$_i$-ga   [Mary-ga   kare$_i$-ni okutta tegami]-o
John-Nom Mary-Nom he-to   sent   letter-Acc
mada yonde inai (koto)
yet   read   not
"John has not yet read the letter Mary sent him"

b.   *Kare$_i$-ga [Mary-ga   John$_i$-ni okutta tegami]-o mada
he-Nom Mary-Nom John-to sent   letter-Acc yet
yonde inai (koto)
read   not
"He has not yet read the letter Mary sent John"

c.   [John$_i$-kara okane-o   moratta hito]-ga   kare$_i$-o
John-from money-Acc received person-Nom he-Acc
suisensita (koto)
recommended
"The person (who) received money from him recommended John"

d.   [Kare$_i$-kara okane-o   moratta hito]-ga   John$_i$-o
he-from   money-Acc received person-Nom John-Acc
suisensita (koto)
recommended
"The person (who) received money from him recommended John"

If Japanese lacks VP, in (8c), we expect that the pronoun *kare* "he" c-commands its antecedent *John*, and therefore, the sentence should be ill-formed. (8c) is, however, well-formed. Whitman (1982/87) and Saito (1985) argue that the grammaticality of (8c) demonstrates that VP exists in Japanese.

1.2.2   Weak crossover

Saito and Hoji (1983) argue for VP in Japanese using data that involve weak crossover (henceforth, WCO). Let us first consider the contrast in (9a–b) and (9c–d). In (9c–d), the intended reading is not available: *his* cannot be construed as a bound pronoun.

(9)   a.   Everyone$_i$ loves his$_i$ mother
b.   Who$_i$ loves his$_i$ mother?
c.   *His$_i$ mother loves everyone$_i$
d.   *Who$_i$ does his$_i$ mother love?

Quantified NPs (henceforth, QNPs) are considered to move at the level of logical form (henceforth, LF) to take a scope. The LF representations of (9) are given in (10).

(10) a. [everyone$_i$ [t$_i$ loves his$_i$ mother]]
      b. [who$_i$ [t$_i$ loves his$_i$ mother]]
      c. *[everyone$_i$ [his$_i$ mother loves t$_i$]]
      d. *[who$_i$ [his$_i$ mother loves t$_i$]]

The ill-formedness of (9c–d) is analyzed in terms of WCO, whose configuration is illustrated in (11).

(11) *[operator$_i$ [... pronoun$_i$ ... t$_i$ ...]] (WCO)
      A variable cannot be the antecedent of a pronoun that it does not c-command.[8]

Note that the existence of VP is also crucial here. If there is no VP, a variable would c-command the pronoun in the ill-formed examples too.

   Let us now observe Japanese examples from Saito and Hoji (1983). In these, an anaphor *zibun* "self" is used instead of a pronoun. This is because the pronoun *kare* "he" cannot have the bound variable interpretation.[9] This is illustrated in (12).

(12) *Dare$_i$-ga   kare$_i$-no hahaoya-o   aisiteiru no
       who-Nom his   mother-Acc love   Q
       "Who loves his mother?"

(13) is an example of *backward reflexivization* in N. A. McCawley (1976): the antecedent of *zibun* is *Mary*. It shows that *zibun* can be bound by the antecedent which does not c-command the anaphor.

(13) [[John-ga   zibun$_i$-no kuruma-o kowasita] koto]-ga
       John-Nom self's   car-Acc   broke   fact-Nom
       Mary$_i$-o   odorokaseta
       Mary-Acc surprised
       "The fact that John broke her car surprised Mary"

(14) shows that the anaphor *zibun* can be a bound anaphor when it is c-commanded by the QNP.

(14) a. Daremo$_i$-ga/Dareka$_i$-ga   [[Mary-ga   zibun$_i$-no kuruma-o
          everyone-Nom/someone-Nom   Mary-Nom self's   car-Acc
          kowasita] koto]-ni odoroita
          broke   fact-Dat be surprised
          "Everyone/someone was surprised by the fact that Mary broke his car"

b. Dare$_i$-ga   [[Mary-ga   zibun$_i$-no kuruma-o kowasita] koto]-ni
who-Nom   Mary-Nom self's   car-Acc   broke   fact-Dat
odoroita   no
was surprised Q
"Who was surprised by the fact that Mary broke his car?"

Now let us observe WCO examples from Saito and Hoji (1983).

(15) a.   ?*[[Mary-ga   zibun$_i$-no kuruma-o kowasita] koto]-ga
           Mary-Nom self's   car-Acc   broke   fact-Nom
           daremo$_i$-o/dareka$_i$-o   odorokaseta
           everyone-Acc/someone-Acc surprised
           "The fact that Mary broke his car surprised everyone/someone"
      b.   ?*[[Mary-ga   zibun$_i$-no kuruma-o kowasita] koto]-ga
           Mary-Nom self's   car-Acc   broke   fact-Nom
           dare$_i$-o   odorokaseta no
           who-Acc surprised   Q
           "Whom did the fact that Mary broke his car surprise?"

Saito and Hoji (1983) argue that although an anaphor is used instead of a pronoun in Japanese examples, the contrast displayed in (14) and (15) is parallel to the contrast in (9a–b) and (9c–d). The configuration of the ill-formed examples, namely (15a–b), is illustrated in (16).

(16) *[Operator$_i$ [. . . anaphor$_i$ . . . t$_i$ . . .]]
      A variable cannot be the antecedent of an anaphor that it does not c-command.

Note that the existence of VP is crucial in order to rule out (15) in terms of WCO. In this light, Saito and Hoji (1983) argue that VP exists in Japanese. The existence of VP argues against the nonconfigurational approach to Japanese.

In this section, we first reviewed the difference between the nonconfigurational hypothesis and the configurational hypothesis for Japanese. We next observed Saito's (1985) argument that VP exists in Japanese. Given that VP exists, we now assume that Japanese is a configurational language.

2   Arguments for Movement Analysis of Flexible Word Order

We assume that the basic word order in Japanese is SOV. We must now account for the other orders. Saito (1985) provides evidence that the flexible word order of Japanese is due to movement, which is called "scrambling" following Ross (1967).

2.1 *Pronominal coreference*

Saito (1985) shows that the OSV order influences pronominal coreference. We observed in section 1.2.1 that the crucial notion in the pronominal coreference is c-command. Let us examine the following examples cited from Saito (1985: 39). In (17b), the object is located in the sentence-initial position.

(17) a. *Kare$_i$-ga [Mary-ga   John$_i$-ni okutta tegami]-o mada
            he-Nom   Mary-Nom John-to sent   letter-Acc yet
            yonde inai (koto)
            read   not
            "He has not yet read the letter Mary sent to John"
      b. [Mary-ga   John$_i$-ni okutta tegami]-o kare$_i$-ga mada
            Mary-Nom John-to sent   letter-Acc he-Nom yet
            yonde inai (koto)
            read   not
            "The letter Mary sent to John, he has not yet read"

In (17a), the pronoun *kare* "he" c-commands its antecedent *John*; it is ruled out by the condition stated in (7), which is repeated in (18).

(18)   A pronoun cannot c-command its antecedent. (Saito, 1985: 36)

The grammaticality difference demonstrated in (17a–b) suggests that the subject does c-command the object in (17a) but not in (17b). The grammaticality of (17b) can be accounted for if we assume that the object moved to the position where the subject cannot c-command it. Saito (1985), therefore, argues that (17b) involves movement and its structure is as illustrated in (19).

(19)

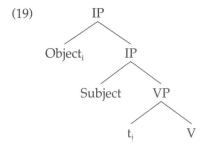

In (19), the object, which was base-generated in the VP, moved to the sentence-initial position, leaving its trace in the original position. The trace is coindexed with the moved constituent and assumed to be the same type as the moved constituent. As illustrated in (19), when the order is OSV, the subject no longer c-commands the moved object. The subject pronoun, therefore, does not c-command its antecedent in the object phrase in (17b).

2.2   Crossover

Saito (1985) also appeals to the crossover data to argue for a movement approach to flexible word order. Let us observe the following examples cited from Saito (1985: 47).

(20) a.   John$_i$-no sensei-ga   kare$_i$-o (zibun-de) syookaisita (koto)
             John's   teacher-Nom he-Acc (herself)   introduced
             "John's teacher herself introduced him"
      b. ??/?*John$_i$-no sensei-o   [kare$_i$-ga (zibun-de) syookaisita] (koto)
             John's   teacher-Acc he-Nom (himself)   introduced
             "John's teacher, he himself introduced"

The subject precedes the object in (20a) and the subject contains the antecedent of the pronoun. The object precedes the subject in (20b) and the object contains the antecedent of the pronoun. As long as the c-command relationship between the pronoun and its antecedent is concerned, there is no difference between (20a) and (20b). However, (20a) is well-formed and (20b) is ill-formed. Moreover, compare (20b) and (17b), which is repeated as (21).

(21) [Mary-ga   John$_i$-ni okutta tegami]-o kare$_i$-ga mada yonde inai (koto)
       Mary-Nom John-to sent   letter-Acc he-Nom yet   read   not
       "The letter that Mary sent to John, he has not yet read"

In both (20b) and (21), the object phrase contains the antecedent of the subject pronoun and precedes the subject. (20b) is ill-formed, whereas (21) is well-formed.

  Saito (1985) proposes to account for the contrast in (20b) and (21) in the same way as the contrast in (22) (see Reinhart 1976, 1983). The verb *put* subcategorizes a locative PP; we consider that PP is moved to the sentence-initial position in (22). The contrast displayed in (22a) and (22b) is parallel to the contrast in (20b) and (21).

(22) a. *[In Ben$_i$'s box]$_j$, he$_i$ put his cigars t$_j$
      b.   [In the box that Ben$_i$ brought from China]$_j$, he$_i$ put his cigars t$_j$

Saito (1985) appeals from the ill-formedness of (20b) to Postal's (1971) "crossover," which is stated in (23).

(23) When a pronoun c-commands its antecedent at D-structure but this c-command relation does not obtain at S-structure due to a movement to an A'-position, the sentence is grammatical only if the antecedent is embedded *deeply enough* in the moved phrase. (Saito 1985: 49)

In (20b), the antecedent of the pronoun is not embedded deeply enough, whereas in (21) the antecedent of the pronoun *is* embedded deeply enough.

Note also that this phenomenon is observed only when movement is involved. In (20a), for example, the antecedent of the pronoun is not deeply embedded; it is, however, well-formed. (20a) does not involve movement. The contrast in the grammaticality in (20b) and (21) suggests that movement of the object phrase is involved in (20b) and (21).

2.3   Quantifier floating

Saito (1985) argues that a subject–object asymmetry found in *quantifier floating*, discussed in Kuroda (1980, 1983) and Haig (1980), argues for scrambling analysis of flexible word order in Japanese.[10] It is known that a floating numeral quantifier (henceforth, NQ) and its host NP comprise a constituent in Japanese (Kamio 1977).

Kuroda (1980) shows that NQs that modify object NPs can be separated from the objects by an intervening subject, whereas NQs that modify subject NPs cannot be separated from the subject by an intervening object. Let us observe Kuroda's (1980: 27) examples. The NQ in (24) modifies the object.

(24) a. Igirisuzin-ga   utide-no   kozuti-o   hutatu   katta
          Englishman-Nom striking-Gen mallet-Acc 2 objects bought
          "An Englishman bought 2 *mallets of luck*"
      b. Utide-no   kozuti-o   igirisuzin-ga   hutatu   katta
          striking-Gen mallet-Acc Englishman-Nom 2 objects bought
          "*Mallets of luck*, an Englishman, 2 pieces, bought"

In (24a), the object and its NQ are adjacent. In (24b), on the other hand, the object and its NQ are not adjacent: there is a subject NP between them. Both (24a) and (24b) are well-formed, however. The NQ in (25), on the other hand, modifies the subject.

(25) a. Igirisujin-ga   sannin   utide-no   kozuti-o   katta
          Englishman-Nom 3 people striking-Gen mallet-Acc bought
          "Three Englishmen bought (the) *mallet of luck*"
      b. *Igirisujin-ga   utide-no   kozuti-o   sannin   katta
          Englishman-Nom striking-Gen mallet-Acc 3 people bought
          "Englishmen bought (the) *mallet of luck*, three people"

In (25a), the subject and its NQ are adjacent, whereas in (25b), they are not. In (25b), there is an object NP between the subject and its NQ, and the sentence is ill-formed. Kuroda (1980) argues that the contrast displayed in (24b) and (25b) indicates that the basic word order in Japanese is Subject–Object–Verb and the other word orders are due to movement.

Saito (1985), moreover, argues that under the hypothesis that (24b) involves movement and syntactic movement leaves a trace, we may say that the floating

NQ is licensed by the trace which is adjacent to the NQ. The generalization that a floating NQ cannot be related to an NP across another NP argument can be maintained and the well-formedness of (24b) can still be accounted for. The structure of (24b) is illustrated in (26).

(26)   [Utide-no kozuti]$_i$-o [igirisuzin-ga t$_i$ hutatu katta]

In this section, we examined Saito's (1985) evidence for a movement approach to flexible word order in Japanese. The OSV order creates a different c-command relationship between the subject and the object. The OSV order, moreover, exhibits the crossover phenomenon (Postal 1971), which is typically observed when A'-movement is involved. The OSV order, furthermore, appears to have a trace in the position between the subject and the verb.

3   Long-Distance Preposing

3.1   *Long-distance scrambling*

Saito (1985), furthermore, shows that long-distance preposing affects the possibility of pronominal coreference. In so doing, he argues for S.-I. Harada's (1977) hypothesis that scrambling is not clause-bound.[11] The relevant examples are cited in (27) from Saito (1985: 161).

(27)   a.   *Kare$_i$-ga [dareka-ga   [Mary-ga   John$_i$-ni okutta tegami]-o
             he-Acc   someone-Nom Mary-Nom John-to sent   letter-Acc
             nusumiyomisita to]   omotte iru (koto)
             took-a-peek-at   that thinking
             "He thinks that someone took a peek at the letter Mary wrote
             to John"
        b.   [Mary-ga   John$_i$-ni okutta tegami]$_j$-o kare$_i$-ga [dareka-ga
             Mary-Nom John-to sent   letter-Acc he-Nom someone-Nom
             t$_j$ nusumiyomisita to]   omotte iru (koto)
             took-a-peek-at   that thinking
             "The letter Mary wrote to John, he thinks someone took a peek at"

In (27b), the complex NP object is scrambled across the clause boundary to the sentence-initial position. The well-formedness of (27b) as opposed to the ill-formedness of (27a) demonstrates that the movement makes the coreference between *John* and *he* possible. Saito, therefore, argues that in the case of long-distance preposing also, the preposed phrase is in a position the matrix subject does not c-command.

Saito (1985), thus, argues that long-distance preposing shares the properties of scrambling discussed in section 2 and it is reasonable to assume that long-distance preposing is a subcase of scrambling.

3.2 Long-distance scrambling of the subject and VP-scrambling

Saito (1985: 192) argues that the subject does not scramble long-distance, on the basis of the ill-formedness of (28b).[12,13,14]

(28) a.   Mary-ga   John-ni   [kono giron-ga   okasii to]   itta
      Mary-Nom John-Dat this   argument-Nom strange that told
      "Mary told John that this argument is strange"
   b. *[Kono giron]$_i$-ga   [Mary-ga   John-ni   [t$_i$ okasii to] itta]
      this   argument-Nom Mary-Nom John-Dat   strange that told
      "This argument, Mary told John that is strange"

In (28b), the embedded subject was scrambled to the matrix sentence-initial position and the sentence is ill-formed. Given that the subject does not scramble long-distance, Saito argues that VP must be a possible adjunction site for scrambling. Let us observe (29) cited from Saito (1985: 225).

(29)   Mary-ga   [sono hon]$_i$-o   Bill-ni   [PRO t$_i$ yomu yooni] itta (koto)
     Mary-Nom that book-Acc Bill-Dat   read   to   told
     "Mary, that book, told Bill to read"

It is not possible for (29) to have a structure like (30).[15]

(30)

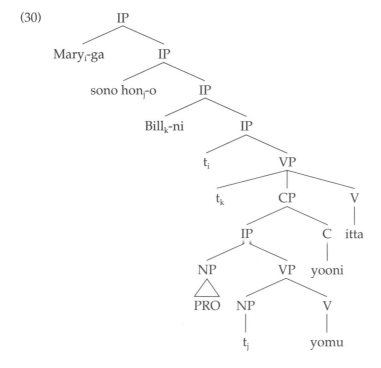

This is because the matrix subject *Mary* cannot be preposed long-distance. Therefore, the well-formedness of (29) demonstrates that VP is a possible adjunction site for long-distance scrambling.

Saito (1985: 267 fn 34) notes that long-distance scrambling from a tensed clause results in marginal grammaticality. His example is cited in (31).

(31)   ??[$_{IP}$John-ga   [$_{VP}$ [sono hon]$_i$-o   [$_{VP}$ minna-ni   [$_{CP}$ Mary-ga   t$_i$
          John-Nom   that book-Acc   everyone-Dat   Mary-Nom
       motte iru to]]] itta] (koto)
       have   that told
       "John, that book, told everyone that Mary has"

In (31), the embedded object is scrambled to VP adjoined position in the matrix clause. This observation of the contrast between (29) and (31) later becomes important in discussing the nature of scrambling.[16]

In this section, we observed long-distance scrambling in Japanese. Saito (1985), however, shows that long-distance scrambling of the subject is not possible. Given that, Saito (1985) argues that VP is a possible scrambling site. He, however, notes that long-distance VP-scrambling from a finite clause results in marginal grammaticality, while long-distance VP-scrambling from a control clause results in perfect grammaticality.

4   The Landing Positions for Scrambled Phrases

We observed the evidence that Japanese has VP and the flexible word order is due to movement. Traditionally, it is considered that there are two types of Maximal Projection movement: A-movement such as Passive and Raising in English (also called NP-movement) and A'-movement such as WH-movement and topicalization in English. A question arises as to whether Japanese scrambling behaves like A-movement or A'-movement.[17] This question amounts to asking where the scrambled phrases land: A-movement is typically to a Case position (N. Chomsky 1986b) such as the Spec of IP, whereas A'-movement is operated either by adjunction or by movement to the Spec of CP.

4.1   Scrambling as semantically vacuous A'-movement (Saito 1989)

Saito (1985, 1989) considers that scrambling is an adjunction operation; therefore, it is an instance of A'-movement. Saito (1989), however, demonstrates that scrambling is different from typical A′-movement such as WH-movement.[18]

Saito (1989) argues that scrambling can be freely undone at LF. First, he shows that the traces created by LF WH-movement in Japanese are subject to the Proper Binding Condition (see also K. Harada 1972). The Proper Binding Condition is stated in (32) (cf. Fiengo 1977, May 1977).

(32)   Traces must be bound.

Now let us examine the relevant examples cited from Saito (1989: 190).

(33)   a.   [$_{NP}$ [$_{CP}$ John-ga   [$_{CP}$ dare-ga   sono hon-o   katta   ka]
                  John-Nom   who-Nom   that   book-Acc bought Q
         siritagatteiru] koto]
         want-to-know the fact
         "the fact that John wants to know who bought that book"
      b.   *[$_{NP}$ [$_{CP}$ Dare-ga   [$_{CP}$ John-ga   sono hon-o   katta   ka]
                  who-Nom   John-Nom that   book-Acc bought Q
         siritagatteiru] koto]
         want-to-know the fact
         "the fact that who wants to know John bought that book"

In Japanese, the Spec of an embedded CP is [+WH] if and only if its head contains the interrogative particle *ka*. Note that in the examples of (33) there are two embedded CPs and only the most deeply embedded C is [+WH]. Since WH-phrases must be at [+WH] CP at LF, in (33b), the WH-phrase *dare* "who" in (33a–b) must move to the most deeply embedded CP at LF.

Saito attributes the ill-formedness of (33b) to an unbound trace of *dare* as illustrated in (34), which is the LF structure of (33b).

(34)   [$_{NP}$ [$_{CP}$ [$_{IP}$ t$_i$ [$_{CP}$ [$_{IP}$ John-ga   sono hon-o   katta]   dare$_i$-ga]
                           John-Nom that   book-Acc bought who-Nom
         siritagatte iru]] koto]
         want-to-know the fact

The trace in (34) is unbound, and it violates the Proper Binding Condition.
   Saito (1989: 192), on the other hand, shows that (35) is well-formed.

(35)   ?[$_{NP}$ [$_{CP}$ [$_{IP}$ Dono hon$_i$-o   [$_{IP}$ Mary-ga   [$_{CP}$ [$_{IP}$ John-ga   t$_i$
                  which book-Acc   Mary-Nom   John-Nom
         tosyokan-kara karidasita] ka] siritagatteiru]] koto]
         library-from   borrowed Q   want-to-know the fact
         "the fact that which book, Mary wants to know John borrowed from the library"

In (35), the embedded object WH-phrase *dono hon* "which book" is scrambled long-distance. At LF, the WH-phrase moves into the embedded Comp marked by *ka*. The LF structure of (35) is given in (36).

(36) [... t_i' [$_{CP}$ ... [... t_i ...] WH$_i$] ...]

We expect the intermediate trace t_i' in (36) to violate the Proper Binding Condition just as t_i in (34) does. (35) is, however, well-formed. Recall that the ill-formedness of (33b) indicates that LF WH-movement in Japanese is subject to the Proper Binding Condition. We must account for the well-formedness of (35).

Saito (1989) argues that unlike other types of A'-movement, such as WH-movement in English, scrambling does not establish a semantically significant operator-variable relation (see also Webelhuth 1989, 1992). This is a reason that scrambling was considered as a *stylistic* movement in Ross (1967), N. A. McCawley (1976), and N. Chomsky and Lasnik (1977). Hence, Saito argues that there should be no trace at the scrambled site at the LF representation. This means that t_i' in (36) should not exist; there is no Proper Binding Condition violation.

Saito (1989) speculates this characteristic of scrambling is related to the nature of its landing position. More specifically, he hypothesizes that the existence of the major subjects (see Kuno 1973, Kuroda 1988, Ueda 1990, Tateishi 1991, among others) in Japanese is related to this phenomenon. An example with major subjects is given in (37).

(37) [$_{IP}$ Nagano-ga   [$_{IP}$ yama-ga   [$_{IP}$ ki-ga   kirei-da]]]
        Nagano-Nom   mountain-Nom   tree-Nom beautiful-is
        "It's Nagano where in mountains trees are beautiful"

The first two nominative phrases *Nagano-ga* and *yama-ga* are major subjects.

Saito (1989) notes that the positions for the major subjects are A'-positions in the sense that they are not assigned a theta role at D-structure. However, they are different from other A'-positions in the sense that they are base-generated in the position adjoined to IP (Shibatani and Cotton 1977, Saito 1982, among others). Japanese has such ambiguous positions. Since scrambling can land in such a position, he argues, it exhibits somewhat different characteristics from typical A'-movement.

4.2 *The VP-internal subject hypothesis*

The VP-internal subject hypothesis, proposed in Koopman and Sportiche (1991), Fukui and Speas (1986), Fukui (1986), Kuroda (1988), and Y. Kitagawa (1986),

among others, raises a new possibility for scrambling. Under this hypothesis, the subject is base-generated at D-structure within VP. In Kuroda's
(1988) hypothesis, for example, the subject is base-generated at the Spec of VP
as illustrated in (38a) at D-structure.[19] Kuroda (1988) further hypothesizes that
in English the subject raises to the Spec of IP to get Case, whereas in Japanese,
the subject can stay at the Spec of VP since INFL has nothing to do with the
subject Case in Japanese.[20]

Moreover, Kuroda (1988) hypothesizes that in Japanese, since the subject
can stay at the Spec of VP, the object can raise to the Spec of IP as illustrated in
(38a). Compare (38a) with (19), which is repeated as (38b). In (38b), scrambling
is considered to be an adjunction. In (38a), on the other hand, scrambling is
not an adjunction.[21]

(38)   a.   b.

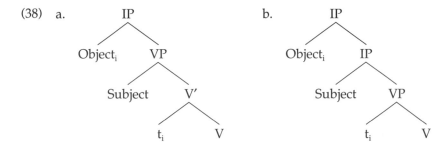

Under the hypothesis that scrambling is an adjunction, it is naturally assumed
that scrambling is A'-movement. Kuroda's (1988) hypothesis, on the other
hand, raises a theoretical possibility for scrambling to be considered as A-
movement.

Note, however, that the VP-internal subject hypothesis makes the status
of the Spec of IP with respect to the A/A' distinction unsettled. This is
because "A-position" had been traditionally defined as a potential theta position (N. Chomsky, 1981a: 47). If the subject receives its theta role within VP as
assumed in the VP-internal subject hypothesis, the Spec of IP is no longer a
potential theta position. On the other hand, the Spec of IP is assumed to be
a Case position at least in English, and A-movement is typically to a Case
position such as the Spec of IP (N. Chomsky 1986b).

4.3   The split IP hypothesis

In the late 1980s to early 1990s, the split IP hypothesis proposed in Pollock
(1989), N. Chomsky (1989, 1992, 1995a), and N. Chomsky and Lasnik (1993)
enabled us to hypothesize that the object raises to a Case position as illustrated
in (39). (See also Mahajan 1989, Déprez 1989, Nemoto 1993, Koizumi 1993, and
Miyagawa 1997a, among many others.)[22]

(39)

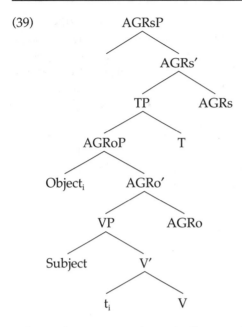

Since A-movement is typically to a Case position (N. Chomsky 1986b), it was not plausible to consider scrambling as A-movement under the hypothesis that the object receives its Case within the VP. The split IP hypothesis and Case checking theory (N. Chomsky 1989, 1992, 1995a, Chomsky and Lasnik 1993), which assumes that the subject and the object raise to a specifier of a functional category to check its Case off, provides a theoretical background for scrambling to be analyzed as movement to a Case position.

5   On the Nature of Clause-Internal Scrambling

In section 5, we examine the data which suggest that clause-internal scrambling has some properties of A-movement and some properties of A'-movement.

5.1   *Scrambling as A-movement*

In this section, we examine data which suggest that clause-internal scrambling has some properties of A-movement. More specifically, we examine data involving anaphor binding and WCO.

5.1.1   *Anaphor binding*

First, let us observe data regarding anaphor binding. Mahajan (1989) shows that anaphors can be bound by a scrambled phrase in Hindi. Saito (1992) shows that that is possible in Japanese too. As is well known, *zibun* "self" exhibits subject-orientation: it cannot be bound by an object phrase. On the other hand, *otagai* "each other" is a local anaphor and does not exhibit subject-orientation.[23] Let us now observe the examples cited from Saito (1992: 74–5). In (40), the anaphor *otagai* is not bound: they violate Condition A of Binding Theory (N. Chomsky 1981a), which requires anaphors to be locally bound by the antecedent which is located in an A-position.

(40) a. ?*Masao-ga otagai$_i$-no sensei-ni karera$_i$-o syookaisita
          Masao-Nom each other's teacher-to they-Acc introduced
          "Masao introduced, to each other, them"
      b. ?*Otagai$_i$-no sensei-ga karera$_i$-o hihansita
          each other's teacher-Nom they-Acc criticized
          "Each other's teacher criticized them"

In (41), the object phrase is scrambled to the sentence-initial position.

(41) a. Karera$_i$-o [Masao-ga otagai$_i$-no sensei-ni t$_i$ syookaisita]
          they-Acc Masao-Nom each other's teacher-to introduced
          "Them, Masao introduced to each other"
      b. ?Karera$_i$-o [otagai$_i$-no sensei-ga t$_i$ hihansita]
          they-Acc each other's teacher-Nom criticized
          "Them, each other's teacher criticized"

(40a–b) differ from (41a–b) only in that the object *karera* "they" is preposed to the sentence initial position. The grammaticality of (41), however, differs sharply from the grammaticality of (40). Saito (1992) argues that if (40a–b) are ill-formed because the anaphor lacks an A-binder, then the well-formedness of (41a–b) indicates that the anaphor has an A-binder. If so, the scrambled object must be in an A-position. This conclusion implies that scrambling can be A-movement.[24]

5.1.2 Weak crossover

Let us next observe WCO examples. There are two problems in WCO with scrambling in Japanese. First, the pronoun *kare* "he" cannot have a bound variable interpretation. Therefore, Saito and Hoji (1983) and Hoji (1985, 1987) use an anaphor or empty pronominal. This problem was solved by the observation that the *so* pronouns such as *sore* "it" and *soitu* "the guy" allow bound variable interpretation (Yoshimura 1989, Hoji 1990, 1991a, and Tada 1990, among others). This is illustrated in (42). In (42a), *kare* cannot have a bound variable interpretation, and therefore is ill-formed under the intended reading. In (42b), on the other hand, *sono hito* "that person" can have a bound variable interpretation.

(42) a.   *Dare$_i$-ga   kare$_i$-no hahaoya-o   aisiteiru no
            who-Nom his   mother-Acc love   Q
            "Who loves his mother?"
      b.   Dare$_i$-ga   [sono hito-]$_i$-no hahaoya-o   aisiteiru no
            who-Nom that person's mother-Acc love   Q
            "Who loves that person's mother?"

Second, the lack of a WCO effect in scrambling has been pointed out as a problem under the hypothesis that scrambling is an adjunction, and therefore, A'-movement (see Saito 1985, Hoji 1985, 1987, and Webelhuth 1989, 1992).

Hoji (1985) presents the following paradigm. Let us assume that both *pro* and *e* are phonetically null pronouns in (43).

(43) a.   ?*[pro$_i$ e$_j$ Hitome mita hito$_i$]-ga   dare$_j$-o   suki-ni natta no
                      a glance saw person-Nom who-Acc fell-in-love   Q
            "A person who saw (him) once fell in love with whom?"
      b.   Dare$_j$-o [[pro$_i$ e$_j$ hitome   mita hito$_i$]-ga   t$_j$ suki-ni natta no]
            who-Acc   a glance saw person-Nom   fell-in-love   Q
            "Whom, a person who saw (him) once fell in love with?"

(43a) is a WCO violation. In (43b), the WH-phrase is scrambled. If scrambling is A'-movement like WH-movement in English, we expect (43b) to be ill-formed just like (44).

(44) ?*Who$_i$ does his$_i$ mother love?

(43b) is, however, well-formed. It appears that scrambling remedies a WCO violation. Under the hypothesis that scrambling is A'-movement, this is not what we expect.[25]

Moreover, using a *so* pronoun, Yoshimura (1989, 1992) shows that scrambling does not yield a WCO violation even with an overt pronoun.[26] The relevant examples are given in (45).

(45) a.   ?*Soitu$_i$-no hahaoya-ga   dare$_i$-o   aisiteiru no
            HIS   mother-Nom who-Acc love   Q
            "His mother loves whom?"
      b.   ?Dare$_i$-o [soitu$_i$-no hahaoya-ga t$_i$ aisiteiru no]
            who-Acc HIS   mother-Nom   love   Q
            "Whom, his mother loves?"

(45a) is a case of WCO violation just like (43a). The object in (45b) is scrambled to the sentence-initial position. If scrambling is necessarily A'-movement, we expect (45b) to be a WCO violation.

A-movement, on the other hand, remedies a WCO violation, as the well-formedness of (46) illustrates.

(46) Who$_i$ [t$_i'$ seems to his$_i$ mother [t$_i$ to be intelligent]]

The difference between (43) and (46) is that (46) undergoes A-movement (Raising) prior to A'-movement (WH-movement). The well-formedness of (46) as opposed to (43) indicates that A-movement remedies a WCO violation. On the basis of WCO data such as (45), Yoshimura (1992) argues that scrambling can be A-movement in Japanese.

5.2 *Scrambling as A'-movement*

In section 5.1, we observed that clause-internal scrambling in Japanese has some properties of A-movement. At the same time, clause-internal scrambling exhibits some properties of A'-movement. This is illustrated in (47), cited from Saito (1992: 76).[27]

(47) Zibun-zisin$_i$-o [Hanako$_i$-ga   t$_i$ hihansita]
      self-self-Acc   Hanako-Nom   criticized
      "Herself, Hanako criticized"

If the object is scrambled to an A-position in (47), it should violate Condition C of Binding Theory (N. Chomsky 1981a), which prohibits referential expressions from being A-bound. The well-formedness of (47), therefore, indicates that scrambling can be A'-movement.

A question arises as to whether clause-internal scrambling can be either A or A'-movement. Tada (1990, 1993) observes that clause-internal scrambling exhibits a strong crossover (henceforth, SCO) effect. It would not be expected if clause-internal scrambling could be A-movement. First, observe SCO examples in English in (48).

(48) a. *[Whose$_i$ mother]$_j$ did he$_i$ love t$_j$
      b. *He$_i$ loves everyone$_i$'s mother.

The examples in (48) yield an SCO violation: the pronoun *he* c-commands either the NP or the trace which contains the QNP coindexed with the pronoun (see Postal 1971, and Higginbotham 1983, among others). It is A'-movement and not A-movement which yields an SCO violation. (49), which includes A movement (Raising) prior to A'-movement, is indeed well-formed.

(49) [Whose$_i$ mother]$_j$ [t$_j'$ seems to him$_i$ [t$_j$ to be intelligent]]

(49) shows that A-movement remedies SCO.

Given that, let us observe SCO examples from Tada (1993: 24). In (50b), the WH object is scrambled.

(50) a.   *Soitu$_i$-ga dare$_i$-no sensei-o   nagutta no
           HE-Nom whose   teacher-Acc hit   Q
           "He hit whose teacher?"
      b.   *[Dare$_i$-no sensei]$_j$-o   [soitu$_i$-ga t$_j$ nagutta no]
           whose   teacher-Acc HE-Nom   hit   Q
           "Whose teacher, he hit?"

Tada argues that if scrambling can be A-movement, (50b) should be grammatical.

In this section, we observed that clause-internal scrambling exhibits mixed properties. It behaves like A-movement with respect to anaphor binding and WCO. On the other hand, it behaves like A'-movement with respect to SCO.

6 Clause-Internal Scrambling vs. Long-Distance Scrambling

Saito (1985) argues that scrambling is not clause-bound. Saito (1992) and Tada (1990, 1993), however, demonstrate that long-distance scrambling behaves differently from clause-internal scrambling.[28] Let us examine similarities and differences between clause-internal scrambling and long-distance scrambling.

6.1 *Weak crossover*

Yoshimura (1989, 1992) shows that long-distance scrambling also remedies a WCO violation.[29] Let us examine the relevant examples. In (51b), the embedded object *dare* "whom" is scrambled long-distance to the sentence-initial position.

(51) a.   *Soitu$_i$-no hahaoya-ga [Hanako-ga   dare$_i$-o   aisiteiru to]
           HIS   mother-Nom Hanako-Nom who-Acc love   that
           itta no
           said Q
           "His mother said that Hanako loves whom?"
      b.   ?Dare$_i$-o [soitu$_i$-no hahaoya-ga [Hanako-ga   t$_i$ aisiteiru to]
           who-Acc HIS   mother-Acc Hanako-Nom   love   that
           itta no]
           said Q
           "Whom, his mother said that Hanako loves?"

The grammaticality difference between (51a) and (51b) indicates, Yoshimura argues, that unlike in Hindi (Mahajan 1989), long-distance scrambling in Japanese can also be A-movement.[30,31,32]

6.2 Anaphor binding

Saito (1992), however, argues that long-distance scrambling cannot be A-movement, on the basis of anaphor binding data.[33] Let us observe the examples from Saito (1992: 76). In (52a), the anaphor *otagai* "each other" is not bound, and therefore, the sentence is ill-formed. In (52b), the embedded object *karera* "they" is scrambled long-distance to the sentence-initial position. (52b), however, remains ill-formed.

(52) a. *Masao-ga   otagai$_i$-no   sensei-ni   [Hanako-ga   karera$_i$-o
        Masao-Nom each other's teacher-Dat Hanako-Nom they-Acc
        hihansita to]   itta
        criticized that told
        "Masao told each other's teacher that Hanako criticized them"
    b. *Karera$_i$-o [Masao-ga   otagai$_i$-no   sensei-ni   [Hanako-ga   t$_i$
        they-Acc   Masao-Nom each other's teacher-Dat Hanako-nom
        hihansita to]   itta]
        criticized that told
        "Them, Masao told each other's teacher that Hanako criticized"

If long-distance scrambling can be A-movement just like clause-internal scrambling in (41b), we expect (52b) to be well-formed too. Saito (1992), therefore, argues that long-distance scrambling cannot be A-movement.

6.3 Additional differences

6.3.1 Quantifier scope relations

Tada (1990, 1993) observes that long-distance scrambling does not change scope relations as opposed to clause-internal scrambling. Kuroda (1970) and Hoji (1985, 1987) note that clause-internal scrambling changes scope relations.[34] The relevant examples are given in (53). (53b) involves scrambling. (53c) is an LF representation of (53b) after Q-raising.

(53) a. Dareka-ga   daremo-o   aisite iru
        someone-Nom everyone-Acc love
        "Someone loves everyone"
    b. Daremo$_i$-o   [dareka-ga   t$_i$ aisite iru]
        everyone-Acc someone-Nom   love
        "Everyone, someone loves"
    c. [Dareka$_j$-ga   [daremo$_i$-o [t$_j$ t$_i$ aisite iru]]]

(53a) is unambiguous: only *dareka* "someone" can take wide scope.[35] Lasnik and Saito (1992) accounts for the unambiguity proposing the rigidity condition on quantifier scope. The condition states that Q_i cannot take wide scope over Q_j if t_i is c-commanded by t_j, where t_i and t_j are variables. (53b) is, however, ambiguous.

Murasugi and Saito (1992) argue that if scrambling is necessarily A'-movement, the ambiguity of (53b) constitutes a counterexample to Lasnik and Saito's rigidity condition. The trace left by scrambling in the object position is asymmetrically c-commanded by the trace left by Q-raising in the subject position as illustrated in (53c). Given these variables, the rigidity condition incorrectly predicts that the subject QNP must take wide scope. They argue that if scrambling can be A-movement, since the trace left by A-scrambling is not a variable, it is irrelevant for the rigidity condition. The ambiguity of (53b), therefore, does not constitute a counterexample to the rigidity condition.

Murasugi and Saito (1992), moreover, argue that if long-distance scrambling is necessarily A'-movement, we expect no quantifier scope change by long-distance scrambling. Tada (1990, 1993) indeed observes that neither (54a) nor (54b) is ambiguous. In (54b), the embedded object is scrambled long-distance to sentence-initial position.

(54) a.   Dareka-ga   [John-ga   daremo-o   aisiteiru to] itta
          someone-Nom John-Nom everyone-Acc love   that said
          "Someone said John loves everyone"
     b.   Daremo$_i$-o   [dareka-ga   [John-ga t_i aisiteiru to] itta]
          everyone-Acc someone-Nom John-Nom   love   that said
          "Everyone, someone said that John loves"

The unambiguity of (54b) indicates that long-distance scrambling is A'-movement.

6.3.2   Licensing NQs

Déprez (1989) observes that when an object phrase is scrambled long-distance, its NQ can occur within the embedded sentence in all the positions in which the object can be scrambled but cannot occur in any position in the matrix sentence. As noted in section 2.3, a trace left by clause-internal scrambling can license an NQ. The relevant example is given in (55).

(55) Hon$_i$-o   [gakusei-ga t_i nisatu katta]
      book-Acc student-Nom 2   bought
      "A student bought two books"

Sportiche (1988: 436) observes that floating quantifiers can modify every kind of empty category except intermediate traces created by WH-movement. Given that, Déprez (1989) examines whether traces created by scrambling can license QNPs. Déprez's (1989: 182) example is cited in (56), where the symbol = is used to mark the positions in which an object NQ such as *ni-satu* "two volumes" can occur and * to mark the position in which an object NQ cannot occur.

(56) Hon$_i$-o   [John-ga   * Mary-ni   * kossorito [= Peter-ga = t$_i$ = katta
book-Acc John-Nom Mary-Dat quietly   Peter-Nom   bought
to] itta]
that told
"John told Mary quietly that Peter bought books"

(56) shows that an object QNP can occur in possible landing sites for clause-internal scrambling but not in possible landing sites for long-distance scrambling. Déprez (1989) argues that her observation, therefore, supports the hypothesis that long-distance scrambling cannot be A-movement.

In this section, we observed that long-distance scrambling behaves somewhat differently from clause-internal scrambling. In addition to what we examined, Tada (1990, 1993) discusses adjunct extraction and A. Watanabe (1992) and Saito (1994a, 1994b) discuss an additional WH effect, and they demonstrate the different behavior of clause-internal scrambling and long-distance scrambling. The data suggest that long-distance scrambling is A'-movement. It remedies WCO, however, just like clause-internal scrambling.

7 VP-Scrambling

We observed in section 6 that clause-internal scrambling and long-distance scrambling behave differently. Note, however, that all the examples we observed so far involve scrambling to the sentence-initial position. As noted in section 3.2, VP is also a possible scrambling site. We explore the nature of VP-scrambling in this section.[36]

7.1 VP-internal structure

Before we discuss VP scrambling, however, we must examine the VP internal structure in Japanese. In section 1, we observed that the basic word order in Japanese is SOV and the OSV order is derived by movement. In this section, we consider the order of the indirect object and the direct object.[37] Hoji (1985, 1987) argues that the basic word order of Japanese is as follows.

(57) Subject (adjunct) Indirect Object Direct Object Verb

7.1.1 Weak crossover

Hoji (1985, 1987) argues that the WCO phenomenon indicates that the indirect object (IO) position is higher than the direct object (DO) position as illustrated in (58).[38]

(58)

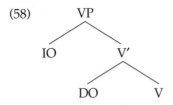

Let us observe the examples cited from Hoji (1987: 178) in (59). In (59a), an empty category e$_j$, which is coindexed with the object WH, cannot have a bound variable interpretation. (59b) indicates that when the direct object WH precedes the indirect object, e$_j$ can have a bound variable interpretation. If in (59b), but not in (59a), the direct object c-commands the indirect object, we can account for the ill-formedness of (59a) in terms of WCO.

(59) a. *Kimi-wa [[pro$_i$ e$_j$ tukutta] kodomo$_i$]-ni [dono ningyoo]$_j$-o ageta no
          you-Top   made   child-to   which doll-Acc   gave Q
          "You gave (it) to the child who made which doll?"
      b. Kimi-wa [dono ningyoo]$_j$-o [[pro$_i$ e$_j$ tukutta] kodomo$_i$]-ni ageta no
          you-Top which doll-Acc   made   child-to   gave Q
          "You, which doll, gave to the child who made?"

Hoji, therefore, concludes that the indirect object is higher than the direct object position in (59a) as illustrated in (58), and (59b) is derived by movement. It follows that the basic order is S–IO–DO–V.

7.1.2 *Quantifier scope*

Hoji (1985, 1987) also appeals to the quantifier scope interpretation to argue for (58). As was noted in section 6.3.1, Kuroda (1970) observes that clause-internal scrambling changes scope relation. Kuno (1973) observes a similar phenomenon. Let us observe Kuno's (1973: 360) examples.

(60) a. Sannin-no onna-ga   hutari-no otoko-o semeta
          3 (people) women-Nom 2 (people) men-Acc blamed
          "Three women blamed two men"
      b. [Hutari-no otoko]$_i$-o [sannin-no onna-ga   t$_i$ semeta]
          2 people men-Acc 3 people women-Nom   blamed
          "Two men, three women blamed"

In (60a), only the subject QNP can take wide scope with respect to the other QNP; in (60b), on the other hand, either the subject QNP or the object QNP can take wide scope with respect to the other.

Given Kuroda's (1970) as well as Kuno's (1973) observation and Saito's (1985) hypothesis that the OSV order derives by movement, Hoji (1987: 182) states:

(61) a. When two quantified NPs are in their D-structure position at S-structure, the quantified NP that c-commands the other takes wide scope with respect to the other.
  b. When a quantified NP is preposed over another quantified NP, the scope interpretation is ambiguous.

Hoji (1987: 183) considers (62), where the indirect object QNP and the direct object QNP interact. (62a) displays IO–DO order and (62b) displays DO–IO order.

(62) a. John-ga   sannin-no onna-ni   hutari-no otoko-o syookaisita
       John-Nom 3   woman-Dat 2   men-Acc introduced
       "John introduced, to three women, two men"
  b. John-ga   hutari-no otoko-o sannin-no onna-ni   syookaisita
       John-Nom 2   men-Acc 3   women-Dat introduced
       "John introduced two men to three women"

He observes that while the indirect object unambiguously takes wide scope over the direct object in (62a), either the indirect object or the direct object can take wide scope over the other in (62b).[39] Hoji, therefore, argues that the indirect object c-commands the direct object at the underlying structure but not vice versa.

7.2 Short-distance VP-scrambling

Given that the basic word order is S–IO–DO–V, let us examine the nature of VP-scrambling. We begin with short-distance VP-scrambling, which we call "S(hort)-scrambling," adopting the term from Tada (1993: 12). Let us also call clause-internal scrambling to the sentence-initial position "M(iddle)-scrambling" and long-distance scrambling to the sentence-initial position "L(ong)-scrambling" as in Tada (1993: 12) for ease of exposition.

7.2.1 VP-scrambling as A-movement

Tada (1990, 1993) observes that S-scrambling differs from M-scrambling and L-scrambling in that only the first remedies an SCO violation. Recall that A-movement neutralizes an SCO violation. Let us observe (63), (64), and (65). (63a), (64a), and (65a) exhibit an SCO effect: WH-in-situ is c-commanded by a coindexed pronoun. The (b) examples of (63–5) involve S-scrambling, M-scrambling, and L-scrambling, respectively.

(63) a. *Taroo-ga soitu$_i$-ni dare$_i$-no sensei-o   syookaisita no
       Taro-Nom HE-Dat whose   teacher-Acc introduced Q
       "Taro introduced, to him, whose teacher?"

b.   Taroo-ga [dare$_i$-no sensei]$_j$-o   [soitu$_i$-ni t$_j$ syookaisita] no
     Taro-Nom whose   teacher-Acc HE-Dat   introduced Q
     "Taro introduced whose teacher to him?"

(64) a.   *Soitu$_i$-ga Hanako-ni dare$_i$-no sensei-o   syookaisita no
           HE-Nom Hanako-Dat whose   teacher-Acc introduced Q
           "He introduced, to him, whose teacher?"
      b.   *[Dare$_i$-no sensei]$_j$-o   [soitu$_i$-ga Hanako-ni t$_j$ syookaisita no]
           whose   teacher-Acc HE-Nom Hanako-Dat   introduced Q
           "He introduced whose teacher to Hanako?"

(65) a.   *Taroo-ga   soitu$_i$-ni [Hanako-ga   dare$_i$-no sensei-o
           Taro-Nom HE-Dat Hanako-Nom whose   teacher-Acc
           syookaisita to] itta no
           introduced that told Q
           "Taro told him that Hanako introduced whose teacher?"
      b.   *[Dare$_i$-no sensei]$_j$-o   [Taroo-ga   soitu$_i$-ni [Hanako-ga   t$_j$
           whose   teacher-Acc Taro-Nom HE-Dat   Hanako-Nom
           syookaisita to] itta no]
           introduced that told Q
           "Whose teacher, Taro told him that Hanako introduced?"

Only (63b) is well-formed. It follows that only S-scrambling remedies an SCO
violation.
   Moreover, Tada and Saito (1991) and Saito (1994b) argue that S-scrambling
is necessarily A-movement, on the basis of examples such as (66).

(66) a.   Masao-ga   [Taroo to   Hanako]$_i$-ni otagai$_i$-o   syookaisita
           Masao-Nom Taro and Hanako-Dat each other-Acc syookaisita
           "Masao introduced, to Taro and Hanako, each other"
      b.   *Masao-ga   otagai$_i$-o   [Taroo to   Hanako]$_i$-ni t$_i$ syookaisita
           Masao-Nom each other-Acc Taro and Hanako-Dat   introduced
           "Masao introduced each other to Taro and Hanako"

In (66b), the direct object is scrambled over the indirect object. Tada and Saito
(1991) and Saito (1994b) compare (66b) and (67b).

(67) a.   [Taroo to   Hanako]$_i$-ga Masao-ni otagai$_i$-o   syookaisita
           Taro and Hanako-Nom Masao-Dat each other-Acc introduced
           "Taro and Hanako introduced, to Masao, each other"
      b.   ?Otagai$_i$-o   [[Taroo to   Hanako]$_i$-ga Masao-ni t$_i$
           each other-Acc   Taro and Hanako-Nom Masao-Dat
           syookaisita]
           introduced
           "Each other, Taro and Hanako introduced to Masao"

Note first that the trace left by scrambling is A-bound in both (66b) and (67b). Tada and Saito (1991) and Saito (1994b) argue that the well-formedness of (67b) indicates that the ill-formedness of (66b) is not due to the fact that the trace is A-bound.

Tada and Saito (1991) and Saito (1994b) account for the ill-formedness of (66b) in terms of a Condition C violation (N. Chomsky 1981a): the scrambled phrase A-binds a coindexed referential expression. This amounts to saying that S-scrambling must be A-movement.[40] If S-scrambling can be A'-movement, we expect (66b) to have the same grammaticality as (67b).

7.2.2   Against short-distance VP-scrambling (S-scrambling)

Miyagawa (1997a), on the other hand, argues that both IO–DO order and DO–IO order are base-generated in Japanese.[41] His argument is based upon Rizzi's (1986) Chain Condition (see also Déprez 1989 and Koizumi 1993, 1995).[42] First, let us observe (68), cited from Miyagawa (1997a: 4). Both (68a) and (68b) involve M-scrambling.

(68)   a.   [John-to   Mary]$_i$-o   [otagai$_i$-no   sensei-ga   t$_i$ mita]
               John and Mary-Acc   each other's teacher-Nom   saw
               "John and Mary, each other's teacher saw"
       b.   ???[John-to   Mary]$_i$-o   [otagai$_i$-ga   t$_i$ mita]
               John and Mary-Acc   each other-Nom   saw
               "John and Mary, each other saw"

We observed that (68a) is well formed. And, based on that, Saito (1992), among others, argues that clause-internal scrambling can be A-movement. A question arises as to how we can account for (68b).

Miyagawa (1997a) argues that (68b) indicates that Japanese observes Rizzi's (1986) Chain Condition. Suppose that the examples in (68) involve A-movement. In (68a), the closest binder for the trace is *John-to Mary* and the chain is well-formed. In (68b), on the other hand, there exists a closer binder, namely *otagai*, between the antecedent and its trace. This yields a Chain Condition violation. As is also noted in Miyagawa, if (68b) involves A'-movement, (68b) violates Condition A of Binding Theory (N. Chomsky 1981a).

Given that, let us now observe (69), cited from Miyagawa (1997a: 5).

(69)   (?)John-ga   [Hanako-to   Mary]$_i$-o   (paatii-de) otagai$_i$-ni
          John-Nom   Hanako and Mary-Acc (party-at)   each other-Dat
          syookaisita
          introduced
          "John introduced Hanako and Mary to each other at the party"

Miyagawa argues that if (69) involves A-movement, we expect to find the same Chain Condition violation as in (68b). (69) is, however, well-formed. Given that, Miyagawa argues that there should be no movement involved in (69), and therefore, both IO–DO and DO–IO are base-generated in Japanese.

7.3 Long-distance VP-scrambling

Let us now observe long-distance VP-scrambling. First of all, recall that as noted in section 3.2, Saito (1985: 267 fn 34) observes that long-distance VP-scrambling from a control clause is perfectly grammatical, while long-distance VP-scrambling from a finite clause results in marginal grammaticality. The relevant examples are repeated in (70).

(70) a.   John-ga   [sono hon]ᵢ-o   minna-ni   [PRO tᵢ yomu
            John-Nom that book-Acc everyone-Dat   read
            yoo(ni)] itta
            to   told
            "John, that book, told everyone to read"
      b.   ??John-ga   [sono hon]ᵢ-o   minna-ni   [Mary-ga   tᵢ
            John-Nom   that book-Acc everyone-Dat Mary-Nom
            motte iru to]   itta (koto)
            have   that told
            "John, that book, told everyone that Mary has"

Tada and Saito (1991) and Saito (1994b) argue that the marginal status in (70b) supports their hypothesis that VP-scrambling, short-distance and long-distance, must be A-movement. A-movement across a CP boundary is prohibited (N. Chomsky 1986b and Lasnik and Saito 1992, among others).[43] They argue that (70b) results in marginal grammaticality (see also Fukui 1992).

Moreover, Nemoto (1993) observes that long-distance VP-scrambling from a control clause remedies SCO as illustrated in (71b).

(71) a.   *Tarooᵢ-wa soituᵢ-ni [PRO dareᵢ-no sensei-o   naguru yooni]
             Taro-Top HE-Dat   whose   teacher-Acc hit   to
             itta no
             told Q
             "Taro told him to hit whose teacher?"
      b.   Taroo-wa [dareᵢ-no sensei]ⱼ-o   soituᵢ-ni [PRO tⱼ naguru yooni]
            Taro-Top whose   teacher-Acc HE-Dat   hit   to
            itta no
            told Q
            "Taro, whose teacher, told him to hit?"

The well-formedness of (71b) suggests that long-distance VP-scrambling can be A-movement.

Nemoto (1993), on the other hand, observes that long-distance scrambling from a control clause to the sentence-initial position does not remedy a SCO violation.

(72) a. *Soitu$_i$-ga Taroo-ni [PRO dare$_i$-no sensei-o   naguru yooni]
     HE-Nom Taro-Dat   whose   teacher-Acc hit   to
     itta no
     told Q
     "He told Taro to hit whose teacher?"

    b. *[Dare$_i$-no sensei]$_j$-o   [soitu$_i$-ga Taroo-ni [PRO t$_j$ naguru yooni]
     whose   teacher-Acc HE-Nom Taro-Dat   hit   to
     itta no]
     told Q
     "Whose teacher, he told Taro to hit?"

Recall that we observed that S-scrambling remedies an SCO violation but M-scrambling does not. It appears, therefore, that the landing position VP is a key for scrambling to be A-movement.

Nemoto (1993), however, argues that long-distance scrambling from a control clause can be A'-movement. The relevant examples are given in (73).

(73) a. John$_i$-ga   Mary-ni [PRO kare$_i$-o homeru yooni] tanonda
     John-Nom Mary-Dat   he-Acc praise to   asked
     "John asked Mary to praise him"

    b. John$_i$-ga [kare$_i$-o [Mary-ni [PRO t$_i$ homeru yooni] tanonda]]
     John-Nom he-Acc Mary-Dat   praise to   asked
     "John, him, asked Mary to praise"

Nemoto (1993) argues that if VP-scrambling is necessarily A-movement as argued in Tada and Saito (1991) and Saito (1994b), (73b) should be ruled out due to a Condition B violation (N. Chomsky 1981a), which prohibits a pronoun from being locally A-bound.[44]

Let us next consider (74). (74b) involves long-distance VP-scrambling. The anaphor in (74a) is not bound: the ill-formedness of (74a) is accounted for in terms of Condition A (N. Chomsky 1981a). The well-formedness of (74b) indicates that the scrambled phrase A-binds the anaphor. This is expected if long-distance VP-scrambling can be A-movement.

(74) a. *Taroo-ga otagai$_i$-ni   [PRO [Hanako-to Masao]$_i$-o
     Taro-Nom each other-Dat   Hanako and Masao-Acc
     hihansuru yoo(ni)] itta
     criticized to   told
     "Taro told each other to criticize Hanako and Masao"

    b. ?Taroo-ga [Hanako-to   Masao]$_i$-o otagai$_i$-ni   [PRO t$_i$
     Taro-Nom Hanako and Masao-Acc each other-Dat
     hihansuru yoo(ni)] itta
     criticize   to   told
     "Taro, Hanako and Masao, told each other to criticize"

Recall that in section 7.2.2, we observed Miyagawa's (1997a) example, which is repeated as (75).

(75)   (?)John-ga   [Hanako-to Mary]$_i$-o   (paatii-de) otagai$_i$-ni
        John-Nom Hanako and Mary-Acc (party-at) each other-Dat
        syookaisita
        introduced
        "John introduced Hanako and Mary to each other at the party"

Miyagawa (1997a) argues that the well-formedness of (75) suggests that there is no movement involved in (75), on the basis of Rizzi's (1986) Chain Condition. Interestingly, however, it appears that (74b) has the same grammaticality as (75). If movement is involved in (74b) as we assume, the well-formedness of (74b) constitutes a counterexample to Miyagawa's (1997a) argument.[45]

In this section, we explored the nature of VP-scrambling. Both short-distance VP-scrambling (S-scrambling) and long-distance VP-scrambling remedy an SCO violation. VP-scrambling is the only kind of scrambling which remedies an SCO violation. VP-scrambling seems to have properties of A-movement. Tada and Saito (1991) and Saito (1994b), moreover, argue that VP-scrambling is necessarily A-movement. Miyagawa (1997a), on the contrary, questions the existence of S-scrambling itself.

8   Concluding Remarks and Future Perspectives

In this chapter, we first observed that flexible word order in Japanese is due to scrambling. We then examined the nature of scrambling. The data we observed demonstrate that scrambling exhibits some properties of traditional A-movement such as Passive and Raising in English and some properties of traditional A'-movement such as WH-movement in English. The nature of scrambling is, however, not yet clear at all. I conclude this chapter with three questions regarding scrambling.

First, we attempted to categorize scrambling within the traditional A/A' distinction using diagnostics such as anaphor binding and WCO. A question arises as to whether these diagnostics distinguish between Case-related movement (so-called A-movement) and nonCase-related movement (so-called A'-movement). For example, Webelhuth (1989, 1992) and Saito (1989, 1992, 1994b) argue that whether or not movement establishes an operator–variable relation at LF is an important distinction. And J. Abe (1993) proposes to analyze scrambling without A/A' distinction.

Second, we observed that both the landing position, whether the sentence-initial position or VP position, and the distance of movement, whether or not movement crosses a clause boundary, are important factors when we discuss the nature of scrambling. Why is this the case? See Saito (1994b), Murasugi and Saito (1995), and Fukui and Saito (1998) for the theory of adjunction in conjunction with the nature of scrambling.

Finally, it is not clear at all why scrambling, which is considered to be optional movement, exists in some languages. Under N. Chomsky's (1995a, 1995b) Minimalist Program, movement of α is possible only when it is necessary for licensing morphological features of α such as Case or [+WH]. Moreover, a question arises as to whether all types of scrambling are optional. Is any scrambling Case-related, for example? See Tada (1993), Fukui (1993), Ura (1996), Takano (1996), Miyagawa (1997a), and Fukui and Saito (1998), among others, for interesting discussion.

NOTES

* I am grateful to Mamoru Saito for his class lectures on scrambling at the University of Connecticut while I was a graduate student there. I would also like to thank Shigeru Miyagawa for making unpublished material available to me. Special thanks go to Thomas Moran and Keiichi Sekiyama for editorial help. I would like to dedicate this chapter to Thomas Moran as a token of my gratitude for his extended help over many years. Needless to say, all shortcomings are mine.

1 It is common practice to add *koto* "the fact that" to some of the Japanese examples to avoid the unnaturalness resulting from the lack of topic in a matrix sentence. The purpose of English translations in quotes is to help readers understand the rough structure of Japanese examples, and they are not intended to be *grammatical* English sentences.

2 Prior to Hale (1980), it was assumed that flexible word order is due to a transformation rule. See Muraki (1974) and S.-I. Harada (1977), among others.

3 See Radford (1988: 120–2) for discussion. He states the following constraint.

(i) No Crossing Branches Constraint (Radford 1988: 121) If one node X precedes another node Y, then X and all descendants of X must precede Y and all descendants of Y (A is a *descendant* of B iff A is dominated by B).

4 Hoji (1985, 1987) argues that Japanese phrase structure is binary. See section 7.1.

5 See also Kuno (1987), among others, who argues that precedence plays some role in Binding Theory.

6 "C-command" is defined as follows:

X c-commands Y if neither X nor Y dominates the other and the first branching node dominating X dominates Y. (Reinhart 1976: 32)

7 The rough meaning of Japanese examples is given in English within quotes. These English sentences are not necessarily grammatical.

8 A "variable" means a trace left by operator movement such as WH-movement and LF-movement.

9   Hoji (1991a) reports that this characteristic of *kare* "he" is discussed in Saito (1981), C. Kitagawa (1981), and S. Nakayama (1982), among others.

10 For more discussion on quantifier floating, see Hoji (1985), Ueda (1990), A. Watanable (1993), Fujita (1994), Ura (1996), Miyagawa (1989b, 1997a), and references cited there.

11 See Saito (1985) and Tsujimura (1996b) for apparent counterexamples for this hypothesis.

12 Takezawa (1987: 129) argues that the *-ga* marked phrase can be preposed long-distance in nonaccusative sentences. His examples are cited in (i).

(i) a. John-ga   [Mary-ni
         John-Nom Mary-Dat
         nihongo-ga   yomeru to]
         Japanese-Nom can read that
         omotteiru
         thinking
         "John thinks Mary can read Japanese"

     b. Nihongo$_i$-ga   [John-ga
         Japanese-Nom John-Nom
         [Mary-ni   t$_i$ yomeru to]
          Mary-Dat   can read that
         omotteiru]
         thinking
         "Japanese, John thinks Mary can read"

13 See also Kuno's (1980) anti-ambiguity device and Saito's (1985) discussion about it.

14 Saito (1985) proposes to relate the nonscramblability of the subject to the Case system in Japanese. See also Saito (1982).

15 It is not clear whether *yoo(ni)* is a complementizer, nor is it clear whether a control clause is CP or IP. See Nemoto (1991, 1993) for some relevant discussion.

16 See Fukui (1992), Nemoto (1993), Saito (1994b), and Fukui and Saito (1998) for relevant discussion.

17 See J. Abe (1993), who argues that it is possible to account for the characteristics of scrambling without A/A' distinction.

18 See also D. Takahashi (1994) for discussion on scrambling of WH-phrases.

19 Koopman and Sportiche (1991) hypothesizes that the subject is adjoined to VP.

20 See also Takezawa (1987), Ueda (1990), and Nemoto (1993), among others, for discussion about whether the subject in Japanese stays at the Spec of VP.

21 Kuroda (1988) also hypothesizes that Japanese IP has multiple Specs, and therefore, can accommodate multiple subjects and multiple scrambling.

22 See also N. Chomsky (1995b) and Ura (1996) for the more recent *agr-less* hypothesis.

23 See Yang (1983) and Y. Kitagawa (1986), among others, for discussion on the nature of *otagai* "each other." See also Fukuhara (1993) for discussion on anaphor binding under Case checking theory.

24 Takano (1996) argues, however, that this does not mean that the scrambled object is in a Case position, since scrambled PPs can bind anaphors.

25 Since Hoji's (1985, 1987) examples are with empty categories, he accounts for this paradox by appealing to "parasitic gaps." He argues that *e* in (43b) need not be a null pronoun but can be a parasitic gap, which is licensed by A'-movement. In this way, the well-formedness of (43b) can be accounted for under the hypothesis that scrambling is A'-movement. For discussion of parasitic gaps,

see also Engdahl (1983), Taraldsen (1981), and N. Chomsky (1982, 1986a), among others.

26 I will use upper-case "HIS," etc. to mark the relevant *so* pronoun, such as *soitu*, for ease of exposition.

27 For the nature of *zibun-zisin*, see Y. Kitagawa (1986) and Katada (1991), among others.

28 See Yoshimura (1992) for a different conclusion.

29 See Tada (1990, 1993) for a different judgment.

30 Cho (1994) attributes the difference between Hindi on the one hand and Japanese/Korean on the other to the fact that in Hindi, overt WH-movement is obligatory in complex sentences, whereas it is optional in Japanese/Korean. Overt WH-movement is optional in simplex sentences in Hindi.

31 See Nemoto (1991, 1993), Yoshimura (1992), and Saito (1992) for more discussion on long-distance A-movement in Japanese.

32 Nemoto (1995) questions the relevance of WCO data as evidence for scrambling to be A-movement. She points out that Lasnik and Stowell (1991) show that in certain A'-movement such as *tough*, parasitic gaps, and topicalization, expected WCO effects do not show up.

33 See Yoshimura (1992) for a different judgment.

34 See also Kuno (1973), Huang (1982), Lasnik and Saito (1992), J. Abe (1993), and Y. Kitagawa (1994), among others.

35 This is different from its equivalent in English. It is known that *someone loves everyone* is ambiguous (May 1977, among others). See Lasnik and Saito (1992) for detailed discussion.

36 Ura (1996) and Takano (1996) discuss VP-scrambling as object-shift.

37 See also Y. Kitagawa (1994), Ura (1996), Takano (1996), and Miyagawa (1997a) for relevant discussion.

38 See also Y. Kitagawa (1994) for relevant discussion. He observes that a WCO violation in double object constructions in Japanese is unexpectedly milder than the subject–object counterpart.

39 See Kuroda (1993b), Y. Kitagawa (1994), and Miyagawa (1997a) for different observation.

40 See Tada (1993) for differences between S-scrambling and *pure* A-movement.

41 Miyagawa (1997a) argues that when the order is IO–DO, *-ni* is a dative Case marker, whereas when the order is DO–IO, *-ni* is a postposition (to). See also A. Watanabe (1995).

42 Chain Condition (Rizzi 1986: 66)

$C = (\alpha_1 \ldots \alpha_n)$ is a chain iff, for $1 \leq i < n$, α_i is the local binder of α_{i+1}

See also N. Chomsky (1981a: 333).

43 See also Yoshimura (1992) and Nemoto (1991) for relevant discussion.

44 Saito (1994b) argues that VP-scrambling can be undone at LF, and therefore, there is no Condition B violation in (73b).

45 Hiroto Hoshi (personal communication) pointed out to me that Y. Matsumoto (1996) has an interesting discussion on the structure of Control constructions in Japanese which might save Miyagawa's (1997a) argument.

6 Reflexives

TAKAKO AIKAWA

0 Introduction

This chapter concerns the binding behavior of Japanese reflexives. Reflexives are used to express one's reflexive action or state. For instance, sentence (1a), in which the English reflexive *himself* occurs as the object, expresses John's reflexive action, that is, "blaming himself." Reflexivization is normally captured through the use of reflexive pronouns. Compare (1a) with (1b–c).

(1) a. John$_i$ blamed himself$_i$.
     b. *John$_i$ blamed John$_i$.
     c. *John$_i$ blamed him$_i$.

In (1b), the subject NP is repeated as the object, and in (1c), the pronominal is used as the object. In both cases, reflexive reading is not possible.

Japanese employs three different types of reflexive words: (i) *zibun* "self," which is morphologically simplex, (ii) *zibun-zisin*, which is composed of *zibun* and *zisin* "self," and (iii) *kare-zisin*, which is composed of the pronominal *kare* "he" and *zisin*. Examples of these three reflexive words are given in (2a–c).

(2) a. Taroo$_i$-ga zibun$_i$-o semeta.
         Taro-Nom self-Acc blamed
     b. Taroo$_i$-ga zibun-zisin$_i$-o semeta.
         Taro-Nom self-self-Acc   blamed
     c. Taroo$_i$-ga kare-zisin$_i$-o semeta.
         Taro-Nom he-self-Acc   blamed
         "Taro$_i$ blamed himself$_i$."

Although Japanese employs the three different reflexives, the literature concerning reflexivization has paid much attention to *zibun*. There are several reasons for this. First, *zibun* exhibits a number of properties different from English reflexives. For instance, consider (3) and (4).

(3) a. Taroo$_i$-ga [Ziroo$_j$-ga zibun$_{i/j}$-o semeta to]   itta.
         Taro-Nom Ziro-Nom self-Acc blamed Comp said
         "Taro$_i$ said that Ziro$_j$ blamed self$_{i/j}$."
     b. John$_i$ said that Bill$_j$ blamed himself$_{*i/j}$.

(4) a. Taroo$_i$-ga Ziroo$_j$-ni zibun$_{i/*j}$-nituite hanasita.
         Taro-Nom Ziro-Dat self-about   told
         "Taro$_i$ told Ziro$_j$ about self$_{i/*j}$."
     b. John$_i$ told Bill$_j$ about himself$_{i/j}$.

In (3a), the matrix subject *Taro* as well as the embedded subject *Ziro* can serve as the antecedent of *zibun*. This means that *zibun* and its antecedent do not have to be in the same clause. In English, by contrast, a reflexive word and its antecedent must be in the same clause, as shown in (3b).

The data in (4), on the other hand, concern the difference between *zibun* and English reflexives with respect to the type of antecedent NP. As in (4a), *zibun* can take only a subject NP as its antecedent. English reflexives do not exhibit such a property as shown in (4b). We will see more differences between *zibun* and English reflexives in section 1.

Another reason why *zibun*-binding has received much attention is that it is claimed to involve pragmatic or discourse factors, not just syntactic ones.[1] As we just saw in (4a), *zibun* is assumed to take only the subject as its antecedent. This subject antecedent condition on *zibun*-binding, however, can be suspended in certain contexts. Take, for instance, the case in (5).

(5) *Taroo$_i$-wa zyuunen mae-ni Mary-ga   zibun$_i$-o tazunete-itta ie-de
      Taro-Top ten years ago   Mary-Nom self-Acc visit-went   house-in
      mada kurasite-iru.
      still   live-ing
      "Taro$_i$ is still living in the house where Hanako went to visit him$_i$ ten years ago." (Kuno 1978b: 206)

In (5), *zibun* takes the subject NP *Taro* as its antecedent. The ungrammaticality of (5) then contradicts the subject antecedent condition. To account for such binding behavior of *zibun*, a number of analyses that resort to pragmatic notions like empathy, perspective, and logophoricity have been explored. *Zibun*-binding thus has invoked not only syntactic analyses but also pragmatic or discourse ones, and the debate concerning which approach is more appropriate has been found extensively in the literature.[2]

Furthermore, *zibun*-binding is used as a diagnostic test for subjecthood in Japanese and it plays a crucial role for analyses of other syntactic phenomena such as passives and causatives. For instance, consider (6).

(6) a. Taroo$_i$-ga Yosiko$_j$-o   zibun$_{i/j}$-no heya-de hatarak-ase-ta.
         Taro-Nom Yosiko-Acc self-Gen   room-in work-Cause-Past
         "Taro$_i$ made Yosiko$_j$ work in self$_{i/j}$'s room."
     b. Taroo$_i$-ga Yosiko$_j$-ni zibun$_{i/j}$-no ofisu-de nak-are-ta.
         Taro-Nom Yosiko-Dat self-Gen   office-in cry-Passive-Past
         "Taro$_i$ was adversely affected by Yoshiko$_j$'s crying in self$_{i/j}$'s room."

(6a) involves the causative construction and (6b) involves the indirect passive
construction. In both examples, *zibun* can be bound to the nonsubject *Yoshiko*
(as well as to the subject *Taro*). Given the subject antecedent condition, this
suggests that *Yoshiko* bears subjecthood, although it is not marked by the
nominative case *-ga*. On the basis of the binding behavior of *zibun* as in (6),
researchers have argued that causatives and indirect passives in Japanese
are underlyingly complex as schematized in (7) (Kuno 1973, K. Inoue 1976b,
Shibatani 1973a, 1976, among others).

(7) a. [$_S$ Taroo [$_S$ Yosiko zibun-no heya-de hatarak-] -aseta]
     b. [$_S$ Taroo [$_S$ Yosiko zibun-no ofisu-de nak-]   -areta]

Given the underlying structures in (7), the nonsubject NP *Yoshiko* in (6) counts
as a subject and hence it can serve as the antecedent of *zibun*. As shown, *zibun*-
binding involves a number of issues, both syntactic and pragmatic. In addition,
zibun-binding plays a crucial role for syntactic analyses of various constructions,
and it is one of the most studied topics in Japanese linguistics.

   The organization of this chapter is as follows: in section 1, I examine
basic properties of *zibun*, while pointing out theoretical issues pertinent to
zibun-binding. Section 2 reviews some syntactic analyses of *zibun*-binding that
have been explored under the framework of Government and Binding Theory
(N. Chomsky 1981a). In section 3, I discuss previous studies of *zibun*-binding
that resort to pragmatic notion(s). In section 4, I examine the nature of the two
Japanese complex reflexives (i.e. *zibun-zisin* and *kare-zisin*). Section 5 discusses
remaining problems concerning Japanese reflexives.

1   *Zibun* "Self"

1.1   *Basic properties of* zibun

Zibun is considered to be the most representative reflexive word in Japanese.
As was mentioned briefly above, *zibun* exhibits a number of properties that are
different from English reflexive words. First, *zibun* lacks specification of person,
gender, and number features (i.e. phi-features). For instance, any subject NP
in (8) can serve as the antecedent of *zibun*.[3] English reflexives, by contrast, must
agree in their phi-features with their antecedents as indicated by the English
translation.

(8) Watasi$_i$/Taroo$_j$/Hanako$_k$/[$_{NP}$Taroo-to Hanako]$_l$-ga zibun$_{i/j/k/l}$-o semeta.
     I   /Taro /Hanako/   Taro-and Hanako-Nom self-Acc   blamed
     "I$_i$/Taro$_j$/Hanako$_k$/[Taroo and Hanako]$_l$ blamed myself$_i$/himself$_j$/herself$_k$/
     themselves$_l$."

Second, only an animate NP can serve as the antecedent of *zibun*. English,
by contrast, has the reflexives, *itself* and *themselves*, for inanimate antecedents.
Consider (9), which is drawn from Kuno (1972b: 178).

(9) a. *Rekisi$_i$-wa zibun$_i$-o kurikaesu.
         history-Top self-Acc repeat
         "History$_i$ repeats itself$_i$."
     b. *Sono sinbun$_i$-wa   kaze-ni zibun$_i$-o hirogeta.
         that newspaper-Top wind-in self-Acc unfolded
         "The newspaper$_i$ unfolded itself$_i$ in the wind."

(9a–b) are ungrammatical because the inanimate NPs *rekisi* "history" and *sono
sinbun* "that newspaper" antecede *zibun*, respectively.

Third, as we saw in (3) above, *zibun* and its antecedent do not have to be in
the same clause, but English reflexives do. (3) is repeated as (10) below.

(10) a. Taroo$_i$-ga [Ziroo$_j$-ga zibun$_{i/j}$-o semeta to]   itta.
          Taro-Nom Ziro-Nom self-Acc blamed Comp said
          "Taro$_i$ said that Ziro$_j$ blamed self$_{i/j}$."
      b. John$_i$ said that Bill$_j$ blamed himself$_{*i/j}$.

In (10a), *zibun* can be bound by the matrix subject *Taro* (as well as the embedded
subject *Ziro*). Cases where a reflexive takes its antecedent outside its local
domain are called long-distance binding (LD-binding). English reflexives cannot
participate in LD-binding as shown in (10b).

Fourth, as seen in (4), the antecedent of *zibun* must be the subject (Kuroda
1965a). English reflexives are not subject to such a constraint. (4) is repeated
as (11).

(11) a. Taroo$_i$-ga Ziroo$_j$-ni zibun$_{i/*j}$-nituite hanasita.
          Taro-Nom Ziro-Dat self-about   told
          "Taro$_i$ told Ziro$_j$ about himself$_{i/*j}$."
      b. John$_i$ talked to Bill$_j$ about himself$_{i/j}$.

Fifth, *zibun* can participate in discourse-binding as illustrated in (12) (Oshima
1979, Koster 1982, Fukui 1984, among others).

(12) A: John$_i$-ga dareka-o soko-ni okutta n-desu-ka?
      B: Iie, zibun$_i$-ga itta n-desu.
      A: "Did John$_i$ send someone there?"
      B: *"No, himself$_i$ (= John) went (there)." (Fukui 1984: 40 with modification)

Zibun in utterance B can refer to *John*, which is introduced in the previous discourse. English reflexives are not allowed to participate in discourse-binding as shown by the ungrammaticality of the English translation.

Sixth, in some dialects of Japanese, *zibun* can be used as the first person pronoun "I" or the second person pronoun "you."[4] This is illustrated in (13) (Gunji 1987, Aikawa 1993, Iida 1996).

(13) a. Masao-ga   zibun-o semeta.
          Masao-Nom self-Acc blamed
          "Masao$_i$ blamed himself$_i$/me."
      b. Yosiko-zyanakute, zibun-ga warui-n-zyanai!
          Yosiko-not   self-Nom bad   it is that
          "It's you, not Yoshiko, who is bad!"

Zibun in (13a–b) can be understood to be the speaker of the sentence and the addressee, respectively. English reflexives, *myself* and *yourself*, do not have such pronominal usage.

Seventh, unlike English reflexives, *zibun* can occur in the possessor position of an NP or in the subject position of an embedded clause as in (14).

(14) a. Taroo$_i$-ga [$_{NP}$ zibun$_i$-no sensee]-o   nagutta.
          Taro-Nom   self-Gen teacher-Acc hit
          "*Taro$_i$ hit himself$_i$'s teacher."
      b. Taroo$_i$-ga [$_S$ zibun$_i$-ga kono kurasu-de itiban   da to]
          Taro-Nom   self-Nom this   class-in   the best be Comp
          omotte-iru.
          think
          "*Taro$_i$ thinks that himself$_i$ is the best in this class."

Last, *zibun* can be modified by some other element. For instance, in (15a), *zibun* is modified by the demonstrative *sono* "that/such" and in (15b), it is modified by the relative clause, *kinoo Mitiko-ni tumetaku atatta* "(who) was hard on Mitiko yesterday." Both these examples are grammatical under the intended readings. Such modification is not possible for English reflexives.

(15) (Context: Usually, Masao is nice to Mitiko but yesterday he was mean to her.)
      a. Masao$_i$-wa sonna zibun$_i$-o semeta.
          Masao-Top such   self-Acc blamed
          "*Masao$_i$ blamed such himself$_i$."
      b. Masao$_i$-wa [$_{NP}$[$_S$ Mitiko-ni   tumetaku atatta] zibun$_i$]-o semeta.
          Masao-Top   Mitiko-Dat was hard   self-Acc blamed
          "*Masao$_i$ blamed himself$_i$, who was hard on Mitiko." (Aikawa 1993:
          55 with modification)

As seen above, the lexical nature of *zibun* and its binding behavior are quite different from those of English reflexives. There are, however, some similarities between *zibun* and English reflexives. One such similarity concerns the c-command requirement. Consider (16).

(16) a. [$_{NP}$ Taroo$_i$-no sensee]$_j$-ga   zibun$_{*i/j}$-o hihansita.
        Taro-Gen teacher-Nom self-Acc   criticized
        "[Taro$_i$'s teacher]$_j$ criticized himself$_{*i/j}$."
      b. [John$_i$'s teacher]$_j$ blamed himself$_{*i/j}$.

In (16a), *Taro*, being embedded in the larger NP, cannot c-command *zibun*, but the whole subject NP, *Taroo-no sensee* "Taro's teacher," can. The contrast in the grammaticality of *zibun*-binding shows that when *zibun* finds its antecedent within the sentence, it observes the c-command requirement. English reflexives behave the same way in this respect, as shown in (16b).

Another similarity between *zibun* and English reflexives is that both of them are incapable of taking a split antecedent, as shown in (17).[5]

(17) a. *Masao$_i$-ga   Taroo$_j$-ni zibun$_{i+j}$-no koto-nituite hanasita.
        Masao-Nom Taro-Dat self-Gen   things-about told
        "*Masao$_i$ told Taro$_j$ things about self$_{i+j}$."
      b. *John$_i$ told Mary$_j$ about themselves$_{i+j}$.

To sum up, *zibun* and English reflexives exhibit the following differences and similarities.

(18)

		Zibun	English reflexives
a.	Phi-feature specification	no	yes
b.	Animacy requirement on the antecedent	yes	no (*itself/themselves*)
c.	Local binding	yes	yes
d.	LD-binding	yes	no
e.	Subject orientation	yes	no
f.	Discourse-binding	yes	no
g.	Pronominal usage of "I"/"You"	yes	no
h.	Possessor position or subject position	yes	no
i.	Modification	yes	no
j.	C-command requirement	yes	yes
k.	Split antecedent	no	no

1.2   Two controversial issues

As we saw in section 1.1, *zibun* exhibits a number of properties different from English reflexives. Among these differences, the following two have received much attention: LD-binding and subject orientation. One reason for this is that these two properties of *zibun* are problematic for the standard Binding Theory (BT) proposed within the framework of Government and Binding Theory (N. Chomsky 1981a). Let us briefly examine the standard BT.

The standard BT concerns the distribution of different types of NPs. Under the standard BT, all NPs are assumed to fall into one of the following three types: (i) anaphors (i.e. reflexives and reciprocals), (ii) pronominals, and (iii) R(eferential)-expressions. The distribution of these three types of NPs is assumed to be regulated by the three binding conditions stated in (19).

(19)   *The Standard Binding Theory* (N. Chomsky 1981a: 188 with some modification)
       Condition A: An anaphor must be bound in its local domain.
       Condition B: A pronominal must be free in its local domain.
       Condition C: An R-expression must be free.

Under the standard BT, α can be bound by β if and only if: (i) α and β are coindexed; (ii) β c-commands α; and (iii) β is in an A-position. Otherwise, α is free. The definition of local domain has several different versions, but we take the one based on the notion of governing category.[6] Informally, this version states that an NP or an S that contains an anaphoric expression α delimits the local domain for α.[7]

Now, using some English examples, let us examine how the standard BT in (19) regulates the distribution of different types of NPs. We focus on Condition A and Condition B, because only these two are relevant to our discussion about *zibun*-binding. Consider (20).

(20)   a. $John_i$ loves $himself_i$/*him_i.
       b. $John_i$ thinks [that Mary loves *$himself_i$/him_i].
       c.   [$_{NP}$ $John_i$'s teacher] hit *$himself_i$/him_i.
       d. $John_i$ like *$herself_{j\ (=Mary)}$/$her_{j\ (=Mary)}$.

Himself/him in (20a) is locally bound by *John*. The occurrence of *himself* satisfies Condition A but the occurrence of *him* violates Condition B. In (20b), by contrast, *himself/him* is free in its local domain. The occurrence of *himself* triggers a Condition A-violation but the occurrence of *him* satisfies Condition B, resulting in the contrast. The contrast in (20c) illustrates the difference in c-command requirement between an anaphor and a pronominal. *John* in (20c), being embedded in the larger NP, fails to c-command *himself/him*. Thus, *himself/him* is not bound by *John*. *Himself* triggers a Condition A-violation but *him* satisfies Condition B. (20d) is an instance of discourse-binding: *herself/her* receives the discourse referent of *Mary*, and these expressions are free. Thus, *herself* triggers a Condition A-violation and *her* satisfies Condition B.

Returning to *zibun*-binding, the fact that *zibun* can participate in LD-binding as well as in local binding is problematic for the standard BT. The possibility of local binding of *zibun* indicates that *zibun* is subject to Condition A and it should be categorized as anaphor. On the other hand, the possibility of LD-binding of *zibun* indicates that *zibun* is subject to Condition B and it should be categorized as pronominal. In short, *zibun* sometimes behaves like an anaphor and sometimes like a pronominal. The standard BT presumes that anaphoric expressions fall into either the category of anaphor or that of pronominal, but not both. Regardless of how *zibun* is categorized, the standard BT cannot provide a satisfactory explanation for this paradoxical nature of *zibun*.

The standard BT also fails to explain the subject orientation because neither Condition A nor Condition B makes any reference to the notion of subjecthood. The two properties of *zibun* mentioned above thus pose serious problems for the standard BT.

The subject orientation of *zibun* has invited yet another debate. As mentioned earlier in (5), the subject antecedent condition on *zibun*-binding faces many counterexamples and its validity is still controversial. (21) presents some counterexamples.

(21) a. [$_S$ Zibun$_i$-ga gan   kamo sirenai koto]-ga   Hirosi$_i$-o
           self-Nom cancer may   Comp-Nom Hiroshi-Acc
          nayam-ase-ta.
          worry-make-Past
          "That he$_i$ might have cancer worried Hiroshi$_i$." (N. A. McCawley
          1976: 63)
      b. *John$_i$-wa Mary-ga   zibun$_i$-o korosita toki, Jane-to
          John-Top Mary-Nom self-Acc killed   when Jane-with
          nete-ita.
          was sleeping
          "*John$_i$ was in bed with Jane when Mary killed him$_i$." (Kuno 1973:
          310)

In (21a), *zibun* is bound to the nonsubject NP, and yet the sentence is grammatical. On the other hand, in (21b), *zibun* is bound to the subject NP, but *zibun*-binding is ungrammatical.[8] These examples are thus problematic for the subject antecedent condition. In fact, such counterexamples are numerous, and many researchers have argued that the nature of *zibun*-binding cannot be fully explained in terms of syntax, and pragmatic factors must be taken into consideration for understanding *zibun*-binding (Kuno 1973, 1978a, Kuroda 1973, Kuno and Kaburaki 1977, Kameyama 1984, 1985, Iida and Sells 1986, Gunji 1987, Sells 1987, Iida 1996, among others). Recall here that *zibun*-binding is used as a diagnostic test for subjecthood in Japanese and analyses of other syntactic phenomena make crucial reference to *zibun*'s subject orientation. Thus, the issue of whether the antecedent condition on *zibun*-binding should be captured in terms of the syntactic notion of subjecthood or in terms of some pragmatic notion(s) is an important one. I will discuss this controversial status of subject orientation in more detail in section 3.

2   Syntactic Analyses of *Zibun*-Binding

We now start examining analyses of *zibun*-binding. In this section, we restrict our attention to those that have been proposed within the framework of Government and Binding Theory (GB) (N. Chomsky 1981a). As mentioned in section 1.2, the paradoxical nature of *zibun* as an anaphor and a pronominal has invited much debate, and the status of *zibun* is still controversial. For this reason, we focus on two types of analyses: (i) those that categorize *zibun* as pronominal, as discussed by Fukui (1984) and Ueda (1986), and (ii) those that categorize *zibun* as anaphor, as in Katada (1988, 1991) and Aikawa (1993).[9]

2.1   Zibun *as a pronominal: Fukui (1984) and Ueda (1986)*

Fukui (1984) and Ueda (1986) argue that LD-binding and discourse-binding of *zibun* indicate that *zibun* bears pronominal-like properties. These two analyses, although implemented with different mechanisms and assumptions, are similar in spirit. They both point toward the conclusion that *zibun* should be categorized as pronominal and that it must function as a bound variable.

Fukui (1984) argues that *zibun* is a special type of pronoun and is subject to Condition B of the standard BT.[10] In addition, he proposes (22) as the antecedent condition on *zibun*-binding.

(22)   *Zibun* must be bound by the closest A'-binder. (Fukui 1984: 27)

In Fukui's analysis, the subject position in Japanese, unlike that in English, is assumed to be an A'-position. (22) then can be paraphrased as saying that *zibun* must be bound by the closest subject. Note that the combination of Fukui's hypothesis that the subject position in Japanese is an A'-position and his condition in (22) implies that *zibun* must function as a bound variable: A'-positions are assumed to be operator positions (cf. N. Chomsky 1981a, 1982) and what is bound by an element in such a position is supposed to function as a bound variable.

Fukui explains local binding of *zibun* in (23) as follows: *Hanako* in (23) is in an A'-position and it is the closest A'-binder for *zibun*. *Zibun*-binding to *Hanako* thus satisfies (22), resulting in grammaticality.

(23)   Hanako$_i$-ga   zibun$_i$-o hihansita.
       Hanako-Nom self-Acc criticized
       "Hanako$_i$ criticized SELF$_i$."

Note that Condition B concerns only cases of A-binding. *Zibun*-binding to *Hanako* in (23) is an instance of A'-binding because *Hanako* is an A'-binder, and so Condition B is not applicable.

Next, consider (24), in which *zibun* in the embedded clause is LD-bound by the matrix subject.

(24) a. Taroo$_i$-ga [zibun$_i$-ga tensai da to] omotte-iru.
Taro-Nom self-Nom a genius be Comp think
"Taro$_i$ thinks that he$_i$ is a genius."

b. Taroo$_i$-ga [Hanako-ga zibun$_i$-o hihansita to] omotte-iru.
Taro-Nom Hanako-Nom self-Acc criticized Comp think
"Taro$_i$ thinks that Hanako criticized him$_i$."

In (24a), *zibun* occurs in the subject position of the embedded clause. The closest A'-binder for this *zibun* is the matrix subject *Taro*. *Zibun*-binding to *Taro* thus satisfies (22), resulting in grammaticality. In (24b), on the other hand, the embedded subject *Hanako* intervenes between *zibun* and the matrix subject. But according to Fukui, this embedded subject is assumed to be in an A-position.[11] The matrix subject *Taro*, but not the embedded subject *Hanako*, counts as the closest A'-binder for *zibun*.[12] Hence, *zibun*-binding to *Taro* in (24b) is grammatical.

Ueda (1986) also argues for the position that *zibun* should be categorized as pronominal. Ueda's characterization of *zibun*, however, is somewhat different from Fukui's. He argues that *zibun* is inherently a bound pronominal. In Ueda's analysis, pronominals are divided into two types: bound pronominals, which have the features of [−anaphor, +pronominal, +bound], and nonbound pronominals, which have the features of [−anaphor, +pronominal, −bound] (cf. N. Chomsky 1982).[13] Ueda claims (1986: 94) that Japanese has two different forms of (overt) pronominals: *zibun*, which bears the features of [−anaphor, +pronominal, +bound], and *kare*, which bears the features of [−anaphor, +pronominal, −bound]. He supports this hypothesis by presenting data such as (25–7). First, consider (25), which involves the quantifier phrase (QP) antecedent, *daremo* "everyone."

(25) a. Daremo$_i$-ga [zibun$_i$-ga sono siken-ni gookaku-suru
everyone-Nom self-Nom that exam.-Dat pass
to] sinzite-iru.
Comp believe

b. *Daremo$_i$-ga [kare$_i$-ga sono siken-ni gookaku-suru
everyone-Nom he-Nom that exam.-Dat pass
to] sinzite-iru.
Comp believe
"Everyone$_i$ believes that he$_i$ will pass that exam." (Ueda 1986: 92 with modification)

QPs do not refer to any specific individuals, and so pronominals cannot be coreferential with them (cf. Geach 1972). Thus, when a QP occurs as the antecedent of a pronoun, that pronoun is forced to be construed as a bound variable.

The contrast in grammaticality between (25a) and (25b) then shows that *zibun* can be construed as a bound variable, but *kare* cannot (S. Martin 1975, Nakai 1976, Oshima 1979, C. Kitagawa 1981, M. Nakayama 1982, Saito and Hoji 1983, Aoun and Hornstein 1986, Hoji 1989, 1990, among others). This is consistent with Ueda's hypothesis above.

Next, consider (26–7), which involve the so-called sloppy identity of pronominals (Sag 1976, Reinhart 1983, among others).

(26)   John$_i$ called his$_i$ mother and Bill, too.
  a.   on the bound variable reading of *his* → sloppy reading
       John called John's mother and Bill called Bill's mother, too.
  b.   on the coreference reading of *his* → strict reading
       John called John's mother and Bill called John's mother, too.

(27) a.   John$_i$-wa zibun$_i$-ga katte-iru inu-o   naguru to, Bill-mo soo sita.
           John-Top self-Nom keep-ing dog-Acc hit when   Bill also so did
           "When John$_i$ hit the dog he$_i$ kept, Bill did so, too."
           (sloppy) "When John hit the dog John kept, Bill hit the dog Bill kept, too."
      b.   John$_i$-wa kare$_i$-no kuruma-ni notta. Bill-mo soo sita.
           John-Top he-Gen car   -in rode Bill also so did
           "John$_i$ got in his$_i$ car. Bill did so, too."
           *(sloppy) "John got in John's car. Bill got in Bill's car, too." (Ueda 1986: 97)

(26) illustrates the sloppy identity test of the English pronoun *his*. The VP in the first conjunct of (26) is assumed to be copied onto the elided VP in the second conjunct. If the pronoun *his* is construed as a bound variable, the predicate of "*x* called *x*'s mother" is copied, resulting in the interpretation of (26a). This type of reading is called sloppy reading. By contrast, if *his* is simply coreferential with *John*, the predicate of "*x* called John's mother" is copied, resulting in the interpretation of (26b).[14] This type of reading is called strict (or nonsloppy) reading. To put these together, variable binding of a pronoun induces sloppy reading whereas coreference of a pronoun induces strict reading, and the availability of sloppy reading tells us whether the pronoun in question can be a bound variable.

Returning to Ueda's analysis, he argues that the result of the sloppy identity test of *zibun/kare* in (27) supports his hypothesis: *zibun* can induce sloppy reading but *kare* cannot. Thus, *zibun* is a [+bound] pronominal and *kare* is a [−bound] pronominal.[15]

In Ueda's analysis, the inherent [+bound] feature of *zibun* plays an important role in accounting for subject orientation. He assumes with Williams (1980) that pronominals can be construed as bound variables only when they are bound by an element that can serve as the subject of predication.[16] He argues

that a subject NP is one of the elements that can serve as the subject of predication and from this, subject orientation follows.

LD-binding, on the other hand, is expected because in Ueda's analysis, *zibun*
is categorized as pronominal. But *zibun*'s ability to participate in local binding
is problematic (as he admits). While Ueda essentially leaves this problem open,
he makes an interesting observation concerning local binding of *zibun*. Compare
(28a) and (28b) below, which are drawn from Ueda (1986).

(28) a. John$_i$-wa zibun$_i$-o nikunde-iru/semeta.
          John-Top self-Acc hate   /blamed
          "John$_i$ hates/blamed himself$_i$." (Ueda 1986: 100)
      b. *John$_i$-wa zibun$_i$-o nagutta/ketta.
          John-Top self-Acc hit   /kicked
          "John$_i$ hit/kicked himself$_i$." (Ueda 1986: 105; originally from Oshima
          1979: 425)

As shown above, local binding of *zibun* is sometimes good but sometimes bad
(cf. N. A. McCawley 1976, Oshima 1979). Ueda notes that there is a semantic
difference between verbs such as in (28a) and those in (28b): the former involves
physical activity whereas the latter involves activity of a more abstract sort.
He suggests that "*zibun* is exempt from the Binding Theory (B) when the verb
of the clause in which *zibun* occurs represents abstract activity" (Ueda 1986:
107). We will come back to this issue later in section 5.

It is important to note that both Fukui and Ueda base their antecedent
conditions on the observation that *zibun* can be bound not only by a subject
NP but also by an element like a topic NP or a discourse referent. In Fukui's
analysis, these potential binders of *zibun* are identified as A'-binders, whereas
in Ueda's, they are identified as elements that can serve as the subject of
predication. Take, for instance, *zibun*-binding to a discourse referent. Both
Fukui and Ueda assume with Huang (1984) that Japanese has an empty topic
and this empty topic is coindexed with some salient discourse referent as
shown in (29).

(29) [$_{Top}$ e$_i$] [$_S$ zibun$_i$ ...] OP$_i$] (where "i" is the index of a discourse referent)

Given Fukui's analysis, discourse-binding of *zibun* in (29) is possible because
zibun is bound by the closest A'-binder (i.e. the empty topic), whereas given
Ueda's, it is possible because the empty topic, just like a regular topic NP, can
serve as the subject of predication. Fukui's antecedent condition and Ueda's,
although stated differently, are thus quite similar.

Fukui's analysis and Ueda's are also similar in that they both use data
involving subject–object asymmetries of *zibun*-binding as supporting evidence.
For instance, examine (30), which involves binding of *zibun* that occurs in an
adjunct clause.

(30) a.   Taroo$_i$-wa [zibun$_i$-ga Ziroo-o   hometa] toki,   Hanako-no
          Taro-Top   self-Nom Ziro-Acc praised   when Hanako-Gen
          soba-ni ita.
          near   was
          "Taro$_i$ was near Hanako when he$_i$ praised Ziro."

     b.   *Taroo$_i$-wa [Ziroo-ga   zibun$_i$-o hometa] toki,   Hanako-no
          Taro-Top   Ziro-Nom self-Acc praised   when Hanako-Gen
          soba-ni ita.
          near   was
          "Taro$_i$ was near Hanako when Ziro praised him$_i$." (Ueda 1986: 99–
          100 with modification)

As noted by Kuroda (1965a), *zibun*-binding in an adjunct clause exhibits a
subject–object asymmetry: the binding of the subject *zibun* by *Taro* in (30a) is
grammatical but that of the object *zibun* in (30b) is not. Such subject–object
asymmetry does not arise when *zibun* occurs in a complement clause as in (31).

(31) a.   Taroo$_i$-wa [[zibun$_i$-ga Ziroo-o   hometa] koto]-o   oboete-iru.
          Taro-Top   self-Nom Ziro-Acc praised Comp-Acc remember
          "Taro remembers that he praised Ziro."

     b.   Taroo$_i$-wa [[Ziroo-ga   zibun$_i$-o hometa] koto]-o   oboete-iru.
          Taro-Top   Ziro-Nom self-Acc praised Comp-Acc remember
          "Taro remembers that Ziro praised him." (Ueda 1986: 100 with
          modification)

In accounting for such subject–object asymmetries, both Fukui and Ueda
make reference to the distinction between a governed S and an ungoverned S.
In Fukui's analysis, this distinction is reflected in the A/A'-distinction of their
subject positions: that is, the subject position of a governed S is an A-position
whereas that of an ungoverned S is an A'-position (see n. 11). Given Fukui's
analysis, *zibun*-binding to *Taro* in (30b) violates (22) because the embedded
subject *Ziro* serves as the closest A'-binder for *zibun*, but the one in (31b) does
not because *Ziro* here is in an A-position and therefore *Taro* counts as the
closest A'-binder for *zibun*. Accordingly, there is a subject–object asymmetry
in (30), but not in (31).

   In Ueda's analysis, such subject–object asymmetries are explained on the basis
of the hypothesis that "the predicate of an ungoverned clause is opaque to the
binding of the overt pronominal, i.e. indices other than that of its own subject
are unavailable for this purpose" (Ueda 1986: 100).[17] Given this, the predicate
of the adjunct clause in (30b) is assumed to be opaque to binding of the object
zibun. This amounts to saying that the index of the matrix subject *Taro* is not
available for the object *zibun* and hence *zibun*-binding to *Taro* is ungrammatical.
The predicate of the complement clause in (31b), on the other hand, is not subject
to his condition above. Accordingly, the binding of the object *zibun* by *Taro* in
(31b) is possible, resulting in the absence of subject–object asymmetry.

2.2 **Zibun** *as an anaphor: Katada (1988, 1991) and Aikawa (1993)*

We now move to the other two proposals of *zibun*-binding that treat *zibun* as an anaphor. They both assume certain LF-mechanisms to explain subject orientation and LD-binding and in this respect, they can be characterized as LF-analyses of *zibun*-binding.[18]

Katada (1988, 1991) argues that *zibun* is an operator anaphor and it raises at LF. She contends that the lack of phi-feature specification of *zibun*, which we saw earlier in (8), implies that *zibun* possesses a "semantic range": just like other operators such as *who/everyone*, *zibun* picks a [+human] referent. She argues that this lexical nature of *zibun* licenses *zibun* to raise at LF. In her analysis, *zibun* is assumed to raise to higher position(s) through VP-adjunction. Examine (32), which schematizes Katada's LF-analysis of *zibun*.

(32) John$_i$-ga [$_S$ Bill$_j$-ga Mary$_k$-ni zibun$_{i/j/*k}$-no koto-o hanasita
John-Nom Bill-Nom Mary-Dat self-Gen things-Acc told
to] omotte-iru.
Comp thinks
"John thinks that Bill told Mary things about self."
a. LF for the coindexation between Bill$_j$-zibun$_j$
[John-Nom ... [$_S$ Bill$_j$-Nom [$_{VP}$ zibun$_j$ [$_{VP}$ Mary-Dat ... t$_j$]]]]
b. LF for the coindexation between John$_i$-zibun$_i$
[John$_i$-Nom [$_{VP}$ zibun$_i$ [$_{VP}$ [$_S$ Bill-Nom ... [$_{VP}$ Mary-Dat ... t$_i$]]]]]

(32a) involves the LF-raising of *zibun* to the VP in the embedded clause and (32b) involves the LF-raising of *zibun* to the VP in the matrix clause.[19] In both cases, *zibun* is bound by the closest c-commanding antecedent (i.e. *Bill*$_i$ in the case of (32a) and *John*$_i$ in the case of (32b)). Thus, not only *zibun*-binding to *Bill* but also *zibun*-binding to *John* satisfies Condition A. Katada argues that this LF-movement of *zibun* makes it possible for *zibun* to participate in LD-binding.

As for subject orientation, she explains it on the basis of the asymmetric c-command relation displayed by subject NPs and nonsubject NPs with respect to *zibun*'s landing site(s). For instance, consider the LF-movement of *zibun* in (32a). After having adjoined to the embedded VP, *zibun* can be c-commanded by the embedded subject *Bill*, but not by the dative NP *Mary*. Hence, *Bill* can antecede *zibun* but *Mary* cannot.

Aikawa (1993), on the other hand, explores an LF-analysis of *zibun* that does not involve any LF-movement of *zibun*. Following Reinhart and Reuland (1991, 1992), she argues that the lack of phi-feature specification in *zibun* forces *zibun* to be associated with Agr (= INFL) at LF: in order for *zibun* to be interpreted, *zibun* must receive phi-features (Bouchard 1984). Agr is the only head that can provide phi-features for *zibun*. She proposes that *zibun* is to be bound to the first accessible Agr (= INFL) at LF so that it can receive phi-features.[20] Examine (33), which schematizes Aikawa's analysis of *zibun*.

(33)

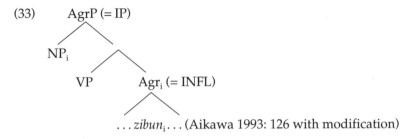

...*zibun*$_i$... (Aikawa 1993: 126 with modification)

In her analysis, *zibun*-binding to the subject NP in (33) occurs in two steps. First, Agr receives the index of the subject NP through spec-head agreement (N. Chomsky 1992).[21] Then, this index is assigned to *zibun* by virtue of *zibun* being bound to Agr. Thus, contrasting with Katada, Aikawa explains subject orientation on the basis of the association between *zibun* and Agr through binding.

Aikawa's explanation of LD-binding also contrasts with Katada's. Recall that under Katada's analysis, LF-raising of *zibun* through VP-adjunction makes it possible for *zibun* to participate in LD-binding. Aikawa's analysis, by contrast, does not invoke any LF-movement of *zibun*. In her analysis, LD-binding of *zibun* is explained on the basis of the mechanism of Agr-chain, which is advanced by Progovac (1992). Following Progovac, she argues that Agr's in Japanese are anaphoric to each other (cf. Borer 1986) and they can form an Agr-chain. This Agr-chain then allows the index of a remote antecedent to be transferred from the Agr associated with the antecedent in question to the Agr closest to *zibun*. As a result, LD-binding of *zibun* becomes possible. Consider, for instance, (34), in which the previous example of (32) is analyzed on the basis of Aikawa's system.

(34) a. John$_i$-ga   [$_s$ Bill$_j$-ga   Mary$_k$-ni zibun$_{i/j/*k}$-no koto-o   hanasita
          John-Nom Bill-Nom   Mary-Dat self-Gen   things-Acc told
          to]   omotte-iru.
          Comp thinks
          "John thinks that Bill told Mary things about self."
      b. [John$_i$ Agr2 [Bill$_j$ Agr-1 Mary$_k$ zibun$_{i/j/*k}$ V] V]

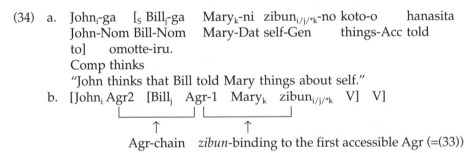

          Agr-chain   *zibun*-binding to the first accessible Agr (=(33))

Zibun-binding to the embedded subject *Bill* can be explained on the basis of (33): the index of *Bill* (i.e. *j*) is assigned to Agr1 through spec-head agreement, and *zibun*, by virtue of its being bound to Agr1, receives this index, resulting in the grammaticality of *zibun*-binding to *Bill*. LD-binding of *zibun* by the matrix subject *John*, on the other hand, involves the Agr-chain composed of Agr1 and Agr2: Agr1 and Agr2, being anaphoric to each other, form an Agr-chain. The index of *John* is first assigned to Agr2 through spec-head agreement and then it is transmitted to Agr1 through the Agr-chain. *Zibun* is bound to Agr1 and *zibun*-binding to *John* is grammatical. Note that the dative NP *Mary* cannot be a potential antecedent for *zibun* because *Mary* is not in spec of Agr1, and so its index is not assigned to Agr1. There is no way for *zibun* to receive the index of *Mary*.

As shown, both Katada and Aikawa utilize LF-mechanisms so that *zibun*-binding can conform to Condition A. In Katada's analysis, LF-raising of *zibun* through VP-adjunction allows *zibun* to be associated with a remote antecedent without violating Condition A, and hence LD-binding of *zibun* becomes possible. This LF-raising also explains subject orientation: the landing site of *zibun* at LF can be c-commanded only by subject NPs, not by nonsubject NPs. Accordingly, *zibun* exhibits the property of subject orientation. In Aikawa's analysis, on the other hand, the mechanism of an Agr-chain allows the binding domain of *zibun* to extend up to some remote antecedent, so that LD-binding of *zibun* becomes possible without violating Condition A. As for subject orientation, she ascribes it to the defective nature of *zibun*: the lack of phi-feature specification in *zibun* forces *zibun* to be associated with Agr for interpretation. *Zibun*, being bound to Agr, then is expected to receive its referent from the subject.

It is hard to assess which LF-analysis would be more viable, because the two analyses above are based on different assumptions and implemented with different LF-mechanisms. However, we wish to point out one problem with Katada's analysis, which has been noted by Hoji (1990). Katada utilizes LF-raising of *zibun* to explain *zibun*'s properties of subject orientation and LD-binding. Thus, for her, it is crucial to show that *zibun* actually raises in LF. Katada, in fact, presents data such as those in (35) as evidence for this hypothesis.

(35) a. ?*[John$_i$-ga [$_{S1}$ zibun$_i$-ga kare$_i$-no hahaoya-o semeta to] itta].
       John-Nom   self-Nom he-Gen mother-Acc blamed Comp said
       "John$_i$ said that zibun$_i$ blamed kare$_i$'s mother." (Katada 1991: 304)
   b. [$_{S2}$ John$_i$ [$_{VP2}$ zibun$_i$ [$_{VP2}$ [$_{S1}$ t$_i$ [$_{VP1}$ ... kare$_i$ ...]]]]]

Given Katada's LF-analysis, *zibun* in the embedded subject position of (35a) is assumed to adjoin to the VP in the matrix clause as in (35b). She assumes that once *zibun* moves to an A'-position, it must stay in that position (Katada 1991: 303). She ascribes the ungrammaticality of (35a) to *kare*'s inability to participate in A'-binding: *zibun*, which in an A'-position, A'-binds *kare*. But *kare* cannot be A'-bound, resulting in ungrammaticality. The problem is, as Hoji (1990) points out, that Katada's analysis above incorrectly predicts a sentence like (36b) to be grammatical.

(36) a.   Daremo$_i$-ga   soitu$_i$-no   hahaoya-o semeta.
            everyone-Nom that guy-Gen mother-Acc blamed
            "Everyone$_i$ blamed that guy$_i$'s mother."
      b.   *?[John$_i$-ga   [zibun$_i$-ga soitu$_i$-no   hahaoya-o semeta
            John-Nom self-Nom that guy-Gen mother-Acc blamed
            to]   itta].
            Comp said
            "John$_i$ said that zibun$_i$ blamed soitu$_i$'s mother."
      c.   [$_{S2}$ John$_i$ [$_{VP2}$ zibun$_i$ [$_{VP2}$ [$_{S1}$ t$_i$ [$_{VP1}$ ... soitu$_i$ ...]]]]]

The sentences in (36) involve the demonstrative *soitu* "that guy." The
grammaticality of (36a), in which *soitu* is bound by the QP antecedent *daremo*
"everyone," simply shows that *soitu* can be a bound variable. (36b) is parallel to
(35a) except that in (36b), *soitu* occurs in place of *kare*. If the ungrammaticality
of (35a) were due to *kare*'s inability to participate in A'-binding as Katada argues,
(36b) should be grammatical because *soitu* can participate in A'-binding. But
this is not the case. The ungrammaticality of (36b) thus casts doubt on Katada's
essential point that *zibun* raises at LF.[22]

3   Pragmatic/Discourse Approach to *Zibun*-Binding

As seen above, under the syntactic approach to *zibun*-binding, subjecthood
condition is taken for granted. However, as mentioned in section 1.2, this
condition faces a number of counterexamples and its validity is still controversial. In order to fully understand the nature of *zibun*-binding, it is essential to
examine in what contexts the subject antecedent condition can be suspended
and what kinds of pragmatic factors are relevant to such contexts. This section
surveys analyses of *zibun*-binding that resort to pragmatic notion(s).

3.1   *Pragmatic factors that affect* **zibun-binding**

We begin by examining in what context(s) *zibun* can take a nonsubject NP as
its antecedent. Consider, first, (37), where *zibun* in the embedded clause is
bound to the nonsubject *Ziro*.

(37)   Taroo-wa Ziroo$_i$-kara [$_S$ Hanako-ga   zibun$_i$-o nikunde-iru
       Taro-Top Ziro-from   Hanako-Nom self-Acc hate
       to]   kiita.
       Comp heard
       "Taro heard from Ziro$_i$ (that): 'Hanako hates me$_i$.'"

To explain such nonsubject *zibun*-binding, Kuno (1973) argues that *zibun* can take a nonsubject NP as its referent if the clause containing *zibun* describes his or her internal feeling or thought. Given Kuno's analysis, *zibun*-binding to the nonsubject *Ziro* in (37) is possible because the embedded clause that contains *zibun* expresses *Ziro*'s internal feeling. Kuno supports this hypothesis by presenting a contrast such as the one between (37) and (38).

(38) *Taroo-ga Ziroo$_i$-ni [$_S$ Hanako-ga zibun$_i$-o nikunde-iru to] itta.
    Taro-Nom Ziro-Dat Hanako-Nom self-Acc hates Comp said
    "Taro said to Ziro$_i$ (that): 'Hanako hates me$_i$.'"

According to Kuno, the interpretation of the first person pronoun in the direct quotation form of an embedded clause can tell us whose internal feeling the embedded clause in question expresses.[23] As shown by the English translations above, the first person pronoun of the direct quotation form in (37) is understood to be Ziro. The embedded clause in (37) represents Ziro's internal feeling, and *zibun*-binding to the nonsubject NP *Ziro* is possible. By contrast, in (38), the first person pronoun is understood to be Taro. The embedded clause represents Taro's internal feeling, and *zibun*-binding to *Ziro* is ungrammatical. Kuno calls this analysis the Direct Discourse Analysis of *zibun*.

Another context where *zibun* can take a nonsubject NP as its antecedent involves a psych-verb (N. A. McCawley 1976). For instance, consider (21a), repeated here as (39), which involves the psych-verb *nayamaseta* "worried."[24]

(39) [$_{NP}$[$_S$ Zibun$_i$-ga gan kamosirenai koto]-ga Hirosi$_i$-o
        self-Nom cancer may Comp-Nom Hiroshi-Acc
    nayamaseta.
    worried
    "That he$_i$ might have cancer worried Hiroshi$_i$." (N. A. McCawley 1976: 63)

Kuno extends the above line of analysis to *zibun*-binding with a psych-verb as in (39). Given Kuno, the constituent that includes *zibun* in (39) (i.e. the whole subject NP) represents *Hiroshi*'s internal feeling. Hence, *zibun*-binding to the nonsubject NP *Hiroshi* is allowed.

The notion of logophoricity is also used to account for nonsubject *zibun*-binding cases as in (37) and (39) (Kuno 1978b, Kameyama 1984, 1985, Iida and Sells 1986, Sells 1987). A logophoric individual is understood to be someone other than the speaker whose speech, thoughts, feelings, or general state of consciousness are reported or reflected in the linguistic context in which a logophoric expression occurs (Clements 1975: 141). Kameyama (1984, 1985), for instance, explores an analysis of *zibun*-binding based on the features of [±sub] and [±log]. She argues that *zibun* can take as its antecedent either an element associated with the feature of [+sub] (a grammatical subject) or one associated with the feature of [+log] (a logophoric individual). Given Kameyama's analysis, the nonsubject *zibun*-binding cases in (37) and (39) are explained as follows. The embedded clause containing *zibun* in (37) reflects Ziro's feeling. Thus, Ziro can be considered to be a logophoric individual and so, *zibun*-binding to *Ziro* is grammatical. The object NP *Hiroshi* in (39) is also considered to be marked as [+log] because the clause containing *zibun* reflects his feeling. Hence, *zibun*-binding to *Hiroshi* is grammatical.

Next, let us examine cases where *zibun*-binding to a subject NP is ruled out. First, compare (21b), repeated here as (40a), and (40b).

(40) a. *John$_i$-wa Mary-ga   zibun$_i$-o <u>korosita</u> toki, Jane-to
         John-Top Mary-Nom self-Acc killed   when Jane-with
         nete-ita.
         was sleeping
         "John$_i$ was in bed with Jane when Mary killed him$_i$." (Kuno
         1973: 310)

     b. John$_i$-wa Mary-ga   zibun$_i$-o <u>korosoo to sita</u> toki, Jane-to
         John-Top Mary-Nom self-Acc tried to kill   when Jane-with
         nete-ita.
         was sleeping
         "John$_i$ was in bed with Jane when Mary tried to kill self$_i$." (Kuno
         1973: 309)

(40a) and (40b) are structurally parallel. But *zibun*-binding in (40a) is ungrammatical whereas that in (40b) is grammatical. The ungrammaticality of (40b), as opposed to the grammaticality of (40a), cannot be explained on the basis of the subject antecedent condition.

To explain such a contrast, Kuno (1973) proposes the Awareness Condition on *zibun*-binding, which roughly states that the referent of *zibun* must be aware of the event or situation in question.[25] Kuno's Awareness Condition explains the contrast between (40a) and (40b) as follows. In (40a), the verb *korosita* "killed" occurs in the *when*-clause. John could not be aware of the event that Mary killed him at the time she killed him. Accordingly, *zibun*-binding to *John* is ungrammatical. By contrast, in (40b), the verb *korosoo to sita* "tried to kill" occurs in the *when*-clause. John could be aware of the state that Mary tried to kill him at the time of her trying to kill him. Hence, *zibun*-binding to *John* is grammatical.

The notion of empathy is also claimed to affect *zibun*-binding (Kuno 1976c, 1978b, Kuno and Kaburaki 1977). Empathy concerns the issue of with whom the speaker identifies himself or herself in describing a given event or state, and it indicates the speaker's position in relation to a particular participant in the event or state described.[26] Kuno and Kaburaki (1977), for instance, argue that *zibun* is an empathy-loaded expression and its referent must be someone with whom the speaker empathizes. Consider, for instance, (41), which is taken from Iida (1996: 46).

(41) a. *Taroo$_i$-wa [Hanako-ga zibun$_i$-ni yatta] okane-o
      Taro-Top Hanako-Nom self-Dat gave money-Acc
      tukatte-simatta.
      use-Perfective
      "Taro$_i$ has used the money that Hanako gave to self$_i$."
   b. Taroo$_i$-wa [Hanako-ga zibun$_i$-ni kureta] okane-o
      Taro-Top Hanako-Nom self-Dat gave money-Acc
      tukatte-simatta.
      use-Perfective
      "Taro$_i$ has used the money that Hanako gave to self$_i$."

The underlined verbs in (41) are giving verbs. Like the case in (40), (41a) and
(41b) are structurally parallel. Yet, *zibun*-binding in (41a) is ungrammatical
whereas *zibun*-binding in (41b) is grammatical. Kuno and Kaburaki argue that
such a contrast cannot be explained on the basis of the syntactic subjecthood
condition, but it can be on that of the notion of empathy. According to Kuno
and Kaburaki, *yatta* "gave" in (41a) signals that the speaker empathizes with
the giver (i.e. *Hanako*), whereas *kureta* "gave" in (41b) signals that the speaker
empathizes with the receiver (i.e. *Taro*). In their analysis, the referent of *zibun*
must be someone with whom the speaker empathizes. *Zibun*-binding to *Taro*
in (41a) then shows that the speaker's empathy is with Taro. But this empathy
relation conflicts with the one signaled by *yatta*. Accordingly, *zibun*-binding in
(41a) is ungrammatical. By contrast, (41b) involves no conflict in the speaker's
empathy: both *zibun*-binding and *kureta* signal that the speaker's empathy is
with Taro. Hence, *zibun*-binding in (41b) is grammatical.
   As seen above, many researchers have explored analyses that resort to different kinds of pragmatic notions. Note, however, that there is one thing in
common among them, namely, they all presuppose that a pragmatic condition
applies to *zibun*-binding only when the subject antecedent condition fails to
explain. That is, as Iida (1996) points out, pragmatic condition(s) are considered
to be secondary to the syntactic subjecthood condition, and in this respect, these
analyses can be characterized as a disjunctive approach to *zibun*-binding.

3.2 Conjunctive theory of **zibun**-binding: Iida (1996)

Recently, Iida (1996) has explored an analysis of *zibun*-binding that stands out
from previous studies. Her analysis stands out because it applies both a syntactic condition and a discourse condition to every instance of *zibun*-binding.
Iida characterizes her analysis as a conjunctive approach to *zibun*-binding. One
immediate consequence of her conjunctive approach is that the power of a
syntactic condition is greatly reduced. Unlike previous analyses, Iida's syntactic condition on *zibun*-binding does not make any reference to the notion
of subjecthood. Instead, it is stated in terms of a coargument relation between
zibun and its antecedent. Informally, her syntactic condition states that *zibun*

may not take a more oblique argument as its referent.[27] Within the framework of Head-Driven Phrase Structure Grammar, arguments of a verb are assumed to hold a certain hierarchy of obliqueness, and a subject is assumed to be the least oblique argument. For instance, the object NP is more oblique than the subject NP in (42). Thus, *zibun*-binding in (42a), where *zibun* is bound to the less oblique argument (i.e. the subject NP), satisfies Iida's syntactic condition, but *zibun*-binding in (42b), where *zibun* is bound to the more oblique argument (i.e. the object NP), violates her condition.[28]

(42)   a.   Taroo$_i$-ga zibun$_i$-o hihansita.
            Taro-Nom self-Acc criticized
            "Taro$_i$ criticized self$_i$."
       b.   *Zibun$_i$-ga Taroo$_i$-o hihansita.
            Self-Nom Taro-Acc criticized
            "Self$_i$ criticized Taro$_i$."

Iida's discourse condition, on the other hand, is based on the notion of deictic perspective. She claims that "the antecedent of *zibun* is understood as the reference point which the speaker chooses in describing the situation in question" (Iida 1996: 163). Thus, in her analysis, the antecedent of *zibun* must have perspective, and *zibun*-binding signals from whose perspective the speaker is describing a given situation. Iida supports this hypothesis on the basis of similarities between the binding behavior of *zibun* and the interpretations of deictic expressions such as *migi* "(on) the right (of)." First, consider (43), which involves the deictic expression *migi*.

(43)   (Situation: Taro and Hanako are standing fact to face)
       Taroo$_i$-wa Hanako$_j$-ni zitensya-o migi-ni ok-ase-ta.
       Taro-Top Hanako-Dat bicycle-Acc right-to put-Cause-Past
       a.   "Taro$_i$ made Hanako$_j$ put the bicycle to his$_i$ right."
       b.   "Taro$_i$ made Hanako$_j$ put the bicycle to her$_j$ right." (Iida 1996: 164)

The deictic expression *migi* in (43) can be ambiguously interpreted either as "Taro's right" or "Hanako's right." This ambiguity, however, disappears once the sentence involves *zibun*-binding as shown in (44).

(44)   Taroo$_i$-wa Hanako$_j$-ni zibun$_j$-no zitensya-o migi-ni ok-ase-ta.
       Taro-Top Hanako-Dat self-Gen bicycle-Acc right-to put-Cause-Past
       a.   ??"Taro$_i$ made Hanako$_j$ put her$_j$ bicycle to his$_i$ right."
       b.   "Taro$_i$ made Hanako$_j$ put her$_j$ bicycle to her$_j$ right." (Iida 1996: 164)

Given Iida's analysis, the referent of *zibun* is assumed to be the one who has perspective. *Zibun*-binding to *Hanako* in (44) thus signals that the speaker describes the situation from Hanako's perspective. The deictic expression *migi* in (44a), however, is interpreted from Taro's perspective. Iida assumes with

Fillmore (1975) that there can be only one perspective in a specified domain. She ascribes the awkwardness of (44a) to the fact that the sentence involves the two different perspectives. (44b), on the other hand, is grammatical because the sentence under this interpretation involves only one perspective (i.e. Hanako's perspective). She argues that data such as in (44) show that *zibun* is in nature similar to deictic expressions and that the referent of *zibun* must be the one who has perspective.

Recall here that Iida's syntactic condition makes no reference to the syntactic notion of subjecthood, and her syntactic condition alone cannot explain a contrast such as that in (45).

(45) Taroo$_i$-ga Hanako$_j$-ni zibun$_{i/*j}$-no ayamati-o   hanasita.
      Taro-Nom Hanako-Dat self-Gen   mistake-Acc told
      "Taro$_i$ told Hanako$_j$ self's$_{i/*j}$ mistake."

In (45), both the subject NP *Taro* and the dative NP *Hanako* are less oblique than *zibun*. Thus, Iida's syntactic condition is met in both cases of *zibun*-binding. However, her discourse condition correctly rules out *zibun*-binding to *Hanako*, while rendering *zibun*-binding to *Taro* grammatical. According to Iida, a subject NP is one of the default possibilities that can have perspective, and the subject's perspective is, in principle, always available. Thus, the subject *Taro* in (45) can be understood as having perspective, but the dative object *Hanako* cannot. Hence, only *zibun*-binding to *Taro* is licensed. In Iida's system, *zibun*'s alleged property of subject orientation is explained in terms of the discourse function of a subject NP, not in terms of subjecthood.

One advantage of Iida's conjunctive approach over a disjunctive approach is that it can explain a contrast such as that in (46). Sample (ia) in n. 28 is repeated here as (46a).

(46) a.   Zibun$_i$-no zitu-no musuko-ga Taroo$_i$-o kurusimete-iru.
          self-Gen   real-Gen son-Nom   Taro-Acc annoys
          "His$_i$ own son annoys Taro$_i$."
      b.   *Zibun$_i$-ga Taroo$_i$-o kurusimete-iru.
          self-Nom Taro-Acc annoys
          (lit.) "Self$_i$ annoys Taro$_i$." (Iida 1996: 98)

As mentioned briefly above, analyses proposed under a disjunctive approach apply the subjecthood condition and a discourse condition independently wherever they are applicable. For instance, recall Kameyama's analysis of *zibun*-binding discussed in section 3.1. Under her analysis, subject *zibun*-binding is explained on the basis of the feature of [+sub] (i.e. a grammatical subject), and nonsubject *zibun*-binding on that of the feature of [+log] (i.e. a logophoric individual). Given her analysis, then, (46a) is grammatical because it reports Taro's internal feeling. Taro is considered to be a logophoric individual and hence *zibun*-binding to *Taro* is allowed. But this line of analysis fails to explain the ungrammaticality of (46b), which also reports Taro's feeling. If the notion of logophoricity is all that matters for nonsubject *zibun*-binding, *zibun*-binding to *Taro* in (46b) should be grammatical, contrary to the fact. The disjunctive approach thus cannot provide a satisfactory explanation of the contrast in (46).

Iida's conjunctive approach, on the other hand, explains the contrast in (46) as follows: her discourse condition is met in (46), because the speaker takes Taro's perspective in both cases. Her syntactic condition, however, rules out *zibun*-binding in (46b) while rendering *zibun*-binding in (46a) grammatical. In (46b), *zibun* is bound to the more oblique argument *Taro*. *Zibun*-binding in (46b) violates her syntactic condition, resulting in ungrammaticality. *Zibun* and *Taro* in (46a), by contrast, do not hold a coargument relation, and *zibun*-binding here is not subject to Iida's condition, resulting in grammaticality.

Another advantage of Iida's conjunctive approach over the disjunctive approach can be seen in data involving multiple *zibun*. Consider (47).

(47)   Taroo-wa [Hanako-ga   zibun-no heya-de zibun-no sigoto-o
       Taro-Top   Hanako-Nom self-Gen   room-in self-Gen job-Acc
       site-ita   to]   itta.
       was-doing Comp said
   a.   Taro said that Hanako was doing his work in his room.
   b.   Taro said that Hanako was doing her work in her room.
   c.   *Taro said that Hanako was doing his work in her room.
   d.   *Taro said that Hanako was doing her work in his room. (Iida 1996:
        80; originally from Howard and Niyekawa-Howard 1976)

As observed in Howard and Niyekawa-Howard (1976), when a sentence contains two instances of *zibun* as in (47), the two *zibun* in question must share the same referent. Thus, sentence (47) can induce the interpretations of (47a–b), but it cannot induce the interpretations of (47c–d). As Iida argues, if a syntactic mechanism and a pragmatic one were to apply disjunctively to *zibun*, the two occurrences of *zibun* in (47) should be able to take two different antecedents and therefore the interpretations in (47c–d) should be available.

Iida's conjunctive approach explains the contrast between (47a–b) and (47c–d) as follows. Her syntactic condition applies to (47) but it has nothing to say about the contrast between (47a–b) and (47c–d): *Taro* and *zibun* are not subcategorized by the same verb. So, *zibun*-binding to *Taro* is not subject to Iida's condition. As for *zibun*-binding to *Hanako*, since *Hanako* is the least oblique argument in the embedded clause, *zibun*-binding to *Hanako* satisfies Iida's condition.[29]

Iida's discourse condition, however, makes the interpretations in (47a–b) available while rendering those in (47c–d) unavailable. As mentioned in (44), the speaker can take only one perspective in describing a given situation. The interpretations in (47a–b) require the speaker to take just one person's perspective to describe the situation, whereas those in (47c–d) require the speaker to take both Taro's perspective and Hanako's. Accordingly, the interpretations in (47a–b) are available but those in (47c–d) are not. Iida argues that data with multiple *zibun* such as those in (47) provide evidence that the conjunctive approach is the right one for *zibun*-binding.

4   Complex Reflexives in Japanese

So far, we have concentrated on *zibun*-binding. In this section, we examine the nature of the complex reflexives, *zibun-zisin* and *kare-zisin*. I first present their basic properties and then examine two analyses of these reflexives, Katada (1988, 1991) and Aikawa (1993).[30]

4.1   Basic properties of zibun-zisin *and* kare-zisin

The two complex reflexives, like *zibun*, are subject to the c-command require-ment. For instance, *Taro* in (48) is embedded in the larger NP and cannot c-command *zibun-zisin/kare-zisin*, but the whole subject NP, *Taroo-no sensee*, "Taro's teacher," can, resulting in the contrast.

(48)   a. $[_{NP}$ Taroo$_i$-no sensee]$_j$-ga   zibun-zisin$_{*i/j}$-o hihansita.
              Taro-Gen teacher-Nom self-self-Acc   criticized
              "[Taro$_i$'s teacher]$_j$ criticized self-self$_{*i/j}$."
        b. $[_{NP}$ Taroo$_i$-no sensee]$_j$-ga   kare-zisin$_{*i/j}$-o hihansita.
              Taro-Gen teacher-Nom he-self-Acc   criticized
              "[Taro$_i$'s teacher]$_j$ criticized he-self$_{*i/j}$."

However, unlike *zibun*, the two complex reflexives cannot participate in LD-binding (Nakamura 1987, Katada 1988, 1991).[31] For instance, consider (49).

(49)   Taroo$_i$-ga [Ziroo$_j$-ga zibun-zisin$_{*i/j}$/kare-zisin$_{*i/j}$-o   semeta
        Taro-Nom Ziro-Nom self-self   /he-self   -Acc blamed
        to]   itta.
        Comp said
        "Taroo$_i$ said that Ziro$_j$ blamed self-self$_{*i/j}$/he-self$_{*i/j}$."

In (49), only the embedded subject *Ziro*, not the matrix subject *Taro*, can ante-cede *zibun-zisin/kare-zisin*.

Although the two complex reflexives are the same with respect to the c-command requirement and their locality, they exhibit different properties in other respects. First, *zibun-zisin* requires no agreement in phi-features with its antecedent, whereas *kare-zisin* does, as exemplified in (50).

(50) a. Taroo$_i$/Hanako$_j$/[$_{NP}$Taroo-to Hanako]$_k$-ga zibun-zisin$_{i/j/k}$-o
           Taro /Hanako   Taro-and Hanako-Nom self-self   -Acc
           semeta.
           blamed
           "Taro$_i$/Hanako$_j$/[Taroo and Hanako]$_k$ blamed self-self$_{i/j/k}$."
      b. Taroo$_i$/Hanako$_j$/[$_{NP}$Taroo-to Hanako]$_k$-ga kare-zisin$_{i/*j/*k}$-o
           Taro /Hanako   Taro-and Hanako-Nom he-self   -Acc
           semeta.
           blamed
           "Taro$_i$/Hanako$_j$/[Taroo and Hanako]$_k$ blamed he-self$_{i/*j/*k}$."

The difference above can be ascribed to the difference in phi-feature specification between the *zibun* part of *zibun-zisin* and the *kare* part of *kare-zisin*: *zibun*
lacks its phi-feature specification, whereas *kare* "he" bears the phi-features of
[+3rd person, +singular, +male]. From this, the contrast in (50) naturally follows.
    Second, the two complex reflexives are different with respect to their subject
orientation: *zibun-zisin* is subject-oriented but *kare-zisin* is not, as shown in (51).

(51) a. Taroo$_i$-ga Ziroo$_j$-ni zibun-zisin$_{i/*j}$-nituite hanasita.
           Taro-Nom Ziro-Dat self-self   -about told
           "Taro$_i$ told Ziro$_j$ about self-self$_{i/*j}$."
      b. Taroo$_i$-ga Ziroo$_j$-ni kare-zisin$_{i/j}$-nituite hanasita.
           Taro-Nom Ziro-Dat he-self   -about told
           "Taro$_i$ told Ziro$_j$ about he-self$_{i/j}$."

Again, we can ascribe this contrast to the difference between *zibun* and *kare*:
zibun is subject-oriented while *kare* is not. Hence, there is a contrast in subject
orientation between *zibun-zisin* and *kare-zisin*.
    Third, the two reflexives under consideration are different with respect to
the type of NP that they can take as their antecedent.

(52) a. Daremo$_i$-ga   zibun-zisin$_i$-o hihansita.
           everyone-Nom self-self-Acc   criticized
           "Everyone$_i$ criticized self-self$_i$."
      b. *Daremo$_i$-ga   kare-zisin$_i$-o hihansita.
           everyone-Nom he-self-Acc   criticized
           "Everyone$_i$ criticized he-self$_i$."

In (52), the QP, *daremo* "everyone," occurs as the antecedent of *zibun-zisin*/*kare-
zisin*. As shown, *zibun-zisin* can take a QP antecedent but *kare-zisin* cannot.
This is predicted, given the fact that *zibun* can be a bound variable but *kare*
cannot (see section 2.1).[32] As shown, differences in binding behavior between
zibun-zisin and *kare-zisin* can be ascribed to the differences in lexical properties
between *zibun* and *kare* (cf. Nakamura 1987).[33]

4.2 Katada's (1988, 1991) unified analysis of the three reflexives

Katada (1988, 1991) explores a unified analysis of the three reflexives in Japanese by extending her LF-analysis of *zibun* to *zibun-zisin* and *kare-zisin*. In so doing, she first distinguishes the complex reflexives from *zibun* on the basis of a difference in their internal structures. Examine (53), which presents Katada's analysis of the internal structures of the three reflexives.

(53)

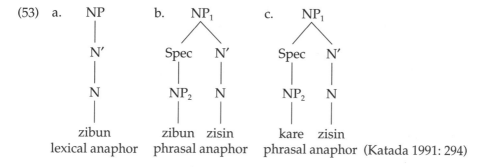

a. NP / N' / N / zibun / lexical anaphor b. NP₁ / Spec N' / NP₂ N / zibun zisin / phrasal anaphor c. NP₁ / Spec N' / NP₂ N / kare zisin / phrasal anaphor (Katada 1991: 294)

Katada characterizes *zibun* as a lexical anaphor and the two complex reflexives as phrasal anaphors. Recall that under Katada's analysis, *zibun* raises to a higher position(s) in LF through VP-adjunction and this LF-raising of *zibun* is unlimited, so that *zibun* can participate in LD-binding (see section 2.2). LF-raising of *zibun* out of *zibun-zisin*, however, is limited. Katada argues that in the case of *zibun-zisin*, what raises is only the *zibun* part, not the entire *zibun-zisin* as schematized in (54).

(54) John$_i$-ga [Bill$_j$-ga zibun-zisin$_{*i/j}$-o semeta to] itta.
John-Nom Bill-Nom self-self-Acc blamed Comp said
"John$_i$ said that Bill$_j$ blamed himself$_{*i/j}$."
Katada's LF-analysis of *Zibun-zisin*

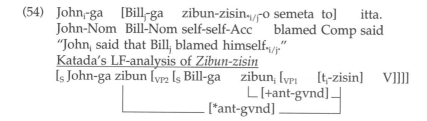

[$_S$ John-ga zibun [$_{VP2}$ [$_S$ Bill-ga zibun$_i$ [$_{VP1}$ [t$_i$-zisin] V]]]]
⌐ [+ant-gvnd] ⌐
⌐_____ [*ant-gvnd] _____⌐

According to Katada, the trace of *zibun* extracted from *zibun-zisin* in the embedded clause of (54) cannot be lexically governed because there is no genitive case marker here.[34] Then, this trace must be antecedent-governed by *zibun* in order to satisfy the Empty Category Principle (N. Chomsky 1981a).[35] LF-raising of *zibun* to the embedded VP allows the trace in question to be antecedent-governed, but LF-raising of *zibun* to the matrix VP does not, as shown above. Accordingly, LD-binding of *zibun-zisin* is not possible.

Zibun-zisin's subject orientation, just like the case in *zibun*-binding, is explained on the basis of the asymmetric c-command relation displayed between a subject NP and a nonsubject NP with respect to the landing site of the *zibun* part of *zibun-zisin*.

As for the binding behavior of *kare-zisin*, Katada argues that *kare-zisin* does not undergo any LF-movement because it possesses the specified phi-features of [+3rd, +singular, +male]. *Kare-zisin* must be interpreted in situ and from this, the unavailability of LD-binding for *kare-zisin* naturally follows. The hypothesis that *kare-zisin* does not undergo LF-movement also explains the absence of the property of subject orientation in *kare-zisin*: *kare-zisin*, being interpreted in situ, can be c-commanded either by a dative NP, if any, or by a subject NP as schematized in (55). Hence, *kare-zisin* exhibits no property of subject orientation.

(55)   ... NP$_i$-ga [$_{VP}$ ... NP$_j$-ni ... [kare-zisin]$_{i/j}$ ...] ...   (Katada 1991: 299 with modification)

As shown, Katada ascribes the differences in binding behavior among the three reflexives to the differences in their LF-movements: LF-raising of (bare) *zibun* is unlimited and so *zibun* can participate in LD-binding. By contrast, LF-raising of *zibun* out of *zibun-zisin* is limited only to the local VP and hence *zibun-zisin* is a local anaphor. The property of subject orientation that these two reflexives exhibit is explained on the basis of the asymmetric c-command relation displayed by subject NPs and nonsubject NPs with respect to the landing site(s) of *zibun*. *Kare-zisin*, on the other hand, does not undergo LF-raising. Hence, neither LD-binding nor subject orientation is available for it.

4.3   **Zibun-zisin** *as a reflexivizer: Aikawa (1993)*

Aikawa (1993) explores yet another type of approach to the distinction between *zibun* and *zibun-zisin*. Following Reinhart and Reuland (1993) (R&R), she characterizes *zibun-zisin* as a reflexivizer and *zibun* as a non-reflexivizer. Since her analysis is largely dependent on R&R's analysis of reflexivity, we will first look at their analysis.

R&R distinguish morphologically complex anaphors (SELF anaphors) from morphologically simplex ones (SE anaphors) on the basis of their functions. They argue that SELF anaphors can function as reflexivizers but SE anaphors cannot. Informally, the function of a reflexivizer is to impose identity between coarguments of a predicate, and the occurrence of a reflexivizer in the reflexivity domain of a predicate (i.e. Theta-grid positions of a predicate) is expected to license the reflexivity of the predicate in question. Thus, in R&R's analysis, only SELF anaphors, not SE anaphors, can license the reflexivity of predicates. Consider, for instance, (56), which involves the two types of Dutch anaphors, *zichzelf* "self-self" and *zich* "self."

(56) a.   Max$_i$ haat zichzelf$_i$.
           "Max hates SELF." (Reinhart and Reuland 1993: 661)
      b.   *Max$_i$ haat zich$_i$.
           "Max hates SE." (Reinhart and Reuland 1993: 665)

As shown, the occurrence of *zichzelf* can induce the reflexive interpretation of
a predicate but the occurrence of *zich* cannot.

It is important to note that under R&R's analysis, the reflexivity of a predicate can also be licensed by the intrinsic (lexical) reflexivity of a predicate. For
instance, consider (57), taken from R&R.

(57) Max schaamt$_{[+reflexive]}$ zich.
          shames   SE
      "Max is ashamed." (Reinhart and Reuland 1993: 666)

According to R&R, the predicate in (57) is intrinsically reflexive and this lexical reflexivity of the predicate can license its reflexivity. This is why (57) is
grammatical without the occurrence of SELF. In R&R's system, not only the
type of anaphor (i.e. SELF or SE) but also the type of predicate (i.e. intrinsically reflexive or not) plays an important role for licensing the reflexivity of
predicates.

Returning to Aikawa (1993), she presents data such as (58) to support the
hypothesis that *zibun-zisin*, but not *zibun*, can function as a reflexivizer. Examine
(58), which involves the interaction between a QP antecedent and the two
reflexives under consideration.

(58) a.   Dareka$_i$-ga   zibun-zisin$_i$/?*zibun$_i$-o tunetta.
           someone-Nom self-self   /self-Acc   pinched
           "Someone$_i$ pinched zibun-zisin$_i$/?*zibun$_i$."
      b.   Daremo$_i$-ga   zibun-zisin$_i$/?*zibun$_i$-o hagemasita.
           everyone-Nom self-self   /self-Acc   encouraged
           "Everyone$_i$ encouraged zibun-zisin$_i$/?*zibun$_i$." (Aikawa 1993: 42 with
           modification)

Aikawa assumes with R&R that the reflexivity of a predicate can be licensed
only through the relationship of variable binding between two arguments of
a predicate. Thus, in her analysis, if an expression x is a reflexivizer and if it
occurs in the reflexivity domain of a predicate, x is expected to be construed as
a bound variable. Aikawa argues that the ungrammaticality of *zibun*-binding in
(58) shows that *zibun* cannot be construed as a bound variable in the reflexivity
domain of a predicate, and as such, it cannot be a reflexivizer. By contrast,
the grammaticality of *zibun-zisin*-binding in (58) shows that *zibun-zisin* in the
reflexivity domain of a predicate can be construed as a bound variable and
hence can be a reflexivizer. She argues that data such as those in (58) support
the hypothesis that Japanese has only one reflexivizer, namely, *zibun-zisin*.

She continues to argue that the strict locality of *zibun-zisin* can be ascribed to the function of *zisin* as a reflexivizer: reflexivity is a matter of the relationship between coarguments of a predicate and it must be licensed locally. The function of *zisin* as a reflexivizer then imposes strict locality on *zibun-zisin*.

As for subject orientation, Aikawa explains it on the basis of the binding relation between the *zibun* part of *zibun-zisin* and Agr: *zibun* of *zibun-zisin*, just like (bare) *zibun*, is expected to be bound to the first accessible Agr in LF for interpretation.

Note that Katada's analysis fails to explain a contrast such as that in (58): her analysis predicts no difference in grammaticality between binding of *zibun-zisin* and local binding of *zibun*. For instance, given her analysis, the *zibun* part of *zibun-zisin* and the bare *zibun* in (58) are both expected to adjoin to the VP at LF. Thus, both binding of *zibun-zisin* and that of *zibun* in (58) are expected to be grammatical. By contrast, Aikawa's analysis, as just seen above, can provide an explanation of such a contrast by making reference to the difference in functions between *zibun-zisin* and *zibun*, and in this respect, Aikawa's analysis is more advantageous than Katada's.

Another advantage of Aikawa's analysis over Katada's can be seen in the contrast between (58) and (59) with respect to the grammaticality of *zibun*-binding. Consider (59).

(59) a. Daremo$_i$-ga   [zibun$_i$-no kodomo]-o tunetta.
          everyone-Nom self-Gen child-Acc pinched
          "Everyone$_i$ pinched self$_i$'s child."
      b. Daremo$_i$-ga   [John-ga   zibun$_i$-o tunetta to]   itta.
          everyone-Nom John-Nom self-Acc pinched Comp said
          "Everyone$_i$ said that John pinched self$_i$." (Aikawa 1993: 43 with modification)

Zibun in (59a) is embedded in the larger NP and *zibun* in (59b) is LD-bound. As shown, once *zibun* gets outside the reflexivity domain, *zibun*-binding to a QP becomes acceptable. Nothing in Katada's system can explain the contrast in grammaticality between *zibun*-binding in (58) and that in (59). Aikawa's analysis, by contrast, can provide an explanation of this contrast: *zibun*, by nature, is capable of being construed as a bound variable and hence *zibun*-binding to the QP in (59) is possible. But in (58), *zibun* occurs inside the reflexivity domain. Aikawa argues that once *zibun* occurs inside the reflexivity domain, because of its inability to function as a reflexivizer, *zibun* cannot be a bound variable. Accordingly, *zibun*-binding to the QP in (58) is ungrammatical.

At this point, one might wonder how her analysis of *zibun* explains the grammaticality of sentences like (60).

(60) Daremo$_i$-ga   zibun$_i$-o hihansita/semeta.
      everyone-Nom self-Acc criticized/blamed
      "Everyone$_i$ criticized/blamed self$_i$."

In (60), *zibun* occurs with the QP antecedent, and unlike in (58), *zibun*-binding to the QP antecedent here is acceptable. Aikawa explains the grammaticality of (60), analogous to R&R's account of (57). She argues that the predicates in (60) are listed in the lexicon both as reflexive and as nonreflexive and that the intrinsic reflexivity of the reflexive entries can license their reflexivity. Accordingly, (60) is grammatical.

5 Remaining Problems

This section discusses some of the remaining problems concerning *zibun*-binding. One problem concerns the binding behavior of local *zibun* as in (61).

(61) a.   Taro$_i$-ga   zibun$_i$-o hihansita/semeta.
             Taro-Nom self-Acc criticized/blamed
             "Taro$_i$ criticized/blamed himself$_i$."
       b. ??/?*Taro$_i$-ga   zibun$_i$-o nagutta/tataita/ketta.
             Taro-Nom self-Acc hit   /hit   /kicked
             "Taro$_i$ hit/hit/kicked himself$_i$."

As was mentioned in section 2.1, the grammaticality of local binding of *zibun* varies, depending on the type of predicate that *zibun* occurs with. The standard BT has no way to explain such varied grammaticality of local *zibun*: if *zibun* is categorized as anaphor, the ungrammaticality of a sentence like (61b) would be problematic for Condition A. But if it is categorized as pronominal, the grammaticality of a sentence like (61a) would be problematic for Condition B. Although this phenomenon of *zibun*-binding has been noted in the literature for quite some time (cf. N. A. McCawley 1976, Oshima 1979, Takezawa 1989, Ueda 1986, Y. Kitagawa 1986, among others), the question of why such varied grammaticality arises for local binding of *zibun* has never been answered in a systematic way.[36]

Note that the pragmatic approach to *zibun*-binding also cannot explain such phenomenon of local binding of *zibun*. For instance, recall Kuno's Awareness Condition that we saw in section 3.1. Taro in (61) must have been aware of his own action, regardless of the type of activity that the verb denotes here. Thus, Kuno's Awareness Condition does not provide a satisfactory account. Iida's conjunctive approach cannot explain the contrast in (61), either: *zibun* is bound to the less oblique argument *Taro*. Thus her syntactic condition is met in both (61a) and (61b). Her discourse condition is also met because Taro, serving as the subject, has perspective. In short, regardless of whether we take a syntactic approach or a pragmatic approach, we have no way to explain the varied grammaticality of local binding of *zibun* in (61).

Recall also Ueda's observation concerning the data in (28), which involve the same kind of contrast observed in (61). He suggests that predicates that allow local binding of *zibun* involve abstract activities whereas those that preclude local binding of *zibun* involve physical activities. One way to capture Ueda's insight is to hypothesize that *zibun* cannot be associated with SELF in a concrete sense. For instance, the activities expressed by the predicates in (61b) affect some body part(s) of the referent of *zibun* in one way or another and in this respect, *zibun* involves SELF in a concrete sense. By contrast, the activities expressed by the predicates in (61a) concern Taro's personality, thought(s), deed(s), etc., rather than Taro's physical body part(s) and in this respect, *zibun* involves SELF in an abstract sense. Thus, it is plausible to assume that the semantic constraint on local *zibun* mentioned above is responsible for the varied grammaticality of local binding of *zibun*.

At this point, one might argue that the reason why (61b) resists local binding of *zibun* is that predicates of the type in (61b) select a body-part NP as their object. As evidence, once a body-part object is inserted, (61b) becomes grammatical as in (62).

(62) Taroo-ga (zibun-no) migi asi-o   nagutta/tataita/ketta.
      Taro-Nom self-Gen   right leg-Acc hit   /hit   /kicked
      "Taro hit/hit/kicked (his) right leg."

The grammaticality of (63), however, indicates that these predicates do not have to take a body-part object.

(63) a. Ziroo-wa sono tukue-o sotto tataita.
          Ziro-Top that desk-Acc softly hit
          "Ziro hit that desk softly."
      b. Hanako-ga   sono booru-o ketta.
          Hanako-Nom that ball-Acc kicked
          "Hanako kicked that ball."

It is important to note that the varied grammaticality of the sort that we saw in (61) disappears if *zibun* occurs in the possessor position of an object NP or in an embedded clause, as shown in (64) and (65).

(64) Taro$_i$-ga   [$_{NP}$ zibun$_i$-no kodomo]-o nagutta/tataita/ketta.
      Taro-Nom   self-Gen child-Acc   hit   /hit   /kicked
      "Taro$_i$ hit/hit/kicked his$_i$ child."

(65) Taroo$_i$-ga [$_S$ Hanako-ga   zibun$_i$-o nagutta/tataita/ketta to]   itta.
      Taro-Nom   Hanako-Nom self-Acc hit   /hit   /kicked Comp said
      "Taro$_i$ said that Hanako hit/hit/kicked him$_i$."

In (64), *zibun* occurs in the possessor position of the object NP, and in (65), it occurs in the embedded clause. In both cases, unlike in (61b), *zibun*-binding is acceptable. A similar pattern can be observed regarding *zibun*-binding to a QP antecedent. (66) illustrates this point.

(66) a. ??/?*Daremo$_i$-ga   zibun$_i$-o nagutta.
           everyone-Nom self-Acc hit
           "Everyone$_i$ hit himself$_i$."
      b.   Daremo$_i$-ga   [$_{NP}$ zibun$_i$-no kodomo]-o nagutta.
              everyone-Nom   self-Gen child-Acc hit
              "Everyone$_i$ hit his$_i$ child."
      c.   Daremo$_i$-ga   [$_S$ Hanako-ga   zibun$_i$-o nagutta to]   itta.
              everyone-Nom   Hanako-Nom self-Acc hit   Comp said
              "Everyone$_i$ said that Hanako hit him$_i$."

The data above then show that an important distinction to be made for *zibun*-binding is whether *zibun* occurs as an argument of a predicate or not. As just seen above, binding of argument *zibun* is affected by types of activities expressed by verbs but binding of nonargument *zibun* is consistently grammatical. Further, argument *zibun* is unstable with respect to variable binding but nonargument *zibun* is not.

The importance of the distinction of argument vs. nonargument for reflexive binding, in fact, is recognized in the traditional view on reflexivization. In traditional linguistics, reflexivization is understood as a property of predicates: that is, use a reflexive if the verb in question expresses a reflexive interpretation (cf. Jespersen 1933, Partee and Bach 1981). Put slightly differently, reflexivization is considered to be about the relationship between coarguments of a predicate.[37] Under the standard BT, however, the phenomenon of reflexivization is subsumed under Conditions A and B and we seem to have "an illusion" that elements called reflexives all concern this phenomenon. But this is clearly not true. To see this more concretely, take *zibun*-binding in (64) and (65). *Zibun* in these examples does not occur as an argument of the predicates, and *zibun*-binding here has nothing to do with reflexivization of the predicates. If we take reflexives literally as elements that concern reflexivization, nonargument *zibun* as in (64) and (65) cannot be a reflexive. The literature has been focusing on the issue of how LD-binding of *zibun* can be accommodated by conforming to the standard BT. But the data above rather point toward the hypothesis that what is crucial is the distinction of argument *zibun* vs. nonargument *zibun* and the theory of *zibun*-binding must make reference to this distinction, which is similar to the position that Iida (1996) takes.

Another problem concerns subject orientation of *zibun*. As seen in section 3, the subject antecedent condition on *zibun*-binding faces counterexamples, and subject orientation is highly controversial. But suppose that subject orientation is not valid as argued by Iida (1996). This hypothesis then may have a significant impact on other phenomena in Japanese. As mentioned at the outset of this chapter, *zibun*-binding has been used as a diagnostic test of subjecthood in Japanese and we saw that researchers have explored analyses of constructions such as causatives or indirect passives on the basis of this diagnosis. But if *zibun*-binding has nothing to do with subjecthood but rather something to do with pragmatic factor(s), as some scholars argue, re-examination of previous analyses of such constructions might be required. In order to shed more light on the grammar of Japanese, the validity of subject orientation should be further investigated.

NOTES

1   Reflexive binding seems to involve pragmatic condition(s) cross-linguistically. See, for instance, Clements (1975), Hyman and Comrie (1981), Kuno (1987), Sells (1987), and Zribi-Hertz (1989), among others.

2   For the syntactic approach to *zibun*-binding, see Kuroda (1965a), Oyakawa (1973, 1974), K. Inoue (1976b), N. A. McCawley (1976), Howard and Niyekawa-Howard (1976), Akmajian and Kitagawa (1976), C. Kitagawa (1981), N. Hasegawa (1981), Oshima (1979), Saito and Hoji (1983), Fukui (1984), Y. Kitagawa (1986), Ueda (1986), M. Nakamura (1987), Katada (1988, 1991), J. Abe (1991), and Aikawa (1993), among others. For the pragmatic approach, see Kuroda (1973), Kuno (1972b, 1973, 1976a, 1976c, 1978a, 1978b, 1986a, 1987), Kuno and Kaburaki (1977), Kameyama (1984, 1985), Iida and Sells (1986), Gunji (1987), Sells (1987), and Iida (1996), among others.

3   It should be noted that when *zibun* takes a plural NP as its antecedent, the sentence induces only a distributive reading, not a collective reading, as shown in (i) (cf. Ishii 1989, J. Abe 1991).

(i)   [_NP_Taro-to   Hanako]_i_-ga
          Taro and Hanako-Nom
      zibun_i_-o semeta.
      self-Acc blamed
      "[_NP_Taro and Hanako]_i_ blamed
      self_i_."

a.   on the distributive reading: Taro blamed himself and Hanako blamed herself.
b.   *on the collective reading: Taro and Hanako (collectively) blamed themselves.

4   Such usage of *zibun* is common in the dialects of the western part of Japan (e.g. Kansai dialect).

5   One might argue that the ungrammaticality of (17) is due to *zibun*'s property of subject orientation: one of the referents of the split antecedent in (17) is the nonsubject *Taro*. However, the following example, which is drawn from J. Abe (1991: 61), shows that this is not the case.

(i)   *Masao_i_-ga   [Yoichi_j_-ga
        Masao-Nom   Yoichi-Nom
        [zibun_i+j_-no syasin-ga
        self-Gen   picture-Nom
        uri-ni deteiru to]   omotte-iru
        be on sale   Comp think
        to]   itta.
        Comp said
        "Masao_i_ said that Yoichi_j_
        thought that a picture of
        themselves_i+j_ would be on
        sale."

The split antecedent in (i) consists of the two subject NPs (i.e. *Masao* and *Yoichi*). Yet *zibun*-binding here is impossible. Data such as (i) show that the ungrammaticality of (17) has nothing to do with the subject orientation of *zibun*.

6 Lasnik (1989) provides a helpful summary of the historical development of the standard BT. We refer to his work for more details on this topic.

7 The definition of governing category (GC) is stated as follows:

> α is the GC for β if and only if α is the minimal category containing β and a governor of β, where α = NP or S. (N. Chomsky 1981a: 188)

8 *Zibun* in (21b) is, in fact, bound to the topic NP *Taro* but this is not problematic if we assume that a topic NP is base-generated in the subject position, and then is topicalized as in (i):

(i) [Taro$_i$ [s   t$_i$ ...]
    ↑_____| (Topicalization)

9 See also Akmajian and Kitagawa (1976), Saito and Hoji (1983), Y. Kitagawa (1986), Farmer et al. (1986), M. Nakamura (1987), and J. Abe (1991), among others.

10 More precisely, Fukui claims that *zibun* is a resumptive pronoun in Japanese.

11 Fukui proposes the following for the distinction of A-subject vs. A'-subject in Japanese:

(i) A-subject: subject of a complement clause
(ii) A'-subject: matrix subject/ subject of an adjunct clause (Fukui 1984: 28)

12 Given Fukui's analysis, the embedded subject *Hanako* is in an A-position (see n. 11). Thus, *zibun*-binding to *Hanako* in (24b) is expected to be ruled out by Condition B. In fact, Fukui notes that this *zibun*-binding is hardly possible. However, many speakers consider such *zibun*-binding acceptable, and

this might be a potential problem for his analysis.

13 N. Chomsky (1982) introduces the features of [±anaphor] and [±pronominal] to categorize different types of NPs, including empty categories, as in (i):

(i)
a. Lexical anaphors, NP-trace → [+anaphoric, −pronominal]
b. Lexical pronominals, pro → [−anaphoric, +pronominal]
c. R-expressions, wh-trace → [−anaphoric, −pronominal]
d. PRO → [+anaphoric, +pronominal]

14 The semantic representations of the two types of readings for the VP in (26) are provided in (i) below:

(i) John$_i$ called his$_i$ mother. (= (26))
a. John (λx (x called x's mother)) (on the bound variable reading of *his*)
b. John (λx (x called John's mother)) (on the coreference reading of *his*)

Informally, (ia) says that whoever is assigned to x, that person x called his (= x's) mother. On the other hand, (ib) says that whoever is assigned to x, that person x called John's mother, not x's mother. The indexing system in syntax cannot encode this distinction between the two types of readings, and therefore it is hard to see the distinction under normal circumstances.

15 Ueda notes that *zibun* in (27a) can induce not only the sloppy reading but also the strict reading, which is contradictory to his analysis. He leaves this problem open.

16 In Williams (1980), the rule of predication is defined as: "coindex NP and X" (Williams 1980: 206), where "X" is the maximal projection of some head. For instance, the

subject predicate relation of the sentence, *John left*, can be indicated as follows: [John]$_{NPi}$ [left]$_{VPi}$.

17   Ueda (1986) stipulates this as a principle specific to Japanese.

18   Since Lebeaux (1983), a series of works has been done to argue for the LF-raising of so-called LD-anaphors. Different types of LF-movement have been proposed for LD-anaphors. See, for instance, Pica (1984, 1987), Battistella (1989), Cole et al. (1990), Huang and Tang (1989), and Koster and Reuland (1991), among others.

19   Katada assumes the following to explain the free extraction of *zibun*:

(i)   The trace of *zibun* can be lexically governed by Case hence the Empty Category Principle (N. Chomsky 1981a) [see n. 35] can always be satisfied;

(ii) Case marker stranding is allowed at LF in Japanese; and

(iii) Subjacency can be violated at LF (Huang 1982). (Katada 1991: 294–5)

20   Reinhart and Reuland (1991, 1992) argue that simplex anaphors (SE anaphors in their terminology) lack phi-features and the acquisition requirement of phi-features forces them to be associated with Agr°. Aikawa, however, argues that adopting their LF-movement analysis for *zibun*-binding is problematic. See Aikawa (1993) for more details.

21   Aikawa assumes with N. Chomsky (1992) that morphological features must be checked off by the head of a functional category (e.g. Agr, Tense, etc.) through spec-head agreement at LF and, in the case of the subject, its features must be checked in spec of Agr (Aikawa 1993: 165).

22   Hoji (1990) points out that the ungrammaticality of (35a) can be explained on the basis of Lasnik's (1986) generalization of referentiality hierarchy, which states that a less referential expression cannot bind a more referential one. *Zibun*, which lacks phi-feature specification, is assumed to be less referential than *kare*, which has the specified phi-features. As such, the ungrammaticality of (35a), in which the less referential *zibun* binds the more referential *kare*, is predicted.

23   It is assumed that a complement clause headed by *to* "that" can be used to represent one's direct speech, thoughts, and feelings (Kuno 1973).

24   Belletti and Rizzi (1988) argue that the surface subject of a psych-verb is the theme of the verb and it originates in the VP. Given this, then, the surface object *Hiroshi* in (39) can c-command the subject NP in the d-structure.

25   Kuno's Awareness Condition on *zibun*-binding is stated as follows:

Zibun in a constituent clause (A) is coreferential with a noun phrase (B) of the matrix sentence only if A represents an action or state that the referent of B is aware of at the time it takes place or has come to be aware of at some later time. (Kuno 1973: 322)

26   The notion of empathy differs from that of logophoricity in the following sense. Empathy encodes whose point of view the speaker is taking in describing a particular event or state, and this notion comes into play in explaining cases where subject *zibun*-binding is ruled out. Logophoricity, on the other hand, concerns whose feeling or thought is reported in the domain that contains

a logophoric expression, and it is used to explain cases of nonsubject *zibun*-binding.

27 Iida proposes the following as a minimal syntactic condition on *zibun*-binding:

   (i) *Zibun* may not "o-command" its antecedent. (Iida 1996: 117)

   (ii) Definition of O-command: Let Y and Z be synsem objects with Y referential, Y "o-commands" Z just in case Y is less oblique than some X that dominates Z. In case X = Z, Y is said to locally o-command Z. (Iida 1996: 115)

Her condition is based on the binding theory of Head-Driven Phrase Structure Grammar (HPSG). See Pollard and Sag (1994) or Iida (1996).

28 According to Iida, *zibun*-binding such as that in (i) below is not subject to her condition.

   (i) a. Zibun$_i$-no zitu-no
        self-Gen real-Gen
        musuko-ga Taroo$_i$-o
        son-Nom Taro-Acc
        kurusimeteiru.
        annoy
        "His$_i$ own son annoys Taro$_i$."

      b. Zibun$_i$-ga Taroo$_i$-nitotte
        self-Nom Taro-for
        yuiitu-no tayori da.
        only-Gen reliance is
        (lit.) "Self$_i$ is only reliable to Taro$_i$." (Iida 1996: 98)

In (ia), *zibun* occurs in the possessive position of the subject. Iida notes that such *zibun* does not enter into an obliqueness relation with the object NP. Thus, her syntactic condition does not rule out *zibun*-binding to the more oblique object NP in (ia). Her condition does not say anything about *zibun*-binding in

(ib), either, because the NP, *Taro-ni totte* "to Taro," is not subcategorized by the verb, and hence no obliqueness relation is held between *zibun* and *Taro*.

29 Note that the first occurrence of *zibun* in (47) (i.e. *zibun* that occurs in the PP, *zibun-no heya-de* "in self's room") does not enter into an obliqueness relation with *Hanako*, because the PP in question is not subcategorized by the embedded verb. Accordingly, the binding of this *zibun* by *Hanako* is not subject to Iida's syntactic condition.

30 Nakamura (1987) also explores an analysis of the two complex reflexives. He takes a parametric approach (cf. Yang 1983, Huang 1983, Manzini and Wexler 1987) to explain their binding behavior.

31 Aikawa (1994) observes that LD-binding of *zibun-zisin/kare-zisin* becomes possible when they occur in the embedded subject position. She analyzes such *zibun-zisin/kare-zisin* as a focus logophor in the sense of Reinhart and Reuland (1993).

32 Note that both *zibun-zisin* and *kare-zisin* can take a referential NP as their antecedent as in (i).

   (i) a. Taroo$_i$-ga zibun-zisin$_i$-o
        Taro-Nom self-self-Acc
        hihansita.
        criticized.

      b. Taroo$_i$-ga kare-zisin$_i$-o
        Taro-Nom he-self-Acc
        hihansita.
        criticized
        "Taro$_i$ criticized himself$_i$."

Given the assumption that *zibun-zisin* can be a bound variable whereas *kare-zisin* cannot, we should predict that (ia) yields only sloppy reading whereas (ib) yields only strict reading. This prediction, however, is not borne out. Examine

(ii) below, which involves the sloppy identity test of *zibun-zisin/kare-zisin*.

(ii) a.   Taroo-ga   zibun-zisin-o
           Taro-Nom self-self-Acc
           hihansita. Kazuo-mo da.
           criticized Kazuo also be
           (sloppy reading) Taro
               criticized himself. Kazuo
               criticized himself, too.
           (strict reading)*Taro
               criticized himself. Kazuo
               criticized him (= Taro),
               too.
      b.   Taroo-ga   kare-zisin-o
           Taro-Nom he-self-Acc
           hihansita. Kazuo-mo da.
           criticized Kazuo also be
           (sloppy reading)(?)Taro
               criticized himself. Kazuo
               criticized himself, too.
           (strict reading) Taro
               criticized himself. Kazuo
               criticized him (= Taro),
               too.

The results in (iia) are consistent with the prediction above, but the availability of the sloppy reading for *kare-zisin* in (iib) is contradictory to it. We leave this problem open here.

33   However, as pointed out by Aikawa (1993), *zibun*'s properties of

modification, pronominal usage, and discourse-binding are not carried over to *zibun-zisin*.

34   Recall that Katada (1991) assumes that the trace of *zibun* can be lexically governed by Case including the genitive case *-no*. See n. 19.

35   The Empty Category Principle (ECP) (N. Chomsky 1981a) states that an empty category must be either lexically governed by a lexical X^0 or antecedent-governed by (i.e. coindexed with and c-commanded by) a category that governs it.

36   N. A. McCawley (1976) proposes that verbs such as *arau* "to wash" obey an Unlike-NP Constraint and that *zibun* cannot occur as an object of such verbs.

37   As we saw briefly in section 4.3, Reinhart and Reuland's (1993) analysis of reflexivity is, in spirit, the same as this traditional view on reflexivization. They argue, among other things, that what Conditions A and B are about can be subsumed under conditions on the wellformedness and the interpretation of reflexive predicates. They propose a revision of BT. Interested readers should refer to them for more details.

7 Passives

HIROTO HOSHI

0 Introduction

Due to the complex properties which Japanese passives display, it has been controversial how many types of passives exist in Japanese and what kind of structure each type of passive construction has. In this chapter, I aim to show that there are three kinds of passive constructions in Japanese and to clarify the structural properties of each passive construction.

(1) is an active sentence and its "direct passive" counterpart is given in (2).[1, 2]

(1) Gakusei-ga   sensei-o   hihans-i-ta.
    student-Nom teacher-Acc criticize-Past
    "The student criticized his teacher."

(2) direct passive:
    Sensei-ga   gakusei-ni hihans-are-ta.
    teacher-Nom student-by criticize-Pass.-Past
    "The teacher$_i$ was affected by his student's criticizing him$_i$."

In the active sentence (1), the logical object of *hihans*, *sensei* "teacher," is in the object position, whereas in the direct passive (2), the logical object appears in the subject position.

Consider example (3), which is an instance of the "indirect passive."

(3) indirect passive:
    Sensei-ga   gakusei-ni kurasu-de   nak-are-ta.
    teacher-Nom student-by classroom-in cry-Pass.-Past
    "The teacher was affected by his student's crying in the classroom."

Unlike the subject of the direct passive, the subject of the indirect passive in (3), *sensei*, does not bear any apparent grammatical relation with the verb *nak* "cry" that is suffixed by the passive morpheme.

Although there has been a consensus as to how to treat the indirect passive, it has been controversial how the direct passive should be analyzed, and two theories of Japanese passives, the "uniform hypothesis" and the "nonuniform hypothesis," have been proposed to account for the properties of the direct passive.[3] Under the uniform hypothesis (K. Hasegawa 1964, Kuroda 1965a, 1979, 1985, Makino 1972, 1973, Howard and Niyekawa-Howard 1976, Kuno 1983, 1986b, Y. Kitagawa 1986, N. Hasegawa 1988, Y. Kitagawa and Kuroda 1992, among others), the direct passive and the indirect passive are analyzed basically in the same way.[4] On the other hand, under the nonuniform hypothesis (N. A. McCawley 1972, Kuno 1973, S.-I. Harada 1973, Perlmutter 1973, K. Inoue 1976a, Kubo 1990, Shibatani 1990, Terada 1990, among others), these passives are treated in two different ways.

More specifically, both approaches agree upon the treatment of indirect passives such as (3) as involving complementation:

(4)

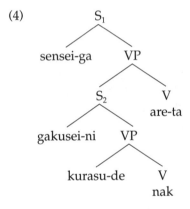

Here, *rare* is considered to be a two-place predicate which takes the subject, *sensei*, and the complement clause, S_2.

However, there has been a crucial disagreement on the analysis of direct passives such as (2). The uniform hypothesis assigns the structure (5) for the direct passive sentence (2),

(5)

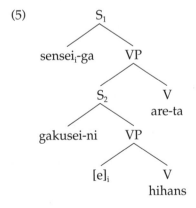

while the nonuniform hypothesis gives the structure (6) to the direct passive
sentence.

(6)

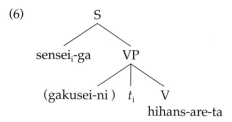

Under the uniform hypothesis, there is basically no difference between the
function of the indirect passive verb *rare* and that of the direct passive verb
rare. *Rare* is considered to be a two-place predicate which takes an external
argument, i.e. a subject, and an internal argument, i.e. a complement clause, as
shown in (4) and (5). The only difference between the direct passive and the
indirect passive is whether or not there is a gap in the direct or indirect object
position in the complement clause which is coindexed with the matrix subject.
If the structure has such a gap as in (5), it represents the direct passive. If, on
the other hand, there is no gap coindexed with the matrix subject as in (4), the
structure represents the indirect passive. That is, the passive verb *rare* is considered to be an optional control verb on the uniform hypothesis. If the matrix
subject controls the object of the complement clause (henceforth, the complement object), then direct passives such as (2) are generated. On the other hand,
if such a control relation between the matrix subject and the complement
object is absent, indirect passives such as (3) are generated.[5]

Under the nonuniform hypothesis, the passive morpheme of the direct passive and that of the indirect passive are considered to be completely different.
The passive morpheme, *rare*, of the indirect passive is considered to be a verb
which requires an external argument and an internal argument as illustrated
in (4), whereas *rare* of the direct passive is considered to be a suffix which
triggers NP movement of the internal argument of the attached verb, as is
shown in (6).[6]

Notice that the uniform hypothesis is conceptually preferable to the nonuniform hypothesis. This is so because the uniform hypothesis assumes only
one passive morpheme *rare* whereas the nonuniform hypothesis recognizes
two different types of *rare*, and yet they do not seem to be naturally related.
What is more important is that both the uniform hypothesis and the nonuniform
hypothesis agree that indirect passives such as (3) involve complementation
as illustrated in (4). Y. Kitagawa and Kuroda (1992) thus argue that given
the availability of a zero/empty pronoun in Japanese, there is no reason to
deny *a priori* the possibility that the gap in the complement object position of
the direct passive is a base-generated empty pronominal coindexed with the
matrix subject under either of these two hypotheses. Hence, even if it is proven
that representation (6) rather than (5) is the correct structure for direct passive
sentence (2) as the nonuniform hypothesis proposes, it still has to be explained

under the nonuniform hypothesis why structure (5) with pro in the complement object position cannot be available for direct passive example (2). Kitagawa and Kuroda conclude that for this reason, more burden of proof is put on the nonuniform hypothesis.[7]

Importantly, Kuroda (1979), while maintaining the uniform treatment of Japanese passives such as (2) and (3), proposes that there exists another type of passive in Japanese, "*ni yotte* passives" such as (7).[8]

(7)   *ni yotte* passive:
　　　Sensei-ga　　gakusei-ni yotte　hihans-are-ta.
　　　teacher-Nom student-to owing criticize-Pass.-Past
　　　"The teacher was criticized by his student."

As seen in (2) and (7), the only difference between *ni* direct passive (2) and *ni yotte* passive (7) appears to be *ni* vs. *ni yotte*. And indeed, Kuno (1973) and others consider the *ni yotte* passive to be a variant of the *ni* direct passive. However, on the basis of K. Inoue's (1976a) and his own semantic observations, Kuroda (1979) argues that *ni yotte* passives are fundamentally different from *ni* passives, and assigns structure (8) to *ni yotte* passive example (7).

(8)

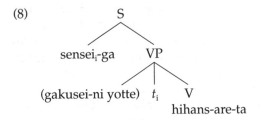

Notice that this structure is significantly different from structure (5), which Kuroda (1965a, 1979)/the uniform hypothesis gives to *ni* direct passive (2). That is, structure (8) for *ni yotte* passive (7) involves NP movement of the logical object of *hihans, sensei*, to the subject position, whereas structure (5) for *ni* direct passive (2) involves complement object deletion. On the other hand, Kuroda's structure (8) has significant similarities with structure (6), which the nonuniform hypothesis assigns to *ni* direct passive sentence (2). In both (6) and (8), the logical object *sensei* moves to the subject position.

In this chapter, I will focus on examining the properties of the most controversial Japanese passives, *ni* direct passives and *ni yotte* passives, and I will show that as Kuroda (1979) argues, *ni yotte* passives involve NP movement as illustrated in (8). At the same time, I will argue that as the uniform hypothesis proposes, *ni* direct passives such as (2) have a theta subject, a subject required by the passive verb *rare*. However, I will demonstrate as well that as the nonuniform hypothesis argues, the *ni* direct passive also involves NP movement, contrary to the claims by the uniform hypothesis. I will thus conclude that both the uniform hypothesis and the nonuniform hypothesis are empirically well founded in one respect or another and that these two competing hypotheses have to be reconciled to account for the properties of the *ni* direct passive properly. Finally, I will present a proposal made in Hoshi (1991, 1994a, 1994b) as a way of incorporating these two theories into one analysis.

In the following section, I will show supporting evidence taken from K. Inoue (1976a) and Kuroda (1979), among others, for Kuroda's dichotomy between *ni* direct passives and *ni yotte* passives. The evidence there indicates that the subject of the *ni* direct passive is an argument of the passive verb *rare*, and thus *ni* direct passives such as (2) have a theta subject as the uniform hypothesis proposes. The evidence in the next section also shows that as Kuroda proposes, the subject position of the *ni yotte* passive is a nontheta position. Based on Lasnik and Fiengo's (1974) proposals on English passives, I will also demonstrate in section 1 that the existence of two types of passives, the theta subject passive and the nontheta subject passive, is not peculiar to Japanese at all because not only Japanese but also English has two kinds of passives. One type of English passive, the *get* passive, has a theta subject exactly like the *ni* direct passive, whereas the other type of English passive, the *be* passive, has a nontheta subject.[9] The discussions in section 1 will thus lead us to the conclusion that there exist at least two types of passives in Japanese, the *ni* direct passive and the *ni yotte* passive.

In section 2, I will first review N. A. McCawley's (1972), Kuno's (1973), and Saito's (1982) arguments for an NP movement analysis of the *ni* direct passive proposed by the nonuniform hypothesis. In so doing, I will show that their arguments pose problems for a theta subject/complement object deletion analysis of the *ni* direct passive by the uniform hypothesis and that the *ni* direct passive is different from the *ni* indirect passive in important respects. This claim will then lead us to conclude that we have to recognize the dichotomy between *ni* direct passives and the *ni* indirect passives proposed by the nonuniform theory, in addition to Kuroda's *ni* vs. *ni yotte* passive dichotomy. That is, Japanese has three distinct types of passives, the *ni* indirect passive, the *ni yotte* passive, and the *ni* direct passive. At the end of section 2, I will also show that as Kuroda proposes, the *ni yotte* passive involves NP movement.

In section 3, on the basis of the discussions of sections 1 and 2, I will first review the structure of the *ni* indirect passive and the *ni yotte* passive. Given strong arguments for both the uniform hypothesis and the nonuniform hypothesis regarding the analysis of the *ni* direct passive, I will then argue that both of these hypotheses must be correct in one respect or another. The passive morpheme of the *ni* direct passive is a predicate which takes an external argument and an internal argument as the uniform hypothesis argues. However, as the nonuniform hypothesis claims, the passive morpheme of the *ni* direct passive also functions as a suffix which suppresses the external theta role and absorbs the accusative Case of the attached verb, triggering NP movement. And I will show an analysis of the *ni* direct passive made in Hoshi (1991) as a way to reconcile the uniform hypothesis and the nonuniform hypothesis. Section 4 presents remaining problems with respect to the analysis of Japanese passives presented in section 3. Section 5 concludes the discussions of this chapter.

1   Evidence for the Uniform Hypothesis/Kuroda's Dichotomy

In this section, I will demonstrate that as the uniform hypothesis proposes, the *ni* direct passive has a theta subject, whereas the *ni yotte* passive has a nontheta subject as Kuroda (1979) argues. Consider again *ni* direct passive example (2) and *ni yotte* passive example (7), which are repeated here as (9a) and (9b), respectively.

(9)   a.   *ni* direct passive:
          Sensei-ga   gakusei-ni hihans-are-ta.
          teacher-Nom student-by criticize-Pass.-Past
          "The teacher$_i$ was affected by his student's criticizing him$_i$."
      b.   *ni yotte* passive:
          Sensei-ga   gakusei-ni yotte   hihans-are-ta.
          teacher-Nom student-to owing criticize-Pass.-Past
          "The teacher was criticized by his student."

At first glance, the only difference between (9a) and (9b) seems to be the use of *ni* vs. *ni yotte*. However, on the basis of K. Inoue's (1976a) and his own semantic observations on *ni* passives and *ni yotte* passives, Kuroda (1979, 1986) proposes different analyses for *ni* direct passives such as (9a) and for *ni yotte* passives such as (9b).

Assuming the uniform treatment of *ni* passives, Kuroda (1979, 1986) maintains his theta subject/complement object deletion analysis of the *ni* direct passive as shown in (10a). Importantly, however, he proposes an NP movement analysis for the *ni yotte* passive as illustrated in (8), which is repeated here as (10b).

(10)   a.   b.

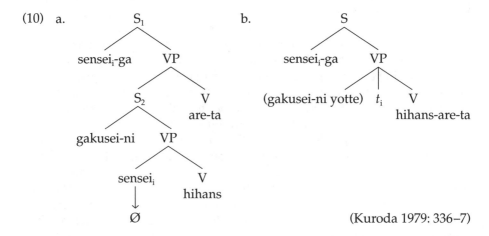

(Kuroda 1979: 336–7)

As illustrated in structure (10a), the uniform hypothesis proposes that the passive morpheme of the *ni* direct passive is a two-place predicate which requires a subject and a complement clause. Kuroda (1979, 1986) further proposes that the external argument, the subject, of the *ni* direct passive is required to be an affectee by the passive verb *rare*.[10] In contrast, Kuroda argues that the passive morpheme in (10b) is an affix which triggers NP movement of the internal argument of the verb *hihans* "criticize." Because it is an affix, the passive morpheme of the *ni yotte* passive does not impose any selectional restriction on the subject and the subject, *sensei*, in (10b) is a nontheta subject. I will show below supporting evidence for these structures for the *ni* direct passive and the *ni yotte* passive.

K. Inoue (1976a) observes that *ni yotte* passives such as (11b) are grammatical, whereas *ni* direct passives such as (11a) are ungrammatical.[11] Kuroda (1979) also observes contrasts such as the one in (12a–b).

(11) a. *Kaikai-ga   gityoo-ni   sengens-are-ta.
          opening-Nom chairperson-by announce-Pass.-Past
          "The opening of the meeting$_i$ was affected by the chairperson's announcing it$_i$."
      b. Kaikai-ga   gityoo-ni   yotte sengens-are-ta.
          opening-Nom chairperson-to owing announce-Pass.-Past
          "The opening of the meeting was announced by the chairperson."
          (K. Inoue 1976a: 83)

(12) a. *Fermat-no   teiri-ga   John-ni syoomeis-are-ta.
          Fermat-Gen theorem-Nom John-by prove-Pass.-Past
          "Fermat's theorem$_i$ was affected by John's proving it$_i$."
      b. Fermat-no   teiri-ga   John-ni yotte syoomeis-are-ta.
          Fermat-Gen theorem-Nom John-to owing prove-Pass.-Past
          "Fermat's theorem was proven by John." (Kuroda 1979: 330–1)

These contrasts are straightforwardly accounted for by Kuroda's theory of Japanese passives. Abstract NPs such as *kaikai* "opening" or immutable NPs such as *Fermat-no teiri* "Fermat's theorem" are in the subject position of the *ni* direct passive in (11a) and (12a). However, those NPs cannot be interpreted as affectees, and hence they fail to satisfy the selectional restriction imposed by the *ni* direct passive verb. Therefore, examples (11a) and (12a) are correctly ruled out by Kuroda's theory/the uniform hypothesis. On the other hand, since there is no selectional restriction imposed on the subject position in the *ni yotte* passive under Kuroda's proposal, (11b) and (12b) are permitted as desired.

S.-I. Harada (1977) first argues that verb phrase idioms can be passivized in Japanese. Hoshi (1991) clarifies that Harada's claim regarding passivizability of verb phrase idioms is correct for the *ni yotte* passive but it is incorrect for the *ni* direct passive, and provides further support for Kuroda's proposal that the *ni* direct passive has a theta subject as the uniform hypothesis argues, whereas the *ni yotte* passive has a nontheta subject. Consider the following examples.

(13)   a.   John-ga   tyuui-o   harat-ta.
            John-Nom heed-Acc pay-Past
            "John paid heed."
       b.   *Tyuui-ga   John-ni haraw-are-ta.
            heed-Nom John-by pay-Pass.-Past
            "Heed$_i$ was affected by John's paying it$_i$."
       c.   Tyuui-ga   John-ni yotte   haraw-are-ta.
            heed-Nom John-to owing pay-Pass.-Past
            "Heed was paid by John."

(14)   a.   John-ga   keti-o   tuke-ta.
            John-Nom fault-Acc attach-Past
            "John found the fault."
       b.   *Keti-ga   John-ni tuke-rare-ta.
            fault-Nom John-by attach-Pass.-Past
            "Fault$_i$ was affected by John's attaching it$_i$."
       c.   Keti-ga   John-ni yotte tuke-rare-ta.
            fault-Nom John-to owing attach-Pass.-Past
            "The fault was found by John." (Hoshi 1991: 70–1)

There are sharp contrasts in grammaticality between *ni* direct passive examples (13b)/(14b) and *ni yotte* passive sentences (13c)/(14c). These contrasts show that verb phrase idioms such as *tyuui-o haraw* "pay heed" or *keti-o tuke* "find a fault" can only be passivized with *ni yotte*, but that verb phrase idioms resist *ni* direct passivization. In Kuroda's analysis, these contrasts are also straightforwardly accounted for. A part of a verb phrase idiom such as *tyuui* "heed" or *keti* "fault" can never be interpreted as an affectee, something that is acted upon or influenced. Thus, (13b) and (14b) are ruled out due to a violation of the selectional restriction imposed on the subject of the *ni* direct passive by *rare* under Kuroda's theory/the uniform hypothesis. In contrast, the passive morpheme of the *ni yotte* passive does not impose any restriction on the subject, and thus both (13c) and (14c) are grammatical.

The contrast in (15a–b) observed by Kuroda (1979) further substantiates his dichotomy of Japanese passives.

(15)   a.   Daitooryoo-ga   orokanimo CIA-ni   koros-are-te
            president-Nom stupidly   CIA-by kill-Pass.
            simat-ta.
            shouldn't have-Past
            "The president stupidly let the CIA kill him, which he should not
            have let happen (*Or, more colloquially*: The president stupidly went
            and got killed by the CIA)."

b. ??Daitooryoo-ga orokanimo CIA-ni yotte   koros-are-te
president-Nom stupidly   CIA-to owing kill-Pass.
simat-ta.
shouldn't have-Past (Kuroda 1979: 325–6)

Subject-oriented adverbs such as *orokanimo* "stupidly" require a theta sub-ject.[12,13] Since the subject of the *ni* direct passive (15a), *daitooryoo* "president," is a theta subject required by the *ni* passive verb, the subject-oriented adverb *orokanimo* is properly licensed in this sentence. However, the subject of the *ni yotte* passive (15b) is moved from the object position to the subject position, taking a parallel structure to (10b), and it is not a theta subject as is argued in Kuroda's theory. Hence, the subject in (15b) fails to license *orokanimo*.[14,15]

Hoshi (1991) provides further support for Kuroda's (1979, 1985) dichotomy between *ni* passives and *ni yotte* passives by showing that not only Japanese but also English has two types of passives, the *get* passive and the *be* passive. Furthermore, it is shown there that the *get* passive has a theta subject exactly like the *ni* direct passive, whereas the *be* passive has a nontheta subject as the *ni yotte* passive.

(16a) is an instance of the *get* passive, and (16b) an instance of the be passive.

(16)   a.   John got arrested by the police.
       b.   John was arrested by the police.

On the surface, it appears as if the only difference between *get* passive (16a) and *be* passive (16b) is *get* vs. *be*. However, Lasnik and Fiengo (1974) propose that there is a selectional restriction on *get* of the *get* passive requiring that its subject not denote an immutable entity, whereas there is no such restriction imposed on the subject by *be* of the *be* passive.

Consider Lasnik and Fiengo's paradigm in (17) and (18).

(17)   a.   *The parallel postulate got chosen by the mathematicians.
       b.   The parallel postulate was chosen by the mathematicians.

(18)   a.   *Heed got paid to our warning.
       b.   Heed was paid to our warning. (Lasnik and Fiengo 1974: 554)

As shown in (17a–b), immutable NPs such as *the parallel postulate* cannot be in the subject position in the *get* passive, whereas those NPs can appear in the subject position of the *be* passive. The contrast between (18a) and (18b) indicates that verb phrase idioms such as *pay heed* can be passivized in the *be* passive, but verb phrase idioms resist *get* passivization. These contrasts are straightforwardly accounted for by Lasnik and Fiengo's (1974) proposal for the *get* passive and the *be* passive. Since immutable NPs or a part of a verb phrase idiom cannot satisfy selectional restrictions imposed by the verb *get* of the *get* passive, (17a) and (18a) are correctly predicted to be ungrammatical.

On the other hand, no such restriction is imposed on the subject position by *be* of the *be* passive. Hence, both (17b) and (18b) are correctly allowed by Lasnik and Fiengo's theory.

Notice that the contrasts in (17) and (18) parallel the contrasts which we observed between the *ni* direct passive and the *ni yotte* passive in (11)/(12) and (13)/(14). Notice further that with respect to the nature of the subject position, the *get* passive shares important properties with the *ni* direct passive, and that the *be* passive and the *ni yotte* passive have the same properties. That is, the *ni* direct passive and the *get* passive have a theta subject required by *rare* and *get*, respectively, while the *ni yotte* passive and the *be* passive have a nontheta subject.

The following contrast that Lasnik and Fiengo also observe lends further support to this parallelism between Japanese passives and English passives.

(19)   a.   Cowens got fouled by Kareem Jabbar on purpose.
      b.   ??Cowens was fouled by Kareem Jabbar on purpose. (Lasnik and Fiengo 1974: 554)

A subject-oriented adverbial phrase like *on purpose* requires a theta subject. As shown in (19a–b), they are compatible with the *get* passive, while those elements cannot be properly licensed in the *be* passive.[16] This contrast is also straightforwardly accounted for by Lasnik and Fiengo's (1974) theory of English passives. Note also that the contrast in (19) parallels the contrast between the *ni* direct passive (15a) and the *ni yotte* passive (15b).

By showing the evidence above, it is thus concluded in Hoshi (1991) that Kuroda's theta/nontheta subject dichotomy of passives is not peculiar to Japanese at all. His type of dichotomy of passives exists not only in Japanese but also in English, and Kuroda's dichotomy of Japanese passives in turn receives cross-linguistic support. The *ni* direct passive and the *get* passive have a theta subject selected by *rare* and *get*, respectively, whereas the *ni yotte* passive and the *be* passive have a nontheta subject.[17] Importantly, this conclusion also provides substantial support for the uniform hypothesis of *ni* passives. Under the uniform hypothesis, it is claimed that not only the subject of *ni* indirect passives such as (3) but also the subject of *ni* direct passives such as (9a) is required by the passive verb *rare* as illustrated in (10a).

Given Kuroda's analysis of *ni* direct passives and *ni yotte* passives, we can thus straightforwardly account for the data in (11–15). And Kuroda's theta subject analysis of the *ni* direct passive under the uniform hypothesis and his NP movement analysis of the *ni yotte* passive, as schematized in (10), receive considerable support. However, a question arises as to why the so-called "affectedness" interpretation is clearly obtained in the *ni* indirect passive (3), whereas such an affectedness interpretation is not evident in the *ni* direct passive (9a).[18]

To answer this question, Kuroda (1979, 1985) and Y. Kitagawa and Kuroda (1992) propose the following plausible hypothesis: the passive morpheme *rare* of *ni* passives, i.e. both *ni* direct passives and *ni* indirect passives, requires the subject to be "affected" by the event or state described by the complement clause, and affectedness interpretations can be of positive, negative or neutral nature, depending on the (lexical) semantics/pragmatics involved in each sentence rather than necessarily being "adversative" (cf. Wierzbicka 1979, Oehrle and Nishio 1980).[19] In the *ni* direct passive (9a), which involves the control relation between the matrix subject and the complement object, what the matrix subject refers to is an "affected" argument in both the matrix and embedded clauses. Thus, an affectedness interpretation imposed by the passive morpheme *rare* is not obvious or such an affectedness interpretation is neutralized in the *ni* direct passive. For this reason, the affectedness interpretation is not evident in *ni* direct passives such as (9a). On the other hand, *ni* indirect passives such as (3) lack such a syntactic basis between the matrix subject and the embedded object. The passive morpheme *rare* therefore requires proper pragmatics that will permit us to establish an affectedness relation between the experiencer argument, i.e. the matrix subject, and the eventuality argument, i.e. the complement clause. Hence, an affectedness interpretation is evident in *ni* indirect passives such as (3).[20,21]

To summarize, I have shown in this section that Kuroda's dichotomy between *ni* direct passives and *ni yotte* passives is correct with respect to the nature of the subject position. That is, as the uniform hypothesis proposes, *ni* direct passives such as (9a) have a subject required by the passive morpheme *rare*, as illustrated in (10a), repeated here as (20a). On the other hand, *ni yotte* passives such as (9b) have a nontheta subject, as shown in (10b), repeated here as (20b).

(20) a.

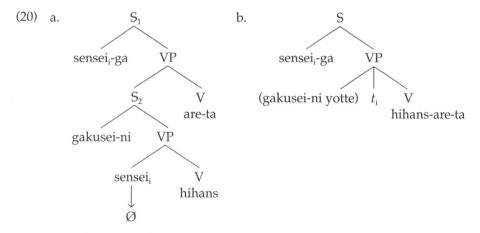

This conclusion clearly indicates that there are at least two types of passive constructions in Japanese, the *ni* direct passive (20a) and the *ni yotte* passive (20b), although we have not yet discussed the nature of *ni* indirect passives such as (3) in detail. Structure (4), which both the uniform and nonuniform hypotheses assign to (3), is repeated here as (21).

(21)

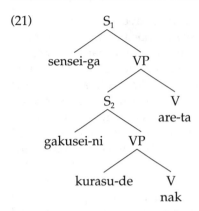

Finally, notice also that the supporting evidence for the uniform treatment of the *ni* direct passive in this section poses problems for the nonuniform hypothesis. This is because under the nonuniform hypothesis, the subject position of the *ni* direct passive is assumed to be a nontheta position, as shown in (6), repeated here as (22).

(22)

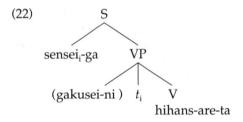

The nonuniform hypothesis thus cannot account for the ungrammaticality of (11a), (12a), (13b), and (14b), or the grammaticality of (15a), as the theta subject analysis of the *ni* direct passive under the uniform hypothesis does.

2   Evidence for the Nonuniform Hypothesis

In the previous section, I have shown that the theta subject analysis/ complement object deletion analysis of the *ni* direct passive by the uniform hypothesis is well founded and that the uniform hypothesis correctly captures the properties of the subject position of the *ni* direct passive. I have also shown that *ni yotte* passives have a nontheta subject as Kuroda proposes. In this section, however, by examining other properties of the *ni* direct passive, I will demonstrate that there is also strong evidence for an NP movement analysis of the *ni* direct passive proposed by the nonuniform hypothesis. I will show here too that *ni yotte* passives involve NP movement, as Kuroda proposes.

The nonuniform hypothesis assigns structure (22), repeated here as (23), to the *ni* direct passive example in (9a).

(23)

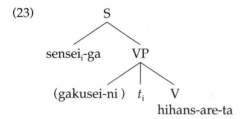

Reinterpreting this NP movement analysis under the principles-and-parameters theory (N. Chomsky 1981a, 1986b, among others), Saito (1982), Marantz (1984), and Miyagawa (1989b), among others, propose that like the passive morpheme *en* in English, the passive morpheme *rare* of the *ni* direct passive is a suffix which suppresses an external argument and absorbs accusative Case from the attached verb.[22] Hence, as illustrated in (23), the logical subject of the attached verb *hihans* appears as an adverbial *ni* "by" phrase, i.e. an adjunct phrase, and the logical object of *hihans* moves from its original position to the subject position to receive nominative Case *ga*.

By reviewing Saito's (1982), N. A. McCawley's (1972), and Kuno's (1973) arguments, I will show below that as the nonuniform hypothesis argues, the gap in the *ni* direct passive is an NP trace left behind by the movement of the object. I will also show that the *ni* phrase in the *ni* direct passive is a suppressed argument, an adjunct, whereas the *ni* phrase in the *ni* indirect passive is an argument. To the extent that this claim is correct, it provides substantial support for the nonuniform hypothesis regarding the treatment of *ni* direct passives and *ni* indirect passives, but poses problems for the uniform hypothesis. This is because the uniform hypothesis proposes the theta subject analysis for the *ni* passive, as illustrated in (20a) and (21). And under the uniform hypothesis, it is not expected that there exists an NP trace in the *ni* direct passive or that the *ni* phrase of the *ni* direct passive is an adverbial *ni* "by" phrase, while the *ni* phrase in the *ni* indirect passive is an argument. The arguments in this section will thus lead us to the conclusion that we have to recognize the dichotomy between *ni* direct passives and *ni* indirect passives proposed by the nonuniform hypothesis besides Kuroda's *ni* vs. *ni yotte* passive dichotomy. That is, there are three different types of passives in Japanese, the *ni* direct passive, the *ni* indirect passive and the *ni yotte* passive.

Saito's (1982) arguments for the NP movement analysis of the *ni* direct passive crucially rely on the "abstract" Double-*o* Constraint in (24).[23]

(24) A verb can assign accusative Case to at most one NP in Japanese.

Let us first consider how we can explain the data in (25a–c) by appealing to the constraint.

(25) a.   Mary-ga   John-o/ni   aruk-ase-ta.
        Mary-Nom John-Acc/to walk-Cause-Past
        "Mary made/let John walk."
    b.   Mary-ga   John-*o/ni   hon-o   yom-ase-ta.
        Mary-Nom John-*Acc/to book-Acc read-Cause-Past
        "Mary made/let John read the book."
    c.   Kono hon$_i$-wa [$_S$ Mary-ga   John-*o/ni   [e]$_i$ yom-ase-ta].
        this   book-Top   Mary-Nom John-*Acc/to   read-Cause-Past
        "This book$_i$, Mary made/let John read it$_i$."

In (25a), the causee, *John*, can be marked with the dative marker *ni* or accusative Case *o*. This is because there is only one NP marked with accusative Case and thus, the abstract Double-*o* Constraint in (24) is irrelevant in this example. In contrast, in (25b), the causee *John* must be marked with the dative marker and cannot be marked with accusative Case. This is because there is an NP, *hon* "book," which requires accusative Case, and thus constraint (24) prevents the causee *John* from receiving accusative Case. Constraint (24) blocks the causee *John* from being marked with accusative Case in (25c) as well, because the empty category in example (25c) is either a base-generated pronominal or a trace left behind by the movement of the topic NP, *kono hon* "this book" (Kuroda 1965a, Kuno 1973, Saito 1985, Hoji 1985, among others). In either case, the empty category requires accusative Case. Therefore, the causee in (25c) cannot receive accusative Case from the complex predicate, *yom-ase*.[24]

Consider Saito's key example (26b).

(26) a.   John$_i$-ga   (damatte) Tom-ni [e]$_i$ sikar-are-ta.
        John-Nom (silently) Tom-by   scold-Pass.-Past
        "John$_i$ was affected by Tom's scolding him$_i$ without saying anything."
    b.   Mary-ga   John$_i$-o /ni (damatte) Tom-ni [e]$_i$
        Mary-Nom John-Acc/to (silently) Tom-by
        sikar-are-sase-ta
        scold-Pass.-Cause-Past
        "Mary made/let John be scolded by Tom without saying anything."
        (Saito 1982: 92)

In (26b), the *ni* direct passive sentence (26a) is embedded in a causative sentence. What is crucial in (26b) is that the causee *John* is allowed to be marked with accusative Case unlike the causee in (25b–c). If the empty category in the *ni* direct passive requires Case as in (25c), then the causee should not be able to receive Case from the complex predicate *sikar-are-sase* due to the abstract Double-*o* Constraint in (24). Saito thus concludes that the gap in the *ni* direct passive must be an NP trace left behind by the movement of the object *John*, which does not bear accusative Case.

More specifically, the NP movement analysis of *ni* direct passives under the nonuniform hypothesis which Saito convincingly defends assigns structure (27) to example (26b).[25]

(27)

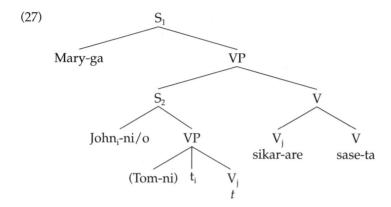

Due to absorption of the accusative Case and suppression of the external argument of *sikar* "scold" by the passive morpheme *are*, the logical subject of *sikar* optionally appears as an adverbial *ni* "by" phrase, *Tom-ni*, and an NP trace, t_i, is created by the movement of the logical object of the verb, *John*. Since an NP trace does not require Case and there is no NP other than the causee *John* in (27) which requires accusative Case, abstract Double-*o* Constraint (24) correctly allows *John* to be marked with accusative Case.[26]

On the other hand, the theta subject analysis/complement object deletion analysis of the *ni* direct passive under the uniform hypothesis assigns structure (28) to example (26b).

(28)

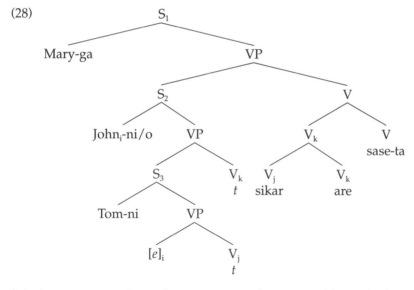

Saito's arguments above do not seem to be compatible with this structure, because it is not immediately clear why the gap in the complement object position has properties of an NP trace. An NP trace in passive is a gap created by the movement of the object to the subject position, but such NP movement is not assumed to take place in (28) under the uniform hypothesis. Further-more, if we assume with Y. Kitagawa and Kuroda (1992) that the gap in the complement object position of the *ni* direct passive is pro, then we incorrectly predict that due to constraint (24), the causee *John* in (28) cannot be marked with accusative Case like the causee in (25b–c). This is crucial because pro is an empty category which requires Case.

The following binding facts concerning the antecedent of *zibun* "self," which N. A. McCawley (1972) and Kuno (1973) independently observe, provide fur-ther support for the NP movement analysis of the *ni* direct passive under the nonuniform hypothesis and for the nonuniform treatment of *ni* direct passives and *ni* indirect passives.

(29) a. John$_i$-ga   Mary$_j$-ni zibun$_{i/*j}$-no uti-de   [e_i] koros-are-ta.
John-Nom Mary-by self-Gen   house-in   kill-Pass.-Past
"John$_i$ was affected by Mary$_j$'s killing him$_i$ in self$_{i/*j}$'s house."

b. John$_i$-ga   Mary$_j$-ni zibun$_{i/j}$-no koto-o   zimans-are-ta.
John-Nom Mary-by self-Gen   matter-Acc boast-Pass.-Past
"John$_i$ was affected by Mary$_j$'s bragging about self$_{i/j}$'s matter."
(N. A. McCawley 1972, Kuno 1973: 299, 304)

In the *ni* direct passive (29a), a subject-oriented long-distance anaphor, *zibun* "self," can take *John* as its antecedent but it cannot take *Mary* as its antecedent. However, in the *ni* indirect passive sentence (29b), *zibun* can take either *John* or *Mary* as its antecedent.

(29b) is an instance of the *ni* indirect passive. Hence, both the uniform hypo-thesis and the nonuniform hypothesis assign the same structure, (30), to the example, and the binding facts in (29b) are straightforwardly accounted for.

(30) [$_{S1}$ John$_i$-ga [$_{S2}$ Mary$_j$-ni zibun$_{i/j}$-no koto-o zimans] are-ta]

In this representation, both *John* and *Mary* are in the subject positions, i.e. the positions immediately dominated by S, and those NPs bind the anaphor, *zibun*. Thus, the possible antecedent of *zibun* in the *ni* indirect passive (29b) is either *John* or *Mary*.

Importantly, however, N. A. McCawley and Kuno argue that the binding facts in the *ni* direct passive (29a) can be successfully accounted for by an NP movement analysis under the nonuniform hypothesis, but those facts cannot be explained by a theta subject analysis under the uniform hypothesis. Compare the structures in (31a–b). (31a) is the structure which a theta subject analysis under the uniform hypothesis assigns to the *ni* direct passive (29a), whereas (31b) is the representation which an NP movement analysis under the non-uniform hypothesis gives to the example.

(31) a. [$_{S1}$ John$_i$-ga [$_{S2}$ Mary$_j$-ni zibun$_{i/j}$-no uti-de [e]$_i$ koros] are-ta]
b. [$_S$ John$_i$-ga [$_{VP}$ Mary$_j$-ni zibun$_{i/*j}$-no uti-de t_i koros-are-ta]]

(30) and (31a) are the structures that the uniform hypothesis assigns to examples (29a) and (29b), respectively, and in both of these structures, *John* is the subject of S₁ and *Mary* is the subject of S₂. Thus, given structure (31a) for (29a), the uniform hypothesis makes a false prediction that in both (29a) and (29b), *zibun* can take either *John* or *Mary* as its antecedent, contrary to fact. Assuming structure (31b) to be the correct structure of (29a), however, we can correctly account for the binding facts in (29a) under the nonuniform hypothesis. In (31b), *John* is the only argument NP which is immediately dominated by S, and thus is in the subject position. This is because under an NP movement analysis by the nonuniform hypothesis, *Mary* is crucially a suppressed external argument, i.e. not a subject but an adverbial *ni* "by" phrase, and it appears immediately below VP. Hence, under N. A. McCawley's (1972) and Kuno's (1973) NP movement analysis of the nonuniform hypothesis, only *John* can be the antecedent of *zibun* in (29a), as desired.[27,28,29]

In summary, I have briefly reviewed arguments for the NP movement analysis of *ni* direct passives proposed under the nonuniform hypothesis by N. A. McCawley (1972), Kuno (1973) and Saito (1982). And I have shown in this section that their arguments lead us to the conclusion that as the non-uniform hypothesis claims, the passive morpheme of the *ni* direct passive is indeed a suffix which triggers NP movement by absorbing accusative Case and suppressing an external argument from the attached verb. This conclusion therefore provides support for structure (23), repeated here as (32a), which the nonuniform hypothesis proposes for *ni* direct passive example (9a). However, it poses serious problems for complement object deletion structure (20a), repeated here as (32b), which the uniform hypothesis assigns to the example.

(32) a.   b.

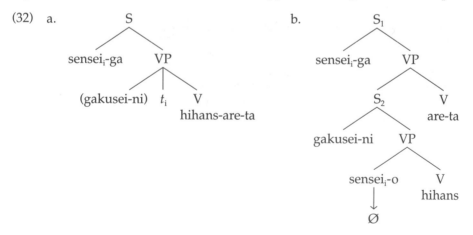

As the nonuniform hypothesis proposes, the *ni* direct passive involves NP movement of the object NP as illustrated in (32a), and thus the causee *John* in (26b) can be marked with accusative Case. Furthermore, the passive morpheme of the *ni* direct passive suppresses an external argument of the attached verb so that the logical subject of the attached verb appears as an adverbial *ni* "by" phrase in this type of passive as shown in structure (32a). Hence, in example (29a), not *Mary* but only *John* can be the possible antecedent of *zibun*. In contrast, a theta subject/complement object deletion analysis by the uniform hypothesis cannot account for the Case facts in (26b) and the binding facts in (29a) as the nonuniform hypothesis does for the reasons explained above.

Notice also that the contrast in (29), which N. A. McCawley and Kuno observe regarding the possible antecedent of *zibun*, strongly indicates that *ni* direct passives are different from *ni* indirect passives. This claim made by N. A. McCawley and Kuno together with Kuroda's dichotomy between *ni* direct passives and *ni yotte* passives discussed in section 1 then leads us to conclude that Japanese has three distinct types of passives, the *ni* direct passive, the *ni* indirect passive and the *ni yotte* passive.

It should also be noted here that the data in (33) indicate that as Kuroda proposes, the *ni yotte* passive involves NP movement and the *ni yotte* phrase is a suppressed external argument, an adjunct.

(33) a. Mary-ga   John$_i$-o /ni Tom-ni yotte [e]$_i$ sikar-are-sase-ta.
          Mary-Nom John-Acc/to Tom-to owing   scold-Pass.-Cause-Past
          "Mary made/let John be scolded by Tom."
      b. John$_i$-ga   Mary$_j$-ni yotte zibun$_{i/*j}$-no uti-de [e$_i$] koros-are-ta.
          John-Nom Mary-to owing self-Gen   house-in   kill-Pass.-Past
          "John$_i$ was killed by Mary$_j$ in self$_{i/*j}$'s house."

As is shown in (33a), the causee *John* can be marked with accusative Case *o* in the *ni yotte* passive counterpart of (26b) as well. This shows that as in the *ni* direct passive (26b), the gap in the *ni yotte* passive is also an NP trace, which does not require Case. Notice also that as in (29b), not *Mary* but only *John* is the possible antecedent for *zibun* in example (33b), thereby suggesting that *John* is a subject, but *Mary-ni yotte* is an adverbial *by* phrase, an external argument suppressed by the passive morpheme *are*.

This conclusion thus provides further support for Kuroda's structure (20b), repeated here as (34), for *ni yotte* passive example (9b).

(34)

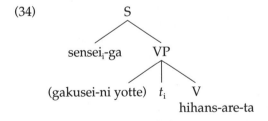

Like the passive morpheme of the *ni* direct passive, the passive morpheme of the *ni yotte* passive absorbs Case and suppresses an external argument from the attached verb, triggering NP movement of the logical object to the subject position for Case reasons.[30]

3 Three Types of Japanese Passives and a Reconciliation of the Uniform Hypothesis and the Nonuniform Hypothesis

In section 2, we reached the conclusion that there are three types of passive constructions in Japanese, the *ni* indirect passive, the *ni* direct passive, and the *ni yotte* passive. In this section, on the basis of the discussions in sections 1 and 2, I will first review the structures which capture properties of the *ni* indirect passive and the *ni yotte* passive. By showing that both the uniform hypothesis and the nonuniform hypothesis capture the properties of the *ni* direct passive in one respect or another but that either of those hypotheses cannot be entirely correct, I will then argue that we need to reconcile the uniform hypothesis and the nonuniform hypothesis to account for the properties of the *ni* direct passive properly. Finally, I will show a proposal made in Hoshi (1991) as a way of subsuming the NP movement analysis by the nonuniform hypothesis under the theta subject analysis by the uniform hypothesis.

Consider first structure (21) for *ni* indirect passive example (3), whose treatment both the uniform hypothesis and the nonuniform hypothesis agree upon. Example (3) and structure (21) are repeated here as (35a) and (35b), respectively.

(35) a. *ni* indirect passive:
Sensei-ga   gakusei-ni kurasu-de   nak-are-ta.
teacher-Nom student-by classroom-in cry-Pass.-Past
"The teacher was affected by his student's crying in the classroom."

b.

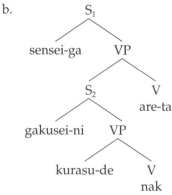

The passive morpheme of the *ni* indirect passive is a two-place predicate which takes the subject *sensei* and the complement clause, S_2, as illustrated in (35b).

Because this type of Japanese passive morpheme does not absorb Case or suppress an external theta role, intransitive verbs such as *nak* "cry," *hur* "fall," or *kur* "come" can be used in the *ni* indirect passive as shown in (35). Furthermore, given structures such as (35b) for the *ni* indirect passive, we can account for the fact that *Mary* can be the antecedent of *zibun* in (29b). This is because in the *ni* indirect passive, the *ni* phrase is analyzed as the subject of the complement clause as shown in (35b).

Consider next structure (34) proposed by Kuroda (1979) for *ni yotte* passive example (9b). Example (9b) and structure (34) are repeated here as (36a) and (36b), respectively.

(36)   a.   *ni yotte* passive:
            Sensei-ga   gakusei-ni yotte   hihans-are-ta.
            teacher-Nom student-to owing criticize-Pass.-Past
            "The teacher was criticized by his student."
         b.

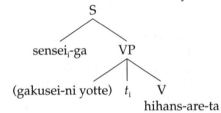

The English *be* passive counterpart of (36a) is in (36c) and its structure is given in (36d).[31]

(36)   c.   The teacher was criticized by the student.
         d.

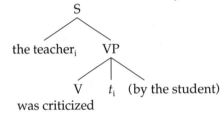

As shown in (36b–c), the subject position of the *ni yotte* passive and the *be* passive is a nontheta position. Therefore, with this structure, we can account for the grammaticality of (11b)/(12b) and (13c)/(14c), the ungrammaticality of (15b), and the parallelisms between *ni yotte* passives and *be* passives which we discussed in section 1. Unlike the passive morpheme of the *ni* indirect passive but like the passive morpheme *-d* in English, the passive morpheme of the *ni yotte* passive, *are*, is a suffix which obligatorily absorbs Case and suppresses an external argument from the attached verb, triggering NP movement of the object to the subject position for Case reasons. Thus, we can also explain the Case facts in (33a) and the binding facts in (33b) as we discussed at the end of the previous section.

Given structures such as (36b) for the *ni yotte* passive, we can account as well for the ungrammaticality of *ni yotte* passive examples such as (37). (Kuno 1973 attributes example (37a) to James McCawley.)

(37) a. *John-ga   ame-ni yotte hur-are-ta.
          John-Nom rain-to owing fall-Pass.-Past
          "John was rained on." (Kuno 1973: 346)
      b. *Sensei-ga   gakusei-ni yotte kurasu-de   nak-are-ta.
          teacher-Nom student-to owing classroom-in cry-Pass.-Past
          "The teacher was cried by the student in the classroom."

This is because the passive morpheme of this type is an obligatory absorber of Case and external theta role so that intransitive verbs such as *hur* "fall" or *nak* "cry" are incompatible with *ni yotte* passives. In this respect, the *ni yotte* passive is significantly different from the *ni* indirect passive (cf. (35a) vs. (37b)).

Recall that it has been controversial how to analyze the *ni* direct passive. To analyze this type of Japanese passive, the uniform hypothesis proposes a theta subject/complement object deletion analysis. On the other hand, the nonuniform hypothesis proposes an NP movement analysis. And we have reached the conclusion in sections 1 and 2 that both the theta subject/complement object deletion analysis under the uniform hypothesis and the NP movement analysis under the nonuniform hypothesis correctly account for properties of *ni* direct passives such as (9b) in one way or another.

The uniform hypothesis assigns structure (32b) to *ni* direct passive example (9b). Example (9b) and structure (32b) are repeated here as (38a) and (38b), respectively.

(38) a. *ni* direct passive:
          Sensei-ga   gakusei-ni hihans-are-ta.
          teacher-Nom student-by criticize-Pass.-Past
          "The teacher$_i$ was affected by his student's criticizing him$_i$."
      b.

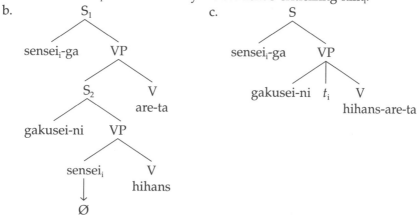

On the other hand, the nonuniform hypothesis assigns structure (32a), repeated here as (38c), to *ni* direct passive example (38a).

In structure (38b) proposed by the uniform hypothesis, the subject *sensei* is a theta subject, because it is selected by the passive verb *are*. With this structure, we can account for the ungrammaticality of (11a)/(12a) and (13b)/(14b), and the grammaticality of (15a). Structure (38c) proposed by the nonuniform hypothesis, on the other hand, cannot account for these data, because the subject position is assumed to be a nontheta position in (38c), as we discussed in section 1.

In contrast, structure (38c) correctly captures the nature of the gap and the status of the *ni* phrase in this type of Japanese passive. That is, in (38c), the gap in the *ni* direct passive is identified as an NP trace, which does not require Case, and the *ni* phrase is claimed to be an adverbial *ni* "by" phrase. We can thus correctly account for the Case facts in (26b) and the binding facts in (29a), as was discussed in section 2. On the other hand, structure (38b) proposed by the uniform hypothesis for the *ni* direct passive cannot account for the facts in (26b) or (29a). This is so, because structure (38b) does not involve NP movement and the *ni* phrase of the *ni* direct passive, *gakusei-ni*, is not analyzed as an adverbial *ni* "by" phrase but is analyzed as the subject of the complement clause in (38b).

It is thus clear that both the uniform hypothesis and the nonuniform hypothesis are correct in one respect or another, but that neither of them can be entirely correct as an analysis of the *ni* direct passive. Therefore, we need to reconcile these two hypotheses, the uniform hypothesis and the nonuniform hypothesis, to account for the properties of the *ni* direct passive adequately. Given this consideration, here, I present a proposal made in Hoshi (1991) as a way of reconciling these two hypotheses. The structure which Hoshi (1991) suggests for the *ni* direct passive sentence (38a) is given in (39a).[32]

(39)   a.

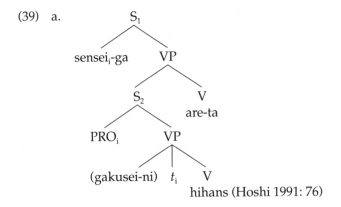

hihans (Hoshi 1991: 76)

Notice that under this proposal by Hoshi (1991), the NP movement analysis by the nonuniform hypothesis is subsumed under the theta subject analysis by the uniform hypothesis. As the uniform hypothesis proposes, the subject of the *ni* direct passive sentence, *sensei*, is a theta subject since it is required by the passive verb *are*. Furthermore, the matrix subject controls the complement object, PRO. On the other hand, as the nonuniform hypothesis argues, NP movement is also involved in this structure. Although the subject, *sensei*, itself does not move, PRO undergoes NP movement from the complement position of the verb, *hihans*, to the subject position of the complement clause, S_2.[33,34] Importantly, given structures such as (39a) for *ni* direct passives, we can account for the properties of all the *ni* direct passive examples in this chapter, i.e. 11(a)/(12a), (13b)/(14b), (15a), (26b), and (29a). Under this PRO movement analysis of the *ni* direct passive, (11a)/(12a) and (13b)/(14b) are straightforwardly ruled out because the subject of the *ni* direct passive is required to be an affectee by the passive verb *rare*, as the uniform hypothesis proposes.

Saito's example (26b) is assigned structure (39b), and the pro movement analysis can also account for the Case facts in the example as the NP movement analysis under the nonuniform hypothesis does.

(39) b.

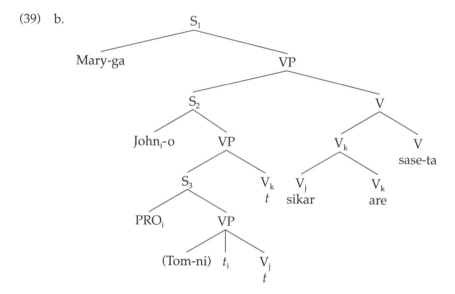

In this representation, the verb *sikar* "scold" first adjoins to the passive verb *are* and then, [$_{Vk}$ *sikar-are*] adjoins to the causative verb *sase*, creating a complex verb [$_V$ *sikar-are-sase*]. The trace left behind by the movement of PRO is an NP trace, which does not require Case, under this proposal, and pro receives null Case but not accusative Case in the subject position of S_2. Hence, in (39b), there is no NP other than the causee *John* which requires accusative Case. Thus, the abstract Double-*o* Constraint is irrelevant in this structure and hence, *John* is allowed to be marked with accusative Case as desired.

Under the assumption that *ni* direct passives such as (29a) are always assigned the PRO movement structure given in (39c), we can correctly account for the binding facts in (29a) as well, as the nonuniform hypothesis does.

(39) c.

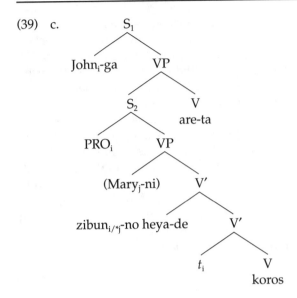

In (39c), the two subject positions, the positions immediately dominated by S_1 and S_2, are occupied by *John* and PRO, which is controlled by *John*. The subject of the embedded clause, *Mary*, appears as an adverbial *ni* "by" phrase due to suppression of an external argument by the passive morpheme *rare*. Furthermore, both of these subject NPs, *John* and PRO, bind a subject-oriented long distance anaphor, *zibun*. Thus, given structure (39c), we can correctly predict that in (29a), not *Mary* but only *John* can be the antecedent of *zibun*, as desired.

Furthermore, as a desirable consequence, this proposal shown in (39a) naturally captures the similarities between the *ni* direct passive in Japanese and the *get* passive in English. (40a) is an instance of the *get* passive, whose properties we discussed in some detail in section 1, and (40b) is the structure Hoshi (1991) proposes for *get* passive examples such as (40a).[35]

(40) a.   The teacher got criticized by his student.
      b.

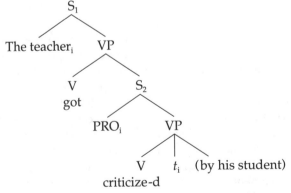

(Hoshi 1991: 85)

Notice that structure (40b) parallels structure (39a) for the *ni* direct passive sentence (38a) in notable respects. The subject NP *the teacher* is a theta subject which is required by the verb *get* of the *get* passive. The subject itself does not undergo NP movement, but PRO which is controlled by the matrix subject moves from the complement position of the embedded verb *criticize-d* to the subject position of S_2 to receive null Case. Furthermore, in both the *ni* direct passive and the *get* passive, the logical subject of the embedded clause appears as an adverbial *by* phrase. Given this theta subject analysis of the *get* passive, we can thus straightforwardly account for the ungrammaticality of (17a)/(18a) and the grammaticality of (19a). Furthermore, structural parallelisms between (39a) and (40b) allow us to capture similarities between the *ni* direct passive and the *get* passive that we discussed in section 1.

In this section, on the basis of the discussions in the preceding sections, I have clarified the structural properties of three types of Japanese passives, the *ni* indirect passive, the *ni yotte* passive and the *ni* direct passive. In particular, I have argued that the uniform hypothesis and the nonuniform hypothesis are both correct in one respect or another in relation to their analyses of the *ni* direct passive and that these two hypotheses must be reconciled. As a way of doing so, I have shown a proposal made in Hoshi (1991) under which the NP movement analysis by the nonuniform hypothesis is subsumed under the theta subject analysis by the uniform hypothesis. In the following section, I will point out remaining problems for the analysis of Japanese passives suggested in this section.

4   Remaining Issues

In this section, I will point out remaining issues concerning the analysis of each type of Japanese passive which is presented in section 3. The first problem concerns the analysis of the *ni* indirect passive in (35), the second one concerns the analysis of the *ni yotte* passive in (36), and the last one concerns the structure of the *ni* direct passive given in (39a).

4.1   Pro/**kare***: passives vs. causatives*

Let us first discuss a problem regarding the structure of the *ni* indirect passive. In section 3, structures (35b) and (39a) were assigned to *ni* indirect passive (35a) and *ni* direct passive (38a), respectively. Representation (35b) is given in (41a), and structure (39a) is repeated in (41b).

(41) a.   b.

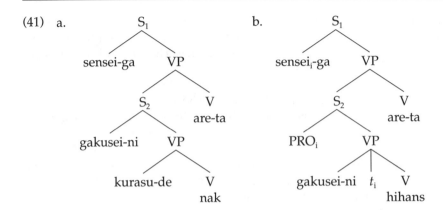

Under the analysis in section 3, the passive morpheme *are* is assumed to be a two-place predicate, taking the subject *sensei* and the complement clause, S_2, in both *ni* indirect passive (41a) and *ni* direct passive (41b), as the uniform hypothesis proposes. However, structure (41b) for the *ni* direct passive is significantly different from structure (41a) for the *ni* indirect passive. As the non-uniform hypothesis argues, structure (41b) for the *ni* direct passive involves NP movement of the logical object of the embedded verb, PRO, while structure (41a) for the *ni* indirect passive does not involve such PRO movement.

Recall, however, that as Y. Kitagawa and Kuroda (1992) point out, if we assume the analysis of Japanese passives like the one in section 3 under which the *ni* indirect passive involves complementation as shown in (41a), we cannot rule out the possibility that the *ni* direct passive example (38a) has also the structure given in (42). And in fact, Kitagawa and Kuroda propose (42) for *ni* direct passive example (38a), where pro coindexed with the matrix subject is base-generated in the complement object position.[36]

(42)

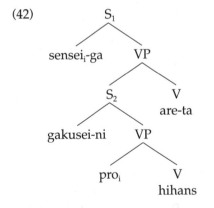

(Kitagawa and Kuroda 1992: 3)

Notice that once we are given either structure (41b) or structure (42) ambiguously for *ni* direct passives such as (38a), we lose our explanation concerning the binding facts in (29a). Recall also that I have shown in sections 2 and 3 that the properties of example (29a) are accounted for only by some type of NP movement analysis like the one shown in (41b), and that a theta subject analysis such as the one in (42) cannot account for those facts in (29a). That is, a theta subject analysis incorrectly predicts that as in (29b), either *John* or *Mary* can be the antecedent of *zibun* in (29a).

Although it is not clear how we can solve this problem under the analysis given in section 3, the consideration above in turn suggests that in contrast with structures such as (41a–b), structures such as (42) are not available as structures for *ni* passives for some principled reason. And the ungrammaticality of examples such as (43), which Mamoru Saito (personal communication, 1990) and Y. Kitagawa and Kuroda (1992: 41) independently observe, at least suggests that this is indeed the case.

(43)   *John$_i$-ga   Bill-ni kare$_i$-o sinyoos-are-ta.
       John-Nom Bill-by he-Acc trust-Pass.-Past
       "John$_i$ was affected by Bill's trusting him$_i$."

Here, we observe that the *ni* passive disallows pronominal elements such as *kare* which is coindexed with the matrix subject in the complement object position. If this is a correct generalization about *ni* passives, structures (42) and (43) are both disallowed and *ni* direct passive examples such as (38a) are unambiguously assigned structures such as (41a).

Importantly, in this respect, the *ni* passive sharply contrasts with the causative in Japanese. Oshima (1979) observes the causative counterpart of the *ni* passive (43) is grammatical as shown below:

(44)   John$_i$-ga   Bill-ni kare$_i$-o sinyoos-ase-ta.
       John-Nom Bill-to he-Acc trust-Cause-Past
       "John$_i$ let/made Bill trust him$_i$." (Oshima 1979: 427)

If we assume with Kuroda (1965a), Kuno (1973), and Shibatani (1973b, 1990), among others, that Japanese causatives such as (44) involve complementation as in (45),

(45)   [$_{S1}$ John$_i$-ga [$_{S2}$ Bill-ni kare$_i$-o sinyoos]-ase-ta]

the grammaticality of example (44) indicates that in contrast with *ni* passives, Japanese causatives allow a pronominal element which is coindexed with the matrix subject to appear in the complement object position. Hence, a remaining problem as to the structure of *ni* passives which we need to solve is why *ni* passives such as (43) do not allow a pronominal element coindexed with the matrix subject in the complement object position as causatives such as (45) do.[37]

4.2   *Double/multiple object structure: passives and ECM*

Consider next Kuroda's structure (36b) again which we assume for the *ni yotte* passive (36a). Structure (36b) is repeated here as (46).

(46)

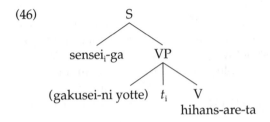

We have seen in the preceding sections that this NP movement structure proposed by Kuroda captures the properties of the *ni yotte* passive. That is, the subject position of the *ni yotte* passive is necessarily a nontheta position, as was shown in (11b)/(12b), (13c)/(14c), and (15b). Furthermore, the *ni yotte* passive always involves NP movement of the logical object and the *ni yotte* phrase is an adverbial *by* phrase, as we observed in the data in (33) (cf. (35a) vs. (37b)).

However, as Kuroda (1979, 1985) and Kuno (1983, 1986b) point out, which noun phrase may be preposed and made the passive subject by *ni yotte* passivization is a potential problem for this type of NP movement analysis of *ni yotte* passives. Consider the following *ni yotte* passive examples from Kuroda (1979).

(47) a.   John-ga   kokumu-syoo-ni   yotte ryoken-o
           John-Nom State-Department-to owing passport-Acc
           toriage-rare-ta.
           take away-Pass.-Past
           "The State Department revoked John's passport."
     b.   Nihon-ga   sihonka-tati-ni yotte utukusii sizen-o
           Japan-Nom capitalist-Pl-to owing beautiful nature-Acc
           hakais-are-te-iru.
           destroy-Pass.-Prog
           "Capitalists are destroying the beautiful nature of Japan." (Kuroda
           1979: 339)

Given that the *ni yotte* passive cannot be analyzed as a variant of the *ni* indirect passive even optionally (cf. (35a) vs. (37b)), Kuroda suggests that the passive subject of (47a) seems to be derived from the source phrase in (48a), *John-kara*, and that the source of the passive subject of (47b) might be the genitive noun phrase in (48b), *nihon-no*, or the locative noun phrase in (48c), *nihon-de*.

(48) a.   Kokumu-syoo-ga   John-kara ryoken-o   toriage-ta.
           State-Department-Nom John-from passport-Acc take away-Past
           "The State Department revoked John's passport."

b. Sihonka-tati-ga   nihon-no utukusii sizen-o   hakais-i-te-iru.
capitalist-Pl-Nom Japan-Gen beautiful nature-Acc destroy-Prog
"Capitalists are destroying the beautiful nature of Japan."

c. Sihonka-tati-ga   nihon-de utukusii sizen-o   hakais-i-te-iru.
capitalist-Pl-Nom Japan-in beautiful nature-Acc destroy-Prog
"Capitalists are destroying the beautiful nature in Japan." (Kuroda 1979: 339)

This possibility suggested by Kuroda regarding target phrases preposed by *ni yotte* passivization is supported by the following data.

(49) a. Gakusei$_i$-ga [$_{VP}$ kokumu-syoo-ni   yotte san-nin t_i (karerano)
student-Nom   State-Department-to owing three-Cl   (their)
ryoken-o   toriage-rare-ta].
passport-Acc take away-Pass.-Past
"The State Department revoked three students' passports."

b. Yooroppa-no kuni$_i$-ga   [$_{VP}$ sihonka-tati-ni yotte   mut-tu t_i
Europe-Gen   country-Nom   capitalist-Pl-to owing six-Cl
(sono) utukusii sizen-o   hakais-are-te-iru].
(its)   beautiful nature-Acc destroy-Pass.-Prog
"Capitalists are destroying the beautiful nature of six European countries."

Under Miyagawa's (1989b) theory of numeral quantifiers in Japanese, a numeral quantifier and its associated NP are required to mutually c-command.[38] Notice that in (49a–b), neither of the numeral quantifiers, *san-nin* or *mut-tu*, can c-command its associated NP in the subject positions, *gakusei* "student" and *yooroppa-no kuni* "European country," due to the existence of VP. The grammaticality of the data in (49) thus indicates that Kuroda's speculation is correct: by *ni yotte* passivization, not only the direct object but also some argument other than the direct object can undergo NP movement to the subject position, leaving a trace behind in its original position. Under his theory, in (49a–b), the numeral quantifiers, *san-nin* and *mut-tu*, are thus associated with the subject NPs through the traces left behind by the NP movement of *gakusei* and *yooroppa-no kuni*, as illustrated in these examples.

A question, however, arises as to why such an argument other than the direct object undergoes NP movement by *ni yotte* passivization. Recall that under the analysis in section 3, it is assumed that the passive morpheme of the *ni yotte* passive absorbs accusative Case and suppresses an external argument from the attached verb, triggering NP movement of the internal argument. One way to solve this problem is to adopt Ishii's (1989) and Shibatani's (1990) proposal that Japanese has a very wide range of double/multiple accusative structure underlyingly as in Korean (H. S. Choe 1987, Yoon 1990, Maling and Kim 1992, among others), and to hypothesize further that predicates in Japanese can take an "additional" object/"affected" argument, typically a theme or patient, depending on the lexical meaning of each predicate.[39] Under this

hypothesis, in *ni yotte* passives such as (47a–b)/(49a–b), the additional object/
affected argument is preposed to the subject position. Hence, in (49a–b),
numeral quantifiers are associated with the subject NPs through the traces left
behind by the movement of those additional objects.

Under this speculation, the following multiple object structures are supposed to exist underlyingly in Japanese. And the ungrammaticality of the
following active examples, where the additional objects *John* and *nihon* appear,
is accounted for by the abstract Double-*o* Constraint in (24).

(50) a. *Kokumu-syoo-ga   John-(o)   ryoken-(o)   toriage-ta.
          State-Department-Nom John-(Acc) passport-(Acc) take away-Past
          "The State Department revoked John's passport."
      b. *Sihonka-tati-ga   nihon-(o)   utukusii sizen-(o)
          capitalist-Pl-Nom Japan-(Acc) beautiful nature-(Acc)
          hakais-i-te-iru.
          destroy-Prog
          "Capitalists are destroying the beautiful nature of Japan."

Notice that there are two NPs marked with accusative Case in these examples.
In contrast, the abstract Double-*o* Constraint in (24) does not rule out examples
such as (49a–b). This is so because the empty categories shown in (49a–b) are
NP traces, which do not require Case.[40,41]

The claim that by *ni yotte* passivization, not only the direct object but also an
additional object/affected argument can undergo NP movement to the subject
position receives further support from the paradigm in (51) and (52).

(51) a. *Nihongo-gakka-no   sinsetu-ga   gakutyoo-ni
          Japanese-Department-Gen new establishment-Nom president-by
          happyoos-are-ta.
          announce-Pass.-Past
          "The president announced the new establishment of the Depart-
          ment of Japanese."
      b. *Nihongo-gakka-no   sinsetu-ga   gakutyoo-ni
          Japanese-Department-Gen new establishment-Nom president-by
          (sono) igi-o   setumeis-are-ta.
          (its)   significance-Acc explain-Pass.-Past
          "The president explained the/its significance of the new establish-
          ment of the Department of Japanese."

(52) a.   Nihongo-gakka-no   sinsetu-ga   gakutyoo-ni
          Japanese-Department-Gen new establishment-Nom president-to
          yotte happyoos-are-ta.
          owing announce-Pass.-Past
          "The president announced the new establishment of the Depart-
          ment of Japanese."

b. *Nihongo-gakka-no   sinsetu-ga   gakutyoo-ni
   Japanese-Department-Gen new establishment president-to
   yotte (sono) igi-o   setumeis-are-ta.
   owing (its) significance-Acc explain-Pass.-Past
   "The president explained the/its significance of the new establishment of the Department of Japanese."

Under Kuroda's theory/the analysis in section 3, we can straightforwardly account for the ungrammaticality of (51a–b) and for the grammaticality of (52a). The subject position of both *ni* direct passive (51a) and *ni* indirect passive (51b) is a theta position, and in these examples, the subject is required to be an affectee by the passive verb *are*. However, abstract NPs such as *sinsetu* "new establishment" cannot be interpreted as affectees, and thus (51a) and (51b) are correctly ruled out. On the other hand, the subject position of the *ni yotte* passive is a nontheta position, and thus there is no selectional restriction imposed on the subject of this type of Japanese passive. Hence, *ni yotte* passive example (52a) is permitted.

Importantly, in grammaticality, *ni yotte* passive example (52b) parallels *ni* passives in (51a–b) but not *ni yotte* passive (52a), and Kuroda's dichotomy between *ni* passives and *ni yotte* passives appears to break down in (51) and (52). Notice, however, that in (52b), the direct object *(sono) igi-o* "(its) significance" is not *ni yotte* passivized. Thus, under the suggestion above, it must be the additional/affected argument, typically a theme or patient, that is preposed to the subject position in *ni yotte* passive example (52b). However, abstract NPs such as *sinsetu* cannot be interpreted as an affected argument, a theme/patient of *setumeis* "explain." Hence, (52b) is correctly ruled out, as desired, and we are led to the conclusion that in contrast with multiple object structures (50a–b), the following multiple object structure does not exist even underlyingly in Japanese:

(53) *Gakutyoo-ga   nihongo-gakka-no   sinsetu-(o)
      president-Nom Japanese-Department-Gen new establishment-(Acc)
      (sono) igi-(o)   setumeis-i-ta.
      (its) significance-(Acc) explain-Past
      "The president explained the significance of the new establishment of
      the Department of Japanese."

Notice further that although (51b) and (52b) are both ungrammatical, they are forced to have similar interpretations. Under the analysis presented in this chapter, we can also account for this observation, while maintaining Kuroda's dichotomy of *ni* passives and *ni yotte* passives. In *ni* passive (51b), the subject NP *nihongo-gakka-no sinsetu* is required to be an "affectee" by the passive morpheme *are*, whereas in (52b), the preposed subject NP, *nihongo-gakka-no sinsetu*, is also required to be interpreted as an "additional" object/"affected" argument of *setumeis* "explain." In either of these two cases, a similar selectional restriction is imposed upon the passive subject *sinsetu*, but the passive subject NP cannot satisfy such restrictions in (51b) or (52b). Hence, (51b) and (52b) are both ungrammatical with violations of similar selectional restrictions.[42]

Given the hypothesis that predicates in Japanese can license an additional object/affected argument depending on its lexical meanings, we can naturally account for the interesting properties of the Japanese "Exceptional Case Marking" (henceforth, ECM) construction like (54).

(54) a. Mary-ga   kare-ga/o   baka   da   to   omot-ta.
          Mary-Nom he-Nom/Acc foolish Cop Comp think-Past
          "Mary thought [s′ that he/*him was foolish]."
      b. Kare-ga Mary-ni yotte baka   da   to   omow-are-ta.
          he-Nom Mary-to owing foolish Cop Comp think-Pass.-Past
          "He$_i$ was thought by Mary [s′ that e_i was foolish]."

In Japanese ECM example (54a), it appears that the embedded subject can surface with either nominative Case or accusative Case. On the other hand, as the English translation indicates, the embedded subject must surface with nominative Case but cannot appear with accusative Case in English. (54b) is the *ni yotte* passive counterpart of (54a). As the English translation indicates, the English *be* passive counterpart of (54b) is totally ungrammatical in contrast with (54b).

Noting these differences between the Japanese ECM construction and the English counterpart, Saito (1982, 1983) suggests that they are different in that in (54a), the NP *kare* can be outside S′ so that *kare* coindexed with pro in S′ can appear with accusative Case, while this is not possible in English (cf. the English translation of (54a)). His structure for (54a) is given in (55).

(55) a. [s Mary-ga [s′ kare-ga baka da to] omot-ta]
      b. [s Mary-ga kare$_i$-o [s′ pro$_i$ baka da to] omot-ta]

More specifically, Saito claims that the predicate, *omow* "think," in Japanese can be a two-place predicate or a three-place predicate as in (55a–b), while *think* in English is a two-place predicate. That is, in his proposal, *kare$_i$-o* and [s′ pro$_i$ *baka da to*] are both analyzed as internal arguments of *omow* in (54a), as illustrated in (55b).[43] Because *kare* is the matrix object, it can be preposed to the matrix subject position by *ni yotte* passivization, as shown in (54b). For this reason, the English counterpart of (55b) does not exist, and the English counterpart of (54b) is ungrammatical.

Notice that the suggestion regarding an additional object/affected argument in Japanese in this section can provide an answer for the question as to why *omow* in Japanese can be a three-place predicate in contrast with *think* in English. This is that the Japanese ECM construction above can be considered as an instance in which the additional object/affected argument licensed by the predicate, *omow*, surfaces with accusative Case.[44] This is because S' does not require Case (N. Chomsky 1981a, Stowell 1981), and thus the abstract Double-*o* Constraint in (24) does not prevent this type of additional object/ affected argument, a theme argument of *omow*, from surfacing in the construction given in (54a–b).

The claim that the NP *kare* in example (54a–b) is the additional/affected argument, a theme argument of *omow*, receives support from the following contrast between (56a) and (56b–c).

(56) a. Mary-ga [$_{S'}$ tyuui-ga taisetu da to] omot-ta.
   Mary-Nom   heed-Nom important Cop Comp think-Past
   "Mary thought that we have to be careful."
   b. *Mary-ga tyuui$_i$-o [$_{S'}$ pro$_i$ taisetu da to] omot-ta.
   Mary-Nom heed-Acc   important Cop Comp think-Past
   "Mary thought that we have to be careful."
   c. *Tyuui$_i$-ga Mary-ni yotte [$_{S'}$ pro$_i$ taisetu da to]
   heed-Nom Mary-to owing   important Cop Comp
   omow-are-ta.
   think-Pass.-Past
   "It was thought that we have to be careful."

While examples (56b–c) are ungrammatical, (54a) and (56a) are grammatical. This is so, because in (56b), abstract NP's such as *tyuui* 'heed' cannot be interpreted as an affected argument of *omow*, a theme. Hence, it cannot appear outside S' as an additional object, and due to unavailability of an additional object, *ni yotte* passive example (56c) is ungrammatical. On the other hand, in (54a), NPs such as *kare* "he" can be interpreted as an affected argument, and thus, (54a) is grammatical. In (56a), the NP *tyuui* is the subject of the embedded clause and thus, affectedness interpretation is not imposed by the matrix verb *omow*. Hence, (56a) is grammatical.[45]

The above speculation regarding the properties of *ni yotte* passive examples such as (47a–b)/(49a–b) thus seems to be a plausible one, but questions still remain as to what the exact nature of an additional object/affected argument is, and exactly what kinds of predicates in Japanese license such an additional object/affected argument.

4.3 Theta role assignment: Japanese passives and Chicheŵa/Romance causatives

Finally, consider again structures (39a) and (40b) which Hoshi (1991) proposes for *ni* direct passive (38a) and *get* passive (40a), respectively. (39a) is given in (57a), and (40b) is repeated here as (57b).

(57)   a.   b.

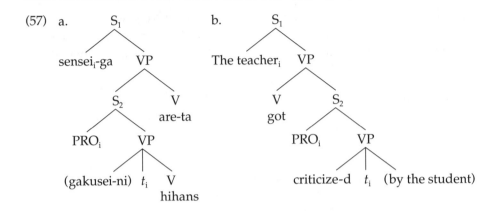

Recall that it was argued in section 3 that given structure (57a) for the *ni* direct passive and structure (57b) for the *get* passive, we can account for the properties of each of these two passives that we discussed in sections 1 and 2. At the same time, we can straightforwardly capture the similarities between them that we also discussed in those sections. First, both *ni* direct passive (57a) and *get* passive (57b) have a theta subject. Second, these two passives involve the NP movement of PRO, which is controlled by the matrix subject, within the complement clause, S_2. PRO undergoes NP movement to the subject position of S_2 to receive null Case. Third, in these two passive constructions, the logical subjects of the embedded verbs, *gakusei* and *the student*, appear as adverbial *by* phrases optionally in S_2.

Notice, however, that a question arises as to the function of the passive morpheme of the *ni* direct passive represented in structure (57a). In *get* passive (57b), *get* of the *get* passive is assumed to be a two-place predicate which takes the subject, *the teacher*, and the complement clause, S_2. And the passive morpheme, *d*, absorbs Case and suppresses an external argument from the attached verb *criticize*, triggering the NP movement of PRO in S_2. In contrast, in structure (57a) for the *ni* direct passive, the passive morpheme *are* is represented simply as a two-place predicate, taking the subject *sensei* and the complement clause, S_2. Therefore, in (57a), it is unclear how the passive morpheme *are* functions as a suffix which absorbs Case and suppresses an external theta role like the English passive morpheme, *d*, in (57b). To put this problem in a different way, (57a) does not express structurally the conclusion in sections 1, 2, and 3: as the uniform hypothesis proposes, the passive morpheme of the *ni* direct passive is a two-place predicate which takes a subject and a complement clause, but at the same time, the passive morpheme of this type is a suffix which triggers NP movement by absorbing Case and suppressing an external argument from the attached verb, as the nonuniform hypothesis argues. In (57a), the passive morpheme of the *ni* direct passive is treated only as a two-place predicate, but it is not treated as a suffix which like the English passive morpheme, *d*, in (57b), is claimed to trigger the NP movement of PRO.

As a way of solving this problem regarding the dual nature of the passive morpheme of the *ni* direct passive, Hoshi (1994a, 1994b) proposes the derivation in (58) for *ni* direct passive example (38a).[46]

(58) a.   b.

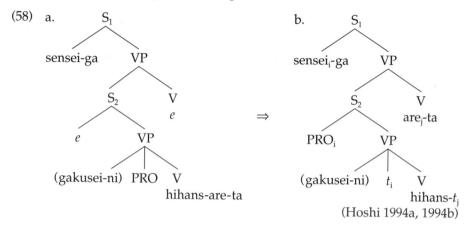

(Hoshi 1994a, 1994b)

Notice that adopting Washio's (1989/90) important proposal, Hoshi (1994a, 1994b) attempts to capture the dual characteristics of the passive morpheme of the *ni* direct passive, *are*, in the course of the derivation, as illustrated in (58).[47] In so doing, Hoshi argues that the similarities between the *ni* direct passive and the *get* passive are captured structurally in the derivation given in (58). Under this proposal, the passive morpheme *are* adjoins to the embedded verb, *hihans*, to absorb Case and suppress an external argument as a suffix without assigning its theta roles at the initial point of the derivation, as shown in (58a). At a later point of the derivation in LF, as illustrated in (58b), the passive verb *are* excorporates/splits off from the embedded verb and raises into the V position of the matrix clause, S_1, discharging a subject theta role to *sensei* and an internal theta role to S_2.[48] In the course of the derivation shown in (58b), PRO controlled by the matrix subject also moves into the subject position of S_2 to receive null Case.[49]

The claim that the passive morpheme of the *ni* direct passive has such dual characteristics might appear quite peculiar to Japanese at first glance. Importantly, however, not only the Japanese passive morpheme of this type but also the causative verb in Romance, Chicheŵa and other languages display the same type of dual characteristics (Alsina 1992, M. Baker 1988, Kayne 1975, Williams 1979, Zubizarreta 1985, Di Sciullo and Williams 1987, Burzio 1986, Guasti 1992, among others).[50] Consider the following Italian *faire-par* constructions:

(59) a. Ho fatto spegnere la   candela da Giovanni.
          (I) made put out   the candle   by Giovanni
          "I made the candle be put out by Giovanni."
      b. Piero fa   riparare la   macchina da Giovanni.
          Piero makes repair   the car   by Giovanni
          "Piero has the car repaired by Giovanni."

In these two Italian causative examples, the external arguments, the subjects of the embedded verbs, appear as an adverbial *da* "by" phrases, although no affixes such as a passive morpheme which suppress an external argument are attached to the embedded verbs.

Given these facts, Williams (1979), Zubizarreta (1982, 1985), and Di Sciullo and Williams (1987), among others, propose that in the *faire-par* construction, the causative verb functions in two different ways: it behaves as a predicate, assigning theta roles; it also behaves as a lexical affix, suppressing the external argument of the verb of the embedded clause. If these similarities between the *ni* direct passive morpheme and the causative morpheme in other languages are real, we can conclude that the dual characteristics displayed by the passive morpheme of the *ni* direct passive are not peculiar to Japanese.[51] A question, however, remains as to why the *ni* direct passive verb and the causative verb in other languages display this type of dual characteristics.

5   Conclusions

In sections 1 and 2, I have shown that Kuroda's dichotomy between *ni* passives and *ni yotte* passives and the dichotomy of *ni* direct passives and *ni* indirect passives proposed by the nonuniform hypothesis are both correct. And I have concluded that there are three different types of passives in Japanese, *ni yotte* passives, *ni* direct passives, and *ni* indirect passives. On the basis of the discussions in sections 1 and 2, I have also demonstrated that Kuroda's NP movement analysis of *ni yotte* passives and the structure which both the uniform hypothesis and the nonuniform hypothesis assign to *ni* indirect passive are basically correct. However, in section 3, by showing that both the uniform hypothesis and the nonuniform hypothesis correctly capture important properties of the *ni* direct passive in one way or another but that neither of these two competing theories can be entirely correct, I have argued that we have to reconcile both of these two hypotheses to analyze the *ni* direct passive properly. As a way of doing this, I have presented a proposal made in Hoshi (1991).

In section 4, I have pointed out remaining problems for the analysis of Japanese passives presented in section 3 together with possible solutions. First, I have pointed out that given the analysis in section 3, *ni* direct passive example (38a) is assigned structure (41b) or structure (42), and thus we lose our account for the binding facts in (29a). Although I did not offer a solution for this problem in this chapter, I suggested the possibility that structures such as (42) involving pro in the complement object position are not available for *ni* direct passives. This claim is based on the fact that pronominal elements such as *kare* in the complement object position cannot be coindexed with the matrix subject in *ni* passives as shown in (43), whereas such pronominal elements can be coreferential with the matrix subject in causatives in Japanese as in (44).

This fact also suggests that although *ni* passives and causatives in Japanese project biclausal structure, they must have some fundamental differences (A. Watanabe 1993, Hoshi 1994a, 1994b).

Second, if the analysis of *ni yotte* passives presented in this chapter is correct, the data in (47), (49), and (51) suggest that the predicate–argument structure in Japanese is significantly different from that in languages such as English. That is, predicates in Japanese can take an additional object/affected argument, typically a theme or patient, like predicates in Korean but unlike predicates in English. This conclusion then lends support to Kuroda's (1988) agreement parameter (cf. Fukui 1986, Takano 1996, Fukui and Takano to appear): English is a forced agreement language, whereas Japanese is a nonforced agreement language. Given the principle of the uniqueness of agreement which requires that agreement inducing base categories such as V agree with at most one X^{max} (Kuroda 1988), it is correctly predicted by Kuroda's theory that there are multiple/double object structures in Japanese, while there aren't such constructions in English.

Third, if the derivation in (58a–b) proposed for the *ni* direct passive is correct, it must be the case that theta role assignment does not have to be completed at the initial point of the derivation, D-structure, as Larson (1988) argues. Thus, to the extent that the proposed derivation in (58a–b) for the *ni* direct passive is correct, it provides support for N. Chomsky's (1992, 1995a) proposal that D-structure, in which all the grammatical relations are represented all at once, does not exist.

NOTES

* I wrote this chapter when I was staying in the Department of Japanese at the Faculty of Foreign Languages at Nanzan University as a guest academic researcher in 1997. Here, I would like to express my gratitude to Nanzan University, which provided me with such a valuable opportunity. This chapter is based on my previous work on Japanese passives (Hoshi 1991, 1994a, 1994b). I would also like to thank Koichi Abe, Yasuaki Abe, Koji Arikawa, Mona Anderson, Naoya Fujita, Hajime Hoji, Yasuo Ishii, Noriko Kawasaki, Ruth Kempson, Chisato Kitagawa, Yoshihisa Kitagawa, S.-Y. Kuroda, Richard Larson, Howard Lasnik, Diane Lillo-Martin, Shigeru Miyagawa, Naoko Nemoto, Shigeo Tonoike, Noriko Yoshimura, Javier Ormazabal, Natsuko Tsujimura, Myriam Uribe-Etxebarria, Saeko Urushibara, and especially Jun Abe and Mamoru Saito for their valuable comments and suggestions, which greatly helped me develop my analysis of Japanese passives. The research that I conducted to write this chapter was supported in part by research funds from the School of Oriental and African Studies at the University of London and the Japan Foundation Endowment Committee.

1   Following Howard and Niyekawa-Howard (1976), Kuroda (1979, 1985), Saito (1982), Kuno (1983, 1986b), Miyagawa (1989b), Y. Kitagawa and Kuroda (1992), and Tsujimura (1996b), among others, I adopt the terms "direct passives" and "indirect passives" and I use these terms simply for the purposes of exposition at the phenomenal level without any commitment to particular analyses.

The present tense form of the passive morpheme in Japanese is *rare-ru*, and the past tense form is *rare-ta*. The initial consonant *r* drops after consonantal verb stems such as *nagur* "punch" or *nak* "cry." Verbs derived from an abstract noun by means of a light verb *su-ru* "do" have the passive form ending *s-are-ru*. Hence, the passive form of *hihansu-ru* "criticize" is *hihans-are-ru* "be criticized."

2   It should be noted that translations I provide for Japanese passive examples do not have any theoretical import.

3   Following Howard and Niyekawa-Howard (1976), Kuroda (1979, 1985), Saito (1982), Kuno (1983, 1986b), Miyagawa (1989b), Y. Kitagawa and Kuroda (1992), and Tsujimura (1996b), among others, I adopt the terms "uniform hypothesis" and "nonuniform hypothesis."

4   See Saito (1982) and Marantz (1984) for different versions of the uniform hypothesis. Some of the important proposals made by them will be discussed later in section 2.

5   More specifically, K. Hasegawa (1964) and Kuroda (1965a, 1979) propose that if the direct or indirect object of the embedded clause is identical with the matrix subject, the embedded object is deleted. Reinterpreting this complement object deletion analysis in the principles-and-parameters theory (N. Chomsky 1981a, 1986b, among others), Kuroda (1983) briefly discusses the possibility that the gap in the embedded object position of direct passives might be pro-controlled by the matrix subject. On the other hand, Y. Kitagawa and Kuroda (1992) assume that the gap in the direct passive is pro in their paper. However, they state that they have not yet attained a complete understanding of the nature of the empty category involved in direct passives (Y. Kitagawa and Kuroda 1992: 42), and imply that the gap in the direct passive which is optionally controlled by the matrix subject has some special properties. See their work for their important discussions about the nature of this gap.

6   Reinterpreting this NP movement analysis in the principles-and-parameters theory, Saito (1982), Marantz (1984), Miyagawa (1989b), and others propose that the passive morpheme of the direct passive suppresses the external theta role and absorbs the Case of the attached verb, triggering NP movement of the logical object. This NP movement analysis of direct passives will be discussed in detail in section 2.

7   We will come back to this issue in section 4.

8   Following K. Inoue (1976a) and Kuroda (1979), among others, I call the passive construction with *ni, ni* passives, and the passive constructions with *ni yotte, ni yotte* passives. Roughly speaking, both *ni* and *ni yotte* correspond to *by* in English.

Given these terminologies, I thus call passive sentences such as (2) the *ni* direct passive, and passive examples such as (3) the *ni* indirect passive in this chapter.

9   Y. Kitagawa and Kuroda (1992) also discuss the parallelism between the *ni* direct passive and the *get* passive. See Washio (1989/90) for a different comparison between Japanese passives and English passives.

10 By the term "affectee," Kuroda (1979) basically means something or someone that is acted upon or influenced. The reader is referred to Kuroda (1979, 1985) and Kuno (1983, 1986b) for the exact definitions of terms such as "affectees," "affect," "affectivity," or "affectedness" which are used in Kuroda (1979).

11 K. Inoue (1976a) first observes contrasts such as the one in (11a–b), and claims that the distinction between *ni* and *ni yotte* is determined by semantic factors. And she has made the following important remark on this point: "*ni* has the meaning of 'influence of the agent' on the passive subject. Its difference from *ni yotte* is: *ni* may be used only in cases where the passive subject and the agent are closely related to each other in this sense." From this, Inoue concludes "if the passive subject is such that it does not feel such influence, or that it does not receive the direct effect of such influence, one cannot use *ni*. Therefore, if the passive subject is inanimate, *ni* is often excluded" (K. Inoue 1976a: 84).

12 Lasnik and Fiengo (1974) show that the following contrast can be accounted for by the same assumption:

(i) a. $John_i$ is intentionally easy to please $[e]_i$.
     b. *$John_i$ is intentionally certain $[t_i$ to win]. (Lasnik and Fiengo 1974: 546–7)

The reader is referred to Perlmutter (1970), Jackendoff (1972), Lasnik and Fiengo (1974), Zubizarreta (1982), and Hoshi (1991), among others, for detailed discussions on this assumption.

13 Although Kuroda (1979) marks * for example (15b), a violation of the requirements imposed by subject-oriented adverbs seems to induce marginal ungrammaticality, as shown in (15b).

14 Kuno (1983, 1986b) abandons the nonuniform analysis of the direct passive and the indirect passive proposed in Kuno (1973), and adopts a uniform analysis of *ni* passives, which is quite similar to Kuroda's (1965a, 1979, 1986) analysis. Kuno (1983, 1986b) also differentiates *ni yotte* passives from *ni* passives, but he does so differently from Kuroda. See Kuno (1983, 1986b) for detailed discussions of his analysis of *ni* passives and *ni yotte* passives. Y. Abe (1985) also argues for Kuroda's dichotomy between *ni* passives and *ni yotte* passives.

15 There is another important difference between *ni* passives and *ni yotte* passives. According to Kuno (1973: 346), James McCawley first observed that there does not exist a *ni yotte* passive counterpart of *ni* indirect passives such as (3).

(i) *Sensei-ga   gakusei-ni yotte
      teacher-Nom student-to owing
      kurasu-de   nak-are-ta.
      classroom-in cry-Pass.-Past
      "The teacher was cried by the student in the classroom."

An account of the ungrammaticality of *ni yotte* passive examples such as (i) will be provided in section 3.

16 Lasnik and Fiengo (1974) marks * for example (19b), but the contrast in (19a–b) seems to be much weaker than the ones in (17a–b) and (18a–b). This is consistent with the claim that a violation of the requirements imposed by subject-oriented adverbs is weak, as was suggested in n. 13.

17   See Cheng and Huang (1994) for more discussions on the *get* passive.

18   Y. Kitagawa and Kuroda (1992) propose the following argument structure for the passive morpheme of the *ni* passive:

(i)   *rare*:
[Experiencer/Agent [Eventuality __]]
[+Affected]
   (Y. Kitagawa and Kuroda 1992: 37)

The term "eventuality," which is intended to cover both events and states, is adopted from Bach (1986).

19   *Ni* indirect passive examples such as (i) which Kuno (1973: 24) observes show that the interpretation of the indirect passive does not have to be adversative.

(i)   Taroo$_i$-ga sensee-ni kare$_i$-no
      Taro-Nom teacher-by he-Gen
      musuko-o home-rare-ta.
      son-Acc   praise-Pass.-Past
      "Taro$_i$ was affected by the teacher's praising his$_i$ son."

In this *ni* indirect passive, the adversative interpretation is not obtained, and the effect on Taro of the teacher's praising his son is positive and beneficial.

20   Kuno (1983, 1986b) independently makes a similar proposal regarding the differences in interpretation between *ni* direct passives and *ni* indirect passives.

21   Through a detailed study of various empirical phenomena including quantifier scope and "reconstruction" effects in *ni* passives, Y. Kitagawa and Kuroda (1992) also convincingly argue for the uniform treatment of *ni* passives.

22   See Saito (1982), Marantz (1984), and Miyagawa (1989b), among others, for relevant discussions of N. Chomsky's (1981a) proposal that passive morphology suppresses an external argument and absorbs Case from the attached verb.

23   See S.-I. Harada (1973), Shibatani (1973b), Kuroda (1978, 1988), Poser (1981), and Saito (1982, 1985), among others, for the nature of the abstract Double-*o* Constraint in Japanese. (24) is Saito's (1985) interpretation of S.-I. Harada's (1973) abstract Double-*o* Constraint. As is clear in the discussion below, a complex predicate counts as a single verb for this constraint.

24   S.-I. Harada (1973) and Kuroda (1978, 1988), among others, observe that examples such as (i) are not as ungrammatical as (25b).

(i)   ??Mary-ga   [John-o
      Mary-Nom [John-Acc
      hamabe-o hasir]-ase-ta.
      beach-Loc run]-Cause-Past
      "Mary made/let John run on the beach."

They propose that this is because example (i) violates the "surface" Double-*o* Constraint, which mildly prohibits multiple occurrence of *o* in a single clause, but (25b) violates abstract Double-*o* Constraint in (24) as well as the surface Double-*o* Constraint. Notice that in (25b), *John* and *hon* are both marked with accusative Case *o*, while in (i), *John* is marked with accusative Case *o* but *hamabe* is marked with the locative marker *o*.

   Harada and Kuroda, among others, further observe that in an important respect, the abstract and surface Double-*o* Constraint violations differ aside from their degrees of deviance. The abstract double-*o* violation obtains even when one of the "*o*-marked NPs" is an empty category, if the empty category requires accusative Case. On the other hand, the surface Double-*o* Constraint violation can be circumvented by dislocating one of them. This is illustrated below as well as in (25c). (See Kuroda 1978, Hoji 1990, and Murasugi 1991 for detailed discussions on the cleft construction in Japanese. In the latter two works, it is assumed that the examples in (ii) and (iii) involve movement of an empty operator to Comp.)

(ii)

a. *[$_{S'}$ [$_S$ Mary-ga   John-o
          Mary-Nom John-Acc
     e_i yom-ase-ta]-no]-wa
          read-Cause-Past-Comp-Top
     hon$_i$-o   da.
     book-Acc Cop
     "It is a book that Mary made John read."

b. *[$_{S'}$ [$_S$ Mary-ga e_i hon-o
          Mary-Nom   book-Acc
     yom-ase-ta]-no]-wa
     read-Cause-Past-Comp-Top
     John$_i$-o   da.
     John-Acc Cop
     "It is John that Mary made read a book."

(iii)

a. [$_{S'}$ [$_S$ Mary-ga   John-o e_i
          Mary-Nom John-Acc
     aruk-ase-ta]-no]-wa
     walk-Cause-Past-Comp-Top
     hamabe$_i$-o da.
     beach-Loc Cop
     "It is the beach where Mary made John walk."

b. [$_{S'}$ [$_S$ Mary-ga e_i hamabe-o
          Mary-Nom   beach-Loc
     aruk-ase-ta]-no]-wa
     walk-Cause-Past-Comp-Top
     John$_i$-o   da.
     John-Acc Cop
     "It is John that Mary made walk on the beach."

As the examples in (ii) have two NPs that require abstract objective Case, they are completely out even when one of them is a trace left behind by empty operator movement. On the other hand, the examples in (iii) show that an accusative NP and an *o* locative NP are compatible as long as one of them is dislocated.

25 Just for ease of exposition, I assume that the Japanese causative verb is a two-place predicate, as illustrated in (27) and (28). Furthermore, I assume Kuroda's (1965a) verb-raising analysis of Japanese causatives. In this chapter, I also assume a slightly modified version of Saito's (1982) theory of Case assignment/licensing in Japanese: nominative case *ga* is structurally assigned to an NP which is immediately dominated by tensed S; accusative Case *o* is assigned to an object; as for the dative marker *ni*, it is assigned to an argument which cannot surface with either nominative case *ga* or accusative Case *o*.

26 In a class lecture at the University of Connecticut in 1989, Mamoru Saito pointed out similarities between the complement object deletion analysis of the Japanese *ni* direct passive by the uniform theory and that of the English *tough* construction proposed by Lasnik and Fiengo (1974). On the basis of the Case properties shown in (26b), he also pointed out a crucial difference between these two constructions: the gap in the *ni* direct passive is an NP trace, whereas the gap of the *tough* construction has the properties of a WH trace (N. Chomsky 1977, among others).

27 The reader is referred to Howard and Niyekawa-Howard (1976) and Kuno (1983, 1986b) for different accounts for the facts in (29a–b) under the uniform hypothesis.

28 N. A. McCawley's (1972) and Kuno's (1973) arguments based on the observations of the possible

antecedent of *zibun* "self" are not as strong as Saito's (1982) argument for the existence of an NP trace in the *ni* direct passive. Y. Kitagawa and Kuroda (1992), for example, cast doubt on the validity of N. A. McCawley's and Kuno's observations that the *ni* phrase in the *ni* direct passive cannot be the antecedent of *zibun*, by observing that *kensatsugawa* "prosecution" is clearly the antecedent of *zibun-tati* in *ni* direct passive (i).

(i)   Kono syookobukken$_i$-ga
      this   evidence-Nom
      kensatugawa$_j$-ni
      the prosecution-by
      zibun-tati#$_i$/$_j$-no
      self-pl-Gen
      tugoo-noiiyooni [*e*]$_i$
      advantageous
      dettiage-rare-ta.
      fake up-Pass.-Past
      "This evidence was faked up by the prosecution to their advantage." (Y. Kitagawa and Kuroda 1992: 17)

I agree with their grammatical judgment shown in (i), but it seems to me that examples such as (i) have some special properties, because we observe basically the same binding facts in the following *ni yotte* passive example:

(ii) Kono syookobukken$_i$-ga
      this   evidence-Nom
      kensatugawa$_j$-ni   yotte
      the prosecution-to owing
      zibun-tati#$_i$/$_j$-no
      self-pl-Gen
      tugoo-noiiyooni [*e*]$_i$
      advantageous
      dettiage-rare-ta.
      fake up-Pass.-Past
      "This evidence was faked up by the prosecution to their advantage."

The fact that the NP *kensatugawa* can also be the antecedent of *zibun-tati* in (ii) implies that a constraint which requires anaphors such as *zibun* be c-commanded by its antecedent can be cancelled in this type of example. This is so, because the *ni yotte* phrase is a pure adverbial phrase, and thus the NP within the *ni yotte* phrase should not be able to c-command anything outside of the phrase. I, thus, leave the exact nature of examples (i–ii) for future research and continue to assume that N. A. McCawley's (1972) and Kuno's (1973) observations regarding the possible antecedent of *zibun* in *ni* passives are basically correct. See J. Abe (1997) for much relevant discussions on special properties of *zibun* such as the one mentioned above.

29 The reader is referred to Miyagawa (1989b) for more arguments for an NP movement analysis of the *ni* direct passives. See also Y. Kitagawa and Kuroda (1992) for counterarguments to Miyagawa's arguments.

30 The *ni yotte* "by" phrase is similar to the passive *by* phrase in languages such as Hebrew in that both of those phrases are clearly adverbial agentive phrases. In *ni yotte* passives, the *ni yotte* "by" phrase means literally "owing to" or "due to", and in Hebrew, the *by* phrase means literally "in the hands of" (Zubizarreta 1985). On the other hand, the *ni* "by" phrase in the *ni* direct passive and the *by* phrase in English as well as in other languages such as French, Spanish, and Italian need not be agentive. That is, those *by* phrases do not restrict semantic role of their complements. Given this, a question arises as to why in the *ni yotte* passive, a suppressed external

argument appears as the agentive *ni yotte* "by" phrase, whereas in the *ni* direct passive, a suppressed argument appears with *ni* "by" which has a dummy status. I leave this question for future research. See Hoshi (1994a, 1994b) for relevant discussions.

31 (36d) is a simplified structure of the *be* passive in English. See N. Chomsky (1981a), Jaeggli (1986), and M. Baker et al. (1989), among others, for detailed discussions of the structure of the *be* passive.

32 This proposal crucially adopts a VP internal PRO movement analysis which Saito and Murasugi (1990) originally propose to explain the nature of some instances of the *be* passive. The reader is referred to Saito and Murasugi (1990) for detailed discussions of their VP internal PRO movement analysis of *be* passives in English. Just for ease of exposition, the structure which Hoshi (1991) proposes of *ni* direct passives such as (38a) is simplified in the text.

33 In this chapter, I assume that PRO undergoes NP movement to receive null Case in the subject position of the complement clause for it to be properly licensed. See N. Chomsky and Lasnik (1993) and R. Martin (1993) for relevant discussions on the theory of null Case for PRO. The reader is referred to Hoshi (1991) for a different motivation for PRO movement.

34 On the basis of different considerations, Nishigauchi (1993) proposes a different type of PRO movement analysis for the direct passive which involves a human subject. The reader is referred to his work for detailed discussions of the proposal.

35 Just for ease of exposition, the structure Hoshi (1991) proposes

for *get* passives such as (40a) is simplified in the text.

36 Just for ease of exposition, I have simplified the structure that Y. Kitagawa and Kuroda (1992) propose for the *ni* direct passive in the text.

37 A. Watanabe (1993) and Hoshi (1994a, 1994b) attempt to solve this problem in terms of Condition B of Binding Theory by assigning different types of biclausal structures for *ni* passives and causatives in Japanese.

On the other hand, to defend structure (42) for the *ni* direct passive, Y. Kitagawa and Kuroda (1992, nn. 29, 46) claim that the ungrammaticality of (43) is due to the interaction between the referential property of *kare* and the optional control involved in Japanese *ni* passives. However, it is not immediately clear how this constraint is derived from independently motivated principles in grammar, and it is not clear under their theory either why the constraint rules out *ni* passive example (43) but permits causative example (44). See Y. Kitagawa and Kuroda (1992) for more detailed discussions of their constraint mentioned above.

38 By making use of numeral quantifiers, Miyagawa (1989b) has convincingly shown where the empty category coindexed with the passive subject syntactically exists in Japanese passives. The reader is referred to Miyagawa (1989b) for his arguments to this effect.

39 This seems to be a reasonable hypothesis, given the claim by Choe (1987) and Yoon (1990), among others, that in Korean multiple object constructions, an "additional" object is subject to some sort of affectedness condition.

40 Like examples (25b–c), examples such as (50a) violate the abstract Double-*o* Constraint. As shown below, the violation in (50a) cannot be circumvented by dislocating one of the *o*-marked NPs. (See relevant discussions in n. 24.)

(i) a. *[$_{S'}$ [$_S$ Kokumu-syoo-ga
       State Department-Nom
       John-o e_i
       John-Acc
       toriage-ta]-no]-wa
       take away-Past-Comp-Top
       ryoken$_i$-o   da.
       passport-Acc Cop
       "It is his passport that the State Department took away from John."

   b. *[$_{S'}$ [$_S$ Kokumu-syoo-ga
       State Department-Nom
       e_i ryoken-o
          passport-Acc
       toriage-ta]-no]-wa
       take away-Past-Comp-Top
       John$_i$-o   da.
       John-Acc Cop
       "It is John from whom the State Department took away a passport."

41 Based on the properties of examples such as (47a–b), Ishii (1989), Terada (1990), Kubo (1990), and Shibatani (1990), among others, propose that Japanese has the "possessor passive." The actual implementation of the idea differs in these works. For example, the possessor NP is claimed to be the underlying specifier of the object NP in Kubo's proposal, but as another (accusative) object in Shibatani's analysis. A possible solution for the problem for Kuroda's NP movement analysis of the *ni yotte* passive in the text, if it is correct, lends support to Ishii's and Shibatani's proposal. The reader is referred to Kuroda (1979, 1985), Kuno (1983, 1986b), Ishii (1989),

Terada (1990), Kubo (1990), Shibatani (1990), and Y. Kitagawa and Kuroda (1992), among others, for more detailed discussions on this issue.

42 Kuno (1983, 1986b) proposes that both *ni* passives and *ni yotte* passives have the same biclausal structure, but that the passive subject of *ni* passives does not have to be "directly involved" in the event or state described by the complement clause, whereas the passive subject of the *ni yotte* passives must be "directly involved" in the event or state described by the embedded clause. (See Kuno 1983, 1986b) for his precise definition of the notion, "direct involvement"; cf. Kuroda 1985.) The analysis of Japanese passives presented in this chapter is clearly incompatible with this analysis. Importantly, however, our analysis provides an answer for the question of why the passive subject of *ni yotte* passives must be directly involved in the event or state described by the complement clause. This is because in *ni yotte* passivization, the direct object or the additional object/affected argument is forced to become the passive subject by NP movement.

43 See Kuno (1976b) for detailed discussions of the properties of the Japanese ECM construction. Ishii (1989) convincingly argues for the structure proposed by Saito (1982, 1983) through a study of the Japanese reciprocal predicates. Hoji (1991b) also argues for Saito's structure (55) for the Japanese ECM constructions such as (54a).

44 Hoji (1991b) calls what I call an additional object/affected argument a major object.

45 The Japanese ECM constructions such as (54a) are different from the

English ECM constructions like (ia–b).

(i) a. We believed [$_S$ him/*he to be honest].
    b. We believed [$_S$ there to be a riot in LA].

First, in contrast with (54a), (ia–b) involve S but not S' as their complement clauses. Second, as shown in (ia), the embedded subject must appear with accusative Case. Third, as illustrated in (ib), there is no selectional restriction imposed on the embedded subject. Hence, expletive elements such as *there* can appear in the subject position of the complement clause (cf. (56b–c)).

46 Just for ease of exposition, I have simplified the structures proposed by Hoshi (1994a) for the *ni* direct passive in the text. Hoshi's (1994b) structures are slightly different from the ones proposed in Hoshi (1994a), but this difference does not affect the discussions of this chapter.

47 Washio (1989/90) proposes that the passive morpheme of the *ni* indirect passive has the dual characteristics. More specifically, he claims that the Japanese passive morpheme of this type not only suppresses the external theta role of the verb in an embedded clause, but also assigns a theta role as a predicate in a matrix clause. To explain this dual nature of *rare* of the *ni* indirect passive, Washio (1989/90) first proposes that *rare* of this type of Japanese passive first functions as a suffix and at a later point of the derivation behaves as a predicate, by adopting Larson's (1988) theory in an innovative way. Although Hoshi (1994a, 1994b) disagrees with Washio (1989/90) in that the passive morpheme of the *ni* indirect passive has such dual characteristics, Hoshi (1994a, 1994b) adopts Washio's ingenious proposal to capture the dual nature of *rare* of the *ni* direct passive as shown in (58). See Y. Kitagawa and Kuroda (1992) and Hoshi (1994a, 1994b) for arguments against Washio's specific proposals about Japanese passives.

48 Saito and Hoshi (1994) also propose that in the Japanese light verb construction, the theta role assigning noun discharges (some of) its theta roles in LF.

49 The reader is referred to Hoshi (1994a, 1994b) for desirable consequences derived from the proposal given in (58).

50 I am very grateful to Mamoru Saito, who brought the interesting properties of Romance causatives to my attention. He pointed out in personal communication in 1990 that the *ni* direct passive and one type of Romance causatives, the *faire-par* construction, have significant similarities. Both of these constructions project biclausal structure; the subject of the embedded clause appears as an adjunct *by* phrase, although it appears that no affix which triggers suppression of an external argument is attached to the embedded verb.

51 See Hoshi (1994b) for a uniform treatment of Japanese passives and Romance causatives.

8 Causatives*

SHIGERU MIYAGAWA

0 Introduction

In this chapter, I will present an analysis of the syntax and morphology of the causative construction in Japanese. Since Kuroda's 1965 MIT dissertation, much of the work on the Japanese causative has focused on the causative construction formed by a verb stem and the morphologically dependent causative morpheme *(s)ase*. By its dependent nature, *(s)ase* attaches to the verb stem, and forms a morphologically and phonologically unitary "word." The causative morpheme takes the shape *sase* if it attaches to a vowel-ending stem (*tabe-sase* "eat-cause") while the initial *s* drops if the verb stem is consonant-ending (*ik-ase* "go-cause"). The deletion of *s* in the latter is forced by the open-syllable property of Japanese. Much of the chapter will be concerned with the syntax of this *V-(s)ase* causative construction. I will, in particular, take up the issues that arise with the operation of Counter Equi, including case marking issues such as the Double-*o* Constraint. Kuroda (1965a) first proposed the operation of Counter Equi, which has the unusual property that the lower of two coreferential noun phrases deletes the higher phrase (the name "Counter Equi" was given by S.-I. Harada (1973)). After reviewing this analysis, I will present a recent analysis by Harley (1995) that captures the intuition behind Counter Equi, but in the form of an abstract NP movement at the level of Logical Form. I will show that this LF movement analysis shares a number of properties with the Counter Equi analysis, hence we can view it as the Minimalist version of Counter Equi. I will give additional evidence for Harley's analysis by showing that it allows us to avoid empirical problems that arise with the Counter Equi analysis. In the last part of this chapter, I will take up some issues having to do with the relationship between the syntactic *V-(s)ase* and lexical causatives. As a part of this discussion, I will deal with the *V-(s)as* form, which often alternates freely with *V-(s)ase*.[1]

1   Syntax of *V-(s)ase*

When we look at the surface structure of a *V-(s)ase* sentence, there is nothing extraordinary compared to sentences with a simple verb. The morphologically complex verb is phonologically a unitary word (Y. Kitagawa 1986), and the case-marking possibilities on the arguments reflect what we find in sentences with simple verbs. The three possibilities for the *V-(s)ase* are given below.

(1)   intransitive stem
      Hanako-ga   Taroo-o   ik-ase-ta.
      Hanako-Nom Taro-Acc go-Cause-Past
      "Hanako made Taro go."

(2)   intransitive stem
      Hanako-ga   Taroo-ni ik-ase-ta.
      Hanako-Nom Taro-Dat go-Cause-Past
      "Hanako let Taro go."

(3)   transitive stem
      Hanako-ga   Taroo-ni piza-o   tabe-sase-ta.
      Hanako-Nom Taro-Dat pizza-Acc eat-Cause-Past
      "Hanako made/let Taro eat pizza."

Each of these case-marking arrays is found with simple verbs. The Nom–Acc sequence in (1) is found with typical transitive verbs such as *naguru* "hit" and *taberu* "eat." The Nom–Dat–Acc sequence in (3) is found with double-object verbs such as *ageru* "give" and *okuru* "send." The Nom–Dat sequence in (2) is found with simple verbs such as *noru* "get on (e.g. a bus, horse)."

The most important syntactic discovery about the *V-(s)ase* construction is that, despite the fact that it appears ordinary on the surface, it exhibits properties associated with a complex structure (Kuroda 1965a). One argument for the complex structure comes from the behavior of the reflexive *zibun* "self," which requires a subject as its antecedent. In a simplex sentence, which contains only one subject, the interpretation of the reflexive is unambiguous.

(4)   Tanaka$_i$-ga   Suzuki$_j$-ni   zibun$_{i/*j}$-no hon-o   ageta.
      Tanaka$_i$-Nom Suzuki$_j$-Dat self$_{i/*j}$-Gen   book-Acc gave
      "Tanaka gave Suzuki self's book."

However, in a *V-(s)ase* sentence, the interpretation of *zibun* is ambiguous (Kuroda 1965a).

(5)   Tanaka$_i$-ga   Suzuki$_j$-ni   zibun$_{i/j}$-no hon-o   yom-ase-ta.
      Tanaka$_i$-Nom Suzuki$_j$-Dat self$_{i/j}$-Gen   book-Acc read-Cause-Past
      "Tanaka made/let Suzuki read self's book."

Because *zibun* requires a subject as its antecedent, this ambiguity suggests a biclausal structure, as illustrated below.

(6)

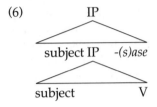

The *V-(s)ase* in (5) above is formed from the transitive-verb stem *yom* "read." The same ambiguity arises with a *V-(s)ase* formed from an intransitive stem, regardless of whether the causee is marked with the accusative *o* or the dative *ni*.[2,3]

(7) a. Tanaka$_i$-ga   Suzuki$_j$-o   zibun$_{i/j}$-no heya-e   ik-ase-ta.
         Tanaka$_i$-Nom Suzuki$_j$-*Acc* self$_{i/j}$-Gen   room-to go-Cause-Past
         "Tanaka made Suzuki go to his room."
     b. Tanaka$_i$-ga   Suzuki$_j$-ni   zibun$_{i/j}$-no heya-e   ik-ase-ta.
         Tanaka$_i$-Nom Suzuki$_j$-*Dat* self$_{i/j}$-Gen room-to go-Cause-Past
         "Tanaka let Suzuki go to his room."

1.1   Case marking and the causee

With the biclausality analysis in place, the central issue for the syntax of *V-(s)ase* is how we account for the case marking of the causee. The causer is always marked with the nominative case marker (or the topic marker *wa*), as expected, and, if the verb stem is transitive, the object of the verb stem is marked with the accusative case marker, again, as expected. It is the analysis of the case marking on the causee that requires further analysis. If the verb stem is intransitive, the causee may be marked with the accusative case marker *o* or the dative case marker *ni*. If the stem is transitive, the causee may only be marked with the dative *ni*.[4] Marking the causee with the accusative case marker leads to a Double-*o* Constraint violation (S.-I. Harada 1973, K. Inoue 1976a, Kuroda 1965a, Poser 1981, Shibatani 1973b), which stipulates that two occurrences of the accusative *o* in a simplex clause are prohibited.

(8) *Hanako-ga   Taroo-o piza-o   tabe-sase-ta.
      Hanako-Nom Taro-*Acc* pizza-*Acc* eat-Cause-Past
      "Hanako made/let Taro eat pizza."

I will discuss the Double-*o* Constraint in detail in the next section.

1.2   *Make vs. let*

Closely tied to the issue of case marking on the causee is the interpretation of the causative sentence. This is most clearly seen in the constructions where the verb stem is intransitive, and the causee may be marked with the accusative or the dative, as in (1) and (2). As originally noted by Kuroda (1965b) and in many subsequent works (e.g. S.-I. Harada 1973, C. Kitagawa 1974, Miyagawa 1984, Shibatani 1973b, 1976, Tonoike 1978), the "accusative" causative implies some sort of direct or coercive causation, while the "dative" causative implies a much less direct or coercive causation. In the transitive-stem *V-(s)ase* con-struction, this difference is not reflected in the case marker between accusative and dative; the causee can only be marked by the dative case marker owing to the Double-*o* Constraint. Nevertheless, we can detect the difference in mean-ing between the "make" and "let" causative.

A natural way to encode this difference between "make" and "let" causative into the syntax of *V-(s)ase* is to postulate two kinds of *(s)ase*. One takes a direct object for the causee, which captures the "make" interpretation. This direct object is coreferential with the embedded subject. The other *(s)ase* does not take a direct object, reflecting the "let" causative interpretation.

(9)   a.   "make" causative   b.   "let" causative

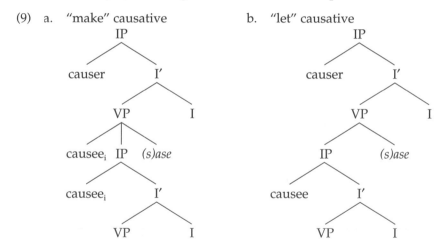

In the "make" causative in (9a) above, the object of *(s)ase* functions semanti-cally in the same way as the object of a simple lexical causative such as *tomeru* "stop." In both, the subject/causer is interpreted to directly affect the referent of the object. In the "let" causative in (9b), *(s)ase* takes a sentential complement without also taking a direct object. The interpretation of this structure is that the causer "let" the situation referred to by the complement clause take place, with-out implying that there is any direct causation directed at the causee. Kuroda (1965a, 1965b) was the first to propose this bifurcation of structure for the "make" and "let" interpretations, and Kuno (1973) and many others followed his lead.

1.3   Counter Equi

The analysis above captures the intuition behind the "make" vs. "let" causative. In terms of the mechanics of case-marking assignment, it works straightforwardly for the "make" causative with an intransitive stem. The direct object, corresponding to the causee, gets the accusative case marker, and the embedded subject, which also corresponds to the causee, is deleted by Equi; in the more recent framework the latter would presumably be a PRO. To assign the dative case on the causee, Kuroda (1965a, 1978) proposes a rule that extracts the embedded subject to the matrix clause, and assigns it the dative case marker *ni*. This rule applies to both intransitive-stem and transitive-stem sentences. For the intransitive-stem sentence, this rule applies without the help of another rule.

(10)   intransitive-stem "let" causative

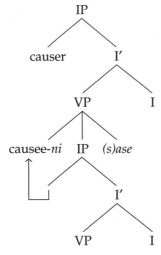

The same operation is responsible for the dative case marking on the causee in a transitive-stem "let" causative. Up to this point, the later system developed by Kuno (1973) is essentially the same, with one fundamental difference. Kuno assumes that at some point in the derivation, the biclausal structure is collapsed into a simplex one, and the original embedded verb raises and attaches to *(s)ase*. The verb-raising analysis is also adopted by Baker (1985), who analyzes a variety of head-raising phenomena cross-linguistically. Unlike Kuno (1973), Baker assumes that the biclausal structure stays intact even after verb raising. I will defend this position.

For the transitive-stem "make" causative, Kuroda (1965a) proposed an unusual rule which is now called Counter Equi (S.-I. Harada 1973). This deletion rule operates in exactly the opposite way from the regular Equi, in that the lower of the two identical phrases deletes the higher phrase.

(11) Counter Equi with transitive-stem "make" causative

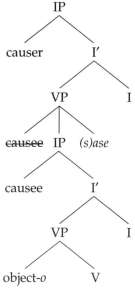

This clears the way for the embedded subject to raise to the matrix VP and receive the dative *ni*. This unusual rule allows the derivation to avoid the Double-*o* Constraint. If, instead of Counter Equi, the normal Equi applies, the causee in the matrix clause would be assigned the accusative *o*. Because the embedded clause also has an object with the accusative *o*, this leads to two occurrences of *o*, in violation of the Double-*o* Constraint.[5]

In contrast, Kuno (1973) analyzes the dative *ni* on the causee of a transitive-stem "make" causative as fundamentally different from the *ni* on the causee of an intransitive-stem "let" causative. He suggests that the former *ni* is an instance of the dative marking that occurs with double-object verbs such as *ageru* "give."

(12) Taroo-ga   kodomo-ni geemu-o   ageta.
     Taroo-Nom child-Dat   game-Acc gave
     "Taro gave his child a game."

In Kuno's system, this dative marking on the causee of a transitive-stem "make" causative is made possible by the fact that after the biclausal structure is collapsed, and verb raising takes place, the complex verb, V-*(s)ase*, ends up with two internal arguments, the causer and the object of the verb stem.

I will defend the analysis that distinguishes between the two kinds of *ni* as originally proposed by Kuno (1973). We will see that the *ni* on the "let" causee in both the transitive-stem and intransitive-stem causatives is a postposition, while the *ni* on the causee of a "make" transitive-stem causative is a case marker (Harley 1995).

2   An Alternative Analysis

Contrary to the analysis by Kuroda (1965a, 1978), and also Kuno (1973) and Shibatani (1973b), there is evidence that the "make" causee is in the embedded subject position, while the "let" causee, or a phrase corresponding to it, is in the matrix clause alongside *V-(s)ase*. This is exactly the opposite of the structure originally proposed by Kuroda (1965a).

(13)   a.   "make" causative   b.   "let" causative

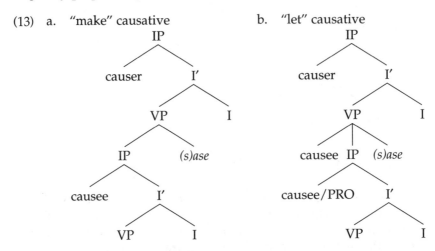

These structures have been proposed as an alternative to Kuroda's analysis by K. Inoue (1976a, 1983), Harley (1995), Terada (1990), and Tonoike (1978). I will give arguments that these structures are correct for the two kinds of causatives under investigation. Later, I will suggest an extension to this analysis proposed by Harley (1995) that captures in an interesting way the original insight by Kuroda (1965a) that the "make" causative has a direct object, while a "let" causative does not. As we will see, with Harley's extension, the two approaches become virtually nondistinct.

I now turn to empirical evidence for the two structures above. I will begin with a discussion of the Double-*o* Constraint, and show that for the "make" causative, we must assume the structure in (a) above, in which the causee is in the embedded subject position.

2.1   *Double-o Constraint and the alternative analysis*

In Kuroda (1965a, 1978) (cf. also S.-I. Harada 1973, Shibatani 1973b), Counter Equi, which deletes the higher of two coindexed NPs, makes it possible to avoid the Double-*o* Constraint. This operation applies to the transitive-stem "make" causative.

(14) Hanako-ga   Taroo-ni/*-o   piza-o   tabe-sase-ta.
     Hanako-Nom Taro-Dat/*-Acc pizza-Acc eat-Cause-Past
     "Hanako made Taro eat pizza."

If the Double-*o* Constraint were not to apply, the derivation with regular Equi, which would result in the causee having the accusative case, should also be grammatical, just as in the intransitive-stem "make" causative.

(15) Hanako-ga   Taroo-o ik-ase-ta.
     Hanako-Nom Taro-Acc go-Cause-Past
     "Hanako made Taro go."

2.1.1 *Evidence for the Double-*o* Constraint*

One problem associated with motivating the Double-*o* Constraint is that it is difficult to construct a minimal pair to show its effect. Thus, in the transitive-stem "make" causative, for which the effect of this Constraint was first detected (Kuroda 1965a), the accusative case marker never shows up on the causee, so that we are left to compare this with the intransitive-stem "make" causative. It is possible that these two constructions involve some independent property that gives an appearance that the Double-*o* Constraint holds. If, for example, Counter Equi is independently motivated as an operation that applies without reference to the Double-*o* Constraint, there would be no need to invoke this Constraint for the causative construction.

S.-I. Harada (1973) motivates the Double-*o* Constraint and Counter Equi using a construction that he terms the *tokoro*-complement. In this construction, a verb takes as its complement a NP headed by the word *tokoro* "occasion."

(16) Keisatu-ga [sono doroboo-ga   nigeru tokoro]-o   tukamaeta.
     police-Nom [that burglar-Nom escape occasion]-Acc arrested
     "The police arrested the burglar trying to escape."

In response to M. Nakau's (1973) analysis, which does not postulate any "extra" elements that do not show up in the surface form, S.-I. Harada (1973) argues that this construction contains a direct object in the matrix clause that is coreferential to the embedded subject.

(17) ... sono doroboo [sono doroboo-ga   ...]-o   tukamaeta
     ... that burglar [that burglar-Nom ...]-Acc arrested

This matrix object never surfaces under normal circumstances because it would lead to a violation of the Double-*o* Constraint.

(18) *Keisatu-ga sono doroboo-o nigeru tokoro-o   tukamaeta.
       police-Nom that burglar-Acc escape occasion-Acc arrested
       "The police arrested the burglar trying to escape."

To derive the grammatical string, Counter Equi applies, which deletes the
matrix object under identity with the embedded subject.

Harada gives several arguments for the existence of this "extra" matrix
object. A particularly striking piece of evidence is the cleft construction, in
which we can see the direct object making its appearance.

(19) Keisatu-ga   sono doroboo-o/*-ga   tukamaeta nowa, nigeru
       police-Nom that burglar-Acc/*-Nom arrested   escape
       tokoro(-o)   datta.
       occasion(-Acc) was
       "It was the moment he tried to escape that the police arrested the burglar."

What is clefted here is the *tokoro* complement. As shown, "the burglar" must
have the accusative case, which identifies the phrase as a part of the matrix
clause, not the clefted complement. It is ungrammatical with the nominative
Case marker because the nominative would identify the phrase as the subject
of the clefted complement, hence fragmenting the structure of the clefted complement.[6] While this argument for the existence of the extra matrix object
is compelling (but see particularly Kuroda 1978), we face the same problem
I noted for the transitive-stem "make" causative: Counter Equi is directly tied
to the Double-*o* Constraint.

Miyagawa (1986) gives evidence for the Double-*o* Constraint using the
purpose expression construction. Because Counter Equi is irrelevant to the
derivation of this construction, it is possible to construct a minimal pair to
show the effect of the Constraint. The purpose expression (PE) is made up of
a motion verb, most commonly "go" or "come," and a tenseless complement
that usually immediately precedes the motion verb.

(20) Taroo-ga [PRO hon-o   kai-ni] itta.
       Taro-Nom [PRO book-Acc buy]   went
       "Taro went to buy a book."

I gave several arguments to show that, while the PE is biclausal to begin with,
an optional rule of restructuring has the effect of collapsing this structure
into a simplex one, very much like the restructuring construction in Romance
(Rizzi 1982). This restructuring operation may apply only if the complement
is adjacent to the matrix motion verb (Miyagawa 1986).

One argument for restructuring has to do with the occurrence of a phrase
that must be construed with the matrix motion verb. In the following example,
the instrumental phrase *zitensya-de* "by bicycle" must be construed with the
matrix "go;" it is semantically anomalous with the embedded verb "buy."

(21) *Kodomo-ga [PRO hon-o   zitensya-de kai-ni] Kanda-ni itta.
   child-Nom [PRO book-Acc bicycle-by buy]   Kanda-to went
   "My child went to Kanda to buy a book by bicycle."

The instrumental "by bicycle" occurs in the complement clause, which is not adjacent to the matrix verb due to the intervention of the goal phrase "to Kanda." This leads to semantic anomaly because "by bicycle" is forced to be construed with the complement VP "buy a book." If the goal phrase "to Kanda" is removed, the complement clause is adjacent to the matrix verb, and restructuring makes it possible to appropriately construe "by bicycle" with the matrix verb "go."

(22) Kodomo-ga hon-o   zitensya-de kai-ni itta.
   child-Nom book-Acc bicycle-by buy   went
   "My child went by bicycle to buy a book."

We can see the effect of the Double-*o* Constraint if we causativize a sentence such as the above. Note that the verb, "go," is intransitive, so the causative counterpart of this is the intransitive-stem causative, which allows either the accusative ("make") or the dative ("let") causee. There is no problem if the causee is dative.

(23) Taroo-ga   kodomo-ni hon-o   zitensya-de kai-ni ik-ase-ta.
   child-Nom child-Dat   book-Acc bicycle-by buy   go-Cause-Past
   "Taro let his child go by bicycle to buy a book."

However, if the causee is accusative, we get a violation of the Double-*o* Constraint.

(24) *Taroo-ga   kodomo-o hon-o   zitensya-de kai-ni ik-ase-ta.
    child-Nom child-Acc book-Acc bicycle-by buy   go-Cause-Past
    "Taro made his child go by bicycle to buy a book."

In contrast, if restructuring is not forced by the occurrence of a phrase such as "by bicycle" in the complement portion of the sentence, the double appearance of *o* is fine because they are in two different clauses.

(25) Taroo-ga   kodomo-o [PRO hon-o   kai-ni] (zitensya-de)
   child-Nom child-Acc [PRO book-Acc buy]   (bicycle-by)
   ik-ase-ta.
   go-Cause-Past
   "Taro made his child go (by bicycle) to buy a book."

(24) and (25) constitute a minimal pair for motivating the Double-*o* Constraint without making reference to Counter Equi.

As a final note about the nature of the Double-*o* Constraint, Poser (1981) shows that the effect of this Constraint shows up with abstract Objective (accusative) Case. In the following transitive-stem "make" causative, the object of the verb stem has been topicalized, so that it does not take *o*. Despite this, the Double-*o* Constraint is violated.

(26) Piza$_i$-wa Hanako-ga Taroo-ni/*-o e_i tabe-sase-ta.
      pizza$_i$-Top Hanako-Nom Taro-Dat/*-Acc e_i eat-Cause-Past
      "Pizza, Hanako made Taro eat."

In the ungrammatical sentence, there is only one accusative *o*, which occurs on the causee. This indicates that the Double-*o* Constraint is sensitive to the Objective Case assigned to the empty category, *e*, in the direct object position. This Case, which is not pronounced, is assigned to the *structural* position of the direct object. I will continue to use the widely used name "Double-*o*" Constraint, with the understanding that *o* here may be the actual accusative case marker or the abstract Objective Case.[7]

2.1.2 Problem with the Counter Equi analysis

A problem arises with the Counter Equi analysis in regard to the Double-*o* Constraint. The Double-*o* Constraint prohibits more than one occurrence of the accusative case marker/Objective Case in a simplex clause. To prohibit the ungrammatical transitive-stem "make" causative, then, it is necessary to assume restructuring (or clause union in Relational Grammar terminology) of the causative, just as we saw for the purpose expression construction. However, there is evidence that restructuring of the type we saw for the purpose expression never applies to the causative construction (Miyagawa 1986). I will give two arguments against a restructuring analysis of the causative construction.

S.-I. Harada (1973) observed that the embedded object in a transitive-stem causative cannot be passivized.

(27) *Kodomo$_i$-ga Taroo-ni (yotte) Hanako-ni t$_i$ yob-ase-rare-ta.
      child$_i$-Nom Taro-by   Hanako-Dat t$_i$ call-Cause-Passive-Past
      "The child was made to call by Taro by Hanako."

S.-I. Harada (1973), who assumed restructuring, proposed a Global Constraint that prohibits an originally embedded NP from being passivized at the matrix level (after restructuring). However, as noted by K. Inoue (1978), if we simply assume that restructuring never applies to the causative construction, we can readily exclude the ungrammatical passive example by appealing to the locality condition on A-movement. One such locality is Condition A of Binding Theory (N. Chomsky 1981a), which states that an anaphor must be bound within its local domain. If NP trace is viewed as an anaphor, the ungrammatical example would constitute a violation of Condition A, because it fails to be bound within its local domain (the embedded IP). There are other locality conditions on A-movement that would give the same result, but I will not pursue them here.

The second argument has to do with the construal of a pronoun. It is possible for a pronoun in the embedded object position to be coreferential with the causer (Oshima 1979).

(28) Taroo$_i$-ga Hanako-ni kare$_i$-o hihans-ase-ta.
Taro$_i$-Nom Hanako-Dat he$_i$-Acc criticize-Cause-Past
"Taro made Hanako criticize him."

This construal is possible because the antecedent and the pronoun are in different clauses, so that the pronoun is not bound in its local domain. It is possible that, even if restructuring applies, we can encode some relevant information into the derivation, along the lines of a Global Constraint, to make the construal still possible. However, Miyagawa (1986) gives evidence from PE to show that if restructuring does apply, the local domain that "protects" the pronoun is destroyed.

(29) Taroo-ga Hanako$_i$-to   [PRO kanozyo$_i$-o syookaisi-ni]
Taro-Nom Hanako$_i$-with [PRO she$_i$-Acc   introduce]
daigaku-ni   itta.
university-to went
"Taro went with Hanako to the university to introduce her."

(30) ???Taroo-ga Hanako$_i$-to   kanozyo$_i$-o zitensya-de syookaisi-ni itta.
Taro-Nom Hanako$_i$-with she$_i$-Acc   bicycle-by   introduce   went
"Taro went with Hanako by bicycle to introduce her."

In (29), restructuring cannot apply because the adjacency condition for it is not met, owing to the occurrence of "to the university" between the complement clause and the matrix motion verb. In this biclausal structure, the pronoun may be construed with the antecedent in the matrix clause. In (30), the occurrence of "by bicycle" forces restructuring, making the intended construal for the pronoun impossible.

Given these arguments, we can assume that the causative construction never undergoes restructuring. On this account, the ungrammatical double-*o* occurrence in a transitive-stem "make" causative becomes a mystery if we follow the widely accepted underlying structure (see below) (S.-I. Harada 1973, Kuroda 1965a, Kuno 1973, Shibatani 1973b) instead of the one we are assuming.

(31) *Hanako-ga   Taroo-o piza-o   tabe-sase-ta.
Hanako-Nom Taro-Acc pizza-Acc eat-cause-Past
"Hanako made Taro eat pizza."

(32)   "make" causative

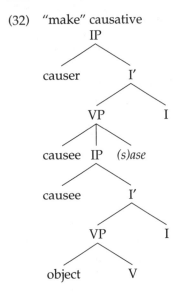

Instead of Counter Equi, it is possible to apply regular Equi to this structure, which would result in the causee in the matrix clause having the accusative *o*. Without restructuring, the two accusative phrases (the second is on the embedded object) occur in different clauses throughout the derivation, thus the Double-*o* Constraint should allow this string. To get the grammatical string, Counter Equi must be forced to apply to this biclausal structure instead of the regular Equi, but that would make the nature of Double-*o* Constraint, and also the operation of Counter Equi, devoid of substance.

On the other hand, the analysis that we are pursuing, which locates the causee of the "make" causative in the embedded subject position (K. Inoue 1976a, Harley 1995, M. Nakau 1973, Terada 1990, Tonoike 1978), can easily account for this ungrammaticality without resorting to restructuring. The two occurrences of *o* are in the same, embedded clause. Below, I will give further evidence for the alternative analysis.

2.2   *Further evidence for the alternative analysis*

I will now give independent evidence that the causee of the "make" causative is in the embedded subject position while the *ni* phrase in a "let" causative is in the matrix clause with *(s)ase*.

In Miyagawa (1996, 1997a), I gave a series of arguments against movement to a VP-adjoined position.[8] We find additional evidence for this in the causative construction if we adopt the proposal that the "make" causee stays in the embedded subject position while the phrase corresponding to the "let" causee appears in the matrix clause. Let us begin with the following "make" and "let" examples.

(33) a. "make"
　　　　Taroo-ga   kodomo-o kooen-e ik-ase-ta.
　　　　Taro-Nom child-Acc park-to go-Cause-Past
　　　　"Taro made his child go to the park."
　　b. "let"
　　　　Taroo-ga   kodomo-ni kooen-e ik-ase-ta.
　　　　Taro-Nom child-Dat   park-to go-Cause-Past
　　　　"Taro let his child go to the park."

Now note the contrast in grammaticality if we scramble the goal phrase "to the park" to the left of the causee.

(34) a. "make"
　　　　　Taroo-ga   kooen-e$_i$ kodomo-o t$_i$ ik-ase-ta.
　　　　　Taro-Nom park-to$_i$ child-Acc t$_i$ go-Cause-Past
　　　　　"Taro made his child go to the park."
　　b. "let"
　　　???Taroo-ga   kooen-e$_i$ kodomo-ni t$_i$ ik-ase-ta.
　　　　　Taro-Nom park-to$_i$ child-Dat   t$_i$ go-Cause-Past
　　　　　"Taro let his child go to the park."

If we assume that the accusative causee in (34a) is in the embedded subject position, the scrambled element, "to the park," adjoins to the embedded IP, a legitimate adjunction site. However, in (34b), the *ni* phrase corresponding to the causee is in the matrix VP, thus, by virtue of the prohibition against the VP-adjunction landing site, "to the park" cannot move to the VP-adjoined site. I conjecture that the reason why this sentence is not completely out is due to the fact that there is a focus position above the VP (Miyagawa 1997a), which is a legitimate landing site for "to the park." One way to view the awkwardness of the example in (34b) is that, due to the prohibition against VP-adjunction, "to the park" is moving to the focus position, but pronounced in a neutral way, without focus, there is no reason for this phrase to move into this position, leading to the awkwardness. We can improve (34b) by placing focus stress on the moved element.

(35) (?)Taroo-ga   **kooen-e**$_i$ kodomo-ni t$_i$ ik-ase-ta.
　　　　　Taro-Nom **park-to**$_i$ child-Dat   t$_i$ go-Cause-Past
　　　　　"Taro let his child go to the park."

No such focus is needed for (34a), in which "to the park" is adjoined to the embedded IP.

　This analysis predicts that a transitive-stem causative example should only have the "make" interpretation if the object is scrambled to the left of the causee. I believe that this is correct with neutral intonation.

(36)　a.　without scrambling
　　　　　Taroo-ga　kodomo-ni piza-o　　　tabe-sase-ta.
　　　　　Taro-Nom child-Dat　pizza-Acc eat-Cause-Past
　　　　　"Taro made/let his child eat pizza."
　　　b.　with scrambling
　　　　　Taroo-ga　piza-o$_i$　　　kodomo-ni t$_i$ tabe-sase-ta.
　　　　　Taro-Nom pizza-Acc$_i$ child-Dat　　t$_i$ eat-Cause-Past
　　　　　"Taro made/???let his child eat pizza."

In (36b), the object phrase, "pizza," has scrambled to the left of the causee, "child." For this movement to be legitimate, the scrambled object must adjoin to the embedded IP. This is only possible if the causee, "child," is in the embedded subject position. It is only in the "make" causative that the causee is positioned as such – in the embedded IP.

　　Terada (1990) argues for the alternative structures for the causative construction on the basis of the interpretation of agent-oriented adverbs such as *hitori-de* "alone" (cf. also Harley 1995). On the assumption that such an adverb must be clausemate with the agentive phrase that it modifies, Terada notes the following difference.

(37)　a.　"make"
　　　　　Hanako-to　Taroo-ga　hitori-de kodomo-o kooen-e
　　　　　Hanako-and Taro-Nom alone　　child-Acc　park-to
　　　　　ik-ase-ta.
　　　　　go-Cause-Past
　　　　　"Hanako and Taro made the child go alone to the park."
　　　b.　"let"
　　　　　*Hanako-to　Taroo-ga　hitori-de kodomo-ni kooen-e
　　　　　Hanako-and Taro-Nom alone　　child-Dat　park-to
　　　　　ik-ase-ta.
　　　　　go-Cause-Past
　　　　　"Hanako and Taro let the child go alone to the park."

As shown, the adverb "alone" may occur to the left of the causee only in the "make" causative example. Terada accounts for this difference by hypothesizing that the accusative causee in the "make" causative is generated in the embedded subject position, and the adverb "alone" to its left may occur in the same IP, possibly by adjunction.

(38)　"make"　[$_{IP}$ . . . [$_{IP}$ *hitori-de* "alone" causee . . .] (s)ase . . .]

On the other hand, in the "let" causative, the *ni* phrase occurs in the matrix clause, and it binds a PRO in the embedded subject position. Because it is PRO that receives the agentive thematic role, by occurring to the left of the *ni* phrase, the adverb cannot be in the same clause with the phrase (PRO) that receives the agentive role.

(39) "let" *[$_{IP}$ ... *hitori-de* "alone" causee$_i$-*ni*. [$_{IP}$ PRO$_i$ ...] *(s)ase* ...]

If the adverb occurs to the right of the *ni* phrase, the sentence is perfect, as predicted.

(40) Hanako-to   Taroo-ga   kodomo-ni hitori-de kooen-e ik-ase-ta.
       Hanako-and Taro-Nom child-Dat   alone   park-to go-Cause-Past
       "Hanako and Taro let the child go alone to the park."

   This analysis predicts, correctly, that a transitive-stem *V-(s)ase* sentence only has the "make" interpretation if the adverb occurs to the left of the causee.

(41) Hanako-to   Taroo-ga   hitori-de kodomo-ni terebi-o mi-sase-ta.
       Hanako-and Taro-Nom alone   child-Dat   TV-Acc watch-Cause-Past
       "Hanako and Taro made/*let the child watch TV alone."

   This analysis of the "make" causative straightforwardly accounts for the Double-*o* Constraint violation if *o* appears on the transitive-stem "make" causee.

(42) *Hanako-ga   Taroo-*o* piza-*o*   tabe-sase-ta.
       Hanako-Nom Taro-*Acc* pizza-*Acc* eat-Cause-Past
       "Hanako made/let Taro eat pizza."

This is bad because both accusative phrases are in the same, embedded clause. In the next section, I will show that this structure for the "make" causative is, in fact, the only way to account for the Double-*o* violation, thus giving further credence to the analysis we are pursuing.

3 Status of *Ni* on the Causee

Sadakane and Koizumi (1995) note that a "floated" numeral quantifier can only occur with the accusative causee, leading them to categorize *ni* on the causee as a postposition.

(43) Taroo-ga   kodomo-o/*-ni futa-ri kooen-e ik-ase-ta.
       Taro-Nom kids-Acc/*-Dat 2-Cl   park-to go-Cause-Past
       "Taro made two kids go to the park."

However, Harley (1995) observes that the dative causee can support a floated numeral quantifier in the transitive-stem "make" causative.

(44) Taroo-ga   kodomo-ni futa-ri yasai-o   tabe-sase-ta.
       Taro-Nom kids-Dat   2-Cl   vegetables-Acc eat-Cause-Past
       "Taro made two kids eat the vegetables."

Following the analysis of "floated" numeral quantifiers (cf. Miyagawa 1989b and references therein), Harley concludes that the *ni* in the "let" causative in both intransitive- and transitive-stem *V-(s)ase* constructions is a postposition, which prohibits a "floated" numeral quantifier, as observed by Sadakane and Koizumi (1995). However, the *ni* in the transitive-stem "make" causative is a case marker. This reflects Kuno's (1973) analysis, in which the *ni* in the transitive-stem "make" causative is a dative marker equivalent to the dative marking on the goal phrase of a double-object verb such as *watasu* "hand." In Miyagawa (1989b, 1996, 1997a), I give evidence that the dative marker on the goal phrase in a double-object construction is a case marker, not a postposition. Thus, for example, it is able to support a floated numeral quantifier.

(45)   Taroo-ga   kodomo-ni futa-ri tyokoreeto-o   watasita.
       Taro-Nom kids-Dat   2-Cl   chocolate-Acc handed
       "Taro handed two kids chocolate."

   The postpositional *ni* phrase in the "let" causative is assigned a thematic role independent of the coreferential embedded subject (Harley 1995).[9] Harley notes that this postposition is invariant, in that the "let" *(s)ase* always selects this postposition, and she equates this with "quirky case" found in languages such as Icelandic, in which a certain case/preposition (often dative) is selected by the verb, and the verb assigns a theta role along with the case/preposition.[10] This theta role assigned by a "let" *(s)ase* indicates the recipient/beneficiary of the act of "let" or "permit." This is reflected in the fact that the causee of the "let" causative must be such that the act being undertaken must be clearly "self-controllable" (S.-I. Harada 1973, Tonoike 1978), or, similarly, that the act must be interpretable in such a way as to allow the intention of the causee to come through (e.g. K. Inoue 1976a), which is not the case with the "make" causative. Thus, for example, S.-I. Harada (1973) notes that the following intransitive-stem causative is natural with the accusative *o* but not with *ni*.

(46)   Taroo-ga   tomodati-o/#-ni   komar-ase-ta.
       Taro-Nom friend-Acc/#-Dat be: bothered-Cause-Past
       "Taro caused his friend to be bothered."

Ni in this example is semantically anomalous on the assumption that the psychological state of being bothered is not something that one naturally obtains intentionally, but is caused by some external force, hence not "self-controllable."[11] Finally, as a postpositional phrase, we would not expect a "let" causee to undergo passivization. As Kuroda (1965a) originally noted, a causative-passive sentence such as the example below only has the "make" interpretation.

(47)   Taroo-ga   hahaoya-ni yasai-o   tabe-sase-rare-ta.
       child-Nom mother-by vegetable-Acc eat-Cause-Pass.-Past
       "Taro was made to eat vegetable by his mother."

For expository purposes, I will continue to call all instances of *ni* "dative," regardless of whether it is the case marker in the "make" causative or the postposition in the "let" causative.

4   LF Movement of the "Make" Causee: A Minimalist Version of Counter Equi[12]

We have seen that there is evidence to support the alternative analysis of the causative construction, in which the causee in the "make" causative resides in the embedded subject position. However, as it stands, there is one glaring disadvantage to this approach. It makes mysterious the distinction between the "make" and "let" interpretations. On this approach, *(s)ase* does not take a matrix object, hence there is no natural way to capture the "make" interpretation that parallels ordinary lexical causatives. Related to this issue is the question of how the "make" causee in an intransitive-stem causative receives accusative case marking, which is normally assigned to a direct object.

Harley (1995) proposes an addition to the alternative analysis that responds to these two, and other, issues. Harley's analysis, which is cast in the Minimalist Program (e.g. N. Chomsky 1993, 1995a), in effect establishes an object position for the "make" causee in the matrix clause associated with *(s)ase*. This appears incompatible with the observation that the "make" causee is in the embedded subject position, an analysis that Harley (1995) herself promotes on the basis of Terada's (1990) work. There are two components to Harley's analysis that get around this problem. First, we can identify an object position in terms of the theta role that it has, and Case. In most sentences, theta role and Case are assigned from the same source. However, in exceptional circumstances, the two diverge. This is the Exceptional Case Marking construction.

(48)   Everyone considers him to be a fool.

The theta role on *him* identifies it to be the embedded subject, but the accusative case identifies it to be the object of the matrix verb *consider*. Even though it is a subject of the embedded clause, identification of it as the matrix object by Case is sufficient for it to undergo passivization.

(49)   He is considered by everyone to be a fool.

What Harley argues is that the "make" *(s)ase* is identified with an object Case position, very much like the ECM verbs. Thus, for all instances of "make" *(s)ase*, the transitive nature of *(s)ase* is characterized by the fact that it assigns Case to the object position. Second, Harley suggests that while the "make" causee is in the embedded subject position at overt syntax, as we have seen, at LF, it moves into the matrix object Case position. In the Minimalist

Program (N. Chomsky 1993), this "object" position is a general position of object–verb agreement. The agreement may be in the form of Case, or it may be another sort of agreement such as gender, as in the Hindi example below (Mahajan 1990).

(50)   Sitaa-ne laRkaa   dekhaa.
       Sita-erg boy-*masc* saw-*masc*
       "Sita saw the boy."

I will use the label AGRo (e.g. N. Chomsky 1993, Mahajan 1990) to indicate the position of this object-agreement position. Thus, Harley's proposal is that at LF, the "make" causee moves into the specifier of AGRoP in the matrix clause.

(51)   LF A-movement for Case checking: "make" causative

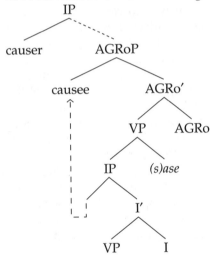

In many ways, this LF-movement analysis captures the intuition of the Counter Equi analysis originally proposed by Kuroda (1965a). In both approaches, there is an object position in the matrix clause containing *(s)ase*, thus characterizing this *(s)ase* as a transitive verb. Furthermore, the "make" causee moves from the embedded subject position to this matrix object position, thus identifying the theta role of this causee with the subject of the embedded verb. In this way, we can view this LF movement analysis as the Minimalist version of Counter Equi.

    Evidence that the "make" causative is associated with an Objective Case position comes from the fact that we see the accusative *o* on the intransitive-stem "make" causee. Without an object (Case) position, the appearance of this case marker is completely mysterious. Furthermore, as Harley (1995) notes, we know that the "make" causee can be passivized in the transitive-stem causative as well as in the intransitive-stem causative (Kuroda 1965a).

(52) Taroo-ga   Hanako-ni   piza-o   tabe-sase-rare-ta.
Taro-Nom Hanako-by pizza-Acc eat-Cause-Pass.-Past
"Taro was made to eat pizza by Hanako."

This is direct passive, as indicated by the fact that a numeral quantifier associated with the derived subject may be stranded, indicating that movement has
taken place that leaves a trace which supports the stranded numeral quantifier
(cf. Miyagawa 1996).

(53) Kodomo$_i$-ga Hanako-ni t$_i$ futa-ri piza-o   tabe-sase-rare-ta.
kids$_i$-Nom   Hanako-by t$_i$ 2-Cl   pizza-Acc eat-Cause-Pass.-Past
"Three kids were made to eat pizza by Hanako."

This kind of direct passive is possible with verbs associated with the object
Case position. Because the "make" causee is in the embedded subject position at
overt syntax, which is not an object Case position, Harley is led to the analysis
that this causee phrase raises to the object Case position (specifier of AGRoP)
at LF.[13]

   The LF-movement analysis has a number of advantages over the Counter Equi
analysis. First, it unifies the derivation of all "make" causatives. The "make"
causee undergoes this LF movement regardless of whether the verb stem of
V-(s)ase is intransitive or transitive. In the Counter Equi analysis, Counter Equi
applies to the transitive-stem "make" causative, while regular Equi applies
to the intransitive-stem "make" causative. Second, the LF-movement analysis
correctly locates the "make" causee in the embedded subject position at overt
syntax. This is made possible by the architecture of the GB/Minimalist model.

(54)

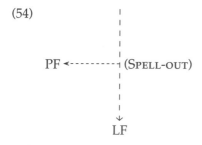

What this design says is that at some point in the derivation of a string prior
to reaching LF, the string is also sent to PF. This is the point called SPELL-OUT.
The string heading for LF may continue to undergo derivation, but once past
the SPELL-OUT, any derivational operation that changes the shape of the string
does not get reflected in the pronunciation (P(honological) F(orm)) of the string.
Thus, under the LF-movement analysis, the "make" causee is in the embedded
subject position at SPELL-OUT, and this is the form that is sent to PF for pronunciation. We have seen evidence that for the overt form, the "make" causee
indeed resides in the embedded subject position.

4.1 Double-o Constraint at PF

The LF-movement analysis makes it possible for us to be precise about where the Double-*o* Constraint applies in the grammar. On the basis of the Minimalist assumption that constraints and principles apply at the two interface levels of PF and LF (N. Chomsky 1995a), we are led to conclude that the Double-*o* Constraint applies at PF. Recall that we detect a violation of this Constraint if the "make" causee in a transitive-stem causative has the accusative *o*.

(55) *Hanako-ga   Taroo-o   piza-o   tabe-sase-ta.
      Hanako-Nom Taro-Acc pizza-Acc eat-Cause-Past
      "Hanako made Taro eat pizza."

If the Double-*o* Constraint applies at PF, the two accusative phrases are in the same clause – the embedded clause – thus the Constraint correctly rules this string out. However, if the Constraint were to apply at LF, the two accusative phrases are in two different clauses owing to the LF movement of the causee, and the Constraint would incorrectly allow this string to go through. The idea that the Constraint applies at PF reflects the intuition that some linguists have had that it is a "fairly surface" one (e.g. K. Inoue 1976a, Shibatani 1973b).

The LF-movement analysis also helps to reveal the PF status of those phrases that are licensed ultimately by Objective Case. In the grammatical transitive-stem "make" causee, the causee is marked with the dative *ni*.

(56) Hanako-ga   Taroo-ni   piza-o   tabe-sase-ta.
      Hanako-Nom Taro-Dat pizza-Acc eat-Cause-Past
      "Hanako made Taro eat pizza."

Setting aside for the moment the status of this *ni*, I assume, following Harley (1995), that this causee is licensed by Objective Case. Recall that Poser (1981) gave a convincing argument that the Double-*o* Constraint applies to Objective Case as well as to the case marker *o*. So, why isn't this example in (56) flagged by the Constraint at PF? One way to view the Case status of the causee here is that the Objective Case is not licensed until it resides in an object position, which, for this causee, is the specifier of AGRo, to which it moves at LF. At SPELL-OUT, and in PF, the Objective Case is unlicensed, thus somehow "inert" for the purposes of the Double-*o* Constraint.[14]

What is the status of the *ni* on the transitive-stem "make" causee? It does not have a function to assign Case because that burden is taken up by Objective Case. It appears to have no function at all in the syntactic (i.e. non-PF) component. One possibility is that it does not exist in the syntactic component, but appears for the first time in PF, to meet some unknown requirement that PF imposes for pronunciation of the phrase.[15] This captures the fact that the "make" causee in the transitive-stem causative functions as a case marker relative to a floated numeral quantifier (Harley 1995). If this *ni* only exists at

PF, there is nothing in the syntactic component to block the association of the causee with a floated numeral quantifier, unlike the postposition *ni* on the "let" causee.[16]

In the remainder of this chapter, I will turn to issues surrounding lexical causatives and their relationship to the syntactic *V-(s)ase*.

5 Multiple Causatives

Given that the causative morpheme *(s)ase* is inserted in syntax, there is, in principle, nothing to block a multiple occurrence of *(s)ase*. However, Kuroda (1993a), following S. Martin (1975), notes that two occurrences of *(s)ase* is only possible if the first instance of *(s)ase* is a part of a lexical causative. If both are "syntactic" *(s)ase*, only one *(s)ase* can appear, although the sentence is interpreted as a double causative. In the following example, *aw-ase* "cause to meet" may function as a lexical causative (Kuroda 1993a, Miyagawa 1980), while *suw-ase* "smoke-cause" can only be a syntactic causative (Kuroda 1993a).[17]

(57) Taroo-ga Hanako-ni Ziroo-o Mitiko-ni   aw-ase-sase-ru.
     Taro-Nom Hanako-Dat Jiro-Acc Mickiko-Dat meet-cause-Cause-Pres
     "Taro will cause (make/let) Hanako to cause Jiro to meet Michiko."

(58) a. *Taroo-ga   Hanako-ni   Ziroo-ni tabako-o
         Taro-Nom Hanako-Dat Jiro-Dat cigarette-Acc
         suw-ase-sase-ru.
         smoke-cause-Cause-Pres
         "Taro will cause Hanako to cause Jiro to smoke."
     b. Taroo-ga   Hanako-ni   Ziroo-ni tabako-o   suw-ase-ru.
         Taro-Nom Hanako-Dat Jiro-Dat cigarette-Acc smoke-Cause-Pres
         "Taro will cause Hanako to cause Jiro to smoke."

For the syntactic double causative exemplified in (58b), the question I wish to ask is which of the two syntactic *(s)ases* is dropped to make it possible for the sentence with the double-causative meaning to form a grammatical sentence. A related question is whether the absence of the second *(s)ase* is some surface morphological phenomenon, or its absence has a syntactic or morphological consequence.

First, note that the passive of the "lexical causative-causative" in (57) is fine, though, admittedly, it is awkward because of the complexity of the structure.

(59) Hanako-ga   Taroo-ni Ziroo-o Mitiko-ni
     Hanako-Nom Taro-by Jiro-Acc Michiko-Dat
     aw-ase-sase-rare-ru.
     meet-cause-Cause-Pass.-Pres
     "Hanako will be made by Taro to cause Jiro to meet Michiko."

Turning to the double syntactic causative, note that the higher causee may host a floated numeral quantifier, indicating that it may function as a "make" causee.

(60) Taroo-ga oya-ni   futa-ri kodomo-ni tabako-o
      Taro-Nom parents-Dat 2-Cl   kids-Dat   cigarette-Acc
      suw-ase-ru.
      smoke-Cause-Pres
      "Taro will make two parents cause their kids to smoke."

Despite this, the passive of this double syntactic causative is quite bad, in sharp contrast to the passive of lexical causative-causative combination in (59).

(61) *Hanako-ga   Taroo-ni Ziroo-ni tabako-o   suw-ase-rare-ru.
      Hanako-Nom Taroo-by Jiro-Dat cigarette-Acc smoke-Cause-Pass.-Pres
      "Hanako will be made to cause Jiro to smoke by Taro."

One way to interpret this example is that it is the higher *(s)ase* that is dropped, so that the passive morpheme is unable to attach to it and carry out the necessary operations. There is obviously enough of the "empty" *(s)ase* to support a "make" causative interpretation (or, possibly, also "let"), but by virtue of being empty, it is not accessible to any syntactic or morphological alterations that are required by the passive morpheme. On this view, the absent *(s)ase* does not have a full status as a verb, because it does not admit to passivization. Consequently, it is not just a matter of blocking the pronunciation of this *(s)ase* to make the sentence grammatical, but its absence in the overt form has tangible syntactic consequences.[18]

6 *V-(s)ase* and *V-(s)as*

Up to now we have only dealt with *(s)ase,* and have ignored a related productive morpheme, *(s)as*. For the most part, the two are interchangeable, as shown below (the vowel *i* is inserted after *sas* to conform to the open-syllable structure of Japanese), although for some speakers, the *(s)as* form has a stronger "direct causative" interpretation (Shibatani 1973b).

(62) Hanako-ga   Taroo-ni piza-o   tabe-sase-ta/tabe-sasi-ta.
      Hanako-Nom Taroo-Dat pizza-Acc eat-Cause-Past
      "Taro made/let Hanako eat pizza."

As shown below, it is possible for the accusative and dative case markers to alternate in an intransitive-stem *V-(s)as* sentence, just as we saw for *V-(s)ase.*[19]

(63) Hanako-ga   Taroo-o/-ni   ik-asi-ta.
     Hanako-Nom Taro-Acc/Dat go-Cause-Past
     "Hanako made/let Taro go."

Shibatani (1973b: 345–9) made an important observation, that a *V-(s)as* may be used interchangeably with the corresponding *V-(s)ase* if there is a corresponding verb stem. For example, the intransitive verb stem *agar-u* "rise" has the transitive lexical-causative counterpart *age-ru* "raise." This lexical causative corresponds (in the number of arguments) to the *V-ase/as* verb *agar-ase/as* "cause to rise." In this situation, *(s)as* alternates freely with *(s)ase*.

(64) Taroo-ga Hanako-o   butai-ni agar-(s)ase-ta/agar-(s)asi-ta.
     Taro-Nom Hanako-Acc stage-on rise-Cause-Past
     "Taro made Hanako rise onto the stage."

However, if there is no lexical-causative counterpart of *V-(s)as*, *V-(s)as* may "be equated" with a lexical causative (Shibatani 1973b). The following is taken from Shibatani (1973b), in which the verb *odorok-u* "surprise," which lacks a lexical causative counterpart, is the *V* in *V-ase/-as*.[20]

(65) a. Eiga   kantoku-ga   zyoyuu-o   odorok-ase-ta.
        movie director-Nom actress-Acc surprise-Cause-Past
        "The movie director made the actress be surprised."
     b. Eiga   kantoku-ga   zyoyuu-o   odorok-asi-ta.
        movie director-Nom actress-Acc surprise-Cause-Past
        "The movie director surprised the actress."

In (65b), *as* in *odorok-as* is a part of the lexical causative on a par with "monomorphemic" lexical causatives such as *age-ru* "raise" we saw earlier.

In Miyagawa (1980), I gave additional evidence for this analysis. Based on the assumption that only lexical causatives may participate in idiomatization, the following example shows that only the *V-(s)as* form, *nar-asu*, has lexical-causative status. *Nar-u* "ring" does not have a "monomorphemic" lexical causative counterpart.

(66) *nar* "ring"
     a. Taroo-ga   fuhei-o   nar-asi-ta/*nar-ase-ta.
        Taro-Nom complaint-Acc ring-Cause-Past
        "Taro complained."
     b. *Fuhei-ga   natta.
        complaint-Nom rang

As shown in (66b), the verb *nar-u* "ring" alone does not participate in this idiomatization, hence the entire lexical causative *nar-as-u* must noncompositionally be construed (along with "complaint") to constitute the idiom. Note that the alternative form with *(s)ase, nar-ase*, is ungrammatical with the idiomatic read-ing, indicating that in this idiom, *(s)as* alone functions as the lexical causativizer. Thus, there are two kinds of *(s)as*, one that alternates with *(s)ase*, and the other a lexical causativizer.

In Miyagawa (1980, 1984, 1989b), I gave evidence that *(s)ase* may also function as a lexical causativizer, precisely in the same environment as when *(s)as* appears as a lexical causativizer – in the absence of a "monomorphemic" lexical causative counterpart. The following idioms from Miyagawa (1989b) are taken from Zenno (1985). In (67a–c), *V-(s)ase* participates in idiomatization because of a lack of a transitive-stem counterpart; in (67d–f) *V-(s)ase* is "blocked" from appearing in an idiom due to the presence of a transitive-stem counterpart.

(67)

	Intransitive stem	*Transitive stem*	*Causative*	
a.	**heru** "lessen"	—	**her-ase**	
	hara-ga heru		hara-o her-ase-ru	
	stomach-Nom lesson		stomach-Acc lesson-Cause	
	"get hungry"		"wait for a meal"	
b.	**hikaru** "shine"	—	**hikar-ase**	
	me-ga hikaru		me-o hikar-ase-ru	
	eye-Nom shine		eye-Acc shine-Cause	
	"be under a watchful eye"		"keep a watchful eye"	
c.	**kiku** "be effective"	—	**kik-ase**	
	haba-ga kiku		haba-o kik-ase-ru	
	width-Nom be effective		width-Acc be effective-	
			Cause	
	"have influence with"		"influence"	
d.	**hairu** "come in"	**ireru** "put in"	**hair-ase**	
	kiai-ga hairu	kiai-o ireru	*kiai-o hair-ase-ru	
	spirit-Nom come in	spirit-Acc put in		
	"be full of spirit"	"put spirit into"		
e.	**itamu** "ache"	**itameru** "hurt"	**itam-ase**	
	mune-ga itamu	mune-o itameru	*mune-o itam-ase-ru	
	heart-Nom ache	heart-Acc hurt		
	"be worried"	"worry oneself"		
f.	**oreru** "break"	**oru** "break"	**ore-sase**	
	hone-ga oreru	hone-o oru	*hone-o ore-sase-ru	
	bone-Nom break	bone-Acc break		
	"require hardwork"	"exert oneself"		

What is striking about the "lexical" *V-(s)ase* in (67a–c) is that these are inter-changeable with *V-(s)as* in the idiomatic reading: *hara-o her-as-u* "wait for a meal;" *me-o hikar-as-u* "keep a watchful eye;" *haba-o kik-as-u* "influence." We thus have an asymmetry between the lexical causativizers *(s)as* and *(s)ase*. A lexical causative formed with *(s)as* may not alternate with *(s)ase* and maintain the lexical-causative status, while a lexical causative formed with *(s)ase* may alternate with *(s)as* freely. Given this asymmetry, the most general statement we can make about *V-(s)ase/V-(s)as* is the following (Miyagawa in press).

(68)   *(s)ase* has as its allomorph *(s)as*.

This statement is true regardless of whether *(s)ase* is a part of a "syntactic" or a "lexical" causative. Along with this allomorph *(s)as*, there is the lexical causativizer *(s)as*, which does not have an allomorph, hence it cannot be interchangeable with *(s)ase*. This *(s)as*, when attached to a verb to form a lexical causative, blocks *(s)ase* from functioning as a lexical causative for the same verb.

6.1   The double-causative test

The double-causative test (Kuroda 1993a, S. Martin 1975) confirms the distribution of *(s)ase* and *(s)as*. Take the two intransitive verb stems *ugok-u* "move" and *hatarak-u* "work." Neither has a "monomorphemic" transitive counterpart. Thus, the *V-(s)as* (or *V-(s)ase*) counterpart should be a candidate for lexical-causative status. However, as Kuroda (1993a), on the basis of S. Martin (1975), notes, only *ugok-as-u* "move" functions as a lexical causative.[21]

(69)   Taroo-ga Hanako-ni kodomo-tati-o heya-no   mae-ni
       Taro-Nom Hanako-Dat kids-Acc   room-Gen front-to
       ugok-as-ase-ta.
       move-cause-Cause-Past
       "Taro made Hanako cause the kids to move to the front of the room."

(70)   *Taroo-ga Hanako-ni kodomo-tati-o hatarak-as-ase-ta.
        Taro-Nom Hanako-Dat kids-Acc   work-cause-Cause-Past
        "Taro made Hanako cause the kids to work."

The fact that *ugok-as-u* cannot alternate with *ugok-ase* in the double-causative construction, as shown below, indicates that *(s)as* here is the lexical causativizer, not the allomorph of *(s)ase*.

(71)   *Taroo-ga Hanako-ni kodomo-tati-o heya-no   mae-ni
        Taro-Nom Hanako-Dat kids-Acc   room-Gen front-to
        ugok-ase-sase-ta.
        move-cause-Cause-Past
        "Taro made Hanako cause the kids to move to the front of the room."

The fact that *ugok-u* "move," but not *hatarak-u* "work," can be lexically causativized is compatible with the observation (e.g. Harley 1995, Levin and Rappaport Hovav 1995, Pustejovsky 1995) that in an intransitive–lexical causative pairing, the intransitive verb is unaccusative. The subject of the intransitive verb "move" is a theme, not an agent, hence semantically, it is an unaccusative verb. In contrast, the subject of "work" is an agent, hence it is an unergative verb. The latter requires an IP with an external subject position, which, in turn, makes it impossible for this V-(s)as to form a lexical causative (Miyagawa 1997b).

We saw in the previous section that the V-(s)ase verb *aw-ase* "meet-cause" may function as a lexical causative, since it can participate in a double-causative construction. On our characterization of the (s)ase~(s)as allomorphy, we predict that it should be possible for the corresponding (s)as form to also be allowed in a double-causative sentence. This prediction is borne out.

(72)   Taroo-ga   Hanako-ni   Ziroo-o Mitiko-ni   aw-as-ase-ru.
       Taro-Nom Hanako-Dat Jiro-Acc Michiko-Dat meet-cause-Cause-Pres
       "Taro will cause (make/let) Hanako to cause Jiro to meet Michiko."

7   Concluding Remarks

In this chapter, I gave evidence for the LF-movement analysis of the syntax of the V-(s)ase causative construction as proposed by Harley (1995). The LF-movement analysis captures the intuition behind the Counter Equi analysis originally proposed by Kuroda (1965a), while avoiding certain empirical problems that the latter analysis faces, particularly with regard to the Double-*o* Constraint. I also treated the lexical/syntactic causative distinction, in particular, showing that in the double syntactic causative construction, in which the causative morpheme (s)ase may only appear once, it is the higher (s)ase that is suppressed from appearing. Finally, we observed that the morphological alternant of (s)ase, (s)as, has two forms, one that is a lexical causativizer, and the other an allomorph of (s)ase.

There are a number of issues that remain unresolved. I will mention a few of these topics for future research.

7.1   *The nature of the Double-o Constraint*

I have argued in this chapter that the Double-*o* Constraint applies at PF. But what, exactly, is the nature of this constraint? It cannot simply be a constraint against any multiple occurrence of *o* in a single clause, since it is well known that "path/locative" type of *o*-phrases may cooccur with the accusative *o* (e.g. Kuroda 1978, Poser 1981).

(73)   Taroo-ga   Hanako-o   hamabe-o aruk-ase-ta.
       Taro-Nom Hanako-Acc shore-Acc walk-Cause-Past
       "Taro made Hanako walk along the shore."

Clearly, the type of *o* that gets flagged by the Double-*o* Constraint is associated with Objective Case (Poser 1981). Why should a PF constraint be sensitive to the type of underlying Case type? Related to this problem is the question why this Constraint should occur in Japanese. In some of the Romance languages (e.g. French), we see a similar phenomenon with "make." Thus, while the causee may be marked in the accusative case if the lower verb is intransitive, it may only be marked in the dative if the verb is transitive.

(74) Je la   fais   manger.
    I   her(Acc) make eat
    "I make her eat."

(75) Je lui   fais   manger la   tarte.
    I   to-her(Dat) make eat   the pie
    "I make her eat the pie."

Is this also a PF constraint? In contrast to "make," the "let" verb allows the double-accusative sequence, showing that the "Double-*o*" Constraint does not apply to "let," in contrast to Japanese.

(76) Je la   laisse manger la   tarte.
    I   her(Acc) let   eat   the pie
    "I let her eat the pie."

Comparative research may yield a very different picture of the Double-*o* Constraint from the view given in this chapter.

7.2 *Lexical causatives*

I touched only briefly on the lexical causatives. As noted, lexical causatives in Japanese are always morphologically distinct from the unaccusative counterpart (e.g. *ak-u* "open$_{intr}$," *ake-ru* "open$_{tr}$"). There are a large number of morphologically distinct alternations, many seemingly quite arbitrary (cf. Jacobsen 1992). For example, the morpheme *-e-* appears in the lexical causative in a number of classes (e.g. *sim-e-ru* "close$_{tr}$"), but it also appears in some unaccusative members of an unaccusative–lexical causative pair (e.g. *nuk-e-ru* "come off"/ *nuk-u* "pull out"). Is the *-e-* in these lexical causative and unaccusative forms the same morpheme? Related to this issue is the direction of derivation. Is the unaccusative basic, and its lexical causative counterpart derived from it? Looking at the unaccusative–lexical causative pairs in Jacobsen's list, it is often not clear which way the derivation goes. If we look only at the V-(*s*)*ase* causative verb, it is clear that the V is basic, and the causative form is derived by adding -(*s*)*ase* to it. But there are other instances in which the opposite appears to hold. We have already seen the pair *nuk-e-ru* "come off"/*nuk-u* "pull out," in which *-e-* appears to be added to the lexical causative member of the pair to derive the unaccusative. Another example is the pair *husag-ar-u* "become obstructed"/*husag-u* "obstruct," in which the morpheme *-ar-* appears to be added to the lexical causative *husag* to derive the unaccusative form (cf. Levin and Rappaport Hovav 1995 for arguments that the lexical causative may function as the basic form). Chierchia (1989) suggests that CAUSE underlies both the unaccusative and the lexical causative (cf. also Levin and Rappaport Hovav 1995, Pustejovsky 1995), which suggests that it does not make sense to talk about one being derived from the other. A close examination of the various morphological classes of unaccusative–lexical causative pairs should yield results that will help us in understanding this issue of derivation.

7.3   *The nature of case marking*

As the final topic, I note that the analysis of case marking given in this chapter raises a number of questions about the nature of case marking in Japanese. I suggested that the dative *ni* associated with the "make" causee appears for the first time in PF. As far as the syntactic side of the derivation is concerned, the Case requirement of the "make" causee is met by Abstract Objective Case. If this turns out to be correct, the appearance of this *ni* at PF is indicating some yet-to-be identified constraint on pronunciation of noun phrases. One might speculate that other case markers (as opposed to postpositions and inherent case) such as the nominative *ga* may also appear only in PF, in order to meet the requirement of the unidentified pronunciation constraint. To ultimately justify the "PF" account of *ni* on the "make" causee, we must identify the exact nature of the pronunciation requirement at PF that is met by adding the *ni* to the noun phrase.

NOTES

*   I am grateful to Marlyse Baptista, Guglielmo Cinque, Olga Fernandez, Ken Hale, Heidi Harley, Alec Marantz, and Natsuko Tsujimura for discussion related to the topic matter in this chapter. An earlier version of the chapter was presented at the seminar on argument structure at MIT in the fall of 1997. I thank those in attendance for numerous useful comments. The research for this work was partially supported by a grant from Fujitsu Limited to MIT.

1   Some of the issues I take up for the syntactic/lexical causative forms originally arose from a controversy between two approaches to the analysis of *V-(s)ase*. Kuroda (1965a, 1981, 1990, 1993a), as well as most linguists, assumes what I term a "different-component" analysis of the causative construction. The "different component" refers to the idea that, in this approach, the syntactic *V-(s)ase* is constructed in the syntactic component, while the lexical causatives exist in the

lexicon. In contrast, Miyagawa (1980) as well as Farmer (1980) propose a "same-component" analysis, in which both the "syntactic" *(s)ase* and the lexical causatives are formed in the same component of the grammar. In Miyagawa (1980, 1984, 1986, 1989b), I assumed that both causative forms are built in the lexicon, thus this approach has come to be termed the "lexical" approach to the causative construction. More recently, I have argued that the "same component" is syntax (Miyagawa in press), on the basis of the design of grammar made possible by Distributed Morphology (Halle and Marantz 1993). The difference between "syntactic" and "lexical" causatives is a function of the phrase structure underlying these two causative forms. In this chapter, I will not attempt to argue for or against either of these approaches (cf. Kuroda 1981, 1990, 1993a, for example, for arguments for the different-component analysis; cf. Miyagawa in press for a "syntactic" same-component analysis). One thing that the "same-component" analysis has done is to call attention to the structure of lexical causatives and their relationship to the "syntactic" *V-(s)ase* form. I will present some of the findings of this line of research, but will stay neutral to the same/different-component approaches.

2 Y. Kitagawa (1986) proposes that the "syntactic" *V-(s)ase* is formed in the lexicon, thus adopting the same-component approach. He has, in addition, a proposal that at LF, the causative morpheme moves to a higher point in the structure by excorporation, thereby effecting a biclausal structure. Miyagawa (1987b) provides independent evidence from Wh-movement for LF excorporation, although the structure that is involved is not the causative construction.

3 See Shibatani (1973b) for arguments based on adverbial scope that also give evidence for the biclausal nature of the *V-(s)ase* sentence.

4 It should be noted that *-(s)ase* may attach to a verbal form "larger" than a verb stem. For example, the aspectual form *hazime* "begin" attaches to a verb stem, *tabe-hazime* "begin to eat," and *(s)ase* may attach to this complex form: *tabe-hazime-sase* "cause to begin to eat."

5 There is a problem here with regard to the domain in which the Double-*o* Constraint applies. The Double-*o* Constraint prohibits two instances of the accusative *o* in a simplex clause. If we adopt Kuno's (1973) analysis that collapses the biclausal structure, then we can readily account for the ungrammaticality that arises if the causee is marked with *o* in a transitive-stem "make" causative. Both the causee with *o* and the accusative object with *o* end up in the same simplex clause after the biclausal structure is restructured into a simplex one. However, under the assumption that this "restructuring" does not apply, which is the position I am assuming, the two occurrences of *o* are always in two different clauses, thus Double-*o* Constraint should not rule this structure out. I will show later that it is in fact possible to keep the "nonrestructuring" analysis and still have the Double-*o* Constraint prohibit only the ungrammatical sentences.

6 Kuroda (1978, 1992) argues that the "regular" *tokoro*-complement sentence in (16) does not contain a matrix object, thus making it unnecessary to invoke Counter

Equi. The direct object shows up in structures that underlie, for example, the cleft.

7   See n. 11 for some possible analyses of Poser's observation.

8   To be precise, the arguments in Miyagawa (1996, 1997a) do not exclude VP-adjunction as an intermediate step in a longer movement, but do prohibit a movement in which the final landing site is a VP-adjoined position.

9   See Miyagawa (1997b) for an alternative analysis in which the causee in both "make" and "let" causative originates in the embedded subject position. The "make" causee undergoes LF raising to the matrix "object" position, as proposed by Harley (1995) and defended in this chapter. For the "let" causee, which always receives the dative *ni*, it raises to the matrix clause to be licensed by Tense. This latter movement occurs at overt syntax, unlike the "covert" LF movement for the "make" causative.

10   This is very close to the characterization of inherent case. With the verb of change of position, the *ni* phrase acts as an inherent case (Sadakane and Koizumi 1995), but the *ni* on the "let" causee is postposition (Harley 1995, Sadakane and Koizumi 1995). It is not clear how we derive this difference.

11   The verb *yurusu* "permit," which is close in meaning to the "let" causative, has a similar structure.

(i)   Hanako-ga   kodomo-ni [PRO
      Hanako-Nom kids-Dat   [PRO
      kooen-e iku koto]-o
      park-to go Compl]-Acc
      yurusita.
      permitted
      "Hanako permitted the kids to go to the park."

This *ni* is a postposition, as shown by the fact that it cannot be associated with a floated numeral quantifier.

(ii) *Hanako-ga   kodomo-ni
      Hanako-Nom kids-Dat
      san-nin [PRO kooen-e iku
      3-Cl   [PRO park-to go
      koto]-o   yurusita.
      Compl]-Acc permitted
      "Hanako permitted three kids to go to the park."

12   This section assumes knowledge of the basic notions in the Minimalist Program (N. Chomsky 1993, 1995a). Readers not familiar with this program are referred to, among others, Marantz (1995). For an introductory discussion of the notion of Logical Form (LF), see Huang (1995), among others.

13   Harley (1995) also gives an argument that the "make" causative raises at LF, on the basis of an observation by Terada (1990) about the scope of "only" relative to the causative morpheme *(s)ase*. Terada notes that if "only" attaches to the "let' causee, it only takes wide scope relative to *(s)ase*, but in the "make" causative, it is scopally ambiguous.

(i)   "make"
      Taroo-ga   Hanako-dake-o
      Taro-Nom Hanako-only-Acc
      suwar-ase-ta.
      sit-Cause-Past
      "Taro made only Hanako sit down."
      only ≫ make, make ≫ only
(ii) "let"
      Taroo-ga   Hanako-dake-ni
      Taro-Nom Hanako-only-Dat
      suwar-ase-ta.
      sit-Cause-Past
      "Taro let only Hanako sit down."
      only ≫ let, *let ≫ only

Suppose that Taro, Michiko, and Ikuko told everyone to sit down (or told everyone they can sit down), including Hanako. For Hanako, she was the only one that Taro had sit down. The others were told by someone other than Taro to sit down. This is the interpretation in which "only" takes wide scope over *(s)ase*, and this interpretation is available in both the "make" and "let" causatives above. Now suppose that there are three people in the room, Hanako, Masako, and Jiro. They were all ready to sit down, and Taro, Michiko, and Ikuko have the authority to permit it. However, Taro, invoking seniority over Michiko and Ikuko, had Hanako sit, and the others not sit. Thus, only Hanako sat down, in contrast to the first interpretation. This situation describes the situation in which "only" takes narrow scope relative to *(s)ase*. Terada claims that this interpretation is available only for the "make" causative. The ambiguity observed in the "make" causative can be captured if we assume that the "make" causee forms a chain, formed by NP movement, whose head is in the matrix clause and the tail in the embedded clause. As Harley herself admits, this distinction in scope between "make" and "let" is quite subtle.

14 This analysis, if correct, leads us to an apparent paradox about Objective Case in Japanese. The Objective Case may be licensed at LF, as in the case of the causative, or at overt syntax, as in the case of Poser's (1981) example given in (26). In Poser's example, which involves topicalization, the Objective Case on the empty element is visible to the Double-*o* Constraint, thus, under the "PF" application of the Constraint,

this Objective Case is licensed at overt syntax. There are a number of possible ways to cope with this apparent paradox. One possibility is that topicalization does not involve movement (e.g. Kuno 1973, Saito 1985), and the empty element is an empty pro, not an A'-bound trace. We can surmise that an empty pro comes equipped with a Case that need not be licensed by AGRo to be visible, very much like the accusative case marker *o*. Another possibility is that the difference between these two "kinds" of Objective Case may be a function of the kind of chain involved, A'-chain (topicalization) or A-chain (LF movement for Case). Yet another possibility is that the Objective Case is licensed as soon as the phrase resides in an object position. For the topicalization example, the empty element resides in the object position of the verb, thus licensed at that position. But the "make" causee only resides in the "object" position – specifier of AGRo – at LF. I will not attempt to resolve this issue in this chapter.

15 If this *ni* indeed has no function in the syntactic component, we are in fact led to conclude that it only appears at PF. All LF objects must be interpretable (N. Chomsky 1995a). If there is an uninterpretable element, it must be checked off, or the string "crashes." There is nothing in the string that could check off *ni* at LF, thus if it were to appear at LF, the string would crash.

16 There are a number of questions that arise for this "PF" analysis of the "case-marker" *ni*. What precisely is the PF condition that requires this *ni* to appear at PF? How is this *ni* assigned to the correct phrase? I do not have an answer to the

first question. For the second, one possibility is to follow Takezawa's (1987) analysis. Takezawa argues that the nominative *ga* is licensed by tense. If tense does not occur, as in the case of the embedded clause in the causative construction, *ni* is inserted as a "default" case marker. If this *ni* only appears at PF, as I have speculated, Takezawa's "default *ni* rule" would apply at PF.

17   I have constructed the first example, with *aw-ase-sase-ru*. The examples with *suw-ase(-ase)* are taken from Kuroda (1993a).

18   There is another way to view the "absentee" double causative. We might say that the higher of the two syntactic causatives is literally missing from the structure. Following Hale and Keyser (1993), the causative interpretation comes purely from the structure of the sentence. On this account, the lack of passivization is straightforwardly explained – there is no verb to passive.

19   There is a regional difference that distinguishes *(s)ase* and *(s)as*. According to Shibatani (1973b: 346), "in the Kansai area, e.g., Osaka, still the *sas* form is much more often used than the *sase* form . . . On the other hand, in the Kantoo area, e.g., Tokyo, the *sas* forms are innovative forms in colloquial speech." In a similar vein, Kuroda (1993a: fn. 4) notes that the dictionary, *Kokugogaku*

ziten, "has *-sase* in the verb paradigm for the Tokyo dialect and *-sas* for the Kyoto [Kansai] dialect." Consequently, some of the distinctions we will draw in this section are pertinent only to the speakers from the Kantoo region. Historically, the *sas* form "gave rise to the *sase* form around the 12–15th century" (Shibatani 1973b: 346; cf. Miyagi 1969).

20   See Jacobsen (1992) for an extensive list of lexical causative verbs and their intransitive (inchoative) counterparts in Japanese.

21   Kuroda (1993a: 14–15) notes that *ugok-as-u* "move" is structurally ambiguous between the lexical causative and the syntactic causative. The syntactic causative is, presumably, the *(s)as* that is the allomorph of *(s)ase*, which in this case is solely syntactic because the lexical causative *(s)as* blocks it from participation in the lexical causative. Thus, Kuroda (1993a: 14) notes that the following example "sounds unacceptable, or at best peculiar . . . [because] the causee of a productive causative is *prototypically* understood as a (secondary) agent."

(i)   Naomi-ga   isu-o
      Naomi-Nom chair-Acc
      ugok-ase-ta.
      move-Cause-Past
      "Naomi caused a chair to move."

9 Quantification and *wh*-Constructions

TAISUKE NISHIGAUCHI

0 Introduction

This chapter attempts to provide an overview of linguistic phenomena in Japanese involving quantification and *wh*-constructions, and various theoretical approaches to these phenomena. Since *wh*-phrases and constructions involving them play major roles in this and related areas, this chapter will focus on the behavior of *wh*-phrases and *wh*-constructions and a variety of theoretical attempts to characterize them.

The first half of this chapter, viz. sections 1–4, will be focused on such syntactic notions as locality restrictions, especially Subjacency and two major effects which are supposed to be subsumed under it, and as we go along, our focus will be on such semantic areas as quantificational variability (section 5), the functional interpretation (sections 6–7), and so on. As the discussion proceeds, however, we will see that some notions which are apparently motivated in syntax play vital roles in what we consider to be semantic phenomena. We will further observe that some notions which have hitherto been considered to be semantic in nature prove to be crucially important in phenomena which have been thought to be purely syntactic. This is a large-scale shift of focus rapidly gaining force in the principles-and-parameters approach in the areas related to Logical Form (LF). What follows is a case study from Japanese.

1 A *wh*-In-Situ Language

Japanese is said to be a "*wh*-in-situ language," that is, a language in which *wh*-phrases appear in any position within a sentence or a clause that may be occupied by regular NPs in the syntactic form or representation relevant to pronunciation ("s-structure" or "pre-Spell-out" structure). In this respect

Japanese differs from many European languages including English in which some or all *wh*-phrases must occupy certain designated positions within a clause containing them. To see this, compare the following sentences with their respective English translations.

(1) a.   John-ga   dare-o   ture-te kuru no?
          John-Nom who-Acc bring   come Q
          "Who will John bring?"
     b.   John-ga   dare-to   ki-ta no?
          John-Nom who-with came Q
          "Who did John come with, With whom did John come?"

In (1a), the *wh*-phrase *dare* "who" appears in the position of a direct object, and in (1b), the same phrase appears as part of a postpositional phrase (PP).

It is possible to have these *wh*-phrases in a clause-initial position, as in:

(2) Dare-o   John-ga   ture-te kuru no?
     who-Acc John-Nom bring   come Q

but the point is that there is virtually no difference in meaning between (1a) and (2), and that (2) is a result of the relative freedom of constituents within a clause that is allowed in this language. Thus, it was the commonly held view in the generative tradition until the early 1980s that no syntactic movement was involved directly in the derivation of *wh* constructions in Japanese and other *wh*-in-situ languages, such as Chinese, Korean, Hindi, and many others.[1]

In the mid-1980s, influenced by the important work of May (1977, 1985) and Huang (1982), the trend of inquiry started gaining force in which the behavior of *wh*-in-situ is analyzed in terms of covert movement that takes place in the process of mapping s-structure to Logical Form (LF). Lasnik and Saito (1984), Nishigauchi (1986, 1990), and Hoji (1985) were among the works that shed new light on various aspects of quantification and *wh*-constructions in Japanese in this theoretical format.

One of the important motivations for treating *wh*-constructions in Japanese this way was the so-called locality effects exhibited by this type of construction. We will look at the relevant phenomena in the next section.

2   Locality

One of the key notions in discussing the behavior of *wh*-constructions is *scope*. In English, scope of a *wh*-phrase is determined by (i) the position that was occupied by a *wh*-phrase in d-structure, and (ii) the position to which the *wh*-phrase has moved at s-structure, which is widely assumed as Spec of CP, since N. Chomsky (1986a). If the *wh*-phrase has the entire sentence as its scope, the sentence is interpreted as a *wh*-question, while if the scope of the *wh*-phrase is limited to an embedded clause, the whole sentence does not necessarily function as a question.

(3) a. *Who*$_i$ does John think that Mary likes *t*$_i$? John は M が 誰を 好いていると 思ってるんだい?
  b. John wants to know *who*$_i$ Mary likes *t*$_i$. John は M が 誰を 好いてるか 知りたいんかい?

In Japanese, scope of the *wh*-phrase is determined by (i) the position of the *wh*-phrase and (ii) the position of the interrogative marker *ka*, whose syntactic category is assumed to be C(omplementizer).

(4) a. John-wa [Mary-ga   *dare-o*   ture-te kuru to] ii   masi-ta *ka*? 言えんだい?
    John-Top Mary-Nom who-Acc bring   come that say Hon-Past Q
    "Who did John say Mary will bring?"
  b. John-wa [Mary-ga   *dare-o*   ture-te kuru *ka*] ii   masi-ta   *ka*? 言ってたかい?
    John-Top Mary-Nom who-Acc bring   come Q   say Hon-Past Q
    "Did John say who Mary will bring?"

In (4a), the *wh*-phrase is in the embedded clause while the interrogative *ka* is at the end of the sentence, so that scope of the *wh*-phrase extends over the whole sentence. Hence the whole sentence is interpreted as a *wh*-question. Sentence (4b) is minimally different from (4a) in that while its *wh*-phrase is in the same position, there is an interrogative marker at the end of the complement clause. Here, scope of the *wh*-phrase is limited to the embedded clause. The interrogative marker *ka* at the end of the sentence does not play any role in determining the scope of the *wh*-phrase, making the entire sentence a yes–no question.[2]
   The fact that we have just seen from the contrast in (4a–b) tells us two things of immediate concern: one is that the "construal" of the *wh*-phrase with the interrogative marker *ka* plays a major role in determining the scope of the *wh*-phrase. The second point, which is more specific, is that this construal process is subject to a locality restriction: the *wh*-phrase has to be construed with the closest interrogative marker *ka*, so in the case of (4b) the *wh*-phrase can only be construed with the interrogative marker at the end of the complement clause, so its scope is limited to the embedded clause.
   In the next subsection, we will discuss this last aspect of the matter from a different theoretical viewpoint.

2.1 wh-*Island Condition*

The property of the *wh*-construction in Japanese that we have just observed can be considered a case of the *wh*-Island Condition, whose effect is exemplified by the following ungrammatical sentence from English.

(5) *What did Bill wonder to whom John gave?

Bill は [John が だれに 何を やった か] 知りたがっているんかい?
*だい?

The ungrammaticality of this sentence is attributed to the fact that the *wh*-phrase *what* has been fronted over a domain (CP) where *wh*-movement of *to whom* has already applied.

(6)   *[_CP_what₂ did [_IP_Bill wonder [_CP_to whom₁ [_IP_John gave t₂ t₁]]]]?

Now let us consider the following sentence.

(7)   Bill-wa [John-ga   dare-ni   nani-o   age-ta ka] oboe-te   i-masu ka?
      Bill-Top John-Nom who-Dat who-Acc gave   Q   remember be-Hon Q
          a.   "Does Bill remember what John gave to whom?"
      not b.   "*What does Bill remember to whom John gave?"

While this sentence is acceptable, its interpretation can only be (7a), where the scope of the two *wh*-phrases is limited to the embedded clause, so that the whole sentence is interpreted as a yes–no question. It cannot be interpreted as (7b), in which one of the *wh*-phrases, *nani* "what," is taken to have the whole sentence as its scope.
    The parallelism between (7) and (5) becomes clearer if we hypothesize, along the lines of Huang (1982), that *wh*-in-situ languages have *wh*-movement in the process of mapping s-structure to LF. In the case of Japanese, Nishigauchi (1990) hypothesizes that the interrogative marker *ka* is of category C with the feature [+wh]. Movement of *wh* to Spec CP, then, is performed to meet the agreement requirement with respect to the [+wh] feature at LF.

(8)   [_CP_ *wh_i_* [_IP_ . . . t_i_ . . .] *ka*]
                                    [+wh]

Along this line, suppose *wh*-movement of *nani(-o)* "what" takes place in the embedded clause of (7). We will obtain the following intermediate structure.

(9)   . . . [_CP_ *nani(-o)_i_* [_IP_ John-ga   dare-ni   t_i_ age-ta] ka] . . .
                              John-Nom who-Dat   gave   Q

Since Spec CP is occupied by a *wh*-phrase, subsequent movement of the remaining *wh* out of this clause is in violation of the *wh*-Island Condition. This accounts for the absence of reading (b) of (7). The only way the remaining *wh*-phrase *dare(-ni)* "who-Dat" can move to satisfy the agreement requirement would be to move within the complement clause, adjoining to the previously-moved *wh*:

(10)   . . . [_CP_ *nani(-o)_i_* *dare-ni_j_* [_IP_ John-ga   t_j_ t_i_ age-ta] ka] . . .
                                 John-Nom   gave   Q

This accounts for the fact that (7) has only the (a) interpretation, in which both *wh*s have the complement scope.

These observations have led the theorists to suppose that the properties of *wh*-constructions in Japanese are identical with those of the English counterpart, and that they involve "covert" *wh*-movement at LF.

On the other hand, it has been observed in the literature that *wh*-in-situ in English has a lot of freedom with respect to the *wh*-Island Condition. It has been acknowledged since C. L. Baker (1970) that the following sentence, with a *wh*-in-situ within a *wh*-island, can be ambiguous with respect to scope.

(11)   Who remembers where John bought *what*?

On one interpretation, the *wh*-in-situ *what* has the same scope as *where*. This interpretation can be elucidated by means of the following answer.

(11)   a.   Mary does. Or
           Mary remembers where he bought what.

The other interpretation is that on which the *wh*-in-situ has the matrix scope and is paired with the *wh*-phrase in the main clause.

(11)   b.   Mary remembers where he bought this, and Jane remembers where
           he bought that.

This fact has been taken to indicate that covert movement of *wh* in English is free from the *wh*-Island Condition effects.

Let us consider whether the same applies in Japanese. Dayal (1996) considers the following Japanese example, which is parallel to (11) in English and differs from (7) in that there is an additional *wh*-phrase in the matrix clause.

(12)   Dare-ga   [Mary-ga   doko-de nani-o   kat-ta   ka] sitte
       who-Nom   Mary-Nom where-at what-Acc bought Q   know
       imasu   ka?   誰が［Mがどこで何を買った⑩］知ってんだい？
       be-Hon Q
       "Who knows where Mary bought what?"

Dayal's observation is that the Japanese speakers that she had consulted had no problem in accepting a pair-list answer to (12), analogous to (11b) (Dayal 1996: 93, fn. 3.) While I find the judgment reported by Dayal reasonable, it is necessary to acknowledge that a list interpretation is not so readily available for (12), if the sentence is pronounced normally. If two *wh*s, *dare* "who" and *nani* "what," are stressed, that makes it easier to obtain the list answer parallel with (11b).

There is one aspect of the matter, not noted by Dayal (1996), that critically distinguishes the *wh*-construction in Japanese from the English counterpart. In English, the *wh*-phrase that has been moved overtly to the initial position of the

1st reading

embedded clause, *where* in the case of (11), is incapable of taking the matrix scope, so that the value filling in *where* cannot be paired with the value filling in the matrix subject *wh*.[3] Therefore, the following list answer is impossible.

(11) c. Mary remembers what he bought at Macy's, and Jane remembers what he bought at Bloomingdale's.

The point about Japanese (12) is that it allows the list interpretation which is elucidated by this answer, if it is read with *dare* "who" and *doko-de* "where" stressed to emphasize the pairing. Such an interpretation is marginal, but it is to the same extent as a list interpretation analogous to (11b) is marginal.

This point is related to the "Superiority" effect observed in English, which basically limits the overt movement to a "higher" or c-commanding *wh* when there are multiple occurrences of *wh* within a single clause.[4] This underlies the ungrammaticality of the following.

(13) *Who remembers [what John bought where]?

What, which originates as the direct object of the V, is selected here as an element to be moved overtly to the initial position of the embedded clause, over and above *where*, which is underlyingly outside VP and hence "higher" than *what*.

The fact that (11c) is available, even marginally, as an answer to (12) can be traced to the absence of the Superiority effect in Japanese. The Superiority effect is quite likely a defining characteristic of languages with overt *wh*-movement and has no force in *wh*-in-situ languages like Japanese.[5] We will see, however, in section 7, some cases in Japanese where a similar effect is at stake.

2.2 Complex NP constraint

One of the important features of *wh*-constructions in Japanese is that sentences like the following are perfectly grammatical.

(14) Kimi-wa [dare-o   egai-ta   hon]-o   yomi masi-ta   ka?
     you-Top who-Acc described book-Acc read Hon-Past Q
     "You read a book such that it described who?" Or
     lit.   "*Who did you read a book that described?"

As the ungrammaticality of the (literal) English translation indicates, overt *wh*-movement out of a complex NP, such as a relative clause as in this case, is generally prohibited in English. This constraint, first discussed in detail by Ross (1967), has been called the Complex NP Constraint (CNPC). Later, N. Chomsky (1973) proposed that both the CNPC and the *wh*-Island Condition are to be reformulated under a unified notion of Subjacency, defined on the notion of "bounding nodes," or "barriers" (N. Chomsky 1986a).

君は、何を書いた本を読んだんだい？
너는 [무엇을 그린]책을 읽었노?

Thus, the *wh*-construction in Japanese exhibits a sharp contrast, if it is supposed that it involves covert movement of *wh*-phrases in the derivation of LF, with overt *wh*-movement in English, in that it appears to allow movement of a *wh*-phrase out of a complex NP, in violation of Subjacency.

3   The Pied-Piping Analysis

The behavior of *wh*-constructions in relation with the CNPC effect that we observed in the previous section poses a serious asymmetry with respect to the relevance of Subjacency in viewing the phenomena in terms of covert movement at LF. On the one hand, we saw in section 2.2 that covert *wh*-movement in Japanese shows obedience to the *wh*-Island effect of Subjacency. On the other hand, the total grammaticality of examples like (14) appears to suggest that the behavior of *wh*-constructions in Japanese is free from the CNPC effect of Subjacency. This poses a problem to the widely accepted idea that the *wh*-Island Condition and the CNPC are subsumed under the general principle of Subjacency.

The analysis of the relevant phenomena proposed by Nishigauchi (1990) provides a solution to this apparent asymmetry with respect to Subjacency. Nishigauchi proposed that sentences involving apparent violations of the CNPC effect of Subjacency should be analyzed in such a way that they do not involve a movement of *wh*-phrases out of complex NPs. How is such an analysis possible? Nishigauchi's suggestion is that movement of the *wh*-phrase occurs only inside the relative clause, and that this movement has the effect of making the entire complex NP identified as a *wh*-phrase. The device which makes this possible is *feature percolation*: the *wh*-feature is percolated through the Spec positions.

(15)

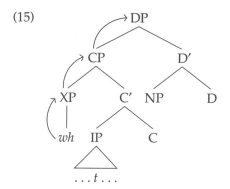

Since the entire DP is now identified as a *wh*-phrase, it can now move to Spec CP of the matrix clause. Its LF-representation is something like the following in essentials.

(16)   [[that described who] book]$_i$[you are reading t_i]

This analysis makes it possible to say that the LF-derivation of sentences like (14) does not (necessarily) mean that it involves real violations of Subjacency.

This analysis claims that the entire complex NP containing the *wh*-phrase is moved together with the *wh*-phrase itself. Such a phenomenon is found in English sentences like the following.

(17)   a.   *In which book* did you find the answer?
       b.   This is the man, *several pictures of whom* you just saw at the post office.

In both these examples, a larger unit containing the *wh*-phrase has undergone overt movement. This phenomenon has been referred to as Pied-Piping since it was first discussed by Ross (1967). On this analogy, the theory of LF-syntax which posits representations like (16) for sentences involving apparent violations of CNPC is referred to as the (large-scale) Pied-Piping analysis.

One of the well-known arguments for the Pied-Piping analysis comes from short answers to *wh*-questions. In general, it is possible to answer a *wh*-question by means of an expression filling in the value for the *wh*, followed by a copula.

(18)   Q.   Dare-ga   ki   masu ka?
            who-Nom come Hon   Q
            "Who is coming?"
       A.   John desu.
            John Cop
            "(It's) John."

Now the point about (14) is that it can be answered by either of the following.

(19)   a.   Gates desu.
            Gates Cop
       b.   Gates-o   egaita   hon desu.
            Gates-Acc described book Cop
            "(It's) the book that describes Gates."

Answer (19b) matches the portion which occupies the Operator position as a result of large-scale Pied-Piping in the LF-representation (16), and hence its acceptability can be accounted for straightforwardly. If, on the other hand, the *wh*-phrase were to move directly out of the complex NP in violation of Subjacency, its acceptability requires an explanation, which, to my knowledge, has never been undertaken. The fact that (19a) is also a possible answer to (14) can be accounted for if we suppose that it is a further truncated form of (19b) by means of a discourse deletion rule.

Although Nishigauchi (1990) did not attempt to make precise the nature of the discourse deletion rule, it is clear that the formulation of this process requires reference to a number of factors, which may be semantic, contextual, etc. One aspect of the matter discussed by Nishigauchi is that if the *wh* and the containing complex NP are of the same kind, say, a person, the truncated answer is much less acceptable than the longer answer.

(20) Dare-ga   suisen-sita   hito-ga   saiyoo sare soo   desu ka?
     who-Nom recommended person-Nom appoint Pass likely Cop Q
     lit. "The person such that who recommended him/her will be appointed?"

(21) a. Suzuki kyoozyu ga   suisen-sita   hito   desu.
        Suzuki Prof.   Nom recommended person Cop
        "(It's) the person who Prof. Suzuki recommended."
     b. #Suzuki kyoozyu desu.
         Suzuki Prof.   Cop
        "(It's) Prof. Suzuki."

In this example, both the *wh*-phrase and the complex NP containing it refer to persons. There seems to be a constraint on shortening of a description, to the effect that deletion is not recoverable where the entire description and a part of it to be left behind by deletion are sufficiently similar in kind. Thus, in (20), if the expression meaning "who" is replaced by "which professor" and the head nominal meaning "person" is replaced by "student," short answer (21b) is expected to be improved in acceptability. And this prediction appears to be borne out.

Kuno and Masunaga (1986), in their attempt to refute the Pied-Piping analysis, present the following contrast.

(22) Kare-wa [nani-o   tuku-ru kaisya]-ni   tutome-te i-masu ka?
     he-Top   what-Acc make   company-Dat work-for Cop   Q
     lit. "He works for a company such that it produces what?"

(23) Kare-wa [nani-o   tuku-ru kaisya]-kara   kane-o   kari-masita ka?
     he-Top   what-Acc make   company-from money-Acc borrowed   Q
     lit. "He loaned from a company such that it produces what?"

(24) a. Pasokon desu.
        PC   Cop
        "(It's) PC."
     b. Pasokon-o tukuru kaisya   desu.
        PC-Acc   make   company Cop.
        "(It's) a company that produces PC."

Kuno and Masunaga's observation is that while (22) allows either of the answers (24), (24b) is preferred as an answer to (23), answer (24a) being rated

"??" in this context. Kuno and Masunaga's explanation for this difference is that while the speaker of (22) is interested in the identity of the referent of the subject, the speaker of (23) is interested in the identity of the company. While it is not clear why this consideration constitutes an argument against the Pied-Piping analysis, I do find some difference between the two examples (though not unanimously supported by the Japanese speakers that I have consulted), and I submit that this type of consideration must be incorporated into the formulation of the discourse deletion rule.

There are many aspects of the Pied-Piping analysis that I have been unable to discuss in this section. Nishigauchi presents other arguments for the Pied-Piping analysis, among which is the one based on quantifier scope. J.-W. Choe (1987) and N. Hasegawa (1986) develop an argument for this analysis based on Weak Crossover effects. Pesetsky (1987) discusses the implications of this hypothesis in the wide context of the derivation of LF. As we will see shortly, A. Watanabe (1992) adopts this analysis in a different format. von Stechow (1996) points out some problems of the Pied-Piping analysis from semantic points of view. Also see Lasnik and Saito (1992) for arguments against it.

4   Debate

The motivation for the Pied-Piping analysis lies in the fact that it eliminates the apparent asymmetry of Subjacency: while covert *wh*-movement in Japanese shows obedience to the *wh*-Island effect of Subjacency, to the same degree that overt *wh*-movement of English is sensitive to it, it appears to show outright violations of the CNPC effect. With the Pied-Piping analysis, it is possible to say that the relevant data do not (necessarily) show that the CNPC is ignored.

On the other hand, it has long been acknowledged that covert *wh*-movement in English is immune from either the *wh*-Island effect or the CNPC effect of Subjacency.

(25)   a.   Who remembers where John bought *what*? (= (11))
      b.   Who read a book that criticizes whom?

As we saw in section 2.1, (25a) allows the reading on which the *wh*-phrase within the *wh*-island takes the matrix scope and is paired with the subject *wh*-phrase. The grammaticality of (25b) indicates that covert *wh*-movement in English is immune from the CNPC effect of Subjacency.

This consideration poses a threat to the idea underlying the Pied-Piping analysis. If covert *wh*-movement in English is immune from any effect of Subjacency, the absence of Subjacency effects may quite likely be a property of covert *wh*-movement in general. If covert *wh*-movement is generally free from Subjacency effects, why do we need the Pied-Piping analysis to show that it is not free from the CNPC effect of Subjacency?

In straightening out this discussion, it helps to take a look at A. Watanabe's (1992) theory of *wh*-movement. Watanabe starts out with the generally held view that only overt *wh*-movement is obedient to Subjacency. Then, Watanabe argues that *wh*-movement takes place both at s-structure and at LF in languages like Japanese as well. Overt *wh*-movement at s-structure involves movement of an empty Operator to Spec CP. This line of analysis is empirically motivated by the contrast between the following.

(26) *?John-wa [Mary-ga   nani-o   kat-ta ka-dooka] Tom-ni osie
       John-Top Mary-Nom what-Acc bought whether   Tom-Dat tell
       masi-ta   ka?   알려주더나?
       Hon Past Q
       "For what *x*, John told Tom whether Mary bought *x*?" Or
       lit.   "What did John tell Tom whether Mary bought?"

(27) John-wa   [Mary-ga nani-o   kat-ta ka-dooka] dare-ni   osie
       John-Top-Nom Mary   what-Acc bought whether   who-Dat tell
       masi-ta   ka?   알려주더노?
       Hon Past Q
       "Who did John tell whether Mary bought what?"

In (26), the only way the Operator of *wh*-phrase in the complement clause to take matrix scope at s-structure is to move directly out of the *wh*-island headed by *ka-dooka* "whether or not," and this is in violation of Subjacency, which accounts for its ungrammaticality. In (27), in contrast, it is possible to apply overt movement of the Operator out of *dare-ni* "who-Dat," a *wh* in the matrix clause, and this is in no violation of Subjacency.[6]

(28) [$_{CP}$ Op$_i$ [$_{IP}$ John-wa [$_{CP}$ . . . *nani* . . . *ka-dooka*] [*t$_i$* dare] . . .] *ka*]

Subsequently at LF, the *wh*-phrase in the complement clause may be moved to the matrix Spec CP. This is all right, since covert *wh*-movement is not affected by Subjacency. This accounts for the acceptability of (27), and a similar analysis holds for the marginal acceptability of the wide-scope interpretation of (12), discussed in section 2.1.

Looked at this way, there is a crucial difference between the *wh*-Island effect and the CNPC effect. While the *wh*-Island effect is eliminated by the presence of an additional *wh*-phrase in a position from which *wh*-movement is not constrained by Subjacency, in the cases related to the CNPC effect, the relevant construction in Japanese is totally independent of the presence or absence of an additional *wh*-phrase: the grammaticality of (14), for example, is not affected whether, say, its matrix clause subject is a *wh*-phrase or not. Yet, in A. Watanabe's (1992) theory, the Operator of the *wh*-phrase in (14) must move at s-structure out of the complex NP in violation of Subjacency, despite the supposition that *wh*-movement at s-structure is universally constrained by Subjacency.

Then, how can we account for the grammaticality of (14)? The answer lies with the Pied-Piping analysis. A. Watanabe (1992) claims that it is possible to have a [+*wh*] Operator originating in the Spec position of the complex NP containing the *wh*-phrase, and it is this Operator that moves to CP Spec at s-structure.

(29)   [$_{CP}$ Op$_i$[$_{IP}$ you are reading [$_{DP}$ t_i [that describes who] book]]]

This has virtually the same effect as the large-scale Pied-Piping of the whole complex NP, saving the s-structure movement of *wh* from violating Subjacency. Although A. Watanabe (1992) does not discuss it in detail, the licensing of the Operator originating in Spec DP of the complex NP should be backed by the feature-percolation mechanism sketched by (15).

In this connection, it is instructive to look at a relevant example from Hindi, another *wh*-in-situ language. Dayal (1996) observes that the following example, parallel in meaning to (14) in Japanese, is ungrammatical.

(30)   *[kitaabeN jo   kis-ne   likhiiN] mez par rakhii haiN
        books   that who-Nom wrote   table on kept   is
        "Who is such that the books s/he wrote are on the table?"

On the basis of this consideration, Dayal (1996: 226) concludes that "Hindi . . . provides clear evidence of Subjacency effects at LF." Dayal further notes that the ungrammaticality of (30) should be attributed to the inapplicability of the Pied-Piping mechanism here, which can be "explained in terms of connectedness in the sense of Kayne (1983), interacting with the feature percolation crucially required for pied-piping to take effect" (1996: 227). And this derives from the structure of relative clause constructions in this language, which Dayal discusses at length in chapter 5 of her book.[7]

In this section, we have seen, drawing much on the analysis of A. Watanabe (1992), that the Pied-Piping analysis at LF is motivated even on the widely held view about the distinction between overt and covert *wh*-movement, only the former of which is supposed to be subject to Subjacency.

5   Quantificational Variability

The focus of this section is on the quantificational nature of *wh*-phrases. It has been recognized, since Kuroda (1965a) and in the traditional studies in Japanese grammar, that the *wh*-phrase in Japanese shows quantificational variability – it can be used as having various quantificational meanings other than as an interrogative pronominal.

This idea has been revived by Nishigauchi (1990), Berman (1991), Lahiri (1991), and Y.-H. Audrey Li (1992), among others, leading to new insights to the nature of *wh*-phrases and constructions.

5.1 *The indeterminate pronominal*

Wh-phrases in Japanese can be used as parts of various quantificational expressions in combination with particles. It is because of this property that the *wh*-phrase in Japanese is termed *hutei-go* "the indeterminate (pronominal)," for the meaning of the *wh* itself cannot be determined without looking at its environment or something else that occurs with it (see Kuroda 1965a). The following, not intended as an exhaustive list, gives a glimpse of this phenomenon.

(31) *"Indeterminates" in Japanese*

dare "who" 누구	dare-ka "someone" 누가	dare-mo 누구를 "everyone" "(not) anyone"	dare-demo "anyone" 누구라를
nani "what" 무엇	nani-ka "something" 무엇이	nani-mo "(not) anything" 무엇를	nan(i)-demo "anything" 무엇이라를

As this paradigm suggests, the particle *ka* yields indefinites with the existential force, *demo* yields "free choice" indefinites, in combination with a *wh*. The particle *mo* yields two outputs combining with *dare* "who": *dāre-mo*, with accent on the first mora, is a universal quantifier, while *dare-mo* with no accent is a negative polarity indefinite.

(32) a. Dāre-mo-ga ki-ta.
　　　　　　　-Nom came
　　　　　"Everyone came."
　　 b. Dare-mo ko　 na-ka-ta.
　　　　　　　　　 come not-Past
　　　　　"Nobody came."

누구가
누구를
누구나
누구가

For discussion of this phenomenon, see Nishigauchi (1990), N. Hasegawa (1991a), and references cited there.

Nishigauchi (1990: chapter 4), inspired by the work of Kuroda (1965a), discusses the "discontinuous" construction involving the *wh*-phrase and the "quantificational particle" (QPt) *mo*.

(33) Dare-ga　 ki-te　mo, hookoku si-te kudasai.
　　　 who-Nom come QPt report　 do　please
　　　 "For all *x*, if *x* comes in, please report that to me."

The speaker of this sentence is requesting that every visitor should be reported. The *wh*-phrase here, thus, is inducing universal quantification in collaboration with the QPt *mo*.

Nishigauchi (1990) claims that this property of the "indeterminate" should be captured by covert *wh*-movement at LF. On this analysis, the *wh*-phrase undergoes movement to Spec CP headed by *mo*, whose category is C with feature [+*qf*] (from "quantificational force").

(34) $[_{CP} wh_i [_{IP} \ldots t_i \ldots] mo]$
         $\uparrow$_____| [+*qf*]

The idea underlying this approach is that a *wh*-phrase, which otherwise is devoid of any semantic content, picks up its meaning by being moved to Spec CP and being in Spec-head agreement with [+*qf*] C.

A piece of evidence for this *wh*-movement analysis comes from the *wh*-Island effect. The construal of *wh* with *mo* is blocked if it occurs within a *wh*-island headed by the interrogative C *ka*.

(35)   ??[Mary-ga   nani-o   kat-ta   ka] wakat-te mo hookoku
         Mary-Nom what-Acc bought Q   found   QPt report
         si-te kudasai.
         do   please
         "Even if you find out what Mary bought, please report that to me."
         not   "For all *x*, if you find out whether Mary bought *x*, please report
              that to me."

In this sentence, the *wh*-phrase has to be associated with the interrogative C *ka* of the embedded clause, and its association with *mo* at the end of the adjunct clause is impossible: this is a *wh*-Island effect. The only way *mo* can act here is as an adjunct head, meaning "even if (though)."

Nishigauchi (1990) further argues that the Pied-Piping analysis is relevant in this construction as well. Consider the following example, in which a *wh*-phrase occurs inside a complex NP.

(36)   [Dare-ga   kai-ta hon]-o   yon-de mo, hitotu hihyoo-o
         who-Nom wrote book-Acc read   QPt one   review-Acc
         kai-te kudasai.
         write please
         "For all *x*, *y*, *x* a person, *y* a book that *x* wrote, please write a review of *y*."

Nishigauchi's analysis claims that the entire complex NP, identified as a *wh*-phrase due to the local *wh*-movement inside the relative clause and the feature-percolation mechanism, gets moved to Spec CP headed by *mo*. What happens then is that the complex NP, as well as the *wh*-phrase inside, picks up its quantificational force as a universal quantifier. Thus, notice that in (36) there is a scope interaction not just between a review and an author, but also between a review and a book written by that author.

This is reminiscent of the *unselective binding* phenomenon, discussed by Heim (1982), as seen in the behavior of indefinite NPs.

(37)   If a man owns a donkey, he loves it.

Heim observes that this sentence can be interpreted as:

(38)   For all x, y, if x is a man, y a donkey, x owns y, then x loves y.

In Heim's theory, indefinite NPs are restricted free variables and are assigned their quantificational force by a quantificational element in their environment which serves as an unselective binder: in the case of (37), the indefinite NPs *a man* and *a donkey* are both assigned the force of universal quantification by *if*, or the necessity operator associated with it.

Nishigauchi's analysis of sentences like (36) claims that the effect of unselective binding is realized by the Pied-Piping of the complex NP containing *wh*: the quantificational force of this complex NP, as well as the *wh*-phrase inside, is determined as universal by means of the Spec-head agreement with *mo*.

Before closing this section, it is worthwhile to point out that the idea of viewing *wh*-phrases as "indeterminates" has significant implications from universal perspectives. Nishigauchi (1990: chapter 5) shows that the *wh*-phrase in English exhibits this property in sentences like the following.

(39)   No matter what he wrote, he sent it to *Linguistic Inquiry*.

This sentence involves universal quantification, and this is effected by the unselective binding of the *wh*-phrase by *no matter*. Thus, Japanese and English show a curious similarity with respect to the quantificational nature of *wh*-phrases: their quantificational force is determined by some external element which serves as unselective binder. Chinese behaves in a different way in this respect. The following example is from Y.-H. Audrey Li (1992).

(40)   Chī diǎn   shénme zài   zǒu ba!
        eat (a) bit what   then go Prt
        "Please eat a little something before you leave."

In Chinese, a *wh*-phrase can serve as an indefinite pronoun on its own, without being construed with some other element in the sentence or clause. In addition, Chinese differs from Japanese and English in that the interpretation of *wh*s as indefinite pronouns is subject to rather severe restrictions in terms of the environments in which they occur: this process favors contexts of uncertainty and inference, while contexts involving factivity generally disallow this use of *wh*s. Thus, this phenomenon is subject to different restrictions in different languages.

Furthermore, quantificational variability with *wh*s does not seem to hold in all languages. Ouhalla (1996) points out that *wh*s in Hindi and Iraqi Arabic can only be used as interrogative pronouns, not allowing quantificational variability. For an extensive cross-linguistic survey of indefinite pronouns, see Haspelmath (1997).

5.2   *Complement types*

There is another way in which *wh*-phrases can show quantificational variability (QV). This has to do with the types of complement clauses in which *wh*-phrases occur. Berman (1991) and Lahiri (1991), among others, discuss the issues involving embedded questions as complement to Vs such as *know, remember*, etc., which semantically define the relation between the subject and the *answer* of the embedded question (as opposed to Vs like *wonder*, which define the relation with the question itself). What has been observed along this thread is that the felicitous utterance of sentences like *John remembers who came to the party* is normally taken as meaning that John remembers *all* the people who came to the party. Use of an adverb of quantification modifying the main V affects the quantificational force of the *wh*-phrase, so that *John mostly remembers who came to the party* means John remembers most of the participants.

The following Japanese example exhibits this property.

(41)   John-wa [dare-ga   paatii-ni kuru ka] (daitai) sit-te iru.
       John-Top who-Nom party-to come Q   mostly know is
       "John (mostly) knows who will come to the party."

Without the Q-adverb *daitai* "mostly," this sentence means John knows every participant of the party, while with the adverb, it means John knows most of them.

In Japanese, *wonder*-type Vs show a peculiar property with respect to the form of the complementizer. *Wonder*-type Vs, but not *know*-type Vs, allow their interrogative complements to be headed by *ka-to*, viz. the interrogative C followed by another C which has hitherto been assumed to correspond to *that* in English.

(42)   [Dare-ga   kuru ka-to] omot-ta / tazune-ta / utagat-ta / ibukat-ta /
        who-Nom come   wondered asked   doubted   wondered
       *sit-ta / *osie-ta / *oboe-te-iru, etc.
        knew   told   remembers

One of the Vs, *omow*, is peculiar in that it requires the complement to be headed by *ka-to* in order to behave as an interrogative-taking V. Otherwise, it selects a non-interrogative complement headed by *to* "that," and behaves in ways parallel with *think* or *believe*. Other *wonder*-type Vs allow their complements to be headed by either *ka* or *ka-to*.[8]

Now, this distinction poses a new research topic in the context of the *wh*-Island effect of Subjacency: complements to *wonder*-type Vs show much stronger resistance to covert *wh*-movement out of them. To see this, consider the following.

(43) *John-wa [Mary-ga   nani-o   kat-ta ka-dooka-to] dare-ni tazune
     John-Top Mary-Nom what-Acc bought whether   who-Dat ask
     masi-ta   ka?
     Hon Past Q
     "Who did John ask whether Mary bought what?"

This sentence, which differs from Watanabe's example (27) in the choice of the matrix V and the complementizer form, is much less acceptable.[9]

In English as well, the *wh*-Island effect turns out to be stringent with the choice of *wonder*-type V in (11), which allowed the *wh*-in-situ within the *wh*-island to take matrix scope.

(44) Who wonders where John bought *what*?

Unlike (11), this sentence does not have the interpretation elucidated by (11b). The same point is observed in the following, which differs from (12) in terms of the matrix V and the complementizer form.

(45) Dare-ga   [Mary-ga   doko-de nani-o   kat-ta ka-to] omotte
      who-Nom Mary-Nom where-at what-Acc bought Q   wonder
      imasu   ka?
      be-Hon Q
      "Who wonders where Mary bought what?"

Thus, there is a significant generalization: the *wh*-Island effect is stringent with *wonder*-type Vs, and this effect is alleviated only in the complement to *know*-type Vs. Then, where does this difference come from?

In the first place, the fact that the LF-movement of *wh* out of a *wh*-island that is a complement to a *wonder*-type V is impossible suggests that Subjacency effects at LF exist, contrary to the view popular in the current literature. On this assumption, burden of explanation lies rather with the behavior of *know*-type Vs.

Dayal (1996) takes just this approach. Dayal argues that the QV phenomenon with *know*-type Vs should be accounted for in such a way that the complement CP to this type of V is subject to QR (Quantifier Raising) at LF, along the lines of Berman (1991) and Lahiri (1991). Unlike Berman and Lahiri, Dayal claims that only multiple *wh*-complement, which can semantically be considered a set of questions, can trigger QR.[10]

(46)   a.   Who remembers where John bought what? ⇒
      b.   [$_{CP}$ where John bought what]$_i$ who remembers t_i

The *wh*-in-situ *what* can be further moved and adjoined to CP.

(46)   c.   [$_{CP}$ *what*$_j$ [$_{CP}$ where John bought t_j]]$_i$ who remembers t_i

In this position, Dayal claims that *what* can have scope interaction with the *wh* of the matrix clause. In Dayal's analysis, it is this scope interaction with a matrix *wh*, effected by QR, that enables a *wh*-in-situ in a *wh*-island to take matrix scope, in apparent violation of the *wh*-Island effect.

    This analysis accounts for the grammaticality of A. Watanabe's (1992) example (27) and its contrast with (43), assuming that the *wh*-Island effects of Subjacency exist uniformly both at s-structure and LF.

6   The Functional Interpretation

One of the central notions in the current study of *wh*-constructions is the *functional* nature of *wh*-phrases, first studied extensively by Engdahl (1986, 1988) and Chierchia (1991, 1992–3). The functional nature of *wh*-phrases is illustrated by examples like the following.

(47)   Which book did every author recommend?

Engdahl and Chierchia observe that the answers to (47) can be classified into the three types exemplified in the following.

(48)   a.   **Individual answer:** *War and Peace.*
      b.   **Pair-list answer:** Bellow recommended *Herzog*, Heller *Catch-22* . . .
      c.   **Functional (relational) answer:** *His* most recent book.

The *individual* answer provides the title of the book that every author mentioned. Of particular relevance to the present discussion are the *pair-list* answer and the *functional (relational)* answer. The pair-list answer often takes the form of a list of pairs related by the predicate of the sentence, as in (48b). The functional (relational) answer supplies the value of *wh* as a *function* with the value of the other quantifier as its argument. Thus, the answer *his most recent book* is thought of as a function mapping from an individual (an author) to an individual (his book).[11]

    On the syntactic side, Chierchia (1991, 1992–3) considers a *wh*-phrase (or its trace) as consisting of a function and an argument, where the value of the argument may be determined by a quantifier that c-commands it. Cast in the framework of N. Chomsky (1993), elements which have undergone movement are "reconstructed" in their original positions at LF. Coupled with the idea examined in the previous section that *wh*-phrases are "indeterminate" expressions, serving essentially as restricted variables, this idea can be illustrated by the following representation, which I suggest as an LF for (47).

(47)   Which book did every author recommend?

(49)   [Which book]$_1$ did [every author]$_2$ recommend [e_2 N]$_1$

This is essentially the position of Hornstein (1995). Here, the "trace" of the moved *wh*-phrase contains an empty NP *e* which is bound by the quantifier in the subject position, together with the nominal content, which I assume is empty. Chierchia (1991, 1992–3) refers to the index assigned to the inner empty category as the "a-index," distinguishing it from the "f-index" assigned to the entire element, now viewed as a function.

On the semantics side, Chierchia views sentences like (47) as questions asking for the function making a certain proposition true. Applied to (47), its semantics is paraphrased as:

(50)   Which function *f* is such that every author *x* recommended *f(x)*?

Chierchia's (1991) account for his observation that the pair-list interpretation is only possible with a universal quantifier is that, since a pair-list is essentially the extension of the function *f*, the extension can be obtainable only when the generator set is identified. Such a situation is possible only when universal quantification is involved.

Hornstein (1995) extends this line of analysis to multiple *wh*-questions, exemplified by the following.

(51)   Who bought what?
       John bought a bicycle, Mary a motorcycle, . . .

As this example indicates, a multiple *wh*-question normally expects a list of pairs related by the predicate as its answer, a pair-list answer, which, according to Engdahl (1986, 1988) and Chierchia (1991, 1992–3), is a special case of functional answers. Pursuing this idea, Hornstein (1995) proposes to treat the *wh*-in-situ as a functional *wh*-element, the *wh* in Spec CP being a quantifier generating the set of pairs (the generator). Thus, the LF that Hornstein proposes for (51) is the following.

(52)   [*Who*$_1$ [t_1 bought [e_1 N]]]

Hornstein (1995) attributes the fact that multiple *wh*-questions expect pair-list answers to his observation that multiple *wh*-questions require exhaustiveness: a full list of pairs must be provided in a felicitous answer to a multiple *wh*-question. Hornstein claims that this exhaustiveness requirement underlies the pair-list interpretation of multiple *wh*-questions, which normally is available only when universal quantification is involved.

A pair-list interpretation is typically obtained in simple multiple questions like the following.

(53) a. Dare-ga   nani-o   mot-te kuru no?
          who-Nom what-Acc bring   come Q
          "Who is bringing in what?"
     b. Taroo-ga hana-o,   Hanako-ga   okane-o, . . .
          Taro-Nom flower-Acc Hanako-Nom money-Acc
          "Taro, flowers, Hanako, money, . . ."

These questions can be naturally answered by listing pairs of individuals related by the predicate of the question sentences.

Nishigauchi (1998) discusses the locality requirement on the binding of the a-index in the functional *wh*: the binding of the a-index takes place most congenially within a local domain.[12] I must use this rather unscientific wording because it appears to be wrong to define the empty category with the a-index as simply anaphoric.

Sentences like the following constitute a case in point.

(54) John-wa dare-ni [Bill-ga   nani-o   tabe-ta to] it-ta no?
       John-Top who-Dat Bill-Nom what-Acc eat-past that said Q
       "Who did John tell that Bill had eaten what?"

Although this is a fine sentence of Japanese, most of the speakers of the language that I check it with find it very hard to answer (54) pair-wise.[13]

The "near-anaphoric" nature of the empty category inside the functional *wh* accounts for the fact that a pair-list interpretation of a multiple *wh*-question is most easily available when the multiple *wh*s occur as clausemates. Further, this analysis gives the following prediction. Even if multiple *wh*s are separated by a clause boundary, a pair-list interpretation should be possible if there is an element, anaphoric or pronominal, that serves to link the binding between them. That this prediction is borne out is shown by the following examples.

(55) a. Who said Mary would bring in what?
     b. *Who*$_1$ said *she*$_1$ would bring in what?

Speakers of English find it easier to answer (55b) pair-wise than (55a). The reason we claim is that the presence of the bound pronoun mediates the binding of the a-index associated with *what*. The following sentence from Japanese shows the same point.

(56) Dare$_1$-ga [zibun$_1$-ga/e_1 nani-o   mot-te kuru to] it-ta no?
       who-Nom self-Nom   what-Acc bring   come that said Q
       "Who said self would bring in what?"

Here, the presence of the reflexive *zibun* "self" or an empty pronominal serves to link the two *wh*s. To use the notation of linking (Higginbotham 1983, etc.), the following linking pattern results.

(57)   *Dare*$_1$ ... [zibun/e_1 ... [e_1 N] ...

However, there is evidence that the binding of the functional *wh* is pronominal in nature, not anaphoric. First, as has been observed by Chierchia (1991, 1992–3) and Hornstein (1995), among others, a functional interpretation involving a quantifier is restricted to sentences in which the quantifier c-commands the trace of *wh*. Thus the following sentence, where the quantifier is c-commanded by *wh* (and its trace), does not have the functional interpretation.

(58)   Who recommended every book?

(59)   a.   Scott Peck.
         b.   *Its author.

This has led the authors to the analysis of relevant phenomena in terms of Weak Crossover (WCO), arguing for the relevance of the a-index, as in the following representation.

(60)   Who$_1$ [e_2 N]$_1$ recommended [every book]$_2$?

On the other hand, notice that the functional interpretation is possible when a definite NP is involved which does not c-command a *wh*-phrase (or its trace).

(61)   a.   Who recommended *Sophie's World*?
         b.   I don't know, maybe *its author*.

Here, the speaker who gives the answer need not know that the author is Jostein Garder, or, for that matter, what the book is all about. (S)he is only supplying the relation that involves the book as the answer – a typical functional answer. This is possible, because WCO does not prevent coindexing involving a definite antecedent.[14]

The following is the LF representation that I suggest for the question sentence.

(62)   *Who*$_1$ [e_2 N]$_1$ recommended *Sophie's World*$_2$

This coindexing pattern suggests that the nature of the empty category is pronominal, for it is parallel with the following, which involves a pronoun.

(63)   *Its*$_1$ author recommended *Sophie's World*$_1$

Coindexing involving an anaphor, such as the reciprocal, in the corresponding position is generally judged as ungrammatical.

(64)   **Each other₁'s teachers recommended [John and Mary]₁.*

Furthermore, the binding of functional *wh*s is highly dependent on contextual information, and it is possible to think of a context which allows a sentence in which pair-list interpretations are possible despite the fact that two *wh*s are separated by a clause-boundary. Such a context may be something like this: imagine Mary has been trying to spread a bad rumor about Bill, her ex-boyfriend, that he is a habitual shoplifter, so she tells a number of people that he has been stealing various things, a different item per addressee. With that context in mind, consider the following multiple *wh*-question.

(65)   Mary-wa dare-ni [Bill-ga   nani-o   nusun-da to] it-ta no?
       Mary-Top who-Dat Bill-Nom what-Acc steal-past that said Q
       "Who did Mary tell that Bill had stolen what?"

This question, in which the *wh*s are clearly not clausemates, can be readily answered pairwise: she told Jane that he had stolen a video game machine, and Sally that he had stolen a Walkman.

   Thus, the "near-anaphoric" nature of functional *wh*s is probably an illusion – while the binding relation is most easily obtainable within a local domain, it can hold across a clause-boundary, provided with appropriate contextual information.[15]

   The functional nature of *wh*-phrases has a number of theoretical consequences, broadening the scope of the research in the field. A recent example is Nishigauchi (1998), which examines various aspects of "Multiple Sluicing," first discussed by D. Takahashi (1994), and later by Nishiyama et al. (1996).

(66)   a.   John-ga [dareka-ga   nanika-o   katta   to] it-ta.
            John-Nom someone-Nom something-Acc bought that said
            "John said someone bought something."
       b.   Mary-wa [dare-ga   nani-o   ka] siri-tagat-te iru.
            Mary-Top who-Nom what-Acc Q   know-want is
            lit.   "Mary wants to know who what."

Sluicing is a kind of ellipsis which derives (67b) from (67a), where a clausal unit (IP) is elided, with a *wh*-phrase left behind.

(67)   a.   John remembers who Mary went out with.
       b.   John remembers who (with).

While in English only one *wh*-phrase can be left behind by this elliptical process, in the Japanese example (66b), two *wh*-phrases are seen to be left behind.[16] This phenomenon is referred to as "Multiple Sluicing." Nishigauchi's analysis is built on the framework of Chung et al. (1995), in which an LF-Copying approach to Sluicing is developed. Nishigauchi claims that the functional interpretation is an essential property of the LF-representation related with sentences like (66b), and shows that a number of theoretical consequences follow from this analysis, which bear not only on this particular ellipsis phenomenon but on *wh*-constructions in general.

7   Approaches to *Naze*

One of the long-standing puzzles in the study of syntax and its relation to the logical structure of Japanese is the contrast seen in the following.

(68) a.   Dare-ga   naze soko-e   itta   no?
          who-Nom why there-to went Q
          "Who went there why?"
     b. *Naze dare-ga   soko-e   itta   no?
          why   who-Nom there-to went Q
          "(no interpretation)"

The relative ordering of the two *wh*-phrases, one corresponding to *why* in English and the other corresponding to *who*, results in a fairly sharp contrast in grammaticality. Following A. Watanabe (1992), we consider this as a case of "anti-superiority," since *why* in Japanese appears to resist a position "superior" to other *wh*-phrases in the sentence.

   Several analyses have been proposed in the literature. A. Watanabe (1992) and Saito (1994a) present analyses based on the ECP applying at the level of LF.

   S. Watanabe (1995) is an attempt to account for the contrast in question from a very different angle. He views the ungrammaticality of (68b) as being a case of Weak Crossover (WCO) violations. In so doing, he draws on the theoretical apparatus of Hornstein (1995), whose ideas have been influenced by Chierchia (1991, 1992–3), and makes crucial reference to the notion of the *functional* interpretation of *wh*-phrases. The key notion there is that a *wh*-phrase can be used as a *functional* element, being itself a function mapping an individual to another individual. The main thrust of S. Watanabe's (1995) analysis is that *why* is an inherently functional operator which needs to be c-commanded by another operator at the relevant level of representation. The ungrammaticality of (68b) is explained in terms of the following LF-representation.

(69)   [(naze =) e N] dare-ga . . .

where the a-index of the functional element *naze* is not c-commanded by the putative generator *dare*, and hence a WCO violation results.

S. Watanabe's analysis accounts for the improvement of the following example, which differs from (68b) minimally in that there is a third *wh*-phrase *doko*.[17]

(70) Naze dare-ga   doko-e itta   no?
      why who-Nom there-to went Q
      "Why who went where?"

S. Watanabe's analysis suggests the following LF-representation for this example.

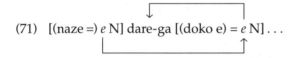

(71) [(naze =) *e* N] dare-ga [(doko e) = *e* N] . . .

Here, the addition of the third *wh*, which serves as another functional element, makes it possible to have this linking (Higginbotham 1983, etc.) pattern: this addition makes it possible for *dare* to serve as generator linked to the third *wh*, a functional element. On the assumption that the empty element in the functional *wh* is pronominal in nature, there is no problem in linking the empty element in *doko* to the empty element within *naze*. Since this representation has two licit linking relations, the grammaticality of (70) is successfully accounted for.

Although S. Watanabe's (1995) analysis suggests a promising line of research towards the understanding of *wh*-constructions, there is one conceptual problem with it. It involves, on the empirical level, the semantic interpretation of (68a): although (68a) is a fine sentence, it does not allow a pair-list interpretation. In other words, it is impossible to answer (68a) by providing pairs each consisting of a person and a reason that that person went there. In contrast, the following sentence, which contains a superficially synonymous expression corresponding to "for what reason" instead of "why," allows for a pair-list interpretation.

(72) Dare-ga   donna   riyuu-de kita no?
      who-Nom what-like reason-for came Q
      "Who came for what reason?"

This suggests that *naze* is not a functional element whose a-index can be bound by an individual-level generator, while such a binding is possible with *donna riyuu-de* "for what reason."

This issue is related, I believe, to the analysis of the following English sentence, which lacks a multiple question reading, explored by Williams (1994).

(73) Why did every boy leave?

Williams (1994) suggests that *why*, being an expression of a higher order than the individual-level expressions, cannot be "dependent" on the universal quantifier, an individual level expression, while such dependence is crucially necessary for a multiple question reading to be available. *(For) what reason*, on the other hand, is an individual-level expression and hence the dependence is possible.

Nishigauchi (1997) discusses the problems involving dependency with various *wh*-phrases of higher order, and suggests difficulties, as well as merits, in this line of analysis. The idea of treating *wh*s as functions is likely on the right track, but what needs to be considered is the nature of the function: in the case of *why*, the function involved here is not one mapping individuals to individuals, as with regular individual-level *wh*s, but one mapping an entity of higher order, such as a proposition, to reason, another entity of higher order.

8   Conclusion

This chapter has been an overview of various aspects of quantification and *wh*-constructions in Japanese and theoretical approaches to these and related phenomena. The first half of this chapter has been a survey of syntactic properties of *wh*-constructions in Japanese, where the emphasis has been on various topics centering on the locality restrictions imposed on these constructions, especially Subjacency, which is supposed to subsume the *wh*-Island Condition effects and the CNPC effects. In the latter half of this chapter we directed our attention to ways in which *wh*-constructions behave and contribute to various semantic phenomena related with quantification.

What we have seen in this short trip is the ways in which aspects of *wh*-constructions which at first sight appear to be best characterized as syntactic in nature show up over again when we look at semantic aspects of constructions involving *wh*-phrases. Recall that the Pied-Piping analysis, which was motivated on the syntactic considerations on locality requirements, was relevant when we discussed the quantificational variability (QV) phenomena involving *wh*-phrases as "indeterminates," or that the QV phenomena involving complement types (*know*-vs. *wonder*-type Vs) were crucially relevant in our discussion of the *wh*-Island effects of Subjacency. The functional nature of *wh*-phrases, whose original motivation had been mostly semantic, has proven to be relevant in various areas where key notions have hitherto been such syntactic machinery as the ECP.

This shift of focus, where semantic notions are seen to play more important roles in broader areas than were recognized in the researches of the 1980s, is a relatively new trend in the principles-and-parameters approach. My hope is that this chapter has shown, even partly, how quantification and *wh* constructions in Japanese contribute to our growing insights into the nature of human language in the new light.

NOTES

1   Takahashi (1993) claims that some cases of fronting of *wh*-phrases in Japanese must be considered as having the properties of *wh*-movement at s-structure.

2   Some speakers of Japanese find it possible to interpret the *wh*-phrase of (4b) as having wide scope. Such an interpretation may be paraphrased by the following English sentence:

(i)   Who did John say whether Mary will bring?

We will consider this matter in greater detail below.

3   This matter is discussed extensively by Lasnik and Saito (1984, 1992).

4   N. Chomsky (1973) first discussed the Superiority Condition. See Hornstein (1995) and Comorovski (1996) for recent approaches to this issue.

5   See Lasnik and Saito (1984), among others, for the relevance of this constraint to a variety of languages.

6   Example (27) is a little modified from Watanabe's original example. We will turn to this in n. 9.

7   The discussion is not quite complete until we discuss the apparent absence of the CNPC effect in LF, displayed by the grammaticality of sentences like the following.

(i)   Who read a book that criticizes whom?

In these cases, the referential property of the complex NP containing the *wh*-phrase is relevant. If the larger complex NP is definite and referential, the acceptability of this type of example is degraded.

(ii) *?Who read this book that criticizes whom?

If the complex NP is definite and referential, it cannot be raised by QR at LF, which accounts for the ungrammaticality of (ii), for here the only way the *wh*-phrase can move to Spec of the matrix CP is to move out of the complex NP. On the other hand, in (i), the complex NP containing the *wh*-phrase has a chance of being raised by QR at LF, since it is indefinite. The fact that the *wh*-phrase in the complex NP may take the matrix clause is quite likely dependent on the position accorded to the complex NP at LF, which is an adjunct position of the matrix IP. Fiengo et al. (1987), who argue against the Pied-Piping hypothesis, explore an analysis along this line.

8   In Spanish, it has been observed that the complementizer *que* "that" may sometimes precede a *wh*-phrase just in case the governing V involved is a *wonder*-type V, and that this is not possible with *know*-type Vs. Consider the following examples from Rivero (1980).

(i)   a.   Te   preguntan que para
           you   ask(3p)   that for
           qué   quieres   el préstamo.
           what want(2s) the loan
           "They ask you what you want the loan for."

      b.   El   detective sabe
           the detective know(3s)
           (*que) quién la   mató.
           that who   her killed(3s)
           "The detective knows who killed her."

It has also been noted that, in Spanish, direct questions can be embedded under *wonder*-type Vs while this is impossible with *know*-type Vs. This property can also be observed in parallel fashion in Japanese *ka-to*. For discussion along this thread in Spanish, see Lahiri (1991) and references cited there.

9 It should be noted that this is not directly due to the complementizer form: *ka-dooka-to* is possible in:

(i) [Mary-ga   kuru ka-dooka-to]
     Mary-Nom come whether
     tazune-ta / ibukat-ta.
     asked   wondered

One other thing which should be noted here is that A. Watanabe's own (1992) example was actually the following, which minimally differs from (43) in that the interrogative complementizer involved is *ka-dooka*.

(ii) John-wa [Mary-ga   nani-o
      John-Top Mary-Nom what-Acc
      kat-ta   ka-dooka] dare-ni
      bought whether   who-Dat
      tazune masi-ta   ka?
      ask   Hon Past Q
      "Who did John ask whether
      Mary bought what?"

And this one differs from (27) in the choice of the V: in (27), the V used was *osie* "tell," while here it is *tazune* "ask." Personally, I find (27) more acceptable than (ii), though I do acknowledge that (ii) is high in acceptability.

Thus, what should be observed here is that *tazune* "ask" is a *wonder*-type V just in case the complement to it is headed by *ka-to*; otherwise it can be a *know*-type V. In fact, the following sentence allows a QV interpretation.

(iii) [Dare-ga   kuru ka] daitai
       who-Nom come Q   mostly
       tazune-ta
       asked
       "(I) mostly asked who will come."

It is possible to interpret this sentence as: "for most people x, I asked whether x would come." So the acceptability of (ii) is by no means contradictory to the generalization discussed in the text.

10 This is based on the fact that multiple *wh*-questions such as *Who bought what?* can be answered by a set of propositions: *John bought this, Bill bought that*, etc. We will turn to this issue in the next section.

11 Engdahl (1986, 1988) uses the term "relational" because the function in this sense serves to specify the relation between individuals.

12 The idea that multiple *wh*-questions involve a clausemate condition is expressed in Kuno and Robinson (1972). Also see Sloan (1990) for a similar idea.

13 It is a nontrivial question what it means to have a multiple *wh*-question when you cannot provide a pair-list answer to it. In fact, in my class discussions on this type of topic, I have noticed that some students reject multiple *wh*-questions in Japanese to which they find pair-list answers unavailable. In the case of (54), however, it is possible to obtain a pair-list interpretation depending on contextual information. We will return to this topic later on.

14 This line of analysis may be further extended to cases such as the following, noted by Srivastav (1992), who has a different approach.

(i) a. Who is looking after these children?
     b. Their (respective) mothers.

15 Cf. Bolinger (1978), who provides counterexamples to Kuno and Robinson's (1972) clausemate condition.

16 Nishigauchi (1998) discusses some English examples where multiple *wh*-phrases are apparently involved in what appears to be Sluicing.

17 This fact is pointed out in Saito (1994a), where in an appendix he proposes to account for it by the operator-movement analysis of A. Watanabe (1992).

10 Word Formation

TARO KAGEYAMA

0 Introduction

A long-standing debate in generative grammar concerns the Lexicalist Hypothesis, the strongest form of which demands complete separation of morphology from syntax, thereby disallowing active interactions of word formation and
syntactic operations (Di Sciullo and Williams 1987). Such a hypothesis confronts
serious challenges from an agglutinative language like Japanese, where one
suffix after another is productively added to a verb stem to give rise to more
and more complex predicates, as in *tabe-hazime(-ru)* "eat-begin" = "begin to eat,"
tabe-hazime-sase(-ru) "eat-begin-cause" = "make (someone) begin to eat," and
tabe-hazime-sase-ta(-i) "eat-begin-cause-want" = "want to make (someone) begin
to eat." This chapter will review issues in Japanese word formation which
directly pertain to the evaluation of the Lexicalist Hypothesis. Included in my
discussion are Verb+Verb compounds, Noun+Verbal Noun compounds, and
Verbal Noun+*suru* compounds. Space limitations prevent me from looking into
other topics of theoretical interest in the realm of lexical morphology, such
as N–N compounding (e.g. *inu-goya* "dog-house"), A–N compounding (e.g. *aka-
boo* "redcap"), nominalization (e.g. *ame-huri* "rainfall"), lexical prefixation and
suffixation (e.g. *sai-kakunin* "re-assure," *niga-mi* "bitterness"), clipping (e.g. *siritu-
daigaku* "private universities" → *si-dai*), and reduplication (e.g. *(biiru-o) nomi-
nomi* "while drinking beer"). For the topics that are not included in this chapter
as well as the basics of Japanese morphology, the reader is referred to Kageyama
(1982), Shibatani (1990: chapter 10), and Tsujimura (1996b: chapter 4).

1 Lexicalism and Transformationalism

Unlike European languages which chiefly employ affixation in deriving new
predicates, Japanese makes extensive use of compounding to produce a rich
variety of complex predicates as exemplified in (1).

(1) a. Noun–Verb: tabi-datu "set out on a journey"
     b. Verb–Verb: tobi-dasu "jump out," tabe-sugiru "eat too much"
     c. Noun–Adjective: te-atui "cordial," sio-karai "salty"
     d. Verb–Adjective: musi-atui "steaming hot," yomi-nikui "hard to read"
     e. Verbal Noun–*suru*: kyuukei-suru "take a rest," huka-oi-suru "chase too far"
     f. Verb–*te* Verb: tabe-te miru "try eating," arat-te oku "finish washing"

In the history of Japanese generative grammar, the approaches to such complex predicates have been split between transformationalism and lexicalism. On the lexicalist side, Miyagawa (1980, 1989b), Farmer (1984), Miyara (1982), Y. Kitagawa (1986), Grignon (1990), Sells (1995), and others attempt to reduce the formations of all or most of the complex predicates to the lexicon. Works in Lexical-Functional Grammar (LFG: A. Ishikawa 1985, Y. Matsumoto 1996) and Head-driven Phrase Structure Grammar (HPSG: Gunji 1996) are also classified under the broad rubric of lexicalism. The approach that has enjoyed more popularity since the inception of transformational grammar, however, is a syntactic one in which causatives and other grammatical-function-changing suffixes are set up as independent predicates taking syntactic complement structures (Kuroda 1965a, Kuno 1973, Shibatani 1973c, K. Inoue 1976a).

While there are radical lexicalists who extend a lexical treatment to all kinds of complex forms including tense inflections and case particles, there does not seem to be anyone who espouses a purely syntactic approach to word formation. Those who recognize causative *-sase* and desiderative *-ta(i)* "want" as syntactic predicates do not deny that certain kinds of complex words are due to lexical formation. Mixed positions along these lines, which grant the word formation capacity to both lexicon and syntax, have been articulated by Shibatani (1975), Sugioka (1984), Shibatani and Kageyama (1988), and Kageyama (1977, 1982, 1989, 1993).

Since the lexicon is an indispensable component for any theory of grammar, the null hypothesis will hold that the principal locus of word formation is the lexicon. Nonetheless, Japanese presents quite a few phenomena which are hard to explain unless word formation is executed directly on syntactic structure. Before we delve into them, however, it is first necessary to pinpoint the notion "word."

2 Lexical Integrity

A hallmark of words is that no part of them can be separated, moved, or deleted by rules of syntax. This universal property, variously referred to as "lexical integrity," "syntactic atomicity," or "lexical island," is illustrated for Japanese by two phenomena.

(2) *Focus particles cannot intrude into a word.*
 a. *Watasi-wa [inu-<u>sae</u>-goya]_N-o   kat-ta.
   I-Top   [dog-<u>even</u>-house]-Acc buy-Past
   "I bought even a doghouse."
 b. *Ueta   hitobito-wa zassoo-o [tabe-<u>sae</u>-hazime]_V-ta.
   starved people-Top weed-Acc [eat-<u>even</u>-begin]-Past
   "The starved people even began to eat weeds."

(3) *Backward gapping cannot delete part of a word.*
 a. Ken-wa sukiyaki-o ~~tabe~~, Naomi-wa susi-o   tabe-ta.
   Ken-Top sukiyaki-Acc eat   Naomi-Top sushi-Acc eat-Past
   "Ken ate sukiyaki, and Naomi sushi."
 b. Ken-wa Furansu-no ~~kuruma-o kai~~, Naomi-wa Itaria-no
   Ken-Top France-Gen ~~car-Acc buy~~   Naomi-Top Italy-Gen
   kuruma-o kat-ta.
   car-Acc   buy-Past
   "Ken bought a car made in France, and Naomi, one made in Italy."
 c. *Ken-wa [inu-~~goya]-o tukuri~~,   Naomi-wa [usagi-goya]-o
   Ken-Top [dog-~~house]-Acc make~~ Naomi-Top [rabbit-house]-Acc
   tukut-ta.
   make-Past
   "Ken made a doghouse, and Naomi a rabbit-house."
 d. *Ken-wa [nomi-~~hazime~~], Naomi-wa [tabe-hazime]-ta.
   Ken-Top [drink-~~begin~~]   Naomi-Top [eat-begin]-Past
   "Ken began to drink, and Naomi began to eat."
   (This is grammatical on the reading "Ken drank, and Naomi began
   to eat.")

Focus particles like *sae* "even," *mo* "also," and *dake* "only," which have the function of focusing or topicalizing a phrase, cannot be attached to part of a word, in much the same way that *wh*-movement in English cannot affect only a portion of a word (*He likes baseball.* → **What does he like __ball?*). The ungrammaticality of (2a–b) thus shows that *inu-goya* "doghouse" and *tabe-hazime(ru)* "begin to eat" qualify as words.

   Another test for lexical integrity is Gapping. As shown in (3), Gapping in Japanese deletes one consecutive string (not necessarily one syntactic constituent) from the end of a clause (Kageyama 1989; *pace* J. D. McCawley and Momoi 1986). Particularly remarkable is the fact that only the head of an NP may be deleted, leaving the genitive modifier stranded (3b). Even so, the deletion cannot encroach on the territory of a compound word (3c–d), as is also the case in English (**John outran Bill and Mary out-swam Pat.*: Bresnan and Mchombo 1995).

   These tests help us grasp the general traits of complex expressions in Japanese: a noun–verb combination without any case particle, as in (2a) and (3c), constitutes a word, and so does a combination of two verbs in the infinitive (traditionally called the *ren'yoo* form), as in (2b) and (3d). In contrast, complex forms with case particles do not count as words by the criteria at hand. Consider honorific verbs as in (4).

(4) a.   yase-ru (plain) → o-yase-ni   nar-u (honorific)
         get thin-Pres   Hon-get thin-Dat become-Pres
     b.   Sensei-wa   o-yase-ni-sae   nat-ta.
         teacher-Top Hon-get thin-Dat-even become-Past
         "My teacher even got thin."
     c.   Sensei-wa   o-yase-ni   ~~nari~~,   okusan-wa o-hutori-ni
         teacher-Top Hon-get thin-Dat become, wife-Top   Hon-get fat-Dat
         nat-ta.
         become-Past
         "My teacher got thin, and his wife got fat."

(4a) shows the general pattern of honorification, where a verb stem is sandwiched by the honorific prefix *o-* (or *go-*) and the dative particle *ni* and the verb *naru* "become" is supplemented after it. Although the whole *o-V-ni naru* is pronounced with one stretch of accent just like ordinary words and *o- . . . ni-naru* is sometimes treated as a single morpheme, yet the applicability of Particle insertion (4b) and Gapping (4c) reveals that the sequence actually comprises two phrases: *o-V-ni* and *naru*.

I have taken the trouble to delineate procedures for identifying a word. This is significant because in lexicalist works, we sometimes encounter confusing claims which insist that honorific verbs and other complex expressions which ought to fall into the domain of syntax should be derived by word formation rules in the lexicon (as witnessed in Y. Kitagawa 1986 and Grignon 1990 for honorific verbs, and Sells 1995 for case particles and inflections). Such claims seem to stem from lack of a well-articulated concept of "word." The fundamental tenet of the theory of lexical phonology is that phonological rules are divided into lexical and postlexical rules, and that the lexical ones apply exclusively in the lexicon. Under this assumption, causatives and other syntactic suffixes are inevitably relegated to the lexicon, because the complex predicates comprising them undergo phonological rules which normally apply word-internally (Miyara 1982, Y. Kitagawa 1986, Clark 1987, Grignon 1990). However, phonological behavior is not a reliable criterion for identifying a morphological word. Since what is crucial to the Lexicalist Hypothesis is the notion of lexical integrity, primary importance should be attached to syntactic clues in deciding whether a given element is a word or not.

We now set out to survey the whole gamut of syntax-related word-formation processes in Japanese. Sections 3 and 4 will respectively deal with compounding in syntax and compounding after syntax. While these two types of compounding create morphological words, section 5 will introduce composite predicate formation which does not involve morphological words.

3 Word Formation in Syntax

As an archetypal case of word formation in syntax, this section will take up Verb–Verb compounds, with particular emphasis on their derivations.

3.1 Lexical and syntactic compound verbs

Japanese has vast numbers of V–V compound verbs, probably on the order of several thousands. These can be classified into two groups (Kageyama 1989, 1993).

(5) Type A (lexical compounds): uti-korosu "shoot-kill = shoot to death," nomi-aruku "drink-walk = tour bars," si-nokosu "do-leave = leave undone," kiki-kaesu "ask-return = ask back," oi-dasu "chase-take-out = send out," nage-suteru "throw-abandon = throw away," tobi-agaru "jump-rise = jump up," naki-yamu "cry-stop = stop crying," naki-sakebu "cry-shout = cry and scream"

Type B (syntactic compounds): kaki-hazimeru "write-begin = begin to write," tabe-oeru "eat-finish = finish eating," hanasi-tuzukeru "speak-continue = continue speaking," ugoki-dasu "move-begin = begin to move," tabe-kakeru "eat-set = be about to eat," tasuke-au "help-join = help each other," tabe-sokoneru "eat-miss = miss eating," tabe-sugiru "eat-pass = overeat," ii-wasureru "say-forget = forget to say," tabe-tukusu "eat-exhaust = eat up"

Having the same composition of "infinitive (V1) + infinitive (V2)", the two groups of compounds are equally qualified as words (cf. (2b) and (3d)).

The two groups display discrepancies in semantic transparency, productivity, and ordering (Kageyama 1989). Type A compounds tend to have lexicalized or conventionalized meanings while type B compounds are semantically transparent. Type A compounds are by and large limited to lexically specified combinations of V1 and V2, whereas type B compounds basically have no lexical idiosyncrasies on the combinations of two components. Additionally, a strict ordering relation is observed between the two types of compounds: type B appears outside type A, but not vice versa.

These discrepancies are not sufficient to establish one group as lexical and the other as syntactic, because proponents of level-ordered morphology could accommodate them in terms of difference of levels within the lexicon. In fact, Grignon (1990) proposes to locate type A compounding at level I and type B compounding, alongside causative and desiderative suffixations, at level II.

It is also difficult to circumscribe the two groups in terms of meanings. Many of the V2s in type B, such as -oeru "finish," *tuzukeru* "continue," and *dasu* "start," denote aspectual meanings, and such aspectual verbs have traditionally been analyzed as originating from biclausal sentential structures on a par with causatives. However, some type A compounds like *huri-yamu* "(rain) fall-stop" have aspectual meanings, and there are nonaspectual verbs like *-kaneru* "hesitate," *-sokoneru* "miss," *-au* (reciprocal), and *-naosu* "do again" which fall into type B (S. Martin 1975, Moriyama 1988, Kageyama 1989, 1993, Y. Matsumoto 1996).

Then, how can we prove that type B compounds are really created in syntactic structure? Kageyama (1989, 1993) adduces several tests, which all take the form of putting certain kinds of syntactic elements on V1. Compare the two types of compounds in their ability or inability to include passivized verbs, honorific verbs, the verbal proform *soo su-* "do so," and VN–*suru* compounds in the V1 position.

(6)   *Passives in V1*
    a.   **kak-are-komu (cf. kaki-komu), *os-are-aku (cf. osi-akeru)
        write-Pass.-insert   push-Pass.-open
        cf. yude-tamago "boiled eggs" vs. *yude-rare-tamago "boil-Pass.-egg"
    b.   ais-are-tuzukeru   koros-are-kakeru
        love-Pass.-continue kill-Pass.-be about to

(7)   *Honorific verbs in V1 (cf. also Kuno 1983)*
    a.   **o-kaki-ni   nari-komu   *(tegami-o)   o-uke-ni   nari-toru
        Hon-write-Dat become-insert (letter-Acc) Hon-get-Dat become-take
        "write in"   "receive"
        cf. tabe-mono "eat-thing = food" vs. *o-tabe-ni nari-mono "Hon-eat-thing"
    b.   o-utai-ni   nari-hazimeru (densya-ni) o-nori-ni   nari-sokoneru
        Hon-sing-Dat become-begin (train-on) Hon-ride-Dat become-miss
        "begin to sing"   "miss the train"

(8)   *Verbal proform in V1 (cf. also Akmajian and Kitagawa 1976–7)*
    a.   naki-sakebu → *soo si-sakebu   kaki-komu → *soo si-komu
        cry-shout   so do-shout   write-insert   so do-insert
        cf. tabe-mono "eat-thing = food" vs. *soo si-mono "so do-thing"
    b.   tabe-tuzukeru → soo si-tuzukeru   tasuke-au → soo si-au
        eat-continue   so do-continue   help-Recipr so do-Recipr
        "continue eating"   "help each other"

(9)   *VN–suru in V1*
    a.   **toonyuu-si-komu cf. nage-komu
        throw-do-insert
        cf. kai-mono "buy-thing = shopping," *koonyuu-si-mono "purchase-do-thing"
    b.   kyooryoku-si-au   tookan-si-wasureru
        cooperate-do-Recipr   mail-do-forget

A sharp demaracation is drawn between (a) and (b) in each set. The crux of this observation is that the elements used in the four diagnoses are syntactically motivated: passivization is traditionally treated as syntactic; honorific verbs and the proform *soo su-* "do so" are not words but phrases; VN–*suru* originates from syntactic structure (section 4.2). Naturally, their syntactic character is incompatible with genuine instances of lexically derived words, as shown in (cf.) above. Since type A compounds reject the syntactic elements, they are judged lexical. In contrast, type B compounds, which can accommodate them, call for syntactic derivation.

Akmajian and Kitagawa (1976–7) also noticed contrasts like (7) and (8). However, they postulated a biclausal syntactic structure for both groups, trying to attribute the difference to the feature [±Aux]. The antithesis of this unitary syntactic account is Grignon's (1990) unitary lexical analysis mentioned above. Apparently, neither analysis could adequately elucidate the nature of the disparities observed above.

While the preceding discussion has been devoted to V–V compounds, I hasten to add that the same diagnoses serve to distinguish compound adjectives of the form V–A. For example, compound adjectives with desiderative -*ta(i)* (e.g. *iki-tai* "eager to go"), *tough*-adjectives (e.g. *yomi-yasui* "easy to read"), and negative -*nai* (e.g. *tabe-nai* "do not eat") are syntactic, while *koge-kusai* "burn-smelly = smell burning," *musi-atui* "steam-hot = sultry," and other fixed compounds are lexical.

3.2 Complementation structures in syntactic compounds

Provided that type B compounds are syntactic, we now ask exactly what structures they are associated with. In the early transformational model, Shibatani (1973c), M. Nakau (1973), K. Inoue (1976a), and Kuno (1983) postulated two kinds of complementation, as in figures 10.1 and 10.2.

The structural distinction is primarily motivated by the selectional restrictions on the main subject. *Oeru* "finish" and other verbs which select volitional agents as their subjects are accorded a transitive structure, whereas *dasu* "begin" and others which are not limited to voluntary actions are construed in the intransitive structure.

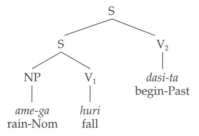

Figure 10.1   Intransitive structure

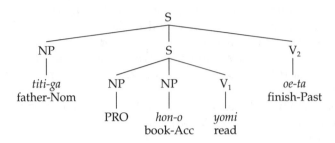

Figure 10.2   Transitive structure

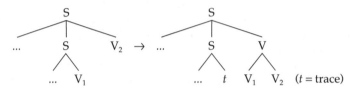

Figure 10.3   Verb Raising

Structures like the above were associated with the rule of Verb Raising, which adjoined the embedded V1 to the main V2 to produce a compound verb, as in figure 10.3.

Later, when clauses were uniformly represented as CP, K. Inoue (1989), in the spirit of M. Baker (1988), hypothesized that head-movement or Incorporation would apply cyclically to raise the complement verb through I and C up to the main verb. Such structures are refuted by Y. Li (1990), who proposes a principle to rule out the incorporation chain of V–I–C–V with functional categories (I, C) intervening between lexical categories (V).

On the basis of the VP-internal subject hypothesis, Nishigauchi (1993) sets up raising (i.e. intransitive) and control (i.e. transitive) structures without I and C, and Kageyama (1993) proposes a further elaboration by dividing transitive structures into two types, one taking a VP complement (figure 10.4) and the other a V′ complement (figure 10.5). This leaves us with a total of three types of complement structures instead of the traditional two.

Kageyama's (1993) primary motivation for distinguishing the two structures resides in the passivization of a whole compound verb or what Nishigauchi (1993) calls "long-distance passive."

(10)   a.   *VP-complement: -sokoneru* "miss," *-sobireru* "miss the chance," *-okureru* "be late," *-akiru* "become weary," *-tukeru* "be accustomed," *-kaneru* "hesitate"

yuusyoku-o tabe-sokone-ta → *yuusyoku-ga tabe-sokone-rare-ta
dinner-Acc eat-miss-Past   dinner-Nom eat-miss-Pass.-Past
"He missed eating dinner."   lit. "Dinner was missed eating."

b. *V'-complement: -naosu* "do again," *-wasureru* "forget," *-oeru* "finish,"
   -tukusu "exhaust, do thoroughly"
   suupu-o atatame-naosi-ta → suupu-ga atatame-naos-are-ta
   soup-Acc heat-do again-Past   soup-Nom heat-do again-Pass.-Past
   "She reheated the soup."   "The soup was reheated."

The head verbs in (10a) are assumed to select a subject NP and a complement VP. Then, in figure 10.4, passivization in the matrix clause cannot move
the embedded object ("dinner") to the matrix subject position because the
complement subject PRO would cause a violation of Rizzi's (1991) Relativized
Minimality Condition. The head verbs in (10b), on the other hand, select V'
complements. Since the structure in figure 10.5 lacks PRO in the embedded
subject, no violation of the Relativized Minimality Condition ensues.

The VP/V' distinction has semantic repercussions. According to Kageyama,
the embedded object in V' complements is theta-marked not only by the

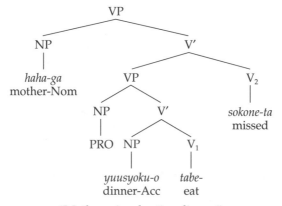

"Mother missed eating dinner."

Figure 10.4 Transitive VP complement

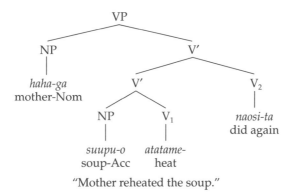

"Mother reheated the soup."

Figure 10.5 Transitive V' complement

embedded V but also by the matrix V – double theta-marking which is made possible by M. Baker's (1989) idea that the theta-marking of internal argument is done within the projection of V'. Put in plain terms, the embedded object of V' structure is predicated jointly by V1 and V2. This is manifested clearly in the meaning of passive sentences.

(11) a.   koozan-o hori-tukus-u → koozan-ga hori-tukus-are-ru
          mine-Acc dig-exhaust   mine-Nom dig-exhaust-Pass.
          "to deplete the mine"
     b.   *okane-o   moti-tukus-u
          money-Acc have-exhaust

The passive in (11a) means that the mine is exhausted as a result of digging it. The double predication explains why sentences like (11b) are illformed: money cannot be exhausted as a result of possessing it.

In contrast, the V2s that select VP complements predicate the whole embedded clause rather than the embedded object alone. For example, *yuusyoku-o tabe-sokoneru* "miss eating dinner" means that the act of eating dinner is not accomplished, without entailing that the dinner itself is spoiled (*sokoneru* "spoil"). In other words, the categorial distinction of VP and V' represents different degrees of semantic affinity between the main verb (V2) and the embedded object. Kageyama further observes that the VP/V' distinction is correlated with variations in honorification: with V'-type compounds, the honorific marker attaches more readily to the entire compound than to V1 alone (*o-kaki-naosi-ni naru* "Hon-write-do again-Dat become vs. ?*o-kaki-ni nari-naosu*), but the reverse is true of VP-type compounds (?*o-kai-kane-ni naru* "Hon-buy-be reluctant-Dat become" vs. *o-kai-ni nari-kaneru*) (cf. Kuno 1983).

Long-distance passives have been studied by other researchers as well. Sugioka (1984) regards the V2s of syntactic compounds as syntactic suffixes that are invariably attached to V', whereas Nishigauchi (1993) puts forth a syntactic analysis based on the assumption that the transitive V2s uniformly select a VP complement. Kageyama's analysis integrates the merits of these predecessors. Those syntactic analyses should be contrasted with Miyagawa's lexical approach. Working under a strong Lexicalist Hypothesis, Miyagawa (1989b) tries to account for long-distance passives by the notions of case-absorption and morphological adjacency: the passive *-rare* absorbs the case feature of the verb it directly attaches to.

(12) a.   (*hon-ga   kodomo-ni) yom -ase   -rare (-ta)
          book-Nom children-Dat read Cause Pass. Past
          lit.   "The book was made children read."
          from   "He made children read the book."
     b.   (Tegami-ga) okuri- tuzuke- rare (-ta)
          letters-Nom send   continue Pass. Past
          lit.   "Letters were continued sending."
          from   "He continued sending letters."

In (12a), the passive is debarred from absorbing the case of the main verb (*yom-* "read") by the intervening causative *-sase*. This, argues Miyagawa, accounts for the ungrammaticality of passivized causative sentences. For aspectual verbs which permit passivization of the embedded object, Miyagawa stipulates that those verbs are "transparent" so that case absorption can ignore their existence. It is not clear why aspectual verbs are transparent; he only suggests that "an aspectual marker does not assign an external thematic role of its own at any time" (1989b: 185). This suggestion is at odds with the fact that the V2s that allow long-distance passives, as in (10b), are transitive verbs taking their own subjects.

Recently Y. Matsumoto (1996) has arrived at a three-way classification which is essentially identical to Kageyama's. Aside from the verbs of intransitive complementation, two groups of transitive-type verbs are distinguished in Matsumoto's LFG framework in terms of a(rgument)-structure and f(unctional)-structure. What Matsumoto calls type II verbs, such as *oe-ru* "finish" and *naos-u* "do again," take Agent and SUBEVENT in a-structure and create a "monoclausal" f-structure, whereas type III verbs, such as *kane-ru* "be reluctant" and *sokone-ru* "miss," take Agent and EVENT in a-structure and have a "biclausal" f-structure. Y. Matsumoto (1996: 19) characterizes SUBEVENT as being "semantically interwoven with the situation described by the upper, embedding argument structure, so that SUBEVENT and its upper structure together represent one complex event," as opposed to EVENT, which is "semantically independent of the situation described by the upper structure." It is not hard to see that these functional characterizations of EVENT and SUBEVENT are tantamount to the semantic effects brought about by Kageyama's VP and V' structures, respectively.

An objection Matsumoto raises to Kageyama's syntactic analysis concerns the interpretation of adjuncts. Y. Matsumoto (1996: 181) points out that in examples like (13), the time adverbial refers unambiguously to the matrix event alone.

(13) Yuusyoku-wa gozi-to rokuzi-no aida-ni   tabe-hazime-rare-ta.
      supper-Top   five-and six-Gen middle-in eat-begin-Pass.-Past
      "Supper was started between 5 and 6."
      *"The eating of supper between 5 and 6 was begun."

Since this example involves a passivized compound verb, it corresponds to Kageyama's V' structure. That syntactic structure, argues Matsumoto, would wrongly predict that the time adverbial should be ambiguous between the reading in which it is attached to the matrix V' and the one in which it is attached to the embedded V'. In Matsumoto's analysis, the time adverbial necessarily designates the matrix event, because V1's SUBEVENT is subsumed under it.

However, given the parallel relations between VP and EVENT on the one hand, and between V' and SUBEVENT on the other, it may be said that the two analyses are notational variants. As mentioned above, the embedded object in Kageyama's V' structure is predicated by V1 and V2, so that the two verbs describe a single event in tandem. Such being the case, it is semantically inappropriate to make only V1 have relations with a time adverbial. Setting aside such semantic problems, the crucial difference between the two authors boils down to the morphological treatment of the syntactic compounds. For Kageyama, they are two separate verbs at D-structure and are amalgamated in syntax; for Matsumoto, the compounds are represented as single verbs in c-structure. For the latter, then, the occurrence of VN–*suru* as V1 in syntactic compounds (9) will pose a new problem.

3.3   Semantic and morphological conditions on lexical compounds

Unlike syntactic compounds, lexical compounds are formed by mere concatenation of two verbs. Accordingly, previous investigations have been centered on what sorts of restrictions govern the concatenations.

The semantic relations holding between two component verbs have been a popular topic of research, and different authors give different classifications (see Nagashima 1976, Tagashira 1978, Tagashira and Hoff 1986, among others). Y. Matsumoto (1996), for example, distinguishes four types: (i) pair compounds (V1 and V2: *hikari-kagayaku* "shine-sparkle = shine brightly"), (ii) cause compounds (V2 because of V1: *obore-sinu* "drown die = be drowned to death"), (iii) manner compounds (V2 while V1: *nagare-otiru* "flow fall = flow down"), and (iv) means compounds (V2 by V1-ing: *naguri-korosu* "strike-kill = strike (someone) to death").

Another vexed problem is how the argument structure of an entire compound is determined (Yamamoto 1984, Kageyama 1993, Y. Matsumoto 1996). In the majority of instances, V2 determines the argument structure of an entire compound, in conformity with the Righthand Head Rule (Williams 1981).

(14) a.   Inu-ga   doroboo-o/*ni   kan-da.
           dog-Nom burglar-Acc/*Dat bite-Past
           "The dog bit the burglar."
      b.   Inu-ga   doroboo-ni/*o   kami-tui-ta.
           dog-Nom burglar-Dat/*Acc bite-stick-Past
           "The dog bit at the burglar."

The verb *kamu* "bite" calls for an accusative object (14a), but when it is compounded with *tuku* "stick" (14b), the whole compound takes a dative object, reflecting the dative marking of V2 *tuku*. While Y. Matsumoto (1996) contends that lexical compound verbs are strictly rightheaded as regards the percolation of argument structure, Kageyama (1993) gives examples in which V1 and V2 jointly contribute to the creation of a complex argument structure.

Lexical compounding is also constrained by the morphological properties of component verbs. Typically observed are combinations of two intransitive verbs (*ukabi-agaru* "float-rise = float up") or two transitive verbs (*hiki-ageru* "pull-raise = pull up"), whereas mixtures of a transitive and an intransitive verb are generally unacceptable, as in **ukabi-ageru* "float-raise" or **hiki-agaru* "pull-rise." Jacobsen (1992) calls this phenomenon "transitive parity."

Kageyama (1993) makes refinements to Jacobsen's transitive parity by formulating the Transitivity Harmony Principle, based on two types of intransitive verbs.

(15) *The Transitivity Harmony Principle*
      Given the three argument structures below, lexical compound verbs are built by combining two verbs of the same type of argument structure.
      (a) transitive verbs: $(x <y>)$
      (b) unergative intransitive verbs: $(x < >)$
      (c) unaccusative intransitive verbs: $<y>$

In the argument structures above, x represents external argument, and y internal argument. Since both transitive and unergative verbs have external argument, their argument structures are deemed of the same type, while unaccusative verbs, lacking external argument, are assumed to constitute a separate type. Kageyama argues that the formation of lexical compound verbs is contingent upon the argument-structure types, on the grounds that in addition to the combinations of transitive–transitive and unergative–unergative, mixed combinations of transitives and unergatives are attested while unaccusatives may be compounded only with unaccusatives.

(16) a. transitive V1 + unergative V2
          (teki-o) mati-kamaeru "(enemies) wait-be prepared"
      b. unergative V1 + transitive V2
          (me-o) naki-harasu "(eyes) cry-cause swell"

(17) a. *transitive V1 + unaccusative V2
          *tuki-otiru "push-fall" (cf. tr.+tr.: tuki-otosu "push-make fall")
      b. *unaccusative V1 + transitive V2
          *ore-mageru "snap-bend" (cf. tr.+tr.: ori-mageru "fold-bend")
      c. *unergative V1 + unaccusative V2
          (me-ga) *naki-hareru "(eyes) cry-get swollen" (cf. (16b))
      d. *unaccusative V1 + unergative V2
          *koroge-oriru "tumble-step down" (cf. unacc.+unacc.: koroge-otiru "tumble-fall")

Kageyama conceives of the Transitivity Harmony Principle as a morphological constraint on the formation of lexical V–V compounds, arguing that this compounding takes place at the level of argument structure. He further points out that this condition is peculiar to Japanese lexical V–V compounding. Thus, combinations of transitive and unaccusative verbs (like *naguri-taoreru* "strike-fall" or *osi-aku* "push-open") are not permitted in Japanese but are attested in Chinese V–V compounds (Y. Li 1993) and Bantu serial verb constructions (M. Baker 1989). Interestingly enough, the resultative constructions in English, such as *to strike a person down* or *to push the door open*, also employ the pattern "transitive verb + (unaccusative) adjective/particle."

The Transitivity Harmony Principle is not without exceptions. Kageyama himself notes examples whose first members appear to have turned into prefixes because of "semantic bleaching," or whose second members have almost become suffixes like *-komu* "go in." Y. Matsumoto (1996), however, questions the general feasibility of the THP by adducing examples like (18).

(18) a. (*) ori-magaru (fold-bend), sui-agaru (suck-go up), tumi-agaru (pile-go up), tatakai-horobiru (battle-be ruined), kui-tubureru (eat-collapse)
      b. uti-agaru (hit-go up), hari-tuku (paste-be attached), yaki-tuku (burn-be attached), musubi-tuku (fasten-be attached)

These consist of unaccusatives and transitives, or unaccusatives and unergatives. It seems to me, however, that these counterexamples are only apparent.

Pinker and Prince (1991) explicate the distinction in the productivity of word formation between fully productive, rule-governed morphology like the English regular inflection (*walked, laughed*) and semiproductive analogical morphology like the English irregular tense (*sang, caught*), and Sugioka (1995–6) shows the significance of the rule/analogy distinction in analyzing Japanese N–V compounds. Considerations of this sort should be brought to bear on lexical V–V compounds as well.

Regarding Matsumoto's counterexamples in (18), I find the compounds in (18a) are not listed in dictionaries. Perhaps some of them are idiosyncratic, not commonly accepted. The examples in (18b), albeit commonly used, are due to back-formation from their transitive counterparts. This is suggested by the fact that the intransitive versions are semantically handicapped in comparison with the transitive counterparts. For example, while the transitive *musubi-tukeru* "tie together" can be applied to both concrete and abstract objects, the intransitive *musubi-tuku* (fasten-be attached) is used only metaphorically: compare the nonliteral *Hutatu-no ziken-ga musubi-tuite-iru* "The two cases are mutually related" with the literal *Nihon-no roopu-ga musubi-tuite-iru* "Two ropes are tied together." There are also reverse cases in which transitive verbs (e.g. *mai-ageru* "flutter-raise") appear to be back-formed from the intransitive counterparts (*mai-agaru* "flutter-rise = soar").

Note finally that the rule/analogy distinction, which characteristically applies to the word formation whose output is listed in the lexicon, does not come into play with syntactic word formation: all syntactic compounds are formed by rule. This confirms the validity of our distinction between lexical and syntactic compounds.

4 Word Formation after Syntax

The kinds of syntactic compounds that we saw in section 3 have the same morphological and phonological shape as lexically derived compounds. The complex predicates to be addressed in this section are markedly different in that they exhibit phrasal rather than compound accents.

4.1 *Postsyntactic compounds*

Japanese has a special syntactic category of Verbal Noun (VN: S. Martin 1975, Kageyama 1976–7, 1982, 1993). Like Nouns, VNs are not inflected in tense, but like verbs they have their own argument structure and are classified into transitives (simple transitives like *benkyoo* "study;" ditransitives like *kihu* "donate") and intransitives (unergatives like *undoo* "exercise;" unaccusatives like *hassei* "occur").

Opinions diverge as to the exact nature of VNs. Many researchers, including Miyagawa (1987a), Iida (1987), Grimshaw and Mester (1988), Terada (1990), Tsujimura (1990b), and Sato (1993), regard VNs as no different from Nouns except that they are equipped with argument structure. This is primarily because they are normally combined with *suru* "do" to realize their arguments with Case particles.

There are, however, syntactic contexts in which VNs appear to directly Case mark their argument NPs.

(19) kyoozyu-ga   Ainu-go-o   kenkyuu-tyuu-ni . . .
      professor-Nom Ainu-language-Acc research-during-Dat . . .
      "while the professor was doing research on Ainu"

In (19), the VN *kenkyuu* "research" takes a nominative subject and an accusative object (for the syntax of this construction, see Iida 1987, Saiki 1987, Tsujimura 1992). While Iida (1987) claims that the aspectual feature of the conjunctive morpheme *-tyuu* "in the middle of" enables the VN to execute its Case marking, Kageyama (1993) observes other syntactic environments without an aspectual morpheme.

(20) a. [sanka-o   go-kiboo] no kata-wa . . .
         [participate-Acc Hon-wish] Gen person-Top
         "Those who wish to participate . . ."
     b. Suiyoobi-made-ni   [repooto-o teisyutu] no   koto.
         Wednesday-by-Dat [report-Acc submit] Gen thing
         "Submit your term paper by Wednesday."

In view of these and other examples, Kageyama (1993) concludes that in those specific constructions, VNs can Case mark their arguments without the aid of *suru.* N. Hasegawa (1991b) and Manning (1993) also analyze VNs as functioning either as Ns or as Vs. An alternative will be to postulate a zero verb corresponding to *suru*, as Sato (1993) does.

We now observe that an interesting thing happens in these constructions.

(21) a. *Incorporation of direct object*
      Sooseki-ga   Rondon-o   hoomon no   ori . . .
      Soseki-Nom London-Acc visit   Gen occasion
      "when Soseki visited London"
      → Sooseki-ga   [Rondon:hoomon]$_{VN}$ no   ori . . .
        Soseki-Nom [London:visit]   Gen occasion
   b. *Incorporation of intransitive (unaccusative) subject*
      Zisin-ga   hassei no   sai   wa . . .
      earthquake-Nom occur Gen occasion Top
      "in case an earthquake occurs"
      → [dai-zisin:hassei]$_{VN}$ no   sai   wa . . .
        [earthquake:occur] Gen occasion Top

Shibatani and Kageyama (1988) discovered that in these adverbial constructions, the predicate VN may incorporate its internal argument to form a compound word (given in the brackets). In (21a), for example, the direct object is adjoined to the VN to yield a compound predicate *[Rondon:hoomon]* "London visit." This type of compound is characterized by the phonological property that the two components (N and VN) are separated by a slight pause (indicated by the colon (:)) and retain their respective lexical accents rather than being unified into one accent. Because of this, Shibatani and Kageyama called this type of compound "postsyntactic compounds."

Shibatani and Kageyama carefully demonstrate that such expressions are not results of mere particle ellipsis but make up genuine words, and that they are constructed from syntactic structure. Like Noun Incorporation in other languages (M. Baker 1988), postsyntactic compounding applies only to NPs which are structurally governed by the predicate, and not to inherently Case-marked PPs such as NP-*kara* "from NP" or NP-*de* "with NP." The syntactic nature is further shown by the fact that the head VN can have an honorific prefix *go-*, as in *[Yooroppa:go-ryokoo] no ori* "when traveling in Europe," which is impossible with the lexical counterpart, **yoOROPPA-GO-RYOkoo* "a European tour." Naturally, the same compounding is applicable to the bracketed parts in the nontime adverbial clauses in (20) above. (But see Sato (1993) for a different analysis of these compounds.)

Subsequently, Kageyama and Shibatani (1989), Kageyama (1989, 1993), and Yumoto (1990) uncovered evidence that this compound formation has a wider range of application, extending to noun phrase structures and to "Adjectival Nouns [AN]" (S. Martin 1975, Kageyama 1982, Miyagawa 1987a). For lack of space, I show only examples involving unaccusative subjects.

(22) *Postsyntactic compounding with VN in Noun Phrase*
Nihon-niokeru zisin-no   hassei
Japan-in   earthquake-Gen occurrence
"the occurrence of earthquakes in Japan"
→ Nihon-niokeru [zisin:hassei]$_{VN}$
   Japan-in   [earthquake:occurrence]

(23) *Postsyntactic compounding with AN*
singi-ga   huzyuubun ni tuki . . .
discussion-Nom insufficient Dat because
"because the discussion is insufficient"
→ [singi:huzyuubun]$_{AN}$ ni tuki
   [discussion:insufficient] Dat because

In the light of the phonological peculiarity, Spencer (1991: 454) suggests that postsyntactic compounds might be regarded as "phonological words." However, I should like to maintain the view that they are *bona fide* morphological words. The wordhood is demonstrated by the inapplicability of Gapping, as in (24a). This should be contrasted with the grammaticality of (24b), where only the Case particle is gapped in a phonological word of noun–particle sequence.

(24) a. *Tookyoo-de [oo-zisin: ~~hassei~~],   Yokohama-de [oo-kazi: hassei]
         Tokyo-in   [big earthquake occur] Yokohama-in [big fire: occur]
         no nyuusu
         Gen news
         "the news that a big earthquake occurred in Tokyo and a big fire broke out in Yokohama"
     b. Kyoo-wa [Ken-~~ga~~ ~~yasumi~~,   asita-wa
         today-Top Ken-Nom have a day off, tomorrow-Top
         [Naomi-ga] yasumu.
          Naomi-Nom have a day off
         "Today Ken takes a day off, and tomorrow, Naomi."

In the next two subsections, we will see that the phrasal accent is not unique to the postsyntactic compounds.

4.2 VN-suru *compounds*

In the postsyntactic compounding introduced above, VNs incorporate their internal argument. Because of their dual character as predicates and nouns, VNs can themselves be targets of incorporation into a predicate, yielding compounds like *undoo-suru* "exercise-do" and *zyoohatu-suru* "evaporate-do." The incorporating hosts in this case are limited to the verb *suru* "do" and its suppletions like the potential *dekiru* "can do" and the honorific *nasaru* (Kageyama 1976–7).

(25)   undoo-o   suru → undoo-suru
       exercise-Acc do   exercise-do "take exercise"
       undoo-ga   dekiru → undoo-dekiru
       exercise-Nom can do   exercise-can do "can take exercise"

In the literature, there are two competing views on the derivation of such VN–*suru* compounds. The lexical approach (K. Inoue 1976a, Miyagawa 1987a, 1989a, Grimshaw and Mester 1988) holds that *suru*, as a verbalizer, is attached to VNs in the lexicon, whereas the syntactic approach (Kageyama 1976–7, 1982, 1993, Tsujimura 1990b, Terada 1990, Sato 1993, Dubinsky 1994) maintains that VN and *suru* are generated as separate constituents and get amalgamated in syntactic structure (although the exact syntactic structures from which incorporation takes place differ from author to author). Needless to say, these two analyses are grounded on the premise that VN–*suru* makes up a compound word. However, Poser (1989, 1992) and Y. Matsumoto (1996) challenge this premise, claiming that the sequence VN–*suru* is a periphrastic expression rather than a word. Before contesting the lexical and syntactic analyses, it is therefore urgent that we clarify the morphological status of VN–*suru*.

The by-now familiar tests yield apparently contradictory results. First, focus particles may be interpolated between VNs and *suru*.

(26)   a.   sanpo-<u>sae</u> suru   b.   bidoo-<u>dani</u> si-nai
            walk-even do   budge-even do-not

There are many other syntactic contexts in which the lexical integrity of VN–*suru* is lost (Poser 1989, Kageyama 1993: 259, Y. Matsumoto 1996: 40).

(27)   a.   seihu-an-ni   <u>sansei mo   hantai mo</u>   si-nai
            government-plan-Dat approve-also disapprove-also do-not
            "neither approve nor disapprove the governmental plan"
       b.   seikoo-site-mo si-nakute-mo
            seikoo-do-also do-not-also
            "no matter whether you succeed or not"
       c.   – Ronbun-o teisyutu-si-masi-ta   ka?
              paper-Acc submit-do-Polite-Past Q
              "Did you submit your paper yet?"
            – Hai, si-masi-ta.
              yes do-Polite-Past
              "Yes, I did."

In (27a), the coordinated parts are obviously phrases since they contain the particle *mo*. In (27b), while the first conjunct involves VN–*suru*, the second one has only *suru* without a VN. If *seikoo-suru* "succeed-do" were to count as a single word, it would have to be assumed that the VN in the second conjunct was deleted, destroying the lexical integrity. The dialog in (27c) presents a similar pattern in which the second person responds only with *suru*. It is important to note that since the Japanese *suru* does not function as an auxiliary verb like the English *do*, the *suru* in the answer of (27c) directly corresponds to the *suru* of *teisyutu-suru* in the question.

The detachability of *suru* and VNs as exemplified above leads Poser (1989, 1992) and Y. Matsumoto (1996: 40) to deny the morphological wordhood of *suru* compounds. They are right as far as examples like (26) and (27) are concerned: VNs and *suru* are discrete constituents in those particular constructions. However, this by no means entails that the simple juxtaposed form (VN–*suru*) is also a phrase. On the contrary, there is evidence that VN–*suru* without any element inside truly makes up a word. Observe how Gapping works (Kageyama 1993).

(28) a. *Tuma-wa daietto-si, otto-wa   kin'en-si-ta.
          wife-Top diet-do,   husband-Top quit smoking-do-Past
          "The wife went on a diet, and the husband quit smoking."
      b. Tuma-wa daietto-sae si, otto-wa   kin'en-sae   si-ta.
          wife-Top diet-even   do, husband-Top quit smoking-even do-Past
          "The wife even went on a diet, and the husband even quit smoking."

As shown by (28a), it is not possible to delete only the *suru* part, leaving behind the VN *daietto* "diet." Here we disagree with Poser (1989, 1992), who regards similar examples to (28a) as grammatical. In our view, (28a) cannot be interpreted as resulting from Gapping of *suru*; if it is accepted at all, its first clause ("The wife went on a diet") will have to be construed as an incomplete tenseless clause like a newspaper headline. This point is confirmed by comparing (28a) with (28b). Gapping of *suru* applies perfectly in this latter sentence, where VN and *suru* are presented as separate constituents. The contrast in (28a–b) will be sufficient to argue against the view of Poser and Matsumoto. Although the VNs and *suru* separated by particles or other syntactic material are phrases, the combined form of VN–*suru* definitely constitutes a morphological word. When VN and *suru* are separated by syntactic material, the VN can stand by itself – technically, Case particles and focus particles (which Sato 1993 assumes to assign oblique case) enable the VN to eschew the Case filter. Without such syntactic support, the VN must lean on the verb *suru* for incorporation.

So far we have seen that VN–*suru* compounds originate from a phrase like VN-*o suru*. The data given above also argue for the syntactic derivation of *suru* compounds. Consider again the examples in (27) where *suru* stands alone in the second conjunct of a clause or the answer part of a discourse. Were the whole VN–*suru* derived in the lexicon, as claimed by Miyagawa (1987a), it would be extremely difficult to explain such cases, because only the VN portion of the compound word would have to be deleted in outright violation of the lexical integrity. In the syntactic analysis (Kageyama 1993), these examples do not involve deletion of VN but have pro in lieu of a lexical VN.

Table 10.1   Syntactic V–V compounds and VN-*suru* compounds

Differences in:	Syntactic V–V compounds	VN-suru compounds
Nominalization	OK (*ne-sugi* "sleep excessively")	*(*suimin-si* "sleep-doing")
-*kata* suffixation	OK (*kaki-hazime-kata* "the way one begins to write")	?*(*undoo-si-kata* "the way one takes exercise")
Reduplication	*(*tasuke-ai-ai* "help-Recipr")	OK (*undoo-sii-sii* "taking exercise repeatedly")

Since this pro is generated as a separate constituent from *suru* (in a non-incorporated structure), no infringement of lexical integrity results.

Provided that VN–*suru* compounds are syntactic, the question we must now ponder is whether they are syntactic in the same way as syntactic V–V compounds are. In point of fact, the two groups of complex predicates exhibit substantial differences with respect to nominalization (Y. Matsumoto 1996), suffixation of -*kata* "the way" (Kageyama 1993, Y. Matsumoto 1996), and verb reduplication (Kageyama 1976–7), as summarized in table 10.1.

Syntactic V–V compounds, like lexical compounds, are readily amenable to nominalization and -*kata* suffixation, while VN–*suru* compounds resist them. On the other hand, reduplication can apply only to the *suru* portion of VN–*suru*, but never to the V2s of syntactic as well as lexical V–V compounds. In addition, as Poser (1989) observes, *suru* compounds have a phrasal accent. These discrepancies indicate that syntactic V–V compounds make up morphologically "tighter" units than VN–*suru*.

The phrase-like character of VN–*suru* compounds will be most reasonably attributed to their formation at the postsyntactic level (s-structure) (Kageyama 1993). The unavailability of nominalization and -*kata* suffixation with VN–*suru* is then accounted for by saying that these rules operate at the levels prior to s-structure (namely, in the lexicon and syntactic cycle: cf. Sugioka 1984, 1992). The state of affairs involving the word-formation processes discussed so far will be schematically represented as in figure 10.6.

In the model sketched in figure 10.6, word-formation rules apply at three different levels of grammar: the lexical component, the syntactic component, and s-structure (i.e. postsyntax). Some rules apply exclusively at a specific level, while others may be spread over different levels. In particular, nominalization and -*kata* suffixation straddle the boundary of the lexical and syntactic components, while verb reduplication as well as VN–*suru* and postsyntactic compounding is situated at the postsyntactic level (this rule is inapplicable to N–VN postsyntactic compounds, since it calls for the V category). The word formation processes at the three levels are globally constrained by an independent module of Morphology Theory which identifies their outputs as morphological words. Kageyama (1993) calls this model of grammar "Modular

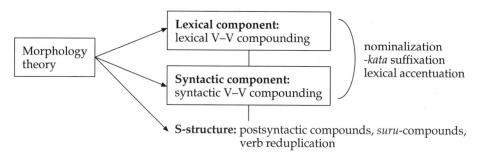

Figure 10.6   Modular Morphology

Morphology." Since Gapping, a rule in the phonological component, applies after all these complex predicate formations are completed, it serves as the infallible test for morphological integrity.

Now the place of the lexical accentuation rule in figure 10.6 deserves special attention. As mentioned earlier, the distinction of lexical and postlexical rules in the framework of lexical phonology is said to mirror the distinction of the lexical and the syntactic component. We have seen, however, that compound words derived from syntactic structure exhibit the same phonological behavior as lexically derived words. A reasonable way to maintain the division of syntax and lexicon while at the same time incorporating the insight of lexical phonology will be to expand the domain of lexical phonology from the lexicon to the syntactic component, as schematized above. What lexical phonologists call "lexical accentuation" now covers word formation in both lexical and syntactic components, and what they call "postlexical phonology" will designate the postsyntactic (s-structure) level.

4.3   *V–te compounds*

Complex predicates involving the gerund (*-te*) form of verbs, such as V–*te morau* "receive the favor of doing," V–*te hosii* "want (someone) to do," V–*te oku* "finish doing, leave done," and V–*te miru* "try doing," are always a nuisance in Japanese grammar. Observe the conflicting results of the two tests.

(29) a. Sono husigi-na buttai-o, Ken-wa ket-te-<u>sae</u>   mɪ-ta.
          that strange   object-Acc Ken-Top kick-Te-even try-Past
          "Ken even tried kicking the strange object."

   b. *Sono husigi-na buttai-o,   Naomi-wa [tatai-te mi], Ken-wa
          that strange   object-Acc Naomi-Top hit-Te try, Ken-Top
          [ket-te   mi-ta].
          kick-Te try-Past
          "Naomi hit and Ken kicked the strange object."

On the one hand, the detachability of the V–*te* portion as in (29a) has forced Sugioka (1984), Ishikawa (1985), Y. Matsumoto (1996), and others to deny the wordhood of V–*te* forms; on the other hand, the inapplicability of Gapping (29b) and other phenomena have led M. Nakau (1973), Kuno (1973), Shibatani (1978), Miyagawa (1989b), and others to identify them as complex predicates. Faced with the conflicting sets of data, J. D. McCawley and Momoi (1986) proposed a special syntactic representation in which V–*te* is dominated simultaneously by the embedded clause and by the matrix verb.

It is evident that V–*te* complexes have the same amphibious nature as VN–*suru* compounds: they originate from phrases and end up with words at the postsyntactic level. This accounts for why V–*te* complexes are pronounced with a phrasal accent just like VN–*suru* compounds. Furthermore, like VN–*suru* compounds, they show resistance to nominalization and -*kata* suffixation.

(30)   a.   *tabe-te mi
             eat-Te trying
       b.   ?*ronbun-no [kaite-mi-kata]
             paper-Acc [write-try-way]

This suggests that the formation of V–*te* complex predicates takes place at the same postsyntactic level as VN–*suru* compounding (Kageyama 1993). In fact, verb reduplication seems applicable to V–*te miru*, as in *tabete mii-mii* "try eating little by little."

5   Nonmorphological Word Formation in Syntax

We have hitherto reviewed word-formation processes applying at three levels: in the lexicon, in syntax, and after syntax. Regardless of the difference in levels, all the complex predicates created by these rules share the fundamental property of being morphological words. However, there are phenomena where composite expressions which are not morphologically identified as words exhibit the same syntactic behavior as words.

5.1   *Light verb constructions with* suru

Let us start with the analysis of the "light verb constructions" with VNs and *suru* proposed by Grimshaw and Mester (1988) (henceforth G&M). The crucial data will be summarized in (31).

(31)   a.   John-wa murabito-ni [[ookami-ga kuru-to]-no
             John-Top villager-to   wolf-Nom come-Comp-Gen
             keikoku]-o sita.
             warn-Acc did
             "John gave the villagers a warning that the wolf was coming."

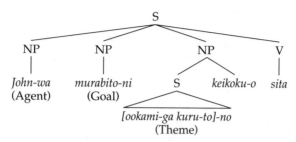

Figure 10.7 Partial argument transfer

b. John-wa murabito-ni [ookami-ga kuru-to]   keikoku-o sita.
   John-Top villager-to [wolf-Nom come-Comp] warn-Acc did
   "John warned the villagers that the wolf was coming."

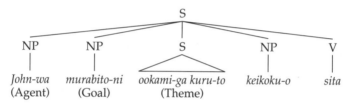

Figure 10.8 Total argument transfer

c. John-wa murabito-ni [ookami-ga kuru-to]   [keikoku-sita]ᵥ.
   John-Top villager-to [wolf-Nom come-Comp] warn-did
   "John warned the villagers that the wolf was coming."

What interests us is that the argument relations of the whole sentences are determined by the VN *keikoku* "warning," rather than the main verb *suru* "do." In particular, the content clause "that the wolf was coming" and the indirect object "villagers" are associated with the ditransitive VN "warning," as is clear from the fact that (31a) and (31b) become unacceptable if the VN is deleted (Sato 1993).

(32) *John-wa murabito-ni ookami-ga kuru-to(-no)   sita.
       John-Top villagers-Dat wolf-Nom come-Comp-Gen did

It appears that the *suru* in such sentences serves no purposes other than just carrying the tense inflection. For this reason, G&M call this *suru* "a light verb."

G&M postulated that the light verb *suru* has an accusative case but is devoid of argument structure as shown in (33a), while the VN *keikoku* has an argument structure like (33b).

(33) a. light *suru*:
          argument structure ( )   case feature <acc>
      b. *keikoku* "warn":
          argument structure (Agent (Goal (Theme)))

Two points should be noted. First, *suru* is held responsible for marking the VN (*keikoku*) with the accusative *-o*. Second, the empty argument structure of *suru* serves as a relay point for transferring the undischarged theta-roles of the VN to the argument NPs in the main clause. Thus in (31a), while the Theme role (i.e. content clause) is satisfied within the NP headed by the VN, the other roles (Agent and Goal) are transferred via the empty argument structure of *suru* to the subject "John" and the indirect object "villagers." This may be called partial argument transfer (Sato 1993). (31b), on the other hand, illustrates a case of total argument transfer, where all of the arguments of *keikoku* appear to be licensed in the main clause. Whether the argument transfer is partial or total, it appears that *suru* works in conjunction with the VN in determining the argument relations of a whole sentence. Although the VN and *suru* in these examples do not make up a morphological word because the VN bears the accusative marker, yet they together function as a composite predicate of the sentences. Of course, precisely the same theta-relations are observed with the incorporated VN–*suru* (31c).

  G&M's analysis was immediately subjected to critical examinations and modifications by various researchers. Two major issues can be sorted out: (i) accusative case on VN and (ii) argument transfer. As to the first issue, while G&M stipulate that *suru* automatically assigns accusative case to the preceding VN, Miyagawa (1989a), Dubinsky (1989), Tsujimura (1990b), and Kageyama (1991) discovered, totally independently of each other, that there is a significant correlation between the transitivity-type of a VN and the availability of accusative marking on it: transitive and unergative VNs can be marked in the accusative but unaccusative VNs cannot.

(34) a. transitive VN: kenkyuu-o suru "do research"
      b. unergative VN: undoo-o suru "do exercise"
      c. unaccusative VN: *sikyo-o suru "pass away"

The unavailability of accusative marking on unaccusative VNs is attributed to Burzio's generalization, which essentially says that predicates which take external argument can assign accusative case to the object NP. Given the argument transfer account, the main verb *suru* can implement accusative marking only if the VN from which it inherits argument structure is transitive or unergative. On this view, the accusative case on VNs in the light verb construction directly reflects the transitivity property of the VNs themselves.

  There are researchers who try to account for the accusative marking of VNs without resorting to Burzio's generalization (Terada 1990, Ahn 1990, Isoda 1991, Uchida and Nakayama 1993). According to them, the instance of *suru* which accompanies the accusative-marked VN is not a light verb but merely an ordinary, "heavy" verb meaning "do;" in other words, argument transfer takes place only when VN is morphologically combined with *suru* as in (31c). This analysis misses the fact that argument transfer does occur when VN and *suru* are clearly separated by focus particles (Sells 1989, Sato 1993, Kageyama 1993, Y. Matsumoto 1996, Dubinsky 1994).

(35) a. Inseki-ga   Taiheiyoo-ni   rakka-wa si-ta   ga ...
      meteorite-Nom Pacific-ocean-Dat fall-Top   do-Past but ...
      "A meteorite fell in the Pacific ocean, but ..."
   b. Keisatu-wa yoogisya-o taiho-wa   si-ta   ga ...
      police-Top   suspect-Acc arrest-Top do-Past but ...
      "The police arrested the suspect, but ..."

Note that *rakka* "fall" in (35a) is an unaccusative VN, so that it would have to be incorporated into *suru* unless accompanied by a focus particle; *taiho* "arrest" in (35b), though transitive and hence compatible with accusative marking, cannot take agentive modifier (**yoogisya-no taiho-o suru* lit. "make an arrest of the suspect") because of certain aspectual conditions on "genitive + VN" phrases (see Tanomura 1988, Kageyama 1991, 1993, Uchida and Nakayama 1993, Dubinsky 1994).

Examples like (35) present unequivocal evidence that argument transfer occurs even when VNs are morphologically distinct from the main verb *suru*. Whether or not VNs are marked in the accusative is a separate matter from the issue of argument transfer. Although linguists normally avoid double accusative marking on VN and theme NP in examples like (35b), Kageyama (1991, 1993) attests actual examples from spontaneous speech which carry accusative markers on both VN and object NP (36a).

(36) a. Kabu-o   zyooto-sita gawa-wa, nanraka-no mikaeri-o
      stocks-Acc sell-did   side-Top   some-Gen   recompense-Acc
      kitai-o   site, ... (TV news)
      expect-Acc do
      "The man who sold the stocks expected some recompense or other"
   b. Zyookyaku-no uti,   19-nin-ga   kyuuzyo-o
      passengers-Gen among 19-people-Nom rescue-Acc
      s-are-masi-ta. (TV news)
      do-Pass.-Polite-Past
      "Of the passengers, nineteen were rescued."

Even more illuminating are passive sentences like (36b) in which the Theme NP is subjectivized with the accusative-marked VN left behind. Of course the same result obtains if a focus particle is added to the VN–*o*, as in *19-nin-ga kyuuzyo-wa s-are-ta*.

While Uchida and Nakayama (1993) assume that only CP can be floated away from NP in non-passive sentences (as in (31b) above), the fact is that ordinary NP objects can also be dissociated from the NP of which the VN is the head, as in (35b) and (36). And when the arguments are embodied outside the VN phrase, an unexpected phenomenon is observed: the VN in such syntactic environments is rendered "syntactically inert." By this I mean the VN resists all sorts of syntactic operations: scrambling (37a), passivization (37b), replacement by pro or a pronoun (37c), and modification (37d) (see Sells 1989, Dubinsky 1990, Kageyama 1991, 1993, Sato 1993).

(37) a.   *Taiho-wa$_i$ keisatu-ga   yoogisya-o t_i si-ta.
             arrest-Top police-Nom suspect-Acc   do-Past
             lit.   "As for the arrest, the police did of the suspect."
     b.   *Taiho-ga$_i$,   keisatu-niyotte yoogisya-o t_i s-are-ta.
             arrest-Nom police-by   suspect-Acc   do-Pass.-Past
             lit.   "The arrest was done the suspect by the police."
     c.   *Keisatu-ga   yoogisya-o   sore-o/pro si-ta.
             police-Nom suspect-Acc it-Acc/pro do-Past
             lit.   "The police did it of the suspect."
     d.   *Keisatu-ga yoogisya-o kinkyuu-no   taiho-o/wa   si-ta.
             police-Nom suspect-Acc on-the-spot-Gen arrest-Acc/Top do-Past
             lit.   "The police did an on-the-spot arrest of the suspect."

These effects are reminiscent of the lexical integrity of morphological words. In other words, *VN–o/wa suru*, albeit formally a phrase, is nonetheless endowed with the same quality as a morphological word. We will call such an expression "a composite predicate."

   Researchers have been seeking possible ways to capture, as it were, the "non-morphological" wordhood of the composite predicate *VN–o suru*. Figures 10.9 and 10.10 show two of them (where we ignore tense inflection).

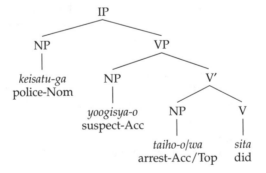

Figure 10.9   Complex V′ predicate

   In figure 10.9, Sato (1993) postulates that VN and *suru* form a complex predicate V′. In figure 10.10, Kageyama (1991, 1993) adopts M. Baker's (1988) idea of Abstract Incorporation (something like "reanalysis"), arguing that VN and *suru* are functionally, though not morphologically, identified as a word

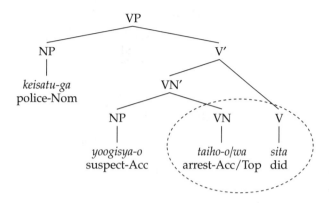

Figure 10.10   Abstract Incorporation

(represented by the dotted circle). Alternative approaches are proposed by Dubinsky in Relational Grammar (1990) and in the Minimalist Program (1994).

5.2   *Light verb constructions with other verbs*

Y. Matsumoto (1996) makes an interesting observation that *suru* is not alone in exhibiting the "argument transfer" effects. According to him, *hazimeru* "begin," *kokoromiru* "attempt," *tsuzukeru* "continue," *kurikaesu* "repeat," and others also behave as light verbs in that they allow arguments of a VN to show up in the matrix clause.

(38)   Karera-wa Tookyoo-e bussi-no   yusoo-o   hazime-ta/kokoromi-ta.
       they-Top   Tokyo-to   goods-Gen transport-Acc begin/attempt-Past
       "They began/attempted to transport the goods to Tokyo."

Matsumoto further points out syntactic parallelisms of these constructions with syntactic complementation structures with *-te morau* "receive the favor of -ing." We can extend Matsumoto's observation a step further to the complementation structures involving syntactic V–V compounds. (Matsumoto does not make this extension because for him, light verb constructions and *-te morau* constructions have syntactically complex structures, while the syntactic V–V compounds are represented as single verbs in the syntactic c-structure.) This will reveal a striking uniformity across different types of complex and composite predicates, as shown in the general schema in figure 10.11.

In figure 10.11, Pred1 represents V1 in syntactic V–V compounds, V–*te* in *-te* complex predicates, and VN in light verb constructions; and Pred2 designates V2 in syntactic V–V compounds, *morau* and other verbs in *-te* complex predicates, and *suru* and other light verbs in light verb constructions.

Given this common structure, the differences between particular constructions are reduced to how the complement and matrix predicate are made into complex or composite words. The differences may be tabulated as in table 10.2.

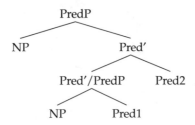

Figure 10.11   General schema of complex and composite predicates

Table 10.2   Predicate and word-formation types

Construction	Types of predicate	Types of word formation
a	Syntactic V–V compounds	Incorporation in syntax
b	*-te* complex predicates	Incorporation at postsyntax
c	VN–*suru* compounds	Incorporation at postsyntax
d	VN–*o suru* construction	Abstract Incorporation in syntax
e	VN–*o hazimeru* as in (38)	(No word formation)

The first three rows (a, b, c) in table 10.2 involve morphological words, and the fourth (d), a composite predicate. In contrast, the last group (e) undergoes neither morphological compounding nor Abstract Incorporation, because the VN remains syntactically active (39a) and the Theme object rejects accusative marking (39b).

(39) a.   John-ga   sono supai-to kokoromi-ta no-wa   sessyoku-da.
           John-Nom the   spy-with attempt-Past Comp-Top contact-Copula
           lit.   "What John attempted with the spy was contact."
      b.   *Karera-wa Tookyoo-e bussi-o   yusoo-sae
           they-Top   Tokyo-to   goods-Acc transport-even
           hazime-ta/kokoromi-ta.
           begin/attempt-Past
           "They even began/attempted to transport the goods to Tokyo."

It is not clear how this last type of light verb construction can be accounted for.

6   Conclusion

This chapter has reviewed several different types of complex and composite predicates which are motivated by syntactic structure. The existence of these syntactically derived words indicates that the strong form of the Lexicalist

Hypothesis is not appropriate for Japanese. Any theory of word formation and morphology must account for the differences and similarities among the varied types of complex and composite predicates in a systematic way. Our discussion in this chapter has been based on a rather traditional view of syntax, where the lexicon and syntax have a balanced division of labor. It remains to be seen how the data that have motivated the distinction between lexical and syntactic word formation can be explicated in a more revealing way in the Minimalist framework or other grammatical models which recognize only one level of syntactic structure. Whatever theory one may adopt, Japanese will surely present challenging problems.

Another fruitful area for future research is the semantics of compound and complex predicates. While lexical semantics tends to be concentrated on lexicalized words, extensive research will be necessary not only in lexical words but also in syntactically derived words, as is hinted at by our discussion on V'-type compounds in section 3.3. Furthermore, while this chapter has been devoted to compounding, semantic effects caused by prefixes and suffixes will pose even more intriguing problems (see Kageyama 1996 for concrete examples).

All those problems emerge from the complex nature of "words." Words constitute the interfaces of syntax, semantics, and phonology (Jackendoff 1997). Because of the multifaceted nature of words, research in word formation should itself be multifarious, and that is why this area is formidably difficult to manage and at the same time endlessly fascinating.

11 Tense and Aspect

TOSHIYUKI OGIHARA

0 Introduction

This chapter is concerned with the semantics of tense and aspect in Japanese. The semantics of tense and aspect has been studied within various theoretical persuasions, and this chapter cannot possibly do justice to every previous research endeavor that concerns the semantics of tense and aspect in Japanese. What I hope to accomplish here is very modest in terms of scope. I restrict my attention to a very small number of issues that I consider to be theoretically important. Furthermore I discuss previous studies only if they are conducted in a formal semantic framework or are interpretable in formal semantic terms. But for the sake of readability, this chapter is written in such a way that the main argumentation can be followed by any linguist who is interested in the issues under discussion.[1]

Before discussing specific issues and examples, I shall provide a general guideline for how the terms "tense" and "aspect" will be used in this chapter. I adopt Comrie's (1976: 1–3) suggestion given in (1) as our guide.

(1) Tense relates the time of the situation referred to to some other time, usually to the moment of speaking. Aspects are different ways of viewing the internal temporal constituency of a situation.

Note that according to (1) the semantic contribution of a tense may be determined in relation to the utterance time (= the moment of speaking) though this is not obligatory. The essential ingredient of a tense morpheme is that it is an external way of looking at some "event" or "situation." Consider the examples in (2).

(2) a. John built a house.
     b. John will build a house.
     c. John was building a house.
     d. John will be building a house (when Mary arrives here next month).

(2a) is in the past tense, while (2b) is in the future tense. Despite the difference in tense form, both of them state that John does something that results in the coming about of a complete house. Let us refer to this information as the "propositional content" of (2a–b). A tense morpheme does not alter the propositional content of the sentence in question and simply locates it at an appropriate position on the time continuum. On the other hand, (2c–d) are progressive sentences. When a native speaker interprets (2c) or (2d), its "propositional content" is different from that involved in (2a) or (2b) in that it does not involve a complete house. The difference between (2a–b) and (2c–d) can be summarized in the following manner: both (2a) and (2b) entail that there will be a complete house built by John at some future time, whereas neither (2c) nor (2d) guarantees this outcome. In other words, a tense morpheme simply locates "the same thing" at different temporal positions, whereas an aspect morpheme such as the progressive changes the propositional content itself. For example, an aspect morpheme looks into the internal structure of the type of situation described by the main predicate and focuses on one particular aspect of the situation described by the predicate, say the beginning, the ending, or the middle.

Given the relatively liberal characterization of tense assumed here, Comrie (1985) distinguishes between absolute tense, which is speech-time oriented, and relative tense, which can relate to other contextually salient times. We adopt the latter for the purpose of this chapter. We will discuss two sets of data in this chapter: one involving the morphemes -*ru* and -*ta*, the other the morpheme -*te iru*.

1   The Morphemes -*ru* and -*ta*

The morphemes -*ru* (present) and -*ta* (past) in Japanese have been studied extensively in the literature. Japanese has no overt present tense morpheme as such, nor does it have a future tense morpheme suffixed to the verb. Japanese is similar to English, at least morphologically, in that it does not have an overt marker on the verb that indicates future time. However, English has the future auxiliary *will*, which is said to be a future tense morpheme. In Japanese, future-oriented interpretations are supplied by sentences in the simple present tense. When needed, explicit reference to future events is made in terms of future-oriented nouns like *tumori* "intention" and *yotei* "plan." We shall take up a number of issues involving these two morphemes. To simplify our discussion and exposition, we will restrict our attention to the behavior of -*ta*. However, the points we will make about -*ta* will be equally valid for -*ru*.

1.1   *The theoretical status of the morpheme* -ta

It is controversial whether -*ta* is a tense morpheme or an aspect morpheme. As far as I know, three arguments (two of which are related) have been presented in the literature for the view that this morpheme is an aspect morpheme, a perfect morpheme to be more specific. One major argument is that a tense morpheme is by definition a deictic expression, which -*ta* is not. A second major argument is that -*ta* has the following two uses: (i) to specify the temporal location of the relevant event or state (a "referential use"), or (ii) to existentially quantify over past times without specifying the location of the relevant event or state. A third view (which is related to the second view) is that -*ta* allegedly carries a result state meaning on a par with the English perfect, which is often regarded as an aspect morpheme. I will show that these three arguments are not strong enough to undermine the claim that -*ta* is a relative tense morpheme.

First, I discuss the view according to which -*ta* is not a tense morpheme because it is not a deictic expression. It is often assumed in the linguistics literature that any tense morpheme is a deictic expression in that its interpretation is made in relation to the temporal deictic center, namely the utterance time. This is not the only viable theory of tense; as mentioned above, Comrie characterizes tense in a slightly different way and distinguishes between absolute tense and relative tense. However, the idea that tense is speech-time oriented has a stronghold in linguistics. This is partly because Reichenbach's theory of tense, which embodies the idea that tense is speech-time oriented, is popular among linguists. For example, Reichenbach's theory is employed by Hornstein (1990) for English and by Ota (1972) for Japanese. According to Reichenbach, the meaning of each tense form is specified in terms of the relation among three temporal entities: S (for speech time), R (for reference time), and E (for event time). The semantic import of E and S is clear. E indicates the time (if there is such a time) at which the event described by the sentence takes place. S indicates the time at which the sentence in question is uttered. The interpretation of R is not immediately clear, but R distinguishes between the simple past and the past perfect in the following way. The simple past tense form in English is indicated by a representation of the form E, R_S (= E and R are simultaneous and S follows them), whereas the past perfect tense form is indicated by E_R_S.[2] The semantic import of R becomes clear when we consider examples like (3a–b).

(3) a. Mary lived in Seattle.
     b. Mary had lived in Seattle.

Reichenbach's proposal accounts for the difference between (3a) and (3b) in the following way. When a sentence is uttered in a normal situation, an assertion is made with regard to an interval that is "in focus." For example, (3a) does not merely say that Mary lived in Seattle at some past time; rather, it asserts that Mary lived in Seattle during some specific past interval that is salient in the context in question. This salient interval is referred to as a "reference time" in Reichenbach's framework. On this interpretation of Reichenbach's system, (3b) is interpreted to mean that Mary's living in Seattle is located entirely before the salient time in question. This clarifies the intuitive difference between (3a) and (3b). Reichenbach's proposal can also account for the behavior of tense and aspect morphemes in verb complement clauses. Consider examples like (4a–b).

(4) a. John found out that Mary lived in Seattle.
    b. John found out that Mary had lived in Seattle.

(4a) means that Mary's living in Seattle overlaps with the time of John's finding out this fact, whereas (4b) says that Mary's living in Seattle wholly precedes the time of John's finding this out. We can account for these facts correctly by adopting Reichenbach's proposal and his assumption that the reference time should be the same for all clauses that belong to the same sentence (referred to as the "permanence of the reference point").[3]

Reichenbach himself does not attempt to say how each tense or aspect morpheme that occurs in a sentence contributes compositionally to the overall interpretation of the sentence. However, we can extract such information from the graphical representations Reichenbach provides for various combinations of tense and aspect morphemes: the morpheme *-ed* indicates R_S, and the perfect (i.e. *have -ed*) indicates E_R.[4] This means that *-ed* is a deictic expression whereas the perfect is not. Given the assumption that the former is a tense morpheme and the latter is not, we can say that Reichenbach's framework as interpreted here reinforces the popular idea that a tense morpheme is necessarily a deictic expression.

On the basis of the above discussion about English, it is often claimed that the morpheme *-ta* in Japanese is an aspect morpheme rather than a tense morpheme because it is a nondeictic temporal morpheme. Let us look at the examples in (5).

(5) a. Taroo-wa [Hanako-ga   hon-o   yon-da] to   it-ta.
       Taro-Top   Hanako-Nom book-Acc read-Past that say-Past
       "Taro said that Hanako had read a/the book."
    b. Taroo-wa [terebi-o mi-ta   ato-de] benkyoo-suru.
       Taro-Top   TV-Acc watch-Past after-at study-Pres
       "Taro will study after watching TV."

(5a) contains a verb complement clause, and the time of Hanako's reading the book is understood to be located before the time of Taro's saying, thanks to the morpheme *-ta* in the verb complement clause. It does not suffice to say that the time of Hanako's reading a book is located earlier than the utterance time because this time *must* be located before Taro's saying. The same is true of (5b), which involves a temporal adverbial clause. The time of Taro's watching TV is understood to be located in the past in relation to the time of his studying because of the morpheme *-ta* in the temporal adverbial clause. Examples like (5a–b) indicate that *-ta* is not a deictic expression in that its interpretation is not necessarily determined in relation to the utterance time, the temporal deictic center. Instead, *-ta* locates an event or state in relation to the time indicated by a tense that locally c-commands it. For those who assume that a tense morpheme is by definition a deictic expression, *-ta* is clearly not a tense. To the extent that the point with respect to which its semantic contribution is determined is not necessarily the utterance time, *-ta* resembles the English perfect (see Ogihara 1987).[5] Thus, if we go along with those who claim that the English perfect is an aspect morpheme and not a tense morpheme, *-ta* is an aspect morpheme.

On the other hand, if we follow Comrie's (1976) suggestion presented in (1), the above Japanese data suggest that *-ta* is a relative tense morpheme. This viewpoint was defended by Soga (1983), K. Matsumoto (1985), and others. Ogihara (1996) executes it in a formal semantic framework and shows that a system in which a sentence denotes a property, and in which the semantics of verbs like *say* (or *iu* "say" in Japanese) is understood in terms of the subject's self-ascription of properties (attitude *de se* in the sense of D. Lewis 1979), accounts for the behavior of tense morphemes in Japanese and English.[6] Thus, according to Comrie's suggestion and Ogihara's semantic account, the morpheme *-ta* is clearly a tense morpheme although it is a relative one unlike *-ed* in English. I believe that this settles the issue raised above concerning the status of the morpheme *-ta*. If *-ta* is regarded as an aspect morpheme just because it is not speech-time oriented, the controversy here is merely a matter of terminology. However, since the term "aspect" is used more commonly for a different meaning characterized as in (1), I think it is much less confusing to use the term "relative tense" for *-ta* and reserve the term "aspect" for such concepts as progressive and inchoative.

Let us now turn to a second major argument for the ambiguity of *-ta*. M. Nakau (1976) and Teramura (1978) (among others) claim that *-ta* is ambiguous between a preterit (*kako*) interpretation and a perfective (*kanryoo*) interpretation. This is a very common view among the researchers of tense and aspect in Japanese. When a sentence with *-ta* is used for a preterit interpretation, it accompanies an adverbial that refers to a definite past interval (e.g. *kinoo* "yesterday"). This adverbial restricts the temporal location of the event or state in question. This resembles the view that tense is a referential expression (e.g. Enç 1987). On the other hand, when a sentence with *-ta* is used for a perfective interpretation, no such adverbial restricts the temporal location of the relevant event or state. In this case, this sentence is interpreted to mean that there was a past time at which a relevant event or state obtained with no specification as to when it obtained. Some relevant examples are given in (6a–b).

(6) a. Taroo-wa kinoo   hon-o   yonda.
         Taro-Top yesterday book-Acc read-Past
         "Taro read the book yesterday."
     b. Taroo-wa hon-o   yonda.
         Taro-Top book-Acc read-Past
         "Taro has read the book."

However, it is arguable that adverbials that refer to definite past intervals merely restrict the quantificational force associated with *-ta*. For example, it is arguable that the semantic difference between (6a) and (6b) stems from the presence or absence of the adverb *kinoo* "yesterday" and that the morpheme *-ta* has a constant meaning in (6a) and in (6b). This is suggested by the translations (7a–b) of (6a–b).

(7) a. $\exists t[t$ is earlier than now $\wedge$ Taro reads the book at $t \wedge t$ is located within yesterday]
     b. $\exists t[t$ is earlier than now $\wedge$ Taro reads the book at $t]$

Therefore, the presence and absence of such adverbials does not substantiate the view that *-ta* is ambiguous between a preterit interpretation and a perfective interpretation. See Ogihara (1996: 16–17) for some relevant discussion.

Lastly, let us discuss a third major reason that *-ta* is regarded as an aspect morpheme. The claim is that it has an aspectual interpretation in the narrow sense of the term as defined in (1). To be more concrete, it is claimed to have a result state interpretation. Let us first consider some English examples that involve the perfect.

(8) a. John lost his passport.
     b. John has lost his passport.

(8a) simply says that an event of John's losing his passport took place in the past relative to the utterance time. On the other hand, (8b) requires for its truth that the passport that John lost have not turned up. One way of understanding this fact is that (8b) contains as part of its truth condition the continuation of a state that results from John's losing his passport, namely the state of John's not having his passport. This claim about the semantics of the perfect has been presented in the literature (e.g. Parsons 1990, Kamp and Reyle 1993).[7]

As mentioned above in connection with the second argument for the ambiguity of *-ta*, M. Nakau (1976), Teramura (1978), and others claim that *-ta* can receive a perfective (*kanryoo*) interpretation. In view of the result state analysis of the English perfect, this claim about *-ta* is subject to a different semantic analysis. That is, it is arguable that *-ta* can receive a result state interpretation on a par with the English perfect. One piece of evidence for this position is that the same type of adverbial occurs in English sentences in the perfect and Japanese sentences in the *-ta* form. Consider examples (9a–d).

(9) a. Taro has already read the book.
     b. Taroo wa moo hono yonda
         Taro-Top already book-Acc read-Past
         "Taro has already read the book."
     c. Taro is already here.
     d. Taroo-wa moo koko-ni iru.
         Taro-Top already here be-Pres
         "Taro is here already."

Since the adverb *already* occurs with the present perfect, the fact that its Japanese equivalent *moo* "already" can occur with the -*ta* form of a verb seems to indicate that -*ta* and the perfect have some meaning in common.[8] Note that (9c–d) are stative sentences in the simple present tense and contain *already* and *moo*. This strongly suggests that *already* or *moo* can make reference to states. For example, (9c) asserts that the state of Taro's being here obtains now and that this is unexpectedly early. Thus, given the assumption that the English perfect is used to indicate a result state, we seem to be justified in claiming that *already* (or *moo*) has the same role to play in sentences like (9a–b). For example, (9a) means that the state of Taro's having read the book obtains now and this is unexpectedly early.

On the other hand, we also find many differences between the -*ta* form in Japanese and the past tense form in English. For one thing, when a present perfect sentence in English is negated, *yet* can occur in it, as shown in (10a). However, as indicated by (10b), its Japanese counterpart cannot occur with *mada* "yet." The contrast between (10c) and (10d) also argues against assigning the same meaning to the morpheme -*ta* and the English perfect.

(10) a. Taro has not seen the movie yet.
  b. *Taroo-wa mada sono eega-o   minakat-ta.
     Taro-Top yet   that movie-Acc see-Neg-Past
     Intended: "Taro has not seen the movie yet."
  c. Taro has visited Hanako three times since the beginning of this year.
  d. ??Taroo-wa kotosi-no   hazime   kara san-kai   Hanako-o
     Taro-Top this-year-Gen beginning from three-times Hanako-Acc
     tazuneta.
     visit-Past
     Intended: "Taro has visited Hanako three times since the beginning of this year."

Note that in order to convey what one might refer to as a "result state" interpretation, one must use the -*te iru* form of the verb in question (in the present tense) as shown in (11).

(11) a. Taroo-wa mada sono eega-o   mi-te i-nai.
     Taro-Top yet   that movie-Acc see-Te iru-Neg-Pres
     "Taro has not seen the movie yet."
  b. Taroo-wa kotosi-no   hazime   kara san-kai   Hanako-o
     Taro-Top this-year-Gen beginning from three-times Hanako-Acc
     tazune-te iru.
     visit-Te iru-Pres
     "Taro has visited Hanako three times since the beginning of this year."

On the basis of the examples like the ones above, Ogihara (1996) concludes that -*ta* in Japanese is a "relative tense" morpheme. The similarity between the

English perfect and *-ta* discussed above can be accounted for if we assume that the Japanese *-ta* construction allows for the possibility that there is no con- textually salient past interval that restricts the quantificational force of the morpheme. When this happens, its interpretation is quite similar to some uses of the English perfect.[9]

Let me caution the reader, however, that the above account of the semantics of the *-ta* form is far from uncontroversial. One strong piece of evidence that some occurrences of this morpheme convey an "aspectual meaning" comes from data involving relative clauses. Consider the examples in (12).

(12) a. Taroo-wa [soko-no   nuke-ta   oke]-o   mot-te iru.
          Taro-Top   bottom-Gen miss-Past pail-Acc have-Pres
          "Taro has a pail that has no bottom."
      b. Taroo-wa [ai-ta mado]-kara nigedasu   tumori-da.
          Taro-Top   open (iv.)-past   window from escape-intend-Past
          "Taro intends to escape from an open window."

In both (12a) and (12b), the morpheme *-ta* indicates a current state rather than a previous event in relation to the matrix clause time. Thus, (12a–b) seem to indicate that *-ta* can produce an aspectual interpretation in relative clauses. The relative tense theory assumed here cannot deal with examples like (12a–b). How to explain an apparent aspectual use of *-ta* remains a problem for future research.[10,11]

1.2 Some problems with the "relative tense theory"

As mentioned in 1.1, Soga (1983), K. Matsumoto (1985), and Ogihara (1996) argue that Japanese has a relative tense system. To put it simply, this proposal suggests that every tense morpheme is interpreted in relation to the tense that locally c-commands it.[12] If this theory is on the right track, every embedded occurrence of the morpheme *-ta* indicates anteriority over the time indicated by the tense in the higher clause. However, there are some examples that indicate that this is not always the case. Let us discuss some such examples. Tadasu Hattori (personal communication) pointed out examples like (13a), whereas Soga (1983), Kudo (1995), and others discussed examples like (13b).

(13) a Taroo-wa zibun-ga gan-dat-ta   to   sitte i-ta.
          Taro-Top self-Nom cancer-be-Past that know-Past
          "Taro knew that he had cancer."
      b. Taroo-wa Tokyo-ni i-ta   toki, apaato-ni   sundei-ta.
          Taro-Top Tokyo-at be-Past when apartment-at live-Past
          "When Taro was in Tokyo, he lived in an apartment."

(13a) involves a verb complement clause that contains a past tense morpheme. Despite the fact that the matrix clause is in the past tense, some native speakers claim that it can receive an interpretation in which the time of his having cancer is simultaneous with the time of his knowing it.[13] On the other hand, (13b) concerns a temporal adverbial clause with a stative verb headed by *toki* "when." It is generally assumed that a temporal adverbial clause is subordinate to the matrix clause. Since the *toki*-clause is in the past tense, it is expected that the entire period of Taro's being in Tokyo precedes the time of his living in an apartment. However, (13b) can only have a simultaneous interpretation as indicated by the English gloss. This is unexpected under the relative tense theory.

One possible account of the data in (13) is that the embedded clause is somehow moved in the syntax and is interpreted independently of the matrix clause tense. It is important to notice that in both (13a) and (13b), the alleged embedded clause is presupposed to be true. If the verb *sitte-iru* "know" is replaced by *sinzi-te iru* "believe" as in (14), no simultaneous interpretation is obtained.[14]

(14)   #Taroo-wa zibun-ga gan-dat-ta   to   sinzi-te i-ta.
       Taro-Top self-Nom cancer-be-Past that believe-Past
       Intended: "Taro believed that he had cancer."

Given this special semantic property of the clauses in question, I do not think we should give up the idea that Japanese is a relative tense language. The fact that clauses that are presupposed to be true behave differently should be explained in terms of the special property of true propositions. In the case of (13a), we could say that the verb complement clause is in fact an NP of the form "the fact that S" and could be scoped out on a par with regular NPs. As for (13b), since *toki* is a noun which literally means "time," it is arguable that the *toki*-clause is an NP that is scoped out of the matrix clause. If this is the case, *toki* "when" simply indicates that the two propositions overlap in time. A. Nakamura (1994) suggests a solution along these lines.

2   The Morpheme *-te iru*

As mentioned in earlier sections, we follow Comrie regarding the distinction between tense and aspect. Japanese has many aspect morphemes, each of which has a unique meaning associated with it. We shall discuss only one representative example here: the morpheme *-te iru*.

The modern study of the aspect morpheme *-te iru* starts with H. Kindaichi's (1950) work.[15] Kindaichi classifies verbs into four groups: stative verbs, durative verbs, instantaneous verbs, and the fourth verbal category. They are exemplified by the sentences in (15).

(15) a. Taroo-wa Tokyo-ni iru. (stative verb)
      Taro-Top Tokyo-at be-Pres
      "Taro is in Tokyo."
   b. Taroo-wa ima ki-o   taosi-te iru. (durative verb)
      Taro-Top now tree-Acc fell-Te iru-Pres
      "Taro is now pushing down/felling a tree."
   c. Taroo-wa (ima asokode)   taore-te iru. (instantaneous verb)
      Taro-Top now over-there fall-Te iru-Pres
      "Having fallen down, Taro is now lying over there."
   d. Yama-ga   takaku sobie-te
      Mountain-Nom tall   become-high-Te
      iru. (the fourth verbal category)
      iru-Pres
      "A mountain stands tall."

Kindaichi uses the morpheme *-te iru* as a diagnostic to obtain this classification. Roughly speaking, Kindaichi's criteria can be described as follows. A stative verb cannot occur in the *-te iru* form. A durative verb can occur in the *-te iru* form for an ongoing process interpretation. When an adverbial that indicates the current time (e.g. *ima* "now") occurs with a durative verb in the *-te iru* form, this is the only interpretation the resulting sentence receives.[16] An instantaneous verb occurs in the *-te iru* form (with an optional current-time-oriented adverbial) to indicate that the result state of the event described by the sentence obtains now. Verbs that belong to the fourth verbal category behave in a rather unexpected way in that they normally occur only in the *-te iru* form and do not seem to have a compositional semantic structure. (15d) simply means that the mountain stands tall and therefore appears to describe a current state. We might expect that this interpretation is obtained by the result state meaning of the verb *sobieru* indicated by the morpheme *-te iru*. By "computing backwards" so to speak, we expect that *sobieru* means "become tall." However, this hypothesis is not empirically supported because the verb *sobieru* must be used in the *-te iru* form as shown by the unacceptability of (16).

(16) *Yama-ga   kyonen sobie-ta.
    mountain-Nom last year become-tall-Past
    Intended interpretation: "A mountain was formed last year."

Thus, Kindaichi posits a separate verb class (or sentence class) for this type of verb.
   An important fact not clearly stated in Kindaichi's work is that most (perhaps all) sentences in the *-te iru* form are ambiguous between two interpretations. Ambiguity is found even with "instantaneous" verbs which do not produce progressive interpretations. Fujii (1966) points out that there is an important difference between "normal" result state interpretations and what he calls "experiential" interpretations. Consider the examples in (17).

(17)   a.   Taroo-wa 1970-nen ni kekkonsi-te iru.
            Taro-Top 1970-year in marry-Te   iru-Pres
            "Taro has the experience of having gotten married in 1970."
       b.   Taroo-wa kyonen   itido hugu-o   tabe-te iru.
            Taro-Top last-year once globefish-Acc eat-Te iru-Pres
            "Taro has the experience of having eaten globefish once last year."

What is interesting about the examples in (17) is that this type of interpretation
can be obtained with either an instantaneous verb (e.g. (17a)) or a durative
verb (e.g. (17b)). Also worthy of note is the fact that each sentence in (17)
contains an adverbial indicating a past interval, as opposed to examples like
(15b–c) which contain a current-time-oriented adverbial. Ogihara (in press)
takes this fact seriously and proposes the following classification of the interpretations associated with the V–*te iru* form.

(18)

Verb class	*"Current situation"*	*"Experiential"*
Durative verbs	Progressive	Experiential
Instantaneous verbs	(Concrete) result state	Experiential

(18) represents the idea that progressive interpretations and (concrete) result
state interpretations should be grouped together as opposed to experiential interpretations. This classification is based upon the distribution of co-occurring
adverbials and leads us to expect that some semantic property is shared by
progressive interpretations associated with durative verbs and (concrete) result
state interpretations associated with instantaneous verbs. It appears at first that
the difference between them is so clear that it is not possible to bring out a
property common to these two "interpretations." The difference can be described as in (19a–b).

(19)   a.   *Durative sentence ϕ*: For any interval t, *ima ϕ-te iru* (where *ima* means
            now) is true at t only if *ϕ-te simatta* (finish doing ϕ) is false at t.
       b.   *Instantaneous sentence ϕ*: For any interval t, *ima ϕ-te iru* (where *ima*
            means now) is true at t only if *ϕ-te simatta* (finish doing ϕ) is true at t.

If (19a–b) are on the right track, we must concede that -*te iru* and a tenseless
sentence interact in different ways in the two cases.

On the other hand, the fact that the same type of adverbial (i.e. current-time-
oriented adverbials) can be used to indicate both of these "interpretations"
shows that they should be captured in a similar way. It is more intuitive to
deal with examples like (20a) and (20b) in the same way because a naïve
native speaker would be unable to distinguish the two "uses" of -*te iru*.[17]

(20)   a.   Taroo-wa ima hasit-te iru.
            Taro-Top now run-Te iru-Pres
            "Taro is now running."

b. Taroo-wa ima taore-te iru.
Taro-Top now fall-Te iru-Pres
"Taro is now lying on the ground (as a result of having fallen down)."

To do justice to the distribution of temporal adverbials and the native speaker's intuitions, Ogihara (in press) proposes that by modifying the lexical semantics of so-called "instantaneous sentences," a unified analysis of the *-te iru* form (or put more accurately, the morpheme *-iru*) becomes possible. Essentially, the idea is that the information that concerns the result state of an instantaneous event sentence is assumed to be part of its lexical meaning. For example, if Taro falls to the ground at 7:00 and lies there until 7:05, then *Taroo-wa taoreru*, which is the tenseless sentence involved in (20b), is said to be true both at 7:00 and "at" the interval that starts at 7:00 and ends at 7:05. By adopting this proposal about the semantics of so-called "instantaneous sentences," we can now say simply that ϕ-*te iru* is true at some time *t* iff there is an eventuality *e* at *t* such that *e* is a proper portion of another eventuality *e'* that is an eventuality that is characterized by ϕ.[18] This provides a solution to the compositionality problem that the *-te iru* form poses. For example, we can now say that (20a) is true at *t* iff there is an eventuality at *t* that could be extended to an eventuality of Taro's running; similarly, (20b) is true at some *t* iff there is an eventuality at *t* that could be extended to an eventuality of Taro's falling. This is illustrated in (21a–b).

(21) a.

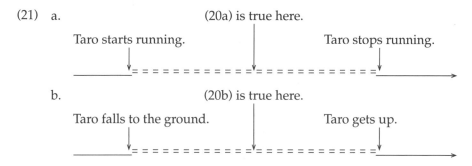

As for the distinction between "current situation" interpretations and "experiential" interpretations, Ogihara (in press) hypothesizes that the morpheme *-te* can bear the feature [+perfect] in some cases, and this is responsible for "experiential interpretations" associated with some sentences in the *-te iru* form. To put simply, a tenseless sentence of the form ϕ-*te* (where *-te* bears the feature [+perfect]) describes an experience associated with ϕ attributed to the denotation of the subject NP.[19] Given the special provision about instantaneous sentences just given, we can say that the semantic role played by the morpheme *-iru* is constant. Put simply, ϕ-*te iru* is true at some time *t* iff there is a current eventuality that could be extended to an eventuality described by ϕ-*te* (ignoring tense). Ogihara (in press) suggests the possibility that the semantic difference between current situation interpretations and experiential interpretations of

-iru is characterized in terms of stage-level vs. individual-level predicates (Milsark 1974, Carlson 1977). That is, a sentence in the *-te iru* form that receives a current situation interpretation is claimed to involve a stage-level predicate, and one that receives an experiential interpretation an individual-level predicate. Matsuda (1997) confirms this hypothesis by presenting examples similar to the ones given in (22).

(22)   a.   Taroo-ga   ima   ki-o   taosi-te iru.
            Taro-Nom now tree-Acc fell-Te   iru-Pres
            "Taro is now felling a tree."
       b.   Taroo-ga   ima   yooroppa-ni it-te   iru.
            Taro-Nom now Europe-to   go-Te iru-Pres
            "Taro is now in Europe (as a result of having gone there)."
       c.   Taroo-ga   imamade-ni hon-o   zyussatu-mo   kai-te   iru.
            Taro-Nom till now-Dat book-Acc ten-as many as write-Te iru-Pres
            "Taro is the one who has the experience of having written as many as ten books."
       d.   Taroo-ga   kyonen yooroppa-ni itte   iru.
            Taro-Nom last year Europe-to   go-Te iru-Pres
            "Taro is the one who has the experience of having gone to Europe last year."

Kuroda (1965a) observes that when a sentence contains a *ga*-marked NP and an individual-level predicate, the *ga*-marked NP must receive a focused interpretation. Note that (22a–b) are "neutral descriptive statements" in that they do not invoke focused interpretations of *ga*-marked NPs. On the other hand, in order to assign a coherent interpretation to (22c) or (22d), the *ga*-marked NP must be interpreted as focused as indicated by the English gloss. Given Kuroda's generalization as a diagnostic, we can conclude that current situation interpretations of *-iru* (exemplified by (22a–b)) involve stage-level predicates, whereas experiential interpretations of *-iru* involve individual-level predicates. This in turn substantiates the classification of various readings of *-te iru* given in (18).

  I believe that Ogihara's (in press) proposal is descriptively adequate and also captures the native speaker's intuition that the progressive interpretation of a durative sentence in the *-te iru* form and the result state interpretation of an instantaneous sentence in the *-te iru* form have something in common. However, the proposal leaves a few things to be desired. One is that the proposal does not say explicitly how the distinction between durative sentences and instantaneous sentences comes about; it simply posits different verb classes and distinguishes these classes by stating the semantic differences between them. As we shall see below, it is clear that the difference is not caused by the difference in temporal duration of the events in question. If so, what is it that is responsible for the difference between these two sentence classes? The proposal also falls short of a true explanation of the phenomenon in question in that it posits a lexical difference between achievement sentences in English and "instantaneous sentences" in Japanese; achievements in English can describe preparatory stages but not result state stages of events, whereas instantaneous sentences in Japanese are exactly the opposite.

Okuda (1977) challenges Kindaichi's proposal by pointing out that Kindaichi uses the wrong criterion to distinguish between durative verbs and instantaneous verbs. Okuda makes two points. One is that the distinction between durative verbs and instantaneous verbs should not be made in terms of the temporal duration of events. That is, a sentence that contains a so-called "instantaneous verb" does not describe an instantaneous event. It describes an event that takes time to complete. The other point, which is clearly related to the first, is that a "durative event sentence" involves an action of an individual, whereas an "instantaneous event sentence" involves a change that an individual undergoes. Okuda suggests that we should pay attention to argument structure when we study semantic properties of the -*te iru* construction. I reinterpret Okuda's claim as follows: the semantic contribution of the -*te iru* form can be explicated in terms of assignment of a property to an entity denoted by the subject NP of the sentence in question. Let us look at examples (23a–b).

(23) a. Taroo-wa ki-o   taosi-te iru.
        Taro-Top tree-Acc fell-Te iru-Pres
        "Taro is now felling a tree."
    b. Ki-ga   taore-te   iru.
        Tree-Nom fall-down-Te iru-Pres
        "A tree is on the ground (as a result of having fallen)."

The striking difference between (23a) and (23b) can be accounted for in terms of the three principles given in (24).

(24) a. In general, a sentence in the -*te iru* form is used to assign a property to the entity denoted by the subject NP and to nothing else. (This is implicit in Okuda's remarks.)
    b. An agentive entity can be assigned a property of "engaging in" the action named by the predicate (i.e. VP), whereas a nonagentive entity cannot.
    c. An entity can be assigned a property of being in some state if its obtaining this state as soon as the event described by the sentence is part of the lexical meaning of the predicate.

Assuming (24a–c), we can explain a number of things that had to be stipulated in Ogihara's (in press) proposal summarized above. Let us see how this account compares with the proposal put forth by Ogihara with regard to the difference between (23a) and (23b), which contain the transitive verb *taosu* "knock down/fell" and the intransitive verb *taoreru* "fall down," respectively. In Ogihara's proposal, the difference between (23a) and (23b) is encoded in terms of types of events they involve. Roughly put, (23a) involves a process part, whereas (23b) involves a result state part. On the other hand, (24a–c) account for why verbs like *taosu* and *taoreru* interact with *-te iru* in different ways. In (23a) the subject NP *Taroo* bears an agentive thematic role. Thus, Taro can be understood to "engage in" an action named by the VP when the VP occurs in the *-te iru* form. This yields a progressive interpretation. On the other hand, *ki* "tree" occurs as the object NP, and this fact prevents (23a) from receiving a (concrete) result state interpretation associated with the tree. By contrast, the NP *ki* "tree" occurs as the subject in (23b) and can be assigned a property by the *-te iru* form. Since this NP has a thematic role associated with an undergoer, it can receive a result state interpretation.

However, (24b–c) raise the following questions: (i) why is it that an agentive subject NP cannot receive a concrete result state interpretation?; (ii) why is it that an undergoer subject NP cannot receive a process (= progressive) interpretation? The first question is easier to answer. When someone fells a tree, this person does not obtain any specific property over and above the property of having felled a tree, but the tree obtains the property of lying on the ground. Thus, a concrete result state reading that is associated with a current-time-oriented adverbial can only be attributed to an entity that obtains a specific property when the event in question is completed.[20] The other question is harder to answer. An event of a tree's falling to the ground could be an extended event that takes a long time. However, the *-te iru* form is incapable of referring to the "process" associated with the event. This is presumably because when we talk about an ongoing process, we usually identify it in terms of the agent rather than by the undergoer. Thus, it makes sense to attribute a property associated with a process to an agent and not to an undergoer. At least in Japanese, this distinction is grammaticized to the extent that only agentive NPs can receive ongoing process interpretations. The fact that this asymmetry between agentive NPs and patient/undergoer NPs is not observed in English suggests that this is possibly a language-specific constraint valid in Japanese. However, the above reasoning seems convincing because it does not require that a sentence containing a transitive verb involve an event that lasts longer than the event associated with a sentence containing an intransitive verb.

As mentioned above, one important point that Okuda makes is that the distinction between durative sentences and instantaneous sentences cannot be drawn in terms of the temporal duration of events in question. Consider examples in (25). (25a) and (25c) are "durative sentences," whereas (25b) and (25d) are "instantaneous sentences." Note that one and the same event can be described in terms of (25a) and (25b).[21] It should also be noted that (25c) generally takes only a few hours to complete, whereas (25d) generally takes years, if it is understood that the paint came off naturally. Yet, the *-te iru* construction would yield a progressive interpretation with (25a) and (25c) but not with (25b) or (25d).

(25) a. Taroo-wa doa-o   ake-ta.
          Taro-Top door-Acc open-Past
          "Taro opened the door."
      b. Doa-ga   ai-ta.
          door-Nom open-Past
          "The door opened."
      c. Taroo-wa kuruma-no penki-o   hagasi-ta.
          Taro-Top car-Gen   paint-Acc remove-Past
          "Taro removed his car's paint."
      d. Kuruma-no penki-ga   hagare-ta.
          car-Gen   paint-Nom come-off-Past
          "The car's paint came off."

Note also that so-called "instantaneous sentences" can occur with adverbials that indicate extended intervals as shown in (26a–b).

(26) a. Ni-nen   de ie-no   penki-ga   hagare-ta.
          two-years in house-Gen paint-Nom come-off-Past
          "The paint of the house came off in two years."
      b. Hanako-wa iti-nen   de gakkoo-ga   iyaninat-ta.
          Hanako-Top one-year in school-Nom get-tired-of-Past
          "Hanako got tired of school in one year."

Okuda's argument is also persuasive when we realize that some sentences allow for both a progressive reading and a (concrete) result state reading as shown in (27).

(27) Taroo-wa ima ki-ni   nobot-te iru.
      Taro-Top now tree-Dat climb-Te iru-Pres
      "Taro is now climbing a tree"
      or "Taro is up the tree (after having climbed it)."

Taro is clearly an active participant in the event described in (27), and this sentence can receive a progressive interpretation as expected. However, it can also receive a result state interpretation as shown in the English glosses. This shows that a result state interpretation is not inherently related to the instantaneous nature of the event. Since it is counterintuitive to posit two different verbs that surface as *noboru*, Okuda's proposal suggests a way out of the dilemma that a Kindaichi-type proposal faces.

But how shall we translate Okuda's insight into a compositional semantic theory? If the temporal trace of events associated with tenseless sentences does not predict the semantics of their *-te iru* counterparts, what does? One possibility is to propose a theory in which events and times play independent roles. In this theory, one can grant that an event of a tree's falling to the ground is an extended event that takes time and claim at the same time that a sentence with a thematic subject that describes this event is true at the final

moment of this event (but not "at" the temporal trace of the entire event).
I believe that this type of proposal enables us to resolve the apparent conflict
between Kindaichi's proposal and Okuda's ideas. I shall sketch here the proposal I have in mind.[22]

In this proposal, the following four predicate types are recognized in Japanese:
stative predicates (e.g. *Tokyo-ni iru* "be in Tokyo"), accomplishment/activity
predicates (e.g. *ie-o tateru* "build a house"), resultative predicates (e.g. *ki-o
taosu* "fell/knock down a tree;" instantaneous verbs in Kindaichi's terms), and
accomplishment+resultative predicates (e.g. *ki-ni noboru* "climb a tree"). They
can be defined as in (28).

(28) a. *In general:* For any predicate ϕ, individual a, eventuality e, and interval t, if $[\![\phi]\!](a)(e)(t) = 1$, then $t \subseteq \tau(e)$ (i.e. t is part of the temporal trace
of e). Note: τ is the temporal trace function which applies to an
eventuality and yields the interval that this event "occupies."
  b. *Stative predicate ϕ:* For any individual a, eventuality e, and interval t,
if $[\![\phi]\!](a)(e)(t) = 1$, then for any $t' \subseteq t$ $[\![\phi]\!](a)(e)(t') = 1$.
  c. *Accomplishment/Activity predicate ϕ:* For any individual a, eventuality
e, and interval t, if $[\![\phi]\!](a)(e)(t) = 1$, then for any $t \subset t$ $[\![\phi]\!](a)(e)(t') = 0$.
  d. *Resultative predicate ϕ:* For any individual a, eventuality e, and interval t, if $[\![\phi]\!](a)(e)(t) = 1$, then there is a $t' \subseteq t$ such that $[\![\phi]\!](a)(e)(t') = 1$
and for any t'' such that it overlaps with t' and $[\![\phi]\!](a)(e)(t'') = 1$, t' is an
initial subinterval of t''.
  e. *Accomplishment+resultative predicate ϕ:* For any individual a, eventuality e, and interval t, if $[\![\phi]\!](a)(e)(t) = 1$, then there is a $t' \subseteq t$ such
that $[\![\phi]\!](a)(e)(t') = 1$ and for any t'' such that it overlaps with t' and
$[\![\phi]\!](a)(e)(t'') = 1$, t' is either an initial subinterval of t'' or a final
subinterval of t''.

(28a) says that a time at which some sentence is true is part of the temporal
trace of the event that it involves. This is a looser relation between events and
times than is normally assumed in the literature. (28b) shows that a stative
sentence has the subinterval property. (28c) takes care of accomplishments and
activities. Although the difference between these two subclasses is important
with regard to the imperfective paradox (Dowty 1979), they can be grouped
together for the purpose of this proposal.[23] (28d) concerns resultative predicates, which correspond to instantaneous verbs in Kindaichi's terminology.
We now assume that they involve events that are possibly extensive but
are characterized in terms of a particular interval (within the temporal trace
of the eventuality in question) at which a relevant state starts to obtain. (28d)
formalizes the idea that a resultative sentence is true with regard to an event
e with respect to an interval t iff e is an eventuality that intuitively represents
the entire resultant state associated with this sentence and t is an initial part of
the temporal trace of e. (28e) takes care of an interesting class of predicates
exemplified by (27) which can produce an ongoing process interpretation as

well as a (concrete) result state interpretation. The characteristic of this class of predicate is that the entity denoted by the subject is an agent that engages in an action and acquires a concrete property as a result of its own action.

Given the definition of various predicate classes in (28), the semantics of *-iru* can be given as in (29).

(29) For any predicate ϕ, individual a, eventuality e, and interval t, $[\![\phi\text{-te iru}]\!]$ $(a)(e)(t) = 1$ iff (i) there is a time $t' \supseteq t$ such that $[\![\phi\text{-te}]\!]$ $(a)(e)(t') = 1$ or (ii) in a world that is reasonably close to the actual one there exist an eventuality $e' \supseteq e$ and an interval $t' \supseteq t$ such that $[\![\phi\text{-te}]\!]$ $(a)(e')(t') = 1$.

I shall say a few words about why the condition (ii) is necessary. The relevant event we find in the actual world is not necessarily a complete one for two reasons. When the sentence is an accomplishment, it can involve the so-called imperfective paradox (Dowty 1979, etc.) as exemplified by (30a). On the other hand, when the sentence is a resultative sentence, it is possible that the event in question does not have a clear beginning as in (30b). That is, (30b) can be true in a situation where the wall has a hole, but this hole was there by design and was there as soon as the wall was built.

(30) a. Taroo-wa ie-o   tate-te   ita-toki   ni sin-da.
       Taro-Top house-Acc build-Te iru-Past when at die-Past
       "Taro died when he was building a house."
     b. Kabe-ni ana-ga   ai-te   iru.
       wall-Dat hole-Nom open-Te iru-Pres
       "The wall has a hole."

(29) is essentially the same as the proposal in Ogihara (in press), which is based upon Landman (1992), except that it accounts for the differences among various sentence classes in terms of thematic properties of subject NPs. I shall now demonstrate this point.

What we want the theory to explain is why different subject NPs produce different aspectual properties of the entire sentence. Let us look at some relevant examples. As I discuss these examples, I will explain why they have the aspectual properties they do. Consider the examples in (31).

(31) a. Taroo-wa ki-o   taosi-te iru.
       Taro-Top tree-Acc fell-Te   iru-Pres
       "Taro is felling a tree."
     b. Ki-ga   taore-te iru.
       tree-Nom fall-Te   iru-Pres
       "A tree is lying on the ground."
     c. Taroo-wa ki-ni   nobot-te iru.
       Taro-Top tree-Dat climb-Te iru-Pres
       "Taro is now climbing a tree"
       or   "Taro is now up the tree having climbed it."

I assume that the three predicates used in (31a–c) translate as in (32a–c), respectively.

(32)   a.   ki-o taosu $\Rightarrow \lambda x \lambda e \lambda t \exists y[\text{AGT}(x)(e)(t) \wedge \text{fell}(e) \wedge \text{tree}(y) \wedge \text{TH}(y)(e)]$
        b.   taore $\Rightarrow \lambda x \lambda e \lambda t[\text{fall}(e) \wedge \text{TH}(x)(e)(t)]$
        c.   ki-ni nobot $\Rightarrow \lambda x \lambda e \lambda t \exists y[\text{AGT-TH}(x)(e)(t) \wedge \text{climb}(e) \wedge \text{tree}(y) \wedge$
             $\text{LOC}(y)(e)]$

AGT stands for agent, TH for theme, LOC for locative, and AGT-TH for agentive theme. I use the label AGT-TH for an argument that is agentive but is also theme-like in that it undergoes some change as a result of its own action. The three types of predicates are distinguished in terms of different thematic roles, which are encoded as three-place relations involving individuals, events, and times. The constraints given in (33) show how this is done.

(33)   a.   For any individual a, eventuality e, and interval t, if $[\![\text{AGT}]\!](a)(e)(t) = 1$
             then for any $t' \subseteq t$ $[\![\phi]\!](a)(e)(t') = 0$.
        b.   For any individual a, eventuality e, and interval t, if $[\![\text{TH}]\!](a)(e)(t) = 1$
             then there is a $t' \subseteq t$ such that $[\![\phi]\!](a)(e)(t') = 1$ and for any t'' such that
             it overlaps with t' and $[\![\phi]\!](a)(e)(t'') = 1$, t' is an initial subinterval of t''.
        c.   For any individual a, eventuality e, and interval t, if $[\![\text{AGT-}$
             $\text{TH}]\!](a)(e)(t) = 1$ then there is a $t' \subseteq t$ such that $[\![\phi]\!](a)(e)(t') = 1$ and for
             any t'' such that it overlaps with t' and $[\![\phi]\!](a)(e)(t'') = 1$, t' is either an
             initial subinterval of t'' or a final subinterval of t''.

With the stipulation that only the thematic role associated with the subject NP is time sensitive, one can account for the transitive-intransitive asymmetry observed in Japanese. To confirm that our proposal accounts for the most crucial data, let us discuss (31a–c).

(34)   a.   *Taroo-wa ki-o taosi-te iru* is true at t in w iff there is an event e' and an
             interval $t' \supset t$ such that $[\![\lambda e \lambda t' \exists y[\text{AGT}(\text{Taro})(e)(t) \wedge \text{fell}(e) \wedge \text{tree}(y) \wedge$
             $\text{TH}(y)(e)]\!](e')(t') = 1$ in w or in a world that is reasonably close to w.
        b.   *Ki-ga taore-te iru* is true at t in w iff there is an event e' and an interval
             $t' \supset t$ such that $[\![\lambda e \lambda t \exists x[\text{fall}(e) \wedge \text{tree}(x) \wedge \text{TH}(x)(e)(t)]\!](e')(t') = 1$ in w
             or in a world reasonably close to w.
        c.   *Taroo-wa ki-ni nobot-te iru* is true at t in w iff there is an event e' and
             an interval $t' \supset t$ such that $[\![\lambda e \lambda t \exists y[\text{AGT-TH}(\text{Taro})(e)(t) \wedge \text{climb}(e) \wedge$
             $\text{tree}(y) \wedge \text{LOC}(y)(e)]\!](e')(t') = 1$ in w or in a world reasonably close
             to w.

(31a) receives an ongoing process interpretation because t' is an interval at which Taro is the agent of the felling event e'. This is understood to mean that Taro is in the process of felling a tree at t. Since the predicate TH does not have a temporal argument, it does not interact with the *-te iru* morpheme. As a result, (31a) does not produce a result state interpretation. (31b) receives a (concrete) result state interpretation because t' is regarded as a time at which the tree in question is the theme of the falling event e'. This is understood to mean that the tree is lying on the ground at t. Finally, (31c) can receive two distinctive interpretations: an ongoing process interpretation and a result state interpretation. This is because t' can be a time at which Taro's climbing of a tree obtains but can also be an initial interval at which Taro's being at the top of the tree obtains.

I have not mentioned how "experiential" interpretations are accounted for in this system. Using Ogihara's (in press) idea, we can let *-te* manufacture a new predicate that behaves like a resultative predicate. I contend that the property denoted by the newly created predicate is one that denotes the most general result state indicated by the original predicate. For example, given the predicate *ie-o tateru* "build a house," *ie-o tate-te* denotes the property of having built a house. Then *-iru* simply shows that the individual denoted by the subject NP has the property of being part of such an eventuality. This is as desired. Although the details of this new proposal are yet to be worked out, I believe that this approach is on the right track.

McClure (1995) offers an alternative way of explaining the complex behavior of the morpheme *-te iru*. He argues that the semantics of the morpheme *-te iru* is accounted for in a unified manner if we posit a new ontological structure for various aspectual classes. Put roughly, the English progressive indicates that no final segment (as defined by McClure) of the eventuality in question is realized, whereas the *-te iru* construction in Japanese indicates that all final segments of the eventuality are realized. If I understand McClure's proposal correctly, it does not account for result state interpretations of *-te iru*. Consider example (35).

(35)   Taroo-wa ima yuka-ni taore-te iru.
       Taro-Top now floor-at fall-Te   iru-Pres
       "Taro is now lying on the floor (after having fallen down)."

According to McClure's proposal, (35) is true iff Taro's falling obtained in the past (perhaps within a contextually salient past interval). However, (35) in fact requires that Taro be lying on the floor now thanks to the adverbial *ima* "now." I take this to mean that the existence of the result state in question is asserted by (35) and is not merely implicated. Thus, McClure's solution is not without problems.

3   Conclusion

This chapter discussed the semantics of tense and aspect with special reference to the morphemes *-ta* and *-te iru*. Two topics were covered in connection with the morpheme *-ta*. I first discussed the issue of whether *-ta* is a tense morpheme or an aspect morpheme. I concluded that it is a relative tense morpheme in the sense of Comrie (1976) in that its interpretation is determined in relation to structurally higher tenses and not necessarily in relation to the utterance time. Although -*ta* conveys a resultant state meaning in some restricted circumstances (e.g. relative clauses), the argument for the view that -*ta* is a "relative tense morpheme" remains very strong. Second, I turned to some apparent problems for the claim that -*ta* is a relative tense morpheme. It was pointed out that *when*-clauses and factive verb complement clauses seem to be problematic for the claim that -*ta* is a relative tense morpheme. As a possible account, I suggested that the fact that the problematic constructions involve clauses that are presupposed to be true. In section 2, I turned to the morpheme -*te iru*. I discussed the problem of accounting for its ambiguity and presented some concrete proposals. Ogihara's (in press) proposal was described in some detail, and its strengths and weaknesses were pointed out. It offers a compositional semantics for the -*te iru* form on the basis of a new analysis of the lexical meaning of so-called instantaneous sentences. But this proposal contains a stipulative and language specific claim about instantaneous sentences in Japanese. Adopting Okuda's (1977, 1984) suggestion, I revised Ogihara's (in press) proposal. This enables us to derive the asymmetry between agentive subjects and nonagentive subjects in -*te iru* sentences in a more principled manner.

Finally, let me say a few words about the direction of future research in tense and aspect. As for the research involving tense morphemes, the interpretation of -*ta* in relative clauses and some other subordinate clauses is not well understood and should be investigated in detail. As for aspect morphemes, in addition to -*te iru*, Japanese has many morphemes that have various specialized and subtle meanings, such as -*te aru*, -*te oku*, whose semantic properties are largely unexplored in formal semantics.[24,25] Since these morphemes have interesting morphological and semantic properties, I hope that many interesting research results will be produced that will deal with these morphemes.

NOTES

1   See Teramura and Inoue (1989) for a survey article on tense and aspect in Japanese.

2   The present perfect in English is indicated by a representation of the form E_R, S.

3   In colloquial speech, the permanence of the reference point is not always followed. For instance, (i) can be used to indicate that the time of Bill's buying a book precedes the time of John's saying.

(i)   John said that Bill bought a book.

However, the permanence of the reference time accounts for examples like (4a–b) which are characteristic of written discourse.

4   To be more accurate and complete, the present tense indicates the

simultaneity of R and S, and the absence of the perfect indicates the simultaneity of E and R.

5   Ota (1972) draws a different conclusion from the observed difference between English and Japanese with regard to tense; he claims that Japanese has no reference time.

6   This generalization requires the proviso that English has a sequence-of-tense rule whereas Japanese does not.

7   See McCoard (1978) for a good overview of various proposals about the English perfect.

8   But note that (9b) can be replaced by *Taroo-wa moo hon-o yonde iru* for approximately the same meaning.

9   For an alternative analysis of embedded tense morphemes, see Mihara (1992).

10 Kinsui (1994) discusses this type of example.

11 M. Nakau (1976) discusses the behavior of tense and aspect morphemes in such constructions as conditionals, complements of perception verbs, etc.

12 Tense morphemes that are embedded within NPs (e.g. relative clauses and noun complement clauses) are not exceptions to this generalization in that these NPs are subject to scoping on a par with "regular" NPs. See Ogihara (1996) for details.

13 The judgment involved is subtle. According to my judgment, (13a) is only marginally acceptable on a simultaneous interpretation and would sound much better with a present tense in the complement clause. However, I concur that (13a) is more acceptable than (14) on a simultaneous reading.

14 This only has a "shifted interpretation," in which the time

of his having cancer precedes the time of his believing.

15 Having been inspired by Kindaichi's work on -*te iru*, many other researchers worked on the same topic. See Fujii (1966), Okuda (1977), Soga (1983), K. Matsumoto (1985), Kinsui (1994), Kudo (1995), McClure (1995), and Shirai (in press) among others. See also Ota (1971) for a comparative study of Japanese and English with regard to aspectual properties of verbs and Jacobsen (1992) for a good English source for a survey of various issues and proposals made about aspectual properties of verbs in Japanese. See also Tsujimura (1996b) for a more concise overview.

16 We shall see below what other interpretations it has when a different type of adverbial occurs in the sentence.

17 Jacobsen (1992) observes that a sentence in the -*te iru* form always has the subinterval property. Jacobsen's observation is obtained as a consequence of the proposal made in Ogihara (in press) or the proposal made in this chapter.

18 See below for a more definitive version of this generalization.

19 When -*te* bears the feature [−perfect], ϕ-*te* has the same interpretation as ϕ.

20 As mentioned above, any sentence in the -*te iru* form can receive an experiential interpretation, but this reading requires an overt or covert past-oriented adverbial as exemplified by (i).

(i)   Taroo-wa kyonen   hei-o
      Taro-Top last-year wall-Acc
      taosi-te   iru.
      knock-down-Te iru-Pres
      "Taro has the property of having knocked down a wall last year."

As the English gloss shows, the interpretation associated with (i) can also be explained in terms of ascription of a property to the individual denoted by the subject NP, though this property is an extremely general one characterized by "having knocked down the wall." This observation is made in Ogihara (in press) and can now be incorporated into the account underlying (24a–c).

21 If Taro opens the door in such a way that he is not visible to the speaker of (25b), this sentence is perfectly acceptable as a description of the situation in question.

22 See Takezawa (1991) for a syntactic proposal that incorporates Okuda's suggestion.

23 The term "imperfective paradox" refers to the fact that when a telic sentence (i.e. achievement or accomplishment) is involved, the entailment relation indicated by (i) does not hold.

(i) NP is VP-ing
$\Rightarrow$ NP will have VP-ed.

For example, *John is building a house* does not entail *John will have built a house*.

24 For papers dealing with such aspect morphemes, see H. Kindaichi (1976b).

25 *-aru* literally means "be" (for non-animate beings), whereas *-oku* literally means "put" or "place."

diathesis alternation

12   Lexical Semantics

NATSUKO TSUJIMURA

0   Introduction

As syntactic theories develop, more attention has been paid to lexical properties of argument-taking elements such as verbs (cf. N. Chomsky 1986b, Pesetsky
1982, Stowell 1981). A great many syntactic phenomena have been accounted
for by referring to the makeup of argument structure. Argument structure,
while its role in syntax is irrefutable, has increasingly been believed to be
derivable from the verb's meaning. Furthermore, when the meaning of a verb
is dissected, a particular meaning component of the verb is often responsible
for certain syntactic behavior. One of our tasks in lexical semantics, then, is not
only to represent verb meaning accurately but also to identify meaning components that may have specific relevance to syntactic phenomena.[1]
    The lexicon contains phonological, morphological, semantic, and syntactic
information of lexical items, but it is not necessary to specify every bit of the
knowledge the speaker has about a word because some properties are predictable from others. Research has certainly verified that this holds for lexical
semantics. For instance, a number of generalizations can be drawn holding
for a semantically coherent set of verbs by looking at verb meaning. This is
clearly exhibited in diathesis alternations where the same verb shows syntactic
and semantic variants that are accompanied by a different distribution and
a different array of arguments. Extensive research on diathesis alternations
has revealed that some syntactic behavior of a verb's arguments and meaning
specific to variants of an alternation and the types of alternation are predictable based on the semantic class of the verb (cf. Levin 1993, Levin and Rappaport
Hovav 1995). This line of research is further motivated by language acquisition since it provides an answer to Plato's problem: how can a child know so
much given so little? A child does not have access to all the information about
all verbs existing in a given language, and yet has the ability to determine
which verbs should have which pattern of arrangement among arguments.

The tight relationship between the verb's meaning and the syntactic realization of its arguments has been confirmed by experimental work on language acquisition (cf. Gropen et al. 1989, Pinker 1989). It is particularly for these reasons that issues in lexical semantics have drawn more attention in recent linguistic investigation of word meaning (cf. Bloom 1993, Gleitman and Landau 1994).

This line of research has influenced various areas in Japanese linguistics, not only the development of the lexical semantic field itself but also syntactic analyses. However, while issues surrounding argument structure have raised a tremendous amount of discussion, as is evidenced by much literature on the light verb construction, for example (cf. Dubinsky 1994, Grimshaw and Mester 1988, Y. Matsumoto 1996, Miyagawa 1989a, Tsujimura 1990a, Uchida and Nakayama 1993), a number of questions related to the exact nature of the interaction between verb meaning and syntax are still to be answered to a greater extent for Japanese. For instance, numerous questions await answers concerning how a verb's meaning, and which component of the meaning, interacts with the way in which its arguments are projected in syntax. Any coherent answer to this question would require a fine-grained analysis of verb meaning that is linguistically relevant and that leads to a well-defined verb classification.

In this chapter I will give an overview that focuses on some of the lexical semantic issues that have been dealt with in Japanese linguistics. The discussion will be centered on lexical semantic properties of verbs, particularly in their interaction with syntax. The survey given in this chapter is by no means comprehensive and deals mostly with sources written in English.[2] In section 1 I shall present a few examples from English that delineate the motivation for the investigation of word meaning in relation to syntax and language acquisition. Subsequent sections introduce several works that deal with some lexical semantic issues for Japanese. As I mentioned briefly above, the research on word meaning in Japanese has yet to be expanded to a larger extent, and I will consider potential areas for further inquiry in the last section.

1   Motivations for Research on Meaning Components

Much research has been conducted for diathesis alternations in English. This is because by examining which verbs allow a particular diathesis alternation and which verbs do not, we can isolate the meaning components for which the alternations are responsible. The relationship between diathesis alternation and verb meaning is, hence, where we can clearly observe the contribution of research on verb meaning and meaning components. Some of the examples of diathesis alternations in English are given below (cf. Levin 1993).

(1)   *Locative alternation*
    a.   John smeared paint on the wall.
    b.   John smeared the wall with paint.

(2)   *Causative/inchoative alternation*
    a.   Mary broke the vase.
    b.   The vase broke.

(3)   *Unspecified object alternation*
    a.   Bill ate a large pizza.
    b.   Bill ate.

(4)   *Conative alternation*   Conative
    a.   Susy kicked the wall.
    b.   Susy kicked at the wall.

(5)   *Dative alternation*
    a.   Howard gave Ann a painting.
    b.   Howard gave a painting to Ann.

Diathesis alternations are important in that the verbs that allow for a particular alternation often turn out to constitute a uniform set of verbs that share a particular semantic component. In order to illustrate the relevance of diathesis alternations, let us single out the causative/inchoative alternation in English.

   As the pair in (2) shows, verbs like *break* can appear either as a transitive verb or as an intransitive verb. The subject of the intransitive is characteristically identical with the object of the transitive variant. The causative/inchoative alternation is quite common in English, but is not available to just any verb. The range of data pertinent to our discussion is given below. The verbs under (c) are other members that share the same alternation behavior.

(6)   *Verbs that allow the causative alternation*   깨다, 녹다, 열다, 잠기다, 끓다.
    a.   Mary broke the vase.
    b.   The vase broke.   tokeru, aku, sizumu, waku
    c.   melt, open, sink, boil, . . .

(7)   *Verbs that do not allow the transitive variant*
    a.   John laughed.
    b.   *The teacher laughed John.
    c.   smile, play, swim, . . .   웃다. 놀다. 헤엄치다.

(8)   *Verbs that do not allow the intransitive variant*
    a.   My father wrote the story.
    b.   *The story wrote.
    c.   cut, bake, murder, . . .   썰다 굽다, 굽다. 죽이다

A question to be asked is whether the lexicon should have all the information as to which verbs should have the alternation, which verbs should have only the intransitive variant, and which verbs should have only the transitive variant as a lexical property of each verb. Such specification, of course, would end up with an enormous amount of listing in the lexicon, and this is where verb meaning plays a crucial role. That is, unnecessary redundancy in the lexicon can be avoided once we capture lexical semantic generalizations holding of the verbs that exhibit uniform behavior.

Levin and Rappaport Hovav (1995), for one, discuss the meaning differences that lead to the range of variation illustrated above. First, they attribute the difference between (6) and (7) to the fine-grained meanings of whether the eventuality denoted by the verb is caused externally or internally. For example, the verbs that allow the alternation, such as those in (6), all share the meaning that the eventuality denoted by the verb is caused externally. In contrast, the verbs in (7), which do not allow the transitive variant, denote an internally caused eventuality. That is, when a vase breaks, the breaking event is caused by some external force, and is not caused by inherent properties that the vase has. When a person smiles, on the other hand, the event is caused by the person's voluntary facial gesture, for instance, and not by an external force that brings about the movement of the person's face in a smiling manner. This difference in external vs. internal causation is shared by the exemplary verbs under (6c) and (7c). Hence, Levin and Rappaport Hovav conclude that the causative alternation makes reference to the verbs' fine-grained meaning difference, namely, external vs. internal causation.

It is important to investigate fine-grained meaning properties of verbs because a broad definition of verbs often does not give a sharp distinction. This can be seen by a pair of verbs that have very close meaning, such as *shake* and *shudder*. Levin and Rappaport Hovav argue that despite the very similar meanings of the two verbs, only *shake* allows the causative alternation, and that this is exactly the difference that external vs. internal causation is expected to account for: *shake* denotes an externally caused eventuality while *shudder* implies an internally caused eventuality. Furthermore, among the verbs in (6), even the same verb does not always allow for the causative alternation when it can denote internal causation. For example, the verb *burn* has two senses, "consume by fire" and "emit heat," but only in the former sense does the verb allow the alternation. This is shown below.

(9)   a.   The leaves burned.
      b.   The gardener burned the leaves.

(10) a.   The fire burned.
      b.   *The campers burned the fire. (Levin and Rappaport Hovav 1995: 101)

The verb *burn* in (9) has the "consume by fire" sense. Under this interpretation, the eventuality of burning the leaves must be brought about by an external force, i.e. the gardener in this case, and hence the alternation is allowed. The

Fine-grained meaning

same verb in (10), in contrast, is used in the "emit heat" sense: emitting heat is internally caused by the fire as its inherent property. The causative alternation is not possible, as predicted. Thus, the external vs. internal causation can account for the difference between verbs in (6) and those in (7). We can furthermore predict whether a verb can show the alternation or not by examining the verb's meaning focusing on where causation comes from.

Fine-grained verb meaning can also explain why not all the transitive verbs that denote external causation display intransitive counterparts. For instance, both the verbs in (6) and (8) denote that the eventuality is caused externally, but only the former exhibit the alternation. Levin and Rappaport Hovav go on to argue that the fundamental meaning difference between the two groups boils down to the question of whether "the eventuality can come about spontaneously without the volitional intervention of an agent" (1995: 102). That is, the eventuality denoted by the verbs in (6) can occur without a volitional agent, as is evidenced by sentences like *The storm broke the door*, where the storm does not bear volition. The verbs in (8), on the other hand, must all take an animate, volitional agent, and by no means can they imply that the eventuality comes about spontaneously. Such restriction is observed by *His brilliance wrote the novel*.

A consequence of the semantic analysis given by Levin and Rappaport Hovav is that when a verb that belongs to (6) above has two senses and the difference between the two has to do with the presence or absence of a volitional entity that brings about the eventuality, the same verb should behave differently regarding the causative alternation depending on the sense that the verb bears. The verb *break* presents one such case. Compare the following pair.

(11) a.   John broke the door.
      b.   The storm broke the door.
      c.   The door broke.

(12) a.   John broke his promise.
      b.   *The storm broke his promise.
      c.   *His promise broke.

The eventuality described in (11) can come about spontaneously without a volitional entity, as is demonstrated by (b). Under such an interpretation, the verb *break* can participate in the alternation. The eventuality represented in (12), however, must come about with an intentional agent, as the ungrammatical sentence in (b) shows. The unacceptable intransitive variant in (c) is the result of the semantic generalization given above. Hence, not all the verbs that denote externally caused eventuality behave uniformly with respect to the causative alternation: of these only the verbs whose eventuality can occur without a volitional agent allow for the alternation.

The illustration of the causative alternation taken from Levin and Rappaport Hovav's work explicitly displays that there is no need in the lexicon for each verb to have the specification as to which diathesis alternations it can allow.

Instead, the recognition of particular meaning components resulting from fine-grained semantic analyses provides an insight into choice of alternations, given a particular set of principles that bridge the meaning components and the syntactic projection of the verb's arguments. Generalizations of the sort discussed above holding between semantically coherent classes of verbs and diathesis alternations can ultimately explain the speaker's innate knowledge about the language.

Related to the remark made immediately above, lexical semantic research of verbs is further motivated by language acquisition issues. Let us take the dative alternation as our example, as is illustrated in (5) above. Additional examples are given below.

(13) a. Damon sent his mother a gift.
      b. Damon sent a gift to his mother.

(14) a. Sally taught the children French.
      b. Sally taught French to the children.

(15) a. Kevin showed the officer the letter.
      b. Kevin showed the letter to the officer.

It has been pointed out by many researchers, such as Green (1974), Oehrle (1976), and Stowell (1981), among others, that there is a subtle difference in meaning between the variants. The double object sentences in (a) imply that the first object actually receives the second object while the (b) variants do not necessarily assume such a possessor change. For example, (14a) implies that the children actually learned the language while (14b) does not. Gropen et al. (1989) show from their experimental work with adults and children that the semantic difference between the variants, namely possession change, is in fact psychologically real and serves as one of the criteria to determine which verbs should undergo the dative alternation. When the verb does not denote change of possession, the alternation is not available. This is why verbs like *drive* cannot show the alternation: *Mary drove the car to Paris* but not **Mary drove Paris the car*. In this ungrammatical alternation Paris cannot be the possessor of the car, and hence the double object sentence is not available.

The relevance of the semantic property in the dative alternation, i.e. possession change, is further confirmed by the kind of errors that children make. In their spontaneous speech children use the double object variant to the verbs that normally do not participate in the alternation in adult speech. For instance, *Don't say me that* (= Don't tell me that) and *You put me just bread and butter* are actual speech that children use, but in their speech, they use the verbs *say* and *put* to mean *tell* and *give*, respectively. The latter two verbs enter into the alternation in adult speech. Gropen et al. explain that even in these errors, children do follow the semantic criterion of possession change although the meanings of the verbs *say* and *put* are not as refined as those that adult speakers assume. That is, children in making these errors interpret verbs to denote possession change and hence form the double object sentences with them.

Another piece of evidence comes from adult speech in their coinage of new verbs such as *fax, xerox, bitnet,* and *e-mail.* These new verbs participate in the dative alternation.

(16) a. Mary faxed me a document.
     b. Mary faxed a document to me.

(17) a. Please xerox me the file.
     b. Please xerox the file to me.

(18) a. I will e-mail you my reply.
     b. I will e-mail my reply to you.

Even new verbs like these can alternate because they meet the semantic criterion of possession change.

In sum, the discussion of two diathesis alternations in English, exemplified in (6–8) and (13–15), has demonstrated that lexical semantics plays an important role in syntax and language acquisition and that research of the type described above is well motivated.

2   Locative Alternation *the hypallage phenomenon*

There have been a few diathesis alternations that have been investigated in Japanese. Perhaps the best described is the locative alternation, also known as the hypallage phenomenon, as discussed extensively by Kageyama (1980b) and Fukui et al. (1985). An example of the locative alternation in English has been given in (1), which is repeated below, with an additional example in (19). The Japanese examples of the alternation are given in (20–2).

(1) a. John smeared paint on the wall.
     b. John smeared the wall with paint.

(19) a. Mary cleared dishes from the table.
     b. Mary cleared the table of dishes.

(20) a. Taroo-ga   penki-o   kabe-ni nutta.
        Taro-Nom paint-Acc wall-on smeared
        "Taro smeared paint on the wall."
     b. Taroo-ga   kabe-o   penki-de   nutta.
        Taro-Nom wall-Acc paint-with smeared
        "Taro smeared the wall with paint."

(21) a. Hanako-ga   hana-o   heya-ni kazatta.
        Hanako-Nom flower-Acc room-in decorated
        "Hanako put flowers (to decorate) in her room."

    b.   Hanako-ga   heya-o   hana-de   kazatta.
        Hanako-Nom room-Acc flower-with decorated
        "Hanako decorated her room with flowers."

(22) a.   Huku-ga   hako-ni tumatteiru.
        clothes-Nom box-in   is filled
        "Clothes are filled in the box."
    b.   Hako-ga huku-de   tumatteiru.
        box-Nom clothes-with is filled
        "The box is filled with clothes."

The (a) variants all have the material NP as the direct object while the location NP is marked with a pre/postposition; the (b) variants, on the other hand, have the location NP as the direct object while the material NP is marked with a pre/postposition. (22) shows that the alternation is not restricted to transitive verbs: *tumaru* "fill, clog" is an intransitive verb, and the same range of Case marking alternation is observed between the Nominative Case and the postpositions.

   There are several other characteristics besides the Case marking pattern of material and location NPs that accompany the two variants of the alternation. First, the two variants convey slightly different meanings, which have been distinguished as the "holistic" vs. "partitive" interpretations (cf. Anderson 1971, 1977, Schwartz-Norman 1976). When the location NP is the direct object, as in the (b) sentences above, the entire location is construed to be affected by the action denoted by the verb. This reading is referred to as the holistic interpretation. The other variant, namely, the (a) sentences, does not imply that the whole location is affected. This interpretation is termed as partitive. In (20b), for example, the entire wall is painted while in (20a) the wall is not necessarily covered with paint in its entirety. Similarly, in (22), the holistic interpretation is obtained in (b) while the partitive interpretation is observed in (a).

   Second, Kageyama (1980b) observes that the adverbial modification reveals the distinct patterning between the two variants. This is shown below (Kageyama 1980b: 44).

(23) a.   Taroo-ga penki-o   kabe-ni **usuku** nutta.
        Taro-Nom paint-Acc wall-on thin   smeared
        "Taro gave the wall a thin coat of paint."
    b.   *Taroo-ga penki-o   kabe-ni **siroku** nutta.
        Taro-Nom paint-Acc wall-on white smeared
        "Taro smeared paint on the wall white."

(24) a.   Taroo-ga kabe-o   penki-de **siroku** nutta.
        Taro-Nom wall-Acc paint-with white smeared
        "Taro smeared the wall with paint white."

   b.   *Taroo-ga   kabe-o   penki-de   **usuku** nutta.
        Taro-Nom wall-Acc paint-with thin   smeared
        "Taro gave the wall a thin coat of paint."

It is interesting to see that an adverbial modifier of a particular type is associated with a particular type of direct object: that is, the adverbial modifiers
usuku "thin" and *siroku* "white" both are predicated of the direct object, but
the former can be predicated only of a material NP, describing the manner in
which the material is applied to the location, while the latter can be predicated
only of a location NP, depicting the resulting state of the location. Hence, the
nature of adverbial modifiers is determined by the choice between a material
NP or a location NP as the direct object.
   Third, Fukui et al. (1985) remark that the locative alternation is not exhibited
with a wide range of verbs in Japanese in comparison with the verbs that allow
the alternation in English. A fairly large number of verbs in English that include
spray/load verbs, *swarm* verbs, and verbs of emission allow for the alternation,
but a parallel situation is not obtained in Japanese. For instance, *nuru* "smear"
and *sasu* "stick" exhibit the alternation, but the verbs in (25) allow only the
material object pattern with the partitive interpretation, as (26) shows.

(25)   *haru* "hang," *maku* "spray," *hanekakeru* "splash," *tumu* "load," *hirogeru*
       "spread," *tumiageru* "pile," . . .

(26)   a.   Susumu-ga   posutaa-o kabe-ni hatta.
            Susumu-Nom poster-Acc wall-on hung
            "Susumu hung posters on the wall."
       b.   *Susumu-ga   kabe-o   posutaa-de hatta.
            Susumu-Nom wall-Acc poster-with hung
            "Susumu hung the wall with posters."

Fukui et al. note, however, that the degree of the locative alternation can be
increased by a morphological means. When the suffix *-tukusu* "exhaust" is
added to some of the verbs in (25), for example, the variant that has a location
NP as its direct object becomes acceptable. This is shown below.

(27)   a.   Susumu-ga   posutaa-o kabe-ni hari-tukusita.
            Susumu-Nom poster-Acc wall-on hang-exhausted
            "Susumu hung posters on the wall."
       b.   Susumu-ga   kabe-o   posutaa-de hari-tukusita.
            Susumu-Nom wall-Acc poster-with hang-exhausted
            "Susumu hung the wall with posters."

Hence, many of the Japanese verbs that potentially show the locative alternation further require a morphological supplement to make the alternation
available.

Fourth, Japanese lacks the locative alternation with verbs of removing exemplified by (19) in English. Consider the following examples along with the list of other verbs that disallow the alternation.

(28) a. Mitiko-ga   sara-o   teeburu-kara katazuketa.
          Mitiko-Nom dish-Acc table-from   cleared
          "Mitiko cleared dishes from the table."
      b. *Mitiko-ga   teeburu-o sara-de   katazuketa.
          Mitiko-Nom table-Acc dish-with cleared
          "Mitiko cleared the table of dishes."
      c. Mitiko-ga   sara-o   katazuketa.
          Mitiko-Nom dishes-Acc cleared
          "Mitiko cleared dishes."
      d. Mitiko-ga   teeburu-o katazuketa.
          Mitiko-Nom table-Acc cleared
          "Mitiko cleared the table."

(29) *ubau* "rob," *nozoku* "expunge," *damashitoru* "con," *akeru* "empty," . . .

As (28c–d) indicate, the occurrence of direct object alone, whether a material NP or a location NP, is not precluded; rather, it is the variant with a location NP as direct object and a material NP marked with a postposition that cannot surface.

Given these characteristics, Kageyama (1980b) and Fukui et al. (1985) provide analyses with different foci: Kageyama's analysis centers on the derivation of one variant from the other while Fukui et al. investigate what semantic component triggers the locative alternation.[3] Assuming that the NPs that appear in the locative alternations bear thematic roles such as Agent and Theme, Kageyama argues that the NP marked with the Accusative Case in each variant is Theme, where Theme is understood as the entity that undergoes change of state. He further proposes an optional rule of Theme Transfer, which applies to the material object variant to derive the location object variant. The Theme Transfer and its applications to verbs of attaching and verbs of removing are taken from Kageyama (1980b: 55–6).

(30) Theme Transfer
      $$\begin{bmatrix} \text{Theme} \\ \text{X} \end{bmatrix} \quad [\text{LOC}] \quad \rightarrow \quad [\text{X}] \quad \begin{bmatrix} \text{LOC} \\ \text{Theme} \end{bmatrix}$$
      (LOC is a cover symbol for Location, Goal, and Source)

(31) a. [Agent] $\begin{bmatrix} \text{Theme} \\ \text{Instru.} \end{bmatrix}$ [Goal] V

          Watasi-ga penki-o   kabe-ni nuru
          I-Nom   paint-Acc wall-on smear
          "I smear paint on the wall."

b. [Agent]   [Instr.] $\begin{bmatrix} \text{Goal} \\ \text{Theme} \end{bmatrix}$ V

Watasi-ga penki-de kabe-o nuru
I-Nom paint-with wall-Acc paint
"I smear the wall with paint."

(32) a. [Agent]   [Theme]   [Source]   V
Watasi-ga garakuta-o heya-kara katazukeru
I-Nom junk-Acc room-from clear
"I clear the junk from the room."

b. [Agent]   [φ] $\begin{bmatrix} \text{Source} \\ \text{Theme} \end{bmatrix}$ V

Watasi-ga φ heya-o katazukeru
I-Nom room-Acc clear
"I clear the room of the junk."

The (b) sentences are obtained as a result of the application of the Theme Transfer to (a). The Theme Transfer strips off the Themehood of the material NP and transfers it to the location NP, thereby turning the location NP into the entity that undergoes change of state. As the comparison between (31) and (32) shows, Kageyama attributes the presence of the two variants in verbs of adding and their absence in verbs of removing to the difference in the array of thematic roles with which each verb class is associated. With verbs of adding such as *nuru* "smear," the material NP bears not only Theme but also Instrument, and after the Theme is transferred to the Goal NP, the role of Instrument is kept to be assigned to the material NP. In contrast, the material NP in verbs of removing bears only Theme, and no thematic role remains after the Theme is transferred. This is why the material NP cannot appear in the location object variant with verbs of removing.

Setting a theoretical debate about thematic roles aside, the analysis using the rule of Theme Transfer may be problematic to certain verbs that meet the condition of the rule but do not allow the alternation. *Oku* "put," for one, is such a verb. Consider the following.

(33). a. [Agent]   [Theme]   [Location] V
Watasi-ga hon-o tana-ni oku
I-Nom book-Acc shelf-on put
"I put a book on the shelf."

b. [Agent]   φ $\begin{bmatrix} \text{Location} \\ \text{Theme} \end{bmatrix}$ V

*Watasi-ga tana-o oku
I-Nom shelf-Acc put
"I put the shelf."

The verb *oku* "put" takes the Theme NP and the Location, and thus it should meet the condition for the Theme Transfer. The result of the rule application, however, is ungrammatical, as (33b) shows. It may suggest, then, that the array of thematic roles that are associated with the arguments of the verb may not be sufficient for the rule of Theme Transfer to apply unless the rule application is strictly limited to verbs of attaching and verbs of removing.

Instead of focusing on the derivational relation between the two variants, Fukui et al. attempt to pursue a meaning component that would account for various types of argument distribution represented by *nuru* "smear," *haru* "hang," and *katazukeru* "clear." The relevant data are given below.

(34) a.   Taroo-ga penki-o   kabe-ni nutta.
           Taro-Nom paint-Acc wall-on smeared
           "Taro smeared paint on the wall."
      b.   Taroo-ga kabe-o   penki-de nutta.
           Taro-Nom wall-Acc paint-with smeared
           "Taro smeared the wall with paint."

(35) a.   Susumu-ga   posutaa-o kabe-ni hatta.
           Susumu-Nom poster-Acc wall-on hung
           "Susumu hung posters on the wall."
      b.   *Susumu-ga   kabe-o   posutaa-de hatta.
           Susumu-Nom wall-Acc poster-with hung
           "Susumu hung the wall with posters."
      c.   Susumu-ga   posutaa-o hatta.
           Susumu-Nom poster-Acc hung
           "Susumu hung posters."
      d.   *Susumu-ga   kabe-o   hatta.
           Susumu-Nom wall-Acc hung
           "Susumu hung the wall."

(36) a.   Mitiko-ga   sara-o   teeburu-kara katazuketa.
           Mitiko-Nom dish-Acc table-from   cleared
           "Mitiko cleared dishes from the table."
      b.   *Mitiko-ga   teeburu-o sara-de   katazuketa.
           Mitiko-Nom table-Acc dish-with cleared
           "Mitiko cleared the table of dishes."
      c.   Mitiko-ga   sara-o   katazuketa.
           Mitiko-Nom dishes-Acc cleared
           "Mitiko cleared dishes."
      d.   Mitiko-ga   teeburu-o katazuketa.
           Mitiko-Nom table-Acc cleared
           "Mitiko cleared the table."

(37) a.   Susumu-ga   posutaa-o kabe-ni hari-tukusita.
           Susumu-Nom poster-Acc wall-on hang-exhausted
           "Susumu hung posters on the wall."

b. Susumu-ga   kabe-o   posutaa-de hari-tukusita.
    Susumu-Nom wall-Acc poster-with hang-exhausted
    "Susumu hung the wall with posters."

The verb *nuru* "smear" in (34) is one of the few verbs that allow the locative alternation. The verb *haru* "hang" in (35), on the other hand, does not alternate and shows only the material object sentence. This verb, however, participates in the alternation when it is suffixed by *-tukusu* "exhaust," as in (37). Verbs of removing in general, as with *katazukeru* "clear" in (36), do not alternate, either. While *haru* in (35) and *katazukeru* in (36) appear to be parallel in their lack of the location object variant, they are indeed different: with *katazukeru*, the material NP and the location NP can each appear in a sentence, as is shown in (36c–d); whereas *haru* seems to block the occurrence of the location NP marked with the Accusative Case whether it is with a material NP or without it, as (35d) suggests.

Fukui et al. claim that the meaning component of "Affect" is a crucial factor to determine whether a given verb can alternate. They assume that the linguistically relevant meaning of a verb is defined at the Lexical Conceptual Structure (LCS). The LCS is a level of representation over which a rough equivalent of a dictionary meaning of a verb is stated, and it is further mapped onto the argument structure of the verb (cf. Hale and Keyser 1986). Under this assumption, the abbreviated LCSs of the three verbs in (34–7) are given below.

(38) a. *nuru*: Realize the action NURU by using the Material x & Affect y
      b. *haru*: Realize the action HARU by using the Material x
      c. *katazukeru*: KATAZUKERU x & Affect y
      d. *hari-tukusu*: Realize the action of HARU by using the Material x & Affect y

Along with the LCS representations of these verbs, they propose the following conditions for the locative alternation.

(39) a. The verb takes two arguments x, y in its LCS; and
      b. One of its argument (y) is affected by the action represented by the meaning of the verb ("Affect y").

First, the verb *nuru* "smear" has two arguments, indicated as x and y in (38), and moreover, its LCS contains the component of "Affect y." Both conditions are met, and the verb can participate in the alternation. The LCS of (38b), on the other hand, clearly shows that neither condition is satisfied with *haru* "hang." There is only one argument, x, which is why (35d) is ungrammatical: the location NP is not an argument required by the verb. Furthermore, the component "Affect y" is not a part of the meaning specification. These two situations account for the difference that *nuru* can alternate but *haru* cannot. Second, the verb *katazukeru* "clear" satisfies both conditions, having two arguments and the "Affect *y*" clause in its LCS, and so we should expect the verb to enter into the alternation. This is not what we actually have, however, as is indicated by (36b). The specification of two arguments in the LCS of *katazukeru* is necessary in order to account for the difference between (35c–d) and (36c–d). What prevents *katazukeru* from alternating, according to Fukui et al., is that there is no Case available to *sara* "dish" in (36b). Unlike the material object with *nuru*, the argument *x* of *katazukeru* is a simple object of KATAZUKERU and does not qualify to receive the Accusative Case. Japanese is also dissimilar to English in that there is no Case like *of* that is assigned to the corresponding NP in English. Hence, Fukui et al. conclude that the alternation is blocked for the Case reason in the instance of *katazukeru*. Third, the suffixation of *-tukusu* plays a role as altering the LCS of verbs like *haru* "hang." As (38b) shows, *haru* requires only one argument in its LCS, but by suffixing *-tukusu*, the verb's LCS can be transformed into the one equivalent to the LCS of *nuru* "smear." This can be seen in (38d). Given the newly derived LCS, both conditions of (39) are met, and *hari-tukusu* participates in the alternation to the same degree as *nuru*. This explains the difference between (35) and (37). Hence, Fukui et al. attempt to capture the availability of the locative alternation with various verbs by identifying the meaning component of "Affect *y*" as a triggering factor.

The locative alternation reveals several interesting characteristics, both syntactic and semantic, and shows that it is quite conceivable to analyze verb meaning and possibly a specific meaning component as strongly linked to the availability of the alternation as we have seen above. Relevance of verb meaning is further confirmed by Kageyama's observation that a single verb that can belong to two different semantic classes displays contrasting behavior with respect to the locative alternation. To illustrate this, he uses the verb *ahureru* "overcrowd, overflow." The following are taken from Kageyama (1980b: 50–1).

(40)   a.   Amerika-no dooro-ni-wa nihonsei-no   kuruma-ga ahurete-iru.
             America-Gen street-on-Top Japanese-Gen car-Nom   overcrowd-be
             "Japanese cars are overcrowding American streets."
       b.   Amerika-no dooro-wa nihonsei-no   kuruma-de ahurete-iru.
             America-Gen street-Top Japanese-Gen car-with   overcrowd-is
             "American streets are overcrowded with Japanese cars."

(41)   a.   Yokusoo-kara yu-ga   ahurete-iru.
             bathtub-from hot water-Nom overflow-is
             "Hot water is overflowing the bathtub."
       b.   Yokusoo-ga (*yu-de)   ahurete-iru.
             bathtub-Nom (hot water-with) overflow-is
             "The bathtub is overflowing."

The intransitive verb *ahureru* clearly has different meanings in these two instances: the one in (40) has a meaning very close to verbs of group existence like *swarm* (cf. Levin 1993); while the one in (41) bears the sense of substance emission like *spill*. The latter in particular can be considered as similar in meaning to verbs of removal, except that *ahureru* is an intransitive verb. Given the contrasting meanings and what we have observed with verbs of removal in Japanese, the alternation patterns in (40) and (41) are a natural consequence.

3 Unaccusativity

Unaccusativity has invited a great deal of discussion in syntax and lexical semantics ultimately centering on what makes a verb unaccusative (cf. Dubinsky 1985, 1989, Kageyama 1991, Kishimoto 1996, Miyagawa 1989a, 1989b, Terada 1990, Tsujimura 1990a, 1990c, 1991, 1994, 1996a, 1997, among many more). Unaccusative verbs, in contrast with unergative verbs, constitute a type of intransitive verb whose sole argument patterns with the direct object of transitive verbs. Some of the primary issues have revolved around the questions of whether unergative and unaccusative should have syntactic representations and whether there are semantic characteristics that determine which verbs belong to which intransitive class. It is this latter question to which lexical semantics has made a direct contribution. Attempts made in Japanese to this end are found in Jacobsen (1992), Kishimoto (1996), and Tsujimura (1991, 1994, 1996a).

The parallel patterning between the subject of an unaccusative verb and the object of a transitive verb in Japanese is often observed with some of the pairs of transitive and intransitive verbs that are morphologically related.[4] Jacobsen (1992) provides an extensive list of such verb pairs in his study of transitivity (cf. Ikegami 1988). A few examples are given below.

(42) a. Taroo-ga kabin-o kowasita.
          Taro-Nom vase-Acc broke
          "Taro broke the vase."

      b. Kabin-ga kowareta.
          vase-Nom broke
          "The vase broke."

(43) a. Yoshio-ga bataa-o tokasita.
          Yoshio-Nom butter-Acc melted
          "Yoshio melted butter."

      b. Bataa-ga toketa.
          butter-Nom melted
          "Butter melted."

(44) a. Sensei-ga siken-no hi-o kimeta.
          teacher-Nom exam-Gen date-Acc decided
          "The teacher decided the date of the exam."

b. Siken-no hi-ga   kimatta.
    exam-Gen date-Nom decided
    "The date of the exam has been decided."

The range of data given above is reminiscent of the English causative alternation discussed in section 1. Japanese, however, departs from English in that the transitive and intransitive verbs have different, although morphologically related, forms. In each case in (42–44), the transitive verb in the (a) variant and the intransitive verb in the (b) variant are morphologically related, sharing the identical root. The subject of the intransitive sentences in (b) is the object of the transitive sentences in (a), as is indicated by the Case markers. In examining a large set of pairs of intransitive and transitive verbs of the sort depicted in (42–4) with respect to the characteristics inherent to intransitive variants, Jacobsen captures the generalization that the eventuality denoted by an unaccusative verb, i.e. the intransitive variant, spontaneously comes about. He explains that unaccusative verbs "express events which simply happen, apart from any agentive involvement, accompanied by some change in state of the syntactic subject" (1992: 129). Note that this semantic characteristic observed with the unaccusative variant of the morphologically related transitive–intransitive pairs in Japanese is not inconsistent with what Levin and Rappaport Hovav (1995) consider as the semantic properties that trigger the causative alternation in English briefly discussed in section 1. Recall that Levin and Rappaport Hovav claim that intransitive verbs whose eventualities are externally caused have transitive variants. They further contend that when the causation that brings about the event can be unspecified, an intransitive variant, namely an unaccusative verb, is derived. Thus, this semantic characterization of unaccusative verbs that enter into the causative alternation in English subsumes what Jacobsen describes for unaccusative verbs, namely, spontaneous change of state.

Another way of viewing spontaneous change of state is lack of agency or volitionality. It is this semantic notion of volitionality, or lack of it, that Kishimoto (1996) takes up in his semantic-based approach to unaccusativity. Kishimoto first demonstrates that deverbal nominals consisting of the suffix *-kake* "be about to, do halfway" modify the direct object of a transitive verb and the subject of an unaccusative verb, but not the subject of an unergative verb and the subject of a transitive verb. On the basis of this observation, he regards the deverbal nominalization as a diagnostic test for unaccusativity. The following paradigm summarizes his point.

(45) *The direct object of a transitive verb*
      Akatyan-ga miruku-o nonda.
      baby-Nom milk-Acc drank
      "The baby drank milk."
      nomi-kake-no   miruku
      drink-KAKE-Gen milk
      "milk, half drunk"

(46) *The subject of a transitive verb*
   *nomi-kake-no   akatyan
   drink-KAKE-Gen baby
   "a baby, almost drinking"

tabe kaketa
mɘk-ul kka haessta

(47) *The subject of an unaccusative verb*
   Doa-ga   aita.
   door-Nom opened
   "The door opened."
   aki-kake-no   doa
   open(intr.)-KAKE-Gen door
   "the door, slightly ajar"

나 갈까 하는 중이다.

de-kakeru tokoro da

na- kal kka ha-nun cung-i-ta.

(48) *The subject of an unergative verb*
   Rannaa-ga   hasitta.
   runner-Nom ran
   "The runner ran."
   *hasiri-kake-no rannaa
   run-KAKE-Gen runner
   "the runner, almost running"

ok — *why*

走りかけたランナー

kal kka
kake

열릴랑 말랑 하는 문

The sample lists that result from this diagnostic test are shown below (taken from Kishimoto 1996: 264–5).

(49) *Unaccusative verbs*

sinu	"die"	oboreru	"be drowned"
umareru	"be born"	nemuru	"sleep"
tissoku-suru	"smother"	furueru	"tremble"
kuruu	"go wrong"	mahi-suru	"paralyze (intr.)"
komu	"be crowded"	moeru	"burn (intr.)"
yowaru	"weaken (intr.)"	katamuku	"lean (intr.)"
naku	"cry"	korobu	"fall down"
kumoru	"get cloudy"	naoru	"cure (intr.)"

(50) *Unergative verbs*

sakebu	"shout"	hasiru	"run"
odoru	"dance"	okiru	"get up"
noboru	"climb"	asobu	"play"
ugoku	"move"	oyogu	"swim"
nigeru	"escape"	hataraku	"work"
hanasu	"talk"	hoeru	"bark"
tatakau	"battle"	tobi-komu	"dive"
tatu	"stand up"	dekakeru	"go out"

Once he classifies intransitive verbs into these two groups on the basis of the deverbal nominalization test, Kishimoto attempts to identify a meaning

notions { volitionality
          telicity

Jacobson ✓

component that may correlate with the unaccusative–unergative dichotomy and claims that it is the notion of volitionality that gives rise to the distinction between the two intransitive classes. On the basis of the observation that the subjects of the verbs in (49) are not agents while their counterparts in (50) are, he concludes that if the sole argument of an intransitive verb is a volitional entity, the verb is unergative; otherwise, the verb is unaccusative. Thus, lack of volitionality as a meaning component crucial to unaccusative verbs is consistent with Jacobsen's analysis of unaccusativity.

Another meaning component that may have relevance to unaccusativity is discussed in Tsujimura (1991, 1994, 1996a), where the notion of delimitedness or telicity is considered in relation to verbs of motion. Motion verbs are not homogeneous in that some are unaccusative while others are unergative, but the dichotomy seems to come from finer-grained meanings that are shared by each class. Among motion verbs, for example, those that specify inherent direction are unaccusative. Motion verbs with inherent direction include *tuku* "arrive," *kuru* "come," *iku* "go," *agaru* "rise," *otiru* "fall," and *kaeru* "return." Underlying the notion of inherent direction is a potential goal of the motion denoted by the verb. That is, motion verbs with inherent direction can be considered as telic, and this is evidenced by the pattern of adverbial modifiers in (51): the adverbial modifier of the type "in an hour" reflects the telicity of the event; while the modifier of the type "for an hour" suggests that the event is atelic. As the Numeral Quantifier (NQ) test shows, these verbs are unaccusative.[5]

(51) a.   Sono kyaku-ga   itizikan-de hoteru-ni tuita.
           that guest-Nom one hour-in hotel-at   arrived
           "That guest arrived at the hotel in an hour."
      b. *Sono kyaku-ga   itizikan-no   aida hoteru-ni tuita.
           that guest-Nom one hour-Gen for   hotel-at   arrived
           "That guest arrived at the hotel for an hour."

(52) Kyaku-ga   hoteru-ni osoku san-nin tuita.
      guests-Nom hotel-at   late   three-Cl arrived
      "Three guests arrived at the hotel late."

Motion verbs with inherent direction are sharply contrasted with motion verbs without the specification of direction. Manner of motion verbs, for example, are subsumed under the latter class. Included in manner of motion verbs are *aruku* "walk," *hasiru* "run," *oyogu* "swim," *tobu* "fly," and many more. These verbs do not denote a potential goal of the motion, and so the event is atelic. Lack of telicity is shown by the distribution of adverbial modifiers, and these verbs are unergative, as the NQ test verifies below.

(53) a. *Gakusei-ga   kooen-de itizikan-de aruita.
           student-Nom park-in   one hour-in walked
           "The student walked at the park in an hour."

  b. Gakusei-ga   kooen-de itizikan-no   aida aruita.
      student-Nom park-in   one hour-Gen for   walked
      "The student walked in the park for an hour."

(54) *Gakusei-ga   kooen-de inu-to   san-nin aruita.
     student-Nom park-in   dog-with three-Cl walked
     "Three students walked with a dog in the park."

Hence, the specification of inherent direction and lack of it, which may ultimately lead to telicity, or delimitedness in the sense of Tenny (1987), can be
claimed to contribute to the determination of unaccusativity.

   Inherent direction or telicity specified as the lexical semantic property of
each verb and its connection to unaccusativity may further be supported by
manner of motion verbs that appear with goal phrases. Manner of motion
verbs that lack inherent direction are unergative, as we have stated above, but
the addition of a goal phrase to these verbs exhibits seemingly unexpected
behavior in the NQ test.

(55) ?Gakusei-ga   inu-to   kooen-made san-nin aruita.
     student-Nom dog-with park-as far as three-Cl walked
     "Three students walked to the park with a dog."

The judgment is subtle, but the improvement is recognizable between (54) and
(55). It suggests that a manner of motion verb accompanied by a goal phrase
can appear in the unaccusative syntactic configuration. Therefore, a strong
specification of a potential goal of the motion denoted by the verb, which can
be characterized as telicity or delimitedness, plays a vital role in unaccusativity.
Together with volitionality discussed by Jacobsen and Kishimoto, then, these
meaning components provide strong grounds in the semantic characterization
of unaccusativity.[6]

4   Aspectual Properties

Aspectual properties[7] constitute an important part of verb meaning since they
refer to temporal constituency internal to the eventuality denoted by a given
verb. Core concepts pertinent to verb aspects are reflected on the four verb
classes that Vendler (1967) and Dowty (1979) propose: state, activity, accomplishment, and achievement. The latter three classes all refer to dynamic
actions, but they can further be divided into two groups based on their telicity.
Activity verbs do not imply a terminal point of the event and are characterized
as atelic. In contrast, events denoted by accomplishment and achievement
verbs have natural ending points and hence they are telic. Jacobsen (1992)
and McClure (1994) follow the Vendler/Dowty tradition in classifying Japanese verbs into the four aspectually natural classes. The aspect-based verb

classification is significant since repercussions of the aspectual properties inherent to each group appear in diverse syntactic and semantic phenomena (cf. Ikegami 1985, Ogihara 1992, Soga 1983).

An example of such an interaction is observed in the verb classification that H. Kindaichi (1976a) offers. Kindaichi categorizes Japanese verbs into four classes in a slightly different manner from the Vendler/Dowty classification. They are listed in (56) with examples.

(56)   a.   *Stative:*
             aru "be," *dekiru* "can do," *hanaseru* "can speak," *mieru* "be visible,"
             yoo-suru "require"
       b.   *Continuative:*
             yomu "read," *kaku* "write," *warau* "laugh," *utau* "sing," *aruku* "walk,"
             miru "look," *nomu* "drink," *osu* "push," *hataraku* "work"
       c.   *Instantaneous:*
             sinu "die," *kieru* "turn off," *sawaru* "touch," *kimaru* "decide," *sameru*
             "wake," *hazimaru* "begin," *tootyaku-suru* "arrive"
       d.   *Type 4:*
             sobieru "tower," *sugureru* "be outstanding," *zubanukeru* "outstand-
             ing," *arihureru* "be common"

Stative verbs describe static situation with no reference to dynamic actions. Continuative verbs refer to dynamic actions that last for an unspecified length of time. Instantaneous verbs denote actions that take place instantaneously. Tape 4 verbs, under Kindaichi's system, receive a separate treatment due to their unique characteristic regarding *-te iru*, as will be discussed below.

Kindaichi's classification is solely based on whether a verb occurs in the *-te iru* form and if it does, which interpretation, progressive or resultative (or perfect), is induced.[8] Stative verbs simply do not appear in the *-te iru* form.[9] Continuative and instantaneous verbs do occur in the *-te iru* form, but the interpretations are different: *-te iru* with a continuative verb is interpreted as progressive while that with an instantaneous verb is construed as resultative. Finally Type 4 verbs are those that must appear in the *-te iru* form.[10] These characteristics with *-te iru* are exemplified in (57–60).

(57)   *Stative*
         *Taroo-ni musuko-ga at-te iru.
          Taro-Dat son-Nom   have
         "Taro has a son."

(58)   *Continuative*
         Hanako-ga   hon-o   yon-de iru. (progressive)
         Hanako-Nom book-Acc read
         "Hanako is reading a book."

(59) *Instantaneous*
      Inu-ga   sin-de iru. (resultative)
      dog-Nom die
      "A dog has been/is dead."

(60) *Type 4*
      Sono gakusei-wa totemo sugure-te iru. (cf. *sugureru/ta)
      that student-Top very   be outstanding
      "That student is outstanding."

Although Kindaichi's verb classification depicted in (56) is determined by how each verb behaves with respect to -*te iru*, the differences between stative, continuative, and instantaneous verbs are also aspectually motivated, as is reflected on the interpretation of -*te iru*.

In comparing Kindaichi's classification with the Vendler/Dowty system, we notice a great similarity between stative verbs and states as well as between instantaneous verbs and achievements. Jacobsen (1992) notes that Kindaichi's continuative class corresponds to Vendler/Dowty's activities and accomplishments. As the examples in (56b) suggest, Kindaichi focuses on aspectual properties of verbs alone while Dowty, in particular, considers the role of direct objects and includes them in his classification. For example, many of the transitive verbs like *kaku* "write" in (56b) can be interpreted as either activity or accomplishment in Dowty's system depending on the range of direct object the verbs take. This ambiguity is indeed reflected in the interpretation of -*te iru*. Compare the following examples.

(61) a. Titi-ga   (ima) hon-o   kai-te iru. (progressive)
          father-Nom (now) book-Acc write
          "My father is writing a book/books now."
      b. Titi-ga   (moo)   hon-o   gosatu-mo kai-te iru. (resultative)
          father-Nom (already) book-Acc five-as many as write
          "My father has already written as many as five books."

The same verb can be classified either as activity, as in (61a), or as accomplishment, as in (61b), depending on the aspectual interpretation of the event in each case. As an activity verb, -*te iru* in (61a) is interpreted as progressive; on the other hand, in (61b), the verb is an accomplishment and the verb in the -*te iru* form refers to the state as a result of the book-writing event. This suggests that under Vendler/Dowty's system of Japanese verbs, too, the interpretation of -*te iru* has a close interaction with the aspect classes: that is, activity and achievement verbs induce the progressive and resultative readings, respectively, while accomplishment verbs can be ambiguous between the two interpretations.

Investigations of aspectual properties of verbs further lead us to a natural account for various linguistic phenomena. An example illustrating this comes from deverbal nominalization with *-kake* "be about to, do halfway," which has been introduced in section 3 in connection with unaccusativity. Below, I will offer an alternative analysis to demonstrate that the notion of telicity may provide a better account for a wider scope of the phenomenon.[11]

Kishimoto (1996) proposes the rule of deverbal nominal modification, which in its essence disallows agent to be modified by a deverbal nominal. The following examples, however, show that agent can be modified by *-kake* nominalization.[12]

(62) Kaeri-kake-no   gakusei-o   hikitomete sigoto-o   tanonda.
      return-KAKE-Gen student-Acc stop   work-Acc asked
      "I stopped the student, almost going home, and asked him to do work."

(63) Tabe-kake-no   hito-made   hasi-o   oite tatiagatta.
      eat-KAKE-Gen person-even chopsticks-Acc put got up
      "Even people who were in the middle of eating put down chopsticks and got up."

(64) Keeki-o tukuri-kake-no   kokku-ga kyuuni   deteitta.
      cake-Acc make-KAKE-Gen cook-Nom suddenly left
      "The cook, in the middle of making a cake, suddenly left."

(65) Aruki-kake-no   akatyan-ni-wa ki-o   tukete kudasai.
      walk-KAKE-Gen baby-to-Top   attention-Acc attach please
      "Please pay attention to babies, almost walking."

The individuals denoted by the heads in the examples above, *gakusei* "student," *hito* "person," *kokku* "cook," and *akatyan* "baby," all undertake the activities volitionally, and the deverbal nominals with these heads are acceptable.

What is shared by the examples above is characterized by telicity: that is, all the eventualities involved in these examples are telic. In (64), for example, in the absence of the overtly expressed direct object, *keeki-o* "cake-Acc," the acceptability of the deverbal nominal decreases, parallel to (46). The presence of the direct object in this example plays a role as a delimiter, in the sense of Tenny (1987), explicitly specifying the telicity of the eventuality. (63), on the other hand, is not accompanied by a direct object, but the grammaticality appears to reside in a contextual information that forces the interpretation in which the direct object is understood. That is, the deverbal noun is acceptable only under the interpretation that the event of eating is telic. I will come back to (65) shortly, as this example is particularly important to demonstrate the relevance of telicity.

When an extended set of data of grammatical and ungrammatical deverbal nominals with *-kake* is examined, a large number of verbs that belong to activity verbs show a strong tendency to derive unacceptable nominals, while accomplishment and achievement verbs generally end in acceptable ones. Compare the following.

(66) *aruki-kake-no hito   "person, halfway walking"
      *warai-kake-no hito   "person, halfway laughing"
      *odori-kake-no hito   "person, halfway dancing"
      *hasiri-kake-no hito "person, halfway running"
      *utai-kake-no hito   "person, halfway singing"

(67) tukuri-kake-no uti   "house, halfway built"
      uti-o tukuri-kake-no hito   "person, in the middle of building a house"
      kaki-kake-no hon   "book, halfway written"
      hon-o kaki-kake-no hito   "person, in the middle of writing a book"

(68) sini-kake-no hito "person, almost dying"
      kie-kake-no hi   "fire, almost being extinguished"

The three groups above correspond to activity, accomplishment, and achievement verbs, respectively. These aspectual classes and the availability of deverbal nominals lead to the generalization that grammatical nominals denote telic events while ungrammatical nominals denote atelic events. The specification of the direct objects in (67) makes it explicit that the events are to be interpreted as telic, as we have observed with (64) above. Of particular interest is the comparison between *aruki-kake-no hito* "person, halfway walking" in (66) and (65). Although the verbs in these two examples are identical, they differ in telicity. In (66), the verb *aruku* "walk" receives the most natural interpretation, namely, atelic. The same verb in (65) bears a slightly different meaning: the verb here views walking as a telic event whose endpoint refers to a steady walking stage, and the transition from a crawling stage, for instance, to the steady walking stage that babies undertake can be considered as a delimited eventuality. It is under such an interpretation of the verb that the deverbal nominal is acceptable in this example.

The role that telicity plays is further confirmed by the following.

(69) eki-made aruki-kake-no   hito
      station-to walk-KAKE-Gen person
      "person, halfway walking to the station"

The activity verb, *aruku* "walk" in this example, does not have a particular meaning that the same verb in (65) implies. That is, the verb meaning is parallel to that of the verb in the first example of (66). However, the presence of the goal phrase *eki-made* "to the station" serves as a delimiter of the action, inducing the telic interpretation. Again, once the event is regarded as telic, the deverbal nominal is acceptable.

5   Language Acquisition Experiments

Experiments on children's language behavior provide interesting testing grounds for many hypotheses proposed to account for linguistic phenomena. This is true in the area of lexical semantics, as is demonstrated by Gropen et al.'s (1989) work mentioned in section 1. Several experimental investigations on semantic properties of verbs in Japanese children's speech have confirmed that this is certainly the case in Japanese.

Rispoli (1990), for instance, examines whether aspectual distinction, especially among state, activity, accomplishment, and achievement, is made in Japanese children's use of verbs.[13] We have discussed above that some verbs cannot co-occur in the *-te iru* form while others do, and that when they do appear in the *-te iru* form, they are interpreted as either progressive or resultative. Recall that the division between the verbs that allow for the *-te iru* form and those that do not is based upon the aspectual class to which an individual verb belongs. The range of data that Rispoli presents can be interpreted to show that the aspectual classification comprising state, activity, accomplishment, and achievement is indeed reflected in the appearance of *-te iru* in children's speech. In his study children properly used the progressive *-te iru* with activities and accomplishments: examples include *motu* "hold," *hasiru* "run," and *taberu* "eat" for the former, and *suwaru* "sit down" and *ireru* "put something in" for the latter. The subjects also displayed the resultative use of *-te iru* with accomplishments, such as *kaku* "write" and *neru* "go to bed," and achievements like *tuku* "turn on," *sinu* "die," and *hairu* "go in." In contrast, stative verbs like *aru* "be" and *dekiru* "be able to," which generally do not appear with *-te iru* under either interpretation in adult speech, were not used in the *-te iru* form by children, either; instead, they appeared in the present tense. This result is consistent with the correlation between the aspectual classification of Japanese verbs and the interpretation of *-te iru*. Rispoli also notes that it is very rare for children to make errors in their association of a particular interpretation of *-te iru* and verb classes. Hence, we can conclude that children, in their use of *-te iru*, know which aspectual class each verb belongs to as a part of the verb's lexical specification.

Rispoli further discusses the question of how children might decide which aspectual class a given verb belongs to, and considers the possibility that they base their judgments on the meanings, and meaning components, of verbs. For instance, many verbs children produced refer to the motion and location of a figure. Of these, verbs of manner of motion, such as *hasiru* "run" and *odoru* "dance," as well as verbs that refer to the manner of the location of a figure, like *motu* "hold," appeared in the progressive *-te iru*. On the other hand, verbs that specify the path of a moving figure, such as *kuru* "come" and *hairu* "go in," are used in the resultative *-te iru* form. Furthermore, when children encounter verbs that are not motion verbs, such as *osieru* "teach," they may treat the verb as analogous to those like *kuru* "come" on the basis of observation that both verbs specify delimiting points as a part of their meanings. In fact, *osieru* "teach" is found in the resultative *-te iru* in his study.

Other experiments along these lines have contributed to the investigation as to how semantic notions including animacy and volitionality play a role in children's distinction between transitive and intransitive verbs (cf. Rispoli 1987, 1989). Thus, what constitutes the meaning of a verb certainly provides potential answers to some of the questions that concern language acquisition.

6 Conclusion

We have illustrated in this chapter that proper characterization of verb meaning and identification of meaning components provide insight into a number of intriguing linguistic phenomena. Representations of fine-grained verb meanings have increasingly been examined from various theoretical perspectives within lexical decomposition (cf. Croft 1991, Dowty 1979, Jackendoff 1990, Foley and Van Valin 1984, Kageyama 1996, 1997, Y. Matsumoto 1996), and we have observed that close examination of verb meaning helps us to establish meaning-based verb classification and to identify particular meaning components that often exhibit direct correlation with certain syntactic phenomena. To this end it will be beneficial to explore diathesis alternations at a more extensive level. Furthermore, language acquisition experiments are a compelling area to confirm theoretical analyses and hypotheses. Emphasis on each of these areas would jointly lead to the elucidation of our innate knowledge of verb meaning.

In the remainder of this final section I would like to discuss what has been known as the "conflation" pattern (also referred to as "lexicalization" by J. D. McCawley 1968a and "incorporation" by Gruber 1965 and Kageyama 1980a), which Talmy (1985) uses to "refer to the representation of meanings in surface forms" (1985: 60). I will take up this issue not only because conflation patterns have direct consequences for verb meaning, but also because conflation seems to be one of the vital aspects bearing a future challenge in the pursuit of lexical properties both from a language-specific and from a typological perspective.

The best sketch of conflation in relation to Japanese may be given from motion verbs. There are a number of motion verbs, but some are different from others in the way in which meaning components such as motion, manner, path, ground, and direction are incorporated in the verb meaning. For example, verbs like *aruku* "walk," *hasiru* "run," and *oyogu* "swim" incorporate the meaning components of motion and manner, while verbs such as *iku* "go," *kuru* "come," and *agaru* "rise" conflate motion and direction. Thus, verbs under the rubric of motion verbs may differ within the language in the way meaning components are conflated. Conflation patterns may also vary across languages. English, for example, allows for the conflation of manner of motion and direction while

Japanese does not, as is demonstrated by the verb *ukabu* "float." Compare the two languages.

(70) a.   Bin-ga   hasi-no   sita-de   ukande-ita.
          bottle-Nom bridge-Gen under-at was floated
          "A bottle was floating under the bridge."
     b.   *Bin-ga   hasi-no   sita-e   ukanda.
          bottle-Nom bridge-Gen under-to floated
          "A bottle floated under the bridge."

(71) a.   The craft floated on a cushion of air.
     b.   The craft floated into the hangar on a cushion of air. (Talmy 1985: 64)

The Japanese verb *ukabu* "float" cannot conflate manner of motion with direction. This is why the verb cannot occur with the expression that signals the direction of the motion, as is shown in (70b), though the meaning with manner of motion is good as in (70a). English, on the other hand, shows that the conflation of manner of motion and direction is allowed: (71b), where *float* displays such an example, refers to the floating manner in which the craft moves as well as the direction of the floating motion. It has been reported that French and Spanish follow the Japanese conflation pattern, disallowing the conflation of manner of motion and direction (cf. Green 1973, Levin and Rapoport 1988, Rapoport 1993, Talmy 1985).

   While Japanese disallows the conflation of manner of motion and direction in the semantic representation of a single verb, it has been often observed that co-occurrence of manner and direction can be achieved by means of periphrastic expressions (cf. Yoneyama 1986, L. Levin et al. 1988, Tsujimura 1990c, 1991, 1994). This is described below.

(72) *Taroo-ga   kooen-e/ni hasitta/aruita.
       Taro-Nom park-to   ran/walked
       "Taro ran/walked to the park."

(73) Taroo-ga   kooen-e/ni hasitte/aruite-itta.
       Taro-Nom park-to   run/walk-went
       "Taro ran/walked to the park."

Direction of motion is not included in the meaning of manner of motion verbs like *hasiru* "run" and *aruku* "walk," and hence a goal phrase cannot co-occur, as (72) suggests. The addition of directed motion verbs like *iku* "go" (and also *kuru* "come") to the gerundive form of the motion verbs, however, makes it possible to represent manner of motion and direction concurrently, as in (73).

   Y. Matsumoto (1996) observes, furthermore, that the conflation of the two meaning components, manner of motion and direction, is in fact found in many compound verbs. His list includes the following (taken from Y. Matsumoto 1996: 277).

(74) kake-agaru   (run-go up)   "run-up"
      kake-noboru   (run-climb)   "run up"
      kake-oriru   (run-go down)   "run down"
      kake-mawaru   (run-go around)   "run about"

      hai-agaru   (crawl-go up)   "crawl up"
      hai-deru   (crawl-go out)   "crawl out"

      aruki-mawaru   (walk-go around)   "walk around"

      hasiri-mawaru   (run-go around)   "run about"
      hasiri-saru   (run-leave)   "run away"

These compound verbs comprise a manner of motion verb as the first member and a directed motion verb as the second. Together, they form a single compound verb that conflates the two meaning components in question. As Matsumoto demonstrates, there are a number of compound verbs that exhibit similar conflation patterns. What this observation amounts to is that while, from the typological aspect, Japanese appears to belong to those languages that display a restricted range of conflation patterns, the language may employ morphological means which compensate for the restricted degree of conflation within simplex verbs. Apparently different languages in this respect, then, could turn out to share similar conflation patterns although the mechanism each language uses to realize them may vary.

Another example suggesting that the investigation of conflation patterns may be a fruitful area for future research is again found in motion verbs. The English manner of motion verb, *walk*, is normally an intransitive verb, but can be used transitively, as in *I walked the dog*. This transitive use of *walk* conflates the causative meaning with manner of motion. So, the example can be paraphrased as *I made/had the dog walk*. This type of conflation is not observed in Japanese, where the causative meaning is expressed with the causative morpheme *-(s)ase*, as in *Inu-o aruk-ase-ta*. The same English verb, *walk*, in *I will walk you home because it's dark*, however, does not have the causative meaning, nor can it find a Japanese equivalent with the causative suffix. The interpretation of this example, namely, "I will accompany you home," can in no way be expressed by some morphological device affecting the manner of motion verb *aruku* in Japanese. This example, thus, suggests that not only the question of whether a certain conflation pattern is available in a language, but also how it is realized and to what degree it is made possible, would be of interest. Hence, further examination of conflation patterns available to Japanese as well as cross-linguistic comparisons would lead to a better understanding of the true nature of verb meaning.

NOTES

*   I would like to thank Clancy
Clements, Stuart Davis, and
Mineharu Nakayama for their
helpful comments and suggestions
on earlier versions of this chapter.
Special thanks go to Beth Levin and
Peter Sells for discussion relevant to
various issues covered here.

1   Approaches to lexical semantic
representation have been divided
into basically two types: they are
what Levin (1995) calls "semantic
role-centered" and "predicate-
centered" approaches. The first
represents the verb's arguments
in terms of thematic roles like
agent and theme, while the
second approach focuses on the
decomposition of the verb meaning
that may involve primitives such
as BECOME and CAUSE. The
discussion of the two approaches
is found in Levin (1995). See also
Fillmore (1968) and Gruber (1965)
for the former approach, and
Carter (1976, 1988), Dowty (1979),
Jackendoff (1983, 1990), and
Pinker (1989) for the latter.

2   It goes without saying that there
are a number of important works
written in Japanese on lexical
semantics of verbs. They include
Ikegami (1981), Kageyama (1996),
Morita (1994), Moriyama (1988),
and Teramura (1982, 1984), to
name just a few.

3   These two analyses also differ in
their lexical semantic representation.
Kageyama adopts the "semantic
role-centered" approach while Fukui
et al. assume the "predicate-
centered" approach, as was
mentioned in n. 1.

4   It should not be assumed that all
morphologically related transitive–

intransitive pairs give rise to
unaccusativity. In order to recognize
intransitive counterparts of such
pairs as unaccusative verbs,
diagnostic tests should be applied to
them. For example, the intransitive
verbs in (42–4) meet the diagnostic
tests of Numeral Quantifiers
(Miyagawa 1989a, 1989b) and/or
the resultative construction
(Tsujimura 1990a) to confirm
their unaccusative status.

5   In the discussion below I assume
that the NQ test constitutes a
reliable diagnostic for unaccusativity
in Japanese. According to Miyagawa
(1989a, 1989b), an NP and its NQ
are required to be in a mutual
c-command relation. In (52) the
NQ and the subject NP *kyaku*
"guest" are not in a mutual
c-command relation, but the
sentence is grammatical. This
suggests that the subject is
underlyingly the direct object
with which the NQ can maintain
a mutual c-command relation.
For details of this test,
see Miyagawa (1989a, 1989b).

6   Telicity and agency are the two
most frequently cited meaning
components in cross-linguistic
research on unaccusativity. See
Van Valin (1990), for example.

7   A detailed discussion of aspect-
based verbal classification and the
aspectual interpretation pertinent to
the *-te iru* construction is found in
chapter 11 of this book. Also, see
Ogihara (in press) for a recent
analysis of the same topic.

8   The progressive interpretation
corresponds to the progressive
(be V-ing) meaning in English.
The resultative (or perfect) reading

refers to the state as a result of the action denoted by the verb.

9 It should be pointed out that verbs that are normally classified as statives, such as *wakaru* "understand" and *dekiru* "can do," do appear in the *-te iru* form, as in *wakat-te iru* and *deki-te iru*, with the resultative interpretation. I agree with Yamagata (1997) in attributing this possibility to the difference between stage-level predicates and individual-level predicates in the sense of Carlson (1977) and Kratzer (1989): that is, by adding *-te iru*, stative verbs like *wakaru* and *dekiru* change their interpretations from individual-level to stage-level.

10 I am excluding the cases where Type 4 verbs appear as prenominal modifiers. In such cases, the verbs can appear in either *-te iru* form or the past tense: e.g. *sugur-te iru/ sugure-ta gakusei* "outstanding student" (cf. Kinsui 1994, Teramura 1984).

11 For a more extensive discussion of Kishimoto (1996), see Tsujimura (1997).

12 I would like to thank Masayo Iida and Yasuko Watt for providing examples (63) and (65), respectively.

13 A related work is found in Cziko and Koda (1987), which also investigates the relation between *-te iru* and aspectual properties of verbs.

13 First Language Acquisition

YUKIO OTSU

0 Introduction

This chapter provides a survey of research on the acquisition of the Japanese language. With the exception of the first section, which is a historical overview, it is highly selective in the sense that it focuses on research which deals with the problem of why Japanese-speaking children are able to acquire the core portion of Japanese grammar despite the fact that relevant experience available to them is severely limited (i.e. under the "poverty of the stimulus" situation (e.g. N. Chomsky 1981b)). In other words, it is an attempt to explore the "logical problem of language acquisition" (Hornstein and Lightfoot 1981, C. L. Baker and McCarthy 1981) or "Plato's problem" (e.g. N. Chomsky 1975) from the perspectives of Japanese grammar.

For example, every adult native speaker of Japanese can tell that (1) is ambiguous in that *sannin* "three people" can be predicated of either *dansi gakusei* "male students" or *hahaoya* "mothers."

(1) Sannin   no dansi gakusei no hahaoya ga   gakkoo e kita.
    three people of male students of mothers Nom school to came
    "Mother(s) of three male students/three mothers of male students came
    to school."

Thus, the subject of (1) *sannin no dansi gakusei no hahaoya* can either mean "mother(s) of three male students" or "three mothers of male students." Notice that in the former case, the number of mother(s) can either be one, two, or three since *sannin* is predicated of *dansi gakusei*, not *hahaoya*, as contrasted with the latter case in which the number of mothers must be three.

When the *sannin*-phrase "floats" to a postsubject position as in (2), it can only be predicated of *hahaoya*.

(2) Dansi gakusei no hahaoya ga   sannin   gakkoo e kita.
    male students of mothers Nom three people school to came
    "Three mothers of the male students came to school."

Thus, in (2) it is not possible to conceive that the number of mother(s) is either one or two; it must be three.

We do not attempt to go into the detailed explanation of why this is so. Instead, in the present context, it is sufficient to point out that these facts follow from the interaction among various phrase structural properties and abstract, probably universal, principles involving such notions as "c-command." If this is so, a very interesting question arises: i.e. where does the relevant knowledge of Japanese come from?

The question is interesting because it is highly unlikely that the knowledge stems from the "general learning mechanism" and experience. Here, we assume that biologically predetermined "Universal Grammar (UG)" plays an important role along with its interaction with experience. Thus, while children exposed to Japanese have to fix many properties of Japanese phrase structure like its head-finalness on the basis of experience, UG provides them with information concerning properties of "operators" such as *sannin*.

In this chapter, we will review some of the relatively recent work on language acquisition that has direct bearing on the correctness of the acquisitional scenario just mentioned. This chapter is also selective in the sense that it is more or less limited to syntax. There has been much work on other areas of Japanese, particularly on phonology and pragmatics, as well. Those readers who wish to obtain a survey from broader perspectives are referred to Clancy (1985).

1   Historical Overview

It may seem a truism that the study of language acquisition should be preceded by a substantial understanding of the nature of grammar in general as well as the nature of particular grammars in order for it to be a serious intellectual endeavor. However, such a truism had not been fully recognized until quite recently in spite of the long history of the study of language acquisition.

C. Chomsky (1969) represents one of the very first such attempts to connect grammatical theory and language acquisition. In her monograph, C. Chomsky takes up four grammatical structures including those related to control and binding that were considered "exceptions" from the perspectives of the then current theory and analyses, and attempted to show experimentally that the acquisition of those structures are in fact delayed beyond five years of age in some instances.

For example, C. Chomsky attempted to show that children encounter difficulties in coming to grasp the fact that the controller of PRO in (3) is the subject of the matrix clause, in contrast with unmarked cases like (4) in which the controller is the object of the matrix.

(3)   John promised Bill PRO to leave

(4)   John told Bill PRO to leave

Tavakolian (1981), which is a collection of reports mainly carried out at the University of Massachusetts under the guidance of Thomas Roeper, represents the opening of the new era of the study of language acquisition trying to bridge language acquisition research and findings of grammatical theory. In these studies, various properties of Universal Grammar including binding and control are taken up, and it has been claimed that it has been shown that those UG-related properties do in fact constrain language acquisition from the very beginning.

Otsu (1981) is another work that represents the new trend from a slightly different perspective. He has taken up the subjacency effect with respect to relative clauses. Subjacency is a universal principle that has been proposed in order to explain some kind of locality effect. Thus, (5) is not grammatical since the extraction of *wh*-phrase has taken place out of a relative clause.

(5)   *What$_i$ is John drawing a monkey [that is drinking milk with t$_i$]?

If subjacency (or some other universal principle(s) from which the subjacency effect follows) is part of UG, and thus innate, children do not have to learn from experience that the extraction of *wh*-phrase out of a relative clause is banned. However, infants would not be able to judge that (5) is bad even if subjacency is part of UG, since there are a number of language-specific properties that they have to learn in order to make such a judgment: the structure of English relative clauses, among other things. However, English-speaking children should be able to judge that (5) is ungrammatical once they learn those language-specific properties if subjacency is part of UG. And this is what Otsu (1981) has shown.

Although properties related directly to UG are generally expected to emerge once necessary learning like the learning of English relative clauses in the above example has taken place, they do not have to. Just like puberty, which is biologically determined, those properties could emerge later if their emergence is controlled by maturation. For example, Borer and Wexler (1987) have suggested that maturational factors should be involved in the emergence of UG-related properties such as A-chain formation, thereby explaining the relatively late emergence of English passives as compared with *wh*-questions.

Those studies mainly use the acquisition of English as their database. In contrast, similar research on the acquisition of Japanese was scarce in those days, partly because the way the properties of UG reflect on the nature of

Japanese grammar was not so transparent despite much important early work on Japanese grammar, notably Kuroda (1965a).

Introduction of the so-called principles-and-parameters approach to Universal Grammar (PP approach to UG) (e.g. N. Chomsky 1981b) has given a very strong impetus to the studies of language acquisition through the notion of parameter setting. Hyams (1986), for example, takes up the so-called null-subject phenomena in the early speech of English children as represented by such utterances as (6) and (7), and attempts to account for the phenomena in terms of the early non-adult-like setting of a relevant parameter.

(6)   Throw it away.

(7)   Want go get it.

More concretely, Hyams claimed that there is a parameter that divides languages into two basic types, i.e. null-subject languages like Italian and non-null-subject languages like English, and the grammar of the children who produce such forms is just like that of Italian-speaking children with respect to the relevant parameter setting. What is intriguing is that such a theory makes very interesting predictions about acquisition. Thus, such children are also expected to produce erroneous, i.e. nonadult, forms as a result of the missetting of the parameter: e.g. lack of expletives such as *it* and *there* and lack of auxiliary *be* and modal auxiliaries. Also, these phenomena are expected to disappear across the board since they stem from a common cause, i.e. parameter missetting. While Hyams's theory had to undergo many revisions because the prediction of the original formulation was not fully borne out, the importance of the research style that she has developed remains unchanged.

These studies have made very important contributions to the study of language acquisition, in particular to the construction of the theory of language acquisition. While it is true that they also contributed to the study of grammatical theory in that they provide grammatical theory with confirming (or disconfirming) evidence from acquisition, the contribution is more or less unidirectional, i.e. from grammatical theory to acquisition.

There are relatively recent contributions in the opposite direction. The most important is the learnability consideration. There is overwhelming evidence that direct negative evidence is not necessary in language acquisition. When a child receives a direct feedback from his or her environment to the effect that a form she or he has produced is ungrammatical and she or he uses such feedback for grammar construction, she or he is said to have used direct negative evidence.

Observation of typical conversations between children and their parents would instantly suggest that parents are in general insensitive to the grammatical properties of children's utterances. They do not correct children's "errors." The following example is a dialogue between a two-year-old and her mother (data collected by Ai Okubo, taken from Kokuritsu Kokugo Kenkyujo 1982: 79–80).

(8) Child: Kondo, syooboo zidoosya.
          this time fire   engine
          "Here comes a fire engine."
  Mother: Hai, kondo wa syooboo zidoosya ne.
          yes
          "Yes, a fire engine this time."
  Child: Kiiro, kiiro zidoosya.
          yellow   car
          "A yellow, yellow car."
  Mother: Hai. Ara?
              oh
          "Yes. Oh!"
  Child: Aoi zidoosya.
          blue
          "A blue car (this time)."

Notice that in his second turn, the child said *kiiro zidoosya* "a yellow car." He should have said *kiiroi zidoosya* because *kiiroi* is the correct prenominal adjectival form while *kiiro* is a noun. In spite of this mistake, the mother did not even try to point that out.

Some adults on some occasions attempt to correct children's mistakes. The typical reaction is that children ignore the correction. The following is a dialogue between a three-year-11-month-old and his father that I collected.

(9) Child: Otoo-tyan, mado   aite.
          Daddy   window open
          "Daddy, the window opens."
  Father: Mado   akete daro.
          window open you mean
          "You mean, open the window."
  Child: Un, mado   aite.
          Yeah window open
          "Yeah, the window opens."
  Father: Mado   akete dayo.
          window open you should say
          "Open the window, you should say."
  Child: Iikara, mado   aite yo, otoo-tyan.
          anyway window open   Daddy
          "Anyway, the window opens, Daddy."

In this dialogue, the child incorrectly used *aite*, the *te*-form of an intransitive *aku* "to open," and the father prompted to use the correct *akete*, the *te*-form of the corresponding transitive *akeru* "to open." In spite of the father's efforts, the child stuck to *aite* until the end of the dialogue.

If direct negative evidence is not necessary for language acquisition, UG must be constructed such that acquisition of particular grammars is possible without direct negative evidence.[1]

With the introduction of the PP approach to UG, Japanese grammar has become one of the most intensely studied particular grammars (e.g. Saito 1985, Fukui 1986). In spite of the progress in research on Japanese grammar within the framework of the PP approach to UG, there has not been a comparable progress in the studies of Japanese acquisition. This chapter is an attempt to survey some of the major findings in these efforts, and at the same time to clarify issues to be studied in the future research.

2   Minimal Linguistic Background

The following discussion provides the minimal linguistic background to read the remainder of this chapter presupposing basic understanding of the nature of Japanese grammar. It is not intended to be a full exposition of Japanese syntax by any means, and hence motivations for the following analysis are not provided.

The basic transitive pattern of Japanese is as exemplified in (10).

(10)   Taroo-ga   sono hon-o   katta.
       Taro-Nom the   book-Acc bought
       "Taro bought the book."

As shown, the subject NP receives the Nominative Case and the object NP receives the Accusative Case. When the verb is an action verb as in (10), the subject NP usually bears the Agent role, and the object NP the Theme role.

We will assume in this chapter that the near-surface phrase structural representation of (10) is (11).

(11)

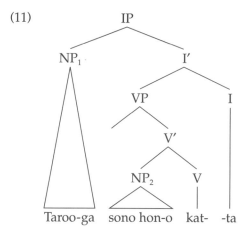

NP$_1$ represents the surface subject position, and NP$_2$ represents the surface object position. We will also assume that the surface subject NP$_1$ originates within VP, more specifically the specifier position of V, but the foregoing discussion does not hinge on this assumption, which is generally called the "VP-internal hypothesis" (e.g. Y. Kitagawa 1986, Kuroda 1988).

In addition to the basic word order exemplified in (10), a "scrambled" version is also possible as in (12).

(12) Sono hon-o   Taroo-ga katta.

The landing site of the scrambled element such as *sono hon o* in (12) is now under heated discussion, but for the purpose of this chapter it suffices only to assume that it lands somewhere higher than VP.

We will assume (13) as the structure of negative sentences.

(13)

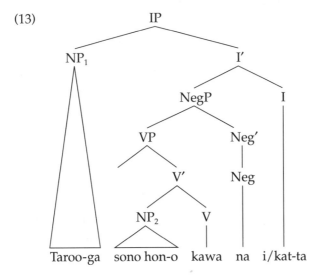

nai is the negative marker, and selects the projection of a non-finite Irrealis verbal form (*mizen-kei*). Notice that tense element such as the past marker *ta* is borne by *nai*, not by the verb.

3   Case Markers and Scrambling

In the late 1970s, there was a group of experimental studies, such as Hayashibe (1975) and K. Sano (1977), among others, concerning children's comprehension of Japanese transitive sentences. Their stimulus sentences contain transitive sentences with the "canonical" (i.e. non-scrambled) word order such as (14) and their scrambled counterpart such as (15).

(14) Kame-san -ga   ahiru-san -o   osimasita.
      turtle   Nom duck   Acc pushed
      "A/The turtle pushed a/the duck."

(15) Ahiru-san-o kame-san-ga osimasita.
      "A/The duck pushed a/the turtle."

The task is act-out: namely, subjects are asked to act out what the stimulus sentence means by manipulating toy animals put on the table in front of them.

Results of these studies have almost consistently shown that there is a group of children, sometimes up to five years old, who have difficulties in comprehending scrambled sentences like (15). Those children typically tend to take the first NP as the agent of the action denoted by the verb, and the second NP as the theme. Those results had generally been considered to indicate that scrambling is acquired fairly late, even as late as children's fifth year.[2]

What Otsu (1994a) has shown is that those results are experimental artifacts. Specifically, it is pointed out that the scrambled NP must have been established as a discourse topic in order to make the use of scrambled sentences natural. In the previous studies, stimulus sentences are given without discourse. As such, use of scrambled sentences like (15) sounds awkward.

Thus, if we add a sentence prior to (15) with a minimal change in (15) itself as well, it sounds perfectly natural:

(16) Kooen ni ahiru-san ga   imasita.
      park   in duck   Nom is-Pol-Past
      Sono ahiru-san o   kame-san ga   osimasita.
      the   duck   Acc turtle   Nom push-Pol-Past
      "There was a duck in a park. A turtle pushed the duck."

In (16), *ahiru-san* "duck" is introduced into the discourse context as a discourse topic by the first sentence. Once it becomes the discourse topic, it is not only all right but even more natural to begin the second sentence with *ahiru-san* fronted by scrambling. Thus, there is a discourse-contextual reason to use scrambled sentences. See also Masunaga (1983) for similar observations.

In Otsu (1994a), subjects in the experimental group received each stimulus sentence with another sentence designed to establish the first NP of the stimulus sentence as the discourse topic, just as we have seen in (16). On the other hand, subjects in the control group received stimulus sentences without any discourses as in the previous studies. As expected, those three-year and four-year subjects in the experimental group virtually had no difficulty in comprehending such sentences, while many subjects in the control group showed the same error pattern as in the previous studies.

This result suggests that the difficulty that children showed in comprehending scrambled sentences in the previous studies are experimental artifacts caused by lack of attention to discourse factors governing the use of scrambled sentences. It also suggests that if we remove those factors that caused the experimental artifact, children as young as three show no difficulty in comprehending scrambled sentences. Such a result is not surprising at all in view of the fact that children do not have to learn much in order to be able to handle scrambled sentences.[3]

4   Case Marker Drop

In colloquial speech, Case markers can sometimes drop. Examples (17) through (20) constitute the basic set of data concerning this Case Marker Drop (CMD) phenomenon.

(17)   Taroo-ga   sono hon-Ø katta.
       Taro-Nom that book   bought

(18)   *Taroo-Ø   sono hon-o katta.

(19)   *Sono hon-Ø Taroo-ga   katta.

(20)   *Sono hon-o Taroo-Ø   katta.

There is still much to be discovered about CMD including possible dialectal variations, but the facts in (17) through (20) seem to be fairly straightforward for speakers of the Tokyo dialect.

Assuming that the basic Japanese phrase structure is (13) and that the landing site of a scrambled element is somewhere outside VP, the above CMD data set can be accounted for by the following surface condition (21).

(21)   When an NP is adjacent to and c-commanded by V, the Case marker attached to it can drop. (Takezawa 1987: 126)

In (17), NP *sono hon* is adjacent to and c-commanded by V *katta*, and therefore the Case marker can drop. In (18), NP *Taroo* is outside VP, and thus is not c-commanded by *katta*. Hence, no CMD is allowed. The same account applies to (19). In (20), the scrambled phrase *sono hon* is outside VP, and is not c-commanded by *katta*. Again, CMD cannot take place. The situation is illustrated in (22) and (23).

(22)

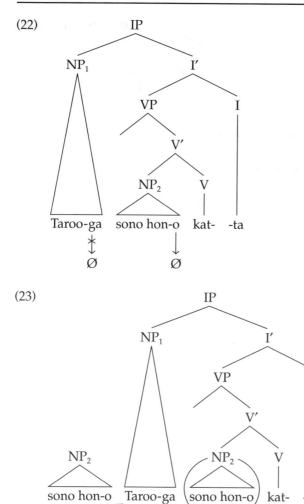

(23)

Otsu (1994b) has attempted to show that young Japanese-speaking children show the same sensitivity to CMD as adults, thereby showing in turn that those children's grammar generates hierarchically organized phrase structures like (22) and (23).

In one of the two experiments reported in Otsu (1994b), ten three-year-olds and ten four-year-olds were interviewed. The task is sentence-completion. The subject is shown a picture of someone involved in some action: e.g. a mother eating a watermelon. The experimenter gives the following instruction to the subject: "Can you tell me about this picture? First, can you begin with X?" X in the instruction is either the word corresponding to the Agent or the Theme of the action denoted by the verb of the sentence that the subject is to produce. No Case marker is added to X. (24) is an example.

(24)   Kono e-   nituite ohanasi-site kureru? Mazu, *okaa-san*-de
       this picture about tell   can you first   *okaa-san*
       hazimete   ne?
       with begin please
       "Can you tell me about this picture? First, can you begin with *okaa-san*?"

If the instruction is (24), the following is the set of possible and impossible answers:

(25)   a.   Okaa-san-ga suika-o   tabeteiru.
            mother-Nom watermelon-Acc eating
            "Mother is eating a watermelon."
       b.   Okaa-san-ga suika-Ø   tabeteiru.
       c.   Okaa-san-ga   tabeteiru.
       d.   *Okaa-san-Ø   tabeteiru.
       e.   *Okaa-san-Ø suika-o   tabeteiru.
       f.   *Okaa-san-Ø suika-Ø   tabeteiru.

In (25c) and (25d), there is no mention of the Theme. Such sentences are possible if the speaker thinks that the hearer, i.e. the experimenter, and the speaker assume that they are talking about the same Theme. Notice that (25d) is illformed because the *ga*-phrase is adjacent to but is not c-commanded by the verb.

When X in (26) is the Theme, e.g. *suika* "watermelon," the following is the set of possible and impossible answers:

(26)   a.   Suika-o   okaa-san-ga tabeteiru.
            watermelon-Acc mother-Nom eating
            "Mother is eating a watermelon."
       b.   *Suika-o   okaa-san-Ø tabeteiru.
       c.   Suika-o   tabeteiru.
       d.   Suika-Ø   tabeteiru.
       e.   *Suika-Ø   okaa-san-ga tabeteiru.
       f.   *Suika-Ø   okaa-san-Ø tabeteiru.

Notice that in (26c) and (26d) there is no mention of the Agent for the same reason that we mentioned for (25c) and (25d). It is assumed that the Theme phrase in (26c) and (26d) remains in the D-structure position, thus making the latter wellformed. Notice also that (26b) is illformed because the Agent phrase is not c-commanded by the verb.

The results succinctly show that there is no single violation of (21). Three-year-olds tend to use shorter forms (for example, while only 3 percent of the responses of the four-year-olds are of the (25c)-type, 30 percent of the responses of the three-year-olds are of that type), but even in those cases they obey (21), a fact that is shown by the contrast between (25d) (0 percent responses of three-year-olds) and (26d) (50 percent responses).

These results, showing that children at least at the age of three obey (21), indicate that those children's grammar generates hierarchically organized phrase structures like (22) and (23). It should also be pointed out that the above results further support the conclusion of Otsu (1994a) that scrambling is acquired much earlier than previous studies indicate.

These experimental results receive support from a production study on CMD reported in Miyata (1992). In her thesis, Miyata reports results of her detailed analysis of production data of children in a wide age range, but her analysis of production of two- and three-year-olds is the most crucial for the present purposes.

Miyata has found 326 utterances with over subjects in her data. In 279 out of those 326 utterances, there is an overt *ga*. In the remaining 47 utterances, there is no overt *ga*: namely, it has dropped. However, Miyata has found that in almost all such cases, the verbs are stative verbs (e.g. (27); cf. Takezawa 1987) or "ergative" verbs which require a Theme subject (e.g. (28); cf. Miyagawa 1989b). In the latter case the subject phrase arguably remains within VP, thus enabling CMD.

(27)   Kimi-ni nani(-ga)   wakaruno.
       you-Dat what-Nom understand-Q
       "What do you understand?"

(28)   Ame(-ga) hutta.
       rain-Nom fell
       "It rained."

If this analysis is correct, there is virtually no example of *ga*-drop where the appearance of *ga* is actually obligatory.

In contrast to *ga*, the *o*-phrase has dropped in as many cases as 124 out of 161 utterances that contain object. In only 37 utterances out of those 161 utterances is there an overt *o*.

If the above analysis is correct, there is overwhelming evidence from production as well that two- and three-year-olds drop Case markers in accordance with (21). This indicates that hierarchically organized phrase structure is already in children's grammar.

5   *Zibun* Binding

Zibun is generally considered to be a Japanese anaphor whose behavior resembles that of *-self* (reflexives) in English. For example, *zibun* must have its antecedent in the same sentence. Thus, (29) is acceptable only when *zibun* refers to John, and is not interpretable when it refers to someone else not mentioned in the sentence.

(29) John$_i$-ga   zibun$_{i/*j}$-no kao-o   kaita.
     John-Nom self-Gen   face-Acc drew
     "John drew his own face."

Also like *-self*, *zibun* must be c-commanded by its antecedent, as illustrated in (30).

(30) John$_i$-no otooto$_j$-ga   zibun$_{*i/j}$ no kao-o   kaita.
     John-Gen brother-Nom self-Gen   face-Acc drew
     "John's brother drew his own face."

Those properties can be explained in terms of Binding Condition A in some form or another. The condition basically states that an anaphor must be bound in its governing category, where the governing categories are Ss and NPs.

However, *zibun* has properties that are distinct from English *-self*. For one thing, the antecedent of *zibun* must be a subject, while *-self* does not show such a restriction.

(31) John$_i$-ga   Bill$_j$-ni zibun$_{i/*j}$-no koto-o   hanasita.
     John-Nom Bill-Dat self-Gen   matter-Acc talked
     "John talked to Bill about himself."

(32) John$_i$ talked to Bill$_j$ about himself$_{i/j}$.

We call this the "subject orientation (SO)" of *zibun*.[4]

Zibun has another interesting property. It can refer to a long-distance subject. For example, (33) is ambiguous.

(33) John$_i$-ga   Bill$_j$-ni [Ned$_k$-ga   Ken$_l$-ni zibun$_{i/*j/k/*l}$-no koto-o
     John-Nom Bill-Dat Ned-Nom Ken-Dat self-Gen   matter-Acc
     hanasita] to   itta.
     talked   that told
     "John told Bill that Ned talked to Ken about himself."

When *zibun* is bound by a long-distance subject, like *John* in (33), the phenomenon is called the "long-distance binding (LDB)" of *zibun*.

Katada (1991) and others have attempted to explain these properties of *zibun* by considering it as an Operator that gets to VP successively. When the sentence contains only one clause and hence one VP, *zibun*, originally located within VP, is adjoined to the VP. The subject c-commands *zibun*, and thus can be the antecedent of *zibun*. On the other hand, the object, which is in VP, does not c-command *zibun*, and hence cannot be its antecedent. This is how the SO of *zibun* is accounted for.

(34)

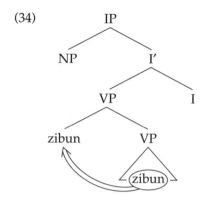

If the sentence containing *zibun* is embedded in other sentence(s), Operator *zibun* raises successively to the upper VP(s), which accounts for the LDB of *zibun*.

There are different analyses of *zibun*, but most, if not all, analyses agree in that the SO and LDB follow in one way or another from properties of UG. From an acquisitional point of view, the early emergence of the SO and LDB is hence expected. Katada's (1991) theory, furthermore, makes a very interesting prediction. That is, it predicts the simultaneous emergence of SO and LDB since they both follow from the Operatorhood of *zibun*.

Otsu (1997) tested 45 subjects in the age range between three and five, 15 subjects in each age group, to test experimentally how these children interpret sentences containing *zibun*. The method is truth-value verification, developed by Stephen Crain (e.g. Crain 1991). Two dolls, Taro (boy) and Hanako (girl), are put behind a screen on the table, and thus they are invisible to the subject. Grover is introduced on the same side of the screen as the subject, and he too cannot see Taro and Hanako. There is an experimenter on the other side of the screen, who is the only one who can see what happens on that side.

Taro and Hanako then perform a certain action. Then, the experimenter on that side whispers to the subject what they did. And the same experimenter asks Grover to guess what they did. Grover, then, says his guess. The subject has been told to give him a cookie if his guess is correct, and a rag if it is incorrect.

After some practice, in the first portion of the test session, the experimenter on the other side of the screen whispers to the subject what Taro and Hanako did by using a simple sentence containing *zibun*, such as (35).

(35) Taroo-ga Hanako-ni zibun-no e-o   miseta.
     Taro-Nom Hanako-Dat self-Gen picture-Acc showed
     "Taro showed Hanako a picture of himself."

Because of its SO, only *Taroo* can be the antecedent of *zibun*, and not *Hanako* or someone else for that matter.

The experimenter then tells Grover that Taro showed a picture to Hanako and asks him to guess whose picture he showed. In this case, if Grover says Taro's picture, he is expected to be given a cookie. If he says someone else's picture, he is expected to be given a rag. We must hasten to add that in the practice session, similar sentences which do not contain *zibun* are given, and in half of the cases it is Taro's picture and in the other half it is Hanako's picture, thereby eliminating the response bias toward either Taro or Hanako.

Twelve three-year-olds, 14 four-year-olds, and 15 five-year-olds were able to understand the procedure, and participated in this portion of the experiment. The result is that all the subjects except one three-year-old responded in an adult-like fashion, thus confirming the early emergence of SO of *zibun*.

The second portion of the experiment employs the same task as the first, but differs in the nature of stimulus sentences. A sample sentence used in this portion is (36).

(36)   Taroo-no otooto-ga   Hanako-ni   zibun-no e-o   miseta.
         Taro-Gen brother-Nom Hanako-Dat self-Gen picture-Acc showed
         "Taro's brother showed Hanako a picture of himself."

In response to the experimenter's request to guess whose picture Taro's brother showed to Hanako, Grover is expected to respond "Taro's brother's," not "Taro's."

The same group of subjects participated in this second portion. Again, almost all the subjects responded in an adult-like fashion. Only one three-year-old (the same subject who failed in the first portion) and one four-year-old failed to do so. This result also confirms the early emergence of the c-command requirement of *zibun* discussed above.

The last portion of the experiment is again like the first two, except for the nature of stimulus sentences. This time, stimulus sentences have an embedded sentence that contains *zibun*, like (37).

(37) Taroo_i-wa [Akira_j-ga Hanako_k-ni $\text{zibun}_{i/j/*k}$-no e-o   miseta]
         Taro-Top   Akira-Nom Hanako-Dat self-Gen   picture-Acc showed
         to   omotta.
         that thought
         "Taro thought that Akira showed Hanako a picture of himself."

The experimenter asks Grover whose picture Taro thought Akira showed to Hanako. Because of LDB of *zibun*, either Taro's picture or Akira's picture is the adult-like response.

In this case, because of the lengthy nature of stimulus sentences, a smaller number of younger subjects (five three-year-olds, 11 four-year-olds, and 15 five-year-olds) were able to participate. This apparently is due to their limited processing capacity, as they also failed in sentences like (38) which do not contain *zibun*.

(38) Taroo-wa [Akira-ga   Hanako-ni   Ziroo-no e-o   miseta]
      Taro-Top   Akira-Nom Hanako-Dat Ziro-Gen picture-Acc showed
      to   omotta.
      that thought
      "Taro thought that Akira showed Hanako Jiro's picture."

However, among those who were able to participate, almost all (four three-year-olds, 10 four-year-olds, and 15 five-year-olds) responded in an adult-like fashion, allowing LDB.

These results show that children as young as three are already aware of SO and LDB. The results strongly suggest that these properties of *zibun* are related to properties of UG, thus requiring no experience for them to emerge.

However, these results do not directly answer the more interesting question of whether SO and LDB of *zibun* emerge at the same time or not. While the results do not conflict with the prediction of the simultaneous emergence of the two properties, it is not clear when these properties, particularly LDB, emerge in acquisition. We have to wait for future research to answer this question.

6 Negation

We mentioned at the beginning of this chapter that *nai* is the negative marker and selects the projection of a nonfinite Irrealis verbal form "mizen-kei." It has been long noticed by researchers of the acquisition of Japanese (e.g. Clancy 1985) that young children produced errors in which a finite verbal form is followed by *nai*. For example, consider (39).[5]

(39) hair-u nai.
      enter not
      "(It) does not enter."

The correct adult counterpart is (40).

(40) hair-a nai.

However, this type of error, named "External Negation (EN)" by T. Sano (1995), had not been given systematic treatment before his work.

Since Bloch (1946), Japanese verbs are classified into two groups with respect to verbal morphology by root-final sounds: consonantal and vocalic. (41) represents the paradigm of consonantal verbs, and (42) that of vocalic verbs.

(41)

	enter	*attach*	*fly*
Nonpast	hair-u	tuk-u	tob-u
Past	hait-ta	tui-ta	ton-da
Irrealis+nai	hair-a nai	tuk-a nai	tob-a nai

(42)
	be/exit	*sleep*	*eat*
Nonpast	i-ru	ne-ru	tabe-ru
Past	i-ta	ne-ta	tabe-ta
Irrealis+nai	i-nai	ne-nai	tabe-nai

A glance at the two paradigms reveals that (42) is much simpler than (41). The Irrealis form of a vocalic verb is identical to its bare root. Furthermore, negative forms can be formed by simply putting *-nai* to the bare root, and the bare root can easily be identified by comparing nonpast and past forms.

T. Sano's (1995) important finding is that there is a dramatic difference between those two types of verbs with respect to the occurrence of the above-mentioned negation errors. Table 13.1, taken from T. Sano (1995: 88), shows this.

On the basis of this observation, T. Sano (1995) proposes the following maturational account.

(43)   Irrealis formation of consonantal verbs matures. At first, children may fail in the formation. After a certain point in development, they become completely competent in it.

Because of this maturational factor being involved, young children have to satisfy themselves with (44) instead of the adult structure in (13), reproduced here for readers' convenience.

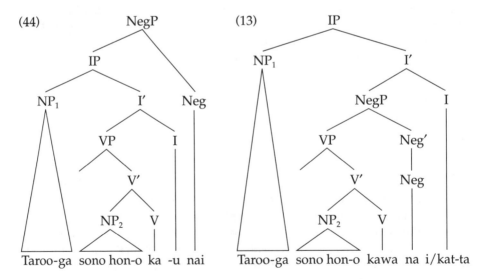

T. Sano (1995) further argues that (43) is a language-specific instantiation of the more general acquisitional principle which he calls "morphological maturation," and attempts to relate EN with "Root Infinitives (RI)" in Indo-European languages (e.g. Wexler 1996).

Table 13.1   Negation errors in consonantal and vocalic verbs reported in
T. Sano (1995: 88)

	Consonantal		Vocalic	
	EN	*Adult-like*	*EN*	*Adult-like*
Toshi (2;3–2;8)[a]	26(72%)	10	0(0%)	25
Ken (2;8–2;10)	30(55%)	25	4(7%)	53
Masanori (2;4)	6(55%)	5	2(6%)	34
Total	62(61%)	40	6(5%)	112

[a] The numbers to the right of the children's names indicate their ages over the period when the experiment was carried out.

(45)   Adjunction-affixation matures. It is not completely operative at first and
       matures at a certain point.

   As mentioned in section 1, there have been proposals concerning maturational factors in language acquisition. However, a caution is needed in introducing the notion of maturation in the theory of language acquisition. The point is that we need to constrain the domain of application as narrowly as possible. Otherwise, the theory could say virtually anything in that there is always room for invoking maturation when allegedly innate properties of language do not seem to operate from the beginning. T. Sano (1995) is apparently aware of this, and attempts to constrain the maturational domain to adjunction-affixation. We need more work, however, to decide if his approach is on the right track.

7   Conclusion

We have discussed some of the recent works that have a direct bearing on the "logical problem of language acquisition." Needless to say, there are other works that were not touched upon here due to space limitation. They include M. Takahashi's (1993) work on verbal nouns, work by a number of people on the "overextended" use of *no* in prenominal position (e.g. Murasugi 1991), M. Nakayama's (1996) work on empty categories, and Imai and Gentner's (1997) work on lexical/cognitive development.
   The studies reviewed in this chapter along with many other recent studies strongly indicate that UG plays an important role in the acquisition of Japanese grammar, guiding children what to look for and where to go. In fact, many abstract grammatical properties do exist in the early grammars of Japanese-speaking children.

With the progress of the PP approach to UG, it has become much easier to put the study of Japanese acquisition into the perspectives of the construction of a general theory of language acquisition. The same applies to studies of the acquisition of other languages as well. "Comparative studies" of language acquisition, just like comparative syntax, will become increasingly important in this context to pin down the role of experience on top of the role of genetically preprogrammed UG.

As mentioned at the outset, work of this sort has just recently begun, and in fact, in spite of all these efforts, we must admit that we are still very far from getting a coherent picture of the development of Japanese grammar as a whole. Much more work along these lines must be carried out for that purpose. To facilitate these attempts, it is now being planned to incorporate Japanese data into the CHILDES database (MacWhinney 1995, Oshima-Takane and MacWhinney 1995). I would like to conclude this chapter by hoping that in the very near future the present chapter will be outdated because of new findings.

NOTES

1   This does not preclude the possibility of inducing negative evidence using positive evidence and children's internal mechanism. This is commonly called "indirect negative evidence" (N. Chomsky 1981a).

Some researchers claim that negative evidence is being provided to children on the basis of grammatical "expansion" following children's incorrect utterances. See G. F. Marcus (1993) for discussion.

2   The interpretation of those results may be less clear. Some authors might have taken the results as showing that an instance of interpretive heuristics then known as "perceptual strategy" (e.g. Fodor et al. 1974) overrides children's grammar in comprehending scrambled sentences. The heuristic in question roughly goes: "If the verb is an action verb, interpret the first NP in a sentence as the Agent and the second as the Patient." Under this interpretation of the experimental

results, scrambling is acquired early but is overridden by the above heuristic.

3   The experimental innovation introduced in Otsu (1994a) may also be useful in studying other constructions whose use is discourse-controlled, such as direct passives.

4   There is a well-known class of "logophoric exceptions" to the generalizations summarized above. The following examples are taken from Kameyama (1984: 230).

(i)   Taroo$_i$ wa   Ziroo$_j$ ni [[zibun$_{i/j}$
      Taro Top/Sub Ziro by   self
      to sokkuri na] otoko ga
      with alike is   man Nom
      iru koto] o   sirasareta.
      exist fact   Acc was informed
      "Taro was informed by Jiro that there is a man who looks just like self."

The outer brackets indicate the clause expressing the content of what Taro was informed of by Jiro, and the inner brackets indicate the relative clause modifying *otoko* "man." Notice that *Ziroo*, which is not a subject in any sense, can be the antecedent of *zibun* in (i).

This class of exceptions is called "logophoric" since nonsubject antecedents in those cases all share the property of being "individuals who inform or report certain information . . . or whose feelings are described" (Kameyama 1984: 230). See Kuno (1986a) and Sells (1987) for related discussion.

How this "logophoric" *zibun* relates to "anaphoric" *zibun* in acquisition and in adult grammar is an extremely interesting question that awaits future research.

For more details of *zibun*, including different analyses from Katada's (1991), and properties of other anaphoric and pronominal elements in Japanese, see chapter 6 in this volume.

5 Examples in this section are taken from T. Sano (1995) unless otherwise mentioned.

14   Sentence Processing

MINEHARU NAKAYAMA

0   Introduction

The field of Japanese processing can be broadly divided into two subfields: word processing (i.e. lexical processing) and sentence processing. The former deals with questions such as how the meaning of a word is retrieved from the lexicon, how the lexicon is organized, and whether or not different orthographies constitute different processing routes. The latter focuses on questions such as how a sentence is parsed, how lexical and syntactic ambiguities are resolved, how a gap is filled in a sentence, and why certain sentences are more difficult to process than others. These are also general questions which one can raise during the investigation of any language and their answers help us understand how the human brain functions.

The above questions become more pertinent cross-linguistically when one considers whether there is a universal processing mechanism in the human brain. While constructing a universal processing model has so far been the predominant approach in the field, one major problem is the fact that universal processing theories were originally constructed solely on the basis of English data. When researchers tried to apply these theories to Japanese, they could not account for Japanese data.[1] We will discuss this in this chapter.

Although the focus of this chapter is Japanese sentence processing, we will first discuss lexical processing briefly because these two subfields are interrelated. For instance, a native speaker of Japanese can recognize words (i.e. can distinguish a word from a nonword in Japanese) very quickly. This suggests that the brain of a native Japanese speaker has a very efficient information retrieval system. Understanding how this system operates is important to understanding how a Japanese comprehends or produces sentences, because the meaning of a sentence requires retrieving information about each word contained in the sentence. The comparison of lexical processing at the word and the sentence levels allows us to understand how the lexical information retrieval system works in addition to making clear other aspects involved in sentence processing. Assuming that the relation between the grammar and the processing mechanism is transparent, understanding how the sentence processing mechanism operates helps us formulate a theory of grammar which is psychologically real. In this view, one can say that the processing mechanism shapes grammar or grammar shapes the processing mechanism, depending on one's point of view.

Understanding an adult's processing mechanism further relates to understanding the language acquisition mechanism. Research questions, such as what the initial state of the processing mechanism is and how children use their parser when formulating their grammar, allow us to understand the initial state of the language faculty and how one's grammar develops. Furthermore, all of the above questions can be addressed to language-impaired subjects as well. The comparison of data from both normal and language-impaired subjects provides us further insights into issues of how the human brain functions. Thus, the processing field is closely connected with theoretical linguistics, language acquisition, neurolinguistics, and other fields included in cognitive science, all of which open a door to the understanding of the human mind.

This chapter is organized into four sections: in section 1, I will briefly discuss the Japanese writing system. Many studies in lexical processing are closely related to issues in Japanese orthography, which is also pertinent to the discussion of sentence processing, since many sentence processing experiments involve reading. In section 2, I present a brief examination of lexical processing. Theories and experiments of sentence processing will be discussed in section 3. During the discussion, I will refer to different processing models and important aspects of the Japanese language which create problems for English-based processing theories. In the final section I will offer concluding remarks. Due to the limitation of space, I cannot exhaustively list or discuss all previous studies. Readers are referred to Kess and Miyamoto (1994) for additional references in Japanese psycholinguistics.

1 The Japanese Writing System

There are two kinds of characters in Japanese, *kana* and *kanji*, beside *roomaji* or romanization. *Kana* is a moraic script form, and there are two kinds, *hiragana* and *katakana*. In present-day Japanese, *hiragana* (cursive *kana*) is primarily used to indicate high-frequency morphemes such as postpositions and inflectional endings. *Katakana* (square *kana*) is used for all loanwords except those of Chinese origin. It is also used for emphasis (e.g. onomatopoetic words and foreigners' conversations in comics). Since these script forms are moraic, their script–sound correspondence is highly regular. There are 46 basic *kana* (71 with the use of diacritics, used for voicing, for example). *Kanji* or Chinese characters, on the other hand, do not have regular script–sound correspondences. They are primarily used for nouns, the roots of adjectives, and verbs. There are 1,945 daily-use *kanji* (or *jooyoo kanji*), most of which are taught during the nine-year compulsory education. Normally, both *kana* and *kanji* are used together in a sentence, although one can in principle choose to write a sentence using only *kana* or romanization. For instance, the same sentence can be written in four ways as shown in (1).

(1) a. Jon-ga   hon-o   yomu.
        John-Nom book-Acc read
        "John reads books."
    b. じょんがほんをよむ。
    c. ジョンガホンヲヨム。
    d. ジョンガ本を読む。

Sentence (1a), which is written in *roomaji*, can be written in *hiragana, katakana,* and mixed script (*hiragana, katakana,* and *kanji*) as in (1b–d), respectively. The standard way of writing is (1d), in which the noun corresponding to John is written in *katakana, hon* "book" and a part of the root of the verb *yom* "read" in *kanji.* Case particles *ga* and *o*, and a part of the root of the verb and tense inflection *mu*, are in *hiragana.* Although the actual root of the verb "read" is *yom*, the *yo* portion is written in *kanji* while *mu* is written in *hiragana* because the readings of *kanji* and *kana* are moraic. Sentences are written vertically (top-down, right to left) or horizontally (left to right, top-down). Generally speaking, vertical writing is more formal and often employed in newspapers and formal letters and documents (Shibatani 1990), while horizontal writing is often found in contemporary governmental documents and scientific work. Horizontal writing is frequently found in readings in social and natural sciences.

Using three different scripts seems complicated enough, but what makes it truly complicated is the fact that there are different readings for each *kanji.* For instance, the *kanji* 行 has three different Chinese readings (*koo, gyoo,* and *an*) as shown in (2). Notice also that (2a) and (2b) are an example of homography.

(2) a. 一行(ikkoo)   "accompanied group of people"
    b. 一行(ichigyoo)   "one line"
    c. 行灯(andon)   "lantern"

These three Chinese readings (*On-yomi*) were brought into Japan from China during three different time periods. In addition, this *kanji* has Japanese readings (*Kun-yomi*) such as "i/yu" as in 行く(i/yu-ku) "go" and "okona" as in 行う(okona-u) "conduct." This means that there are more than four readings for this *kanji.* See Shibatani (1990) on the history of *kanji* and *kana.*

The reading of *kanji* becomes even more complex when the regular reading does not apply to a compound word, a phenomenon known as *jukujikun* (熟字訓). Examples are shown in (3).

(3) 今日(kyoo) "today," 紅葉(momiji) "maple," 大人(otona) "adult"

The Japanese reading is given to a compound word which consists of two or more than two *kanji* characters. Each character often relates to the meaning of the word. For instance, the first character of *kyoo* means "now" and the second character means "day." Hence, the word is "today."[2] In these *jukujikun* cases, one can guess the meaning of words although one may not know how to read them.

Just the opposite of *jukujikun* is *ateji* (当て字), in which the reading of each *kanji* character was borrowed regardless of the meaning of the *kanji* character. Examples are in (4).

(4) 丁度(choodo) "exactly," 矢張(yahari) "as I thought"

Each character of these compound words retains its regular reading. However, their meanings do not obviously constitute or relate to the compound word's meanings. For instance, in the first word, *choo* is a counter and *do* means "degree" in (4). The two characters of the second word mean "arrow" and "paste, affix, or extend," respectively. Unlike *jukujikun*, one can apply regular readings to these *kanji* and understand the meanings of the words.[3]

Not every *kanji* character has more than one reading. The number of readings depends on the individual *kanji*. Therefore, native speakers of Japanese as well as non-native speakers must learn how to read *kanji* on a case-by-case basis. Because of the complicated physical composition of *kanji* characters and their multiple readings, many researchers are engaged in the investigation of the visual recognition process of *kanji* (e.g. Flores d'Arcais and Saito 1993, Flores d'Arcais et al. 1995) and the *kanji* acquisition process by children and L2 learners (e.g. Flaherty 1991, J. Yamada 1992). However, one of the most explored aspects of Japanese orthography has been how both *kana* and *kanji* are processed. We will now turn our discussion to this issue. For more about the Japanese writing system, see M. Paradis et al. (1985), Shibatani (1990), and Taylor and Taylor (1995).

2   Lexical Processing: Direct and Indirect Access

In previous studies on visual word recognition in Japanese, there have been two views on the relationship between script forms and word meanings, namely, direct and indirect access to word meanings. Direct access means that word meanings are directly retrieved from the visual representation of the words without phonological mediation. Indirect access means that phonological mediation is used. Since *kana* has a regular script–sound correspondence, many researchers have proposed that it is likely to need indirect access (i.e. phonological mediation). On the other hand, *kanji* may take the direct route because they do not have obvious regular script–sound correspondences (i.e. word meanings are directly retrieved from the visual representation of the words without phonological mediation). Evidence that the two scripts are accessed differently can be found in the aphasic literature. Impairment of *kana* processing, for instance, has been reported in Sasanuma and Fujimura (1971) among aphasic subjects with the additional symptom of apraxia of speech (see also Sasanuma and Fujimura 1972, Sasanuma 1974, 1980, 1984) and impairment of *kanji* processing was found among *gogi* (word-meaning) aphasics in Sasanuma and Monoi (1975) (see also Imura 1943). The findings in aphasics indicate that the readers use different routes to access the lexicon depending on the script types. Morton and Sasanuma (1984) suggest that *kanji* access the lexicon by their physical form alone (i.e. visual route), while *kana* require the reader to recode phonologically (i.e. phonological route) before the access occurs.[4]

However, it has been reported that both *kana* and *kanji* words have direct and indirect access to meaning. For instance, Besner and Hildebrandt (1987) report that words normally written in *katakana* were named (i.e. read aloud) more quickly among normal subjects when presented in *katakana* than either *katakana* nonwords or *kanji* words presented in *katakana*. Response times (i.e. the duration of the presentation of the word and the onset of naming) for *katakana* nonwords set baseline data since it requires phonological recoding. Since response times for *katakana* words were faster than those that involved the phonological recoding process, it was interpreted that *kana* can access the lexicon directly. Thus, Besner and Hildebrandt conclude that orthographically familiar *kana* words can achieve lexical access on the basis of orthographic code without recourse to phonological recoding. Similar conclusions are found in Hirose (1984, 1985) and Sasanuma et al. (1988).

As for *kanji*, phonological processing is also observed in Horodeck (1987), Wydell et al. (1993), Leong and Tamaoka (1995), and Matsunaga (1995a, 1995b), among others. For instance, Wydell et al. (1993) claim that reading *kanji* is characterized by parallel access to semantics from orthographic and phonological representations. Matsunaga (1995a, 1995b) reports that Japanese readers noticed both homophonic and nonhomophonic *kanji* errors, but that they noticed nonhomophonic errors more frequently than homophonic errors. Furthermore, Kondo and Kakehi (1994) find no difference between *kanji* and *kana* for the interaction between auditory and visual processing, and Gashuu (1994) reports that a familiar *kanji* character is as easily pronounced as *hiragana*. These all suggest that a dual or parallel approach is most plausible.[5] They also suggest that lexical access is very much influenced by the familiarity of the orthographic representation of a particular word.[6]

The role of orthographic familiarity in the processing of Japanese nouns is examined in Darnell et al. (1994) by using a word-by-word reading paradigm. In this task, each word was presented and replaced by another word as soon as a subject pushed a button. In their experiments, the familiarity of *kana* and *kanji* words (i.e. *hiragana* and *kanji* dominant words) in sentences was controlled and their contextual bias was manipulated. That is, the words lexically associated with the target words were presented before the targets in the contextually biased sentences (i.e. semantic priming). They find that (i) the orthography does not affect the reading time unless the sentence is contextually biased, in which case the most familiar orthography is faster; and (ii) *kanji* and *kana* can be processed at the same rate if familiarity is controlled or contexts are nonbiasing.[7] On the basis of these findings, Darnell (1995) compares the logogen model (Morton 1969), the search model (Forster 1976), and the connectionist model (Seidenberg and McClelland 1989) and concludes that the connectionist model can account for the Japanese data more easily.[8]

In sum, the previous findings indicate that any lexical processing model should allow for the dual processing of both *kana* and *kanji*. However, many research questions remain unanswered. For instance: how does *kanji*'s visual lexical access differ from that of other symbols'? How is lexical access in isolation different from in a sentence? When familiarity is controlled, is there any difference in the response time of the lexical decision task (i.e. the judgment as to whether or not what is presented is a word in the language) in terms of the numbers of moras and characters? How do phonetic and semantic primings affect lexical access? Answers to these questions would bring us a better understanding of how lexical access works.[9] I will come back to these research questions in my concluding remarks.

3   Sentence Processing

The field of Japanese sentence processing is still young and more work must be carried out in order to understand how the human brain processes Japanese sentences. However, recent developments provide us with many exciting findings. They have a direct impact on the theory of a universal human language comprehension mechanism.[10] Since most research has been conducted on reading, not listening, our discussion will focus on the findings in reading, although we will refer to some auditory work, where relevant. It is important to note that the test sentences are visually presented with both *kana* and *kanji* in the reading experiments in order to achieve a natural presentation for native speakers.

The task of structure building, i.e. building from a sequence of words to a syntactic representation of how these words are combined, is often called sentence or syntactic parsing. Thus far, the majority of research has been on parsing, although there are different aspects that can be investigated in sentence processing. Therefore, our discussion is also limited to parsing. There are three basic parsing models to which we refer from time to time below. They are a serial model, a parallel model, and a delay model. A serial model builds a single phrase structure as each word comes by (i.e. online) and a parallel model computes all possible structures with equal speed and ranking (i.e. the preference of the structures built). A delay model does not compute any syntactic structures until enough information is provided. Strict versions of these models and any parsing theory developed based on English all have difficulty dealing with the following characteristics of Japanese: (i) it is a head-final language, (ii) it has no relative pronouns, (iii) it has empty pronouns, and (iv) it allows scrambling. I will discuss these points in sections 3.1 through 3.4.

Particular sentence types, garden path and filler-gap sentences, will be referred to in sections 3.5 and 3.6. Sentence (5a) is a well-known English garden path sentence from Bever (1970: 316) and (5b) is an English filler-gap sentence from Frazier et al. (1983: 203).

(5) a. The horse raced past the barn fell.
     b. Everyone liked the woman who$_i$ the little child$_j$ started [PRO$_j$ to sing those stupid French songs for [t]$_i$ last Christmas].

In sentence (5a), a parser (or a syntactic processor) processes words from left to right and considers all elements up to *the barn* as belonging to one sentence with the main verb *raced*. However, when it proceeds to *fell*, it realizes that *fell* is the main verb. When the parser makes a wrong guess, it has been led up the garden path. So it is forced to reanalyze the sentence structure. When a sentence with a temporal ambiguity causes a problem for the parsing mechanism, it has a garden path effect. This implies that the parser makes its decisions incrementally online (i.e. in real-time processing) as the words are received. This suggests the plausibility of a serial processing model. We will look at what kind of garden paths are possible in Japanese and how different models can account for the different garden path effects. See Mazuka and Itoh (1995) for the term "garden path."

The examination of filler-gap sentences allows us to look at how a filler and a gap are linked online. For instance, the filler-gap sentence (5b) contains two different types of gaps (or empty categories), PRO and [t], which are coindexed with their fillers (or antecedents), *the little child* and *who*, respectively. Since *the little child* is interpreted as the subject of *sing*, it is coindexed with the empty subject PRO, and the relative pronoun *who* is related to the gap [t] (trace). To have the correct interpretation, the parser must appropriately locate those gaps and link them with the correct fillers. We will look at how the filler-gap relationship operates in Japanese.

3.1   Japanese, a head-final language

It has been considered that English is a head-initial language while Japanese is a head-final language. Consider the sentences in (6).

(6) a. John [ate an apple].
     b. John-ga   [ringo-o   tabeta].
         John-Nom apple-Acc ate

As shown in (6a), the verb (i.e. the head of the verb phrase) precedes the direct object in English (SVO word order). However, it follows the object in Japanese as in (6b) (SOV word order). This means that the verb which carries the complement information, i.e. subcategorization information, comes first in English, whereas in Japanese it comes at the end of the sentence. This raises the following question: does a Japanese parser wait for the verb in order to build phrase structures while reading? The head-final characteristic of Japanese creates many ambiguities before the verb because the parser cannot figure out how phrases are combined. Although case particles such as *-ga* (Nominative marker), *-ni* (Dative marker), *-o* (Accusative marker), and *-no* (Genitive marker) indicate grammatical functions and help the parser figure out the structure (e.g. A. Inoue 1991, Yamashita 1994, 1997a, 1997b, A. Inoue and Fodor 1995, Mazuka and Itoh 1995, Walenski and Sakamoto 1997), some syntactic ambiguities do not disappear. Consider the following.

(7) a. John-ga Mary-ga . . .
      b. [John-ga   [Mary-ga   ringo-o   tabeta to] itta]
          John-Nom Mary-Nom apple-Acc ate   that said
          "John said that Mary ate an apple."
      c. [John-ga   Mary-ga   suki-da]
          John-Nom Mary-Nom like
          "John likes Mary."

When one reads the sentence from left to right up to *Mary-ga* as in (7a), one cannot simply assume that both *John-ga* and *Mary-ga* are the subjects of different clauses as in (7b). This is because the object of the stative predicate can also take *-ga* as in (7c). That is, when we disregard the discourse context, we can never know which path (7a) will take. Then, what does the parser do?

The parsing model that has been referred to as a serial model builds the phrase structure as each word comes along. If the structure is built incorrectly, the parser must reanalyze the sentence according to this model. On the other hand, the parsing model that does not compute any syntactic structures until enough information is provided is called a delay model. A strict serial model predicts that processing Japanese is difficult because it requires reanalyses due to the structural ambiguities as we saw in (7). On the other hand, a strict delay model does not face this problem because the structure is not built until the combination of the words becomes clear. However, the delay model may cause memory overload because the sentence can be long. Considering the problem the serial model poses, Prichett (1988, 1991, 1992), for instance, proposes a somewhat restricted delay model, which is called a Head-Driven Parser. In this head-driven model, the head projects or builds the structure up to its maximal projection. For example, *Mary-ga* and *ringo-o* are combined with *tabeta* only when the verb *tabeta* is processed in (7b). Since the parser waits until the head, it does not require as much memory as does the strict delay model, which waits until *itta* in (7b) (cf. M. P. Marcus et al.'s 1983 D-theory model).

Another approach that takes into consideration the head-initial vs. head-final structural difference is discussed in Frazier and Rayner (1988), Mazuka and Lust (1989, 1990), and Mazuka (1990, 1998). These studies suggest that the parsing mechanism is affected by a head-initial vs. head-final parameter setting in the grammar. For instance, Mazuka (1990) claims that bottom-up (creating a phrase structure from the word level to the higher S-node level) and top-down (creating a phrase structure from the higher S-node level to the word level) organization of processing strategies is associated with the grammatical parameter setting of left- and right-branching languages. In other words, the parser does not experience difficulty as a consequence of the parameter setting in Universal Grammar when children start forming a grammar. Since subordinate clauses branch out leftward in Japanese and rightward in English, the parser takes the bottom-up and the top-down structure building strategies, respectively. This means that there are two ways the parsing mechanism works.[11]

These theories were proposed because previous theories formulated based on English predicted that Japanese would be quite difficult to process, but in reality, it is not. Berwick and Fong (1995) report that the head-final characteristic alone does not cause much difficulty to the parser, but it is a combination of different characteristics such as empty pronouns and scrambling in Japanese which produces parsing difficulties. We will look at these issues in sections 3.3 and 3.4 below.

3.2   No relative pronouns

Japanese does not have relative pronouns (such as English *who*). This makes processing of Japanese relative clauses different from processing those of English. Furthermore, Japanese does not have different verbal endings in matrix and relative clauses as in Korean. Consider the following sentences. Sentences in (9) and (10) are Japanese and Korean counterparts of the English sentences in (8), respectively. The Korean sentences are from Yamashita (1994: 47–8).

(8) a. John gave Mary an apple.
     b. John saw [the child [who gave Mary an apple]].

(9) a. John-ga   Mary-ni ringo-o   ageta.
         John-Nom Mary-Dat apple-Acc gave
     b. John-ga   [[Mary-ni   ringo-o   ageta] kodomo]-o mita.
         John-Nom   Mary-Dat apple-Acc gave   child-Acc   saw

(10) a. John-i   Mary-eykey sakwua-lul chuwo-ssta.
         John-Nom Mary-to   apple-Acc gave
     b. John-i   [[Mary-eykey sakwua-lul chwu-n] ai-lul]   powassta.
         John-Nom   Mary-to   apple-Acc gave-Rel child-Acc saw

As seen in (9b), Japanese does not have a relative pronoun equivalent to English *who* in (8b). Since there is no relative pronoun between *ageta* "gave" and *kodomo* "child," it is not clear if *ageta* is the verb in the matrix or relative clause. In addition, unlike the Korean sentences in (10b), Japanese verbal endings do not differ depending on whether the verb appears in the matrix or relative clause.[12] This makes the reader not certain if *ageta* is the matrix verb or the relative verb (i.e. the verb in the relative clause). Japanese verbs also do not show gender, person, and number agreement with the subject. This is shown in (11).[13]

(11) a. Mary-ga   John-ni   ringo-o   ageru.
         Mary-Nom John-Dat apple-Acc give
         "Mary gives John an apple."
      b. Boku-ga Mary-ni   ringo-o   ageru.
         I-Nom   Mary-Dat apple-Acc give
         "I give Mary an apple."
      c. Boku-to John-ga   Mary-ni   ringo-o   ageru.
         I and   John-Nom Mary-Dat apple-Acc give
         "John and I give Mary apples."

The lack of agreement in verbal morphology poses another problem for the theory of parsing. For instance, when the parser comes to the verb *ageru* "give" in (12a), it cannot tell if the sentence will end like (12b) or continues like (12c).

(12) a. John-to   Bill-ga   Mary-ni   ringo-o   ageru.
         John and Bill-Nom Mary-Dat apple-Acc give
      b. John-to Bill-ga Mary-ni ringo-o ageru.
         "John and Bill give/will give Mary an apple."
      c. John-to   Bill-ga   [[Mary-ni   ringo-o   ageru] kodomo]-o kimeru.
         John and Bill-Nom Mary-Dat apple-Acc give   child-Acc decide
         "John and Bill decide the child who gives/will give an apple to Mary."

If the parser is building a single structure as it processes each word (i.e. an online serial processing model), it creates a complete simple sentence structure at the verb. However, if (12a) continues like (12c), then it is required to change the structure that has been built. That is, *John-to Bill-ga* is no longer the subject of *ageru*, and it has to be removed from the clause that contains *ageru*. In addition, the subject gap within the relative clause must be created in the structure so that it can be coindexed with the head of the relative clause, i.e. *kodomo*.

In this kind of serial model, the parser processes words from left to right online and attaches the coming word to the previously built structure. For instance, Frazier and Fodor's (1978) parsing model called the Sausage Machine employs the Minimal Attachment strategy for structure building. In this strategy, the structure building/attachment is accomplished with the creation of the smallest number of nonterminal nodes. So when the parser is process-ing (12a), it builds a simple ditransitive structure since creating an alternate relative clause structure requires more nodes (cf. Kimball 1973, Frazier 1978, Frazier and Rayner 1982, Ferreira and Clifton 1986). This can be seen in rough structures in (13), where the ditransitive structure is (13a) and the relative clause structure is (13b).[14]

(13)   a.   b.

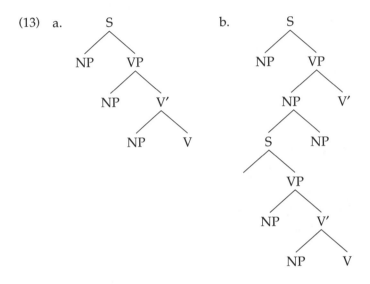

Extending this idea, A. Inoue (1991) proposes the Information Paced Parser, which is a left-to-right, online, serial model with a look-back (i.e. it checks the analysis at the verb and the head NP of a relative clause). Minimal Attachment is operative in this model, but since the information that the parser receives at each point of decision making (i.e. the ambiguous point) is less than that in English, a Japanese parser is less confident. This model is later modified as a Ranked Flagged Information Paced Parser (Inoue and Fodor 1995). In this model, the parser records what alternative parses are and how highly the alternative is valued (flagging). The most heavily weighted flag is parsed first and the decision is made with a confidence proportional to what kind of information the parser received concerning the structural choice and the necessity of reanalysis. For instance, the main clause analysis (12b) is taken as the first parse, but as soon as the relative head noun *kodomo* is read in (12c), the relative clause analysis is taken. This means that although the parser takes the main clause analysis up to the point of the verb *ageru* in (12), it does not strongly commit itself to that particular analysis because of the possibility of the relative clause analysis.

A strict parallel model requires all possible structures to be computed with equal speed and weight, and sent to the semantic module (Altmann and Steedman 1988, but cf. Gorrell 1989, Gibson 1991, Hickok 1993, and MacDonald et al. 1994). Thus, in the case of Japanese, it would create a memory overload due to an overwhelming number of possible structures (particularly in Altmann and Steedman's model). However, a Ranked Parallel Model (Kurtzman 1985, Gorrell 1987) provides possible structures only in the ambiguous region (not every word) and hence restricts the number of structures computed. In Gorrell's model, the computed structures are ranked based on complexity (i.e. the simpler, the higher ranking) and the highest-ranked structure is passed to the semantic processing system first. This model is different from the above-mentioned Ranked Flagged Information Paced Parser in that the former builds the alternate structures while the latter does not. But they are the same in that they both require some memory (i.e. the former needs to keep all alternate structures whereas the latter keeps track of the flags). According to Yamashita (1994), who examines both Japanese and Korean relative clauses employing a lexical decision task (i.e. judging whether or not a particular word presented is a real word) and a grammatical judgment task (i.e. judging whether or not the sequence of the words is grammatical), a serial model with a tentative attachment more accurately accounts for both Japanese and Korean data. See also Hirose and Chun (1998), Hirose and Inoue (in press), and Kamide and Mitchell (1997). At this point in the research, however, it is not clear whether one of these models is substantially superior.

Although the structural ambiguity in the relative clause sentences is found in reading, Venditti and Yamashita (1994) claim that listeners reliably predict the structural difference even before the end of clause is revealed. For instance, they contrasted the following four types of sentences (1994: 376).

(14) a. Mari-ga   [e] yonda.
          Mari-Nom   read
          "Mari read (it)."
      b. [Mari-ga   [e]$_i$ yonda] hakusho$_i$-wa omokatta.
          Mari-Nom   read   report-Top heavy was
          "The report which Mari read was heavy."
      c. [Mari-ga   [e]$_i$ [e] yonda] hanare$_i$-wa kurakatta.
          Mari-Nom   read   room-Top dark was
          "The room in which Mari read (it) was dark."
      d. [Mari-ga   [e] yonda] handan-wa   tadashikatta.
          Mari-Nom   read   decision-Top correct was
          "The decision due to Mari's reading (it) was correct."

Sentence (14a) is a simple sentence with an empty object (see section 3.3 below) while (14b–d) contain complex NPs, i.e. NPs with the argument relative clause and the PP adjunct relative, and the "pragmatic" complex NP (or NP with the gapless relative clause), respectively. All of these sentences include the sequence *Mari-ga yonda* "Mari read." Venditti and Yamashita report that there are robust acoustic differences between simple sentences and subordinate clauses of complex NPs in Japanese, i.e. sentence (14a) vs. (14b) through (14d). Those differences come from different prosodic structures of the two constructions. This suggests that there is online information, namely prosody, which plays a large role in cueing the intended structure of a segmentally ambiguous phrase. Therefore, what is predicted in reading may not actually happen in listening. See also Kondo and Mazuka (1996) and Misono et al. (1997) for prosody.

It is worthwhile mentioning another experimental finding on complex NPs here. Yamashita (1995) examines the following three different types of complex NPs: a gapless complex NP, an adjunct PP relative, and an argument relative.

(15) a. [Yuumei-na haiyuu-ga nesshin-ni shashin-o totta] sakuhinshuu-ga
            famous   actor-Nom ardently   photo-Acc took collection-Nom
            saikin   chuumoku-sareta.
            recently attention-was-paid
            "The collection of the photos the famous actor took recently attracted attention."
      b. [Yuumei-na haiyuu-ga nesshin-ni [e]$_i$ shashin-o totta] kooen$_i$-ga
            famous   actor-Nom ardently   photo-Acc took part-Nom
            saikin   chuumoku-sareta.
            recently attention-was-paid
            "The park where the famous actor took the picture recently attracted attention."
      c. [Yuumei-na haiyuu-ga nesshin-ni kooen-de [e]$_i$ totta] shashin$_i$-ga
            famous   actor-Nom ardently   park at   took photo-Nom
            saikin   chuumoku-sareta.
            recently attention-was-paid
            "The photos that the famous actor took at the park recently attracted attention."

(15a) is an example of a pragmatic complex NP, in which the embedded clause does not contain any gaps, but is pragmatically associated with the head noun *sakuhinshuu* "collection." On the other hand, (15b) and (15c) are instances of the adjunct PP and the argument relative clauses, respectively. All these sentences are similar in that the Minimal Attachment strategy discussed above does not predict any differences in them. Examining the self-paced reading times of these sentences, Yamashita (1995) finds that the verb's argument information is utilized very quickly in Japanese. The effect of the verb information was observed outside the clause, though there was no significant effect inside the clause. That is, as soon as the head noun is read, the gap is created if it is required by the verb in the relative clause. According to Yamashita, the verb argument information functions as an important source of information in online processing and the difference between English and Japanese is that in Japanese both overt and empty arguments are counted and the parser keeps track of them; if all the arguments are in the clause, the parser expects to end the sentence there. See also Yamashita et al. (1993) for these three types of complex NPs, and Horii (1990) for relative clauses with Ga/No conversion.

Another important study on relative clauses concerns center embedding. For instance, Mazuka et al. (1989) find that the reading time per character for (16b) is longer than that for (16a).

(16) a. Hiroshi-ga   [Masao-ga   katta] pan-o   tabeta.
          Hiroshi-Nom Masao-Nom bought bread-Acc ate
          "Hiroshi ate the bread Masao bought."
      b. Yoko-ga   [Hiromi-ga   [Asako-ga   kaita] genkoo-o
          Yoko-Nom Hiromi-Nom Asako-Nom wrote draft-Acc
          kakinaoshita] shorui-o   yonda.
          rewrote   paper-Acc read
          "Yoko read the papers that Hiromi rewrote based on the draft Asako wrote."

Sentence (16a) contains one relative clause while (16b) has two relative clauses, creating the center embedding structure (as the clausal brackets indicate). This processing difficulty appears to be related to the complexity of the structure and memory. For accounts of the processing difficulty, see Gibson (1991), Babyonyshev and Gibson (1995), R. L. Lewis (1996), and Uehara (1997).

3.3   Empty pronouns

There are different kinds of empty categories. Recall sentences (14a) and (14b) and consider them with (17).

(14) a. Mari-ga   [e] yonda.
          Mari-Nom   read
          "Mari read (it)."
      b. [Mari-ga   [e]$_i$ yonda] hakusho$_i$-wa omokatta.
          Mari-Nom   read   report-Top heavy was
          "The report which Mari read was heavy."

(17) a. Mari-ga   kyoo-no   shinbun-o   yonda.
          Mari-Nom today-Gen newspaper-Acc read
          "Mari read today's newspaper."
      b. [e] kyoo-no   shinbun-o   yonda.
              today-Gen newspaper-Acc read
          "She read today's newspaper."
      c. [e] [e] yonda.
                  read
          "She read it."

A relative clause contains an empty category (or a gap) that is associated with the head noun. This is shown in (14b). In addition to this type of the empty category, there is another type as seen in sentence (14a). This empty category is not coindexed with anything. Its reference is taken extrasententially, unlike the empty category in the relative clause. For instance, suppose the context for (14a) is like (17a). When it is clear what Mari read, the object may be unpronounced as in (14a). This empty object is pronominal in nature and called an empty pronoun (often written as pro). Japanese allows such empty pronouns in both the subject and the object positions as is demonstrated in (17b) and (17c).[15]

In order to observe the complexity that empty pronouns raise, consider the sequence in (18a) and possible structures (18b) through (18h).

(18) a.   John-ga   Mary-ni   ringo-o . . .
          John-Nom Mary-Dat apple-Acc
      b.   [John-ga   Mary-ni   ringo-o   (ageta]).
          John-Nom Mary-Dat apple-Acc (gave)
          "John (gave) Mary an apple."
      c.   [John-ga   Mary-ni   ringo-o   (Bill-ga   Sue-ni
          John-Nom Mary-Dat apple-Acc (Bill-Nom Sue-Dat
          orenji-o   ageta]).
          orange-Acc gave)
          "John (gave) Mary an apple (and Bill gave Sue an orange)."
      d.   [John-ga   [[[e]$_i$ Mary-ni   ringo-o   (ageta] kodomo$_i$-ni]
          John-Nom   Mary-Dat apple-Acc gave   child-Dat
          orenji-o   ageta]).
          orange-Acc gave
          "John (gave an orange to the child who gave) Mary an apple."
      e.   [John-ga   [[e] Mary-ni   ringo-o   (ageta] to   itta]).
          John-Nom   Mary-Dat apple-Acc gave   that said
          "John (said that he gave) Mary an apple."
      f.   [[e] [John-ga]   Mary-ni   ringo-o   (ageta] to   itta]).
                John-Nom Mary-Dat apple-Acc gave   that said
          "(He said that) John (gave) Mary an apple."
      g.   [John-ga   Mary-ni   [[e] ringo-o   (katta]   to   itta]).
          John-Nom Mary-Dat   apple-Acc bought that said
          "John (told) Mary (that he bought) an apple."
      h.   [John-ga   Mary-ni   [[e] [[e]$_i$ ringo-o   (katta]   kodomo$_i$-ni]
          John-Nom Mary-Dat   apple-Acc bought child-Dat
          orenji-o   ageta] to   itta).
          orange-Acc gave   that said
          "John (told) Mary (that he gave an orange to the child who bought) an apple."

The sentences in (18) maintain the basic word order and all share the sequence (18a). (18b) is a simple monoclausal sentence. (18c) is a coordinate structure. (18d) shows a relative clause in which the empty category is coindexed with the head noun. (18e) through (18g) contain complement clauses, but (18e) and (18g) differ depending on what type of verb follows *ringo-o*. In these sentences, the empty categories are empty pronouns. (18h) also shows another possible relative clause structure containing two empty categories, one of which is an empty pronoun and the other of which is an empty category that is coindexed with the incoming head noun *kodomo*. The structures in (18b) through (18h) are only some of the possible structures which might occur when one or two verbs, with or without an empty category, appear in a sentence following the sequence (18a). Imagine how many possible structures must be postulated before the end of the sentence if the parser uses a strict parallel model. It would have to postulate an enormous number of logically possible structures for the portion of (18a) shared by (18b) through (18h). Such a model would hardly account for Japanese sentence processing. See Mazuka (1991) on processing empty categories.

3.4   *Scrambling*

We have seen the head position and empty categories create potential problems to a parsing theory. According to Berwick and Fong (1995), empty pronouns and scrambling, in addition to the head position, provide even greater challenges to processing theories. So let us look at scrambling here. Observe the sentences in (19).

(19)   a.   John-ga   ringo-o   tabeta.
John-Nom apple-Acc ate
"John ate an apple/apples."
b.   Ringo-o   John-ga   tabeta.
apple-Acc John-Nom ate
c.   [$_S$ Ringo$_i$-o [$_S$ John-ga [$_{VP}$ [e]$_i$ tabeta]]]

Sentence (19b) is a scrambled counterpart of (19a): the order of the subject and the object is reversed. It has been argued that the structure of (19b) is reflected by (19c), which contains the empty category (i.e. trace) coindexed with the preposed object (cf. Saito 1985).

   Scrambling increases the structural ambiguity of the sentence. For instance, the following structure becomes possible for (18a) in addition to (18b) through (18h). In sentence (20), [t] indicates a trace (i.e. an empty category) of the scrambled element *ringo-o*.

(20)   [John-ga   Mary-ni   [ringo$_i$-o   (Bill-ga   [t]$_i$ katta]   to   itta])
John-Nom Mary-Dat apple-Acc   Bill-Nom   bought that said
"John (told) Mary (that Bill bought) an apple."

Scrambling takes place in the complement clause in (20). Even when *Bill-ga* is read after *ringo-o*, there is no guarantee that the sentence ends like (20) because of the possibility of (18c). Now we can clearly understand why strict serial, delay, and parallel models all have difficulty accounting for Japanese sentence processing.

Although we have mentioned that scrambling creates ambiguities, Yamashita (1997a) claims that the parser is tolerant of scrambling. In a self-paced reading experiment, she found no extra processing load in reading scrambled sentences. In addition, no effect of word order was found on the parser in making syntactic decisions before reaching the verb in the experiment with the lexical decision task. On the other hand, the parser seemed sensitive to Case marking, identifying the grammatical functions of the parsed elements (see also Yamashita 1997b). These results suggest that what we predict theoretically seems different from the empirical findings.

Another interesting experimental finding on scrambling is presented in M. Nakayama (1995). The author reports that scrambled elements do not seem to create traces at the level of representation where empty categories (anaphorically dependent elements) access their antecedents. This finding is different from other types of empty categories such as empty pronouns and NP-traces (cf. M. Nakayama 1990, 1991). If scrambling does not leave a trace, the structure of (19b) is not reflected by (19c) and it suggests that as long as the verb and its arguments are linked together, the order of the arguments does not matter. We will come back to this issue in section 3.6 below (also see Prichett and Whitman 1995 and Ichio 1997).

3.5   Garden path effects and parsing models

If scrambled sentences do not create an extra processing load, the head-final characteristic and empty categories still seem to challenge the parsing theories that have been proposed based on English. Although English-based parsing theories predict processing difficulties in Japanese, the predicted difficulty is often undetected in online experiments. However, some sentences are found to be difficult to process. We now turn the discussion of sentences with different degrees of difficulty (i.e. garden path effects). First, let us consider Nagata's (1993) sentences with giving and receiving verbs (i.e. *kureru* and *ageru/yaru*). For giving and receiving verbs, for instance, see Kuno (1973) and Tsujimura (1996b). The *kureru* sentences were originally considered as garden path sentences by Mazuka et al. (1989).

(21)   a.   Koochi-ga   kantoku-ni   hinansareta toki   bengoshite kureta.
            coach-Nom   manager-by   criticized was when defend   gave
            "When I was blamed by the manager, the coach spoke up for me."
       b.   Koochi-ga   kantoku-ni   hinansareta toki   bengoshite yatta.
            coach-Nom   manager-by   criticized was when defend   gave
            "When the coach was blamed by the manager, I spoke up for him."

The sentences in (21) are the same except for the last verbs, *kureta* in (21a) and *yatta* in (21b), but their interpretations are very different as their translations indicate. Their rough structures can be shown with the brackets as in (22).

(22) a. [Koochi-ga [[e] kantoku-ni hinansareta toki] [e] bengoshite kureta]
       b. [[Koochi-ga kantoku-ni hinansareta toki] [[e] [e] bengoshite yatta]]

Both sentences require two empty pronouns, but what these refer to differs due to the nature of the verbs. *Kureru* requires the referent of its object noun to be "in-group," i.e. the speaker or someone related to the speaker, while *ageru/yaru* does not. Therefore, the two empty pronouns are interpreted as the speaker in (22a) while the empty subject and object are interpreted as the speaker and the coach, respectively, in (22b). The postulation of these empty categories and their interpretations become possible only when the parser reaches the verbs *kureta* and *yatta*. Assuming online serial processing, the preferred structure of *Koochi-ga kantoku-ni hinansareta toki* is that of (22b). Thus, (22b) is considered as the non-garden path control sentence. In Nagata's experiments, the subjects were asked to identify the subject of the verb (either *hinansareta* or *bengoshite*), which was presented after the end of the sentence with different intervals. The higher error rate was observed in the garden path sentences such as (21a) even when the verb was presented four seconds after reading the sentences. That is, (21a) is more difficult to parse than (21b). It was also found that the parser was not able to immediately reconstruct the previous syntactic structure, requiring a certain period of time to reach a final decision. Although this was Nagata's interpretation of the results, he himself questions whether this kind of experimental task reveals the nature of syntactic processing. We will return to this issue in the next section, but for now, suffice it to say that making the subjects answer such questions seems to tap into offline semantic processing, not online syntactic processing. If this is indeed correct, then it is difficult to estimate what degree of difficulty *kureru* sentences create in online syntactic processing.

Mazuka and Itoh (1995) discuss different degrees of reanalyses in garden path sentences.[16] For instance, the sentences in (23) are examples of noncostly reanalysis while (24) and (25) exemplify costly reanalysis. A costly reanalysis here means that a different structural analysis must be taken and the change from the old structure to the new one involves difficulty for the parser.

(23) a. [Hiroshi-ga   [[e]$_i$ Masao-o   mita] otoko$_i$-o . . .
            Hiroshi-Nom   Masao-Acc saw   man-Acc
            "Hiroshi . . . the man who saw Masao . . ."
       b. [Hiroshi-ga   [[e]$_j$ [[e]$_i$Masao-o   mita] otoko$_i$-o
            Hiroshi-Nom   Masao-Acc saw   man-Acc
            yobidashita] onna$_j$ . . .
            called   woman
            Hiroshi . . . the woman who called the man who saw Masao . . ."

(24) a. [Yooko-ga   kodomo-o koosaten-de   mikaketa]
          Yoko-Nom Child-Acc intersection at saw
          "Yoko saw the child at the intersection."
      b. [Yooko$_i$-ga   kodomo-o [[e]$_i$ [e]$_j$ koosaten-de mikaketa]
          Yoko-Nom Child-Acc   intersection saw
          takushii$_j$-ni noseta
          taxi-Dat   put-on
          "Yoko put the child in the taxi which she saw at the intersection."

(25) a. Mukoogawa-o [osu-to   mesu]-no   nihonzaru-no shashin-ga . . .
          over there-Acc male and female-Gen monkey-Gen picture-Nom
          ". . . the picture of the male and female monkey . . . over there . . ."
      b. [[e] Mukoogawa-o osu-]to mesu-no   nihonzaru-no shashin-ga
          over that side-Acc push if female-Gen monkey-Gen picture-Nom
          demasu
          appear
          "If you push the other side, the picture of the female monkey
          appears."

(23b) requires reanalysis after creating a structure like (23a). The parser needs
to construct an additional relative clause. However, since *Masao-o mita otoko* is
intact, the revision is not costly. On the other hand, (24b) requires reanalysis
from the simple clausal structure (24a) to the relative clause structure with two
empty categories. Since *kodomo-o mikaketa* is not intact, it is costly. Sentences in
(25) involve lexical ambiguity. *Osu* is taken as the noun "male" in (25a) but as
the verb "push" in (25b). Because of the different categories, the lexical homonyms create a costly reanalysis.[17] See Mazuka et al. (1997) on the experimental
results of the lexical homonym sentences.

   Although the question of how garden path effects differ must be determined
experimentally, let us assume different degrees of processing load in the above
garden path sentences. Those differences must be explained by the parsing
model. As we discussed in the previous section, a strict serial model fails to
differentiate the different degrees of garden path effects (cf. deterministic models
in M. P. Marcus 1980 and Berwick and Weinberg 1983; but see M. P. Marcus,
et al. 1983 and Weinberg 1995 for different kinds of deterministic models).
Neither a strict delay model nor a strict parallel model can account for the
different degrees of garden path effects. A. Inoue's (1991) and A. Inoue and
Fodor's (1995) Ranked Flagged Information Paced Parser as a serial processing
model and Prichett's (1988, 1991, 1992) Head-Driven Parser as a delay model are
all modified models that account for Japanese data, but they are by no means
problem-free. Mazuka and Itoh (1995) employ a serial model with a tentative
attachment strategy and attempt to explain the different degrees of the effects.
That is, each node attachment is temporal during the structure building process
(cf. Yamashita 1994). All of these models attempt to explain the different garden

path effects, but it is not clear how each precisely calculates the cost for each of the garden path sentences considered.

A different approach is taken in Fodor and Inoue's (1994) Diagnosis Model. It suggests that the recovery from the garden path consists in repairing the structure that was built rather than reparsing the input. In order to repair it, the parser must diagnose its error. If the error is clear from the nature of the symptom (i.e. if the error signaled by the incoming word is incompatible with the structure built), recovery is easy and less costly. This model assumes that the first- and the second-pass parses do not differ fundamentally, but revision difficulty varies depending on the symptom. Consider the following "double relative" sentence (originally from A. Inoue 1991: 71).

(26) Mary-ga   shinseihin-o   kaihatsushita amerikajin-ga
      Mary-Nom new product-Acc developed   American-Nom
      keieishiteiru mise-ga   tsubureta.
      be running   shop-Nom went bankrupt
      a. "*Mary, the shop which the American who developed the new
          product runs went bankrupt."
      b. "The shop which an American runs, where Mary developed the new
          product, went bankrupt."

Sentence (26) means (26b). The (26a) interpretation is not possible. However, the first reading one takes is (26a). This shows a severe garden path effect. The parser starts building the sentence structure from the first word and when *amerikajin-ga* is reached, it reanalyzes the previous clause *Mary-ga shinseihin-o kaihatsushita* as the matrix subject (*Mary-ga*) and a relative clause (*shinseihin-o kaihatsushita*) modifying *amerikajin*. Furthermore, *shinseihin-o kaihatsushita amerikajin-ga keieishiteiru* becomes another relative clause that modifies *mise*. However, this structural analysis fails when the parser faces *tsubureta*. This verb is an intransitive verb, taking *mise* as its subject. Now *Mary-ga* is left out. It cannot be attached to anything. This is the reading (26a). Since it is not a possible interpretation, the parser tries to find another way.

The difficulty of (26) suggests that building a coordinate structure or raising a relative clause appears to be costly. However, it is not always so, suggesting that raising operations are not inherently costly for revisions. Consider the following sentences from Fodor and Inoue (1994: 423).[18]

(27) Oosama-ni-taishite burei dearu kokkai-giin-ni-taishite   burei dearu
      king-Dat-against   rude is   diet-member-Dat against rude is
      otoko-ga   okotta.
      man-Nom became angry
      a. "The man who was rude to [the member of parliament who was
          rude to the king] became angry."
      b. "The man [who was rude to the member of parliament] (and) [who
          was rude to the king] became angry."

(28)   Oosama-ni-taishite burei dearu kokkai-giin-ni-taishite-mo   burei
       king-Dat-against   rude is   diet-member-Dat-against also rude
       dearu otoko-ga   okotta.
       is   man-Nom became angry
       a.   ??"The man who was rude to [the member of parliament who also
            was rude to the king] became angry."
       b.   "The man [who was rude to the member of parliament] (and)
            [who also was rude to the king] became angry."

Sentences (27) and (28) are different in that (28) contains *mo* "also" after *taishite*
"against." These sentences have basic structures comparable to that of (26) (i.e.
two relative clauses). Sentence (27) is ambiguous, but (28) is not. This suggests
that changing from the relative clause analysis to the coordinated relative
clause analysis is not inherently difficult. Then, why is (26) difficult? Fodor
and Inoue claim that it is because detecting the symptom is difficult. In (28),
there is *mo*, which is a symptom that allows the parser to diagnose the problem. Therefore, it is easier to reanalyze (28) than (26), which does not contain
an apparent symptom. The idea that the presence or absence of the symptom
(i.e. positive or negative symptom) affects the reanalysis is crucially different
from other models. This diagnosis model predicts that revision difficulty can
vary with the symptom. See also Hirose and Chun (1998).

3.6   Filler-gap sentences

Sakamoto (1991, 1995a, 1995b, 1996, 1997c) investigates Frazier et al.'s (1983)
Most Recent Filler (MRF) strategy in Japanese control sentences (cf. English
(5b)).[19] According to this strategy, a detected gap (an empty category) is initially
and quickly taken to be coindexed with the most recent potential filler during
comprehension. And in such a case, the parser does not recognize the empty
category as a possible antecedent (the Lexical Fillers Only hypothesis, hereafter
LFO). MRF and LFO make interesting predictions when applied to Japanese.
Let us consider their predictions in two types of Japanese control sentences
used in Sakamoto's experiments.

(29)   a.   Toshio$_i$-ga   ototoi   Junko-ni [PRO$_i$
            Toshio-Nom the day before yesterday Junko-Dat
            Tookyoo-iki]-o   tegami-de hakujooshita.
            Tokyo going-Acc letter-by   confessed
            lit.   "The day before yesterday, Toshio confessed to Junko by mail
                   that he would go to Tokyo."
       b.   Jiroo-ga   senshuu Kazumi$_i$-ni [PRO$_i$ Tookyoo-iki]-o
            Jiroo-Nom last week Kazumi-Dat   Tokyo going-Acc
            denpoo-de   tanonda.
            telegram-by requested
            lit.   "Last week, Jiroo requested of Kazumi by telegram that she go
                   to Tokyo."

Sentences (29a) and (29b) are Subject and Object control sentences, respectively. The empty subject PRO of the nominal clause *Tookyoo-iki* is obligatorily interpreted (i.e. controlled) as the same referent as the subject in (29a) and as the object in (29b). That is, the person who goes to Tokyo is Toshio (the matrix subject) in (29a) but Kazumi (the matrix indirect object) in (29b).[20] In these sentences, the MRF strategy predicts that Junko and Kazumi will be the fillers of the gaps (PROs) because they are the closest fillers to the gaps in (29a) and (29b), respectively. If the MRF strategy is employed, (29a) evokes an incorrect answer to the question, "Who is supposed to go to Tokyo?"

Next, let us consider the scrambled counterparts.

(30) a. Junko$_i$-ni Toshio$_j$-ga ototoi   [t]$_i$ [PRO$_j$
          Junko-Dat Toshio-Nom the day before yesterday
          Tookyoo-iki]-o   tegami-de hakujooshita.
          Tokyo going-Acc letter-by   confessed
          lit. "The day before yesterday, Toshio confessed to Junko by mail
                that he would go to Tokyo."

      b. Kazumi$_i$-ni Jiroo-ga   senshuu [t]$_i$ [PRO$_i$ Tookyoo-iki]-o
          Kazumi-Dat Jiroo-Nom last week   Tokyo going-Acc
          denpoo-de   tanonda.
          telegram-by requested
          lit. "Last week, Jiroo requested of Kazumi by telegram that she go
                to Tokyo."

(30a) and (30b) are scrambled counterparts of (29a) and (29b), respectively. The MRF strategy predicts that either Toshio and Jiroo or traces of Junko and Kazumi will be the fillers of PROs. Since the LFO hypothesis says that empty categories (traces) do not become potential fillers, only Toshio and Jiroo can be the fillers. Then, only (30a) evokes the correct answer to the above question. Because of scrambling, Japanese offers an interesting test to evaluate the MRF strategy and the LFO hypothesis.

Sakamoto presented these types of sentences and asked native subjects to name the person who was supposed to be in Tokyo as soon as they finished listening to them. He measured the time from the presentation of the end of the sentence to the voice onset. He found that their response times for Subject control sentences consistently were longer for both scrambled and unscrambled sentences. This means that scrambling had no effect. If the MRF strategy and the LFO hypothesis are correct, (30a) should not take longer than (30b).

Oda et al. (1997) and Ninose et al. (1998) used Sakamoto's test material with the dichotic listening task and found the opposite results. In their experiments, the subjects were requested to push either a yes or a no button after listening to the name of the person who was supposed to be in Tokyo. The response times for the Object control sentences were longer than those of the Subject control sentences for both scrambled and unscrambled sentence types. There were no scrambling effects in these studies, either.

In Frazier et al. (1983), the subjects were instructed to read the test sentences presented one word at a time on a cathode ray tube (CRT), and at the end of the sentence, they were required to answer whether they understood the sentence ("got it") or whether they had to go back and reread it ("missed it"). Their response times and the percentages of the sentences that were successfully understood were computed. Their experimental task was different from those of Sakamoto, Oda et al., and Ninose et al. Therefore, it may be possible that these different experimental tasks brought different results. In particular, Sakamoto's elicitation task seems to appeal more to semantic processing than to syntactic processing because the subjects must say the person's name instead of choosing yes or no as in Oda et al. and Ninose et al. The comparison of Mazuka et al. (1989) and Nagata (1993) also suggests that the elicitation task seems to tap on much deeper processing (not online syntactic processing). Since it is not clear what experimental tasks are appropriate for the aspects of processing one attempts to investigate, I leave my definite interpretation of the above findings on the Japanese filler-gap sentences for future research (cf. Walenski and Sakamoto 1997). However, their results at least suggest the following: (i) the MRF strategy and the LFO hypothesis seem incorrect, (ii) scrambling has a null effect, and (iii) different tasks bring different results.

Note that the above finding on scrambling is very important. Despite different experimental tasks, no scrambling effects were found in either experiment. As we discussed earlier, scrambling was assumed to increase the structural ambiguity and the processing load for the parser. However, the findings from these experiments as well as M. Nakayama (1995) and Yamashita (1997a) suggest that scrambled sentences are not processed differently from unscrambled sentences. This is an important finding for a theory of a universal human language processing mechanism. However, we must remember that this finding comes from the optional scrambling of sentences without any prior context. That is, short-distance (or clause-internal) scrambling in those sentences does not change the grammaticality or the meaning of the sentence. Therefore, to confirm the present finding, it is necessary to investigate cases in which scrambling changes the grammaticality and the meaning of the sentence as well as cases in which there is a discourse.[21]

4   Concluding Remarks

I have discussed various topics in the field of Japanese processing in this chapter. In lexical processing, I discussed lexical access by different script forms, *kana* and *kanji*. The current finding suggests that a correct lexical access model must allow for the dual processing of both characters. However, there remain many unanswered questions: how is lexical access in isolation different from that in a sentence? Does it bring any orthographic differences? Most of the previous experiments dealt with words in isolation. Therefore, it is important to find out how lexical access differs in isolation from that in a sentence. In this context, we also need to investigate how phonetic and semantic priming affect lexical access (see Ainsworth-Darnell 1998). In particular, semantic priming at the word level and at the sentence level would shed some light on how lexical access is done in a sentence. The question of how *kanji*'s visual lexical access differ from that of other symbols allows us to see the mechanism of visual perception and lexical access. When word familiarity is controlled, is there any difference in the response time of the lexical decision task in terms of the numbers of moras and characters? Can we obtain the same kind of results with different experimental tasks? Answers to these questions would bring us a better understanding of how lexical access works and the structure of the lexicon in our brains.

In sentence processing, we discussed different characteristics of Japanese that would bring processing difficulties to the strict serial, parallel, and delay parsing models theoretically. Given different degrees of garden path effects in Japanese sentences, a correct model must be one of those models with some modification. It must also account for differing degrees of difficulty. In relation to this, one must explore a theory of memory as well. There has been a claim that the source of the processing difficulty lies in memory (e.g. R. L. Lewis 1996). Therefore, the parsing mechanism together with the limitation of memory may possibly create differing degrees of difficulty. In addition, various studies find that there seems to be no difference between scrambled and unscrambled sentences. This is a very important finding in that it has a direct implication for a theory of grammar, assuming the transparency hypothesis, namely, that there is no trace of a scrambled element in the relevant structural representation. If one denies the transparency hypothesis, then one must answer the question of how the grammar and the processing mechanism interact. I have also discussed filler-gap sentences, in which I could not conclude how the control sentences are processed. Conflicting experimental results derived from different tasks in control sentence studies suggest that we need to find out what aspects of grammar a particular task is relevant to.

Finally, my discussion of sentence processing was limited to syntactic processing. This is because literature on semantic and pragmatic aspects of sentence comprehension and production is extremely scarce (cf. M. Walker et al. 1994). Therefore, keeping the above questions in mind, more experimental studies must be carried out which address different aspects of processing. Then, future research would certainly provide a much better understanding of how the language faculty is organized and how it functions (cf. Mazuka and Nagai 1995 and Sakamoto 1997a).

NOTES

*   I would like to thank Julie Boland, Yuki Hirose, Scott Langton, Rick Lewis, Tsutomu Sakamoto, Rumiko Sode, James M. Unger, Hiroko Yamashita, and especially the editor of this book, Natsuko Tsujimura, for commenting on the earlier version of this chapter. Any shortcomings are, of course, mine.

1   For a general history of processing theories in relation to the development of linguistic theories, see Carlson and Tanenhaus (1989) and Frazier (1991).

2   Note that the first two example words in (3) have regular readings, "konnichi" "these days" and "kooyoo" "red leaves/autumn colors." The third word, however, does not have another reading, though the meanings of the characters are "big" and "person."

3   When two *kanji* are combined to form a word, the possible reading patterns are four as shown below. In (ia), for example, both characters are given the Chinese readings; and in (ic), the first character has the Chinese reading while the second has the Japanese reading.

(i)   a.   Chinese–Chinese reading
           古書 (kosho) "old books"
      b.   Japanese–Japanese reading
           古里 (furusato) "hometown"
      c.   Chinese–Japanese (Juubako-yomi)
           本箱 (honbako) "book shelf"
      d.   Japanese–Chinese (Yutoo-yomi)
           古本 (furuhon) "used book"

4   See also M. Paradis et al. (1985). For involvement of the right hemisphere in semantic processing of *kanji*, see Aoki (1990).

5   As for *kanji* phonology, see Wydell et al. (1995) and for the relationship between the experimental tasks and results, see Gashuu (1994) and Hino and Lupker (1996).

6   As for the *kanji* familiarity, Amano and Kondo (1995) and Kondo and Amano (1996a) report that word familiarity ratings depend on the least familiar *kanji* in the word, and Kondo and Amano (1996b) claim that the familiarity ratings are correlated very weakly with the physical complexity of *kanji*. However, they found that the more complex *kanji* tend to be less familiar *kanji*. See also Kondo et al. (1996).

7   Their results need to be compared with those of the lexical access experiment that tests the same words in isolation.

8   Due to space limitations, I cannot discuss these models in detail here. Readers are encouraged to read the original papers cited in the text. However, very roughly speaking, the logogen model is the model that contains a feature recognizer (i.e. logogen) which represents various linguistic information (e.g. semantic and syntactic information) of a word, and it attempts to capture the different characters with the same feature specification. The search model contains one lexicon with the master file and three peripheral files: one organizing words by orthographic properties, one by phonological properties, and one by semantic and syntactic properties. Darnell (1995) points out that this model fails to account for the contextual bias. The connectionist model explains lexical processing via the activation of different nodes such as orthographic, phonemic, and semantic nodes, which have multiple levels of nodes that are all linked in a network. The information flows on the basis of how frequently the connection is used between the nodes. Thus, different accessibilities to particular information are explained.

9   For other research on orthography and lexical processing, for example, see Koda (1990), Wells (1995), and Chikamatsu (1996).

10 There are very few studies on production. See N. Iwasaki et al. (1997).

11 Mazuka's (1998) work is very important in that it addresses the relationship between the processing mechanism and how children shape their grammar. What is the initial state of the processing mechanism? When children do not have adult grammar or when they are formulating grammar, how do they use their parser? What kind of interaction do the processor and the grammar have? These are all serious questions to be answered by the theory of parsing. Although Mazuka attempts to answer these questions, it is not clear to me how her proposal works in detail. See also Weinberg (1993, 1995), Gorrell (1995), and A. Inoue and Fodor (1995), and N. Hasegawa's (1990) comments on Mazuka and Lust (1990).

12 See Yamashita (1994), Hirose and Chun (1998), and Hagstrom and Rhee (1997) for processing Korean relative clauses.

13 Note that the noun does not indicate number, either. This is observed in (11). There are some plural suffixes that can attach to nouns (e.g. *boku* vs. *boku-ra* or *boku-tachi*), which are only used with nouns that refer to people. However, these are not pure pluralizers as discussed in Tsujimura (1996b: 156 fn. 2) and S. Martin (1975). That is, one can say *Tanaka-tachi*, which means a group of people including Tanaka.

14 Although their precise structures may not be like those in (13), the point is clear in that the relative clause structure requires more nodes than the ditransitive structure.

15 Although there are other kinds of empty categories (e.g. PRO, NP-

traces in passives and *wh*-traces in *wh*-questions), we will not go into them here. However, one of them (PRO) will be discussed in Section 3.6. Note that though there are different types of empty categories, there are a couple of characteristics that are common among them. One is that their existence becomes clear by information carried by other elements in the sentence. For instance, an empty pronoun is detected when one reads a transitive verb with one overt argument. It becomes clear by the verb's subcategorization. Thus, they are inferred indirectly. Another characteristic is that they all have their antecedents. They are referentially dependent elements (i.e. anaphoric expressions). For empty categories and sentence processing, see Fodor (1989).

16 As the word 'reanalyses" indicates, they assume a serial processing model. However, I am not certain if they consider that the parser repairs the previously built structure or the parser discards the structure built, but keeps it in memory as the unwanted structure and forces itself to construct another structure by reparsing the sentence.

17 If (25) is presented orally or *osu* is written in *kanji*, the lexical ambiguity does not occur in (25) because *su* in *osu* "male" is accented and written as 雄 or 牡 while *osu* "push" is unaccented and written 押す.

18 Fodor and Inoue's original examples did not contain -*ga* after *otoko*, which might be a typo.

19 By testing the MRF strategy in the control sentences, Sakamoto was also investigating the degree of transparency in the relationship between the mental grammar

and performance theory
(i.e. Transparency Hypothesis).
According to this hypothesis, the
grammar–parser relation is neither
equal nor independent, but is rather
transparent (e.g. Berwick and
Weinberg 1984). Although the
results did not support the MRF
strategy, they did not refute the
hypothesis, either.

20   Sentences in (29) are slightly
different from regular control
sentences. For instance, (29a) can
be paraphrased as follows.

(i)   Toshio$_i$-ga
      Toshio-Nom
      ototoi
      the day before yesterday
      Junko-ni [PRO$_i$
      Junko-Dat
      Tookyoo-e iku koto]-o
      Tokyo to   go fact-Acc
      tegami-de hakujooshita.
      letter-by   confessed
      lit. "The day before yesterday,
            Toshio confessed to Junko
            by mail that he would go
            to Tokyo."

This sentence contains a clause
with the Subject controlled PRO.
If it does not contain the temporal
phrase *ototoi* "the day before
yesterday," the scrambled
sentence will cause the following
ambiguity.

(ii) a. Junko$_j$-ni Toshio$_i$-ga [t]$_j$
          [PRO$_i$ Tookyoo-e iku koto]-
          o tegami-de hakujooshita.
          "Toshio confessed to Junko
          by mail that he would go
          to Tokyo."
      b. [e] Junko-ni [Toshio-ga
          Tookyoo-e iku koto]-o
          tegami-de hakujooshita.
          "Toshio confessed to Junko
          by mail that he would go
          to Tokyo."

Sentence (iib) indicates that the
sentence is not a Subject control
sentence since there is no PRO in
the embedded clause. Because of
this ambiguity and the fact that
the number of temporal phrases is
limited, the scrambled counterparts
of the regular control sentences cannot
be tested. This is why Sakamoto
uses nominal clause sentences.
However, he did test the sentences
with full clauses such as (i) in one
of his experiments. See Sakamoto
(1995c, 1997b) on the nature of
Japanese control sentences.

21   Having said this, I realize that it is
sometimes difficult to test these
cases because of the lack of
appropriate experimental control
sentences against which those
scrambling sentences can be
contrasted. See Ichio (1997) on the
acceptability test of long-distance
scrambling sentences.

15 Discourse Analysis and Pragmatics

SENKO MAYNARD

One tends to simplistically think that the speaker is in the center of place, and the place passively receives the effect from the speaker. But this view is contrary to how the place of talk functions. The speaker is the one influenced by place; place is acting and the speaker is receiving. The place influences, and in fact defines, the speaker. Speaker does not merely speak "in" the place; the speaker is defined "by" the place.

Mio 1948: 21, my translation

0 Introduction: Definition and Organization

Discourse analysis is usually defined in two related ways. First, discourse analysis examines linguistic phenomena of real-life communication beyond the sentence level. Second, discourse analysis views functions of language as primary rather than its form. These two aspects are emphasized in two different books (both bearing the title *Discourse Analysis* and published in 1983). Stubbs (1983: 1) aligns with the first position by saying that discourse analysis refers "mainly to the linguistic analysis of naturally occurring connected spoken or written discourse" and it "attempts to study the organization of language above the sentence or above the clause." G. Brown and Yule (1983: 1) take the second position, stating that discourse analysis is "the analysis of language in use," and "it cannot be restricted to the description of linguistic forms independent of the purposes or functions which those forms are designed to serve in human affairs."

Although discourse analysis is notoriously broadly defined, embedded in even the fluctuating definitions are the insistence on analysis of naturally occurring language and a desire to understand the functions of language. Studies introduced in this chapter all adopt this position, although in differing varieties and degrees.

A note on the term "discourse" should be added here. I use this term in the broadest sense referring to a piece of written, spoken (including nonverbal) communication created in a particular sociocultural context. Although some linguists use the term "text" as synonymous with discourse, I use "text" primarily in reference to the written versions of communication. "Text" also appears in reference to past studies using this term in their theories (e.g. text linguistics and textual tie).

The basic tenet of discourse analysis and pragmatics (and other humanistic/ social research such as sociolinguistics) notably fills in the gap created by formal analysis dominating the field of linguistics since 1960s. Given the current academic milieu of postmodernism, however, to view language as socially situated – both being created in context and creating its context – and to view language as functioning in multiple ways in human cognition and connection seem to be more readily accepted today than ever before. The history of linguistics is rife with contests between obedient and rebellious students. Shifts from American behaviorism to Chomskyan formalism and on to humanistic paradigms seem to follow this inevitable cycle of academic dissent followed by new insurgent moves challenging the now-established former rebels.

This chapter is organized as follows. In section 1, I trace the theoretical sources in the West as well as in Japan that form the background for contemporary discourse analysis and pragmatics research on Japanese. Then, sections 2–4 divide the research effort into three related agendas: discourse structure, language in fact-to-face interaction, and functions of language in discourse. These three concerns reflect some of the key issues of discourse analysis – discourse organization, discourse as interactional event, discourse as language in use, discourse functions, and discourse as being both context-defined and context-defining.

I should add that this chapter touches upon only a limited number of studies in Japanese discourse analysis and pragmatics, primarily focusing on publications available in English. Accelerated developments in Japanese discourse studies conducted in Japan in recent years are not included; the reader is encouraged to consult *Gengo*, *Nihongogaku*, *Nihongo Kyooiku*, and other scholarly journals for additional information concerning current discourse-related research.

The study of discourse structure in Japanese is limited at this point, but the research within contrastive rhetoric has produced interesting results. Research in face-to-face interaction in Japanese has proliferated in recent years and it offers a fertile ground where one can begin to ask the question of how language interacts with culture and society as well as with the identity of self and other. Conversation analysis in Japanese has revealed many ways in which language plays a role in giving meaning to human interaction and vice versa.

The third agenda, examination of language's functions, has been the interest of many linguists with varied theoretical backgrounds. Although discourse researchers are not the only group of scholars pursuing this path, functions on the level of discourse have become the territory charted by discourse researchers. Many of the Japanese language phenomena – thematic *wa*, connectives, interactional particles, to mention a few – function not only within a sentence, but across and beyond sentences in critical ways.

Since discourse analysis and pragmatics incorporate varied views, perspectives, and methods for analyzing data drawn from varied genres, under the heading "functions of language in discourse" I introduce six areas of research with different methodological orientations. The study of discourse function is inherently pragmatics-oriented, and research in Japanese pragmatics has become an important ingredient in Japanese discourse studies.

After reviewing past and current research activities, in section 5 I share some of the concerns and hopes of discourse analysis and pragmatics in Japanese. As a researcher one needs to reflexively ask the rationale for conducting one's own research. Accordingly, I hope to provide some answers, if only to raise more meaningful questions.

1   Background

1.1   *Theoretical sources*

Discourse analysis and pragmatics in Japanese as we see them today can be traced back to several of the linguistic schools in both the West and Japan. One of the most important is the Prague School, whose work has influenced both European and Japanese contemporary discourse analysis. Earlier studies of Japanese grammar by Kuno (1972a) and my own work on the theme marker *wa* (Maynard 1980), for example, have been influenced by the Praguean concept of functionalism (especially Functional Sentence Perspective) which has necessitated the study of Japanese beyond the sentence.

In Europe, text grammar emerged in the 1970s (e.g. van Dijk 1972) and so did text linguistics in the early 1980s (e.g. Beaugrande and Dressler 1981), though, in retrospect, they produced only limited results. Text grammar influenced by generative grammar was unable to account sufficiently for nonformal aspects of text, and text linguistics seems to have suffered from awkwardness stemming from complex network models. Perhaps more influential is the functional systemic grammar led by M. A. K. Halliday. Halliday and other linguists who find text analysis their main interest (e.g. Halliday and Hasan 1976, P. H. Fries 1983, J. R. Martin 1992) have continued analyzing primarily English texts and produced (often pedagogically) useful results.

Two key concepts that emerge in analyzing discourse are "cohesion" and "coherence." "Cohesion occurs when the interpretation of some element in the discourse is dependent on that of another" (Halliday and Hasan 1976: 4). Cohesion is usually limited to the connection (or textual tie) that can be traced through some surface forms. Accordingly, Halliday and Hasan (1976) list the following five types of cohesion: substitution, ellipsis, reference, conjunction, and lexical cohesion. This surface-dependent view of cohesion has become the target of criticism (e.g. G. Brown and Yule 1983). Interpretation of text requires more than mere surface connection; it depends on the reader's broad-based knowledge of how things work, including presupposition, analogy, and logical relations. This knowledge outside the text itself is "coherence." Halliday and Hasan (1976) did not fully discuss coherence, although they suggested that text requires "macrostructure of the text that establishes it as a text of a particular kind" (1976: 324).

More recently, Halliday and Hasan (1989) discuss the concept of "cohesive harmony" where similarity chains and identity chains displaying different ties of cohesion are displayed, and coherence is identified in the way chains are developed and interconnected. Beaugrande and Dressler (1981) take a broad view of text comprehension and include cohesion and coherence as members of seven criteria for textuality (cohesion, coherence, intentionality, acceptability, informativeness, situationality, and intertextuality). Scholars such as J. E. Martin (1992) and Renkema (1993) adopt these criteria for defining and analyzing discourse.

In the United States, the field of sociolinguistics has offered a place where traditional ethnomethodology, anthropology, and sociology are embraced and their views toward language and their analytical frameworks welcomed. Although the interests of ethnomethodologists, anthropologists, and sociologists do not lie in the analysis of language *per se*, many studies (e.g. Goffman 1955, 1981, Sacks et al. 1974, Gumperz 1982a, 1982b) influenced future conversation analysis (and what later came to be called "interactional sociolinguistics").

Issues that have attracted ethnomethodologists' attention include the system of turn-taking, cases of other- and self-repair, the concept of adjacency pair (such as greeting–greeting, question–answer), and the idea of conditional relevance (certain utterances are relevant because they offer what is preferred and expected in the current interactional sequencing).

Out of this context, Tannen (1984) offers a new direction in the study of conversation with a greater attention given to linguistic expressions and strategies. Tannen (1984) microanalyzes extended conversational discourse and identifies an overall conversation style called "high-involvement style." Using interview data, Schiffrin (1987) analyzes chunks of verbal interaction by focusing on discourse-segmenting devices. Rather than identifying conversational style as evidenced in turn-taking and narrative participation as Tannen (1984) does, Schiffrin (1987) concentrates on the analysis of discourse markers (connectives and interjections such as *because, well,* and *I mean*) in an interactional context. Like a series of Tannen's works (1984, 1989), Schiffrin's works (1987, 1994) continue to influence contemporary discourse analysis in the United States, including their students who conduct research on Japanese discourse.

More recently, the study of discourse in Europe has focused on socially and politically significant data, such as political debates, mass media, and professional discourse. Critical discourse analysis, as it is called, refers to a special approach to the study of text and talk, with an aim of discovering discourse structures and strategies of dominance and resistance in social relationships (of class, gender, ethnicity, race, sexual orientation, religion, age, nationality, etc.) (van Dijk 1995).

1.2 Japanese traditional studies

Although researchers of Japanese discourse outside Japan (or trained outside Japan and currently working in Japan) have generally followed theoretical frameworks similar to those mentioned above, it is important to recognize that the Japanese *bunshooron* (in a broad sense resembling discourse analysis) has had a long tradition. In fact *bunshooron* had become a serious concern to Japanese language scholars by the late 1940s, as represented by Mio's work (1948). Mio (1948) emphasized the importance of *hanashi no ba* "place of talk," resonating with the tenet of contemporary sociolinguistics, discourse analysis, and pragmatics. It was Tokieda (1950), however, who endorsed language study beyond the level of sentence in his book on Japanese grammar.

Unfortunately, Tokieda (1950) fails to provide actual analysis of text, and despite his aspiration, Japanese *bunshooron* (as Tokieda envisioned it) did not come into existence. In fact in his next significant work on *bunshooron* titled *Bunshoo Kenkyuu Josetsu* (1977 [1960]), the idea of *bunshooron* becomes somewhat muddled. As indicated by the title *bunshoo kenkyuu*, the contents of this book resemble those earlier studies of *kokugogakusha* (national language studies scholars), concentrating on the interpretation of classical literature. Despite the lack of vigorous textual analysis, Tokieda's ideas of how *bunshoo* should be viewed and studied within his theory of language (i.e. *gengo kateisetsu* "theory of language as process") offer inspiration and motivation.

Following but going beyond Tokieda (1977 [1960]), in a series of publications, Nagano (1972, 1986, 1992) proposes what he refers to as *bunpooronteki bunshooron* (grammar-based discourse analysis). Nagano approaches Japanese discourse (mostly written text taken from school textbooks) from three perspectives, i.e. *rensetsuron* (connection), *rensaron* (chaining), and *tookatsuron* (organization). For example, Nagano makes explicit discourse development (*tenkai*) through the chaining of predicate types based on Mio's (1948) *genshoobun* "sentences of immediate description" and *handanbun* "sentences of judgement."

Recent developments in the study of Japanese discourse include Kaneoka (1989), Sakuma (1981, 1992), and Morita (1995), among others. Briefly, Kaneoka (1989), using the narrative voices of *The Tale of Genji*, analyzes the author's three different positions – observer, teller, and narrator. Sakuma (1981, 1992) uses the discourse unit *bundan* (or *dan*) for the interpretation of discourse. Sakuma points out that one understands the thread of discourse (*bunshoo no bunmyaku*) more accurately and efficiently by noting the connection between *bundan* rather than noting the connection between sentences. Morita (1995) emphasizes the importance of understanding the perspective the language user takes toward the description, and analyzes strategies (e.g. Japanese tense shift and connectives) as a marker of perspective. These three research directions offer significant insight into discourse studies in the West, i.e. narrative voice, discourse units, and discourse functions.

Given the general background mentioned above, research in Japanese discourse analysis and pragmatics continues to grow and change. In the following three sections, I discuss some of the prominent issues the field has concentrated on in recent years.

2   Discourse Structure

The earliest effort in Japanese discourse structure outside Japan is offered by Hinds in his 1976 book. Using what he calls the "reticulum" model, Hinds schematically displays how both written and spoken discourse samples are structured. This schematic model combines the top-down hierarchy for topic development and the linear approach for showing participants in conversation by plotting them along the performative line, story line, and event line.

In his 1983 article Hinds shifts his focus on the structure of expository writings within the field of contrastive rhetoric. Arguing against Kaplan's (1972) work, which has spurred the field of contrastive rhetoric ever since, Hinds analyzes the *Tensei Jingo* column and argues that Japanese rhetorical structure in expository discourse differs from that of English in that it follows the traditional *ki-shoo-ten-ketsu* principle.

More recently, again using *Tensei Jingo* and its English translation as data, Hinds (1990) contrasts expository writings in Japanese, Chinese, Thai, and Korean and concludes that these writings follow an organizational pattern of "quasi-inductive." In quasi-inductive discourse, (i) the thesis statement appears in the final position, (ii) the presentation of the writer's purpose is delayed, (iii) pieces of information contained in the writing are related loosely to a general topic, and (iv) the concluding statement does not necessarily tightly follow the direction of the preceding statements.

English readers usually assume deductive discourse, and if that assumption fails, they will assume that the discourse follows the inductive process. "[I]nductive writing is characterized as having the thesis statement in the final position whereas deductive writing has the thesis statement in the initial position" (Hinds 1990: 89). Hinds (1990) further suggests that the purpose of writing in Japanese may sometimes be simply to introduce a set of observations related loosely to a general topic, leaving a rather heavy burden for readers who are to evaluate those observations on their own terms.

Some empirical evidence supports Hinds's view, one example of which is Kobayashi (1984). On the basis of an examination of 676 writing samples written by 226 Japanese and American students, Kobayashi reports the following.

US students use the general-to-specific rhetorical sequencing, while Japanese students in Japan show a tendency to follow the specific-to-general sequencing. Japanese ESL (English as Second Language) students studying in the US follow a style somewhere between these two sequencing preferences.

Kubota's (1992) analysis of ESL discourse offers an interesting critical view. Kubota compares expository and persuasive essays of both American and Japanese students, incorporating how the writers themselves evaluate their own writings. Although some Japanese ESL students use Hinds's quasi-inductive style, they intimated that they actually prefer (in fact evaluate highly) the deductive style. Students reportedly learned to devalue the Japanese style writing for being ambiguous, roundabout, illogical, digressive, and so on. Kubota points out that students' judgments reflect the West's hegemony over Japanese rhetoric, endorsed, in fact, by Japanese people through the superiority/inferiority complexes they experience in the modernization process. These complexes are in part results of social, political, and academic relations of power within and between Japan and the West.

Discourse structure is a topic whose serious study has only begun. Since strategies of discourse organization are expected to differ from one genre to another, and from one communicational mode to the next, much more attention is required in the future. Other studies that discuss sequencing of information in discourse include Honna (1989), Nishilhara (1990), and Maynard (1996b).

3 Language in Face-to-Face Interaction

3.1 Conversation analysis

Linguistics-oriented analysis of face-to-face interaction began with the publication of Tannen's (1984) book. Using a tape-recorded Thanksgiving dinner conversation as data, Tannen identifies "conversational style," which broadly includes linguistic expressions and interaction-managing strategies. Tannen's analytical steps are: (i) tape-recording of conversation, (ii) transcription, (iii) observation and analysis of data, (iv) hypothesis, (v) incorporation of input from conversation participants and others, and (vi) verification of hypothesis. After observing the New York Jewish style (called the machine-gun question) and analyzing how it functions in narratives, Tannen characterizes this conversation style as "high-involvement style."

Given that Tannen's study concentrates on a particular occasion of talk (a single event of conversation with multiple participants including Tannen herself), in my own work (Maynard 1986, 1987a, 1989b, 1993b) I examine multiple Japanese (and American English) conversations by using video- and audio-taped casual conversations (20 pairs of Japanese and 20 pairs of American) among college students. Both qualitative and quantitative methods are used for analysis, and both global and local levels of structure and conversation management are investigated. From the global perspective I examine thematic structure by focusing on strategies such as mode of reference and repetition which help structure the interaction-based themes of conversation. I also analyze narratives appearing in the data and show that the narrative is emergent in the conversation, and it is co-created by both story teller and story recipient. Focus is placed on interactional management strategies, turn-taking, back-channeling, and head movement. Functions and frequencies of these interactional behaviors are identified and discussed, and it is emphasized that all are significant in structuring the self-contextualization processes of Japanese interaction.

In general, conversation analysis adopts the analytical method developed by ethnomethodologists. Rather than sentences or utterances, conversation analysis considers primary the units of interaction (e.g. turns, back-channels) and their sequencing in conversation. Particularly useful are related concepts of adjacency-pair, conditional relevance, and preference organization. Interaction in conversation is locally organized as a connected pair, such as a question followed by an answer. This expected preferred sequencing of action (i.e. one example of preference organization) creates a place in the conversational sequence where a certain response becomes relevant. Thus, conditional relevance means that "given the first, the second is expectable; upon its occurrence it can be seen to be a second item to the first; upon its non-occurrence it can be seen to be officially absent – all this provided sheerly by the occurrence of the first item" (Schegloff 1968: 1083). The concept of sequenced and situated action is the key for analyzing conversational interaction.

In recent years, some aspects of Japanese conversation have continued to be investigated. One of the topics often discussed (especially in Japan) is the back-channel. For example, Kita (1996) elaborates on back-channel-like utterances jointly sent by participants during the inter-turn pause. Ikeda and Ikeda (1996) offer a descriptive system in which different degrees of head nods as well as the duration of eye gaze are plotted along with the transcript, making it easier to describe both verbal and nonverbal behavior.

Another topic in conversation analysis involves the phenomenon of co-construction. Conversation researchers have often emphasized the collaborative nature of utterance production in English (e.g. conversation as "achievement" as explained by Schegloff 1982). Following this line of inquiry, Ono and Yoshida (1996) investigate co-construction in Japanese informal conversation. It turns out that the co-construction of syntactic units is rare in Japanese, perhaps leaving the collaboration strategies to means other than syntax.

3.2   Specific interactional context

Analysis of face-to-face interaction in Japanese has also led to the investigation of specific situations of talk. Three areas in particular have produced interesting results – business negotiation, conflict situation, and the invitation-refusal process.

H. Yamada (1990, 1992) examines communication strategies used in Japan–US business discourse. On the basis of tape-recorded multi-party conversations of American, Japanese, and American–Japanese business meetings, Yamada contrasts topic-opening strategies, talk distribution, and back-channel strategies across these settings. Using the idea of "cross-talk," Yamada analyzes data by adopting interpretive, comparative, and quantitative methods.

According to H. Yamada (1990, 1992), in cross-cultural business communication Japanese and Americans optimize different cultural strengths – the Japanese strength is shown in the group and the American strength in the individual. For example, "American participants take long monologic turns, distribute their turns unevenly among participants, and take the highest proportion of turns in the topics they initiate; Japanese participants take short turns, distribute their turns relatively evenly among participants, and continue to distribute their turns evenly regardless of who initiates a topic" (1990: 271). Yamada's study illustrates the difficulties arising from cross-cultural talk where meaning-in-context is created in the mutually interactive context of culture, encounter and conversation.

Jones (1990, 1992) examines how Japanese people linguistically handle conflict situations. Using audio- and video-taped conversations between friends and acquaintances, Jones identifies occasions of conflict and microanalyzes three such conversations – television debate, father–daughter conflict in a family, and office communication between co-workers. Jones (1990, 1992) reports that Japanese conflicts often occur in "ratified" situations, and when the conflict is not socially ratified, participants must work hard to ratify it.

A case in point: after a few minutes of strained conversation the co-workers in conflict abruptly stopped talking and turned away from each other. But even under this circumstance, participants strove for a playful tone, introducing laughter and jokes. Co-workers placed the conflict situation into a framework of "play" by using strategies such as style-switching, repetition, parallelism, and laughter. If the conflict is still not ratified after all reframing strategies, Jones (1990: 306) concludes that "it seems . . . impossible for the participants to dispute with each other comfortably," suggesting that perhaps the Japanese themselves have bought into the "myth of harmony."

Szatrowski (1992, 1993) concentrates on the Japanese invitation and refusal interaction taken from recorded telephone conversations, and offers detailed analysis of 13 conversations of invitation. Using the concept of *wadan*, similar to *bundan*, Szatrowski shows that, instead of simple adjacency-pair, Japanese invitation-refusal negotiation is enacted by the invitation *wadan* stage and the response *wadan* stage, which may take several turn exchanges.

Szatrowski (1993) reports that when compared with the English invitation-refusal exchange, Japanese participants rely more on their co-participants in the conversation, which results in co-produced stages. For example, Szatrowski (1992, 1993) provides interaction examples in which an invitee, whose goal may be to refuse, leaves open the possibility of accepting while developing the conversation toward a refusal. A Japanese inviter will go through several "invitation stages;" he or she shows sympathy for the invitee by always leaving some option for a refusal. In the invitee's "answer stages," he or she gradually develops a story, always gauging the inviter's response, trying to convince the inviter that he or she cannot accept the invitation after all. Through this prolonged give-and-take negotiation process, both participants successfully avoid losing "face" (Goffman 1955).

The three studies mentioned above represent analysis of real-life conversation with related but differing contributions – insight into cross-cultural communication, language understood within a larger interactional frame (e.g. play), and the use of discourse units (e.g. *wadan*) for understanding the meaning of utterance clusters.

4   Functions of Language in Discourse

Researchers in Japanese discourse and pragmatics have identified varied functions in various genres of contemporary Japanese. Since methodological frameworks vary, this section develops around major methods along with example representative research. I must point out that topics covered in the following are limited and I do not mean in any way that those studies omitted here are insignificant.

4.1   *Conditions and effects in discourse: thematic marker* wa

Japanese *wa* has been extensively studied in Japan and elsewhere. Earlier research on Japanese *wa* within Western linguistics tradition was conducted by Kuno (1972a). Kuno (1972a), appealing to the Praguean concept of given/new information and the Functional Sentence Perspective, offers four hypotheses regarding *ga* and *wa*, two of which are particularly relevant. Hypothesis 1 states that "-*[g]a* as subject marker in matrix clauses always signals that the subject conveys new information" (1972a: 296), and hypothesis 4 states that "[t]he thematic NP-*wa* in the subject position in embedded clauses becomes NP-*ga* obligatorily" (1972a: 296). Since then Japanese *wa* and *ga* have been associated with given and new information, and are understood to be theme marker and subject marker, respectively.

Examination of *wa* in discourse, however, reveals that the concept of given/new information by itself cannot adequately explain the use (thematization) and nonuse of *wa*. In my own work (Maynard 1980, 1987b), I contrast how characters are marked in similar narratives. For example, in the beginning of Japanese old tales, *Momotaroo* and *Urihimeko*, the "old woman" is marked first by *ga* and consequently by *wa* in the former, but the "old woman" continues to be marked by *ga* in the latter.

Observe data (1) and (2). The data are presented in English; Japanese particles *wa* and *ga* are inserted immediately following the phrases (that are underlined) marked by these particles. (The original Japanese version is available in Maynard 1987b.)

(1) a. Once upon a time there lived <u>an old man and an old woman</u> (*ga*).
     b. Now, it happened one summer day.
     c. <u>The old man</u> (*wa*) went to the mountain to collect firewood.
     d. "See you later."
     e. <u>The old woman</u> (*wa*) saw the old man off,
     f. and (said), "Well, I'll go to the river to get some washing done,"
     g. and went out to the river carrying a washing tub.
     h. Scrub, scrub, scrub.
     i. <u>The old woman</u> (*wa*) worked hard washing clothes.
     j. After a while, something came floating down the stream. (Tsubota 1975: 24)

(2) a. Once upon a time there lived <u>an old man and an old woman</u> (*ga*).
     b. One day <u>the old woman</u> (*ga*) went to the river to do the washing.
     c. From upstream, two boxes approached floating down the stream.
     d. They came bobbing down the river.
     e. Seeing this, <u>the old woman</u> (*ga*) called out,
     f. "Hey, the box filled with things, come this way! Empty boxes, go away from me!"
     g. The box with content approached her.
     h. So the old woman picked it up and returned home.
     i. That evening when the old woman opened the box with the old man, a cucumber came out of the box. (Tsubota 1975: 18)

In (2c) and (2e), despite the fact that "the old woman" appears as given information, it continues to be marked with *ga*. This cannot be explained by Kuno's (1972a) hypotheses, since *ga* is shown to mark given information (as well as new information) in matrix clauses.

Methodologically, the following steps are taken: (i) paragraphs in which relevant linguistic devices appear are contrasted, (ii) distributional differences are identified, (iii) in order to solve the inadequacies of available models, a new framework/perspective is introduced, (iv) other cases are examined to find out if the proposed framework adequately explains the use and nonuse. In this process one is able to discover the conditions in which relevant linguistic devices appear as well as the related effects these forms bring to discourse.

Concretely, after identifying different ways in which characters are thematized and nonthematized, I conclude that the *wa/ga* marking strategy, although often coinciding with the given/new distinction, involves more than the given/ new status of information. I present the concept of "staging" strategy through which the narrator expresses his or her perspective toward the narrative event. The narrator places the thematized participants on the stage for a longer period of time, and consequently thematized characters provide points of reference for the development of the thematic flow. Thematized participants remain activated, evoked, and stored in the reader's consciousness, and they provide a flow of thought to which new and unexpected information may be integrated along the way. The examination of thematization in the unit larger than sentence has led to the new understanding of the thematic *wa* unavailable otherwise.

4.2   *Information and action in conversation: connectives* **dakara** *and* **datte**

Studies of Japanese connectives reveal the importance of analyzing linguistic devices in interactional context. The traditional view of connectives as logi- cally connecting clauses has been shown to be untenable once conversations are examined. The methodology adopted here is that of conversation analysis, especially the idea of conditional relevance. This is most clearly presented in Schiffrin's (1987) analyses of discourse markers which include English connec- tives *and, but, or, so, because*, and *then*.

In my own work (Maynard 1989a, 1992b, 1993a), I analyzed the use of Japanese connectives *dakara* and *datte* in casual conversation and in dialogues of fiction. *Dakara* in [X. *dakara* Y] connects discourse segments [X] and [Y] in that [X] provides semantic and/or interactional reason for [Y]. *Dakara's* function connecting the cause/result semantic relationship is limited to approximately 63 percent in conversation and 87 percent in fiction dialogues, respectively. Elsewhere, *dakara* functions as a marker for explanation related to [X], the turn claim and the turn yield, as well as repetition of already mentioned information.

Datte in [X. *datte* Y] signals that the speaker intends to justify position [X] in the context of opposition/contrast. The "but" and "because" readings usually associated with *datte* are then explained in terms of the turn-taking context (if [X] is the position taken across turns, "but" reading; if [X] is within the turn, "because" reading).

Japanese connectives in conversation have been analyzed by more than a few scholars since. For example, Mori (1994) examines *datte* in multi-party con- versation and concludes that *datte* is used across speakers in collaboration when they together face a third party. On such an occasion, a speaker employs *datte* as a device for displaying alignment with another speaker, while dis- agreeing with the third party. Karatsu (1995) contrasts connectives *dewa, dakara*, and *shikashi*. Karatsu reports that *dakara* functions to (i) add an explanation and (ii) reiterate what the speaker has mentioned previously, while *dewa* (i) paraphrases, (ii) introduces a new topic, or (iii) summarizes the previous discourse, and *shikashi* interrupts the conversation and initiates the topic's conclusion in a certain context. Other studies on Japanese connectives include Takahara (1990) and Hudson (1996).

These functions of connectives are not semantic (or logic-based) but inter-action-related. Herein lies the importance of examining linguistic devices in conversational interaction, which allows identification of functions otherwise unexplained.

Another interesting piece of research on Japanese connectives takes a historical perspective. Onodera (1993), on the basis of analysis of Japanese spanning over 1,200 years – from *Kojiji, Noo,* and *Kyoogen* scripts to *Shinjuu ten no Amijima,* to conversation segments from modern novels (such as *Ukigumo* and *Yukiguni*) and present-day conversation – explores the pragmatic change that conjunctions (*demo* and *dakedo*) and interjections (*ne* and its variants) underwent. According to Onodera, changes in these connectives and conjunctions roughly follow the direction from ideational, to textual, and to more expressive. Her findings confirm Traugott's (1982) hypothesis on semantic change, i.e. less to more personal. The understanding that language foregrounds different aspects of meaning through time offers insights to diachronic discourse analysis.

4.3   Between grammar and pragmatics: clause chaining and complex noun phrases

Some of the studies that fall under Japanese pragmatics and discourse analysis explore the theoretical boundaries of where grammar and discourse interact. Often these studies aim to explain traditionally unexplainable grammatical process by appealing to pragmatic concepts. Two such studies are introduced here; S. Iwasaki's (1988, 1993) analysis of *te* and *tara* clause connection and Yoshiko Matsumoto's (1989a, 1993) analysis of complex noun phrases.

S. Iwasaki (1993), using the concept of the switch reference (whether or not the subject of the following clause is the same as that of the current clause), explains the choice between *te* and *tara* clause chaining. Iwasaki appeals to the concept of "speaker subjectivity" in discourse and introduces the "perspective principle," which distinguishes two types of speaker subjectivity, S-perspective (speaker describes own experience) and O-perspective (speaker describes the other person's experience). After statistically examining *te* and *tara* appearing in 16 personal narratives, Iwasaki concludes that *te* is used when the first person continues to be the subject in the next clause, *tara* when the subject changes in the next clause, i.e. *tara* marks the shift from S- to O-perspective (this also involves change from a higher to a lower degree of information accessibility). For example, observe (3) taken from S. Iwasaki (1993: 61).

(3)   soshite hairenakute, okoshite, de hai . . . haittara yakkosan moo . . . shikata
      nai ttena kanji-de nee
      and (I) couldn't enter (*te*), (I) woke him up (*te*), and (I) entered (*tara*), the
      guy, appearing annoyed, came (*te*)

   S. Iwasaki (1993) finds the perspective principle to be relevant for the selection of internal state predicate forms and tense forms as well. By contrasting *te*
and *tara* in discourse, and by appealing to the pragmatics-motivated concept
of perspective, Iwasaki explicates the grammar of Japanese clause chaining.
Statistical analyses accounting for the speaker's grammatical choice are included in the research design, shedding light on pragmatics/discourse-based
factors in grammar.
   Japanese complex noun phrases offer another problematic area, especially
in accounting for seemingly unexplainable ways of their production and use.
Unlike English, Japanese relative clauses and noun complement constructions seem to more extensively involve pragmatics-based principles. Yoshiko
Matsumoto (1993) makes this point by analyzing commonly used Japanese
expressions such as *atama no yoku naru hon* "the book (by reading) which
(one's) head improves" from Fillmore's frame semantics. Matsumoto identifies
the condition for the Japanese complex noun phrases (i.e. her adnominal clauses)
in terms of the frame evoked by the clause. These frames (or scenes) offer a
pragmatic context in which the clause and the head noun can be appropriately
connected. This study again illustrates that grammatical structure is not ex-
plainable in terms of grammar alone. Instead it is determined by semantic and
pragmatic forces as well.

4.4   *Rhetorical effects and their sources: repetition*

Study of repetition in Japanese began in the early 1980s (Makino 1980, Maynard
1983), but interest in repetition among American discourse researchers in
the 1990s has added renewed impetus. M. Ishikawa (1991), analyzing a 30-
minute conversation among four students, concentrates on self-repetition and
allo-repetition of exact word(s) within the same turn or in the immediately
following turns. Functions of repetition are identified as intensity, iteration,
and continuation (for self-repetition), and as joint idea construction (for allo-
repetition).
   The significant point of Ishikawa's study is the iconicity she observes not
only of the linguistic sign of repetition – argumentation in form (i.e. repetition)
iconically represents argumentation of degree (intensity) – but also between
the form and interactional function. The latter is what Ishikawa refers to as
"interactional iconicity," which is supported by the iconic meaning of identification of the idea and stance toward that idea between participants (i.e.
self and other). The observed correspondence between form and interactional

meaning, along with many other studies on iconicity (e.g. Haiman 1985), offers evidence to refute the commonly accepted arbitrary nature of signs.

Nishimitsu (1990) contrasts repetition in Japanese writings and in their (multiple versions of) English translations. Although the original repetition is translated into English repetition to varying degrees, the closer to the semantic effect of Japanese original the translation is, the more repetition appears. Given the well-known tendency toward deletion, Nishimitsu raises the question of observed frequent repetition in Japanese, and speculates that the Japanese language's high dependency on context allows frequent deletion of various elements, and at the same time, leaves some room for repetition for the purpose of subjective emphasis.

Indeed, repetition and deletion are two sides of the same coin, and as Makino (1993) emphasizes, it is important to recognize positive reasons for repeating and deleting. It is not enough to find conditions for ellipsis; rather it is necessary to identify rhetorical effects of these strategies in discourse.

4.5 *Manipulating information across participants: sentence-final forms*

How sentences and utterances end in Japanese has caught discourse and pragmatics researchers' attention. Frequently studied are the interactional (sentence-final) particles and the nominal predicate (*no da, wake da*, etc.).

Ever since Tokieda (1951) advanced the idea that the fundamental function of sentence-final particles is *"taijinkankei o koosei suru"* "to form an interpersonal relationship," studies of particles have led to the expansion of analysis from the formal framework to the interpersonal expressive domain. In Tokieda's view, *ne* represents a subjective expression seeking to make the addressee a sympathizer, while *zo* and *yo* are expressions forcing upon the addressee the speaker's will and judgment.

In recent years, many scholars have analyzed the functions of interactional particles (e.g. Tsuchihashi 1983, Oishi 1985, Cook 1988). C. Kitagawa (1984) points out that *ne* marks the fact that the utterance is related to the second person, as opposed to *na* which is related to the first person, and *yo* marks the new information, as opposed to *sa* which marks old information.

Kamio (1979, 1990), on the basis of the "theory of the territory of information," summarizes the use of *ne* as the following: (i) *ne* is a marker for *kyoooooteki taido* "co-responding attitude," and the speaker actively encourages the listeners to adopt an identical cognitive state toward the relevant information; (ii) when the speaker assumes that the speaker and the listener possess the identical information as already learned information, the speaker's utterance must accompany *ne*; (iii) when the speaker especially wants to express a co-responding attitude by one's own expression, the speaker's utterance can be accompanied by *ne*; (iv) but *ne* cannot be used when the information provided by the speaker is more deeply involved with the speaker than it is with the listener.

While Kamio's study is based on the types of information status (within or outside of the speaker's and the listener's territory), Masuoka (1991) focuses more closely on the speaker–listener communication. Masuoka states that *ne* and *yo* mark the agreement and the opposition, respectively, of the inner (cognitive) world between the speaker and the listener. By this characterization, Masuoka explains why *yo* and *ne* can be used for both emphasis and softening purposes (*Mini kite kudasai yo.* vs. *Mini kite kudasai ne.*).

The information status and the speaker–listener alignment, however, are not the only ways the information across speakers plays a role in determining some use of *ne*. In my own work (Maynard 1993a, 1993b), I point out that *ne* and *yo* foreground different aspects of communication, interaction versus information. Observe the following conversation (taken from data collected for Maynard 1989b) where originally *yo* appears. *Ne* can appear instead – *Eh, uso, itte nai ne* – although this response is interpreted as an offensive or defiant answer.

(4)　A:　Okuyama ga itta n ja-nai no, are.
　　　　Didn't you, Okuyama, say that?
　　B:　Eh, uso, itte-nai yo. (Eh, uso, itte-nai ne.)
　　　　What, no, not at all, I didn't say that.

A similar question *Okuyama ga itta n daro?* can also be answered either affirmatively – *Aa, itta yo* or *Aa itta ne* – or negatively – *Eh, itte nai yo* or *Eh, itte nai ne.* In all these answers the use of *ne* adds the speaker's defiant attitude. This use of *ne* does not mark Kamio's co-responding attitude and in fact seems to violate its condition described under (4) above. This use of *ne* also does not align the speaker and listener with the sense of agreement as suggested by Masuoka.

Noting the complementary distribution of *ne* and *yo* in conversation (*ne* and *yo* followed by back-channels approximately 58 percent and 33 percent, respectively; followed by new turns approximately 31 percent and 45 percent, respectively), and introducing the scale of relative degree of information availability and accessibility between the speaker and the addressee, I propose (Maynard 1993a, 1993b) that *ne* and *yo* emphasize different aspects of communication (i.e. Discourse Modality), interaction versus information. In answer to a yes/no question, under normal circumstances information is to be foregrounded since that is something being sought. The use of *ne* fails to meet the expectation since it foregrounds the interpersonal feelings instead, and thus resulting in a disengaged interaction.

Researchers will continue investigating the functions of these and other particles in various interactional contexts. Such effort will also necessitate analyses of nominal predicates such as *no da* and *wake da* as well as other sentence-final complementizers (e.g. *koto*) and particles (e.g. *tte*). Other studies investigating sentence-final forms include McGloin (1983), Noda (1990), C. Kitagawa (1995), Okamoto (1995), and Maynard (1992a, in press).

4.6 Acquisition of pragmatic competence: directives and style shifts

Some aspects of Japanese discourse have been studied from the psycholinguistic perspective (especially first-language acquisition). Particularly significant is the role of language in the children's socialization process. For example, Clancy (1986) examines the mother's communicative style in socializing Japanese children into important cultural values. Based on examination of tape-recorded interactions between five mother–child pairs (children approximately two years old), Clancy (1986) concludes that Japanese mothers strongly emphasize sensitivity to the needs, wishes, and feelings of others through what Clancy calls empathy training and conformity training.

The mothers used indirect expressions for making and refusing requests toward two-year-olds. In fact some directives were extremely indirect; for example, in response to the child who said there was nowhere for him to write (on a piece of paper that still had some room), the mother said, *Omeme aru n ja nai* "You have eyes, don't you?" (Clancy 1986: 227). Mothers also incorporated direct instruction or "lessons" of how to use and interpret language.

The close observation of mother–child interactions has revealed a variety of directives used in communication, and more importantly, it has brought into the open how sentences such as *Omeme aru n ja nai* function as a directive in real-life communication.

Cook (1996) studies the language of the school and analyzes polite forms in the Japanese classroom. She finds that third- and fourth-grade teachers shift between *-masu* and plain forms, using *-masu* forms mainly when addressing the entire class to present important information and introduce class activities, and plain forms to address an individual child. The phenomenon of Japanese style and style mixing has been studied extensively (S. Martin 1964, Makino 1983, Maynard 1991, 1993a), but Cook's study documents in detail the classroom interaction and provides statistical results of the *masu* vs. plain forms used by the teachers. Cook also incorporates Rosenberger's (1989) modes of self, i.e. "disciplined" mode, and concludes that "*masu* form used in elementary schools indexes the disciplined mode of self, which is contrasted with the spontaneous mode indexed by the plain form" (Cook 1996: 79). Again, as in Clancy's study, close observation of interaction has led to an understanding of the interactionally regulated style shifts in Japanese.

5 Discourse Analysis: Concerns and Directions

As is made evident by the preceding discussion, discourse analysis and pragmatics adopt data-based analyses. Language is not out there *a priori*; it is given life when used in real human communication. Consequently it becomes important to investigate language in use in interaction and in context, and to build the kind of theory answerable to whatever we find. I maintain that observation of data – and the more of it the better– must be the starting point for linguistic research. Moreover, its theoretical and analytical adequacy must ultimately be evaluated against the data.

The relationship between data and theory in linguistics has evolved through different stages in the latter half of the twentieth century. During the 1950s and early 1960s, observation of data was considered a virtue; in the 1970s, linguists avoided the criticism of being "data-centered;" and in the 1980s, critics complained that there was simply too much theory in linguistics. Today, data and theories seem to go hand in hand; and we witness a variety of interpretive theories thriving in the field.

The instantiation (that is, the utterance) of language is observable, whereas the system of language is not. The system lies somewhere unseen, hiding behind the data. And yet, the data, in turn, are not truly observable without evoking some system-based analytical framework. There is a certain amount of circularity involved in this relationship between data and analytical framework. And yet, the parts of the process – (i) data analysis, (ii) theory building, and (iii) discovering significance in the research – must go hand in hand, in a spiral of repeated inquiries.

Provided that the observation is guided by some emerging analytical framework, and provided that this framework is answerable to data, the results are expected to be meaningful. Obviously, one must not indulge oneself with *ad hoc* observations. Such observations are little more than a mass of unorganized facts, which contribute little, if anything, to our understanding of language and its use.

Yet, we must remain cautious not to be lured into a neat "theory" – however elegant and appealing it may be. Given that theory building sometimes involves ignoring certain aspects of real-life language phenomena, we must remind ourselves that what we discard along the way may turn out to be critical for understanding language.

The nature of meaning and function revealed through discourse analysis and pragmatics suggests that a theory of meaning must in some way be able to account for nonreferential semantics, interpersonal expectations, and discourse effects. Establishing a general theory to account for all these simultaneously is indeed a formidable, if not impossible, task. This is partly because once one rescues and (re)introduces the concept of the social person into the study of linguistics, his or her sociocultural diversity comes into play. Sweeping generalizations that were once possible at the expense of the obscured speaker now become almost impossible.

More to the point, the linguistic theory itself is conceived by each researcher bound by his or her time and space. Thus, ultimately theory building must be conducted in such a way as to answer possible diverse views toward language. Forcing a ready-made theory on another language can invite a distorted view of that language. Since researchers are products of different cultures and academic philosophies of the time, linguistic theories are themselves embedded within culture and society. For this reason, differing views toward language – including the view discussed in this chapter – ought to be considered fairly, with a mind toward openness.

And yet, studies of Japanese discourse have a long way to go. Serious studies in many subfields have only begun. The current trends in critical discourse analysis (representative works including van Dijk 1987, 1993, 1995, Fairclough 1989, Hodge and Kress 1993) offer potential for Japanese discourse (Maynard in preparation). Analysis of personal narrative has also been a major field of discourse analysis, and Japanese contribution in this field has only begun (see, for example, Matsuki 1995 and Kinjo 1996, in which the concept of a narrating self is explored). Ultimately, linguistic research must add to our understanding of how one understands oneself in relation to the other, that is, how language interacts with our concepts of self and society. Incorporating literary criticism is another potential approach in the analysis of Japanese discourse, especially quotation in relation to textual voices (Maynard 1996a).

Research in discourse analysis and pragmatics necessitates the understanding of the Japanese culture and society as context (e.g. Tokunaga 1988 and Maynard 1997, among others). Here, for understanding the Japanese language as a part of the cultural semiotic system, Ikegami's (1981, 1991) works are relevant. Ikegami notes the Japanese language's preference for describing events as "become"-ing (in contrast with English being a "do" language), and identifies a Japanese poetics of "become" not only in the language but in aesthetics, literature, and culture. Understanding language in this way may lead to the understanding of culture from the linguistic perspective. It is also true that through discourse analysis one appreciates that language (which is a part of culture) provides context for itself. Linguistic expressions sharpen the contour of context while the very context encourages the use of expected expressions, resulting in their reciprocal interaction (see Maynard in press for a case study).

As a final note I should point out that Japanese research in discourse analysis and pragmatics should not be an end in itself, and instead, it should develop a critical perspective that goes beyond discovering particularities of the Japanese language. Theories of language nurtured by analyzing Japanese should contribute to a general understanding of language and communication. One possibility lies in typological discourse analysis (Myhill 1992), in which certain parameters (e.g. referential distance, topic persistence) are used to examine discourse across languages. Still, generalizing universal discourse features requires discovery of parameters based on analysis of an individual language. Japanese discourse research is likely to put to the fore some of the features not prominently observed in other languages, thereby expanding the scope of parameters for achieving a fuller understanding of language universals and the nature of language in general.

16 Sociolinguistics: Honorifics and Gender Differences

SACHIKO IDE AND MEGUMI YOSHIDA

0 Sociolinguistics in Japan

This chapter focuses primarily on two issues of relevance for the discussion of sociolinguistics: i.e. politeness and gender issues. However, a short overview of sociolinguistics in Japan may prove useful, since scholars there developed research methods and programs distinct from the Western tradition.

Japanese sociolinguistics developed independently of the Western discipline. Research in this field started in 1949, when the National Language Research Institute was founded with the stated purpose of "doing scientific research on the Japanese language and on the speech behavior of the Japanese people in their daily lives, as well as establishing a solid basis for improving the Japanese Language" (article one of the legal document establishing the Institute).

The main interest of this research institution is concentrated on dialectology and *gengo seikatsu*, which could be literally translated as "language life," and by which is meant the study of speech behavior in daily life. Language varieties according to the speaker's regional background, social status, age, sex, and education are investigated. The aim of such study is to provide a total description of the speech behavior of the people in a community. This work serves to provide the scientific foundation for solving current language problems.

Large-scale projects on dialectology and *gengo seikatsu* have been completed. These projects are ordinarily conducted by choosing a community and collecting data from several hundred subjects picked by random sampling. Usually a team of 10 to 20 researchers and a number of assistants participate in a project, and various kinds of statistical analysis are applied to the data collected.

There is an assumption basic to Japanese sociolinguistics that language differs from individual to individual, rather than from group to group. Researchers do not begin their research by looking into the varieties of language used by people, but look for the factors which cause language varieties by analyzing the massive data reflecting an individual's speech behavior. This runs contrary to the assumption of sociolinguistics in the West, which investigates linguistic varieties while focusing on predetermined linguistic and social variables.

It has often been pointed out that, in the study of *gengo seikatsu* or dialectology, there are few attempts to construct theoretical frameworks as a basis for the design of the surveys, as is usual for sociolinguistic studies in the West. If individual Japanese surveys were based on theoretical frameworks or models, more general descriptions about local speech behavior could be achieved, and more general conclusions about communication patterns in Japanese could be drawn. Therefore, attempts to set up such original frameworks for the analysis of the Japanese language and society have to be undertaken. On the other hand, the Japanese approach to the study of language could make a contribution to the development of more encompassing theories for use by scholars in the West by providing multiple descriptions of analyzed data.

1 Politeness

Human interaction always has the potential to lead to conflict between the participants, and human behavior involves a variety of devices to avert these crises. A key concept at the heart of all of these devices is politeness, which is the speaker's consideration for the addressees in order to make communication among them smooth. Politeness is realized through various verbal and non-verbal devices, and this section discusses the verbal devices, termed linguistic politeness.

Linguistic politeness may be approached through the investigation of language use and of language expressions.

1.1 The aspect of language use

There are two modes for the realization of the aspect of language use: *wakimae* (discernment) and volition.

1.1.1 Wakimae (*discernment*)

Wakimae (the closest equivalent term in English is discernment) refers to behavior based on socially expected norms. In Japanese society, all speakers are expected to assess and acknowledge their sense of place in relation to both the situational context and the social context.

This acknowledgment of one's sense of place in relation to the situational context involves the participants' interpersonal relationship and the formality of the situation. The interpersonal relationship is affected by the social and psychological distance between the participants. Various factors such as differences in age, status, and power and the degree of intimacy all play a role in determining social and psychological distance. The speaker's sense of belonging, which is realized as the categorization of the addressee/referent into *uchi* (in-group) or *soto* (out-group), also relates to social and psychological distance. This sense of belonging goes beyond formal group memberships, and the speaker recognizes *uchi* or *soto* whether the addressee or referent belongs to an actual group such as a company or circle or not. In other words, *uchi* refers to a sense of a close relationship, as with people who belong, in some sense, to the same group, whereas *soto* refers to a sense of a more distant relationship. The speaker uses language to acknowledge both a sense of place in the situational setting, in concordance with the social and psychological distance between participants, as well as the formality of the situation.

The speaker's acknowledgment of the sense of place in relation to society as a whole is reflected through self-presentation. People evaluate their place in society in terms of their age, status, role, gender, ethnicity, culture, and regional background. The speaker's self-presentation is related to a concern for demeanor. Through language use according to *wakimae*, the speakers are able to present themselves as well-demeaned persons in the society.

Social convention requires that a speaker manifests an acknowledgment of this sense of place in relation to the situational context and the society through the choice of linguistic expressions. *Wakimae* in Japanese society means people's discernment of their own place.

This behavior according to *wakimae* can be considered polite behavior for two reasons. One reason stems from the speaker's observation of the socially expected norms. This behavior puts the addressee at ease, since it establishes that the speaker will not threaten the addressee. Furthermore, the observation of the common norm creates an atmosphere of sharedness with the addressee. Therefore, behavior according to *wakimae* functions as a realization of politeness.

1.1.2   Volition

The second mode of linguistic politeness is the volitional use of expressions. This can be described as the use of a strategy to achieve politeness. Speakers use strategies intentionally in order to allow their messages to be received favorably by the addressee. Unlike language use according to *wakimae*, language use according to volition allows the speaker's creative use of strategies toward the addressee.

Language use according to volition forms the core of linguistic politeness, particularly in Western societies. This perspective comes from the basic assumption in Western societies that speaking is the realization of the speaker's intention. Speech act theories (Austin 1962, Searle 1969, 1975) and conversational maxims (Grice 1975) are established on this tacit assumption, which we call here the speaker's volitional use of language. It is in this context that *wakimae* is proposed as the other type of speaking by Ide (1989). In contrast to the volitional use of language, *wakimae* is not determined by volition.

being

Studies of politeness from a western perspective discuss the strategies to achieve politeness assuming the speaker's volitional use of language. P. Brown and Levinson's (1978, 1987) illustrations in their framework are all from the category of volitional strategies of politeness. On the basis of the concept of face wants and the idea that all human begins share them, Brown and Levinson present two kinds of politeness strategies: positive politeness and negative politeness strategies. Positive face wants are those relating to the need for approval or the establishment of a cooperative relationship, and are addressed by positive politeness strategies. Negative face wants have to do with the need not to feel hindered, pressured, or coerced, and are addressed by negative politeness strategies. In addition to these two kinds of politeness strategies, the strategy of "off record" should also be counted as a strategy of politeness. Speakers plan their language behavior so as to realize their intention of maintaining the face of both participants. Thus, language use according to volition means the speaker can make an active choice of expressions from an almost unlimited range of possibilities to achieve the desired politeness. *Creativity?*

1.1.3 The relationship between the two modes of politeness; wakimae *and* volition

Both language use according to *wakimae* and language use according to volition are modes of behavior employed to achieve politeness. The speaker focuses on prescribed social norms in the former behavior, but on the intention in the latter. While the goal is the same in both cases, the means to achieve it are different. *Wakimae* is oriented toward the need for acknowledgment of the positions or roles of all the participants as well as adherence to the prescribed norms of formality appropriate to the particular situation. Volition, on the other hand, is oriented toward the need to maintain the face of all the participants.

Weber's typology of human actions and its reformulation by Habermas (1982) provide a useful framework for the discussion of these two modes of language use. According to Weber (1972), human actions can be classified into four categories and these are characterized by their degree of rationality. Habermas (1982) added a two-dimensional mode of action: action oriented to success, that is, strategic action, and action oriented to understanding, that is, communicative action. The relative positions of language use according to *wakimae* and volition in this framework are as in figure 16.1.

Language use according to volition is an example of strategic behavior in which the speaker intentionally chooses the most effective means to achieve politeness, and this is considered to be the most rational action. This behavior reflects (1) instrumental-rational action, which is determined by consciously calculated attempts to attain the desired ends by the choice of appropriate means. On the other hand, language use according to *wakimae* is motivated by the observation of socially expected norms, and is considered to be non-rational action. This behavior reflects the least rational and most communicative action, (4) traditional/conventional action, which is determined by ingrained

非理性好行等。 ?

Degree of rationality \ Mode of action	Strategic (oriented to success)	Communicative (oriented to understanding)
Rational	*Volition* (1) instrumental-rational (interest)	(2) value-rational (value)
Nonrational	(3) affectual (drive/feeling)	*Discernment* (4) traditional (convention)

Figure 16.1 Framework incorporating *wakimae* and volition in terms of Weber's typology of actions and its reformulation by Habermas
Source: Ide 1989: 232

habituation. Weber's other two categories of human action are (2) value-rational action, which is determined by a conscious belief in the intrinsic value of acting in a certain way, and (3) affectual action, which is determined by specific affects and feeling status. In addition to *wakimae* and volition, there may well be other modes of language use employed in other language to achieve politeness which could fall within these categories.

1.2   The aspect of language expressions

1.2.1   Language expressions used according to wakimae

Wakimae is realized through the choice of appropriate language expressions in concordance with the situational and social context. Because speakers are expected to show their acknowledgment of their sense of place in relation to the situational and the social context, the use of proper linguistic forms correspondent to the situations expresses the speakers' politeness according to *wakimae*. Formal forms are the representative linguistic expressions for manifesting politeness according to *wakimae*, because their use presupposes sociopragmatic concord with the situation.

Formal forms used according to *wakimae* are typically realized as honorifics. Every speaker has a sense of place *vis-à-vis* the addressee or referent, and this place is acknowledged through the use of the appropriate linguistic forms, honorifics. Honorifics are linguistic forms to index the speaker's acknowledgment of this sense of place toward the addressee/referent. If honorifics are used, they index the deferential relations of the speaker, addressee, and referent. They constitute the core of the devices for linguistic politeness in Japanese and many other Asian languages as evidenced by the morphologically well-defined systems developed in these languages. In addition to honorifics, there are some formulaic and other expressions used according to *wakimae*.

Japanese honorifics are mainly of two kinds: one is expressed by means of changing the shape of nominal elements, and the other by predicative elements. Honorifics expressed by means of changing the shape of nominal elements are used to refer to people or objects. There are three types of honorifics which modify person referents: personal pronouns, names with titles, and professional ranks. In personal pronouns, *watakusi* is the honorific form of the first person pronoun, compared to the plain forms *watasi* for women's speech or *boku* for men's speech. In addition, *ano kata* (that person Ref Hon) is the honorific form to refer to the third person, while *ano hito* (that person) or *kare* (he) or *kanozyo* (she) are the plain forms.

The notable aspect of honorifics of personal pronouns is that there are no second person honorifics. *Anata*, the second person plain form, is not used to refer to the addressee to whom the speaker is expected to show deference. It is considered impolite to refer to a person toward whom deference is due by using pronouns in their presence. This is a conspicuous example of avoiding direct reference to the addressee, or that person's belongings or behavior, and constitutes an important characteristic of honorifics. Instead of a personal pronoun, the last name with title or professional rank is generally used in such cases.

Titles attached to names also have honorific expressions. There are varieties of these titles.

(1) LN/FN/kinship terms + *sama***
     (e.g. *Satoo-sama, Hanako-sama, otoo-sama* "father")
     LN/FN/kinship terms + *san**
     (e.g. *Satoo-san, Hanako-san, otoo-san*)
     LN/FN/ + *kun*
     (e.g. *Satoo-kun, Taroo-kun*)

(2) (LN) + *sensei*** (e.g. *Satoo-sensei*)
     (LN) + *senpai*** (e.g. *Satoo-senpai*)

(LN: last name; FN: first name. Asterisks show the honorific forms; two of them indicate a higher degree of honorification.) *Sensei* literally means a "teacher," and it is used for various high-status professionals such as doctors, politicians, and writers as well as ordinary teachers. *Senpai* literally means a senior colleague, and is used for senior colleagues in organizations.

Professional ranks are used independently or with last names.

(3) (LN) *syatyoo*   "president (of a company)"
     (LN) *senmu*   "executive director (of a company)"
     (LN) *butyoo*   "division chief (of a company)"
     (LN) *katyoo*   "department chief (of a company)"
     (LN) *gakutyoo*   "president (of a university)"
     (LN) *gakubutyoo* "dean (of a university)"
     (LN) *kyoozyu*   "professor"

These professional ranks and names with titles are used both as address terms and as nominal elements of sentences such as subjects or objects.

The honorific prefixes *o* or *go* are attached to nouns that refer to objects that are possessed or produced by persons who are worthy of the speaker's respect; for instance, *sensei no go-hon* "teacher's book," or *sensei no o-hanasi* "teacher's talk." *Go* is generally used with Japanese nouns derived from Chinese, while *o* occurs with other nouns.

Honorifics expressed by means of changing the shape of predicative elements can be divided into two types: referent honorifics and addressee honorifics. Referent honorifics occur when the noun phrases of a sentence refer to someone toward whom respect is due. Addressee honorifics occur when the speaker's respectful attitude toward the addressee is expressed.

Referent honorifics are further divided into two types: subject honorifics and object honorifics. The former represents the speaker's respectful attitude toward the subject referents, while the latter represents the speaker's humble attitude toward the object referents.

Subject honorifics are used when the subject noun phrase refers to a person toward whom the speaker is expected to show great respect. They involve the prefix *o* (*go*) and the ending *ni naru*, which is attached to the infinitive form of a verb. Only the prefix is attached when the predicate is an adjective or a nominal adjective, as in (5) and (6).

(4)   Satoo-sensei   wa eki   made o-aruki ni nat-ta.
      Satoo teacher(Title Hon) Top station to   walk Ref Hon Past
      "Professor Sato walked to the station."

(5)   Satoo-sensei   wa o-isogasii.
      Satoo teacher(Title Hon) Top busy Ref Hon
      "Professor Sato is busy."

(6)   Satoo-sensei   wa go-rippa-da.
      Satoo teacher(Title Hon) Top admirable Ref Hon Cop
      "Professor Sato is admirable."

In addition to this honorific form, there are a number of irregular or suppletive subject honorific forms. When verbals which consist of Japanese nouns derived from Chinese and the verb *suru* "do" undergo subject honorification, *suru* is supplemented by *nasaru*.

(7)   Satoo-sensei   wa go-ryokoo nasat-ta.
      Satoo teacher(Title Hon) Top travel Ref Hon Past
      "Professor Sato traveled."

The usual *o* (*go*) . . . *ni naru* form does not attach to some verbs. These verbs inflect idiosyncratically and need to be learned separately.

(8) iku   "go"   o ide ni naru
                         irassyaru
     iru   "exist"   irassyaru
     kuru   "come"   irassyaru
     miru   "see"   go ran ni naru
     iu   "say"   ossyaru

There is a productive subject honorifics verb ending beside *o . . . ni naru*. The suffix *(r) are* (homophonous with the passive suffix) may be attached to a verb to obtain a subject honorific.

(9) Satoo-sensei   ga   go-hon o   kak-are-ta.
     Satoo teacher(Title Hon) Nom Ref Hon book Acc write Ref Hon Past
     "Professor Sato wrote a book."

Along with subject honorifics, an adverb may be converted into an honorific form by the prefixes *o* and *go* when it modifies the activity of a person toward whom special respect is due.

(10) Satoo-sensei   wa o-hayaku   o-kaeri ni nat-ta.
      Satoo teacher(Title Hon) Top early Ref Hon return Ref Hon Past
      "Professor Sato returned early."

Another type of referent honorifics is object honorifics. Object honorifics occur in connection with nonsubject noun phrases. They involve the prefix *o* (*go*) and the ending *suru* attached to the infinitive form of a verb.

(11) Watasi wa Satoo-sensei   ni   sono wake o
      I   Top Satoo teacher(Title Hon) Dat that reason Acc
      o-tazune si-ta.
      ask Ref Hon Past
      "I asked Professor Sato the reason."

When verbals which consist of Japanese nouns derived from Chinese and the verb *suru* "do" undergo object honorification, the prefix *o* is replaced by *hai*.

(12) Watasi wa Satoo-sensei   no o-syasin   o
      I   Top Satoo teacher(Title Hon) of photo Ref Hon Acc
      hai-ken si-ta.
      see Ref Hon Past
      "I saw Professor Sato's photo."

There are some idiosyncratic suppletive forms.

(13) iku   "go"   ukagau
      kiku   "hear"   ukagau
      au   "meet"   omenikakaru
      morau   "receive" itadaku
                          tyoodaisuru
      siru   "know"   zonziageru
      yaru   "give"   sasiageru

Another type of honorifics expressed by means of changing the shape of predicative elements are the addressee honorifics. The addressee honorifics are used when the speaker's deference toward the addressee is expressed. They can be applied independently of the referent honorifics.

(14) Taroo ga   ki-ta. (plain)
      Taro Nom come Past
      "Taro came."

(15) Taroo ga   ki   masi-ta. (addressee honorific)
      Taro Nom come Add Hon Past
      "Taro came."

(16) Satoo-sensei   ga   ki-ta. (plain)
      Sato teacher(Title Hon) Nom come Past
      "Professor Sato came."

(17) Satoo-sensei   ga   irassyat-ta. (subject honorific)
      Sato teacher(Title Hon) Nom come Ref Hon Past
      "Professor Sato came." (Professor Sato's behavior is indexed as honorified.)

(18) Satoo-sensei   ga   ki   masi-ta. (addressee honorific)
      Sato teacher(Title Hon) Nom come Add Hon Past
      "Professor Sato came." (The addressee is indexed as honorified, and/or the situation is indexed as a formal one.)

(19) Satoo-sensei   ga   irassyai   masi-ta.
      Sato teacher(Title Hon) Nom come Ref Hon Add Hon Past
      (subject and addressee honorifics)
      "Professor Sato came." (Professor Sato's behavior and the addressee are indexed as honorified, and/or the situation in indexed as a formal one.)

In actual speech events, the addressee and the referent are often one and the same person, as in (20).

(20) Anata wa irassyai   masu   ka. (subject and addressee honorifics)
      you   Top come Ref Hon Add Hon Q
      "Are you coming?

Besides referent and addressee honorifics, there are forms which neither exalt the referent nor show special respect to the addressee, but humble the speaker. The typical honorific of humility is *itasu*, which replaces the verb *suru* (do) or *suru* of the regular object honorific from *o . . . suru* as in (21) and (22).

(21) Watasi ga   itasi   masu.
      I   Nom do Hum Hon Add Hon
      "I will do (it)."

(22) Watasi wa Satoo-sensei   ni sono wake o   o-tazune
      I   Top Sato teacher(Title Hon) Dat that reason Acc ask Ref Hon
      itasi   masi-ta.
      Hum Hon Add Hon Past
      "I asked Professor Sato the reason."

Humble forms are used in referring to the speaker's behavior, and by using these humble forms, the speaker's own status is lowered with the consequence that the status of the other participant is relatively raised.

In actual utterances, these honorifics attached to predicative elements are used together with the ones attached to nominal elements. Just as the English speaker must obey the grammatical rule of concord when constructing a sentence, the choice of linguistic forms of honorifics is obligatory in the light of social conventions. Example (23) is pragmatically incorrect, while (24) is appropriate in Japanese society.

(23) #Sensei   wa kaetta.
      teacher(Title Hon) Top return Past
      "The teacher returned."

(24) Sensei   wa okaeri ni natta.
      teacher(Title Hon) Top return Ref Hon Past

Because the subjects in these sentences are people due respect and the honorific title *sensei* is used for them, the predicative elements must also be modified by honorifics. Thus, the concord of honorifics is sociopragmatically obligatory.

These honorifics function as indexical signs to express speakers' *wakimae*, that is, the acknowledgment of their sense of place in the situation and in the society to which they belong. For example, the use of honorific titles or professional ranks in addressing or referring to a person shows the speaker's assessment that the person is of a higher position in status or role relationship or that the person has power in the relationship with the speaker. Examples would be subordinates who address their bosses with their professional rank, such as (LN) *butyoo* "a division chief," or students who refer to their supervisors with the appropriate honorific title, such as (LN) *sensei*. In response, the boss may address the subordinate with a plain title, for instance LN+*kun*. This shows that the speakers are observing *wakimae* by showing their acknowledgment of their sense of place in the society to which they belong and in relation to others. However, the same phenomena could be interpreted as the speaker's expression of power in relation to the addressee/referent.

In general, people who are objectively in a lower position cannot shorten the psychological distance by not using honorifics, because that behavior is considered rude according to the politeness of *wakimae*. Therefore, when a subordinate wants to express solidarity with the boss, this cannot be conveyed by avoiding honorifics. It can be expressed by using modal linguistic devices such as sentence-final particles in addition to the honorifics used.

The choice of honorifics or plain forms also shows the speaker's acknowledgment of the *uchi* (in-group) or *soto* (out-group) membership of the addressee or referent. This sense of belonging sometimes takes priority over other factors in determining the choice of linguistic forms, especially in the workplace. For example, a subordinate would refer to the boss without any honorific titles (the last name alone in many cases) when talking with a person who does not belong to the same company. In this case, the speaker intentionally avoids using honorifics, which shows the speaker's categorization of the boss as an in-group person, while the addressee is an out-group person. The speaker's manifestation of this distinction between *uchi* and *soto* is considered important polite linguistic behavior in this situation. The same speaker would of course use the appropriate honorifics when speaking to the boss directly.

The speaker's acknowledgment of the degree of formality of the situation might affect linguistic choices. The boss may address the subordinate with an honorific title, such as (LN) *katyoo* "a department chief" and use honorifics in direct address in an official meeting. This boss's use of honorifics toward a subordinate shows an acknowledgment of the fact that the situation is formal. Another example of this social meaning of honorifics is the speaker's use of high-level honorifics or the honorific first person pronoun *watakusi* at a job interview or in a speech at a wedding reception. Both situations are considered rather formal, and the speaker's choice of honorifics indicates an acknowledgment of it.

The speaker's acknowledgment of the sense of place in relation to the society relates to a personal sense of demeanor, and it often appears in the reciprocal use of honorifics between persons with different status, age, or power in the relationship. For instance, customers may use honorifics when speaking to sales assistants even if they are much older than those assistants, although it is the customer who has power in this relationship. In this case, customers consider their place in the society in terms of their social status, age, role, gender, etc. and choose honorifics as appropriate linguistic forms according to their personal qualities. This use of honorifics indexes their demeanor. The customer's self-portrayal is thus of a desirable person in the society, an end achieved through the linguistic forms chosen. The fact that women use honorifics more frequently than men might also be attributed to their manifestation of demeanor.

These examples have illustrated the various functions of honorifics in indexing speakers' acknowledgment of their sense of place in relation to both the situational and the social context. Interactions in which formal linguistic forms are used repeatedly may appear somewhat stiff, especially to people in Western societies in which volitional language use forms the core of linguistic politeness, because the use of formal forms causes a formal, stiff attitude in the participants. However, such formality is socially expected when there is a large social and/or psychological distance between participants in the interactions in Japanese society, and is considered to be polite. In fact, a lack of honorifics in a situation in which they are expected, which Westerners would feel to be more casual and thus more comfortable, would be decidedly less comfortable for Japanese, since their expectations would not be met.

A person's observation of *wakimae* is also shown by the use of formulaic expressions. For example, people say *Itadaki-masu* (eat Ref Hon Add Hon) "I am going to eat" and *Go-tisou-sama (desita)* (Ref Hon feast Ref Hon (Cop Add Hon Past) "Thank your for your good food" before and after a meal. These are formulaic expressions which are expected to be used in those situations. Another example is *Tumaranai mono desu ga* (trifling thing Cop but) "This is a trifle, (but please accept it)." This expression is often used when the speaker gives a present to someone, especially to a person who is of a higher position in status or role or a casual acquaintance. The speaker does not think that the present is a trifle, but this expression simply shows a humble attitude toward the addressee.

The observation of *wakimae* may constrain the use of a formulaic expression, *Go-kurou-sama (desita)* (trouble Ref Hon Cop Add Hon Past) "Thank you for your hard work," in some situations. This expression would be impolite if used toward an addressee in a higher position. This is because this utterance has an implication of paternal care for the addressee, which the superior is expected to show toward the inferior, not the other way around.

Furthermore, language use according to *wakimae* is concerned with constraints with regard to when to speak or what to say. For example, students in a seminar in a university keep listening to the professor without uttering a word until the professor yields the floor to the students. Similarly, students are not expected to compliment the professor on the lecture by saying something such as *Sensei no ohanasi wa omosirokatta desu* (teacher (Hon Title) of lecture Ref Hon Top interesting Past Cop Add Hon) "Your lecture was interesting." The students are not allowed to interrupt the professor or to make comments on the professor's behavior.

1.2.2   *Language expressions used according to volition*

Language use according to volition is the speaker's active use of strategies to achieve politeness, and there are various possibilities for their realization as shown in P. Brown and Levinson (1978, 1987). The strategies to achieve politeness proposed in this work, as "off record," "positive politeness," and "negative politeness," are all applied to politeness according to volition in Japanese.

Honorifics are categorized as one of the negative politeness strategies, "give deference" in Brown and Levinson's framework. Although the use of honorifics according to *wakimae*, which indexes the social and psychological distance between the speaker and the addressee, is the basic rule of use, honorifics can be used creatively according to the speaker's volition in order to manipulate the psychological distance in some situations. For example, when speakers use honorifics to addressees toward whom they do not normally use them, psychological distance is created through the choice of linguistic forms. Examples are mothers' scolding their children with honorifics, creating distance to assert their awareness of the children's good behavior, and making expensive requests to spouses with honorifics.

Honorifics can also be used as a tool to expand the psychological distance toward the addressee when honorific forms of a high level inappropriate to the situation are employed. In this way the speaker can make *ingin burei* (which literally means "polite impoliteness").

On the other hand, when people want to shorten the psychological distance to the addressee, they can intentionally avoid using honorifics. Ikuta's (1983: 46) example from natural conversations in TV talk shows showed that the interviewer, who generally spoke with honorifics to suit the formal situation appropriate to TV audiences, expressed her attitudinal closeness to the addressee by dropping the honorifics. This strategy of dropping honorifics creates empathy between speakers and addressees, thus making it possible for the interviewee to open up and talk about personal topics in depth.

1.3   *A cross-cultural comparison of linguistic politeness*

Every language has some devices for the realization of politeness, although the systems may be radically different. This section compares the concepts of "politeness" and "linguistic politeness" in American English and Japanese.

1.3.1   *Japanese and American linguistic politeness*

As has already been pointed out, there are two different modes of language use for the realization of linguistic politeness, *wakimae* and volition. A large-scale quantitative analysis led Hill et al. (1986) to the conclusion that Japanese linguistic politeness, as compared to American linguistic politeness, tends to be determined by the *wakimae* type of language use.

Hill's research focused on the comparison of the *wakimae* type of language use in Japanese and American English. In their study, subjects were presented with language expressions and potential addressees. The expressions, all connected with borrowing a pen, showed various degrees of politeness, while the potential addressees were distinguished by power and status. In a questionnaire, the subjects were asked three questions: (i) the level of politeness of each expression, rated on a scale of 1 to 5; (ii) the appropriate politeness level due the various addressees, also rated on a scale of 1 to 5; and (iii) which linguistic form they would use for each type of addressees.

Comparing figures 16.2 and 16.3, it is found that, although both Japanese and American English speakers show the graded responses in which the relative ranking of an addressee correlates with the relative politeness of the linguistic form, Japanese subjects' responses cluster more tightly than do those of the Americans. This might reflect the Japanese subjects' strong observation of *wakimae*.

Furthermore, Japanese responses cluster more tightly within two larger groupings. This means that Japanese subjects tend to categorize the addressees into two groups, as evidenced by their choice of linguistic forms. The linguistic forms judged as relatively circumspect are used with addressees toward whom subjects report being relatively careful, while the forms judged to be relatively informal are used toward those with whom subjects felt relatively relaxed. The addressees in the former group are those considered to belong to the *soto* (out-group) for those subjects, such as people with higher status or strangers, while those in the latter group belong to their *uchi* (in-group), which includes people of equal status or familiar persons. The linguistic forms used toward the former group of addressees contain addressee honorifics such as *desu* or *masu*, while the forms employed toward the latter group do not.

This result provides a clue to finding the key factor which characterizes Japanese language use according to *wakimae*. Although there are a number of variables which determine people's perception of social and psychological distance, Japanese people recognize distance primarily by their sense of grouping people as either *uchi* or *soto*. Among various linguistic components which affect the degree of politeness of an expression, the use of addressee honorifics functions as a clear-cut device for differentiating the degree of politeness of linguistic forms. In other words, typical Japanese language use in accordance with *wakimae* is realized by the use of addressee honorifics toward out-group (*soto*) people and the lack of addressee honorifics toward in-group (*uchi*) people.

1.3.2 The difference in the concept of "politeness" in Japanese and American English

This section compares a definition of the concept of "politeness" between Japanese and American English. Although "politeness" is usually recognized

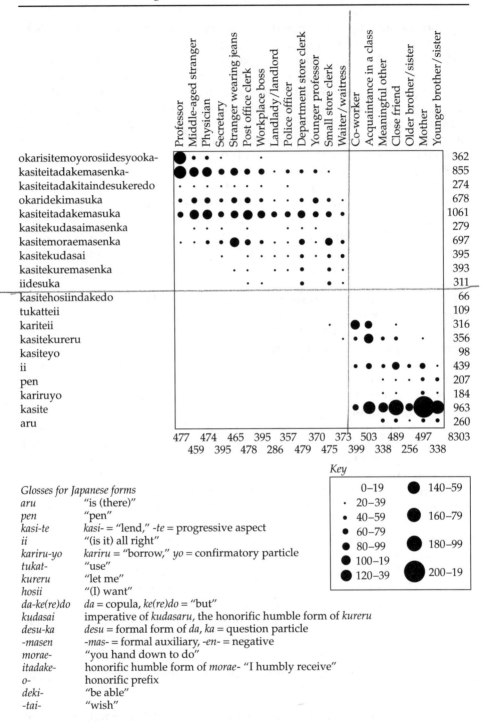

Figure 16.2   Correlation of linguistic forms and addressees: Japanese
Source: Hill et al. 1986: 357

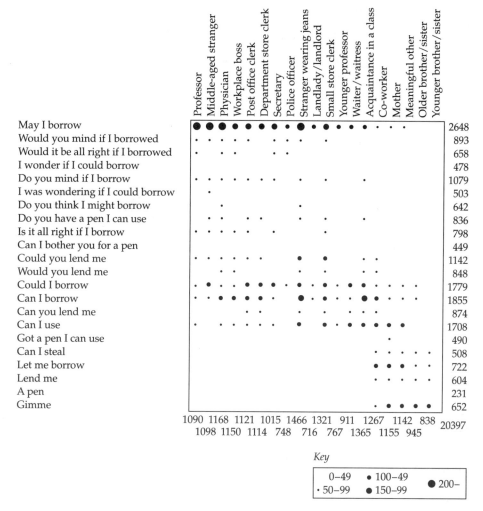

Figure 16.3 Correlation of linguistic forms and addressees: Americans
Source: Hill et al. 1986: 358

as a positive concept associated with smooth communication, the presumption that what is "good" for people's communication is the same in different cultures needs to be questioned. Ide et al. (1992) used quantitative analysis to investigate how politeness is conceptualized by Americans and Japanese.

In that survey, each subject was given a grid containing descriptions of 14 interactional situations and a list of ten adjectives evaluating human behavior, including "polite" and "*teineina*" (polite). The subjects were asked to connect the adjectives which would best represent their own evaluations with the interactional situations. Through multivariate analysis of the data, researchers compared the position of the terms "polite" and "*teineina*" relative to the other

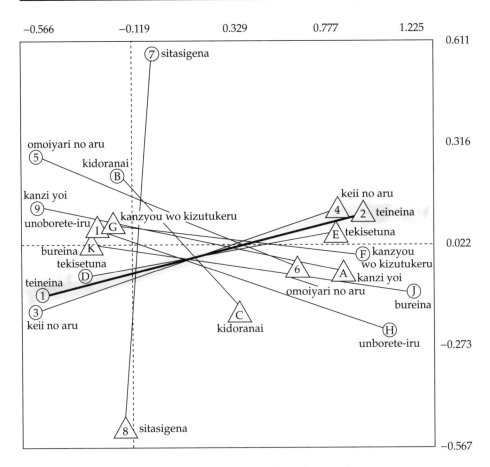

Figure 16.4   Multivariate analysis of adjectives related to politeness: Japanese
Source: Ide et al. 1992: 288

nine terms in a two-dimensional Euclidean space. Comparing figures 16.4 and 16.5 shows that the American case is clearly one-dimensional, while the Japanese case is more or less two-dimensional. This means that Americans exhibit unilateral judgment of various concepts of evaluation, while the Japanese judge in terms of two dimensions. The meaning of the common axis of Japanese and American evaluations can be consistently interpreted as "good" on the left half of the axis and "bad" on the right half. For Japanese responses, another axis can be postulated, the meaning of which could be characterized as "friendly" (upper half) and "nonfriendly" (lower half).

This result clarifies two important differences in the way Americans and Japanese conceptualize politeness. One is in the evaluation of the two concepts, "polite" and "friendly" (*teineina* and *sitasigena* respectively). Americans evaluate them on the same axis; "polite" and "friendly" are "good" concepts, while minus "polite" and minus "friendly" are "bad" concepts. On the other hand,

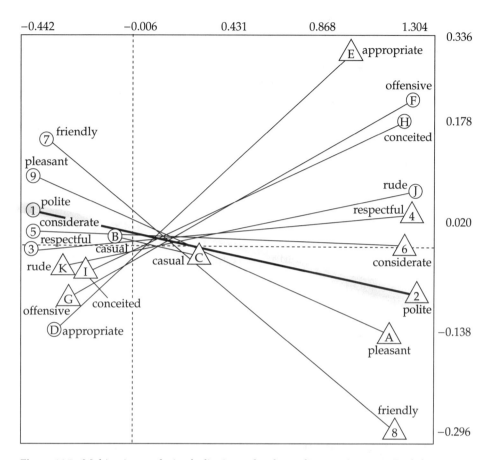

Figure 16.5 Multivariate analysis of adjectives related to politeness: American English
Source: Ide et al. 1986a: 286

Japanese evaluate them as discrete but not opposing concepts. This means that, for Japanese, the concepts *"teineina"* (polite) and minus *"sitasigena"* (friendly) are distinct but not contradictory concepts.

The second difference concerns the degree of correlation between seemingly equivalent concepts. The concept "respectful" (or *"keiinoaru"*) has the highest degree of correlation with the key concept "polite"/*"teineina."* However, this degree of correlation does not obtain between the second and third concepts; "pleasant" and *"kanjiyoi"* (pleasant) are corresponding adjectives, and correlate closely, but "considerate" and *"tekisetuna"* (appropriate) do not. This difference appears to highlight the difference between Americans and Japanese in their preference for two different modes of polite language use, volition and *wakimae*, discussed in the section above. While *"tekisetuna"* (appropriate) is used in Japanese to evaluate behavior in the light of worldly criteria, i.e. *wakimae*, "considerate" is used in English to evaluate behavior represented by one's

volitional exhibition of consideration to others. This difference in the orientation of highly correlated concepts can be seen to exemplify the orientation of
politeness in the two languages; "polite" is oriented towards volition, while
"*teineina*" (polite) is oriented towards *wakimae*.

From these results, the foundation of Japanese linguistic politeness can be
described as behavior according to *wakimae*, which includes a focus on the
appropriate distance between participants in the relationship. However, as
shown in the distinct but not opposing concepts "*teineina*" (polite) and
"*sitasigena*" (friendly), Japanese people can express friendliness toward others
while observing *wakimae*. This is done through the use of modal devices
such as sentence-final particles which co-occur with the use of honorifics, as
mentioned in the section above. For example, students may say to a professor
something like, *Sensei, kono hon omosiroi desu ne* (teacher(Hon Title used as an
address term), this book interesting Cop Add Hon FP) "Professor, this book is
interesting, isn't it?" The speakers show their observation of *wakimae* by using
the honorific title *sensei* or an addressee honorific *desu* toward their professors,
but at the same time they express friendliness by using a sentence-final particle
ne, which seeks confirmation from the addressees.

2   Women's Language

2.1   *Features of women's language*

2.1.1   *Phonological features*

Women speak with a higher pitch than men. Physiological differences between
men and women undoubtedly play a role, but are not the only factor involved.
Results of empirical research led Ohara (1997) to argue that, in Japanese society,
there are sociolinguistically analyzable reasons for the difference in voice pitch
between men and women.

Ohara's experiment (1997) examined the pitch of voice of male and female
speakers, both in naturally occurring conversations and while reading sentences in Japanese and English. The results show that women speak and read
with a higher pitch in Japanese than in English, while men's pitch did not
change significantly in the different situations or languages. The physiological
differences between men and women do not explain women's change of pitch
between the two languages.

Ohara's second experiment clarified the meaning of women's higher pitch
in Japanese. In the experiment, two women uttered some greeting words such
as *konnitiwa* (hello) and *sayounara* (goodbye). With the aid of a computer, these
recordings were altered to produce three different pitches for the greetings.
These recordings were then played for male and female subjects, who were
asked to assess the various characteristics of the two women. As the pitches
became lower, the rating of the characteristics "stubbornness," "selfishness,"

and "strength" rose; while as the pitches became higher, the rating of such characteristics as "cuteness" (like a little girl), "kindness," and "politeness" rose. Thus, this experiment showed clearly that pitch level is closely associated with characteristics of the speaker; in particular, that high pitch is associated with characteristics that are highly valued in Japanese society, characteristics such as "cuteness," "kindness," and "politeness."

2.1.2 *Morphological features*

2.1.2.1 <u>Sentence-final particles</u> Sentence-final particles express the speaker's nonpropositional modal attitude, and they are heard most frequently in informal spoken discourse. They are linguistic features that index the speaker's various cognitive and emotional assessments concerning the contextual factors. Some sentence-final particles characterize male or female speech because of their exclusive use by one sex or the other.

McGloin (1991, 1993) and Ide (1982a, 1991, 1992a) discuss some of the sentence-final particles used exclusively or primarily by one sex. McGloin investigated *zo, ze, sa, wa,* and *no.* She argues that *zo, ze,* and *sa,* which are used primarily by men, express the speaker's insistence on the propositional statement.

(25) Kore kara issyookenmei yaru zo.
      now from one's best   do   FP
      "I will do my best from now on. I strongly insist."

(26) Kore kara issyookenmei yaru ze.
      now from one's best   do   FP
      "I will do my best from now on. I insist."

(27) Kore kara issyookenmei yaru sa.
      now from one's best   do   FP
      "I will do my best from now on. That's the way it goes." (McGloin 1991: 27)

In examples (25) to (27), the speaker adds insistence to his propositional statement that he will do his best. McGloin also discusses the different meanings of these three particles: both *zo* and *ze* add strong emphasis to the speaker's statement, although *ze* is milder than *zo.* Thus, examples (25) and (26) both express the speaker's determination. They also imply that the speaker takes full responsibility for his statement. On the other hand, *sa* lacks such commitment and gives the sense that the speaker is portraying the proposition as an objective description.

While *zo, ze,* and *sa* are the sentence-final particles of insistence, *wa* and *no* indicate rapport and are used mainly by women. McGloin (1991: 33, 34) explains that *wa* and *no* create emotional rapport between the speaker and the addressee, as illustrated in (28) and (29).

(28) Watasi mo iku wa.
      I   also go FP
      "I will go too."

(29) Watakusi kore ga   daisuki   desu   no.
      I Sup Hon this Nom like very much Cop Add Hon FP
      "I just love this."

In (28), the speaker adds emotional emphasis directed toward the addressee and thus creates for the participants an emotional common ground. *No* in (29) engenders a feeling of shared knowledge.

Ide (1982a, 1991, 1992a) discusses the sentence-final particles *wa* and *kasira*, both of which are considered to be items of the feminine vocabulary. In examples (30) and (31), both *wa* and *kasira* indicate the speaker's uncertainty and soften the speech.

(30) Watasi wa Taroo ga   suki da   wa. (Ide 1982a: 381)
      I   Top Taro   Nom like Cop FP
      "I like Taro."

(31) Sensei wa o-kaeri-ni naru kasira. (Ide 1982a: 381)
      teacher Top return Ref Hon FP
      "I wonder if the teacher will return."

According to McGloin and Ide, the feminine sentence-final particle *wa* seems to have two different functions. On the one hand, it establishes empathy between speaker and addressee, which is a positive politeness strategy. On the other hand, it expresses deference to the feelings of the addressee, and thus softens the statement, which is a negative politeness strategy. In fact, *wa* should be considered to have a dual nature. Ide (1992a: 126) explains that "it is the softening function of the particle *wa* (the effect of negative politeness strategy) that makes it possible to create an atmosphere of relaxation because of its function of no-imposition and respect for the other, which in turn creates an atmosphere of the sharedness (the effect of positive politeness strategy)."

Ide's (1979) quantitative analysis shows general tendencies concerning the frequency of use of various sentence-final particles. The survey was based on data collected by recording naturally occurring conversations of university students. Figure 16.6 shows the ratios of frequency of various sentence-final particles used by men and women.

As the figure shows, some particles are used exclusively by men or by women, while others are merely preferred by either men or women. The meaning of this exclusive or preferred use of particular sentence-final particles is

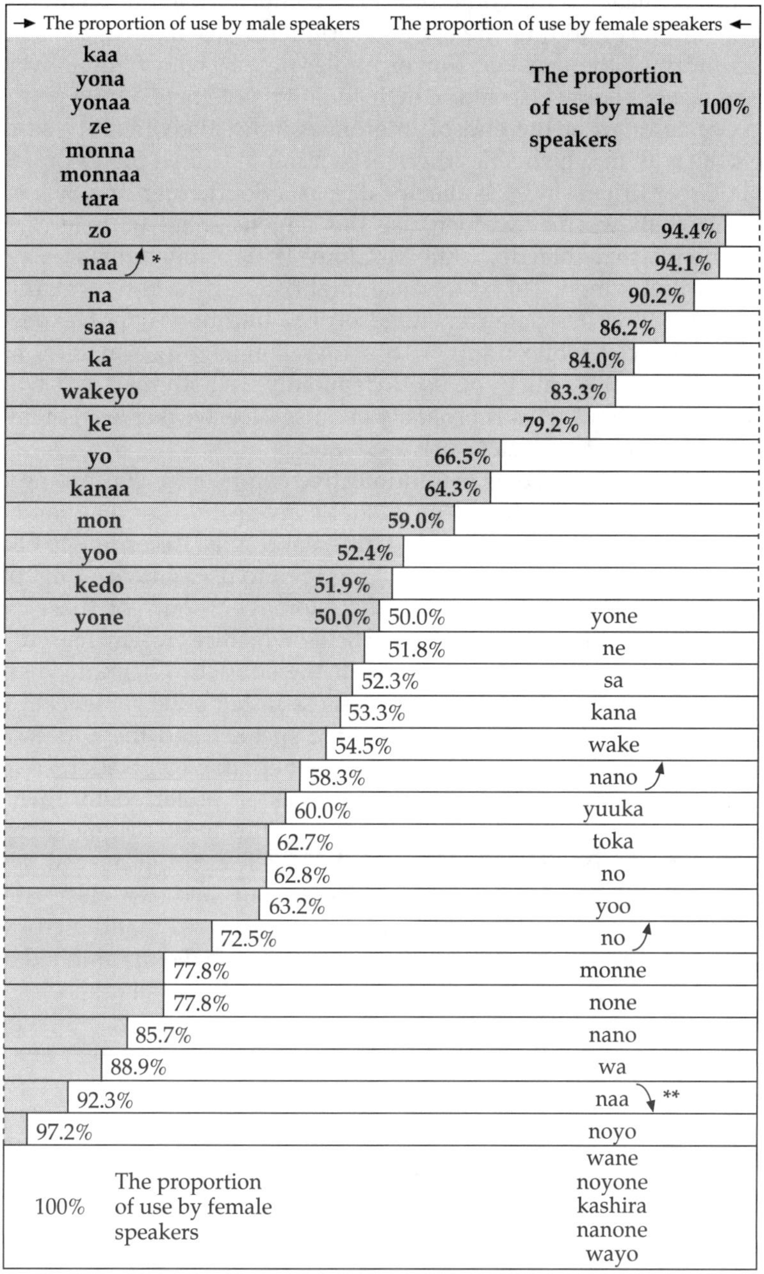

→ The proportion of use by male speakers	The proportion of use by female speakers ←
kaa yona yonaa ze monna monnaa tara	**The proportion of use by male 100% speakers**
zo	94.4%
naa ↗ *	94.1%
na	90.2%
saa	86.2%
ka	84.0%
wakeyo	83.3%
ke	79.2%
yo	66.5%
kanaa	64.3%
mon	59.0%
yoo	52.4%
kedo	51.9%
yone	50.0%

(female side)	particle
50.0%	yone
51.8%	ne
52.3%	sa
53.3%	kana
54.5%	wake
58.3%	nano ↗
60.0%	yuuka
62.7%	toka
62.8%	no
63.2%	yoo
72.5%	no ↗
77.8%	monne
77.8%	none
85.7%	nano
88.9%	wa
92.3%	naa ↘ **
97.2%	noyo
100% The proportion of use by female speakers	wane noyone kashira nanone wayo

Key: *↗ indicates rising tone   ** ↘ indicates falling tone

Figure 16.6 Frequency of the use of sentence-final particles according to the gender of the speakers
Source: Ide 1979: 8–9

great, since it relates to the communicative competence of all members of the speech community and thus the use of a certain particle indexes the femininity or masculinity of the speaker. For example, people who frequently use *wa*, *wane*, and *wayo* thereby also index their identity as female, while people who tend to use *zo* or *na* at the end of utterances index their identity as male. It parallels the way in which a Southern accent in the United States or a Scottish accent in Great Britain indexes the speaker as a Southerner or a Scot.

Figure 16.6 shows that women use the sentence-final particle *sa* slightly more frequently than men do, while McGloin (1991) claimed this was a particle used primarily by men. This difference might stem from the formality of the speech style; McGloin's data depended on her intuition, which expected the rather formal style, while figure 16.6 shows language use in informal conversations. Thus, *sa* seems to be used frequently by both men and women in informal conversations. This is probably because of its weaker level of insistence as compared to other particles such as *zo* and *ze*.

Although figure 16.6 shows communicative competence concerning the use of sentence-final particles based on casual conversation by male and female speakers, Okamoto's (1997) work led to different results. According to Okamoto, some women (especially younger ones) tend not to use sentence-final particles such as *wa*, which represent femininity. Moreover, some of these younger female speakers sometimes use the particles which represent masculinity in informal situations. From interviews with the subjects, Okamoto discovered that the indirectness and lack of assertiveness in feminine sentence-final particles are felt to create distance between the speaker and the addressee, and so the younger speakers are not likely to use them in conversations with close friends. For them, the use of particles such as *yo* preferred by men shows intimacy toward the addressees because of their directness. Okamoto explained that the use of the particles such as *zo* which index strong masculinity were intentionally used by young female speakers only between close friends in order to reinforce their solidarity. It should also be noted that these pragmatic phenomena are observed in informal situations where the uninhibited attitude of the speaker makes it possible to ignore gender identity markers.

Crossing the border of gender-linked usage and using sentence-final particles normally associated with the other sex creates a new identity, that of a person acting outside the conventional gender category.

2.1.2.2   <u>Honorifics and polite expressions</u>   Women tend to use honorifics and polite expressions more frequently than men. This tendency has been examined by several quantitative studies. For example, Ide et al. (1986a), reports on quantitative research focused on women's polite language use. It was found that the politeness level of the linguistic forms women use toward various types of addressees is generally higher than the linguistic forms men would use toward the same addressees.

Table 16.1 shows the average politeness level of the linguistic forms used toward a variety of different addressees. This score is presented based on the

Table 16.1 Average politeness level used for a category of addressees as rated by 500 male and female subjects each (Ide et al. 1986a: 30)

Types of addressee	*Men*	*Women*
a. Child	1.39	1.15
b. Spouse	1.41	1.85
c. Delivery person	2.19	2.39
d. Friend	2.15	2.55
e. Workplace inferior	1.91	2.39
f. Same-status colleague	2.41	2.45
g. Neighbor	3.72	3.25
h. Spouse's friend	3.53	3.99
i. Parent at PTA meeting	3.83	3.50
j. Instructor of hobby group	3.99	4.31
k. Daughter's or son's professor	4.19	4.40
l. Workplace superior	4.31	4.39

analysis of the answers to two questions. The first asked that the respondents rank the level of politeness of a number of variants of "to go" on a scale of 1 (the least polite) to 5 (the most polite). The second asked respondents to choose the most appropriate linguistic expression of "to go" for use when talking with 12 types of addressees. Except in the case of children, the politeness level of the linguistic forms chosen by women is always higher than that of the forms chosen by men. This means that women choose higher-level linguistic forms toward each addressee.

Ogino (1986) also studied honorific usage based on the data collected in interviews based on questionnaires. In his survey, the respondents were asked which of the linguistic variations of *shitte iru* (I know) they would use toward various types of addressees. Ogino quantified the level of politeness of each type of addressee by analyzing the frequency of each expression used toward each addressee. The level of politeness used toward each addressee is judged to be higher when expressions rated as showing higher-level politeness are employed. Figures 16.7 and 16.8 show the relative politeness level used toward different addressees. A block in figure 16.8 is always higher than the corresponding block in figure 16.7. This means that, compared to men, women use more formal expressions with honorifics toward these addressees.

The use of honorifics and polite expressions indexes the speaker's recognition of the particular relationship with the addressee. Therefore, women's frequent use of higher-level polite expressions in these studies might show that women categorize these addressees as being both higher in social status and out-group people. At the same time, the use of polite expressions can be considered as the speakers' display of their own desirable characteristics of good demeanor. Women therefore seem to present themselves as well-demeaned persons by

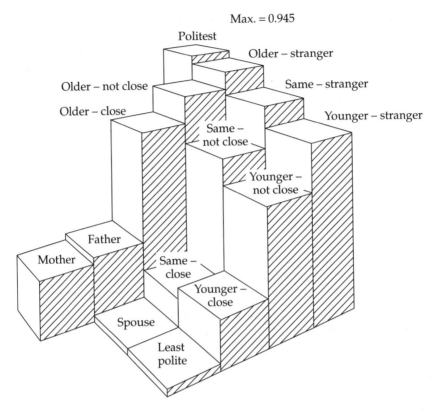

Figure 16.7   The politeness level of linguistic forms used towards addressee by male speakers
Source: Ogino 1986: 45

their linguistic behavior, i.e. by using more polite expressions than those used by men.

Ide and Inoue (1992) present an example of the use of high-level honorifics by women in higher positions in companies in Tokyo. They showed that those women use higher-level honorifics than office ladies who hold lower positions. This use of higher-level honorifics by women in higher positions contradicts the basic pragmatic rule of politeness in Japanese society, because it is the person in the lower position who is required to use honorifics toward the person in the higher position. Why does this opposite phenomenon happen? The use of formal language by those women in higher positions shows their demeanor in their positions, and indexes their identity as well-brought-up persons. The use of formal language becomes a tool in their exercising power, and by doing so, they maintain their high positions in the company.

2.1.2.3   <u>Beautification/hypercorrected honorifics</u>   Beautification honorifics and hypercorrected honorifics are most likely to occur in female speech. Beautification honorifics are used, not to express a respectful attitude toward addressees/

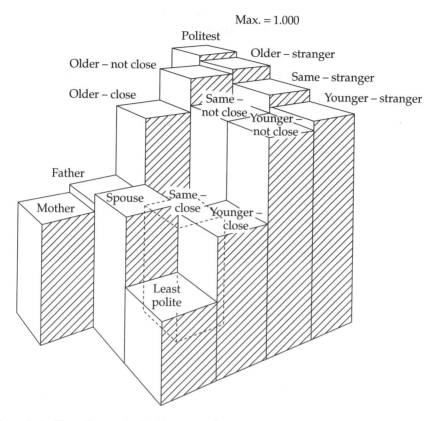

Figure 16.8 The politeness level of linguistic forms used towards addressee by female speakers
Source: Ogino 1986: 46

referents, but to beautify the speech. The prefix *o* (and *go* for Japanese nouns derived from Chinese) is generally attached to nouns as in *o-kane* instead of *kane* (money) and *o-yasai* instead of *yasai* (vegetable). They are different from referent and addressee honorifics even though the same linguistic form of the prefix *o* is employed.

(32)   sensei no o-heya   (honorification)
      teacher of Ref Hon room
      "teacher's room"

(33)   *watasi* no o-heya   (beautification)
      I   of Bea Hon room
      "my room" (Ide 1982a: 379)

The prefix *o* in (32) functions as a referent honorific in that it shows the speaker's respectful attitude toward the referent, *sensei*, but *o* in (33) prefixed to the speaker's own belongings beautifies the speech. Women use these beautification honorifics much more frequently than men do, and many of the beautification nouns are used exclusively by women.

Honorifics are sometimes used indiscriminately. Although their use is expected in connection with an addressee or referent who is to be treated respectfully, they are sometimes used incorrectly with people toward whom the speaker is not expected to show a deferential attitude. This is the case when speakers use honorifics, for instance, toward their own mother or husband.

(34)   Haha   ga   o-kaeri ni nari   masita.
       mother Nom return Ref Hon Add Hon Past
       "My mother returned."

(35)   Syuzin   ni   mousiage te oki masu.
       husband Dat talk Hum Hon   Add Hon
       "I will talk (about it) to my husband."

It goes against the rules to use honorifics in connection with one's mother or husband, since these individuals belong to the speaker's in-group in Japanese society. If honorifics are used in such situations, they are considered to be hypercorrected honorifics. These hypercorrected honorifics are often used by women.

Beautification honorifics and hypercorrected honorifics index the speaker's intention of displaying demeanor. Honorifics are considered to be prestigious linguistic forms, and are generally associated with high social class. Women are likely to have the intention of showing themselves as well-demeaned persons by displaying a higher social class than that to which they actually belong, which leads to their using these prestigious linguistic forms excessively.

2.1.3   Lexical features

2.1.3.1   <u>Personal pronouns</u>   The repertoires of personal pronouns used by men and by women tend to be different. Table 16.2 shows the most frequently used personal pronouns. In addition to the differences in the linguistic forms, a difference in the levels of formality of the same linguistic form can be observed. The first person pronoun *watasi*, which is women's most commonly used first person pronoun in informal speech, is used only in formal speech by men. Moreover, in formal speech, men use the pronoun *watasi* more frequently than *watakusi*, which is more formal first person pronoun, while women use *watakusi* more frequently than *watasi*. The level of the formality of the first person pronoun *watasi* is assessed as being higher by men than by women. In addition, this first person pronoun *watasi* is considered to be in the repertoire of female children's formal forms, while male children do not have a parallel form. This might indicate that only female children develop a sensitivity to the formal attitude of the adults around them as characterized by language use.

Table 16.2   Sociolinguistic structure of personal pronouns

Person	Speaker / Style	Adult Male	Adult Female	Young child Male	Young child Female
First person pronoun	Formal	*watakusi, watasi*	*watakusi, watasi*	None	*watasi*
	Normal	*boku*	*watasi, atasi*	*boku*	FN**+*tyan*
	Deprecatory	*ore*	None	*ore*	None
Seond person pronoun	Formal	*anata**	*anata**	(*kimi*)***	(*anata*)
	Normal	*kimi*	*anata*	FN + *kun* FN + *tyan*	FN + *kun* FN + *tyan*
	Deprecatory	*omae*	None	*omae*	None

  * not applicable in addressing superiors
 ** FN represents first name
*** ( ) begins to appear around the age of five

Another difference concerns the repertoire of deprecatory pronouns. There are pronouns on a deprecatory level in both male adult and male child repertoires: *ore* as a first person pronoun, and *omae* as a second person pronoun, while there are no such pronouns in both women's and girls' speech. Contrary to the female children's sensitivity, male children develop a sensitivity to the deprecatory attitude of the male adults.

These differences in the levels of formality of certain pronouns and even in the existence of certain deprecatory pronouns exemplify the sociolinguistic structure in the repertoires of male and female personal pronouns. This socio-linguistic structure represents the cultural understandings which may seem sexist from a feminist's perspective. Women's more polite first person pronoun in formal settings may reflect women's more polite linguistic behavior in society in general, as may the fact that women's speech lacks deprecatory pronouns. Women's use of personal pronouns in conformity with this repertoire inevitably shows their acceptance of this sociolinguistic structure and indexes "female" as part of the speakers' identity. In addition, the fact that these differences are also evident in female children's repertoires indicates that this system forms a part of the communicative competence which is acquired as part of the process of socialization. Women index their femininity and display their own good demeanor through their polite linguistic behavior.

2.1.3.2   Vulgar expressions   Women do not normally use vulgar expressions. The deprecatory suffix *yagaru*, as in *utai-yagaru* (sing), is likely to be used only by men. Profanities, such as *tikusyoo* (damn), obscenities, and rough expressions, for example, *dekai* for *ookii* (big) or *kuu* for *taberu* (eat), are all expected to be limited to men's speech. Phonological reduction forms, such as *dekee* for *dekai* or *sugee* for *sugoi* (great), are also considered to be unfeminine vocabulary. These forms have a lower level of politeness than the normal expressions.

The exclusive use of these vulgar expressions by men is recognized in both the speaker's and the addressee's mind as part of their normal communicative competence. When men use these expressions, they often acquire the positive value of "covert prestige" (Trudgill 1975: 102) since they display masculinity because of their uninhibited quality. On the other hand, vulgar expressions are seldom heard in women's speech, and women show themselves as well-demeaned persons by not using them. The lack of vulgar expressions indexes the display of demeanor.

2.1.4   Syntactic features

Shibamoto (1987) discussed syntactic differences between men's and women's speech. The syntactic phenomena at the center of her inquiry are the inversion of subjects and verbs and the deletion of subject noun phrases, both of which are conversational features found in informal speech. She tabulated the occurrences of these syntactic features and concluded that it is women who tend to employ inversion and deletion most frequently. However, it could be argued that these phenomena are observed in the data from conversations in less formal situations, and they are not systemic features of women's language.

The conversational data from both the male groups and the female groups were collected by the researcher who observed the conversation. The difference in the networks of the subjects who participated in the conversations might be a problem that could affect the results. The male subjects were workers at a city hall in a suburb of Tokyo, and their conversations took place during the lunch break in the dining room at the workplace, while the female subjects were all housewives, and their conversations took place at the subject's apartment amid children running in and out and interruptions by the phone. It must be noted that there is an apparent difference in the networks of the male and the female subjects, and this may affect the subjects' choice of topics in the conversations; the topics of the female subjects' conversations at their apartments are less formal than those of male subjects' conversations during lunch time at the workplace. Another problem may concern the gender of the participants of the conversations. Because a female researcher collected all the data, the events became male–female on the one hand and female–female on the other hand. It could be argued that the existence of the female researcher as an observer in the conversations made the context more formal for the male subjects who participated in the conversations.

As for the inversion including the subject's postverbal shift, a survey conducted by Ide (1979) indicates that it is a frequent feature in a male college student's mixed conversations. How can these different results with respect to the inversion of subjects and verbs be accounted for?

An analysis of the occurrence of subject and verb inversion, which is in effect merely loose syntax, reveals that it occurs in relaxed conversations when the speaker is paying less attention to form than to content. It could therefore be argued that, in Shibamoto (1987), the females are conversing in a relatively relaxed situation, since the subjects are in their home setting, whereas in Ide (1979) in the mixed-gender conversations, the males felt the situations were more relaxed than the females felt them to be. This means that the issue of inversion is a factor that reflects the perceived formality of the situation. Does this phenomenon mean anything significant about gender differences in the Japanese language? No. This highlights the important question as to what exactly the linguistic features are that are relevant to the gender and language issue, and are thus worth investigating.

2.1.5   *Pragmatic features*

The role of women in conversations is likely to be different from that of men. K. Abe (1989) noted several differences in communicative functions of utterances according to the sex of the speaker.

In that study, a communicative function is defined as the function that each utterance fulfills in response to the previous utterance in order to carry the conversation forward. Abe classified the communicative functions into four groups: (i) carrying forward the conversation by explaining or adding details, (ii) interrupting the conversation by introducing different facts or denying the previous utterance, (iii) showing reactions, and (iv) suggesting a new direction for the conversation by offering new topics or letting new participants join. Using the data collected in recordings of naturally occurring informal conversations of college students, the communicative functions of men's and women's utterances in conversations of groups of men, of women, and of men and women were examined.

The analysis showed that both men's and women's utterances fulfill different functions according to the sex of the participants of the conversation. Women's utterances tend to have the communicative functions of showing reactions and suggesting a new direction for the conversation in mixed groups (iii) and (iv), while utterances are more likely to have the functions of carrying the conversation forward and interrupting the conversation in groups of the same sex (i) and (ii). This pattern is opposite to the functions of men's utterances. Abe concluded that, in mixed-group conversations, men play an important role in carrying the current topic forward or reiterating it, while the role of women is primarily to support the men's role by reacting to their utterances or offering further topics. This difference in men's and women's roles in conversations can be considered a reflection of their role differences in society. Men's leadership in advancing or reiterating the conversation is likely to show that they have power in social relationship with women, while women's supporting role for men in conversations tends to be a manifestation of their supplementary role in social relationships with men.

2.2 Politeness and women's language

The previous section offered an overview of various features of women's speech. This section focuses on politeness as one of the most noticeable features in women's language. As mentioned in the section above, women tend to use higher-level honorifics and to use these more frequently than men, and this means that women's language is more polite than that of men. Why do women use polite language?

Ide et al. (1986a) provided statistical evidence for the factors involved in women's frequent use of polite linguistic forms in their analysis of questionnaires about language use. The survey was conducted by asking more than 500 middle-class, middle-aged men and women about their use of polite linguistic forms. The men were mostly businessmen; the women mostly housewives. The questionnaires presented the subjects with a list of 12 addressees of different ages and degrees of familiarity with the subjects as well as with the variants of *iku* (go) in the context of "when do you go?" Three questions were asked concerning the person category and the linguistic forms: the politeness level of the variants of the linguistic form of "go" (Q1), the politeness level due each addressee in the person category (Q2), and the choice of the linguistic form of "go" the subject would use in conversation with these addressees (Q3). The politeness level in Q1 and Q2 were established on a scale of 1 to 5, with 1 being least and 5 most polite. Q3 was asked after a few weeks' interval from Q1 and Q2.

It was the analysis of the answers to Q3 that showed that women choose more polite linguistic forms for each addressee than those that men choose. Three factors concerning women's polite language use become clear: (i) women assess the politeness level of linguistic forms as being lower than men do; (ii) women assess the appropriate politeness level due to different types of addressees as being higher than men do; (iii) women use the kind of interactional patterns which call for higher linguistic forms more frequently than men do.

From the analysis of the answers to Q1, it was found that women ascribe to each linguistic form a lower politeness level than men do. This appears to influence women's choice of linguistic forms because, as a consequence of the lower politeness level attributed to the various forms, they must choose higher-level politeness forms to achieve the same politeness effect that men achieve with lower-level forms. The second reason for women's more polite language use compared to men's is that women assign each addressee the necessity to use a higher politeness level than men do. This also influences women's choice of linguistic forms, because it results in their use of a polite form of a higher level in connection with the same addressee.

The third reason for women's choosing more polite linguistic forms stems from women's interactional patterns. This factor could be found in the results of Q2 and Q1 × Q3 as shown in figure 16.9. The horizontal lines represent

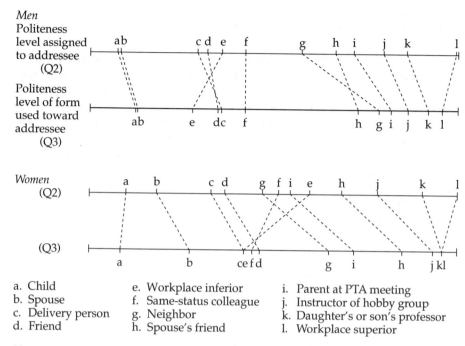

a. Child
b. Spouse
c. Delivery person
d. Friend

e. Workplace inferior
f. Same-status colleague
g. Neighbor
h. Spouse's friend

i. Parent at PTA meeting
j. Instructor of hobby group
k. Daughter's or son's professor
l. Workplace superior

Figure 16.9 Comparison of two kinds of politeness level: politeness level assigned to addressees and politeness level of linguistic forms used toward addressees
Source: Ide et al. 1986a: 32

scales of politeness, with politeness increasing toward the right. On the upper lines, the politeness level assigned to addressees (the results of Q2) are plotted and on the lower lines the politeness level of the linguistic forms actually used toward addressees (the results of Q1 × Q3) are plotted. By comparing these two kinds of politeness level, researchers found that these two politeness levels were not parallel. For some addressees, both men and women chose more polite linguistic forms than the politeness level they assigned toward these addressees in Q2 would indicate. These addressees are the ones with whom one is required to be sociable, for example, the people in the domain of the neighborhood, hobbies, and the home. For other addressees, they chose equal or less polite linguistic forms than the politeness level they assigned to them in Q2. These are addressees in the domain of the workplace with whom solidarity is sought. The grouping of addressees is similar for men and for women, the only exception being the case of children, with whom women choose less polite forms and men choose more polite ones.

Taking men's and women's interaction in their daily lives into account, women in this study had more frequent interaction with people with whom they employ higher-level politeness forms than the politeness level these addressees would require. This is another reason for women's use of more polite speech.

These results can account for the observed differences in the politeness level of linguistic forms and for women's relatively frequent use of beautification and hypercorrected honorifics. Since women engage more frequently in interactions which calls for higher linguistic forms, they employ higher linguistic forms more frequently. It is a general tendency that the frequent use of specific linguistic forms will gradually exhaust their politeness value. Women's lower assessment of the politeness level of the linguistic forms in question can be considered as an example of such a case. Moreover, the frequent use of beautification and hypercorrected honorifics can be traced to this exhaustion of the politeness value of linguistic forms. Since women do not recognize the high politeness level of some linguistic forms, they consequently seek even higher-level linguistic forms, and this can account for their frequent use of beautification honorifics and indiscriminate use of honorifics, that is, hypercorrected honorifics.

3   How Politeness Forms and Women's Language Represent the Speaker's Identity

The previous sections discussed the structure and the social meaning of politeness forms and women's language. The choice among these linguistic forms is associated with the representation of one's identity.

In addition to expressing referential meaning, language has a function of indexing some situational information. In order to interpret this situational information, the speaker and the addressee must have shared knowledge about the situation and language use. This shared knowledge forms a part of the communicative competence of the speaker and of the addressee. When the proper linguistic forms are selected in accordance with the situation, addressees can interpret the social meaning of these linguistic forms because of their communicative competence. This mechanism shows the indexicality of language. The linguistic forms chosen by the speaker function as indexical signs reflecting the speaker's assessment and acknowledgment of the contextual situation for the addressee. Silverstein (1976: 27) explained these indexes as "signs where the occurrence of a sign vehicle token bears a connection of understood spatio-temporal contiguity to the occurrence of the entity signaled. That is, the presence of some entity is perceived to be signaled in the context of communication incorporating the sign vehicle."

The structure of communicative competence contains some cultural understanding of or presuppositions about the society in which it is used. The use of honorifics according to *wakimae* or women's use of polite language, for example, might reflect people's presuppositions concerning behavior conforming to *wakimae* or women's polite behavior in Japanese society. The choice of one linguistic form over another reflects a perception of the structure of cultural understandings and represents the speaker's identity as a member of the society. Therefore, using honorifics or women's language appropriate to the contextual situation exhibits speakers' behavior in accordance with the cultural understandings inherent in honorifics or women's language, and indexes their identity as a person who observes *wakimae* both in the situation and in the society in general. On the other hand, young women's use of language forms which show masculinity, such as the first person pronoun *boku* or the sentence-final particle *ze*, manifests the face that the speakers are violating the sociolinguistic structure realized through women's language.

Furthermore, the appropriate linguistic choice has the effect of avoiding conflict or misunderstandings in the interaction. This effect stems from the fact that the speaker and the addressee confirm for each other that they have shared knowledge about sociopragmatic language usage and that they both conform to those rules of language use. This confirmation in turn engenders a sense of security for both the speaker and the hearer in that they belong to the same speech community and conform to the same cultural understandings realized by the sociolinguistic structure. Thus, the proper use of politeness forms or men's or women's language indexes the speaker's identity as a proper member of the Japanese speech community.

The indexical function of politeness forms and women's language is related to the representation of the speaker's demeanor. Demeanor is explained by Goffman (1967) as an element of a person's ceremonial behavior, typically conveyed through deportment, dress, and bearing, which serves to express the personal quality of desirability. The use of high-level politeness forms is associated with the speech of people in higher social classes, and this sociolinguistic structure concerning the use of politeness forms is shared by people in Japanese society as a part of the structure of the communicative competence. The customer's use of honorifics toward the sales assistants as explained in section 1.2.1 shows the speaker's demeanor. The use of honorifics by a male speaker in higher position, for example, or the fact that women use honorifics more frequently than men would also represent the speakers' demeanor.

The following example shows the representation of a speaker's identity through her language use. This is to review the politeness forms and women's language used in natural conversations. How the speaker represents her identity as a well-demeaned woman of the upper middle class through her choice of honorifics and other linguistic features is revealed in this example.

The data (Ide et al. 1984) was collected by recording naturally occurring conversations. In this conversation, the participants A, C, and D are housewives (and mothers) in their forties, and B is the husband of a novelist. The speaker A visits the famed novelist's house with two other mothers to pay their respects. The novelist and her husband made a donation to the charity event the mothers had held for their daughters' high school. They are all in the entrance hall of the novelist's house, and the three mothers are about to leave.

(36)   1A: (to B)   Mata doozu, ano   sensei   ni   mo
                      again please (Filler) teacher(Title Hon) Dat too
                      yorosiku otutae   kudasai   mase.
                      regard   tell Ref Hon give Ref Hon Add Hon Imp
                      "Please give sensei our best regards."
       2B: (to A)   Ee.
                      yes
                      "Yes."
       3A: (to B)   Siturei itasi   masi   ta.
                      impolite do Hum Hon Add Hon Past
                      "It was impolite of us to have bothered you."
       4A: (to C, D) Aa, irasite   yokatta   wa nee.
                      Ah be Ref Hon good Past FP FP
                      "It was good that he was at home."

In this conversation, A at first speaks to B, who is the husband of the novelist, with many honorific expressions. This use of honorifics shows A's acknowledgment of the fact that B is of higher position and status, and thus is a person who is not considered familiar, and therefore belongs to the *soto* (out-group). It also acknowledges that B has power in the relationship as the result of being the benefactor. A's formal speech style also manifests her demeanor and indexes her femininity. In utterance 1, A says *sensei* (a term used as an honorific referent) to refer to the novelist. The addressee B and the bystanders C and D interpret the meaning of A's formal style. After the three mothers leave the house (in utterance 4), A speaks to other mothers C and D without honorific expressions, using *yokatta* (good Past) instead of *yokatta desu* (good Past Add Hon). A's change of speech style shows her acknowledgment of the change in the situational setting. This time the addressees are two other mothers, and the speech style of A indexes her close relationship with them, since they belong to the *uchi* (in-group) for her. However, in this utterance, A still uses a honorific form, *irasite* (be Ref Hon) instead of *ite* (be). This is because A is referring to B's behavior with *irasite*. The choice of *irasite* instead of other honorific forms such as *oide ni natte* (be Ref Hon) shows A's femininity. The hearers C and D understand the social meaning of this change of A's speech style to plain forms toward them, of A's use of honorifics toward B, and of A's use of the form *irasite*.

4   Further Problems and a Future Agenda

The goal of this chapter has been to present a description of fundamental sociolinguistic issues focusing on politeness and women's language. Further problems and a future agenda should be noted for the development of research in this field.

Situational constraints play a central role in any discussion of Japanese sociolinguistics. However, insufficient attention has been paid to the crucial influence of context/setting/situational factors in pragmatic and sociolinguistic research. The determining factors are far more complex than what has so far been investigated. Factors concerning the speaker, interpersonal factors such as the relationship between the speaker and the addressee, factors of the situational context, and discursive factors should all be considered as important factors of great relevance in Japanese pragmatics. Unlike most European languages, it is a feature of the Japanese language itself to have rich pragmatic constraints at the core of the appropriate use of the language.

Further research should be concerned with the intricate mechanism of these pragmatic factors relevant to the choice of linguistic forms. The determining factors need to be defined rigorously by carefully observing them at each moment of speaking in natural conversations. It is only after we have a clearer picture of the interrelationship of these determining factors that we can establish a comprehensive analysis of the gender-related differences in language use.

The second set of questions revolves around language and the speaker's identity. The indexicality of language allows the speaker to express the ideology of the shared knowledge of the speech community through the choice of particular linguistic forms and expressions. This language ideology comes from the sociolinguistic structure inherent in the linguistic forms and expressions. The speakers recognize the sociolinguistic structure of their language as their communicative competence and choose the appropriate linguistic forms and expressions from the sociolinguistic varieties. The speaker's choice shows the speaker's identity as a person who shares the language ideology in that speech community.

Sociolinguistic research has not yet connected the problem of the speaker's linguistic choice with the speaker's identity. However, language should also be discussed from the perspective of a marker indexing the speaker's identity. In the study of women's language, for instance, the description and interpretation of gender-related differences in language use and the questions of women's inferior social power have been the main concern of the research. However, the more important question requiring investigation should be the indexical function of women's language as a gender identity marker. The study of the indexicality of language which represents the shared ideology of the speech community will clarify the dynamic system of the speaker's identity and language use.

The third problem is the need for an historical approach to gender-related language issues in Japanese society. Women's language in Japan used to refer to special languages used by court ladies, nuns, or courtesans in their secluded worlds, and were studied in these contexts by Japanese philologists long before the surge of research on this topic that began in the 1970s. Contemporary Japanese women's language, which has borrowed a large amount of vocabulary from these earlier special languages, continues the image of high culture carried by educated women in traditional worlds. The studies of gender and language of contemporary Japanese that are based on the perspectives of gender research that have originated in Western research fail to do justice to the issue as it is generally understood in Japanese society.

These problems amount to a confirmation of the importance of research based on the careful observation of language use in each speech community. Sociolinguistic studies must become useful tools for everyone to understand both their own and other cultures by way of clarifying the mechanism of the language, the ideology, and the identity of those who speak the language. This is essential for mutual understanding between peoples of differing cultures.

Bibliography

Abdel-Jawad, H. (1981). Phonological and Social Variation in Arabic in Amman. PhD dissertation, University of Pennsylvania.

Abe, J. (1991). *Zibun* as distributor and its interpretation with pronominal kare. MS, University of Connecticut.

Abe, J. (1993). Binding Conditions and Scrambling Without A/A' Distinction. PhD dissertation, University of Connecticut.

Abe, J. (1997). The locality of *zibun* and logophoricity. Grant-in-Aid for COE Research Report (1) (No. 08CE1001), *Researching and Verifying an Advanced Theory of Human Language: Explanation of the Human Faculty for Constructing and Computing Sentences on the Basis of Lexical Conceptual Features.* Graduate School of Language Sciences, Kanda University of International Studies.

Abe, K. (1989). Seiyakuwari to hatsuwa no kinoo [Roles according to sex and functions of utterances]. *Eibeibungaku Kenkyuu* [Studies of English and American Literature], 24, 75–93.

Abe, Y. (1985). A Theory of Categorial Morphology and Agglutination in Japanese. PhD dissertation, University of Massachusetts.

Ahn, H. (1990). On light verb constructions in Korean and Japanese. *Japanese/Korean Linguistics*, 221–37.

Aikawa, T. (1993). Reflexivity in Japanese and LF-Analysis of Zibun-Binding. PhD dissertation, Ohio State University, Columbus OH.

Aikawa, T. (1994). Logophoric use of the Japanese reflexive zibun-zisin "self-self." In M. Koizumi and H. Ura (eds), *Formal Approaches to Japanese Linguistics 1: MIT Working Papers in Linguistics 24* (pp. 1–22). Cambridge MA: MIT Press.

Ainsworth-Darnell, K. (1998). The Effects of Priming on Recognition Latencies to Familiar and Unfamiliar Orthographic Forms of Japanese Words. PhD dissertation, Ohio State University.

Akinaga, K. (1981). Akusento shuutoku hoosoku [Laws of accent learning]. In the appendix to *Meikai Nihongo Akusento Jiten* [Japanese Accent Dictionary]. Tokyo: Sanseido.

Akmajian, A. and Kitagawa, C. (1976). Deep-structure binding of pronouns and anaphoric bleeding. *Language*, 52, 61–77.

Akmajian, A. and Kitagawa, C. (1976–7). A justification of the feature [+Aux] in Japanese. *Papers in Japanese Linguistics*, 5, 1–25.

Allen, W. S. (1973). *Accent and Rhythm*. Cambridge: Cambridge University Press.

Alsina, A. (1992). On the argument structure of causatives. *Linguistic Inquiry*, 23, 517–55.

Altmann, G. and Steedman, M. (1988). Interaction with context during human sentence processing. *Cognition*, 30:3, 191–238.

Amano, S. and Kondo, T. (1995). Nihongo-ni okeru moji shinmitsudo-to tango shinmitsudo-no sookan [Correlation between the character familiarity and the word familiarity in Japanese]. Paper presented at the 59th meeting of the Japanese Psychological Association.

Anderson, S. R. (1971). On the role of deep structure in semantic interpretation. *Foundations of Language*, 7, 387–96.

Anderson, S. R. (1977). Comments on the paper by Wasow. In P. Culicover, T. Wasow, and A. Akmajian (eds), *Formal Syntax* (pp. 361–77). New York: Academic Press.

Aoki, C. (1990). Hemispheric Lateralization of Japanese *Kanji* and *Kana*: Evidence from Right Hemisphere Involvement in Semantic Processing of *Kanji*. PhD dissertation, Northeastern University.

Aoun, J. and Hornstein, N. (1986). Bound and referential pronouns. MS, University of Southern California and University of Maryland.

Arisaka, H. (1959). *On'inron* [Phonology]. Tokyo: Sanseido.

Árnason, K. (1980). *Quantity in Historical Linguistics*. Cambridge: Cambridge University Press.

Aronoff, M. (1994). *Morphology by Itself*. Cambridge MA: MIT Press.

Austin, J. L. (1962). *How to do Things with Words*. Harvard: Harvard University Press.

Babyonyshev, M. and Gibson, E. (1995). Processing overload in Japanese. In C. T. Schütze, J. B. Ganger, and K. Broihier (eds), *Papers on Language Processing and Acquisition: MIT Working Papers in Linguistics* 26 (pp. 1–36). Cambridge MA: MIT Press.

Bach, E. (1986). The algebra of events. *Linguistics and Philosophy*, 9, 5–16.

Bailey, C.-J. N. (1973). *Variation and Linguistic Theory*. Washington DC: Center for Applied Linguistics.

Baker, C. L. (1970). Note on the description of English questions: the role of an abstract question morpheme. *Foundations of Language*, 6, 197–219.

Baker, C. L. and McCarthy, J. J. (eds), (1981). *The Logical Problem of Language Acquisition*. Cambridge MA: MIT Press.

Baker, M. (1985). The mirror principle and morphosyntactic explanation. *Linguistic Inquiry*, 16, 373–416.

Baker, M. (1988). *Incorporation: A Theory of Grammatical Function Changing*. Chicago: University of Chicago Press.

Baker, M. (1989). Object sharing and projection in serial verb constructions. *Linguistic Inquiry*, 20, 513–53.

Baker, M., Johnson, K., and Roberts, I. (1989). Passive arguments raised. *Linguistic Inquiry*, 20, 219–51.

Battistella, E. (1989). Chinese reflexivization: a movement of INFL approach. *Linguistics*, 27, 987–1012.

Baugh, J. (1979). Linguistic Style-Shifting in Black English. PhD dissertation, University of Pennsylvania.

Bayley, R. (1991). Variation Theory and Second Language Learning: Linguistic and Social Constraints on Interlanguage Tense Marking. PhD dissertation, Stanford University.

Bayley, R. (1994). Consonant cluster reduction in Tejano English. *Language Variation and Change*, 6, 303–26.

Beaugrande, R. de and Dressler, W. (1981). *Introduction to Text Linguistics*. London: Longman.

Beckman, J. N. (1998). Positional Faithfulness. PhD dissertation, University of Massachusetts, Amherst. [ROA-234-1297]

Beckman, M. E. (1982). Segmental duration and the "mora" in Japanese. *Phonetica*, 39, 113–35.

Belletti, A. and Rizzi, L. (1988). Psych-verbs and theta theory. *Natural Language and Linguistic Theory*, 6, 291–352.

Benua, L. (1995). Identity effects in morphological truncation. In J. Beckman, S. Urbanczyk, and L. Walsh (eds), *Papers in Optimality Theory* (pp. 77–136). Amherst MA: GLSA.

Benua, L. (1997). Transderivational Identity: Phonological Relations between Words. PhD dissertation, University of Massachusetts, Amherst. [ROA-259-0498].

Berman, S. (1991). On the Semantics and Logical Form of wh-Clauses. PhD dissertation, University of Massachusetts.

Berwick, R. C. and Fong, S. (1995). Madam Butterfly redux: parsing English and Japanese with a Principles and Parameters approach. In R. Mazuka and N. Nagai (eds), *Japanese Syntactic Processing* (pp. 177–208). Hillsdale NJ: Lawrence Erlbaum Associates.

Berwick, R. C. and Weinberg, A. (1983). The role of grammars in language use. *Cognition*, 13:1, 1–61.

Berwick, R. C. and Weinberg, A. (1984). *The Grammatical Basis of Linguistic Performance*. Cambridge MA: MIT Press.

Besner, D. and Hildebrandt, N. (1987). Orthographic and phonological codes in the oral reading of Japanese *kana*. *Journal of Experimental Psychology: Learning, Memory, and Cognition*, 13:2, 335–43.

Bever, T. G. (1970). The cognitive basis for linguistic structures. In J. R. Hayes (ed.), *Cognition and the Development of Language* (pp. 279–362). New York: Wiley.

Bloch, B. (1946). Studies in colloquial Japanese I: inflection. *Journal of the American Oriental Society*, 66, 97–109.

Bloch, B. (1950). Studies in colloquial Japanese IV: phonemics. *Language*, 26, 86–125.

Bloom, P. (ed.), (1993). *Language Acquisition*. Cambridge MA: MIT Press.

Bolinger, D. (1978). Asking more than one thing at a time. In H. Hiż (ed.), *Questions* (pp. 151–63). Dordrecht: Kluwer.

Borer, H. (1986). I-subjects. *Linguistic Inquiry*, 17, 375–416.

Borer, H. (1989). Anaphoric AGR. In O. Jaeggli and K. Safir (eds), *The Null Subject Parameter* (pp. 69–109). Dordrecht: Kluwer.

Borer, H. and Wexler, K. (1987). The maturation of syntax. In T. Roeper and E. Williams (eds), *Parameter Setting* (pp. 123–72). Dordrecht: D. Reidel.

Bouchard, D. (1984). *On the Content of Empty Categories*. Dordrecht: Foris.

Bresnan, J. and Mchombo, C. (1995). The lexical integrity principle: evidence from Bantu. *Natural Language and Linguistic Theory*, 13, 181–254.

Brown, G. and Yule, G. (1983). *Discourse Analysis*. Cambridge: Cambridge University Press.

Brown, P. and Levinson, S. C. (1978). Universals in language usage: politeness phenomena. In E. N. Goody (ed.), *Questions and Politeness* (pp. 56–289). London: Cambridge University Press.

Brown, P. and Levinson, S. C. (1987). *Politeness: Some Universals in Language Usage.* Cambridge: Cambridge University Press.

Burzio, L. (1986). *Italian Syntax: A Government and Binding Approach.* Dordrecht: D. Reidel.

Burzio, L. (1997). Cycles, non-derived-environment blocking, and correspondence. MS, Johns Hopkins University.

Campbell, W. N. and Sagisaka, Y. (1991). Moraic and syllable-level effects on speech timing. (In Japanese.) *IEICE Technical Report* SP90-106, 35–40.

Carlson, G. N. (1977). Reference to Kinds in English. PhD dissertation, University of Massachusetts, Amherst.

Carlson, G. N. and Tanenhaus, M. K. (1989). Introduction. In G. N. Carlson and M. K. Tanenhaus (eds), *Linguistic Structure in Language Processing* (pp. 1–26). Dordrecht: Kluwer.

Carter, R. (1976). Some constraints on possible words. *Semantikos*, 1, 27–66.

Carter, R. (1988). *On Linking: Papers by Richard Carter.* Lexicon Project Working Papers 25. MIT.

Cedergren, H. (1973). The Interplay of Social and Linguistic Factors in Panama. PhD dissertation, Cornell University.

Chamberlain, B. H. (1888). *A Handbook of Colloquial Japanese.* Tokyo: Imperial University of Tokyo.

Chambers, J. K. (1992). Dialect acquisition. *Language*, 68, 673–705.

Chambers, J. K. (1995). *Sociolinguistic Theory.* Oxford: Blackwell.

Cheng, L. and Huang, C.-T. J. (1994). Three ways to get passives. MS, University of California, Irvine.

Chierchia, G. (1989). A semantics for unaccusatives and its syntactic consequences. MS, Cornell University.

Chierchia, G. (1991). Functional *wh* and weak crossover, *West Coast Conference of Formal Linguistics*, 10, 75–90.

Chierchia, G. (1992–3). Questions with quantifiers. *Natural Language Semantics*, 1, 181–234.

Chikamatsu, N. (1996). The effects of L1 orthography on L2 word recognition. *Studies in Second Language Acquisition*, 18:4, 403–32.

Cho, J. H. (1994). On scrambling: reconstruction, crossover, and anaphor binding. In Y.-K. Kim-Renaud (ed.), *Theoretical Issues in Korean Linguistics* (pp. 255–74). Stanford: Center for the Study of Language and Information.

Choe, H. S. (1987). Syntactic adjunction, A-chain and the ECP: multiple identical case construction in Korean. *North East Linguistic Society*, 17, 100–20.

Choe, J.-W. (1987). LF-movement and pied-piping. *Linguistic Inquiry*, 18, 348–53.

Chomsky, C. (1969). *The Acquisition of Syntax in Children from 5 to 10.* Cambridge MA: MIT Press.

Chomsky, N. (1973). Conditions on transformations. In S. R. Anderson and P. Kiparsky (eds), *A Festschrift for Morris Halle* (pp. 232–86). New York: Holt, Rinehart and Winston.

Chomsky, N. (1975). *Reflections on Language.* New York: Pantheon Books.

Chomsky, N. (1977). On wh-movement. In P. Culicover, T. Wasow, and A. Akmajian (eds), *Formal Syntax* (pp. 71–132). New York: Academic Press.

Chomsky, N. (1981a). *Lectures on Government and Binding.* Dordrecht: Foris.

Chomsky, N. (1981b). Principles and parameters in syntactic theory. In N. Hornstein, and D. Lightfoot (eds), *Explanation in Linguistics: The Logical Problem of Language Acquisition* (pp. 32–75). London: Longman.

Chomsky, N. (1982). *Some Concepts and Consequences of the Theory of Government and Binding*. Cambridge MA: MIT Press.

Chomsky, N. (1986a). *Barriers*. Cambridge MA: MIT Press.

Chomsky, N. (1986b). *Knowledge of Language: Its Nature, Origin and Use*. New York: Praeger.

Chomsky, N. (1989). Some notes on economy of derivation and representation. *MIT Working Papers in Linguistics*, 10, 42–74. Reprinted in N. Chomsky (1995), *The Minimalist Program* (pp. 129–66). Cambridge MA: MIT Press.

Chomsky, N. (1992). A minimalist program for linguistic theory. *MIT Occasional Papers in Linguistics*, 1, 1–52. Reprinted in N. Chomsky (1995), *The Minimalist Program* (pp. 167–218). Cambridge MA: MIT Press.

Chomsky, N. (1993). A minimalist program for linguistic theory. In K. Hale and S. J. Keyser (eds), *The View from Building 20: Essays in Linguistics in Honor of Sylvain Bromberger* (pp. 1–52). Cambridge MA: MIT Press.

Chomsky, N. (1995a). *The Minimalist Program*. Cambridge MA: MIT Press.

Chomsky, N. (1995b). Bare phrase structure. In G. Webelhuth (ed.), *Government and Binding Theory and the Minimalist Program* (pp. 383–439). Cambridge MA: Blackwell.

Chomsky, N. and Halle, M. (1968). *The Sound Pattern of English*. New York: Harper and Row.

Chomsky, N. and Lasnik, H. (1977). Filters and control. *Linguistic Inquiry*, 8, 425–504.

Chomsky, N. and Lasnik, H. (1993). The theory of principles and parameters. In J. Jacobs, A. von Stechow, W. Sternefeld, and T. Vennemann (eds), *Syntax: An International Handbook of Contemporary Research* (pp. 506–69). Berlin: de Gruyter. Reprinted in N. Chomsky (1995), *The Minimalist Program* (pp. 13–128). Cambridge MA: MIT Press.

Chung, S., Ladusaw, W. A., and McCloskey, J. (1995). Sluicing and Logical Form. *Natural Language Semantics*, 3, 239–82.

Clancy, P. M. (1985). The acquisition of Japanese. In D. I. Slobin (ed.), *The Crosslinguistic Study of Language Acquisition, Vol. 1: The Data* (pp. 373–524). Hillsdale NJ: Lawrence Erlbaum Associates.

Clancy, P. M. (1986). The acquisition of communicative style in Japanese. In B. Schieffelin and E. Ochs (eds), *Language Socialization Across Cultures* (pp. 213–50). Cambridge: Cambridge University Press.

Clark, M. (1987). Japanese as a tone language. In T. Imai and M. Saito (eds), *Issues in Japanese Linguistics* (pp. 53–105). Dordrecht: Foris.

Clements, G. N. (1975). The logophoric pronoun in Ewe: its role in discourse. *Journal of West African Languages*, 2, 141–77.

Cofer, T. (1972). Linguistic Variability in a Philadelphia Speech Community. PhD dissertation, University of Pennsylvania.

Cohn, A. and McCarthy, J. J. (1994). Alignment and parallelism in Indonesian phonology. MS, Cornell University and University of Massachusetts, Amherst.

Cole, P., Hermon, G., and Sung, L.-M. (1990). Principles and parameters of long distance reflexives. *Linguistic Inquiry*, 21:1, 1–22.

Comorovski, I. (1996). *Interrogative Phrases and the Syntax–Semantics Interface*. Studies in Linguistics and Philosophy. Dordrecht: Kluwer.

Comrie, B. (1976). *Aspect*. Cambridge: Cambridge University Press.

Comrie, B. (1985). *Tense*. Cambridge: Cambridge University Press.

Cook, H. M. (1988). Sentential Particles in Japanese Conversation: A Study of Indexicality. PhD dissertation, University of Southern California.

Cook, H. M. (1996). The use of addressee honorifics in Japanese elementary classrooms. *Japanese/Korean Linguistics*, 5, 67–81.

Crain, S. (1991). Language acquisition in the absence of experience. *Behavioral and Brain Sciences*, 14, 597–650.

Croft, W. (1991). *Syntactic Categories and Grammatical Relations*. Chicago: University of Chicago Press.

Cziko, G. and Koda, K. (1987). A Japanese child's use of stative and punctual verbs. *Journal of Child Language*, 14, 99–111.

Darnell, K. (1995). Word recognition and reading acquisition in Japanese: the interaction of orthography and expectation. MS, Ohio State University.

Darnell, K., Boland, J., and Nakayama, M. (1994). The influence of orthography and sentence contrast on the processing of nouns in Japanese. In J. Venditti (ed.), *OSU Working Papers in Linguistics* 44 (pp. 92–104). Columbus OH: Ohio State University.

Davidson, L. and Noyer, R. (1997). Loan phonology in Huave: nativization and the ranking of faithfulness constraints. *West Coast Conference of Formal Linguistics*, 15, 65–79.

Davis, S. and Tsujimura, N. (1991). An autosegmental account of Japanese verbal conjugation. *Journal of Japanese Linguistics*, 13, 117–44.

Dayal, V. (1996). *Locality in wh-Quantification*. Dordrecht: Kluwer.

Déprez, V. (1989). On the Typology of Syntactic Positions and the Nature of Chains: Move α to the Specifier of Functional Projections. PhD dissertation, MIT.

Di Sciullo, A.-M. and Williams, E. (1987). *On the Definition of Word*. Cambridge MA: MIT Press.

Dowty, D. (1979). *Word Meaning and Montague Grammar: The Semantics of Verbs and Times in Generative Semantics and in Montague's PTQ*. Dordrecht: D. Reidel.

Dubinsky, S. (1985). Japanese Union Constructions: A Unified Analysis of -*Sase* and -*Rare*. PhD dissertation, Cornell University.

Dubinsky, S. (1989). Compound suru verbs and evidence for unaccusativity in Japanese. *Chicago Linguistic Society*, 25, 98–111.

Dubinsky, S. (1990). Light verbs and predicate demotion in Japanese. In K. Dziwirek, P. Farrell, and E. Mejías-Bikandi (eds), *Grammatical Relations* (pp. 127–45). Stanford: Center for the Study of Language and Information.

Dubinsky, S. (1994). Syntactic underspecification: a minimalist approach to light verbs. In M. Koizumi and H. Ura (eds), *Formal Approaches to Japanese Linguistics 1: MIT Working Papers in Linguistics* 24 (pp. 61–81). Cambridge MA: MIT Press.

Enç, M. (1987). Anchoring conditions for tense. *Linguistic Inquiry*, 18, 633–57.

Engdahl, E. (1983). Parasitic gaps. *Linguistics and Philosophy*, 6, 5–34.

Engdahl, E. (1986). *Constituent Questions*. Dordrecht: Kluwer.

Engdahl, E. (1988). Relational interpretation. In R. Kempson (ed.), *Mental Representations* (pp. 63–82). Cambridge: Cambridge University Press.

Fairclough, N. (1989). *Language and Power*. London: Longman.

Farmer, A. K. (1980). On the Interaction of Morphology and Syntax. PhD dissertation, MIT.

Farmer, A. (1984). *Modularity in Syntax*. Cambridge MA: MIT Press.

Farmer, A. K., Hale, K., and Tsujimura, N. (1986). A note on weak crossover in Japanese. *Natural Language and Linguistic Theory*, 4, 33–42.

Fasold, R. W. (1972). *Tense marking in Black English: A Linguistic and Social Analysis*. Arlington, VA: Center for Applied Linguistics.

Ferreira, F. and Clifton, C. (1986). The independence of syntactic processing. *Journal of Memory and Language*, 25:3, 348–68.

Fiengo, R. (1977). On trace theory. *Linguistic Inquiry*, 8, 35–61.

Fiengo, R., Huang, C.-T. J., Lasnik, H., and Reinhart, T. (1987). The syntax of *wh*-in-situ. *West Coast Conference of Formal Linguistics*, 7, 81–98.

Fillmore, C. (1968). The case for case. In E. Bach and R. T. Harms (eds), *Universals in Linguistic Theory* (pp. 1–88). New York: Holt, Rinehart and Winston.

Fillmore, C. (1975). *Santa Cruz Lectures on Deixis*. Bloomington: Indiana University Linguistics Club.

Flaherty, M. (1991). Do second-language learners of Japanese process *kanji* in the same way as Japanese children? *Japanese Language Education around the Globe*, 1, 183–200.

Flemming, E. S. (1995). Auditory Representations in Phonology. PhD dissertation, University of California, Los Angeles.

Flores d'Arcais, G. B. and Saito, H. (1993). Lexical decomposition of complex *kanji* characters in Japanese readers. *Psychological Research*, 55:1, 52–63.

Flores d'Arcais, G. B., Saito, H., and Kawakami, M. (1995). Phonological and semantic activation in reading *kanji* characters. *Journal of Experimental Psychology: Learning, Memory, and Cognition*, 21:1, 34–42.

Fodor, J. D. (1989). Empty categories in sentence processing. In G. T. M. Altmann (ed.), *Parsing and Interpretation* (pp. 155–210). Hove: Lawrence Erlbaum Associates.

Fodor, J. D. and Inoue, A. (1994). The diagnosis and cure of garden paths. *Journal of Psycholinguistic Research*, 23:5, 407–34.

Fodor, J. D., Bever, T. G., and Garrett, M. F. (1974). *The Psychology of Language: An Introduction to Psycholinguistics and Generative Grammar*. New York: McGraw-Hill.

Foley, W. and Van Valin, R. Jr. (1984). *Functional Syntax and Universal Grammar*. Cambridge: Cambridge University Press.

Forster, K. I. (1976). Accessing the mental lexicon. In R. J. Wales and E. Walker (eds), *New Approaches to Language Mechanisms* (pp. 257–87). Amsterdam: North-Holland.

Frazier, L. (1978). On Comprehending Sentences: Syntactic Parsing Strategies. PhD dissertation, University of Connecticut.

Frazier, L. (1991). Foreword. In M. De Vincenzi, *Syntactic Parsing Strategies in Italian* (pp. xi–xxiii). Dordrecht: Kluwer.

Frazier, L. and Fodor, J. D. (1978). The sausage machine: a new two-stage parsing model. *Cognition*, 6, 291–325.

Frazier, L. and Rayner, K. (1982). Making and correcting errors during sentence comprehension: eye movements in the analysis of structurally ambiguous sentences. *Cognitive Psychology*, 14:2, 178–210.

Frazier, L. and Rayner, K. (1987). Resolution of syntactic category ambiguities: eye movements in parsing lexically ambiguous sentences. *Journal of Memory and Language*, 26:5, 505–26.

Frazier, L. and Rayner, K. (1988). Parameterizing the language processing system: left- vs. right-branching within and across languages. In J. Hawkins (ed.), *Explaining Language Universals* (pp. 247–79). Oxford: Blackwell.

Frazier, L., Clifton, C., and Randall, J. (1983). Filling gaps: decision principles and structure in sentence comprehension. *Cognition*, 13:2, 187–222.

Fries, C. C. and Pike, K. (1949). Coexistent phonemic systems. *Language*, 25, 29–50.

Fries, P. H. (1983). On the status of theme in English: arguments from discourse. In P. H. Fries and M. Gregory (eds), *Micro and Macro Connexity of Texts* (pp. 116–52). Hamburg: Helmut Buske Verlag.

Fromkin, V. (1973). *Speech Errors as Linguistic Evidence*. The Hague: Mouton.

Fujii, T. (1966). Dooshi+te iru no imi [The Meaning of V-te iru]. *Kokugo Kenkyuushitsu* 5. Tokyo University. Reprinted in H. Kindaichi (1976), *Nihongo Dooshi no Asupekuto* [Aspect in Japanese Verbs] (pp. 87–116). Tokyo: Mugi Shoboo.

Fujita, N. (1994). On the Nature of Modification: A Study of Floating Quantifiers and Other Related Constructions in Japanese. PhD dissertation, University of Rochester.

Fukazawa, H. (1998). Multiple input–output faithfulness relations in Japanese. MS, University of Maryland, College Park. [ROA-260-0598].

Fukazawa, H., Kitahara, M., and Ota, M. (1998). Lexical stratification and ranking invariance in constraint-based grammars. MS, University of Maryland, College Park, Indiana University, and Georgetown University. [ROA-267-0698].

Fukuhara, M. (1993). Case-Checking in Japanese. MA Thesis, University of Connecticut.

Fukui, N. (1984). Studies on Japanese anaphora I: the adjunct subject hypothesis and zibun. MS, MIT.

Fukui, N. (1986). A Theory of Category Projection and its Applications. PhD dissertation, MIT.

Fukui, N. (1992). A note on the uniformity of form-chain. MS, University of California, Irvine.

Fukui, N. (1993). Parameter and optionality. *Linguistic Inquiry*, 24, 399–420.

Fukui, N. and Saito, M. (1998). Order in phrase structure and movement. *Linguistic Inquiry*, 29, 439–74.

Fukui, N. and Speas, P. (1986). Specifiers and projection. *MIT Working Papers in Linguistics*, 8, 128–72.

Fukui, N. and Takano, Y. (to appear). Symmetry in syntax: merge and demerge. *Journal of East Asian Linguistics*.

Fukui, N., Miyagawa, S., and Tenny, C. (1985). *Verb Classes in English and Japanese: A Case Study in the Interaction of Syntax, Morphology and Semantics*. Lexicon Project Working Papers 3, MIT.

Gashuu, H. (1994). *Nihongo-no Hyookikeitai-no Hyoojunka-to Sono Ninchishinrigakuteki Datoosei-no Kenkyuu: Report* [Studies on the standardization of the Japanese writing system and its validity from the perspectives of Cognitive Psychology]. Kwansei Gakuin University.

Geach, P. (1972). *Logic Matters*. Oxford: Blackwell.

Gibson, E. A. F. (1991). A Computational Theory of Human Linguistic Processing: Memory Limitations and Processing Breakdown. PhD dissertation, Carnegie Mellon University.

Gleitman, L. and Landau, B. (eds), (1994). *The Acquisition of the Lexicon*. Cambridge MA: MIT Press.

Goffman, E. (1955). On face-work: an analysis of ritual elements in social interaction. *Psychiatry*, 18, 213–31.

Goffman, E. (1967). *Interaction Ritual*. New York: Doubleday.

Goffman, E. (1981). *Forms of Talk*. Philadelphia: University of Pennsylvania Press.

Gorrell, P. (1987). Studies of Human Syntactic Processing: Ranked-Parallel Versus Serial Models. PhD dissertation, University of Connecticut.

Gorrell, P. (1989). Establishing the loci of serial and parallel effects in syntactic processing. *Journal of Psycholinguistic Research*, 18:1, 61–73.

Gorrell, P. (1995). Japanese trees and the garden path. In R. Mazuka and N. Nagai (eds), *Japanese Syntactic Processing* (pp. 331–50). Hillsdale NJ: Lawrence Erlbaum Associates.

Green, G. (1973). A syntactic syncretism in English and French. In B. Kachru, R. B. Lees, Y. Malkiel, A Pietrangeli, and S. Saporta (eds), *Issues in Linguistics: Papers in Honor of Henry and Renee Kahane* (pp. 257–78). Urbana: University of Illinois Press.

Green, G. (1974). *Semantics and Syntactic Regularity*. Bloomington: Indiana University Press.

Grice, H. P. (1975). Logic and conversation. In P. Cole and J. L. Morgan (eds), *Syntax and Semantics 3* (pp. 41–58). New York: Academic Press.

Grignon, A.-M. (1990). Japanese complex predicates and lexical phonology. *Journal of Japanese Linguistics*, 12, 1–33.

Grimshaw, J. and Mester, A. (1988). Light verbs and θ-marking. *Linguistic Inquiry*, 19, 205–32.

Gropen, J., Pinker, S., Hollander, M., Goldberg, R., and Wilson, R. (1989). The learnability and acquisition of the dative alternation in English. *Language*, 65, 203–57.

Gruber, J. (1965). *Studies in Lexical Relations*. Bloomington: Indiana University Linguistics Club.

Guasti, M. T. (1992). Causative and Perception Verbs. PhD dissertation, University of Geneva.

Gumperz, J. (1982a). *Discourse Strategies*. Cambridge: Cambridge University Press.

Gumperz, J. (1982b). *Language and Social Identity*. Cambridge: Cambridge University Press.

Gunji, T. (1987). *Japanese Phrase Structure Grammar: A Unification-Based Approach*. Dordrecht: Foris.

Gunji, T. (ed.), (1996). *Studies on the Universality of Constraint-Based Phrase Structure Grammars*. Osaka University: Toyonaka.

Guy, G. R. (1980). Variation in the group and the individual: the case of final stop deletion. In W. Labov (ed.), *Locating Language in Time and Space* (pp. 1–36). New York: Academic Press.

Guy, G. R. (1981). Syntactic and Phonetic Variation in Carioca Portuguese. PhD dissertation, University of Pennsylvania.

Guy, G. R. (1991a). Explanation in variable phonology: an exponential model of morphological constraints. *Language Variation and Change*, 3, 1–22.

Guy, G. R. (1991b). Contextual conditioning in variable phonology. *Language Variation and Change*, 3, 223–39.

Guy, G. R. (1993). Lexical phonology and the problem of variation. *Berkeley Linguistics Society*, 19, 171–81.

Guy, G. R. (1994). The phonology of variation. *Chicago Linguistic Society*, 30:2, 133–49.

Guy, G. R. (1997). Violable is variable: optimality theory and linguistic variation. *Language Variation and Change*, 9, 333–47.

Guy, G. R. and Boberg, C. (1997). Inherent variability and the obligatory contour principle. *Language Variation and Change*, 9, 149–64.

Guy, G. R. and Boyd, S. (1990). The development of a morphological class. *Language Variation and Change*, 2, 1–18.

Habermas, J. (1982). Goorisei no yukue: kyoiku kaikaku shinhosyusyugi seikatsusekai [The future of rationality: Reformation of education, the new conservatism, and life world]. (interview). *Sisoo*, 6, 54–85.

Haeri, N. (1991). Sociolinguistic Variation in Cairene Arabic: Palatalization and the qaf in the Speech of Men and Women. PhD dissertation, University of Pennsylvania.

Hagstrom, P. and Rhee, J. (1997). Differences between Korean and Japanese processing overload. *Journal of Psycholinguistic Research*, 26:2, 189–206.

Haig, J. (1980). Some observations on quantifier floating in Japanese. *Linguistics*, 18, 1065–83.

Haiman, J. (1985). *Iconicity in Syntax*. Amsterdam: John Benjamins.

Hale, K. (1980). Remarks on Japanese phrase structure: comments on the papers on Japanese syntax. *MIT Working Papers in Linguistics*, 2, 185–203.

Hale, K. (1982). Preliminary remarks on configurationality. *North East Linguistic Society*, 12, 86–96.

Hale, K. (1983). Warlpiri and the grammar of non-configurational language. *Natural Language and Linguistic Theory*, 1, 5–47.

Hale, K. and Keyser, S. J. (1986). *Some Transitivity Alternations in English*. Lexicon Project Working Papers 7, MIT.

Hale, K. H. and Keyser, S. J. (eds), (1993). *The View from Building 20: Essays in Linguistics in Honor of Sylvain Bromberger*. Cambridge MA: MIT Press.

Halle, M. and Idsardi, W. J. (1995). General properties of stress and metrical structure. In J. A. Goldsmith (ed.), *The Handbook of Phonological Theory* (pp. 404–43). Oxford: Blackwell.

Halle, M. and Marantz, A. (1993). Distributed morphology and the pieces of inflection. In K. H. Hale and S. J. Keyser (eds), *The View from Building 20: Essays in Linguistics in Honor of Sylvain Bromberger* (pp. 111–76). Cambridge MA: MIT Press.

Halle, M. and Vergnaud, J.-R. (1987). *An Essay on Stress*. Cambridge MA: MIT Press.

Halliday, M. A. K. and Hasan, R. (1976). *Cohesion in English*. London: Longman.

Halliday, M. A. K. and Hasan, R. (1989). *Language, Context, and Text: Aspects of Language in a Socio-Semiotic Perspective*. Oxford: Oxford University Press.

Hamano, S. (1986). The Sound-Symbolic System of Japanese. PhD dissertation, University of Florida, Gainesville.

Hammond, M. (1997). Underlying representations in Optimality Theory. In I. Roca (ed.), *Derivations and Constraints in Phonology* (pp. 349–65). Oxford: Clarendon Press.

Han, M. S. (1962). The feature of duration in Japanese. *Study of Sounds*, 10, 65–75.

Han, M. S. (1994). Acoustic manifestations of mora timing in Japanese. *Journal of the Acoustical Society of America*, 96:1, 73–82.

Harada, K. (1972). Constraints on WH-Q Binding. *Studies in Descriptive and Applied Linguistics*, 5, 180–206.

Harada, S.-I. (1973). Counter equi NP deletion. *Annual Bulletin of the Research Institute of Logopedics and Phoniatrics*, 7, 113–47.

Harada, S.-I. (1977). Nihongo-ni henkei-wa hitsuyoo da [Transformations are needed in Japanese]. *Gengo*, 6, 88–103.

Haraguchi, S. (1977). *The Tone Pattern of Japanese: An Autosegmental Theory of Tonology*. Tokyo: Kaitakusha.

Haraguchi, S. (1979a). Nihongo onchoo no shosoo [Aspects of Japanese tonal systems]. *Gengo no Kagaku* [Science of Language], 7, 21–69.

Haraguchi, S. (1979b). Tonology of Japanese dialects. In G. Bedell, E. Kobayashi, and M. Muraki (eds), *Explorations in Linguistics: Papers in Honor of Kazuko Inoue* (pp. 125–46). Tokyo: Kenkyuusha.

Haraguchi, S. (1991). *A Theory of Stress and Accent*. Dordrecht: Foris.

Haraguchi, S. (1996). Syllable, mora and accent. In T. Otake and A. Cutler (eds), *Phonological Structure and Language Processing: Cross-Linguistic Studies* (pp. 45–75). Berlin: Mouton de Gruyter.

Haraguchi, S. (1998). *Aspects of Japanese Accent*. Report of the COE Project.

Harley, H. (1995). Subjects, Events, and Licensing. PhD dissertation, MIT.

Harris, J. (1985). *Phonological Variation and Change: Studies in Hiberno-Irish*. Cambridge: Cambridge University Press.

Hasegawa, K. (1964). Nihongo bunpoo shiron [An essay on Japanese grammar]. *Gengobunka*, 1, 3–46.

Hasegawa, N. (1981). The VP complement and "control" phenomena: beyond trace theory. *Linguistic Analysis*, 7, 85–120.

Hasegawa, N. (1986). More arguments for the pied-piping analysis of *wh*-questions in Japanese. *University of Massachusetts Occasional Papers in Linguistics 11: Oriental Linguistics*, 79–108.

Hasegawa, N. (1988). Passives, verb raising, and the affectedness condition. *West Coast Conference of Formal Linguistics*, 7, 99–113.

Hasegawa, N. (1990). Comments on Mazuka and Lust's paper. In L. Frazier and J. De Villiers (eds), *Language Processing and Language Acquisition* (pp. 206–24). Dordrecht: Kluwer.

Hasegawa, N. (1991a). Affirmative polarity items and negation in Japanese. In C. Georgopoulos and R. Ishihara (eds), *Interdisciplinary Approaches to Languages: Essays in Honor of S.-Y. Kuroda* (pp. 271–85). Dordrecht: Kluwer.

Hasegawa, N. (1991b). On head movement in Japanese: the case of verbal nouns. *Proceedings of Sophia Linguistic Society*, 6, 8–32.

Haspelmath, M. (1997). *Indefinite Pronouns*. Oxford: Clarendon Press.

Hattori, S. (1954). On'inron kara mita kokugo no akusento [Japanese accent considered from a phonological viewpoint]. Reprinted in S. Hattori (1960), *Gengogaku no Hoohoo* [Methods in Linguistics] (pp. 240–75). Tokyo: Iwanami Shoten.

Hattori, S. (1960). *Gengogaku no Hoohoo* [Methods in Linguistics]. Tokyo: Iwanami Shoten.

Hayashi, O. (ed.), (1982). *Zusetsu Nihongo* [Illustrated Japanese]. Tokyo: Kadokawa Shoten.

Hayashi, O. and Kakehi, K. (1990). An experimental study on basic perceptual units of speech based on reaction time. Paper presented at the Spring Meeting of the Acoustical Society of Japan.

Hayashibe, H. (1975). Word order and particles: a developmental study in Japanese. *Descriptive and Applied Linguistics*, 8, 1–18.

Hayes, B. (1989). Compensatory lengthening in moraic phonology. *Linguistic Inquiry*, 20:2, 253–306.

Hayes, B. (1995). *Metrical Stress Theory: Principles and Case Studies*. Chicago: University of Chicago Press.

Hayes, B. (1996). Phonetically driven phonology: the role of Optimality Theory and inductive grounding. MS, University of California, Los Angeles.

Heim, I. (1982). *The Semantics of Definite and Indefinite Noun Phrases*. PhD dissertation, University of Massachusetts.

Hepburn, J. C. (1872). *Japanese–English and English–Japanese Dictionary*. (2nd edn). Tokyo: Z. P. Maruya.

Herold, R. (1990). *Mechanisms of Merger: The Implementation and Distribution of the Low Back Merger in Eastern Pennsylvania*. PhD dissertation, University of Pennsylvania.

Hibiya, J. (1988). *A Quantitative Study of Tokyo Japanese*. PhD dissertation, University of Pennsylvania.

Hibiya, J. (1990). Akusento no henka to hen'i -2, 3, 4, 5, 6ppaku keiyoshi- [Tonal variation in Tokyo Japanese: 2, 3, 4, 5, 6 morae adjective]. *Sophia Linguistica*, 28, 25–35.

Hibiya, J. (1991). Keiyoshi akusento no henka to hen'i -randamu sampuringu choosa no kekka kara [Variation in the tone pattern of Japanese adjectives: the sociolinguistic study of Nezu, Tokyo]. *Keio Gijuku Daigaku Gengo Bunka Kenkyuujo Kiyoo* [Reports of the Keio Institute of Cultural and Linguistic Studies], 23, 133–46.

Hibiya, J. (1993). Keiyoshi akusento no henka to hen'i -jitsujikan ni okeru henka to genjiten ni okeru hen'i [The tonal pattern of Japanese adjectives: variation in apparent time and change in real time]. *Keio Gijuku Daigaku Gengo Bunka Kenkyuujo Kiyoo* [Reports of the Keio Institute of Cultural and Linguistic Studies], 25, 207–18.

Hibiya, J. (1995a). The velar nasal in Tokyo Japanese: a case of diffusion from above. *Language Variation and Change*, 7, 139–52.

Hibiya, J. (1995b). Denasalization of the velar nasal in Tokyo Japanese: observations in real time. In G. R. Guy, C. Feagin, D. Schiffrin, and J. Baugh (eds), *Towards a Social Science of Language. Vol. 1: Variation and Change in Language and Society* (pp. 161–70). Amsterdam and Philadelphia: John Benjamins.

Hibiya, J. (1997). Linguistic variation in Japanese-Canadian English: a case study of /-t, d/ deletion. In M. Ukaji, T. Nakao, M. Kajita, and S. Chiba (eds), *Studies in English Linguistics: A Festschrift for Akira Ota on the Occasion of His Eightieth Birthday* (pp. 902–11). Tokyo: Taishuukan.

Hickok, G. (1993). Parallel parsing: evidence from reactivation in garden-path sentences. *Journal of Psycholinguistic Research*, 22:2, 239–50.

Higginbotham, J. (1983). Logical form, binding, and nominals. *Linguistic Inquiry*, 14, 395–420.

Hill, B. Ide, S., Ikuta, S., Kawasaki, A., and Ogino, T. (1986). Universals of linguistic politeness: quantitative evidence from Japanese and American English. *Journal of Pragmatics*, 10, 347–71.

Hindle, D. (1980). The Social and Structural Conditioning of Phonetic Variation. PhD dissertation, University of Pennsylvania.

Hinds, J. (1973). On the status of VP node in Japanese. MS, Tokyo University and Seishin Joshi Daigaku. Reproduced by the Indiana University Linguistics Club, 1974.

Hinds, J. (1976). *Aspects of Japanese Discourse Structure*. Tokyo: Kaitakusha.

Hinds, J. (1983). Contrastive rhetoric: Japanese and English. *TEXT*, 3, 183–95.

Hinds, J. (1990). Inductive, deductive, quasi-inductive: expository writing in Japanese, Korean, Chinese, and Thai. In U. Connor and A. M. Jones (eds), *Coherence in Writing Research and Pedagogical Perspectives* (pp. 89–109). Alexandria VA: Teachers of English to Speakers of Other Languages.

Hino, Y. and Lupker, S. J. (1996). The effects of word frequency for Japanese *kana* and *kanji* words in naming and lexical decision. Paper presented at the 37th annual meeting of the Psychonomic Society, Chicago.

Hirayama, T. (1960). *Zenkoku Akusento Jiten* [All-Japan Accent Dictionary]. Tokyo: Tookyoodoo.

Hirose, T. (1984). The effect of script frequency on semantic processing of *kanji* and *kana* words. *Japanese Journal of Psychology*, 3, 173–6.

Hirose, T. (1985). The effects of orthographic familiarity on word recognition. *Japanese Journal of Psychology*, 56, 44–7.

Hirose, T. and Chun, S. (1998). Attachment ambiguity in head final languages. In N. Akatsuka, H. Hoji, S. Iwasaki, S. Sohn, and S. Strauss (eds), *Japanese/Korean Linguistics*, 7, 311–27. Stanford: CSLI Publications. Distributed by Cambridge University Press.

Hirose, T. and Inoue, A. (in press). Ambiguities in parsing complex sentences in Japanese. In D. Hillert (ed.), *Syntax and Semantics. Vol. 31*. New York, Academic Press.

Hockett, C. (1950). Age-grading and linguistic continuity. *Language*, 26, 449–57.

Hodge, R. and Kress, G. (1993). *Language as Ideology*. London: Routledge.

Hoji, H. (1985). Logical Form Constraints and Configurational Structures in Japanese. PhD dissertation, University of Washington.

Hoji, H. (1987). Weak crossover and Japanese phrase structure. In T. Imai and M. Saito (eds), *Issues in Japanese Linguistics* (pp. 163–201). Dordrecht: Foris.

Hoji, H. (1989). Nominal categories in Japanese and binding conditions. Paper presented at the Workshop on Japanese Syntax and Universal Grammar on Issues Pertaining to Movement, Ohio State University, Columbus OH.

Hoji, H. (1990). Theories of anaphora and aspects of Japanese syntax. MS, University of Southern California, Los Angeles.

Hoji, H. (1991a). Kare. [He]. In C. Georgopoulos and R. Ishihara (eds), *Interdisciplinary Approaches to Language: Essays in Honor of S.-Y. Kuroda* (pp. 287–304). Dordrecht: Kluwer.

Hoji, H. (1991b). Raising-to-object, ECM and the major object in Japanese. Paper presented at the Japanese Syntax Workshop, University of Rochester, New York.

Holden, K. (1976). Assimilation rates of borrowings and phonological productivity. *Language*, 52, 131–47.

Homma, Y. (1981). Durational relationships between Japanese stops and vowels. *Journal of Phonetics*, 9, 273–81.

Hong, Y. (1991). *A Sociolinguistic Study of Seoul Korean*. Seoul: Research Center for Peace and Unification of Korea.

Honna, N. (1989). Nihongo no buntai to eigo no buntai [Japanese style and English style]. *Kooza Nihongo to Nihongo Kyooiku* [Japanese Language and Japanese Language Education], 5, 363–85.

Horii, K. (1990). GA/NO Conversion and Japanese Sentence Processing. MA thesis, Ohio State University.

Hornstein, N. (1990). *As Time Goes By*. Cambridge MA: MIT Press.

Hornstein, N. (1995). *Logical Form: From GB to Minimalism*. Oxford: Blackwell.

Hornstein, N. and Lightfoot, D. (eds), (1981). *Explanation in Linguistics: The Logical Problem of Language Acquisition*. London: Longman.

Horodeck, R. A. (1987). The Role of Sound in Reading and Writing *Kanji*. PhD dissertation, Cornell University.

Horvath, B. M. (1985). *Variation in Australian English: The Sociolects of Sydney*. Cambridge: Cambridge University Press.

Hoshi, H. (1991). The generalized projection principle and its implications for passive constructions. *Journal of Japanese Linguistics*, 13, 53–89.

Hoshi, H. (1994a). Theta role assignment, passivization, and excorporation. *Journal of East Asian Linguistics*, 3, 147–78.

Hoshi, H. (1994b). Passive, Causative and Light Verbs: A Study on Theta Role Assignment. PhD dissertation, University of Connecticut.

Howard, I. and Niyekawa-Howard, A. M. (1976). Passivization. In M. Shibatani (ed.), *Japanese Generative Grammar: Syntax and Semantics 5* (pp. 201–37). New York: Academic Press.

Huang, C.-T. J. (1982). Logical Relations in Chinese and the Theory of Grammar. PhD dissertation, MIT.

Huang, C.-T. J. (1983). A note on binding theory. *Linguistic Inquiry*, 14, 554–61.

Huang, C.-T. J. (1984). On the distribution and reference of empty pronouns. *Linguistic Inquiry*, 15, 531–74.

Huang, C.-T. J. (1995). Logical form. In G. Webelhuth (ed.), *Government and Binding Theory and the Minimalist Program* (pp. 125–76). Oxford: Blackwell.

Huang, C.-T. J. and Tang, C.-C. J. (1989). The local nature of the long-distance reflexive in Chinese. *North East Linguistic Society*, 19, 191–206.

Hudson, M. E. (1996). So? (Japanese connectives sorede, dakara and zya). Paper presented at the Tenth New England Japanese pedagogy workshop, Harvard University.

Hyams, N. M. (1986). *Language Acquisition and the Theory of Parameters*. Dordrecht: D. Reidel.

Hyman, L. M. (1985). *A Theory of Phonological Weight*. Dordrecht: Foris.

Hyman, L. and Comrie, B. (1981). Logophoric reference in Gokana. *Journal of African Languages and Linguistics*, 3, 19–37.

Ichio, A. (1997). Kuuhanchuu-o kateishinai bunrikai moderu – Nihongo-no kakimaze genshoo-o chuushin-ni [The sentence comprehension model without empty category through the examination of Japanese long distance scrambling phenomena]. *Osaka Daigaku Gengobunka-gaku* [Osaka University Language and Culture], 6, 177–89.

Ide, S. (1979). Daigakusei no hanashikotoba ni mirareru danjosai [The differences according to sex in university students' speech]. Handout for the 6th ICU symposium of the study of language and society.

Ide, S. (1982a). Japanese sociolinguistics: politeness and women's language. *Lingua*, 57, 357–85.

Ide, S. (1982b). Dan/josei go no hikaku [A comparison of men's and women's language]. In *Nichieigo Hikaku Kooza Dai 5 Kan: Bunka to Shakai* [Lectures on Comparison of Japanese and English 5: Culture and Society]. Tokyo: Taishuukan.

Ide, S. (1982c). Taiguu hyoogen no hikaku [A comparison of polite expressions]. In *Nichieigo Hikaku Kooza Dai 5 Kan: Bunka to Shakai* [Lectures on Comparison of Japanese and English 5: Culture and Society]. Tokyo: Taishuukan.

Ide, S. (1986). Introduction: the background of Japanese sociolinguistics. *Journal of Pragmatics*, 10, 281–6.

Ide, S. (1989). Formal forms and discernment: two neglected aspects of Japanese linguistic politeness. *Multilingua*, 8, 223–48.

Ide, S. (1991). How and why do women speak more politely in Japanese. In S. Ide and N. H. McGloin (eds), *Aspects of Japanese Women's Language* (pp. 63–80). Tokyo: Kuroshio Publishers.

Ide, S. (1992a). Gender and function of language use: quantitative and qualitative evidence from Japanese. In L. F. Bouton and Y. Kachru (eds), *Pragmatics and Language Learning Monograph Series*, 3 (pp. 117–29). Urbana: University of Illinois.

Ide, S. (1992b). Nihonjin no uchi soto ninchi to wakimae no gengo shiyoo [Japanese recognition of *uchi* and *soto*, and the language use according to wakimae]. *Gengo* [Language], 16, 26–31.

Ide, S. (1992c). On the notion of wakimae: toward an integrated framework of linguistic politeness. In *Kotoba no Mozaiku* [A Mosaic of Language: Essays in Honor of Professor Natsuko Okuda]. Tokyo: Meziro Linguistic Society.

Ide, S. (1993). Sekai no zyosei go nihon no zyosei go [Women's language in the world and Japan]. *Nihongogaku* [Japanese Linguistics], 12, 4–12.

Ide, S. (1995). Goyooron kara mita keigo: wakimae wo shihyoo suru modaritii hyoogen to shite no teineigo [Honorifics from the perspective of pragmatics: addressee honorifics as expressions of modality indexing wakimae]. *Kokubungaku: Kaishaku to Kyoozai no Kenkyuu* [Japanese Literature: Studies of Interpretation and Teaching Materials], 40, 10–17.

Ide, S. (1997). *Zyoseigo no Sekai.* [The World of Women's Language]. Tokyo: Meiji Shoin.

Ide, S. and Inoue, M. (1992). Zyosei kotoba ni miru aidentitii [Identity in women's language]. *Gengo* [Language], 21, 46–7.

Ide, S., Ogino, T., Kawasaki, A., and Ikuta, S. (1986b). *Nihonjin to Amerikajin no Keigo Koodoo* [The Honorific Behavior of Japanese and American People]. Tokyo: Nanundoo.

Ide, S., Hill, B., Carnes, Y. M., Ogino, T., and Kawasaki, A. (1992). The concept of politeness: an empirical study of American English and Japanese. In R. J. Watts, S. Ide, and K. Ehlich (eds), *Politeness in Language: Studies in its History, Theory and Practice* (pp. 281–97). Berlin, New York: Mouton de Gruyter.

Ide, S., Hori, M., Kawasaki, A., Ikuta, S., and Haga, H. (1986a). Sex difference and politeness in Japanese. *International Journal of the Sociology of Language*, 58, 25–36.

Ide, S., Ikuta, S., Kawasaki, A., Hori, M., and Haga, H. (eds), (1984). *Shuhu no Isshuukan no Danwa Shiryoo* [A Corpus of Discourse by a Housewife for a Week]. Report for the Ministry of Education.

Idsardi, W. J. (1992). The Computation of Prosody. PhD dissertation, MIT.

Iida, M. (1987). Case-assignment by nominals in Japanese. In M. Iida, S. Wechsler, and D. Zec (eds), *Working Papers in Grammatical Theory and Discourse Structure* (pp. 93–138). Stanford: Center for the Study of Language and Information.

Iida, M. (1996). *Context and Binding in Japanese.* Stanford: Center for the Study of Language and Information.

Iida, M. and Sells, P. (1986). Discourse factors in the binding of zibun. Paper presented at the Second SDF Workshop in Japanese Syntax, Stanford University CA.

Ikeda, Y. and Ikeda, T. (1996). Nihonjin no taiwa koozoo [Structure of Japanese conversation]. *Gengo*, 25:1, 48–55.

Ikegami, Y. (1981). *Suru to Naru no Gengogaku* [Linguistics of Do and Become]. Tokyo: Taishuukan.

Ikegami, Y. (1985). "Activity" – "accomplishment" – "achievement" – a language that can't say "I burned it, but it didn't burn" and one that can. In A. Makkai and A. Melby (eds), *Linguistics and Philosophy* (pp. 265–304). Amsterdam: John Benjamins.

Ikegami, Y. (1988). Transitivity: intransitivization vs. causativization: some typological considerations concerning verbs of action. In C. Duncan-Rose and T. Vennemann (eds), *On Language* (pp. 389–401). London: Routledge.

Ikegami, Y. (1991). "DO-language" and "BECOME-language": two contrasting types of linguistic representation. In Y. Ikegami (ed.), *The Empire of Signs* (pp. 258–326). Amsterdam: John Benjamins.

Ikuta, S. (1983). Speech level shift and conversational strategy in Japanese discourse. *Language Sciences*, 57, 37–53.

Imai, M. and Gentner, D. (1997). A cross-linguistic study of early word meaning: universal ontology and linguistic influence. *Cognition*, 62, 169–200.

Imura, T. (1943). Shitsugo: Nihongo-ni okeru tokusei [Aphasic, ihre eigenartigen Erscheinungen in der japanischen Sprache]. *Seishin Shinkei-gaku Zasshi* (Psychiatrian et Neurologia Japonica), 47, 30–52.

Inkelas, S., Orgun, O., and Zoll, C. (1997). The implications of lexical exceptions for the nature of grammar. In I. Roca (ed.), *Derivations and Constraints in Phonology* (pp. 393–418). Oxford: Oxford University Press.

Inoue, A. (1991). A Comparative Study of Parsing in English and Japanese. PhD dissertation, University of Connecticut.

Inoue, A. and Fodor, J. D. (1995). Information-paced parsing of Japanese. In R. Mazuka and N. Nagai (eds), *Japanese Syntactic Processing* (pp. 9–64). Hillsdale NJ: Lawrence Erlbaum Associates.

Inoue, K. (1976a). *Henkei-Bunpoo to Nihongo* [Transformational Grammar and Japanese]. 2 vols. Tokyo: Taishuukan.

Inoue, K. (1976b). Reflexivization: an interpretive approach. In M. Shibatani (ed.), *Japanese Generative Grammar: Syntax and Semantics 5* (pp. 117–200). New York: Academic Press.

Inoue, K. (1978). *Nihongo no Bunpoo Kisoku* [Grammatical Rules in the Japanese Language]. Tokyo: Taishuukan.

Inoue, K. (1983). *Nihongo no Kihon Koozoo* [The Basic Structure of the Japanese Language]. Tokyo: Sanseido.

Inoue, K. (1989). Shugo no imi-yakuwari to kaku-hairetsu [The semantic roles of subject and case alignment]. In S. Kuno and M. Shibatani (eds), *Nihongogaku no Shintenkai* [New Developments in Japanese Linguistics] (pp. 79–101). Tokyo: Kuroshio.

Ishii, Y. (1989). Reciprocal predicates in Japanese. *Eastern States Conference on Linguistics*, 6, 150–61.

Ishikawa, A. (1985). Complex Predicates and Lexical Operations in Japanese. PhD dissertation, Stanford University.

Ishikawa, M. (1991). Iconicity in discourse: the case of repetition. *TEXT*, 11, 554–80.

Isoda, M. (1991). The light verb construction in Japanese. *Chicago Linguistic Society*, 27, 261–75.

Itô, J. (1986). Syllable Theory in Prosodic Phonology. PhD dissertation, University of Massachusetts, Amherst. Published (1988), Outstanding Dissertations in Linguistics series. New York: Garland.

Itô, J. (1989). A prosodic theory of epenthesis. *Natural Language and Linguistic Theory*, 7, 217–59.

Itô, J. (1990). Prosodic minimality in Japanese. *Chicago Linguistic Society*, 26:2, 213–39.

Itô, J. and Mester, A. (1986). The phonology of voicing in Japanese: theoretical consequences for morphological accessibility. *Linguistic Inquiry*, 17, 49–73.

Itô, J. and Mester, A. (1992). Weak layering and word binarity. *University of California at Santa Cruz, Linguistics Research Center Report*, 92–109.

Itô, J. and Mester, A. (1994). Reflections on CodaCond and Alignment. In J. Merchant, J. Padgett, and R. Walker (eds), *Phonology at Santa Cruz* (pp. 27–46). Santa Cruz: Linguistics Research Center.

Itô, J. and Mester, A. (1995a). The core–periphery structure of the lexicon and constraints on reranking. In J. Beckman, S. Urbanczyk, and L. Walsh (eds), *Papers in Optimality Theory* (pp. 181–210). Amherst: GLSA.

Itô, J. and Mester, A. (1995b). Japanese phonology. In J. A. Goldsmith (ed.), *The Handbook of Phonological Theory* (pp. 817–38). Cambridge MA: Blackwell.

Itô, J. and Mester, A. (1996). Stem and word in Sino-Japanese. In T. Otake and A. Cutler (eds), *Phonological Structure and Language Processing: Cross-Linguistic Studies* (pp. 13–44). Berlin: Mouton de Gruyter.

Itô, J. and Mester, A. (1997a). Correspondence and compositionality: the ga-gyo variation in Japanese phonology. In I. Roca (ed.), *Derivations and Constraints in Phonology* (pp. 419–62). Oxford: Oxford University Press.

Itô, J. and Mester, A. (1997b). Featural sympathy. In D. Karvonen, M. Katayama, and R. Walker (eds), *Phonology at Santa Cruz (PASC) 5* (pp. 29–36). Santa Cruz: Linguistics Research Center.

Itô, J. and Mester, A. (1997c). Sympathy theory and German truncations. In V. Miglio and B. Moreen (eds), *University of Maryland Working Papers in Linguistics 5. Selected Phonology Papers from Hopkins Optimality Theory Workshop 1997/University of Maryland Mayfest 1997* (pp. 117–39). [ROA-211-0897].

Itô, J. and Mester, A. (1998). Realignment. In R. Kager, H. van der Hulst, and W. Zonneveld (eds), *The Prosody–Morphology Interface* (pp. 188–217). Cambridge: Cambridge University Press.

Itô, J., Mester, A., and Padgett, J. (1995). Licensing and underspecification in Optimality Theory. *Linguistic Inquiry*, 26, 571–614.

Itô, J., Mester, A., and Padgett, J. (1998). Lexical classes in Japanese: a reply to Rice. MS, University of California, Santa Cruz.

Itô, J., Kitagawa, Y., and Mester, A. (1996). Prosodic faithfulness and correspondence: evidence from a Japanese argot. *Journal of East Asian Linguistics*, 5, 217–94.

Ito, T. and Tatsumi, I. (1997). The development of metalinguistic awareness of mora-phonemes in Japanese young children. (in Japanese). *Japan Journal of Logopedics and Phoniatrics*, 38:2, 196–203.

Iwasaki, N., Vigliocco, G., and Garrett, M. F. (1997). Adjectives and adjectival nouns in Japanese: psychological processes in sentence production. Paper presented at the Eighth Annual Japanese/Korean Linguistics Conference, Cornell University.

Iwasaki, S. (1988). A Study of Speaker's Perspective in Japanese Spoken Discourse. PhD dissertation, University of California, Los Angeles.

Iwasaki, S. (1993). *Subjectivity in Grammar and Discourse*. Amsterdam: John Benjamins.

Jackendoff, R. S. (1972). *Semantics in Generative Grammar*. Cambridge MA: MIT Press.

Jackendoff, R. (1983). *Semantics and Cognition*. Cambridge MA: MIT Press.

Jackendoff, R. (1990). *Semantic Structure*. Cambridge MA: MIT Press.

Jackendoff, R. (1997). *The Architecture of the Language Faculty*. Cambridge MA: MIT Press.

Jacobsen, W. M. (1992). *The Transitive Structure of Events in Japanese*. Tokyo: Kuroshio.

Jaeggli, O. (1986). Passive. *Linguistic Inquiry*, 17, 587–622.

Jespersen, O. (1933). *Essentials of English Grammar*. London: Allen and Unwin (1983).

Jones, K. A. (1990). Conflict in Japanese Conversation. PhD dissertation, University of Michigan.

Jones, K. A. (1992). Ratifying conflict in Japanese interactions. Paper presented at the Association for Asian Studies Annual Meeting, Washington DC.

Kageyama, T. (1976–7). Incorporation and Sino-Japanese verbs. *Papers in Japanese Linguistics*, 5, 117–55.

Kageyama, T. (1977). Lexical Structures: A Comparative Study of Japanese and English. PhD dissertation, University of Southern California.

Kageyama, T. (1980a). *Goi no Koozoo: Nichi-ei Hikaku* [The Structure of the Vocabulary: A Comparison of Japanese and English]. Tokyo: Shoohakusha.

Kageyama, T. (1980b). The role of thematic relations in the spray paint hypallage. *Papers in Japanese Linguistics*, 7, 35–64.

Kageyama, T. (1982). Word formation in Japanese. *Lingua*, 57, 215–58.

Kageyama, T. (1989). The place of morphology in the grammar. In G. Booij and J. van Marle (eds), *Yearbook of Morphology 2* (pp. 73–94). Dordrecht: Foris.

Kageyama, T. (1991). Light verb constructions and the syntax-morphology interface. In H. Nakajima (ed.), *Current English Linguistics in Japan* (pp. 169–203). Berlin: Mouton de Gruyter.

Kageyama, T. (1993). *Bunpoo to Gokeisei* [Grammar and Word Formation]. Tokyo: Hitsuji Shoboo.

Kageyama, T. (1996). *Dooshi Imiron* [Verb Semantics]. Tokyo: Kuroshio.

Kageyama, T. (ed.), (1997). *Verb Semantics and Syntactic Structure*. Tokyo: Kuroshio.

Kageyama, T. and Shibatani, M. (1989). Mojuuru bunpoo no gokeisei-ron: meishiku kara no hukugoogo keisei [A theory of word formation in modular grammar: compound formation from noun phrases]. In S. Kuno and M. Shibatani (eds), *Nihongogaku no Shintenkai* [New Developments in Japanese Linguistics] (pp. 139–66). Tokyo: Kuroshio.

Kameyama, M. (1984). Subjective/logophoric bound anaphor zibun. *Chicago Linguistic Society*, 20, 228–38.

Kameyama, M. (1985). Zero Anaphora: The Case of Japanese. PhD dissertation, Stanford University.

Kamide, Y. and Mitchell, D. C. (1997). Relative clause attachment: nondeterminism in Japanese parsing. *Journal of Psycholinguistic Research*, 26:2, 247–54.

Kamio, A. (1977). Suuryooshi no shintakkusu [The syntax of numeral quantifier]. *Gengo*, 8, 83–91.

Kamio, A. (1979). On the notion speaker's territory of information: a functional analysis of certain sentence-final forms in Japanese. In G. Bedell, E. Kobayashi, and M. Muraki (eds), *Explorations in Linguistics: Papers in Honor of Kazuko Inoue* (pp. 213–31). Tokyo: Kenkyuusha.

Kamio, A. (1990). *Joohoo no Nawabari Riron: Gengo no Kinooteki Bunseki* [Theory of the Territory of Information: Functional Analysis of Language]. Tokyo: Taishuukan.

Kamp, H. and Reyle, U. (1993). *From Discourse to Logic: Introduction to Modeltheoretic Semantics of Natural Language, Formal Logic and Discourse Representation Theory*. Dordrecht: Kluwer.

Kanamaru, F. (1993). Ninshoo daimeishi koshoo [Person pronouns and address terms]. *Nihongogaku* [Japanese Linguistics], 12, 109–19.

Kaneoka, T. (1989). *Bunshoo ni Tsuite no Kokugo Gakuteki Kenkyuu* [Study on Discourse from the Japanese Linguistics Perspective]. Tokyo: Meiji Shoin.

Kaplan, R. B. (1972). *The Anatomy of Rhetoric: Prolegomena to a Functional Theory of Rhetoric*. Philadelphia: Center for Curriculum Development.

Karatsu, M. (1995). A functional analysis of dewa, dakara and shikashi in conversation. *Japanese Discourse*, 1, 107–30.

Karvonen, D. (1998). Finnish loanword phonology and the core-periphery structure of the lexicon. MS, University of California, Santa Cruz.

Katada, F. (1988). LF-binding of anaphors. *West Coast Conference of Formal Linguistics*, 7.

Katada, F. (1990). On the representation of moras: evidence from a language game. *Linguistic Inquiry*, 21, 641–6.

Katada, F. (1991). The LF representation of anaphors. *Linguistic Inquiry*, 22, 287–314.

Katayama, M. (1995). Loanword accent and minimal reranking in Japanese. In R. Walker, O. Lorentz, and H. Kubozono (eds), *Phonology at Santa Cruz: Papers on Stress, Accent, and Alignment* (pp. 1–12). Santa Cruz: Linguistics Research Center.

Katayama, M. (1998). Optimality Theory and Japanese Loanword Phonology. PhD dissertation, University of California, Santa Cruz.

Kayne, R. (1975). *French Syntax*. Cambridge MA: MIT Press.

Kayne, R. (1983). *Connectedness and Binary Branching*. Dordrecht: Foris.

Kerswill, P. (1996). Children, adolescents, and language change. *Language Variation and Change*, 8, 177–202.

Kerswill, P. and Williams, A. (1992). Some principles of dialect contact: evidence from the New Town of Milton Keynes. In I. Philippaki-Warburton and R. Ingram (eds), *Working Papers 1992* (pp. 68–90). University of Reading.

Kess, J. F. and Miyamoto, T. (1994). *Japanese Psycholinguistics: A Classified and Annotated Research Bibliography*. Amsterdam: John Benjamins.

Kimball, J. (1973). Seven principles of surface structure parsing in natural language. *Cognition*, 2:1, 15–47.

Kindaichi, H. (1950). Kokugo dooshi no ichibunrui [A classification of Japanese verbs]. *Kokugo Kenkyuu*, 15, 48–65. Reprinted in H. Kindaichi (ed.), (1976), *Nihongo Dooshi no Asupekuto* [Aspect in Japanese Verbs] (pp. 5–26). Tokyo: Mugi Shoboo.

Kindaichi, H. (1967). Gagyo bionron [Velar nasal]. In *Nihongo On'in no Kenkyu* [Studies in Japanese Phonology] (pp. 168–97). Tokyo: Hanawa Shoboo.

Kindaichi, H. (1976a). Kokugo dooshi no ichibunrui [A classification of Japanese verbs]. In H. Kindaichi (ed.), *Nihongo Dooshi no Asupekuto* [Aspect in Japanese Verbs] (pp. 5–26). Tokyo: Mugi Shoboo.

Kindaichi, H. (ed.), (1976b). *Nihongo Dooshi no Asupekuto* [Aspect in Japanese Verbs]. Tokyo: Mugi Shoboo.

Kindaichi, K. (1976). *Nihongo no Hensen* [Historical development of Japanese]. Tokyo: Koodansha.

Kinjo, K. (1996). An indecent call from a man: narrative as revelation of framework. *Pragmatics*, 6, 465–89.

Kinsui, S. (1994). Rentai-shuushoku no -ta ni tsuite [On the prenominal -ta modifier]. In Y. Takubo (ed.), *Nihongo no Meishi-shuushoku Hyoogen* [Noun Modifiers in Japanese] (pp. 29–65). Tokyo: Kuroshio.

Kiparsky, P. (1965). Phonological Change. PhD dissertation, MIT.

Kiparsky, P. (1968). How abstract is phonology? In O. Fujimura (ed.), *Three Dimensions of Linguistic Theory* (pp. 5–56). Tokyo: TEC.

Kiparsky, P. (1971). Historical linguistics. In W. Dingwall (ed.), *A Survey of Linguistic Science* (pp. 577–649). College Park: University of Maryland.

Kiparsky, P. (1982). Lexical morphology and phonology. In I.-S. Yang (ed.), *Linguistics in the Morning Calm* (pp. 3–91). Seoul: Hanshin.

Kiparsky, P. (1985). Some consequences of lexical phonology. *Phonology Yearbook*, 2, 83–138.

Kishimoto, H. (1996). Split intransitivity in Japanese and the unaccusative hypothesis. *Language*, 72, 248–86.

Kita, S. (1996). Aizuchi to unazuki kara mita nihonjin no taimen komyunikeeshon [Japanese face-to-face communication from the perspective of back channels and nods]. *Nihongogaku*, 15, 58–66.

Kitagawa, C. (1974). Case marking and causativization. *Papers in Japanese Linguistics*, 3, 43–57.

Kitagawa, C. (1981). Anaphora in Japanese: kare and zibun. In A. K. Farmer and C. Kitagawa (eds), *Coyote Papers 2: Proceedings of the Arizona Conference on Japanese Linguistics: The Formal Grammar Sessions* (pp. 61–75). Tucson: University of Arizona.

Kitagawa, C. (1984). Hatsugen no kaisookoozoo to kotoba no shutaisei [Structure of levels of utterance and the subjectivity of language]. *Nihongogaku*, 3, 31–42.

Kitagawa, C. (1995). *Wake* as discourse modality indicator: a type of speaker orientation in Japanese. *Japanese Discourse*, 1, 55–81.

Kitagawa, Y. (1986). Subjects in Japanese and English. PhD dissertation, University of MA, Amherst. Published (1994), New York: Garland.

Kitagawa, Y. (1994). Shells, yolks, and scrambling E.g.s. *North East Linguistic Society*, 24, 221–39.

Kitagawa, Y. and Kuroda, S.-Y. (1992). Passive in Japanese (v. 5). MS, University of Rochester and University of California, San Diego.

Kitahara, M. (1996). Consonant gemination and accent in Japanese loanwords. Paper presented at Proceedings of Formal Approaches to Japanese Linguistics 2.

Kobayashi, H. (1984). Rhetorical patterns in English and Japanese. *TESOL Quarterly*, 18:4, 737–8.

Koda, K. (1990). The use of L1 reading strategies in L2 reading. *Studies in Second Language Acquisition*, 12:4, 393–410.

Koizumi, M. (1993). Object agreement and the split VP hypothesis. *MIT Working Papers in Linguistics*, 18, 99–148.

Koizumi, M. (1995). Phrase Structure in Minimalist Syntax. PhD dissertation, MIT.

Kokuritsu Kokugo Kenkyujo. (1982). *Yooji no Kotoba Shiryoo, Vol. 4: Nisai-ji no Kotoba no Kiroku* [Child Speech Data. Vol. 4: Record of a Two-Year Old]. Tokyo: Shuuei Shuppan.

Kondo, T. and Amano, S. (1996a). Nihongo-no moji-ni taisuru shinmitsudo [Familiarity of Japanese characters]. Abstract for the 60th meeting of the Japanese Psychological Association.

Kondo, T. and Amano, S. (1996b). Familiarity ratings of Japanese *kanji* characters. Paper presented at XXVIth International Congress of Psychology.

Kondo, T., Amano, S. and Mazuka, R. (1996). Japanese lexicon database for psycholinguistic research. Paper presented at CUNY conference on Human Sentence Processing.

Kondo, T. and Kakehi, K. (1994). Effects of phonological and semantic information of *kanji* and *kana* characters on speech perception. *International Conference on Spoken Language Processing 94*, 3, 535–8.

Kondo, T. and Mazuka, R. (1996). Prosodic planning while reading aloud: on-line examination of Japanese sentences. *Journal of Psycholinguistic Research*, 25:2, 357–81.

Koopman, H. and Sportiche, D. (1991). The position of subjects. *Lingua*, 85, 211–58.

Koster, J. (1982). Counter-opacity in Korean and Japanese. In *Tilburg Papers in Language and Literature*. Tilburg: Tilburg University.

Koster, J. and Reuland, E. (eds), (1991). *Long Distance Anaphora*. Cambridge: Cambridge University Press.

Kratzer, A. (1989). Stage-level and individual-level predicates. In E. Bach, A. Kratzer, and B. Partee (eds), *Papers on Quantification*. NSF Report. University of Massachusetts, Amherst.

Kubo, M. (1990). Japanese passives. MS, MIT.

Kubota, R. (1992). Contrastive Rhetoric of Japanese and English: A Critical Approach. PhD dissertation, University of Toronto.

Kubozono, H. (1985). Speech errors and syllable structure. *Linguistics and Philology*, 6, 220–43.

Kubozono, H. (1989). The mora and syllable structure in Japanese: evidence from speech errors. *Language and Speech*, 32:3, 249–78.

Kubozono, H. (1990). Phonological constraints on blending in English as a case for phonology-morphology interface. *Yearbook of Morphology*, 3, 1–20.

Kubozono, H. (1993). *The Organization of Japanese Prosody*. Tokyo: Kuroshio.

Kubozono, H. (1995a). Constraint interaction in Japanese phonology: evidence from compound accent. *Phonology at Santa Cruz*, 4, 21–38.

Kubozono, H. (1995b). Perceptual evidence for the mora in Japanese. In B. Connell and A. Arvaniti (eds), *Phonology and Phonetic Evidence: Papers in Laboratory Phonology IV* (pp. 141–56). Cambridge: Cambridge University Press.

Kubozono, H. (1995c). *Gokeisei to On'in Koozoo* [Word Formation and Phonological Structure]. Tokyo: Kuroshio.

Kubozono, H. (1995d). The phonetic basis of phonological foot: evidence from Japanese. *Proceedings of the 13th International Congress of Phonetic Sciences, Stockholm, Sweden*, 4, 372–5.

Kubozono, H. (1996a). Speech segmentation and phonological structure. In T. Otake and A. Cutler (eds), *Phonological Structure and Language Processing: Cross-Linguistic Studies* (pp. 77–94). Berlin: Mouton de Gruyter.

Kubozono, H. (1996b). Syllable and accent in Japanese: evidence from loanword accentuation. *Bulletin of the Phonetic Society of Japan*, 211, 71–82.

Kubozono, H. (1997). Lexical markedness and variation: a nonderivational account of Japanese compound accent. *West Coast Conference of Formal Linguistics*, 15, 273–87.

Kubozono, H. and Mester, A. (1995). Foot and accent: new evidence from Japanese compound accentuation. Paper presented at the annual LSA meeting, New Orleans.

Kubozono, H. and Ohta, S. (1998). *On'in Koozoo to Akusento* [Phonological Structures and Accent]. Tokyo: Kaitakusha.

Kubozono, H., Itô, J., and Mester, A. (1997). On'in koozoo kara mita go to ku no kyookai [The phonological boundary between the word and the phrase]. In Onsei Bunpoo Kenkyuukai (ed.), *Bunpoo to Onsei* [Speech and Grammar] (pp. 147–66). Tokyo: Kuroshio.

Kudo, M. (1995). *Asupekuto, Tensu Taikei to Tekusuto: Gendai Nihongo no Jikan no Hyoogen* [Aspect, Tense, and Text: Temporal Expression in Modern Japanese]. Tokyo: Hitsuji Shoboo.

Kuno, S. (1972a). Functional sentence perspective – a case study from Japanese and English. *Linguistic Inquiry*, 3, 269–320.

Kuno, S. (1972b). Pronominalization, reflexivization, and direct discourse. *Linguistic Inquiry*, 3, 161–95.

Kuno, S. (1973). *The Structure of the Japanese Language*. Cambridge MA: MIT Press.

Kuno, S. (1976a). The speaker's empathy and its effects on syntax: a re-examination of yaru and kureru in Japanese. *Journal of the Association of Teachers of Japanese*, 11, 249–71.

Kuno, S. (1976b). Subject raising. In M. Shibatani (ed.), *Syntax and Semantics 5: Japanese Generative Grammar* (pp. 17–49). New York: Academic Press.

Kuno, S. (1976c). Subject, theme, and the speaker's empathy: a re-examination of relativization phenomena. In C. Li (ed.), *Subject and Topic* (pp. 417–44). New York: Academic Press.

Kuno, S. (1978a). Theoretical perspectives on Japanese linguistics. In J. Hinds and I. Howard (eds), *Problems in Japanese Syntax and Semantics* (pp. 213–85). Tokyo: Kaitakusha.

Kuno, S. (1978b). *Danwa no Bunpoo* [Grammar of Discourse]. Tokyo: Taishuukan.

Kuno, S. (1980). A (further) note on Tonoike's intra-subjectivization hypothesis. *MIT Working Papers in Linguistics*, 2, 171–84.

Kuno, S. (1983). *Shin Nihon-Bunpoo Kenkyu* [New Studies in Japanese Grammar]. Tokyo: Taishuukan.

Kuno, S. (1986a). Anaphora in Japanese. In S.-Y. Kuroda (ed.), *Working Papers from the First SDF Workshop in Japanese Syntax* (pp. 11–70). San Diego: University of California at San Diego.

Kuno, S. (1986b). Ukemi bun-no imi: kuroda setsu-no sai-hihan [The meaning of passive sentences: a reply to Kuroda]. *Nihongogaku*, 5, 70–87.

Kuno, S. (1987). *Functional Syntax*. Chicago: Chicago University Press.

Kuno, S. and Kaburaki, E. (1977). Empathy and syntax. *Linguistic Inquiry*, 8, 627–72.

Kuno, S. and Masunaga, K. (1986). Questions with *wh*-phrases in islands. *University of Massachusetts Occasional Papers in Linguistics 11: Oriental Linguistics*, 139–66.

Kuno, S. and Robinson, J. (1972). Multiple *wh* questions. *Linguistic Inquiry*, 3, 463–87.

Kurisu, K. (1998). Richness of the base and root fusion in Sino-Japanese. MS, University of California, Santa Cruz.

Kuroda, S.-Y. (1965a). Generative Grammatical Studies in the Japanese Language. PhD dissertation, MIT. Published (1979), New York: Garland.

Kuroda, S.-Y. (1965b). Causative forms in Japanese. *Foundations of Language*, 1, 30–50.

Kuroda, S.-Y. (1970). Remarks on the notion of subject with reference to words like Also, Even, or Only (Part 2). *Annual Bulletin of the Research Institute of Logopedics and Phoniatrics 4*. University of Tokyo. Reprinted in S.-Y. Kuroda (1992) (pp. 78–113).

Kuroda, S.-Y. (1973). On Kuno's Direct Discourse Analysis of the Japanese reflexive zibun. *Papers in Japanese Linguistics*, 2, 136–47.

Kuroda, S.-Y. (1978). Case marking, canonical sentence patterns, and counter Equi in Japanese. In J. Hinds and I. Howard (eds), *Problems in Japanese Syntax and Semantics* (pp. 30–51). Tokyo: Kaitakusha. Reprinted in S.-Y. Kuroda (1992), *Japanese Syntax and Semantics, Collected Papers* (pp. 222–39). Dordrecht: Kluwer.

Kuroda, S.-Y. (1979). On Japanese passives. In G. Bedell, E. Kobayashi, and M. Muraki (eds), *Exploration in Linguistics: Papers in Honor of Kazuko Inoue* (pp. 305–47). Tokyo: Kenkyusha.

Kuroda, S.-Y. (1980). Bunpoo-no hikaku. [Comparative grammar]. In T. Kunihiro (ed.), *Nichieigo Hikaku Kooza 2: Bunpoo* (pp. 23–62). Tokyo: Taishuukan.

Kuroda, S.-Y. (1981). Some recent trends in syntactic theory and the Japanese language. In A. K. Farmer and C. Kitagawa (eds), *Coyote Papers 2: Proceedings of the Arizona Conference on Japanese Linguistics* (pp. 103–22). Tucson: University of Arizona Linguistics Circle.

Kuroda, S.-Y. (1983). What can Japanese say about government and binding? *West Coast Conference of Formal Linguistics*, 2, 153–64.

Kuroda, S.-Y. (1985). Ukemi nitsuite no Kuno setsu o kaishaku suru: hitotsu no han-hihan [Reconsideration of Kuno's account of passives: a rebuttal]. *Nihongogaku*, 4, 69–76.

Kuroda, S.-Y. (1986). Movement of noun phrases in Japanese. In T. Imai and M. Saito (eds), *Issues in Japanese Linguistics* (pp. 229–71). Dordrecht: Foris. Reprinted in S.-Y. Kuroda (1992), *Japanese Syntax and Semantics, Collected Papers* (pp. 235–92). Dordrecht: Kluwer.

Kuroda, S.-Y. (1988). Whether we agree or not: a comparative syntax of English and Japanese. In W. J. Poser (ed.), *Papers from the Second International Workshop on Japanese Syntax* (pp. 103–43). Stanford: Center for the Study of Language and Information. Reprinted in S.-Y. Kuroda (1992), *Japanese Syntax and Semantics, Collected Papers* (pp. 315–57). Dordrecht: Kluwer.

Kuroda, S.-Y. (1990). Shieki no jodooshi no jiritsu-sei ni tsuite [The independence of the causative morpheme]. In *Bunpoo to Imi no Aida* [Interface of grammar and meaning] (pp. 93–104). Tokyo: Kuroshio.

Kuroda, S.-Y. (1992). *Japanese Syntax and Semantics, Collected Papers*. Dordrecht: Kluwer.

Kuroda, S.-Y. (1993a). Lexical and productive causatives in Japanese: an examination of the theory of paradigmatic structure. *Journal of Japanese Linguistics*, 15, 1–82.

Kuroda, S.-Y. (1993b). On the scope principle and scope ambiguities in Japanese. MS, University of California at San Diego.

Kurtzman, H. (1985). Studies in Syntactic Ambiguity Resolution. PhD dissertation, MIT.

Laberge, S. (1977). Étude de la variation des pronoms sujets définis et indéfinis dans le français parlé à Montréal [Study of the variation of definite and indefinite pronouns in spoken French in Montreal]. PhD dissertation, Université de Montréal.

Labov, W. (1963). The social motivation of a sound change. *Word*, 19, 273–309.

Labov, W. (1966). *The Social Stratification of English in New York City*. Washington DC: Center for Applied Linguistics.

Labov, W. (1969). Contraction, deletion, and inherent variability of the English copula. *Language*, 45, 715–62.

Labov, W. (1975). The quantitative study of linguistic structure. In K.-H. Dahlstredt (ed.), *The Nordic Languages and Modern Linguistics* (pp. 188–244). Stockholm: Almqvist and Wiksell.

Labov, W. (1984). Field method of the project on linguistic change and variation. In J. Baugh and J. Sherzer (eds), *Language in Use* (pp. 28–53). Englewood Cliffs NJ: Prentice Hall.

Labov, W. (1989). The child as linguistic historian. *Language Variation and Change*, 1, 85–98.

Labov, W. (1994). *Principles of Linguistic Change. Vol. 1: Internal Factors*. Oxford: Blackwell.

Labov, W., Cohen, P., Robins, C., and Lewis, J. (1968). *A Study of the Non-Standard English of Negro and Puerto Rican Speakers in New York City*. Philadelphia: US Regional Survey.

Labov, W., Yaeger, M., and Steiner, R. (1972). *A Quantitative Study of Sound Change in Progress*. Report on NSF Project no. GS-3287. Philadelphia: US Regional Survey.

Labov, W., Bower, A., Hindle, D., Dayton, E., Kroch, A., Lennig, M., and Schiffin, D. (1980). *Social Determinants of Sound Change*. Final report to NSF on SOC 75-00245. Philadelphia: US Regional Survey.

Lahiri, U. (1991). Embedded Questions and Predicates that Embed Them. PhD dissertation, MIT.

Landman, F. (1992). The Progressive. *Natural Language Semantics*, 1, 1–32.

Larson, R. (1988). On the double object construction. *Linguistic Inquiry*, 19, 335–91.

Lasnik, H. (1986). On the necessity of binding conditions. MS, University of Connecticut.

Lasnik, H. (1989). A selective history of modern binding theory. In H. Lasnik (ed.), *Essays on Anaphora* (pp. 1–36). Dordrecht: Kluwer.

Lasnik, H. and Fiengo, R. (1974). Complement object deletion. *Linguistic Inquiry*, 5, 535–71.

Lasnik, H. and Saito, M. (1984). On the nature of proper government. *Linguistic Inquiry*, 15, 235–89.

Lasnik, H. and Saito, M. (1992). *Move α: Conditions on its Application and Output*. Cambridge MA: MIT Press.

Lasnik, H. and Stowell, T. (1991). Weakest crossover. *Linguistic Inquiry*, 22, 687–720.

Lavandera, B. (1975). Linguistic Structure and Sociolinguistic Conditioning in the use of Verbal Endings in si-Clauses (Buenos Aires Spanish). PhD dissertation, University of Pennsylvania.

Lebeaux, D. (1983). A distributional difference between reciprocals and reflexives. *Linguistic Inquiry*, 14, 723–30.

Lennig, M. (1978). Acoustic Measurement of Linguistic Change: The Modern Paris Vowel System. PhD dissertation, University of Pennsylvania.

Leong, C. K. and Tamaoka, K. (1995). Use of phonological information in processing *kanji* and *katakana*. *Reading and Writing: An Interdisciplinary Journal*, 7, 377–93.

Levin, B. (1993). *English Verb Classes and Alternations: A Preliminary Investigation*. Chicago: University of Chicago Press.

Levin, B. (1995). Approaches to lexical semantic representation. In D. E. Walker, A. Zampolli, and N. Calzolari (eds), *Automating the Lexicon* (pp. 53–91). Oxford: Oxford University Press.

Levin, B. and Rapoport, T. (1988). Lexical subordination. *Chicago Linguistic Society*, 24, 275–89.

Levin, B. and Rappaport, M. (1989). An approach to unaccusative mismatches. *North East Linguistic Society*, 19, 314–29.

Levin, B. and Rappaport Hovav, M. (1995). *Unaccusativity: At the Syntax–Lexical Semantics Interface*. Cambridge MA: MIT Press.

Levin, L., Mitamura, T., and Mahmoud, A. T. (1988). Lexical incorporation and resultative secondary predicates. Paper presented at the LSA winter meeting.

Lewis, D. (1979). Attitudes *de dicto* and *de se*. *Philosophical Review*, 88, 513–43.

Lewis, R. L. (1996). Interference in short-term memory: the magical number two (or three) in sentence processing. *Journal of Psycholinguistic Research*, 25:1, 93–115.

Li, Y. (1990). X^0-binding and verb incorporation. *Linguistic Inquiry*, 21, 399–426.

Li, Y. (1993). Structural head and aspectuality. *Language*, 69, 480–504.

Li, Y.-H. Audrey (1992). Indefinite *wh* in Mandarin Chinese. *Journal of East Asian Linguistics*, 1, 125–56.

Lightner, T. (1972). Some remarks on exceptions and on coexistent systems in phonology. In D. S. Worth (ed.), *The Slavic Word* (pp. 426–42). The Hague: Mouton.

Lombardi, L. (to appear). Positional faithfulness and voicing assimilation in Optimality Theory. *Natural Language and Linguistic Theory*.

Lovins, J. B. (1975). *Loanwords and the Phonological Structure of Japanese*. Bloomington: Indiana University Linguistics Club.

McCarthy, J. J. (1997). Sympathy and phonological opacity. Handout of talk given at Hopkins Optimality Theory Workshop 1997/University of Maryland Mayfest 1997.

McCarthy, J. J. and Prince, A. S. (1993a). Generalized alignment. In G. Booij and J. van Marle (eds), *Yearbook of Morphology 1993* (pp. 79–153). Dordrecht: Kluwer.

McCarthy, J. J. and Prince, A. S. (1993b). Prosodic morphology I: constraint interaction and satisfaction. MS, University of Massachusetts, Amherst, and Rutgers University.

McCarthy, J. J. and Prince, A. S. (1994a). The emergence of the unmarked: optimality in prosodic morphology. *North East Linguistic Society*, 24, 333–79.

McCarthy, J. J. and Prince, A. S. (1994b). Two lectures on prosodic morphology. Rutgers Optimality Archive-59.

McCarthy, J. J. and Prince, A. S. (1995). Faithfulness and reduplicative identity. In J. Beckman, S. Urbanczyk, and L. Walsh (eds), *University of Massachusetts Occasional Papers in Linguistics*, 18 (pp. 249–384). University of Massachusetts: Amherst MA.

McCarthy, J. J. and Prince, A. S. (1998). Faithfulness and identity. In R. Kager, H. van der Hulst, and W. Zonneveld (eds), *The Prosody–Morphology Interface* (pp. 218–309). Cambridge: Cambridge University Press.

MacCaulay, R. (1977). *Language, Social Class, and Education.* Edinburgh: Edinburgh University Press.

McCawley, J. D. (1968a). Lexical insertion in a transformational grammar without deep structure. *Chicago Linguistic Society,* 4, 71–80.

McCawley, J. D. (1968b). *The Phonological Component of a Grammar of Japanese.* The Hague: Mouton.

McCawley, J. D. (1978). What is a tone language? In V. Fromkin (ed.), *Tone: A Linguistic Survey* (pp. 113–31). New York: Academic Press.

McCawley, J. D. and Momoi, K. (1986). The constituent structure of -te complements. *Papers in Japanese Linguistics,* 11, 1–60.

McCawley, N. A. (1972). On the treatment of Japanese passives. *Chicago Linguistic Society,* 8, 256–70.

McCawley, N. A. (1976). Reflexivization: a transformational approach. In J. Hinds and I. Howard (eds), *Problems in Japanese Syntax and Semantics* (pp. 51–115). Tokyo: Kaitakusha.

McClure, W. (1994). Syntactic Projections of the Semantics of Aspect. PhD dissertation, Cornell University.

McClure, W. (1995). *Syntactic Projections of the Semantics of Aspect.* Tokyo: Hitsuji Shoboo.

McCoard, R. (1978). *The English Perfect: Tense-Choice and Pragmatic Inferences.* Amsterdam: North-Holland.

MacDonald, M. C., Pearlmutter, N. J., and Seidenberg, M. S. (1994). Lexical nature of syntactic ambiguity resolution. *Psychological Review,* 101:4, 676–703.

McGloin, N. H. (1983). Some politeness strategies in Japanese. In S. Miyagawa and S. Kitagawa (eds), *Studies in Japanese Language Use* (pp. 123–45). Edmonton, Alberta: Linguistic Research.

McGloin, N. H. (1991). Sex difference and sentence-final particles. In S. Ide and N. H. McGloin (eds), *Aspects of Japanese Women's Language* (pp. 23–42). Tokyo: Kuroshio.

McGloin, N. H. (1993). Shuujoshi [Sentence final particles]. *Nihongogaku* [Japanese Linguistics], 12, 120–4.

MacWhinney, B. (1995). The CHILDES Project: Tools for Analyzing Talk. 2nd edn. Hillsdale NJ: Lawrence Erlbaum Associates.

Maddieson, I. (1985). Phonetic cues to syllabification. In V. Fromkin (ed.), *Phonetic Linguistics: Essays in Honor of Peter Ladefoged* (pp. 203–21). Orlando: Academic Press.

Mahajan, A. (1989). On the A/A-bar distinction: scrambling and weak crossover in Hindi. MS, MIT.

Mahajan, A. (1990). The A/A-bar Distinction and Movement Theory. PhD dissertation, MIT.

Makino, S. (1972). Adverbial scope and the passive construction in Japanese. *Papers in Linguistics,* 5, 73–98.

Makino, S. (1973). The passive construction in Japanese. In B. B. Kachru, R. B. Lees, Y. Malkiel, A. Pietrangeli, and S. Saporta (eds), *Issues in Linguistics: Papers in Honor of Henry and Renee Kahane* (pp. 588–605).

Makino, S. (1980). *Kurikaeshi no Bunpoo* [Grammar of Repetition]. Tokyo: Taishuukan.

Makino, S. (1983). Speaker/listener orientation and formality marking in Japanese. *Gengo Kenkyuu,* 84, 126–45.

Makino, S. (1993). Shooryaku no nichiei hikaku [Contrasting Japanese and English ellipsis]. *Nihongogaku*, 12, September, 41–9.

Maling, J. and Kim, A. S. (1992). Case assignment in the inalienable possession construction in Korean. *Journal of East Asian Linguistics*, 1, 37–68.

Manning, C. (1993). Analyzing the verbal noun: internal and external constraints. *Japanese/Korean Linguistics*, 3, 236–53.

Manzini, M. R. and Wexler, K. (1987). Parameters, binding theory and learnability. *Linguistic Inquiry*, 18, 413–44.

Marantz, A. (1984). *On the Nature of Grammatical Relations*. Cambridge, MA: MIT Press.

Marantz, A. (1995). The minimalist program. In G. Webelhuth (ed.), *Government and Binding Theory and the Minimalist Program* (pp. 349–82). Oxford: Blackwell.

Marcus, G. F. (1993). Negative evidence in language acquisition. *Cognition*, 46, 53–85.

Marcus, M. P. (1980). *A Theory of Syntactic Recognition for Natural Language*. Cambridge MA: MIT Press.

Marcus, M. P., Hindle, D., and Fleck, M. M. (1983). D-theory: talking about talking about trees. Proceedings of the 21st Meeting of the Association of Computational Linguistics, 129–36.

Martin, J. E. (1992). *Towards a Theory of Text in Contrastive Rhetoric*. New York: Peter Lang.

Martin, J. R. (1992). *English Text: System and Structure*. Amsterdam: John Benjamins.

Martin, R. (1993). On the distribution and case features of PRO. MS, University of Connecticut.

Martin, S. E. (1952). *Morphophonemics of Standard Colloquial Japanese*. Language Dissertation No. 47. Baltimore: Linguistic Society of America.

Martin, S. (1964). Speech levels in Japan and Korea. In D. Hymes (ed.), *Language in Culture and Society* (pp. 407–15). New York: Harper and Row.

Martin, S. (1972). Nonalphabetic writing systems: some observations. In J. P. Kavanaugh and I. G. Mattingly (eds), *Language by Ear and by Eye* (pp. 81–102). Cambridge MA: MIT Press.

Martin, S. (1975). *A Reference Grammar of Japanese*. New Haven and London: Yale University Press.

Martin, S. E. (1987). *The Japanese Language through Time*. New Haven and London: Yale University Press.

Masunaga, K. (1983). Bridging. In S. Hattori and K. Inoue (eds), *Proceedings of the XIIth International Congress of Linguistics* (pp. 455–60). Tokyo: Proceedings Publishing Committee.

Masuoka, T. (1991). *Modaritii no Bunpoo* [Grammar of Modality]. Tokyo: Kuroshio.

Mathesius, V. (1929). La structure phonologique du lexique du tchèque moderne [Phonological structure of the lexicon of modern Czech]. *Travaux du Cercle Linguistique de Prague*, 1, 67–84.

Matsuda, Y. (1997). Representation of Focus and Presupposition in Japanese. PhD dissertation, University of Southern California.

Matsuki, K. (1995). Creating Showa Memories in Contemporary Japan: Discourse, Society, History and Subjectivity. PhD dissertation, University of Arizona.

Matsumoto, K. (1985). A Study of Tense and Aspect in Japanese. PhD dissertation, University of Southern California.

Matsumoto, Yo. (1996). *Complex Predicates in Japanese: A Syntactic and Semantic Study of the Notion "Word."* Stanford: Center for the Study of Language and Information/Tokyo: Kuroshio.

Matsumoto, Yoshiko. (1988). Reexamination of the universality of face: politeness phenomena in Japanese. *Journal of Pragmatics*, 12, 403–26.

Matsumoto, Yoshiko. (1989a). Grammar and Semantics of Adnominal Clauses in Japanese. PhD dissertation, University of California, Berkeley.

Matsumoto, Yoshiko. (1989b). Politeness and conversational universals: observation from Japanese. *Multilingua*, 8, 207–21.

Matsumoto, Y(oshiko). (1993). Nihongo meishiku koozoo no goyooronteki koosatsu [Pragmatic study of Japanese nominal phrase structure]. *Nihongogaku*, 12, November, 101–14.

Matsunaga, S. (1995a). The Linguistic and Psycholinguistic Nature of *Kanji*: Do *Kanji* Represent and Trigger Only Meanings? PhD dissertation, University of Hawaii at Manoa.

Matsunaga, S. (1995b). *The Role of Phonological Coding in Reading Kanji: Technical Report 6*. Manoa: Second Language Teaching and Curriculum Center, University of Hawaii at Manoa.

May, R. (1977). The Grammar of Quantification. PhD dissertation, MIT.

May, R. (1985). *Logical Form*. Cambridge MA: MIT Press.

Maynard, S. K. (1980). Discourse Functions of the Japanese Theme Marker *Wa*. PhD dissertation, Northwestern University.

Maynard, S. K. (1983). Repetition in Japanese discourse: functions and pedagogical implications. Paper presented at Conference on Japanese and Korean Linguistics and Language Teaching, Harvard University.

Maynard, S. K. (1986). On back-channel behavior in Japanese and English casual conversation. *Linguistics*, 24, 1079–108.

Maynard, S. K. (1987a). Interactional functions of a nonverbal sign: head movement in Japanese dyadic casual conversation. *Journal of Pragmatics*, 11, 589–606.

Maynard, S. K. (1987b). Thematization as a staging device in Japanese narrative. In J. Hinds, S. K. Maynard, and S. Iwasaki (eds), *Perspectives on Topicalization: The Case of Japanese Wa* (pp. 57–82). Amsterdam: John Benjamins.

Maynard, S. K. (1989a). Functions of the discourse marker *dakara* in Japanese conversation. *TEXT*, 9, 389–414.

Maynard, S. K. (1989b). *Japanese Conversation: Self-Contextualization Through Structure and Interactional Management*. Advances in Discourse Processes, vol. 35. Norwood NJ: Ablex.

Maynard, S. K. (1991). Pragmatics of discourse modality: a case of *da* and *desu/masu* forms in Japanese. *Journal of Pragmatics*, 15, 551–82.

Maynard, S. K. (1992a). Cognitive and pragmatic messages of a syntactic choice: a case of the Japanese commentary predicate n(o) da. *TEXT*, 12, 563–613.

Maynard, S. K. (1992b). Speech act declaration in conversation: functions of the Japanese connective *datte*. *Studies in Language*, 16, 63–89.

Maynard, S. K. (1993a). *Discourse Modality: Subjectivity, Emotion and Voice in the Japanese Language*. Pragmatics and Beyond, New Series, vol. 24. Amsterdam: John Benjamins.

Maynard, S. K. (1993b). *Kaiwa Bunseki* [Conversation Analysis]. Nichieigo Taishoo Shiriizu, vol. 2. Tokyo: Kuroshio.

Maynard, S. K. (1996a). Multivoicedness in speech and thought representation: the case of self-quotation in Japanese. *Journal of Pragmatics*, 125, 207–26.

Maynard, S. K. (1996b). Presentation of one's view in Japanese newspaper columns: commentary strategies and sequencing. *TEXT*, 16, 391–421.

Maynard, S. K. (1997). *Japanese Communication: Language and Thought in Context.* Honolulu: University of Hawai'i Press.

Maynard, S. K. (in press). Shifting contexts: the sociolinguistic significance of nominalization in Japanese television news. *Language in Society*, 26:3.

Maynard, S. K. (in preparation). *Danwa Bunseki no Kokoromi: Riron, Bunseki, Nihongo no Hyoogensei* [Discourse Analysis: Theory, Analysis, and Japanese Expressivity]. Tokyo: Kuroshio.

Mazuka, R. (1990). Japanese and English Children's Processing of Complex Sentences: An Experimental Comparison. PhD dissertation, Cornell University.

Mazuka, R. (1991). Processing of empty categories in Japanese. *Journal of Psycholinguistic Research*, 20:3, 215–31.

Mazuka, R. (1998). *The Development of Language Processing Strategies: A Cross-Linguistic Study between Japanese and English.* Hillsdale NJ: Lawrence Erlbaum Associates.

Mazuka, R. and Itoh, K. (1995). Can Japanese speakers be lead down the garden path? In R. Mazuka and N. Nagai (eds), *Japanese Syntactic Processing* (pp. 295–329). Hillsdale NJ: Lawrence Erlbaum Associates.

Mazuka, R. and Lust, B. (1989). Why is Japanese not difficult to process? A proposal to integrate parameter setting in UG and parsing. *North East Linguistic Society*, 18:2, 333–56.

Mazuka, R. and Lust, B. (1990). On parameter setting and parsing: predictions for cross-linguistic differences in adult and child processing. In L. Frazier and J. De Villiers (eds), *Language Processing and Language Acquisition* (pp. 163–206). Dordrecht: Kluwer.

Mazuka, R. and Nagai, N. (1995). Japanese sentence processing: an interdisciplinary approach. In R. Mazuka and N. Nagai (eds), *Japanese Syntactic Processing* (pp. 1–8). Hillsdale NJ: Lawrence Erlbaum Associates.

Mazuka, R., Itoh, K., and Kondo, T. (1997). Processing down the garden path in Japanese processing of sentences with lexical homonyms. *Journal of Psycholinguistic Research*, 26:2, 207–28.

Mazuka, R., Kondo, T., Hayashi, A., and Suzuki, L. (1996). Learning the sound system of a language: acquisition of a special mora in Japanese. MS, Duke University and NTT Basic Research Labs.

Mazuka, R., Itoh, K., Kiritani, S., Niwa, S., Ikejiri, K., and Naitoh, K. (1989). Processing of Japanese garden path, center-embedded, and multiply left-embedded sentences. *Annual Bulletin of the Research Institute of Logopedics and Phoniatrics*, 23, 187–212.

Mester, A., and Itô, J. (1989). Feature predictability and underspecification: palatal prosody in Japanese mimetics. *Language*, 65, 258–93.

Mester, R. A. (1990). Patterns of truncation. *Linguistic Inquiry*, 21, 478–85.

Mihara, K. (1992). *Jisei Kaishaku to Toogo Genshoo* [The Interpretation of Tense and Syntax]. Tokyo: Kuroshio.

Miller, R. A. (1967). *The Japanese Language.* Chicago: University of Chicago Press.

Milroy, J. (1992). *Linguistic Variation and Change: On the Historical Sociolinguistics of English.* Oxford: Blackwell.

Milroy, L. (1980). *Language and Social Networks.* Oxford: Blackwell.

Milroy, L. (1987). *Observing and Analyzing Natural Language.* Oxford: Blackwell.

Milsark, G. L. (1974). Existential Sentences in English. PhD dissertation, MIT.

Mio, I. (1948). *Kokugohoo Bunshooron* [Discourse Theory of Japanese Language]. Tokyo: Sanseido.

Misono, Y., Mazuka, R., Kondo, T., and Kiritani, S. (1997). Effects and limitations of prosodic and semantic biases on syntactic disambiguation. *Journal of Psycholinguistic Research*, 26:2, 229–46.

Miyagawa, S. (1980). Complex Verbs and the Lexicon. PhD dissertation, University of Arizona.

Miyagawa, S. (1984). Blocking and the Japanese causatives. *Lingua*, 64, 177–207.

Miyagawa, S. (1986). Restructuring in Japanese. In T. Imai and M. Saito (eds), *Issues in Japanese Linguistics* (pp. 273–300). Dordrecht: Foris.

Miyagawa, S. (1987a). Lexical categories in Japanese. *Lingua*, 73, 29–51.

Miyagawa, S. (1987b). LF affix raising in Japanese. *Linguistic Inquiry*, 18, 362–7.

Miyagawa, S. (1989a). Light verbs and the ergative hypothesis. *Linguistic Inquiry*, 20, 659–68.

Miyagawa, S. (1989b). *Structure and Case Marking in Japanese*. Syntax and Semantics, vol. 22. San Diego: Academic Press.

Miyagawa, S. (1996). Word order restrictions and nonconfigurationality. In M. Koizumi, M. Oishi, and U. Sauerland (eds), *Formal Approaches to Japanese Linguistics 2: MIT Working Papers in Linguistics 29* (pp. 117–41). Cambridge MA: MIT Press.

Miyagawa, S. (1997a). Against optional scrambling. *Linguistic Inquiry*, 28, 1–26.

Miyagawa, S. (1997b). Light verb *make* and the notion of cause. MS, MIT.

Miyagawa, S. (in press). *(S)ase* as an elsewhere causative and the syntactic nature of words. Ms, MIT. To appear in *Journal of Japanese Linguistics*.

Miyagi, H. (1969). Seru, saseru – shieki [seru and saseru – causatives]. In A. Matsumura (ed.), *Kotengo, Gendaigo, Joshi, Jodooshi Shosetsu* [Case Marking and Auxiliary Verbs in Classical and Modern Language] (pp. 89–96). Tokyo: Gakutosha.

Miyara, S. (1982). A categorial analysis of morphologically complex predicates in Japanese (I). *Papers in Japanese Linguistics*, 8, 79–127.

Miyata, H. (1992). A Study of the Acquisition of the Case Particles in Japanese with Special Reference to *Ga* and *Wo*. MA thesis, Osaka University, Japan.

Modaressi, Y. (1978). A Sociolinguistic Analysis of Modern Persian. PhD dissertation, University of Pennsylvania.

Mohanan, K. P. (1986). *The Theory of Lexical Phonology*. Dordrecht: D. Reidel.

Mori, J. (1994). Functions of the connective *datte* in Japanese conversation. *Japanese/Korean Linguistics*, 4, 147–63.

Morita, Y. (1994). *Dooshi no Imironteki Bunpoo Kenkyuu* [A Study of Verbal Semantics]. Tokyo: Meiji Shoin.

Morita, Y. (1995). *Nihongo no Shiten* [Point of View in the Japanese Language]. Tokyo: Sootakusha.

Moriyama, T. (1988). *Nihongo Dooshijutsugobun no Kenkyuu* [A Study of Verbal Predicates in Japanese]. Tokyo: Meiji Shoin.

Morton, J. (1969). Interaction of information in word recognition. *Psychological Review*, 76, 165–78.

Morton, J. and Sasanuma, S. (1984). Lexical access in Japanese. In L. Henderson (ed.), *Orthographies and Reading: Perspectives from Cognitive Psychology, Neurology, and Linguistics* (pp. 25–42). London: Lawrence Erlbaum Associates.

Muraki, M. (1974). *Presupposition and Thematicization*. Tokyo: Kaitakusha.

Murasugi, K. (1991). Noun Phrases in Japanese and English: A Study in Syntax, Learnability and Acquisition. PhD dissertation, University of Connecticut.

Murasugi, K. and Saito, M. (1992). Quasi-adjuncts as sentential arguments. *Western Conference on Linguistics*, 22, 251–64.

Murasugi, K. and Saito, M. (1995). Adjunction and cyclicity. *West Coast Conference of Formal Linguistics*, 13, 302–17.

Myers, S. (1987). Vowel shortening in English. *Natural Language and Linguistic Theory*, 5, 485–518.

Myhill, J. (1992). *Typological Discourse Analysis*. Oxford: Blackwell.

Nagano, M. (1972). *Bunshooron Shoosetsu* [Detailed Accounts of the Theory of Discourse]. Tokyo: Asakura Shoten.

Nagano, M. (1986). *Bunshooron Soosetsu* [General Theory of Discourse]. Tokyo: Asakura Shoten.

Nagano, M. (1992). Bunpooron toshite no bunshooron [Theory of discourse as theory of grammar]. *Nihongogaku*, 11, April, 12–15.

Nagano-Madsen, Y. (1992). *Mora and Prosodic Coordination: A Phonetic Study of Japanese, Eskimo and Yoruba*. Lund: Lund University Press.

Nagashima, Y. (1976). Hukugoodooshi no koozoo [The structure of compound verbs]. In T. Suzuki (ed.), *Nihongo no Goi to Hyoogen* [Vocabulary and Expressions of Japanese] (pp. 63–104). Tokyo: Taishuukan.

Nagata, H. (1993). Unimmediate construction of syntactic structure for garden path sentences in Japanese. *Journal of Psycholinguistic Research*, 22:3, 365–81.

Nagy, N. (1996). Language Contact and Language Change in Faetar Speech Community. PhD dissertation, University of Pennsylvania.

Nagy, N. and Reynolds, W. (1996). Accounting for variable word-final deletion within optimality theory. In J. Arnold, R. Blake, B. Davidson, S. Schenter, and J. Solomo (eds), *Sociolinguistic Variation, Data, Theory, and Analysis* (pp. 151–60). Stanford: Center for the Study of Language and Information Publications.

Nagy, N. and Reynolds, W. (1997). Optimality theory and variable word-final deletion in Faetar. *Language Variation and Change*, 9, 37–55.

Nakai, S. (1976). A study of anaphoric relations in Japanese. MS, University of Massachusetts, Amherst.

Nakamura, A. (1994). On the tense system of Japanese. *Japanese/Korean Linguistics*, 4, 363–77.

Nakamura, M. (1987). Parameterized extension of binding theory. *MIT Working Papers in Linguistics*, 9, 193–223.

Nakao, T., Hibiya, J., and Hattori, N. (1997). *Shakai Gengogaku Gairon* [Introduction to Sociolinguistics]. Tokyo: Kuroshio.

Nakau, M. (1973). *Sentential Complementation in Japanese*. Tokyo: Kaitakusha.

Nakau, M. (1976). Tense, aspect, and modality. In M. Shibatani (ed.), *Syntax and Semantics 5: Japanese Generative Grammar* (pp. 421–82). New York: Academic Press.

Nakayama, M. (1990). Accessibility to the antecedents in Japanese sentence processing. MS, Ohio State University.

Nakayama, M. (1991). Japanese motion verbs and probe recognition. MS, Ohio State University.

Nakayama, M. (1995). Scrambling and probe recognition. In R. Mazuka and N. Nagai (eds), *Japanese Syntactic Processing* (pp. 257–73). Hillsdale NJ: Lawrence Erlbaum Associates.

Nakayama, M. (1996). *Acquisition of Japanese Empty Categories*. Tokyo: Kuroshio.

Nakayama, S. (1982). On English and Japanese Pronouns. MA Thesis, University of Tokyo.

Nasu, A. (1996). Niji-kango ni okeru sokuon-ka genshoo: Saitekisei-riron niyoru bunseki [Gemination in Sino-Japanese words: an analysis based on Optimality Theory]. *Bulletin of the Phonetic Society of Japan*, 213, 27–40.

Nemoto, N. (1991). Scrambling and condition on A-movement. *West Coast Conference of Formal Linguistics*, 10, 349–58.

Nemoto, N. (1993). Chains and Case Position: A Study from Scrambling in Japanese. PhD dissertation, University of Connecticut.

Nemoto, N. (1995). Scrambling in Japanese, AGRoP, and economy of derivation. *Lingua*, 97, 257–73.

Nessly, L. (1971). Anglicization in English phonology. *Chicago Linguistic Society, 7*, 499–510.

Neu, H. (1980). Ranking of constraints on /-t, d/ deletion in American English: a statistical analysis. In W. Labov (ed.), *Locating Language in Time and Space* (pp. 37–54). New York: Academic Press.

NHK [Japan Broadcasting Association]. (1985). *Nihongo Hatsuon Akusento Jiten* [Japanese Pronunciation and Accent Dictionary]. Tokyo: Nihon Hooso Kyookai.

Ní Chiosáin, M. and Padgett, J. (1997). Markedness, segment realization, and locality in spreading. MS, University of California, Santa Cruz. LRC-97-01. [ROA-188-0497].

Ninose, Y., Oda, J., Sakaki, Y., Sakamoto, T., and Gyoba, J. (1998). On the real-time processing of empty subjects in Japanese using a dichotic-listening method (2): the word order effect. *Cognitive Studies*, 5:1, 82–8.

Nishigauchi, T. (1986). Quantification in Syntax. PhD dissertation, University of Massachusetts.

Nishigauchi, T. (1990). *Quantification in the Theory of Grammar*. Dordrecht: Kluwer.

Nishigauchi, T. (1993). Long distance passive. In N. Hasegawa (ed.), *Japanese Syntax in Comparative Grammar* (pp. 79–114). Tokyo: Kuroshio.

Nishigauchi, T. (1997). Wh yooso-no kansuu-teki kaishaku ni tsuite. [On the functional interpretation of *wh*-phrases]. *Shoin Literary Review*, 30, 37–56.

Nishigauchi, T. (1998). "Multiple sluicing" in Japanese and the functional nature of *wh*-phrases. *Journal of East Asian Linguistics*, 7:2, 121–52.

Nishihara, S. (1990). Nichiei taishoo shuujihoo [Japanese and English contrastive rhetoric]. *Nihongo Kyooiku*, 72, 25–41.

Nishimitsu, Y. (1990). Kurikaeshi no nichiei taishoo danwa koozoo [Contrasting discourse structure of Japanese and English repetition]. In Kakehi Hisao Kyooku Kanreki Kinen Ronshuu Henshuu Iinkai (ed.), *Kotoba no Kyooen–Utage* [Linguistic Fiesta] (pp. 523–49). Tokyo: Kuroshio.

Nishiyama, K., Whitman, J., and Yi, E.-Y. (1996). Syntactic movement of overt wh-phrases in Japanese and Korean. *Japanese/Korean Linguistics*, 5, 337–51.

Noda, M. (1990). The Extended Predicate and Confrontational Discourse in Japanese. PhD dissertation, Cornell University.

Oda, J., Ninose, Y., Sakaki, Y., Gyooba, J., and Sakamoto, T. (1997). Ryooji bunri choohoo-ni yoru kuushugo hantei-no purosesu-no bunseki [On the real-time processing of empty subjects in Japanese using a dichotic-listening method]. *Ninchi Kagaku* [Cognitive Science], 4:2, 58–63.

Oehrle, R. (1976). The Grammatical Status of the English Dative Alternation. PhD dissertation, MIT.

Oehrle, R. and Nishio, H. (1980). Adversity. In A. K. Farmer and C. Kitagawa (eds), *Coyote Papers 2: Proceedings of the Arizona Conference on Japanese Linguistics* (pp. 163–85). Tucson: University of Arizona.

Ogihara, T. (1987). On "past tense" in Japanese. *Texas Linguistic Forum*, 28, 73–90.

Ogihara, T. (1992). *Temporal Reference in English and Japanese*. Bloomington: Indiana University Linguistics Club.

Ogihara, T. (1996). *Tense, Attitudes, and Scope*. Dordrecht: Kluwer.

Ogihara, T. (in press). The ambiguity of the -te iru form in Japanese. *Journal of East Asian Linguistics.*

Ogino, T. (1986). Quantification of politeness based on the usage patterns of honorific expressions. *International Journal of the Sociology of Language*, 58, 37–8.

Ohara, Y. (1997). Syakaionseigaku no kanten kara mita nihonjin no koe no kootei [The high and low pitch of the voice of Japanese from the viewpoint of sociophonetics]. In S. Ide (ed.), *Zyoseigo no Sekai* [The World of Women's Language] (pp. 42–58). Tokyo: Meiji Shoin.

Oishi, T. (1985). A Description of Japanese Final Particles in Context. PhD dissertation, University of Michigan.

Okamoto, S. (1995). Pragmaticization of meaning in some sentence-final particles in Japanese. In M. Shibatani and S. Thompson (eds), *Essays in Semantics and Pragmatics* (pp. 219–46). Amsterdam: John Benjamins.

Okamoto, S. (1997). Social context, linguistic ideology, and indexical expressions in Japanese. *Journal of Pragmatics*, 28, 795–817.

Okuda, Y. (1971). Accentual Systems in the Japanese Dialects. PhD dissertation, University of California, Los Angeles. Revised version published (1975), Tokyo: Bunka Hyouronsha.

Okuda, Y. (1977). Asupekuto no kenkyuu o megutte – Kindaichi teki dankai [On the study of aspect – the kindaichi stage]. *Miyagi Kyooiku Daigaku Kokugo Kokubun* 8. Reprinted in Y. Okuda (1984), *Kotoba no Kenkyuu Josetsu* [An Introduction to the Study of Language] (pp. 85–143). Tokyo: Mugi Shoboo.

Okuda, Y. (1984). *Kotoba no Kenkyuu Josetsu* [An Introduction to the Study of Language]. Tokyo: Mugi Shoboo.

Ono, T. and Yoshida, E. (1996). A study of co-construction in Japanese: we don't finish each other's sentences. *Japanese/Korean Linguistics*, 5, 115–29.

Onodera, N. O. (1993). Pragmatic Change in Japanese: Conjunctions and Interjections as Discourse Markers. PhD dissertation, Georgetown University.

Oshima, S. (1979). Conditions on rules: anaphora in Japanese. In G. Bedell, E. Kobayashi, and M. Muraki (eds), *Explorations in Linguistics: Papers in Honor of Kazuko Inoue* (pp. 423–48). Tokyo: Kenkyuusha.

Oshima-Takane, Y. and MacWhinney, B. (eds) (1995). *CHILDES Manual for Japanese.* Ms, McGill University.

Ota, A. (1971). Comparison of English and Japanese with special reference to tense and aspect. *Working Papers in Linguistics 3*, No. 4, 121–64. Department of Linguistics, University of Hawaii, Honolulu.

Ota, A. (1972). Tense correlations in English and Japanese. In J. E. Alatis (ed.), *Studies in Honor of Albert H. Marckwardt* (pp. 1221–34). Washington DC: Teachers of English to Speakers of Other Languages (TESOL). Also published in *Studies in English Linguistics*, 2, 108–21.

Otake, T., Hatano, G., Cutler, A. and Mehler, J. (1993). Mora or syllable? Speech segmentation in Japanese. *Journal of Memory and Language*, 32, 258–78.

Otsu, Y. (1981). Universal Grammar and Syntactic Development in Children: Toward a Theory of Syntactic Development. PhD dissertation, MIT.

Otsu, Y. (1994a). Early acquisition of scrambling in Japanese. In T. Hoekstra and B. D. Schwartz (eds), *Language Acquisition Studies in Generative Grammar* (pp. 253–64). Amsterdam: John Benjamins.

Otsu, Y. (1994b). Case-marking particles and phrase structure in early Japanese acquisition. In B. Lust, M. Suner, and J. Whitman (eds), *Syntactic Theory and First Language*

Acquisition: Cross-Linguistic Perspectives. Vol. 1: Heads, Projections and Learnability (pp. 159–69). Hillsdale NJ: Lawrence Erlbaum Associates.

Otsu, Y. (1997). *Zibun* hutatabi [*Zibun* revisited]. In Program Committee (ed.), *Ninchi/ Gengo no Seiritsu: Ningen no Kokoro no Hattatsu* [Emergence of Cognition and Language: Development of Human Mind] (pp. 113–22). Tokyo: Kuba Pro.

Ouhalla, J. (1996). Remarks on the binding properties of *wh*-pronouns. *Linguistic Inquiry*, 27, 676–707.

Oyakawa, T. (1973). Japanese reflexivization I. *Papers in Japanese Linguistics*, 2, 94–135.

Oyakawa, T. (1974). Japanese reflexivization II. *Papers in Japanese Linguistics*, 3, 129–201.

Padgett, J. (1995). Partial class behavior and nasal place assimilation. *Proceedings of the Arizona Phonology Conference: Workshop on Features in Optimality Theory.*

Paradis, C. (1985). An Acoustic Study of Variation and Change in the Vowel System of Chicoutimi and Jonquiere (Quebec). PhD dissertation, University of Pennsylvania.

Paradis, C. and Lebel, C. (1994). Contrasts from the segmental parameter settings in loanwords: core and periphery in Quebec French. In *Proceedings of the Conference on Contrast in Phonology.*

Paradis, M., Hagiwara, H., and Hildebrandt, N. (1985). *Neurolinguistic Aspects of the Japanese Writing System.* Orlando FL: Academic Press.

Parsons, T. (1990). *Events in the Semantics of English: A Study in Subatomic Semantics.* Cambridge MA: MIT Press.

Partee, B. and Bach, E. (1981). Quantification, pronouns, and VP-anaphora. In *Formal Methods in the Study of Language* (pp. 445–81). Amsterdam: Matematisch Centrum, Amsterdam University.

Pater, J. (1995). On the nonuniformity of weight-to-stress and stress preservation effects in English. MS, McGill University. [ROA-107-0000].

Pater, J. (1996). *NC. *North East Linguistic Society*, 26, 227–39.

Patrick, P. L. (1991). Creoles at the intersection of variable processes: -t, d deletion and past-marking in the Jamaican mesolect. *Language Variation and Change*, 3, 171–90.

Patrick, P. L. (1992). Linguistic Variation in Urban Jamaican Creole: A Sociolinguistic Study of Kingston, Jamaica. PhD dissertation, University of Pennsylvania.

Payne, A. (1976). The Acquisition of the Phonological System of a Second Dialect. PhD dissertation, University of Pennsylvania.

Perlmutter, D. (1970). The two verbs *begin*. In R. A. Jacobs and P. S. Rosenbaum (eds), *Readings in English Transformational Grammar* (pp. 107–19). Waltham MA: Binn and company.

Perlmutter, D. (1973). Evidence for the cycle in Japanese. *Annual Bulletin of the Research Institute of Logopedics and Phoniatrics*, 7, 187–210.

Pesetsky, D. (1982). Path and Categories. PhD dissertation, MIT.

Pesetsky, D. (1987). *Wh*-in-situ: movement and unselective binding. In E. Reuland and A. ter Meulen (eds), *The Representation of (In)definiteness* (pp. 98–129). Cambridge MA: MIT Press.

Pica, P. (1984). Subject, tense and truth: toward a modular approach to binding. In J. Guéron, H. G. Obenauer, and J.-Y. Pollock (eds), *Grammatical Representation* (pp. 259–91). Dordrecht: Foris.

Pica, P. (1987). On the nature of the reflexivization cycle. *North East Linguistic Society*, 17, 483–99.

Pike, K. L. (1947). *Phonemics: A Technique for Reducing Languages to Writing.* Ann Arbor: University of Michigan Press.

Pinker, S. (1989). *Learnability and Cognition: The Acquisition of Argument Structure*. Cambridge MA: MIT Press.

Pinker, S. and Prince, A. (1991). Regular and irregular morphology and the psychological status of rules of grammar. *Berkeley Linguistics Society*, 17, 230–51.

Pollard, C. and Sag, I. (1994). *Head-Driven Phrase Structure Grammar*. Chicago: University of Chicago Press/Stanford: Center for the Study of Language and Information.

Pollock, J.-Y. (1989). Verb movement, universal grammar, and the structure of IP. *Linguistic Inquiry*, 20, 365–456.

Poplack, S. (1979). Function and Process in a Variable Phonology. PhD dissertation, University of Pennsylvania.

Port, R. F. (1981). Linguistic timing factors in combination. *Journal of the Acoustical Society of America*, 69, 262–74.

Port, R. F., Dalby, J., and O'Dell, M. (1987). Evidence for mora timing in Japanese. *Journal of the Acoustical Society of America*, 81, 1574–85.

Poser, W. (1981). The "Double-o Constraint": evidence for a direct object relation in Japanese. MS, MIT.

Poser, W. (1984). The Phonetics and Phonology of Tone and Intonation in Japanese. PhD dissertation, MIT.

Poser, W. (1989). Japanese periphrastic verbs and noun incorporation. MS, Stanford University.

Poser, W. (1990). Evidence for foot structure in Japanese. *Language*, 66, 78–105.

Poser, W. (1992). Blocking of phrasal constructions by lexical items. In I. Sag and A. Szabolcsi (eds), *Lexical Matters* (pp. 111–30). Stanford: Center for the Study of Language and Information Publications.

Postal, P. (1968). *Aspects of Phonological Theory*. New York: Harper and Row.

Postal, P. (1971). *Crossover Phenomena*. New York: Holt, Rinehart and Winston.

Prichett, B. L. (1988). Garden path phenomena and the grammatical basis of language processing. *Language*, 64, 539–76.

Prichett, B. L. (1991). Head position and parsing ambiguity. *Journal of Psycholinguistic Research*, 20:3, 251–70.

Prichett, B. L. (1992). *Grammatical Competence and Parsing Performance*. Chicago: University of Chicago Press.

Prichett, B. L. and Whitman, J. B. (1995). Syntactic representation and interpretive preference. In R. Mazuka and N. Nagai (eds), *Japanese Syntactic Processing* (pp. 65–76). Hillsdale NJ: Lawrence Erlbaum Associates.

Prince, A. (1996). Aspects of mapping under OT. Handout of talk given at University of California, Santa Cruz, October 1996.

Prince, A. (1997). Elsewhere and otherwise. MS, Rutgers University. [ROA-217-0997].

Prince, A. and Smolensky, P. (1993). *Optimality Theory: Constraint Interaction in Generative Grammar*. Technical Report No. 2, Rutgers Center for Cognitive Science, Rutgers University. New Brunswick NJ: MIT Press.

Progovac, L. (1992). Relativized SUBJECT, long-distance reflexives without movement. *Linguistic Inquiry*, 23, 671–80.

Pustejovsky, J. (1995). *The Generative Lexicon*. Cambridge MA: MIT Press.

Radford, A. (1988). *Transformational Grammar: A First Course*. Cambridge: Cambridge University Press.

Rapoport, T. (1993). Verbs in depictives and resultatives. In J. Pustejovsky (ed.), *Semantics and the Lexicon* (pp. 163–84). Dordrecht: Kluwer.

Reichenbach, H. (1947). *Elements of Symbolic Logic*. New York: Macmillan.

Reinhart, T. (1976). The Syntax Domain of Anaphora. PhD dissertation, MIT.

Reinhart, T. (1983). *Anaphora and Semantic Interpretation*. London: Croom Helm.

Reinhart, T. and Reuland, E. (1991). Anaphors and logophors: an argument structure perspective. In J. Koster and E. Reuland (eds), *Long-Distance Anaphora* (pp. 283–321). Cambridge: Cambridge University Press.

Reinhart, T. and Reuland, E. (1992). Reflexivity. MS, Tel Aviv and Groningen.

Reinhart, T. and Reuland, E. (1993). Reflexivity. *Linguistic Inquiry*, 24, 657–720.

Renkema, J. (1993). *Discourse Studies*. Amsterdam: John Benjamins.

Reynolds, W. T. (1994). Variation and Phonological Theory. PhD dissertation, University of Pennsylvania.

Reynolds, W. T. and Nagy, N. (1994). Phonological variation in Faetar: an optimality account. *Chicago Linguistic Society*, 30:2, 277–92.

Rice, K. (1997). Japanese NC clusters and the redundancy of postnasal voicing. *Linguistic Inquiry*, 28, 541–51.

Rispoli, M. (1987). The acquisition of the transitive and intransitive action verb categories in Japanese. *First Language*, 7, 183–200.

Rispoli, M. (1989). Encounters with Japanese verbs: caregiver sentences and the categorization of transitive and intransitive action verbs. *First Language*, 9, 57–80.

Rispoli, M. (1990). Lexical assignability and perspective switch: the acquisition of verb subcategorization for aspectual inflections. *Journal of Child Language*, 17, 375–92.

Rivero, M.-L. (1980). On left-dislocation and topicalization in Spanish. *Linguistic Inquiry*, 11, 363–93.

Rizzi, L. (1982). A restructuring rule. In *Issues in Italian Syntax* (pp. 1–48). Dordrecht: Netherlands. Also appears in S. J. Keyser (ed.), (1978). *Recent Transformational Studies in European Languages* (pp. 113–58). Cambridge MA: MIT Press.

Rizzi, L. (1986). On chain formation. In H. Borer (ed.), *Syntax and Semantics 19* (pp. 65–95). New York: Academic Press.

Rizzi, L. (1991). *Relativized Minimality*. Cambridge MA: MIT Press.

Roberts, J. (1994). Acquisition of Variable Rules: (-t, d) Deletion and (ing) Production in Pre-School Children. PhD dissertation, University of Pennsylvania.

Roberts, J. (1996). Acquisition of Variable Rules: (-t, d) Deletion and (ing) Production in Pre-School Children. *Institute of Research in Cognitive Science Report* 96–09. Philadelphia: University of Pennsylvania.

Roberts, J. (1997a). Hitting a moving target: acquisition of sound change in progress by Philadelphia children. *Language Variation and Change*, 9, 249–66.

Roberts, J. (1997b). Acquisition of variable rules: a study of (-t, d) deletion in preschool children. *Journal of Child Language*, 24, 351–72.

Roberts, J. and Labov, W. (1995). Learning to talk Philadelphian: acquisition of short a by preschool children. *Language Variation and Change*, 7, 101–12.

Romaine, S. (1984). The sociolinguistic history of t/d deletion. *Folia Linguistica Historica*, 2, 221–55.

Rosenberger, N. (1989). Dialectic balance in the polar model of self: the Japan case. *Ethos*, 17, 88–113.

Ross, J. R. (1967). Constraints on Variables in Syntax. PhD dissertation, MIT.

Russell, K. (1995). Morphemes and candidates in Optimality Theory. MS, University of Manitoba.

Saciuk, B. (1969). The stratal division of the lexicon. *Papers in Linguistics*, 1, 464–532.

Sacks, H., Schegloff, E., and Jefferson, G. (1974). A simplest systematics for the organization of turn-taking for conversation. *Language*, 50, 696–735.

Sadakane, K. and Koizumi, K. (1995). On the nature of the "dative" particle in Japanese. *Linguistics*, 33, 5–33.

Sag, I. (1976). Deletion and Logical Form. PhD dissertation, MIT.

Saiki, M. (1987). Grammatical Functions in the Syntax of Japanese Nominals. PhD dissertation, Stanford University.

Saito, M. (1981). Notes in anaphora in Japanese (I). MS, MIT.

Saito, M. (1982). Case marking in Japanese: a preliminary study. MS, MIT.

Saito, M. (1983). Comments on the papers on generative syntax. In Y. Otsu, H. van Riemsdijk, K. Inoue, A. Kamio, and N. Kawasaki (eds), *Studies in Generative Grammar and Language Acquisition: A Report on Recent Trends in Linguistics* (pp. 79–89). Tokyo: International Christian University.

Saito, M. (1985). Some Asymmetries in Japanese and their Theoretical Implications. PhD dissertation, MIT.

Saito, M. (1989). Scrambling as semantically vacuous A'-movement. In M. R. Baltin and A. S. Kroch (eds), *Alternative Conceptions of Phrase Structure* (pp. 182–200). Chicago: University of Chicago Press.

Saito, M. (1992). Long distance scrambling in Japanese. *Journal of East Asian Linguistics*, 1, 69–118.

Saito, M. (1994a). Additional *wh*-effects and the adjunction site theory. *Journal of East Asian Linguistics*, 3, 195–240.

Saito, M. (1994b). Improper adjunction. In M. Koizumi and H. Ura (eds), *Formal Approaches to Japanese Linguistics 1: MIT Working Papers in Linguistics 24* (pp. 263–93). Cambridge MA: MIT Press.

Saito, M. and Hoji, H. (1983). Weak crossover and move α in Japanese. *Natural Language and Linguistic Theory*, 1, 245–59.

Saito, M. and Hoshi, H. (1994). Japanese light verb construction and the Minimalist Program. MS, University of Connecticut.

Saito, M. and Murasugi, K. (1990). N'-deletion in Japanese. *University of Connecticut Working Papers in Linguistics*, 3, 87–107. Department of Linguistics, University of Connecticut.

Sakai, H. (1994). Alignment with place nodes: an analysis of lexical domain distinctions in Japanese. *West Coast Conference of Formal Linguistics*, 13, 106–21.

Sakamoto, T. (1991). Processing Empty Subjects in Japanese: Implications of the Transparency Hypothesis. PhD dissertation, City University of New York.

Sakamoto, T. (1995a). Transparency between parser and grammar: on the processing of empty subjects in Japanese. In R. Mazuka and N. Nagai (eds), *Japanese Syntactic Processing* (pp. 275–94). Hillsdale NJ: Lawrence Erlbaum Associates.

Sakamoto, T. (1995b). Koobun kaiseki-ni okeru toomeisei-no kasetsu – Kuushugo-o hukumu bun-no shori-ni kanshite [The transparency hypothesis for parsing: on the processing of sentences with empty subjects]. *Ninchi Kagaku* [Cognitive Science]. 2:2, 77–90.

Sakamoto, T. (1995c). Nihongo-no seigyobun-ni kansuru oboegaki [Some notes on control sentences in Japanese]. *Ningen Kagaku* [Human Science], 1, 31–41.

Sakamoto, T. (1996). *Processing Empty Categories in Japanese: Implications for the Transparency Hypothesis*. Kyushu University Press.

Sakamoto, T. (1997a). Toogo kaiseki kenkyuu-no shomondai [Problems in syntactic processing]. In T. Sakamoto (ed.), *Kuushugo-o Hukumu Bun-no Rikaikatei-no Riaru Taimu Bunseki: Report* [On the Real Time Processing of Empty Subject Sentences in Japanese] (pp. 1–10). Kyushu University.

Sakamoto, T. (1997b). Nihongo seigyobun-ni tsuite [On Japanese control sentences]. In T. Sakamoto (ed.), *Kuushugo-o Hukumu Bun-no Rikaikatei-no Riaru Taimu Bunseki: Report* [On the Real Time Processing of Empty Subject Sentences in Japanese] (pp. 1–10). Kyushu University.

Sakamoto, T. (1997c). Kuushugo kaiseki-to toomeisei-no kasetsu [Parsing empty subjects and transparency hypothesis]. In T. Sakamoto (ed.), *Kuushugo-o Hukumu Bun-no Rikaikatei-no Riaru Taimu Bunseki: Report* [On the Real Time Processing of Empty Subject Sentences in Japanese] (pp. 1–10). Kyushu University.

Sakuma, K. (1929). *Nihon Onseigaku* [Japanese Phonetics]. Tokyo: Kazama Shoboo. Reprinted 1963.

Sakuma, M. (1981). The structure of the *bundan* in modern Japanese argumentative discourse: an analysis based on the reader's sense of paraphrasing. In S. Makino (ed.), *Papers from the Middlebury Symposium on Japanese Discourse Analysis* (pp. 200–75).

Sakuma, M. (1992). Bunshoo to bun: dan no bunmyaku no tookatsu [Discourse and sentence: integration of the discourse thread of paragraphs]. *Nihongogaku*, 11, April, 41–8.

Sano, K. (1977). An experimental study on the acquisition of Japanese simple sentences and cleft sentences. *Descriptive and Applied Linguistics*, 10, 213–33.

Sano, T. (1995). Roots in Language Acquisition: A Comparative Study of Japanese and European Languages. PhD dissertation, University of California, Los Angeles.

Sansom, G. (1928). *A Historical Grammar of Japanese*. Oxford: Clarendon Press.

Santa Ana, A. O. (1991). Phonetic Simplification Processes in the English of the Barrio: A Cross-Generational Sociolinguistic Study of the Chicanos of Los Angeles. PhD dissertation, University of Pennsylvania.

Santa Ana, A. O. (1992). Chicano English evidence for the exponential hypothesis: a variable rule pervades lexical phonology. *Language Variation and Change*, 4, 275–89.

Sasanuma, S. (1974). *Kanji* versus *kana* processing in alexia with transient agraphia: a case report. *Cortex*, 10, 89–97.

Sasanuma, S. (1980). Acquired dyslexia in Japanese: clinical features and underlying mechanisms. In M. Coltheart, K. Patterson, and J. C. Marshall (eds), *Deep Dyslexia* (pp. 48–90). London: Routledge and Kegan Paul.

Sasanuma, S. (1984). Can surface dyslexia occur in Japanese? In L. Henderson (ed.), *Orthographies and Reading: Perspectives from Cognitive Psychology, Neurology, and Linguistics* (pp. 43–55). London: Lawrence Erlbaum Associates.

Sasanuma, S. and Fujimura, O. (1971). Selective impairment of phonetic and non-phonetic transcription of words in Japanese aphasic patients: *kana* vs. *kanji* in visual recognition and writing. *Cortex*, 7, 1–18.

Sasanuma, S. and Fujimura, O. (1972). An analysis of writing errors in Japanese aphasic patients: *kanji* versus *kana* words. *Cortex*, 8, 265–82.

Sasanuma, S. and Monoi, H. (1975). The syndrome of Gogi (word-meaning) aphasia. *Neurology*, 25, 627–32.

Sasanuma, S., Sakuma, N., and Tatsumi, I. (1988). Lexical access of *kana* words and words in *kana*. *Annual Bulletin of the Research Institute of Logopedics and Phoniatrics*, 22, 117–23.

Sato, Y. (1993). Complex Predicate Formation with Verbal Nouns in Japanese and Korean: Argument Transfer at LF. PhD dissertation, University of Hawaii.

Schegloff, E. (1968). Sequencing in conversational openings. *American Anthropologist*, 70, 1075–95.

Schegloff, E. (1982). Discourse as an interactional achievement: some use of "uh huh" and other things that come between sentences. In D. Tannen (ed.), *Analyzing Discourse: Text and Talk* (pp. 71–93). Washington DC: Georgetown University Press.

Schiffrin, D. (1987). *Discourse Markers*. Cambridge: Cambridge University Press.

Schiffrin, D. (1994). *Approaches to Discourse*. Oxford: Blackwell.

Schwartz-Norman, L. (1976). The grammar of "content" and "container." *Journal of Linguistics*, 12, 179–87.

Searle, J. (1969). *Speech Acts*. Cambridge: Cambridge University Press.

Searle, J. (1975). Indirect speech acts. In P. Cole and J. L. Morgan (eds), *Syntax and Semantics 3* (pp. 59–82). New York: Academic Press.

Seidenberg, M. S. and McClelland, J. L. (1989). A distributed, developmental model of word recognition and naming. *Psychological Review*, 96, 523–68.

Sells, P. (1987). Aspects of logophoricity. *Linguistic Inquiry*, 18, 445–81.

Sells, P. (1989). More on light verbs and q-marking. MS, Stanford University.

Sells, P. (1995). Korean and Japanese morphology from a lexicalist perspective. *Linguistic Inquiry*, 26, 277–325.

Sells, P., Rickford, J., and Wasow, T. (1996). Variation in negative inversion in AAVE: an optimality theoretic approach. In J. Arnold, R. Blake, B. Davidson, S. Schenter, and J. Solomo (eds), *Sociolinguistic Variation, Data, Theory, and Analysis* (pp. 161–76). Stanford: Center for the Study of Language and Information.

Sherer, T. D. (1994). Prosodic Phonotactics. PhD dissertation, University of Massachusetts, Amherst.

Shibamoto, S. J. (1987). The womanly woman: manipulation of stereotypical and non-stereotypical features of Japanese female speech. In S. V. Phillips, S. Steele, and C. Tauz (eds), *Language, Gender, and Sex in Comparative Perspective* (pp. 26–49). Cambridge: Cambridge University Press.

Shibatani, M. (1972). The non-cyclic nature of Japanese accentuation. *Language*, 48, 584–95.

Shibatani, M. (1973a). A Linguistic Study of Causative Constructions. PhD Dissertation, University of California.

Shibatani, M. (1973b). Semantics of Japanese causativization. *Foundations of Language*, 9, 327–73.

Shibatani, M. (1973c). Where morphology and syntax clash: a case in Japanese aspectual verbs. *Gengo Kenkyuu*, 64, 65–96.

Shibatani, M. (1975). Pre-lexical versus post-lexical raising in Japanese. *Chicago Linguistic Society*, 11, 514–28.

Shibatani, M. (1976). Causativization. In M. Shibatani (ed.), *Syntax and Semantics 5: Japanese Generative Grammar* (pp. 239–94). New York: Academic Press.

Shibatani, M. (1978). *Nihongo no Bunseki* [An Analysis of Japanese]. Tokyo: Taishuukan.

Shibatani, M. (1990). *The Languages of Japan*. Cambridge: Cambridge University Press.

Shibatani, M. and Cotton, C. (1977). Remarks on double nominative sentences. *Papers in Japanese Linguistics*, 5, 261–77.

Shibatani, M. and Kageyama, T. (1988). Word formation in a modular theory of grammar: postsyntactic compounds in Japanese. *Language*, 64, 451–84.

Shinohara, S. (1997). Analyse phonologique de l'adaptation japonaise de mots étrangers [Phonological analysis of the adaptation of foreign words in Japanese]. Thèse pour le doctorat, Université de la Sorbonne nouvelle Paris III. [ROA-243-0298].

Shirai, Y. (in press). Where the progressive and the resultative meet: a typology of imperfective morphology in Japanese, Korean, Chinese and English. *Japanese/ Korean Linguistics*, 7.

Silverstein, M. (1976). Shifters, linguistic categories, and cultural description. In K. H. Basso and H. A. Selby (eds), *Meaning in Anthropology* (pp. 11–55). Albuquerque: University of New Mexico Press.

Sloan, K. (1990). Quantifier–*wh* Interaction. *MIT Working Papers in Linguistics*, 13, 219–37.

Smolensky, P. (1995). On the internal structure of the constraint component Con of UG. Handout of talk given at University of Arizona, March 1995.

Smolensky, P. (1996). The initial state and "Richness of the Base" in Optimality Theory. MS, Johns Hopkins University. [ROA-154-1196].

Soga, M. (1983). *Tense and Aspect in Modern Colloquial Japanese*. Vancouver, British Columbia: University of British Columbia.

Spaelti, P. (1997). Dimensions of Variation in Multi-Pattern Reduplication. PhD dissertation, University of California, Santa Cruz.

Spaelti, P. (1998). Notes on mimetics. MS, Kobe Shoin Woman's University.

Spencer, A. (1991). *Morphological Theory*. Oxford: Blackwell.

Sportiche, D. (1988). A theory of floating quantifiers and its corollaries for constituent structure. *Linguistic Inquiry*, 19, 425–49.

Srivastav, V. (1992). Two types of universal terms in questions. *North East Linguistic Society*, 22, 443–57.

Steriade, D. (1997). Lexical conservatism and its analysis. MS, University of California, Los Angeles.

Stowell, T. (1981). Origins of Phrase Structure. PhD dissertation, MIT.

Stubbs, M. (1983). *Discourse Analysis: The Sociolinguistic Analysis of Natural Language*. Chicago: University of Chicago Press.

Sugioka, Y. (1984). Interaction of Derivational Morphology and Syntax in Japanese and English. PhD dissertation, University of Chicago. Published (1986), New York: Garland.

Sugioka, Y. (1992). On the role of argument structure in nominalization. *Language, Culture and Communication*, 10, 53–80.

Sugioka, Y. (1995–6). Regularity in inflection and derivation: rule vs. analogy in Japanese deverbal compound formation. *Acta Linguistica Hungarica*, 43, 231–53.

Sugito, M. (1989). Haku ka onsetsu ka [mora or syllable]. In M. Sugito (ed.), *Nihongo no Onsei On'in* [Japanese Phonetics and Phonology]. Tokyo: Meiji Shoin.

Suzuki, K. (1995). NN: Rendaku and Licensing Paradox. *Japanese/Korean Linguistics*, 6, 215–28.

Szatrowski, P. (1992). Invitation-refusals in Japanese telephone conversations. Paper presented at the Association for Asian Studies Annual Meeting, Washington DC.

Szatrowski, P. (1993). *Nihongo no Danwa no Koozoo Bunseki: Kan'yuu no Sutoratejii no Ichi Koosatsu* [Structural Analysis of Japanese Discourse: A Study of Invitation Strategy]. Tokyo: Kuroshio.

Tada, H. (1990). Scrambling(s). Talk presented at the Japanese Syntax Workshop, Columbus OH.

Tada, H. (1993). A/A′ Partition in Derivation. PhD dissertation, MIT.

Tada, H. and Saito, M. (1991). VP-internal scrambling. Talk presented at University of Massachusetts at Amherst.

Tagashira, Y. (1978). Characterization of Japanese Compound Verbs. PhD dissertation, University of Chicago.

Tagashira, Y. and Hoff, J. (1986). *Handbook of Japanese Compound Verbs.* Tokyo: Hokuseidoo Press.

Takahara, P. O. (1990). Semantic and pragmatic function of causal connectives in English and Japanese. Paper presented at the International Pragmatics Association Conference, Barcelona.

Takahashi, D. (1993). Movement of *wh*-phrases in Japanese. *Natural Language and Linguistic Theory,* 11, 655–78.

Takahashi, D. (1994). Sluicing in Japanese. *Journal of East Asian Linguistics,* 3, 265–300.

Takahashi, M. (1993). The acquisition of verbal-nouns in Japanese. In H. Nakajima and Y. Otsu (eds), *Argument Structure: Its Syntax and Acquisition* (pp. 152–84). Tokyo: Kaitakusha.

Takano, Y. (1996). Movement and Parametric Variation in Syntax. PhD dissertation, University of California, Irvine.

Takezawa, K. (1987). A Configurational Approach to Case Marking in Japanese. PhD dissertation, University of Washington.

Takezawa, K. (1989). NP movement, anaphoric binding and aspectual interpretation. Presented at Ohio State University Workshop on Japanese Syntax and UG, Columbus OH.

Takezawa, K. (1991). Judootai, nookakubun, bunri-hukanoo shoyuu koobun to -te iru no kaishaku [Passive, ergative case, inalienable possession, and the interpretation of *-te iru*]. In Y. Nitta (ed.), *Nihongo no boisu to tadoosei* [The Voice and Transitivity in Japanese] (pp. 59–81). Tokyo: Kuroshio.

Talmy, L. (1985). Lexicalization patterns: semantic structure in lexical forms. In T. Shopen (ed.), *Language Typology and Syntactic Description 3: Grammatical Categories and the Lexicon* (pp. 57–149). Cambridge: Cambridge University Press.

Tannen, D. (1984). *Conversational Style: Analyzing Talk among Friends.* Norwood NJ: Ablex.

Tannen, D. (1989). *Talking Voices: Repetition, Dialogue and Imagery in Conversational Discourse.* Cambridge: Cambridge University Press.

Tanomura, T. (1988). "Heya-o sooji-suru" to "heya-no sooji-o suru" [*Heya-o soozi-suru* and *hoya-no soozi-o suru*]. *Nihongogaku,* 7:11, 70–80.

Taraldsen, K. T. (1981). The theoretical interpretation of a class of "marked" extraction. In A. Belleti, L. Brandi, and L. Rizzi (eds), *Theory of Markedness in Generative Grammar: Proceedings of the 1979 GLOW Conference* (pp. 475–516). Pisa: Scuolo Normale Superiore.

Tarallo, F. (1983). Relativization Strategies in Brazilian Portuguese. PhD dissertation, University of Pennsylvania.

Tateishi, K. (1989a). Phonology of Sino-Japanese morphemes. *University of Massachusetts Occasional Papers in Linguistics,* 13, 209–35.

Tateishi, K. (1989b). Theoretical implications of Japanese musicians' language. *West Coast Conference of Formal Linguistics,* 8, 384–98.

Tateishi, K. (1991). The Syntax of Subjects. PhD dissertation, University of Massachusetts, Amherst.

Tavakolian, S. (1981). *Language Acquisition and Linguistic Theory.* Cambridge MA: MIT Press.

Taylor, I. and Taylor, M. M. (1995). *Writing and Literacy in Chinese, Korean, and Japanese.* Amsterdam: John Benjamins.

Tenny, C. (1987). Grammaticalizing Aspect and Affectedness. PhD dissertation, MIT.

Terada, M. (1990). Incorporation and Argument Structure in Japanese. PhD dissertation, University of Massachusetts, Amherst.

Teramura, H. (1978). *Nihongo no Bunpoo* [The Grammar of Japanese]. Tokyo: Kokuritsu Kokogo Kenkyuujo.

Teramura, H. (1982). *Nihongo no Shintakkusu to Imi* [The Syntax and Semantics of Japanese] Vol. 1. Tokyo: Kuroshio.

Teramura, H. (1984). *Nihongo no Shintakkusu to Imi* [The Syntax and Semantics of Japanese] Vol. 2. Tokyo: Kuroshio.

Teramura, H. and Inoue, K. (1989). Tensu, asupekuto [Tense and Aspect]. In K. Inoue (ed.), *Nihon Bunpoo Shoojiten* [A Mini-Encyclopedia of Japanese Grammar] (pp. 165–90). Tokyo: Taishuukan.

Tesar, B. and Smolensky, P. (1998). Learnability in optimality theory. *Linguistic Inquiry*, 29, 229–68.

Tokieda, M. (1950). *Nihon Bunpoo Koogohen* [Japanese Grammar, the Spoken Language]. Tokyo: Iwanami Shoten.

Tokieda, M. (1951). Taijin kankei o koosei suru joshi, jodooshi [Particles and auxiliary verbs that construct interpersonal relationship]. *Kokugo Kokubun*, 29:9, 1–10.

Tokieda, M. (1977 [originally 1960]). *Bunshoo Kenkyuu Josetsu* [An Introduction to the Study of Discourse]. Tokyo: Meiji Shoin.

Tokunaga, M. (1988). A paradox in Japanese pragmatics. *Papers in Pragmatics*, 2, 84–105.

Tonoike, S. (1978). On the causative construction in Japanese. In J. Hinds and I. Howard (eds), *Problems in Japanese Syntax and Semantics* (pp. 3–29). Tokyo: Kaitakusha.

Traugott, E. C. (1982). From propositional to textual and expressive meanings: some semantic-pragmatic aspects of grammaticalization. In W. P. Lehmann and Y. Malkiel (eds), *Perspectives on Historical Linguistics* (pp. 289–307). Philadelphia: John Benjamins.

Treiman, R. (1986). The division between onsets and rimes in English syllables. *Journal of Memory and Language*, 25, 476–91.

Trubetzkoy, N. S. (1969). *Principles of Phonology* (trans. C. A. M. Baltaxe). Los Angeles: University of California Press. Original work (1958).

Trudgill, P. (1974). *The Social Differentiation of English in Norwich*. Cambridge: Cambridge University Press.

Trudgill, P. (1975). Sex, covert prestige and linguistic change in the urban British English of Norwich. In B. Thorne and N. Henly (eds), *Language and Sex: Difference and Dominance* (pp. 88–104). Rowley MA: Newbury House.

Tsubota, J. (1975). *Nihon Mukashibanashishuu* [Collection of Japanese Old Tales]. Tokyo: Shinchoosha.

Tsuchihashi, M. (1983). The speech act continuum: an investigation of Japanese sentence final particles. *Journal of Pragmatics*, 7, 361–87.

Tsujimura, N. (1990a). Ergativity of nouns and case assignment. *Linguistic Inquiry*, 21, 277–87.

Tsujimura, N. (1990b). The unaccusative hypothesis and noun classification. *Linguistics*, 28, 929–57.

Tsujimura, N. (1990c). Unaccusative mismatches in Japanese. *Eastern States Conference on Linguistics*, 6, 264–76.

Tsujimura, N. (1991). On the semantic properties of unaccusativity. *Journal of Japanese Linguistics*, 13, 91–116.

Tsujimura, N. (1992). Licensing nominal clauses: the case of deverbal nominal in Japanese. *Natural Language and Linguistic Theory*, 10, 477–522.

Tsujimura, N. (1994). Unaccusative mismatches and resultatives in Japanese. In M. Koizumi and H. Ura (eds), *Formal Approaches to Japanese Linguistics 1: MIT Working Papers in Linguistics 24* (pp. 335–54). Cambridge MA: MIT Press.

Tsujimura, N. (1996a). Another look at unaccusative mismatches in Japanese. *Berkeley Linguistics Society*, 22, 406–16.

Tsujimura, N. (1996b). *An Introduction to Japanese Linguistics*. Oxford: Blackwell.

Tsujimura, N. (1997). Deverbal nominalization and split intransitivity in Japanese. MS, Indiana University.

Tsujimura, N. and Aikawa, T. (1996). Intrinsic reflexivity and inalienable possession in Japanese. In M. Koizumi, M. Oishi, and U. Sauerland (eds), *Formal Approaches to Japanese Linguistics 2: MIT Working Papers in Linguistics 29* (pp. 267–82). Cambridge MA: MIT Press.

Uchida, Y. and Nakayama, M. (1993). Japanese verbal noun constructions. *Linguistics*, 31, 623–66.

Ueda, M. (1986). Notes on a Japanese (reflexive) pronoun zibun. MS, University of Massachusetts, Amherst.

Ueda, M. (1990). Japanese Phrase Structure and Parameter Setting. PhD dissertation, University of Massachusetts, Amherst.

Uehara, K. (1997). Judgments of processing load in Japanese: the effect of NP-ga sequences. *Journal of Psycholinguistic Research*, 26:2, 255–64.

Ujihira, A. and Kubozono, H. (1994). A phonetic and phonological analysis of stuttering in Japanese. *ICSLP 94*, 3, 1195–9.

Ura, H. (1996). Multiple Feature-Checking: A Theory of Grammatical Function Splitting. PhD dissertation, MIT.

van Dijk, T. A. (1972). *Some Aspects of Text Grammar*. The Hague: Mouton.

van Dijk, T. A. (1987). *Communicating Racism*. Newbury Park CA: Sage.

van Dijk, T. A. (1993). *Elite Discourse and Racism*. Newbury Park CA: Sage.

van Dijk, T. A. (1995). Aims of critical discourse analysis. *Japanese Discourse*, 1, 17–27.

van Valin, R. D. (1990). Semantic parameter of split intransitivity. *Language*, 66, 221–60.

Vance, T. (1987). *An Introduction to Japanese Phonology*. Albany: State University of New York Press.

Venditti, J. and Yamashita, H. (1994). Prosodic information and processing of complex NPs in Japanese. In M. Koizumi and H. Ura (eds), *Formal Approaches to Japanese Linguistics 1: MIT Working Papers in Linguistics 24* (pp. 375–91). Cambridge MA: MIT Press.

Vendler, Z. (1967). *Linguistics in Philosophy*. Ithaca NY: Cornell University Press.

von Stechow, A. (1996). Against LF-pied-piping. *Natural Language Semantics*, 4, 57–110.

Wada, M. (1942). Kinki akusento ni okeru meishi no hukugoogo keitai [The accentuation of compound nouns in Kansai dialects]. *Onseigaku Kyookai Kaihoo* [Bulletin], 71, 10–13.

Walenski, M. and Sakamoto, T. (1997). Processing of empty subjects in English and Japanese. In T. Sakamoto (ed.), *Kuushugo-o Hukumu Bun-no Rikaikatei-no Riaru Taimu Bunseki: Report* [On the Real Time Processing of Empty Subject Sentences in Japanese] (pp. 45–57). Kyushu University.

Walker, M., Iida, M., and Cote, S. (1994). Japanese discourse and the process of centering. *Computational Linguistics*, 20:2, 193–231.

Walker, R. (1998). Nasalization, Neutral Segments, and Opacity Effects. PhD dissertation, University of California, Santa Cruz.

Washio, R. (1989/90). The Japanese passive. *Linguistic Review*, 6, 227–63.

Watanabe, A. (1992). Subjacency and S-structure movement of *wh*-in-situ. *Journal of East Asian Linguistics*, 1, 255–91.

Watanabe, A. (1993). AGR-Based Case Theory and its Interactions with the A-bar System, PhD dissertation, MIT.

Watanabe, A. (1995). Nominative-genitive conversion and AGR in Japanese: a crosslinguistic perspective. MS, Kanda University of International Studies, Chiba, Japan.

Watanabe, S. (1995). Aspects of Questions in Japanese and their Theoretical Implications. PhD dissertation, University of Southern California.

Webelhuth, G. (1989). Syntactic Saturation Phenomena and the Modern Germanic Languages. PhD dissertation, University of Massachusetts, Amherst.

Webelhuth, G. (1992). *Principles and Parameters of Syntactic Saturation*. Oxford: Oxford University Press.

Weber, M. (1972). *Shakaigaku no Konpongainen* [The Fundamental Concept of Sociology] [Soziologische Grundbegriffe]. Tokyo: Iwanami Shoten. Japanese trans. I. Shimizu.

Weinberg, A. (1993). Parameters in the theory of sentence processing: minimal commitment theory goes east. *Journal of Psycholinguistic Research*, 22:3, 339–64.

Weinberg, A. (1995). Licensing constraints and the theory of language processing. In R. Mazuka and N. Nagai (eds), *Japanese Syntactic Processing* (pp. 235–56). Hillsdale NJ: Lawrence Erlbaum Associates.

Weinreich, U., Labov, W., and Herzog, M. (1968). Empirical foundations for a theory of language change. In W. P. Lehmann and Y. Malkiel (eds), *Directions for Historical Linguistics* (pp. 97–195). Austin: University of Texas Press.

Wells, S. I. (1995). A speech error investigation of the impact of orthography on Japanese speech production. *Chicago Linguistic Society*, 31, 478–89.

Wexler, K. (1996). The development of inflection in a biologically based theory of language acquisition. In M. L. Rice (ed.), *Toward a Genetics of Language* (pp. 113–44). Hillsdale NJ: Lawrence Erlbaum Associates.

Whitman, J. (1979). Scrambled, over easy, or sunny side up? *Chicago Linguistic Society*, 15, 342–52.

Whitman, J. (1982/87). Configurationality parameters. In T. Imai and M. Saito (eds), *Issues in Japanese Linguistics* (pp. 351–74). Dordrecht: Foris.

Wierzbicka, A. (1979). Are grammatical categories vague or polysemous? (The Japanese "adversative" passive in a typological context). *Papers in Linguistics*, 12, 111–62.

Williams, E. (1979). French causatives. MS, University of Massachusetts.

Williams, E. (1980). Predication. *Linguistic Inquiry*, 11, 203–38.

Williams, E. (1981). On the notions "lexically related" and "head of a word." *Linguistic Inquiry*, 12, 245–74.

Williams, E. (1994). *Thematic Structure in Syntax*. Cambridge MA: MIT Press.

Wolfram, W. (1969). *A Sociolinguistic Description of Detroit Negro English*. Washington DC: Center for Applied Linguistics.

Wolfram, W. (1972). Overlapping influence and linguistic assimilation in second generation Puerto Rican English. In D. Smith and R. Shuy (eds), *Sociolinguistics in Cross-Cultural Analysis* (pp. 15–46). Washington DC: Georgetown University Press.

Wolfram, W. and Christian, D. (1976). *Appalachian Speech*. Arlington VA: Center for Applied Linguistics.

Wydell, T. N., Patterson, K., and Humphreys, G. W. (1993). Phonologically mediated access to meaning for *kanji*: is a ROWS still a ROSE in Japanese *kanji*? *Journal of Experimental Psychology: Learning, Memory, and Cognition*, 19:3, 491–514.

Wydell, T. N., Butterworth, B., and Patterson, K. (1995). The inconsistency of consistency effects in reading: the case of Japanese *kanji*. *Journal of Experimental Psychology: Learning, Memory, and Cognition*, 21, 1155–68.

Yamada, E. (1990). Stress assignment in Tokyo Japanese (1): parameter settings and compound words. *Hukuoka Daigaku Jinbun Ronsoo* [Bulletin of Department of Humanities, Fukuoka University], 21:4, 1575–604.

Yamada, H. (1990). Topic management and turn distribution in business meetings: American versus Japanese strategies. *TEXT*, 10, 271–95.

Yamada, H. (1992). *American and Japanese Business Discourse: A Comparison of Interactional Styles*. Norwood NJ: Ablex.

Yamada, J. (1992). Asymmetries of reading and writing *kanji* by Japanese children. *Journal of Psycholinguistic Research*, 21:6, 563–80.

Yamagata, A. (1997). The stage-level/individual-level distinction: an analysis of *-te-iru*. *Japanese/Korean Linguistics* 8.

Yamamoto, K. (1984). Hukugoodooshi no kaku-shihai [Case relations in compound verbs]. *Toodai Ronkyuu*, 21, 32–49.

Yamashita, H. (1994). Processing of Japanese and Korean. PhD dissertation, Ohio State University.

Yamashita, H. (1995). Verb argument information used in a pro drop language: an experimental study in Japanese. *Journal of Psycholinguistic Research*, 24:5, 333–47.

Yamashita, H. (1997a). The effects of word-order and case marking information on the processing of Japanese. *Journal of Psycholinguistic Research*, 26:2, 163–88.

Yamashita, H. (1997b). On the role of surface morphological markings in the processing of Japanese. MS, University of Illinois at Urbana-Champaign.

Yamashita, H., Stowe, L., and Nakayama, M. (1993). Processing of Japanese relative constructions. *Japanese/Korean Linguistics*, 2, 248–64.

Yang, D.-W. (1983). The extended binding theory of anaphors. *Language Research*, 19:2, 169–92.

Yoneyama, M. (1986). Motion verbs in conceptual semantics. *Bulletin of the Faculty of Humanities*, 22, 1–15.

Yoon, J. H.-S. (1990). Theta theory and the grammar of inalienable possession construction in Korean, Mandarin and French. *North East Linguistic Society*, 20, 502–16.

Yoshimura, N. (1989). Parasitic pronouns. Paper presented at Southern California conference on Japanese-Korean Linguistics, University of California, Los Angeles.

Yoshimura, N. (1992). Scrambling and Anaphora in Japanese. PhD dissertation, University of Southern California.

Yumoto, Y. (1990). Nichiei-taishoo hukugoo-keiyooshi no koozoo [The structure of compound adjectives in Japanese and English]. *Studies in Language and Culture*, 16, 353–70. Osaka University.

Zec, D. (1995). The role of moraic structure in the distribution of segments within the syllable. In J. Durand and F. Katamba (eds), *Frontiers of Phonology* (pp. 149–79). New York: Longman.

Zenno, Y. (1985). Paradigmatic Structure and Japanese Idioms. MA thesis, Ohio State University.

Zribi-Hertz, A. (1989). A-type binding and narrative point of view. *Language*, 65, 695–727.

Zubizarreta, M. L. (1982). On the Relationship of the Lexicon and Syntax. PhD dissertation, MIT.

Zubizarreta, M. L. (1985). The relationship between morphology and morphosyntax: the case of Romance causatives. *Linguistic Inquiry*, 16, 247–89.

Zubritskaya, K. (1994). The Categorical and Variable Phonology of Russian. PhD dissertation, University of Pennsylvania.

Zubritskaya, K. (1997). Mechanism of sound change in optimality theory. *Language Variation and Change*, 9, 121–48.

Index

Errata

447 line 5,   begins→ being
457 Hill's   → Hill et al's